WRISTWATCH ANNUAL

2025

THE CATALOG

of

PRODUCERS, PRICES, MODELS,

and

SPECIFICATIONS

BY PETER BRAUN

WITH MARTON RADKAI

ABBEVILLE PRESS PUBLISHERS

New York   London

FREDERIQUE CONSTANT
GENEVE

Live your passion

MANUFACTURE
Classic Perpetual Calendar

BEYOND CONVENTIONS

CONTENTS

CONTENTS

Advertisers

Alexander Shorokhoff
Alpina
Aristo
Claude Meylan
Colorado Watch Company
Curtis Australia
Detroit Watch Company
Eberhard & Co.
Ernst Benz
Franck Muller
Frederique Constant
Hong Kong Watch
Itay Noy
JS Watch Co.
Louis Moinet
Milus
Ming
Mk II
Orbita
Parmigiani Fleurier
Phoenix Watch Company
Pilo & Co. Genève
Porsche Design
Tourby Watches
Tutima
Vario
Vortic Watch Company
Wempe Glashütte I/SA
Zeitwinkel
Zeroo Time Co

CELEBRATE YOUR TIME

CHRONO 4
21-42

Eberhard & Co. protagonist of time
with Chrono 4 "21-42", the automatic chronograph
celebrating the collection that revolutionized
the reading of time in the Third Millennium.

SHIELD
EBERHARD & CO. WARRANTY
ACTIVATION

AVAILABLE ONLY AT AUTHORISED RETAILERS

EBERHARD1887.COM

EBERHARD & CO

Manufacture Suisse d'Horlogerie depuis 1887

LA CHAUX-DE-FONDS

ZEITWINKEL°

Dear Reader,

Thank you for acquiring this new edition of *Wristwatch Annual.* As you leaf through its pages, you will notice not only that many watches have been updated, but that the layout and the font have also been refreshed. Hybrid being the word of the year, we have made use of QR codes to enhance your experience with an easy connection to the Internet.

Once again, *Wristwatch Annual* has taken a dive into this remarkable industry that straddles engineering, fashion, art, and human emotion. For all involved in manufacturing all those grand timepieces, it's a special industry indeed. First, they are tyrannized by the "economy," which is tied, Gulliver-like, to interest rates, global events, financial ideologies that may or may not work, and ultimately to finicky consumers (the market) who must be willing to buy a product that is of no immediate use—or so say the pragmatists. Check out the story on page 40 for an exploration of watches and lifestyle.

The market is indeed choppy. The post-pandemic boom, driven by accumulations of money that could not be spent on frills and thrills like travel pushed up prices and production. Pre-owned watches became popular thanks to new safeguards and additionally became an asset class for investors. So, people started hunting for "deals" to flip and earn a buck. When friends started asking me about "investing," I declined to give advice. The collectors I have had the privilege to meet love their watches not as assets, just as beautiful objects.

The market crested and 2024 turned out disappointing overall. The cause could be economic, since the younger generation is not yet earning enough to pull in a big fish. However, it could also be the aesthetics and the aura of unattainability that surrounds many of the major players, who are not ready to risk straying from their tried-and-true codes. More agile brands are striving for some diversification by inviting outsiders to participate in their designs. "Collaborations are a way to see our own brand in a different light and to refresh our ideas," one person told me at the Watch Days in September.

The past years have seen a plethora of these innovative ideas, like the Louis Erard collaborations with Label Noir, Vianney Halter,

and The Horophile. After their successful project with MB&F on the LM101, H. Moser & Cie. turned to Studio Underd0g, a brand that "doesn't take itself too seriously." This resulted in timepieces in pinkish-orangish-yellowish hues. Some may not like the style, but they do attract attention.

This book was put together with the idea of exhibiting as wide a spectrum of watches as possible, from the top of the line to affordable but well-made timepieces. I did this as a way to re-mind readers that luxury is not measured by the size of the price tag but rather by the intensity of the relationship a person has with a particular object. That dialogue is totally subjective and unique; it can be rich in associations and memories, or simply fun.

Having said that, you will of course find the venerable stars of the industry in the following pages, but you will also discover many brands that normally pass under the radar, like CIGA Design, Hedone, Shanghai, and Vario, a brand from Singapore. Also new to the book are Elka and Baltic, two companies that create a vintage look without looking old-fangled. The presence of Curtis Australia and Bausele also reveals what's happening down under. Between all these are many fine American brands, such as Vortic, RGM, MKII, Detroit Watches, and the new Phoenix.

As usual, Elizabeth Doerr canvassed the independent scene for us (page 10) and found some exceptional pieces by young and old watchmakers alike. The minute repeater is a pinnacle of watchmaking and is described on page 20. And the Masters and Mavericks section includes, among others, the portrait of a genuine "farmer watchmaker."

Finally, do not forget that after the brands section, we present some of the calibers (page 330) that drive the watches, followed by practical information.

A word of thanks to close: Cindi Barton, Stephanie Sarkany, Kourtnay King, Erin Morris, and others helped review the text, managed the workflow in difficult times, laid out the chapters, and remained calm under pressure. Many thanks, too, to the brands that advertise with *Wristwatch Annual* and who trust in the power of a real book filled with images and original copy. I would encourage you to visit them and check out their goods. Errors do occur, and if you run into one, please make gentle note of it so we correct it. If you don't see your favorite watch or brand here, maybe next year! Have a great read.

Marton Radkai

WRISTWATCH ANNUAL
2025

The Catalog of Producers, Prices, Models & Specifications

This year's Wristwatch Annual cover features Franck Muller's **Vanguard Crazy Hours Vegas Racing**, a watch that commemorates the arrival of Formula One racing in Las Vegas. The hallmark tonneau case is generously dimensioned at 44 mm x 53.7 mm with a height of 15.1 mm. It is cut out of a compressed block of carbon with inserts of Ergal, an aluminum alloy, and polished to reveal a wavy pattern. For the first time, Franck Muller presents the MVD-2800-CHR-SQ Crazy Hours caliber in a skeletonized version. This particular complication has the hour hand jumping to correct numerals, which are arranged in a seemingly haphazard fashion, while the minute and second hands glide over the gambling-themed dial. The Vanguard Crazy Hours Vegas Racing delivers 42 hours of power reserve and is water-resistant to 3 atm.

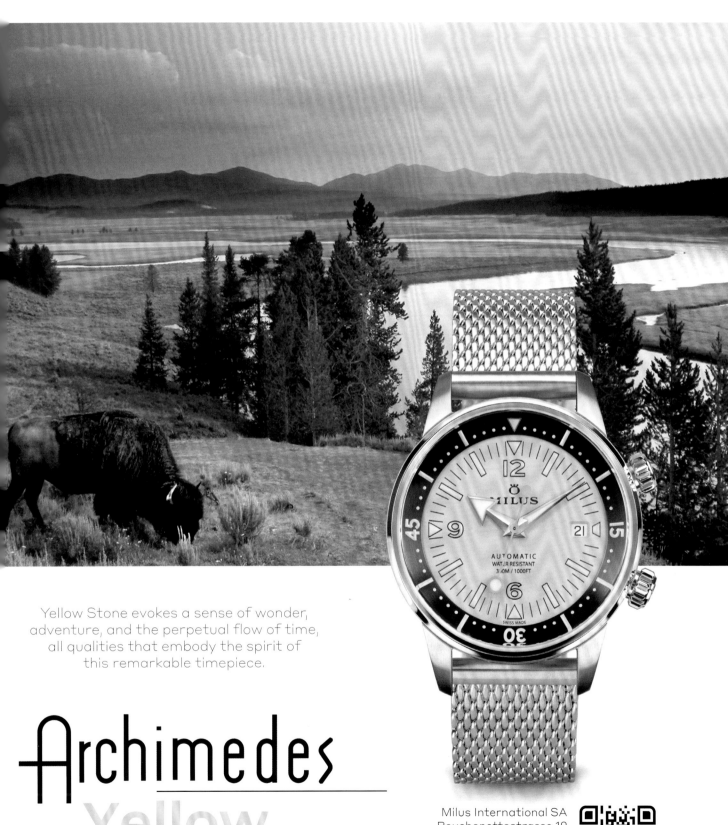

THE INDEPENDENT SCENE 2024

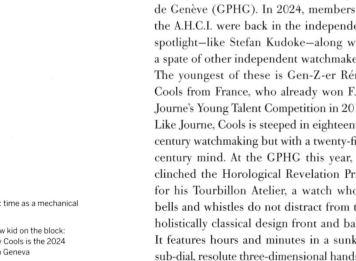

1

BY ELIZABETH DOERR

The world of independent watchmaking has been welcoming "new" faces and talents over the last few years and in pretty much every price class. In fact, our world of ticks and tocks is now graced with more independents than ever before.

The upwind experienced by the independent watchmakers is partially due to the success and reputation of the A.H.C.I.—and perhaps, at least, to the fact that so many of its members get extra attention through awards like those given at the Grand Prix d'Horlogerie de Genève (GPHG). In 2024, members of the A.H.C.I. were back in the independent spotlight—like Stefan Kudoke—along with a spate of other independent watchmakers. The youngest of these is Gen-Z-er Rémy Cools from France, who already won F. P. Journe's Young Talent Competition in 2018. Like Journe, Cools is steeped in eighteenth-century watchmaking but with a twenty-first century mind. At the GPHG this year, he clinched the Horological Revelation Prize for his Tourbillon Atelier, a watch whose bells and whistles do not distract from the holistically classical design front and back. It features hours and minutes in a sunken sub-dial, resolute three-dimensional hands, a 13.2-millimeter tourbillon, all on a luminous, sandy yellow-gold backdrop.

1. Miki Eleta: time as a mechanical game

2. and 3. New kid on the block: Gen-Z Rémy Cools is the 2024 revelation in Geneva

4. Louis Vuitton's spiraling Prize designed to attract dreamers

4

LOUIS VUITTON BOOSTS INDEPENDENT CREATIVES

Another boost came from an unusual quarter, too. Louis Vuitton, as it happens, is now the proud force behind the modern brands founded by previous independent watchmakers Gérald Genta and Daniel Roth. "The Louis Vuitton Watch Prize exists because we believe that the future of watchmaking belongs to the dreamers and rule-breakers who meet the highest standards of craftmanship," said Jean Arnault, director of watches at Louis Vuitton, who called the prize to life.

2

3

INDEPENDENT WATCHMAKING

From around 1,000 submissions, Louis Vuitton preselected twenty semifinalists. Of these, the committee of experts chose five deserving finalists: Petermann Bédat and Simon Brette as well as A.H.C.I. members Andreas Strehler, Raúl Pagès, and John-Mikaël Flaux. The winner, announced on February 6, 2024, was Raúl Pagès with his RP1—Régulateur à Détente. Pagès received a year-long mentorship with Louis Vuitton's team of experts at La Fabrique du Temps as well as a substantial financial prize. "Being honored by the jury of the Louis Vuitton Watch Prize for Independent Watchmakers is the best possible recognition of my work as an independent watchmaker," Pagès said.

A.H.C.I. NEWS

The heart of the independent scene is—and always has been in the modern era—the A.H.C.I. (Académie Horlogère des Créateurs Indépendants/Horological Academy of Independent Creators), a group of independent creators founded in 1985. The way of these individualistic watchmaker-inventors is indeed anachronistic, and though the products that emerge may not be everyone's cup of tea all of the time, they do attract the attention of collectors of rare taste who follow not only the horological escapades of these thirty-odd watchmakers of varying age and nationality, but also the passion and personality that goes into each extremely limited timepiece.

OUT OF THIS WORLD

The year 2024 was marked by surprising launches for some of the group's members and ex-members. Let's start with Christiaan van der Klaauw (CVDK), the only watchmaking outfit in the world completely devoted to astronomical watches. It was founded 50 years ago by one of the first A.H.C.I. members, self-taught Dutch watchmaker Christiaan van der Klaauw. That same year, 1974, van der Klaauw presented his first clock with astronomical complications. In 1996, he introduced his first wristwatch and three years later (1999) the Planetarium, a watch comprising the world's smallest mechanical planetarium (the watch that later formed the basis of the Grand Prix d'Horlogerie de Genève-winning Van Cleef & Arpels watch of the same name).

1. The Référence 2941 monopusher split-seconds chronograph by Gaël Petermann and Florian Bédat reached the finals for the Louis Vuitton Prize

2. and 3. The finalists for the prize (left) and Raul Pagès, the happy winner (right)

3. Christiaan van der Klaauw, master of astronomical clockworks

12

A STRONG CHARACTER CAN BE IDENTIFIED BY THE WRIST.

Exemplify Character and Strength in a New York Minute
with the Wempe Iron Walker 36mm or 40mm.

WEMPE
IRON WALKER

Glashütte i/SA | self-winding movement | Certified Chronometer | stainless steel | from $3,170

TIME AND STONES

An original A.H.C.I. member, Vianney Halter had a big year with a new watch called Art Deco Metropolis and a surprising collaboration. The rather ornamental Art Deco Metropolis is his ode to the design movement of the 1920s and uses a variety of materials and textures to achieve his vision—and purposefully break away from the earlier designs of his *Futur Antérieur* era, which his reputation was built upon. Measuring a very wearable 39.8 mm x 8.2 mm, the titanium case with gold rivets protects his automatic Caliber VH122 with patented "mysterious" rotor.

Van der Klaauw semi-retired in 2009, selling his company to designers Daniël and Maria Reintjes, who have carried on in the independent vein to a great deal of niche success, focusing only on the astronomical and adding to the collection with watches like the Real Moon Joure with the most accurate 3D moon phase in the world and 2020's incredible Planetarium Eise Eisinga, which won a prize at the 2021 GPHG.

Christiaan van der Klaauw celebrated its fiftieth anniversary in 2024 with the Grand Planetarium Eccentric Manufacture, which features an astronomical complication that has never been made or seen before in the world of watchmaking: the only mechanical planetarium watch in the world that displays all eight planets of the Solar System, showing the real-time orbits of Mercury, Venus, Earth, Mars, Jupiter, Saturn, Uranus, and Neptune around the sun. It runs on a new in-house-developed CVDK manufacture movement that is exquisitely finished.

Halter's collaboration with Canadian lapidary artist Beauregard was big news at Watches and Wonders 2024: Ulysse is the unexpected product of these two artisans finding mutual vision, and while it feels like the timepiece's name should represent their journey due to its mythological connotations ("Ulysse" is the French name for "Odysseus"), its origins hit much closer to home for Beauregard, who was the adventure's creative lead. "Ulysse being a legendary sailor, the name came to me naturally," Alexandre Beauregard explained. "But perhaps even more importantly, my son is named Ulysse."

1. and 2. Van der Klaauw's wrist-borne solar systems transform time

3. Vianney Halter's timeless Art Deco Metropolis

4. Vianney Halter and Alexandre Beauregard: form + function = beauty

5. Beauregard's delicate dahlia of stone, each cut by hand

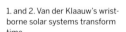

Hong Kong
Watch & Clock Fair
香港鐘表展

SALON de TIME
國 際 名 表 薈 萃

E⁺PLUS

THE WORLD'S PREMIER TIMEPIECE EVENT

2-6 SEP 2025
Hong Kong Convention and
Exhibition Centre

26 AUG-13 SEP 2025
Click2Match (Online)

☎ (852) 1830 668
▢ HKTDC Marketplace

@ exhibitions@hktdc.org
🌐 hkwatchfair.hktdc.com

See More !

1

2

1. and 2. The essence of time: "All wound, the last one kills" inscribed on the Ulysse by Beauregard and Halter

3. Beauregard's prepares the stones, each cut for a perfect fit

This watch is not only Beauregard's first collaboration, but also his first male-oriented timepiece, and it is as unconventional and decorative as every other watch he has created, with its bold dial comprising 68 delicately hued yet perfectly pure hand-cut aquamarines. They are first press-fit in gold latticework only 0.3 mm in thickness and then cemented to mother-of-pearl on the back, which shimmers through the opaque stones. The hands, which recall Beauregard's introductory Dahlia tourbillon, are among the most complicated elements of the watch, involving 24 individual components that Halter assembled with great care since there

is only 0.2 mm space between the dial and the sapphire crystal covering it.

Halter contributed the technology to the ten-piece limited edition in the form of his automatic Caliber U30A, first seen in his Anniversary piece of 2018, which boasts a signature transparent mystery rotor so we can see the beauty of the mechanics, including 30 transparent bearing jewels (synthetic corundum instead of the more typical ruby); beautifully polished and decorated German silver plates and bridges; and an exceptional degree of finishing and beveling aesthetics that must satisfy Beauregard's aesthetic eye.

3

THE MOST AMERICAN MADE WATCH AT SCALE

INSPIRED BY WORLD WAR II HISTORY

1

2

1. – 4. On the race to ultimate thinness, the current champion is the ThinKing by Konstantin Chaykin, which clocks in at 1.65 millimeters

THE RUSSIAN GENIUS

And even though the Beauregard x Vianney Halter launch in April was unexpected, A.H.C.I. member, inventor, and the only Russian watchmaker in the group, Konstantin Chaykin, managed to top the surprise by introducing the ThinKing timepiece prototype in August. This is the thinnest mechanical wristwatch in the world, coming in at just 1.65 mm.

Despite its paper-thin profile, it is bursting with innovations such as an ultra-thin winding barrel with no covers, which sees the winding mechanism directly integrated into the barrel arbor, allowing the inclusion of a functional mainspring in an exceptionally slim space without compromising stability. Another is a double balance wheel, a first in ultra-thin watches. It comes in an ultra-hard stainless-steel case with ultra-light design and feels almost like a piece of paper, weighing just 13.3 grams without the strap. Finally, its special strap includes flexible titanium supports and elastic inserts that absorb shocks and reduce stress on the watch case, enhancing durability while maintaining the watch's ultra-thin profile.

Creativity is alive and very well in the world of independent watchmakers!

Elizabeth Doerr is a freelance journalist specialized in watches and was senior editor of *Wristwatch Annual* until the 2010 edition.

3

4

CLAUDE MEYLAN

VALLÉE DE JOUX

sculpteur du temps

Tortue de Joux

With its pure and timeless curves associated with a proven mechanical, "Tortue de Joux" introduces a new sculpture of time.

THE SOUND OF TIME

BY MARTON RADKAI

On the surface, we human beings rely primarily on our eyes to go about our daily business. But our other senses, notably our ears, pick up subtle cues that we silently process, sometimes even to survive. This is the charm of the repeater watches, a summit in horology not every brand can climb.

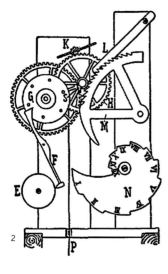

In 2019, Moser & Cie. released a remarkable watch in its curious Swiss Alp line: an 11-millimeter slim, rectangular platinum case, a deep black dial giving pride of place to a flying tourbillon. No hands, no logo, and a six-figure price tag. The company, known for occasionally creating bold tongue-in-cheek pieces, like the "cheese watch," was once again gently poking fun at the eminently fashionable digital wrist technology. The only way to read time on this watch was to push the slider on the side and listen to chimes.

When it comes to complications, chimers (see mini glossary) are considered by many to be the absolute apex of *haute horlogerie*. At their core, all they do is repeat for the ear what is on the dial. Technically, however, they represent an enormous challenge, and as with every complication they are the product of centuries of imagination, inspiration, competition, trial and error, persistence, and sheer skill.

FROM BELL TO GONG

One milestone in the development of the wristwatch was a large, unwieldy contraption built by smithies, bellmakers, and carpenters for church spires. Research suggests that the first repeater dates to 1283, when a clock with a bell (*clocca* in Latin) was installed in the priory of Dunstable, England. Financing for the machine came from the Catholic

Church, which was eager to use this new technology, not to give people the time of day free of charge, but rather to remind them of their canonical duties.

That mechanism inspired generations of inventors, physicists, savant-tinkerers, and, at some point, bona-fide watchmakers. The pocket watch repeater mechanism was invented some time in the seventeenth century as a way to read time in the dark. It was then perfected by Daniel Quare (1647–1724) and, separately, by Edward Barlow (1639–1719). The system was based on a snail-shaped part with twelve segments connected to the hour gear. As it rotates, it passes that information by way of a cam to a toothed rack, which in turn will set off the chiming mechanism. The 12 o'clock snail segment is on the inside of the spiral, meaning the cam has a longer path to follow,

1. Parmigiani's L'Armoriale Répétition Mystérieuse on its special sounding box

2. Edward Barlow's repeater: the rack (M) drops and is stopped by the hour snail cam (N)

3. The four-branched minute repeater cam (from Chopard)

4. Daniel Quare's quarter repeater mechanism (lower segment)

4

1. and 2. The long gongs of the Jaeger Lecoultre Caliber 950 (left), trebuchet hammer on the Speake Marin on the Minute Repeater Carillon (right)

3. Chopard's "stacked-up" minute repeating mechanism

4. Pocket watch with multiple complications including a minute repeater (late nineteenth century)

5. – 7. Parmigiani's L'Armoriale Répétition Mystérieuse: Doric columns (the inspiration for the Doric case), rippling guilloché, classical decorations

8. and 9. The Armoriale's clock side (top) and a look behind the dial (bottom)

so the rack's teeth will trigger the hammer twelve times. After that, the system resets to 1 o'clock so the cam is then indexed on the widest segment of the snail and travels a shorter distance, so when the cam pushes the rack, it will move just enough for one hammer blow on the bell. Quare and Barlow also added a mechanism to shut down the repeater so it did not ring through the night.

Other watchmakers picked up on this rudimentary idea and expanded it to repeat quarter hours and then minutes. The repetition à toc allowed the user to mute the ringing, while still feeling the shocks of the hammers. A century after Quare, Abraham-Louis Breguet improved on the cumbersome bells by using long coils discreetly positioned inside the case. It was a major step towards miniaturization and it ultimately led to the first repeater wristwatch in 1892. It was built by Audemars Piguet for Louis Brandt & Frère, which later became Omega.

CHAMPIONS' LEAGUE

Centuries later, the rudimentary snail and rack system has evolved into a hardly recognizable jumble of cams, wheels, racks, springs, gongs, and hammers that have to be assembled inside a watch case. The enormous development in tools and engineering has allowed brands to not only miniaturize, but also to combine repeaters with other high complications, like a tourbillon, chronograph, or GMT. And the simple chimes have also evolved greatly to include up to four gongs.

The technical advances haven't made building minute repeaters any easier, because those who create watches consider "complication"

a really positive word. And since fitting this mechanism into a movement like some chimera is difficult when using off-the-shelf calibers, many companies design and build dedicated calibers, like the massive JLC 950 used in the Master Grande Tourbillon, for instance. Patek Philippe should also be mentioned as the company that revived the repeater wristwatch in 1989.

The challenges do not stop at assembling hundreds of parts. Because the human ear is in many ways more sensitive than the eye, the gongs must be perfectly tuned. Bulgari even used the famous and strange tritone interval (diminished fifth). Furthermore, a special regulator must ensure that the hammer blows are perfectly even and do not lag on the gongs to ensure a clear sound. The quality of the sound, loudness, and timbre, are determined by a host of factors, like the material used for the gongs and the case. And like one of those heaven/hell jokes, the watchmaker will only find out if all these factors are functional once the watch has been assembled. Needless to say, the aesthetics must also be considered.

What follows is only a small selection of these special watches that truly test the skills and patience of watchmakers.

5 6

PARMIGIANI: SIGHT AND SOUND

The **Armoriale Répétition Mystérieuse** is the latest minute repeater by Parmigiani. It was released on December 2, 2024, on the birthday of founder Michel Parmigiani and is part of the Objets d'Art collection. This model is special for a holistic blending of sound and visuals. Let me explain.

Comfortably mounted in the classic Parmigiani notched white-gold case inspired by Doric columns, the dial of this striking watch—in every sense of the term—does not have hands. Instead, it consists of a complex guilloché with crisscrossing lines that radiate from a central circle with an antique design borrowed from the Palazzo del Te in Mantua, Italy. The guilloché is covered in a green Grand Feu enamel that recalls the clear water of a mountain lake. Gazing at it when time is rung out by pressing the slider, it's as if the vibrations were causing the surface of that lake to ripple.

What enhances the impact is the unusually rich sonority produced by the cathedral gongs. These are extra long and need to be carefully wrapped around the movement, allowing the sound to linger for a while once the hammers have done their job. And you don't have to wear this watch to hear it, since it comes with a specially designed resonating box.

For reading and setting time, the Armoriale Répétition Mystérieuse has a special watch face on the back. Through the sapphire crystal shines a white Guatemalan jade disk engraved with a regular guilloché. Peeking out along the rim of the disk are a gold "M" and "H."

SECRETS

What you don't see is the very complex hand-wound movement built of 392 parts by the famous atelier Renaud et Papi (APRP). Nor can you see 2nd century BCE secret formula behind the calm, dare one say perfect, proportions of this watch. They derive from Michel Parmigiani's long-time infatuation with the Fibonacci sequence, which was known in India in the 2nd century BCE, and emerged in Europe in the 13th century thanks to the brilliant mathematician Leonardo Bonacci (known as Fibonacci, a shortening of "son of Bonacci"). On the surface, it seems merely like a game with numbers, whereby one adds the last two numbers in a series: $1+1=2$; $2+3=5$; $3+5=8$, etc. This sequence, as it turns out, is like an algorithm of nature. One sees it expressed in the arrangement of flower petals, the shape of seashells, the seedheads of sunflowers, and the scales of pinecones. It is so ubiquitous in the Jura Mountains and the true inspiration of the guilloché on the Armoriale dial. These numbers, when divided in pairs, also deliver the Golden Ratio, that proportion that seems most pleasing to the human eye.

POWER CHIMES

In addition to a wholesome timbre and harmony, makers of minute repeaters go to great lengths to develop innovative ways to amplify the sound of their gongs. The fundamental idea is always to add a resonating soundboard.

MASTERS OF SOUND: PATEK PHILIPPE

In 1989, Patek Philippe revived the idea of a minute repeater in a watch and has meanwhile become quite the specialist for this complication—one thinks of such extraordinary creations as the **Grandmaster Chime** of 2014, which added an alarm function to the repeater, plus many other complications. At some point, Patek Philippe's Advanced Research Department, which had been created to work on materials and mechanisms, went to work on amplifying repeaters. They collaborated with, among others, the eminent Federal Institute of Technology in Lausanne and produced the fortissimo "ff" amplifier module in 2021. It consists of a sapphire wafer fit on the underside of the caliber and insulated from the movement by a composite ring. A sound lever shaped like a tuning fork transmits the vibrations to the wafer and spreads throughout the case. Four slits with anti-dust protection located at the cardinal points of the watch let out the sound. This revolutionary mechanism was first used in the **Ref. 5750 "Advanced Research,"** which was presented in 2021.

ULTIMATE AMPLIFICATION: AUDEMARS PIGUET

Marketing these days is often boosted by overtaxed exclamation marks and use of the word "innovative." Audemars Piguet has a history with minute repeaters, having been the first to manufacture repeater wristwatches at the end of the nineteenth century, when wristwatches were not yet fashionable. In 2015, AP, as it is known familiarly, really did bring a novelty to the table at the SIHH with the Royal Oak Concept RD#1. That watch introduced the Supersonnerie, the product of eight years of research together with EPFL in Lausanne and some musicians. The central element was a copper alloy soundboard to which the gongs were fastened rather than to the mainplate. This permits a longer and stronger sound. The key part of the striking mechanism, the regulator, was also reengineered to work silently and to strike the time without interruption. Finally, the problem of skin dampening the sound was overcome by cutting slits into the back of the case.

The Supersonnerie has continued evolving slightly and has appeared in a number of Audemars Piguet models, like the **Royal Oak Supersonnerie** (2021), the **Code 11.59 trilogy Grande Sonnerie Carillon Supersonnerie**, and the **Code 11.59 Ultra-Complication Universelle (RD#4)**, which won the highest prize of the GPHG, the Aiguille D'Or, in 2023.

1. and 3. Patek Philippe's minute repeater with the "fortissimo" module for better sounds

2. The Grandmaster Chime, with twenty complications

4. – 6. Audemars Piguet's Code 11.59 Grande Sonnerie Carillon Supersonnerie (top) with flinqué enamel by Anita Porchet and guilloché expert Yann Von Kaenel; and the Ultra-Complication Universelle RD #4 (bottom)

SIGHT AND SOUND: ULYSSE NARDIN

Ulysse Nardin has always skirted the modern techno-yet-steampunkish design world. But chiming watches with automatons have also appeared regularly among the collections. In 2021, it unveiled its **Blast Hourstriker**, a tourbillon-regulated model with, as the name suggests, grande sonnerie that rings half-hours as well. It has a silencing mechanism, which is a good idea because the chiming is quite loud. To achieve this, Ulysse Nardin approached Devialet, a high-end maker of speakers from France, to develop some way to amplify the sound of the watch. As with the Patek Philippe mentioned above, the basis was a hair-thin membrane made of titanium. It is connected by a spring-like lever to the gongs allowing for maximum vibration. Completing the system is a second cover on the back with chevron slits for the sound. A pusher at 10 o'clock activates the chiming mechanism so the user can observe the hammers, the hour rack, and the regulator in motion on the dial.

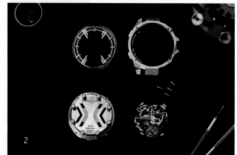

1. – 3. Ulysse Nardin's Blast Hourstriker: a caliber with an amplifier

4. – 6. Chopard's Full Strike uses the sapphire crystal as a sounding element

CRYSTALLINE CLARITY: CHOPARD

In 2017, the Aiguille d'Or was awarded to the Genevan luxury brand Chopard for the **L.U.C Full Strike** timepiece. It's a thin watch, considering the complication, at just 11.55 millimeters thick with an especially intense repeater. Rather than integrate some resonating membrane, the designers experimented with letting the sound come out on the dial side thanks to a remarkable idea that required thousands of hours of work to get just right: the gongs and the sapphire crystal are machined from a single block. This material has not only excellent acoustic properties, but due to its hardness, the sound coming from the gongs is perfectly uniform.

The Full Strike mechanism—which has since appeared in other cases—has two other clever solutions to improve the acoustic experience. First, there is the silent governor that controls the strikes. The second is the stacking up of the racks for the hours, minutes, and quarter hours, so that there is no interruption between the different chimes. It also means the listener has to count quickly.

BIVER

No one in the industry believed that Jean-Claude Biver, the genius of guerilla advertising in horology who turned Hublot into an international sensation, would really retire to a life of making cheese. As many suspected he would do, he founded his own brand. And not surprisingly, his two first launches were minute repeaters. The **Catharsis**, a name that might reflect his feeling about abandoning life in the rough and tumble of business, is a titanium minute repeater with no hands on the dial. Instead, it shows in naive style, a sea of invisibly set, unevenly cut sapphires that give the impression of moving water, a sky spangled with opal stars, and a meteorite moon showing the Widmanstätten pattern. The open case back reveals the movement and a single serpentine hours hand of blue steel to assist in setting the time.

The second model, **Carillon Tourbillon**, has a mysterious, obsidian guilloché dial. It was the first in a series with stone or mother-of-pearl dials, all simple and effective, not what one might have expected from Jean-Claude Biver. The indices are baguette-cut diamonds.

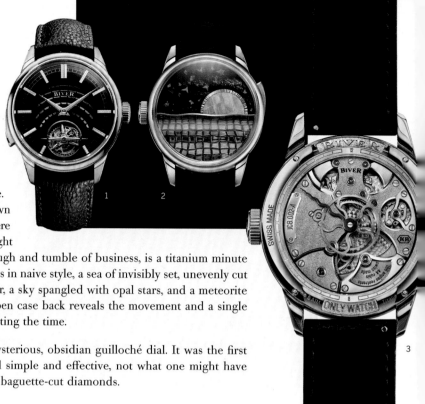

MORE IS EVEN MORE: FRANCK MULLER

In 2009, Franck Muller released the **Aeternitas Mega 4**, a watch that was created to make its way into the annals of horological history as the most complicated wristwatch ever built. A total of 1,438 components are packed into the generously proportioned 61 mm x 42 mm x 23.05 mm platinum case.

The automatic caliber alone measures 40.8 mm x 33.8 mm. It drives thirty-six complications for up to ninety-six hours at 21,600 vph. Twenty-two indications are visible on the dial depending on how one counts. They drive, among others, a stop-seconds chronograph with a monopusher; a dual time function; perpetual calendar; a retrograde date; displays for day, month, year, and leap year; an equation of time; a moon phase; and a one-minute flying tourbillon.

The chiming functions, however, are the acoustic cherry on top of all this. They are led by a remarkable Westminster carillon on four gongs and a programmable grande and petite sonnerie, which are controlled by pushers that show the status on the dial (at about 10:30 and 1:30). This function can be silenced as well.

1. – 3. Jean-Claude Biver's coming-out: The Carillon Tourbillon (left) and his first-born, the Catharsis, (right and bottom)

4. – 6. Franck Muller's mind-blowing Aeternitas Mega 4: Thirty-six complications including a Westminster carillon

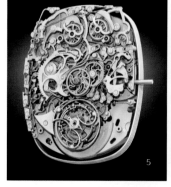

AVANTGARДE

EMOTION • INNOVATION • PROVOCATION

Babylonian Hand winding. Hand engraved movement. Three levels open dial with MOP ring. Blued hands. Stainless steel. 5 ATM. 500 pcs limited Edition.

BULGARI: RINGING IN STYLE

Some time around 2012, Bulgari was raising eyebrows by making watches that were getting thinner by the year. The collection was appropriately named **Octo Finissimo**, and since watchmakers have to make things complicated, they made one with a tourbillon, and soon another with a minute repeater. It was a mere 6.85 millimeters thick. While many brands have invested a great deal in amplifying the sound, Bulgari took a logical shortcut. First, the case was made of brushed titanium, one of the top metals for resonance. Second, they cut very elegant slits in the dial to give the sound space to amplify itself under the sapphire crystal. It all looks simple, but it took years to conceive, prototype, and then build.

GONGS FOR THE PEOPLE: CHRISTOPHER WARD

Those who always wanted a minute repeater but could simply not afford one were pleasantly surprised in November 2022 when the British company Christopher Ward released its **C1 Bel Canto**. It is a *sonnerie au passage*, meaning it rings at the top of the hour, so it is not quite so complicated a repeater, but at least it makes a nice sound. Plus, the design is attractive to those who seek a talking piece. The actual chiming mechanism is visible on a three-dimensionally conceived dial that comes with different background colors. And the price tag is just over $4,000, putting it within range of most any real watch fan.

How did Christopher Ward do it? First, they used a robust off-the-shelf Sellita SW200-1 caliber. They reworked an existing jumping hour module, which is designed to store and then release energy, and used it to power the hammer striking the gong. They also were able to lower costs by only doing perfect finishing on the visible elements of the dial. In fact, finding the right gong was one of the more trying tasks. The work and careful calculations paid off. In 2023, the C1 Bel Canto won the Petite Aiguille Prize at the GPHG for watches between 2,000 and 8,000 Swiss francs.

NEW KIDS ON THE BLOCK: LUCKY HARVEY

To close this incomplete list: a blast from the East. No one can deny the energy of the Chinese watch industry (see *Wristwatch Annual 2024*). Its brands are young, often daring and enthusiastic beyond reason, and backed by a large and very effective industrial machine. It was only a matter of time before Lucky Harvey, founded in 2021 in Guangzhou by Lin Xiaolin, a man with an outspoken passion for watches, produced a chiming watch using an in-house movement. The first is a *sonnerie au passage* that comes with an elegant guilloché dial in various colors and features a silencing mechanism with an indicator on the dial (it costs $1,199). It also has a large date. The second slightly more expensive offering celebrates 2025, the Year of the Snake. Cleverly, the gong curls over the guilloché dial as if it were an extension of the very prominent snake that occupies much of the space. A surprise awaits the beholder: when the watch chimes, the snake sticks out its tongue. Indeed, Lucky Harvey is a new brand, but their genetic make-up already contains a lot of humor. And at $1,999, who can complain?

1. and 2. Sheer elegance: Bulgari combined strong sound with the thin Octo Finissimo case

3. – 6. Christopher Ward's affordable C1 Bel Canto shows its petite sonnerie up front

7. and 8. Lucky Harvey's first chiming watch (left), with bold guilloché; for the Year of the Snake, the serpent on the dial rings the hour in passing (right)

T9 & T9-01 UFO
AUTOMATIC TOURBILLON

Imagined in space. Made in Japan.

ZEROO TIME Co.
Tokyo Japan

MING

37.09 BLUEFIN

WWW.MING.WATCH

GPHG
GRAND PRIX D'HORLOGERIE DE GENÈVE
— 2024 —
SPORTS
WATCH PRIZE

WATCH FACES

BY MARTON RADKAI

The world of watchmaking is reminiscent of an immense tableau that might have been painted by a coalition of artists, from the Brueghels and Jacques-Louis David, to René Magritte and Salvador Dalí. We often see the finished product, but it's good to meet the people who have their "hands in the dough," to use a French expression.

THE DREAMER

When romancing the watch, you will often hear marketers talking airily about "tradition." One figure occasionally mentioned in the great myths of horology in Switzerland is the *paysan-horloger*, the peasant watchmaker. In the narrative, this figure, a kind of Johnny Appleseed, lives in a big farmhouse in the Jura Mountains. He tends to flocks and meager fields in the warm season, and in winter turns to that special window sill where the southern sun pours in, and makes tiny wheels, hands, crowns, cases, cams, springs,

dials, and even straps that are then assembled and ferried to the elites as *accessoires* to their embroidered waistcoats, fluffy jabots, pannier dresses, and lacy petticoats.

It's a wonderfully poetic image, a fairytale of sorts, long gone with the arrival of electricity, central heating, and the factory floor. Thanks to the engraver Ismael Nikles (see *Wristwatch Annual 2024*), though, I found one. His name is Frédéric "Fredy" Jourdain and he is mostly unknown, and apparently happily so. He gave up his sheep and horses a while ago, but he still makes watches and clocks in his farmhouse just outside Tramelan, a town of about 5,000, lying at 1016 meters in the Jura Mountains above Neuchâtel.

We meet on an icy day. His home is simple yet cozy, with a wood stove in the kitchen that warms the house thanks to a modern heat pump. The furnishings are understated and practical. Witnesses to his life are spread liberally on walls, shelves, and table tops: large quartz clocks, a few books, statuettes and drawings from Africa—his companion is from Togo. A poster advertises a younger Fredy Jourdain sporting a beard with a woolly sheep with the announcement: "The Jourdains' dairy sheep."

We sit in his living room with Ismael Nikles, tearing at a fluffy *panettone* with our hands, drinking coffee, chatting about unsettling world news, about Tramelan and how it used to have over a hundred companies involved in watchmaking. A few cross-country skiers slice by outside the window. On the edge of the table is a do-it-yourself clock made of wood

1. and 2. The real thing: Frédéric Jourdain, watchmaker (top), at work and as a sheep farmer in younger years (bottom)

3. The purist: Jourdain with his detent escapement for a table clock

1. and 2. The wooden table clock tourbillon Jourdain assembled and fixed (left); the tinkerer's table (right)

3. and 4. Jourdain's freewheeling watchmaking begins with a drawing on paper

that he finds funny. "Someone sent it to me, I assembled," he says casually. "It didn't work well, so I fixed it." That is the gift of experience.

Getting him to talk about himself and his life is not easy, though I gather that he also taught at the local vocational institute. This region of Switzerland is still imbued with the spirit of the Anabaptists, who had sought refuge in the remote Jura after being attacked by other churches for their beliefs, notably in a personal relationship with God, in real humility, and in communal living, which might explain the deep sense of solidarity among the local watch-working caste. They are not well-disposed toward the showiness that pervades segments of the industry.

We get around to chatting about his work. For the past twenty years or so—he doesn't quite remember when this began—he has had a single mysterious client. "One day, our local antique dealer showed up with an Italian fellow, who asked me if I could make him some watches and clocks," he recalls. Sometimes this man, whose anonymity Jourdain maintains assiduously, suggested ideas, sometimes Jourdain proposed ideas or had some creation ready to go. The agreement means that Jourdain is free to create his timepieces without any brand constraints. The Italian comes at least once a year, picks up what he requested or what Jourdain has made on his own. Who knows where his clocks and watches are now? Jourdain shrugs.

The atelier is in a neighboring room and faces south, as it should. On his workbench stand two brass table clock mechanisms. One is topped by a large rotating tourbillon. These are current projects. In the middle of the room is a simple table strewn pell-mell with drawings of watches, a few of the typical plastic trays, prototypes, tools. It's a tinkerer's paradise. Two watches lie there, casually. One has a white dial, a 24-hour subdial, and a small seconds dial. The other is far more complicated, with retrograde minutes and hours. The only machine I see is an old lathe. There is no computer. He draws and sketches by hand.

While chatting quietly, Jourdain walks around picking up various constructions, like a perpetual calendar coarsely made of brass, and a *détente* escapement held between transparent plates, both prototypes for a clock. This is where ideas and inspirations begin to take shape. He shows me two plastic female arms taken from a doll that will be worked into a clock. He shows me a plan for an animation featuring a man walking around the earth and laughs.

I ask him what makes a good watch. He gives a no-frills answer. "First, you put everything in place and it runs," he says. "Secondly, it has to run accurately." And what about the movement? "I use Unitas. They are tractors, they are my darlings [*mes chouchous*], because they were made right here in Tramelan," he says, his bright blue eyes smiling. "All movements have their childhood diseases, to be honest," he adds, "but they should have as few as possible." I ask for examples, and he points to the gearwheels that are sometimes not perfectly round. And just in case, he keeps an antique topping tool handy.

SEVEN-DAY CYCLE

 Independent Timepiece Maker | www.itay-noy.com | studio@itay-noy.com

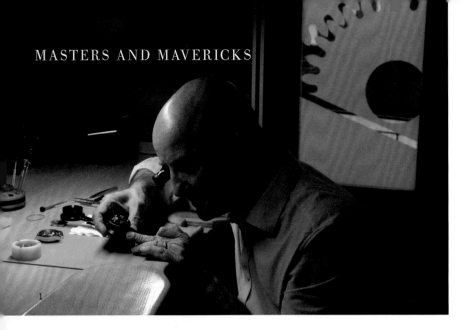

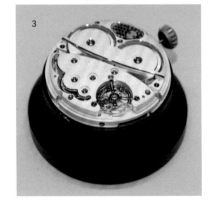

THE ARCHITECT

Some people with a musical gift think in terms of melodies. Others have an unfailing ear for the harmonic sequences underlying those melodies. The composer combines the two. Watchmakers are in some way similar when it comes to aesthetics and mechanics. When Emmanuel Bouchet began considering the life of a creator of timepieces, he wasn't thinking of a dial and hands, "those things from the 1920s and 1930s that have not really evolved," he says with a sightly ironic *moue*, as the French would say. "I was thinking of mechanical systems, and honestly, they would keep me up at night."

Bouchet, who grew up in France and began his career working with his father repairing watches and clocks, first made a splash as the creator of the hyper-complicated Opus 12, released in 2012 by Harry Winston. The first watch he released under his own name, however, was appropriately called the Aleph, the first letter of the Hebrew alphabet. It symbolizes the beginning and Oneness, which is appropriate, since time is at the beginning of all creation and it can be seen as a single dimension humans cut into pieces for convenience.

At first glance, the Aleph looks like one of those modern "machines" with an outsized double escape wheel with inner teeth right in the middle of three subdials. Strangely, though, it only ticks over once every fifteen seconds. "I wanted to make the escapement show the birth of time," says Bouchet. To achieve this effect, he found a clever solution. The pallet fork visible under the central subdial, is controlled by a ruby Reuleaux triangle. This unusual geometric shape looks like a pumped-up equilateral triangle, but it

has the constant width properties of a circle, i.e., the diameter will always be the same, so it provides continuous and equal impulses.

The surprises do not stop there. While the seconds turn smoothly over a day-night disk at 12 o'clock, the subdial at 8 o'clock delivers jumping hours. But the one at 4 o'clock demands more attention: the shorter jumping hand indicates ten-minute increments, so when it reaches 5, its next single step is back to 0. The longer hand is for the minutes. In other words, you have to read it like a digital clock that tells you exactly where you stand now in the continuity of time, not how much time you either have left or have used up. It's really saying *carpe diem*!

What looks simple is mechanically very complex: the system needs two barrel springs, one to drive the gear train to the pallet fork, while the other drives the slow escapement on the dial, including the Reuleaux triangle and maintains the tension of the system.

Bouchet is a man of deep faith and it might well be this that guides his awe of time itself as the invisible ghost in the cosmological machine. When he speaks of his mechanisms, he becomes visibly animated and his speech accelerates as he tries to explain how all the disparate parts of the Aleph actually fit together as one concept.

By the same token, his extensive experience has given him an unerring eye for detail. This talent landed him a job at the complications department of Jaeger-LeCoultre at 21. "When I see a technical blueprint, I immediately see the errors," he tells me, apologizing for what sounds like boasting. Later, as I am leaving, one of his employees confirms this ability, remembering when his boss looked at a movement that wasn't working perfectly, found the problem, did some filing, and all was well. It's the kind of cellular knowledge that transcends mere engineering. He is like one of those divine virtuosos who become their instrument.

1. Emmanuel Bouchet: an ecstatic watchmaker who dreams his mechanisms

2. and 3. The meticulously crafted Aleph shows time passing in slow motion

4. – 6. The Reuleaux Triangle with mysterious fractals (image by Paul Bourke) (top left); guiding the pallet fork (right), and cut from different materials for a unique look (bottom left)

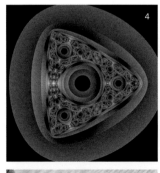

PILO & C°
GENÈVE

CORLEONE SUPERLEGGERA

WE BUILD THE WATCHES
YOU DREAM OF

www.pilo-watches.com

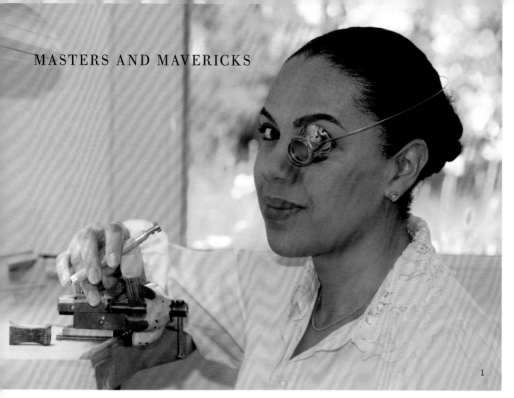

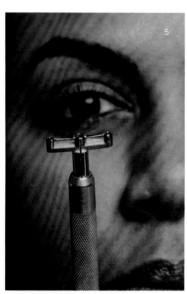

1. – 3. Nathalie Jean-Louis, artist at heart and in deed, breathes life into tiny components (©Stefan Beyler Deutor, left; ©Simon Brette, right)

4. Jean-Louis's art looks free but is very deliberate

5. The beveler's guiding tool (©Stefan Beyler Deutor)

6. Jean-Louis uses her art to enliven the tools of the watchmaking trade

THE MIDWIFE

She started out as an artist, and still paints while also beveling bridges, cams, wheels, and other tiny components. Her work is not just technical, it is art in the Aristotelian sense, representing "not the outward appearance of things, but their inward significance; for this is true art, not the external mannerism and detail."

Nathalie Jean-Louis, of Swiss-Martinique parentage, felt the calling of art early on and went to a specialized school. Later, as an adult, when necessity knocked at her door, she found a job at Piaget in La Côte aux Fées. The word "decoration" in the description triggered her imagination. She was put on a CNC machine to do the initial semi-industrial beveling. But from there, she gazed at the women on the other side of the room using their hand-guided files, microscopes, and machines to polish edges. "I really felt like doing that," she recalls, "and when I feel the impulse, I do whatever I can to reach my goal."

During the next three years she learned everything about *anglage*, both the techniques, like outward and inward beveling, and the reasons for them. In the process, she heard that some were doing this entirely by hand. "That was the Holy Grail in decoration, and I had the great luck to get hired by Greubel Forsey," she remembers. "It nourished my artistic side, my love of challenges, my perfectionism as well," she tells me. And then, in 2011, she took a big step towards another childhood dream by going freelance.

It gave her time to get back to her creative roots. Her artwork is effusive, abstract, and pop. She does jewelry, and even opened a

sideline putting lots of color in the monochrome tools of the watchmaker's trade. I wonder aloud if the highly focused filing gestures are contradictory or complementary. "What looks very free brush is in fact done very deliberately," she responds. And while she is speaking, I suddenly think of Michelangelo's famous *Creation of Adam*, in particular the section with the two hands. As I mention this, she tells me that the Renaissance was her favorite period, notably Carravagio, the master of *chiaroscuro*. "Over time, I realized that there are similarities between the chiaroscuro in Italian painting and the play of light in a watch."

Nathalie Jean-Louis's strict training has drawn major brands as clients. Over the years, improvements in machining have made the work easier, but the human hand is still a requirement for the best results. "With regards to the technical plans, the watches will be terrific, but you will see the traces of machining and that creates no emotion," she points out. "Our work is to give life to the movement. We will transport our energy and our know-how through our hands, and we will embellish the timepieces, magnify them, modify them, create polished and matt surfaces, contrasts."

The watchmaker makes watches with a beating heart, and Nathalie Jean-Louis and the collective of decorating midwives give it the breath that makes each of them speak to us in a unique language.

6

YOUR WATCH, YOUR TRIBE

BY MARTON RADKAI

The primary function of a watch is to coordinate our activities during available time. The other, however, is to signal, maybe unconsciously, something about our persona, our strivings, our lifestyle wish list, even, at times, our alter ego.

1. Pilots' watches seduce real and secret flyers (here is IWC's Mark XVIII)

2. and 3. TAG Heuer's Autavia wristwatches (left) and vintage dash clocks (right) are catnip for car fans

4. Death-defiers: Bomberg's bracelet of skulls

The relationship between consumers and the goods they buy is complex. The objects, accessories, or clothing we acquire, sometimes at great expense, say as much about our relation to the outside world as they do about our inner psychological states, our private self, and how we would like to be seen. Simply put, the extrovert might seek out ostentatious fashions whereas the introvert may try not to be noticed. Yet colorful garb, such as flashy cars and watches, and total understatement both reveal something. This follows from the axioms of communication theory by Paul Watzlawick, the first of which says: "You can't not communicate."

The consumer economy is the great beneficiary of the complex nonverbal dialogue we engage in daily and which is powered by three existential questions: "Who am I?", "Where do I fit in?" and, crucially, "Who is gazing at me?" In his *Being and Nothingness*, Jean-Paul Sartre answered the questions pithily: "We are ourselves only in the eyes of others, and it is through the eyes of others that we assume ourselves as ourselves." Myriad businesses are prepared to help ease the relationship between ourselves and others and shape our individuality, from hairdressers to fashion designers, from tattoo artists to automakers, and naturally (what concerns us here), watchmakers. All these enterprises, service or manufacturing, turn the utilitarian and necessary into a key element of our agency.

UNDER YOUR SLEEVE

Generally speaking, most watch brands are eager to connect their product to a lifestyle, real or desired. Their target group, to use a coarse marketing word, is often revealed in their taglines and slogans, which, in order to be effective, should actually harmonize in some way with the look of the product. For example, guess which brand says "A Crown for Every Achievement" and has become a symbol of success? Why, that would be Rolex. Or take Patek Philippe, essentially a family-owned business, whose image is one of stability, discreet wealth, success in business, a person anchored in a generational continuity; they say: "Begin your own tradition."

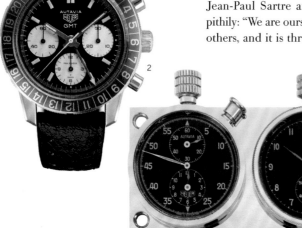

1

The watches appearing in *Wristwatch Annual* do in fact fall into several broad categories of appeal: divers, pilots, military style, the chronograph (with tachymeter), and so forth. They are aimed at the sports fan, the athlete, the car lover, the warrior, the intellectual, the fun-lover, and even the art lover. The many dress watches presented, some of which can intersect with other categories, are the ones collectors might puzzle over before going out to a concert or a dinner, or simply out with friends. They all share one thing in common: they are companions in our daily life and their presence on our wrists is a conscious and sometimes unconscious choice.

COMMUNITY-BUILDING

The brands broadly known as "lifestyle" brands take a different approach. Their watches are purposely made for a particular "tribe" of people who share a particular way of life, or a hobby, for example. Hager Watch (see page 162) founder Pete Brown, for example, is a Freemason and has dedicated one collection to his brother Masons. Some, like the now defunct Jaermann & Stübi, targeted golf players.

Another brand in this category would be Bausele, which stands for Beyond Australian Elements. The brand's founder and CEO, Christophe Hoppé, who goes by the name Christo, was born in Alsace, France. As a watch fan from an early age, he naturally ended up in Switzerland working for, among others, TechnoMarine, but he dreamt of designing watches.

Passion has its own magnetism. He fell in love with an Australian dancer in Geneva and followed her back to Australia. It was

2

3

a revelation. "I was struck by how little the country was represented in the global watch industry despite its incredible natural beauty and lifestyle," he told me in an interview. "My motivation was to combine Swiss craftsmanship with the vibrant, adventurous spirit of Australia and create timepieces that not only tell time but also tell a story about this incredible country."

He launched Bausele in 2011 and now has four main collections, each of which celebrates the continent. The design is always visually simple but with gently modern angles on the cases and bright colors. This tall, wiry man, who walks with a feline gait, is an avid swimmer and does a mile-long lap every morning at Manly Beach near Sydney. In other words, water sports are a core focus of the brand's watches.

The Endless Sunrise and the Infinite Sunset models of the Sydney Diver collection have a bit of sand from the beach in the crown, and the round Oceanmoon collection boasts a crown-activated inner bezel. The more recent Field Good models pay tribute to other Australian sights, like the famous Sydney Opera House and, of course, the orange-red Ayers Rock, known as Uluru by the Aborigines. The crown has some red earth inside. The mission statement of those who join the Bausele Clan is written on the website: "Our watches will not help you become George Clooney or win a Grand Slam, but they can remind you everyday to breathe, focus, invest in yourself and become a better version of who you are. Who that is, is up to you…"

1. Audemars Piguet's Royal Oak series: a Taylor Swift of watch lovers

2. Jaermann & Stübi created the Time to Play for golf players

3. – 5. If you love Australia and the laid-back, sportive lifestyle, join the Bausele clan

4

A PIECE OF WORLD WAR II
HISTORY ON YOUR WRIST

COMING VETERANS DAY 11/11

1. – 3. Chic, relaxed, self-aware, modern: SevenFriday is for the cool crowd of all ages

4. – 6. Gréco's clan meets to dance wherever there is a UV light to reveal the designs of their watches

FRIENDLY TIME

Like Christo Hoppé, Daniel Niederer spent years on the road working for the watch industry. At some point he got the nagging feeling that "something was missing in the world of watches." It might simply have been a sense of humor and an easygoing attitude, but he didn't say specifically.

Back in Zurich, where he lives with his family, he and a friend, Arnaud Duval, launched SevenFriday, a provocative name in the busy world of work or constant self-optimization. Friday is the end of the work week, and seven of them is an admonition to get away from what Niederer curtly calls "bulls**t and a**holes" and go enjoy life, either by doing sports, or going out with the family and friends.

They chose a square case with rounded corners, because, says Dan, "square watches are hard to sell." Time on the dials is delivered by disks driven by a Miyota caliber, which kept the price down. The first models were indeed strange, with a dial embraced by two 3D-printed clamps. After that—it was liked in the Asia–Pacific region, but less in Europe—Dan and Arnaud streamlined the design, keeping the square case, which gave them ample space for the dial disks. The M series released in 2024 is casual sportive and with a more focused dial, thanks to an aperture showing the hours. The M2/05 model is not for those who like to sit around, though, because whenever you look at the time, you're faced with the words "ACTION TALKS, BULLSHIT WALKS."

TRIPPING THE LIGHT

Night owls need watches. Occasionally, at least. Watchmaker Stéphane Gréco has known quite a few of these people. He runs Rhodior near Geneva, which specializes in treating metal surfaces by various processes, like galvanoplasty, rhodium-plating, or chemical coloring. And he has his own brand, Gréco, which makes a renowned hexagonal timepiece, the ultimate in steampunk. The hands of his appropriately named Les Temps Modernes collection (a reference to the Charlie Chaplin movie) are wrenches and they are driven by a solid ETA movement.

Among his many friends and acquaintances, he spotted a target group that was not being properly served by the industry: night owls who go from disco to disco, club to club, or other UV-lit haunts, to commune till the wee hours. Doing a bit of research, he found a fluorescent ink of many colors and, being the expert in such things, invented a process to fix it onto the dials. It was a very expensive product, but he could get free samples online. During the day these watches just tell the time. But give them a dose of ultraviolet light, and they suddenly display complex filigree decorations or drawings in vivid colors. This was around 2001, and his brand found its tribe, even if they need a UV flashlight for daytime demonstrations.

PORSCHE DESIGN

Speed wins races.
Time creates legends.

THE CHRONOGRAPH 1 –
ALL BLACK NUMBERED EDITION.

Worn by Orlando Bloom.
Originally designed by Prof. F. A. Porsche.

#MadeForRacers

Little did he know, however, that he had stumbled on a unique selling point. One day he received a visit from four serious gentlemen, representatives from the European and Swiss Central Banks. They had come to inform him that he could no longer use that terrific ink because it had become a key security feature for the new euro banknotes. He argued that he had gotten it first and that his business depended on it. After some negotiations he was able to make a final purchase of this magic liquid. "I scratched together as much money as I could and bought enough for several generations," he says with a grin. And so, he continued creating surprising dial designs for his tribe.

PARADOX OF COMMUNITY

Fashionable and unique is a contradiction that many brands overcome either by personalization methods, by dazzling taglines, or by making truly unique pieces. Some brands, though, manage to attract individuals who by their very character and lifestyles do not fit into any convenient drawer. They are life polymaths. My friend Michael W. is one: a medium-sized man, limber, clean-shaven, mostly balding, with studious round glasses, and who wears Bermuda shorts and sandals in summer. He paints his fingernails in different colors. His conversation covers many subjects. Major events in his life are boldly tattooed on his body, like the time he was accidentally hit on the head with a two-by-four and suddenly decided he needed a music studio to explore his musical self. He also has a Ph.D. in mathematics from ETH in Zurich, Switzerland's counterpart to MIT.

The watch he wore when we met was thin but large. It had a prominent crown at 12 o'clock and a colorful dial with huge numerals and the lugs sprawled out like a turtle's flippers. It was a Gagà Milano, a brand from Milan, Italy, that was launched twenty years ago by an Italian entrepreneur named Ruben Tomella. The models are inspired by pocket watches and run on a mix of quartz and mechanical movements. They range from the bejeweled Manuale; to the Crystal, made of K9 glass; or the Quirky Tourbillon, for which the company partnered with Hysek. Like them or not, the products are intriguing.

A *gagà*, Cristina Bonetti explained, is a term in the Milanese dialect for a kind of dandy, a man about town who is always chic, yet bold. She went on to describe my friend Michael without knowing him: "A true *gagà* is someone with a taste for the unconventional and the refined, who finds joy in life's details, appreciates artistry, and embodies kindness and charm. It reflects a mindset: seeking beauty in unexpected places, valuing quality over quantity, and standing out not for attention, but as an authentic expression of self."

1. Gréco lights up thanks to exclusive inks used for paper money

2. – 5. Gagà Milano: timepieces for the brash, extroverted, individual, unconventional, and even lighthearted, intellectual people

ARISTO

since 1907

Time and Tradition

www.aristo-watch.de

1. and 2. A double-sided reversible tourbillon by Antoine Preziuso, or a timepiece swamped in precious stone: highest-level bling for the celebrity crowd

3. – 5. Agent-provocateur Chris Long's Azimuth collections telegraph to the industry not to take itself too seriously

6. Charismatic wrist machine: the Volcano by the Chinese company Agelocer

DEAL WITH IT

Gagà Milano attracted some celebrities, naturally. The watches are large, gaudy, and visible. Soccer star Neymar wore one with a big skull on a yellow background, a partnership that was initially serendipitous. Following a different approach, Daniel Lazar, a partner at Jacob & Co., decided in 2004 to directly address the horological needs of celebrities, commercially successful artists, sportspeople, and so forth. He has some imitators, but his unabashed "bling" does fascinate. These huge oval cases dripping with precious stones, especially diamonds, and bulging time-giving objects do say a lot about their buyers and about the zeitgeist, in the spirit of Nero's fiddling while Rome burned. The aesthetics are in the eye of the beholder, but the mechanics cannot be denied. The world of watchmaking, so imbued with Calvinistic self-effacement, might deplore bling as being a touch vulgar, but for the great Antoine Preziuso, for example, making a 65-millimeter behemoth for Jay-Z was just another challenge in extremely *haute horlogerie*. It includes a tourbillon front and rear and Preziuso's signature device to turn the watch over without having to take it off.

It takes a certain courage to wear these "lifestyle" watches. Ask around, and they get anything from a disparaging nod to real anger. At the 2024 Time to Watches show in Geneva, I passed the Azimuth booth along with a friend, a long-time insider of the industry. Founder Chris Long was explaining how his Mr. Roboto had been inspired by old toys. "They are ridiculous," my friend said with genuine disapproval. Maximilian Büsser of MB&F might disagree, as his favorite quote is "The creative adult is a child who has survived."

I couldn't help but think of the nineteenth-century music critic Eduard Hanslick who lambasted the emotional, disruptive creations of the likes of Hector Berlioz and Franz Liszt as "not serious." If the industry wants to really be "disruptive," as its marketers often tell us, it might have to take a less judgmental

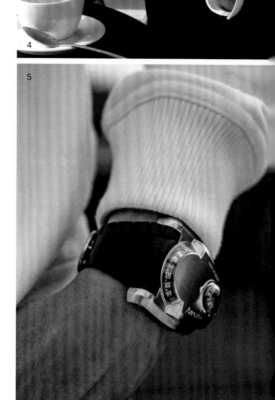

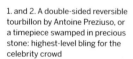

look at these gentle iconoclasts before they are actually at the gates with their entertaining creations. Many of them, like Chris Long, are from Asia, where watchmaking, I have found out during my annual visit to the Hong Kong Watch and Clock Fair, is youthfully exuberant and unconstrained, and where, thanks to a powerful industrial machine, prices are affordable. They may have caught on to something vital for an industry struggling to address younger generations. Society is tribal, and people young and old want something that will speak to them besides that monolithic rectangle that keeps them tethered to data miners.

ACCUTRON

Well before quartz regulators blew up the watch market, engineers were tinkering with the idea of building an electric watch. There is some debate as two who succeeded first, but it was probably the Elgin 725, a collaboration with the French company Lip, that was the first. It had a traditional mechanical movement with a button cell battery-run mechanism. It failed to thrill the market, however. But it did get another company, Bulova Watch Company, interested in the technology. Over the next few years, with the aid of a Swiss engineer named Max Hetzel, the company came up with a clever system using a tiny 360 Hertz tuning fork and a transistor. The Accutron, a combination of the terms accurate and electronic, was unveiled in 1960 as the world's first fully electronic watch. It was an instant success and even attracted NASA among others.

In 2020, Accutron was relaunched as a separate brand with its iconic Spaceview design. The company's design and engineering team based in Tokyo reworked the engine and the design to create a brand-new proprietary electrostatic energy movement. It is run by twin turbines that rotate very fast between two electrodes using the wearer's movements. The energy, stored in an accumulator, powers two motors. One drives the sweep-second hand, and a step motor powers the hour and minute hands. Both motors are synchronized through integrated circuits to provide accuracy to +/- 5 seconds a month.

Accutron decided to steer close to the original when it comes to design. Fans will easily recognize the cherished dial-less model with its green accents. As for the Spaceview, it was in its time a landmark achievement, with its case stripped down to expose the unique tuning fork movement. Accutron also features automatic timepieces inspired from the brand's most iconic historical timepieces.

ACCUTRON C/O CITIZEN WATCH AMERICA
Empire State Building
350 Fifth Avenue, 29th Floor
New York, NY 10118

WEBSITE:
https://www.accutronwatch.com

FOUNDED:
1960 (relaunched in 2020)

DISTRIBUTION:
Accutron
customercare@accutronwatch.com
866-419-84-63

MOST IMPORTANT COLLECTIONS/PRICE RANGE:
Spaceview 2020, Spaceview Evolution and Accutron DNA / $3,500 to $5,000; Astronaut / $3,500; Legacy / $1,290 to $1,600

DNA Casino
Reference number: 28A205
Movement: Accutron caliber NS30; quartz resonator with dual stepper motor and electrostatic drive system for the hands; ø 36 mm, height 6.48 mm; 28 jewels
Functions: hours, minutes, sweep seconds
Case: stainless steel, ø 45.1 mm, height 15.6 mm; sapphire crystal; water-resistant to 5 atm
Band: rubber, double folding clasp
Price: $3,500; limited edition of 100 pieces

DNA Casino
Reference number: 28A206
Movement: Accutron caliber NS30; quartz resonator with dual stepper motor and electrostatic drive system for the hands; ø 36 mm, height 6.48 mm; 28 jewels
Functions: hours, minutes, sweep seconds
Case: stainless steel, ø 45.1 mm, height 15.6 mm; sapphire crystal; water-resistant to 5 atm
Band: rubber, double folding clasp
Price: $3,500; limited edition of 100 pieces

DNA Casino
Reference number: 28A207
Movement: Accutron caliber NS30; quartz resonator with dual stepper motor and electrostatic drive system for the hands; ø 36 mm, height 6.48 mm; 28 jewels
Functions: hours, minutes, sweep seconds
Case: stainless steel, ø 45.1 mm, height 15.6 mm; sapphire crystal; water-resistant to 5 atm
Band: rubber, double folding clasp
Price: $3,500; limited edition of 100 pieces

DNA Casino

Reference number: 28A208
Movement: Accutron caliber NS30; quartz resonator with dual stepper motor and electrostatic drive system for the hands; ø 36 mm, height 6.48 mm; 28 jewels
Functions: hours, minutes, sweep seconds
Case: stainless steel, ø 45.1 mm, height 15.6 mm; sapphire crystal; water-resistant to 5 atm
Band: rubber, double folding clasp
Price: $3,500; limited edition of 100 pieces

Spaceview Evolution

Reference number: 26A209
Movement: Accutron caliber NS30; quartz resonator with dual stepper motor and electrostatic drive system for the hands; ø 36 mm, height 6.48 mm; 28 jewels
Functions: hours, minutes, sweep seconds
Case: stainless steel, ø 43.5 mm, height 15.9 mm; sapphire crystal; water-resistant to 5 atm
Band: reptile skin, double folding clasp
Price: $3,950

Spaceview Evolution

Reference number: 26A210
Movement: Accutron caliber NS30; quartz resonator with dual stepper motor and electrostatic drive system for the hands; ø 36 mm, height 6.48 mm; 28 jewels
Functions: hours, minutes, sweep seconds
Case: stainless steel, ø 43.5 mm, height 15.9 mm; sapphire crystal; water-resistant to 5 atm
Band: reptile skin, double folding clasp
Price: $3,950

Astronaut

Reference number: 2SW8A002
Movement: automatic, Sellita caliber SW330, ø 26.20 mm, height 4.10 mm; 25 jewels; 28,800 vph; 56-hour power reserve
Functions: hours, minutes, sweep seconds; second time zone with GMT hand
Case: stainless steel, ø 41 mm, height 13.85 mm; sapphire crystal; partial transparent case back; water-resistant to 10 atm
Band: stainless steel, double folding clasp
Remarks: the Astronaut "T" design first launched in 1968 features a distinctive day/night bezel.
Price: $3,500; limited to 300 numbered pieces

Legacy x Le Kool

Reference number: 2SW6A002LK
Movement: automatic, Sellita caliber SW200-1, ø 25.60 mm, height 4.6 mm; 26 jewels; 28,800 vph; 42-hour power reserve
Functions: hours, minutes, sweep seconds
Case: stainless steel, ø 34 mm, height 12.6 mm; Football Cross Hatch case design; sapphire crystal; partially transparent case back; water-resistant to 3 atm
Band: metallic leather, pin buckle
Remarks: "565" known as the Football Cross Hatch watch in 1966
Price: $1,550
Variations: comes with two extra black and gold metallic leather straps

Legacy x Le Kool

Reference number: 2SW7A004LK
Movement: automatic, Sellita caliber SW200-1, ø 25.60 mm, height 4.6 mm; 26 jewels; 28,800 vph; 42-hour power reserve
Functions: hours, minutes, sweep seconds
Case: gold-tone stainless steel, ø 34 mm, height 12.6 mm; crown placement at 4 o'clock; sapphire crystal; partial transparent case back; water-resistant to 3 atm
Band: metallic leather, pin buckle
Remarks: historical "412" case design, the original case design for Accutron's iconic Spaceview
Price: $1,600
Variations: comes with two extra black and bronze metallic leather straps

A. LANGE & SÖHNE

A. Lange & Söhne exemplifies the steady, careful, and effective way Germans tend to develop their businesses, in particular family-run ones. Walter Lange, who died in January 2017, actually re-registered the brand A. Lange & Söhne in its old hometown of Glashütte. He did so on December 7, 1990, on the exact day 145 years after the firm was originally founded by his great-grandfather, Ferdinand Adolph Lange. Ferdinand Adolph had originally launched the company to provide work for the local population. And shortly after German reunification in 1990, that is exactly what Glashütte needed again.

Lange is known for its unique aesthetic and mechanical codes, which are at the heart of the Glashütte tradition. There is the three-quarter plate made of German silver (an alloy that looks like silver but is harder and more durable) and the hand-engraved balance cock. The company's growing inventory of outstanding calibers number sixty-nine now and have all been developed and manufactured in-house. They are decorated and assembled by hand with the fine adjustment done in five positions. Patented innovations include the Lange large date, the automatic "zero reset" for the second hand, and the three different patented constant force escapements, notably one for the Lange 31, whose mainspring provides a power reserve of 744 hours. Materials for the cases have grown as well and now include platinum, various golds plus the company's own "Honeygold," stainless steel, and titanium.

The entry-level family is the classic, visually balanced, two-hand Saxonia, while the Lange 1, introduced in 1994, is considered the collection flagship. And the company has continued to innovate in all sorts of ways. Take, for example, the "Honeygold" cases introduced in 2020, or using the Zeitwerk as the home for a minute repeater. In 2019, the company created a stir among watch fans by staking a claim in the very crowded field of sports watches with blue dials by releasing the Odysseus, with a custom automatic movement and weekday and date display. The stainless-steel model has now been joined by a white gold model with an integrated leather or rubber strap, taking daily sports routine to the high end, as it were. The Odysseus's journey continued in 2023 with a chronograph model in a limited edition.

LANGE UHREN GMBH
Ferdinand-A.-Lange-Platz 1
D-01768 Glashütte
Germany

TEL.:
+49-35053-44-0

E-MAIL:
info@lange-soehne.com

WEBSITE:
www.alange-soehne.com

FOUNDED:
1990

NUMBER OF EMPLOYEES:
750 employees, almost half of whom are watchmakers

U.S. DISTRIBUTOR:
A. Lange & Söhne
645 Fifth Avenue
New York, NY 10022
800-408-8147

MOST IMPORTANT COLLECTIONS/ PRICE RANGE:
Lange 1 / $40,300 to $359,400; Saxonia / $19,700 to $287,800; 1815 / $27,300 to $253,500; Richard Lange / $36,800 to $247,800; Zeitwerk / $89,200 to $141,300; Odysseus / $34,900 to $56,500

Odysseus

Reference number: 363.179
Movement: automatic, Lange caliber L155.1 Datomatic; ø 32.9 mm, height 6.2 mm; 31 jewels; 28,800 vph; swan-neck fine adjustment, hand-engraved escapement bridge, 1 screw-mounted gold chaton, parts hand-finished and assembled; 50-hour power reserve
Functions: hours, minutes, subsidiary seconds; date and weekday
Case: stainless steel, ø 40.5 mm, height 11.1 mm; sapphire crystal; transparent case back; water-resistant to 12 atm
Band: stainless steel, folding clasp
Price: $34,900
Variations: in titanium ($56,500; limited to 250 pieces)

Odysseus

Reference number: 363.068
Movement: automatic, Lange caliber L155.1 Datomatic; ø 32.9 mm, height 6.2 mm; 31 jewels; 28,800 vph; swan-neck fine adjustment, hand-engraved escapement bridge, 1 screw-mounted gold chaton, parts hand-finished and assembled; 50-hour power reserve
Functions: hours, minutes, subsidiary seconds; date and weekday
Case: white gold, ø 40.5 mm, height 11.1 mm; sapphire crystal; transparent case back; water-resistant to 12 atm
Band: rubber, pin buckle
Price: $55,200
Variations: with calfskin strap

Odysseus Chronograph

Reference number: 463.178
Movement: automatic, Lange caliber L156.1 Datomatic; ø 34.9 mm, height 8.4 mm; 52 jewels; 28,800 vph; swan-neck fine adjustment, hand-engraved escapement bridge, 4 screw-mounted gold chatons, parts hand-finished and assembled; rapid rotation reset of the seconds and minute chronograph counters; 50-hour power reserve
Functions: hours, minutes, subsidiary seconds; chronograph; date and weekday
Case: stainless steel, ø 42.5 mm, height 14.2 mm; sapphire crystal; transparent case back; water-resistant to 12 atm
Band: stainless steel, folding clasp
Remarks: limited to 100 pieces
Price: $150,000

Lange 1

Reference number: 191.039
Movement: hand-wound, Lange caliber L121.1;
ø 30.6 mm, height 5.7 mm; 43 jewels; 21,600 vph; swan-neck fine adjustment, hand-engraved balance cock, 8 screw-mounted gold chatons, hand-finished and assembled parts; 72-hour power reserve
Functions: hours, minutes, subsidiary seconds; power reserve indicator; large date
Case: white gold, ø 38.5 mm, height 9.8 mm; sapphire crystal; transparent case back; water-resistant to 3 atm
Band: reptile skin, pin buckle
Price: $42,000
Variations: red gold ($42,000); in platinum ($47,900)

Grand Lange 1

Reference number: 137.033
Movement: hand-wound, Lange caliber L095.1;
ø 34.1 mm, height 4.7 mm; 42 jewels; 21,600 vph; 7 screw-mounted gold chatons, swan-neck fine adjustment, hand-engraved balance cock, parts hand-finished and assembled; 72-hour power reserve
Functions: hours, minutes, subsidiary seconds; power reserve indicator; large date
Case: red gold, ø 41 mm, height 8.2 mm; sapphire crystal; transparent case back; water-resistant to 3 atm
Band: reptile skin, pin buckle
Price: $48,100
Variations: in white gold ($48,100)

Lange 1 Moon Phase

Reference number: 192.029
Movement: hand-wound, Lange caliber L121.3;
ø 30.6 mm, height 6.3 mm; 47 jewels; 21,600 vph; 8 screw-mounted gold chatons, swan-neck fine adjustment, hand-engraved balance cock, hand-finished and assembled parts; 72-hour power reserve
Functions: hours, minutes, subsidiary seconds; power reserve indicator; large date, moon phase
Case: white gold, ø 38.5 mm, height 10.2 mm; sapphire crystal; transparent case back; water-resistant to 3 atm
Band: reptile skin, pin buckle
Price: $54,800
Variations: in red gold

Lange 1 Time Zone

Reference number: 136.025
Movement: hand-wound, Lange caliber L141.1;
ø 34.1 mm, height 6.7 mm; 38 jewels; 21,600 vph; 3 screw-mounted gold chatons; hand-assembled and -finished movement; 72-hour power reserve
Functions: hours, minutes, subsidiary seconds; additional 12-hour display (second time zone), double day/night indication, power reserve indicator, daylight savings indication; large date
Case: platinum, ø 41.9 mm, height 10.9 mm; crown-activated ring with city references; sapphire crystal; transparent case back; water-resistant to 3 atm
Band: reptile skin, pin buckle
Price: $74,000
Variations: in red or white gold

Lange 1 Perpetual Calendar

Reference number: 345.036
Movement: automatic, Lange caliber L021.3;
ø 35.8 mm, height 8.8 mm; 63 jewels; 21,600 vph; off-center escapement, 5 screw-mounted gold chatons, hand-engraved balance cock, gold rotor platinum oscillating mass; 50-hour power reserve
Functions: hours, minutes, subsidiary seconds; day/night indication; perpetual calendar with large date, weekday, month, moon phase, leap year
Case: platinum, ø 41.9 mm, height 12.1 mm; sapphire crystal; transparent case back; water-resistant to 3 atm
Band: reptile skin, pin buckle
Price: $139,800
Variations: in red or white gold

Saxonia Thin

Reference number: 201.027
Movement: hand-wound, Lange caliber L093.1;
ø 28 mm, height 2.9 mm; 21 jewels; 21,600 vph; screw balance, swan-neck fine adjustment, hand-engraved balance cock, 3 gold chatons; 72-hour power reserve
Functions: hours, minutes
Case: white gold, ø 37 mm, height 5.9 mm; sapphire crystal; transparent case back; water-resistant to 3 atm
Band: reptile skin, pin buckle
Remarks: silver dial
Price: $23,500
Variations: in red gold ($23,500)

Datograph Up/Down

Reference number: 405.028
Movement: hand-wound, Lange caliber L951.6;
ø 30.6 mm, height 8.1 mm; 46 jewels; 18,000 vph;
4 screw-mounted gold chatons, swan-neck fine
adjustment, hand-engraved balance cock; 60-hour
power reserve
Functions: hours, minutes, subsidiary seconds; power
reserve indicator; flyback chronograph with precisely
jumping minute counter; large date
Case: white gold, ø 41 mm, height 13.1 mm; sapphire
crystal; transparent case back; water-resistant to 3 atm
Band: reptile skin, pin buckle
Remarks: limited to 125 pieces
Price: $93,000
Variations: in pink gold or platinum

Datograph Perpetual

Reference number: 410.038
Movement: hand-wound, Lange caliber L952.1;
ø 32 mm, height 8 mm; 45 jewels; 18,000 vph; off-
center balance; in-house balance wheel, column wheel
control of chronograph functions; 4 screw-mounted
gold chatons; 36-hour power reserve
Functions: hours, minutes, subsidiary seconds; day/
night indication; flyback chronograph with precisely
jumping minute counter; perpetual calendar with large
date, weekday, month, moon phase, leap year
Case: white gold, ø 41 mm, height 13.5 mm; sapphire
crystal; transparent case back; water-resistant to 3 atm
Band: reptile skin, pin buckle
Price: on request in the boutique

Datograph Perpetual Tourbillon Honeygold "Lumen"

Reference number: 740.055
Movement: hand-wound, Lange caliber L952.4;
ø 32.6 mm, height 9 mm; 58 jewels; 18,000 vph;1-
minute tourbillon; 1 diamond capstone, 5 screw-
mounted gold chatons, swan-neck fine adjustment;
50-hour power reserve
Functions: hours, minutes, subsidiary seconds; day/
night indication, power reserve indicator; flyback
chronograph with precisely jumping minute counter;
perpetual calendar with large date, weekday, month,
moon phase, leap year
Case: yellow gold ("Honeygold"), ø 41.5 mm, height
14.6 mm; sapphire crystal; transparent case back
Band: reptile skin, folding clasp
Remarks: sapphire crystal-dial
Price: $145,000; limited to 50 pieces

Zeitwerk

Reference number: 142.031
Movement: hand-wound, Lange caliber L043.6;
ø 33.6 mm, height 8.9 mm; 61 jewels; 18,000 vph; swan-
neck fine adjustment, 2 screw-mounted gold chatons,
constant force mechanism (remontoir), hand-engraved
balance cock; hand-finished and assembled parts;
72-hour power reserve
Functions: hours and minutes (digital, jumping),
subsidiary seconds; power reserve indicator
Case: pink gold, ø 41.9 mm, height 12.2 mm; sapphire
crystal; transparent case back; water-resistant to 3 atm
Band: reptile skin, pin buckle
Price: $121,100
Variations: in platinum

Zeitwerk Minute Repeater

Reference number: 147.050
Movement: hand-wound, Lange caliber L043.5;
ø 37.7 mm, height 10.9 mm; 93 jewels; 18,000 vph;
3 screw-mounted gold chatons, three-quarter plate,
constant force mechanism (remontoir); 36-hour power
reserve
Functions: hours and minutes (digital, jumping),
subsidiary seconds; power reserve indicator, minute
repeater (strikes the digital time indication)
Case: yellow gold ("Honeygold"), ø 44.2 mm, height
14.1 mm; sapphire crystal; transparent case back; water-
resistant to 3 atm
Band: reptile skin, folding clasp
Price: $440,000; limited to 100 pieces
Variations: in white gold or platinum

1815 Up/Down

Reference number: 234.032
Movement: hand-wound, Lange caliber L051.2;
ø 30.6 mm, height 4.6 mm; 29 jewels; 21,600 vph;
7 screw-mounted gold chatons, three-quarter plate,
screw balance, hand-engraved balance cock, parts
hand-finished and assembled; 55-hour power reserve
Functions: hours, minutes, subsidiary seconds; power
reserve indicator
Case: pink gold, ø 39 mm, height 8.7 mm; sapphire
crystal; transparent case back; water-resistant to 3 atm
Band: reptile skin, pin buckle
Price: $34,500
Variations: in white gold ($34,500)

1815 Annual Calendar

Reference number: 238.032
Movement: hand-wound, Lange caliber L051.3;
ø 30.6 mm, height 5.7 mm; 26 jewels; 21,600 vph;
3 screw-mounted gold chatons, hand-engraved balance
cock, parts hand-finished and assembled; 72-hour
power reserve
Functions: hours, minutes, subsidiary seconds; annual
calendar with date, weekday, month, moon phase
Case: red gold, ø 40 mm, height 10.1 mm; sapphire
crystal; transparent case back; water-resistant to 3 atm
Band: reptile skin, pin buckle
Price: $53,100
Variations: in white gold ($53,100)

1815 Chronograph

Reference number: 414.028
Movement: hand-wound, Lange caliber L951.5;
ø 30.6 mm, height 6.1 mm; 34 jewels; 21,600 vph;
4 screw-mounted gold chatons, hand-engraved balance
cock, hand-finished and -assembled parts; 60-hour
power reserve
Functions: hours, minutes, subsidiary seconds; flyback
chronograph
Case: white gold, ø 39.5 mm, height 11 mm; sapphire
crystal; transparent case back; water-resistant to 3 atm
Band: reptile skin, pin buckle
Price: $78,100
Variations: in red gold

1815 Rattrapante Perpetual Calendar

Reference number: 421.056
Movement: hand-wound, Lange caliber L101.1;
ø 32.6 mm, height 9.1 mm; 43 jewels; 21,600 vph;
4 screw-mounted gold chatons; 42-hour power reserve
Functions: hours, minutes, subsidiary seconds; power
reserve indicator; split-seconds chronograph; perpetual
calendar with date, weekday, month, moon phase, leap
year
Case: white gold, ø 41.9 mm, height 14.7 mm; sapphire
crystal; transparent case back; water-resistant to 3 atm
Band: reptile skin, folding clasp
Remarks: red gold-dial
Price: $319,000; limited to 100 pieces

Richard Lange

Reference number: 232.029
Movement: hand-wound, Lange caliber L041.2;
ø 30.6 mm, height 6 mm; 26 jewels; 21,600 vph; hand-
engraved balance cock, 2 screw-mounted gold chatons,
hand-finished and assembled parts, in-house hairspring
with patented mounting clamp; 38-hour power reserve
Functions: hours, minutes, sweep seconds
Case: white gold, ø 40.5 mm, height 10.5 mm; sapphire
crystal; transparent case back; water-resistant to 3 atm
Band: reptile skin, pin buckle
Price: $24,900
Variations: in pink gold

Richard Lange Jumping Seconds

Reference number: 252.029
Movement: hand-wound, Lange caliber L094.1;
ø 33.6 mm, height 6 mm; 50 jewels; 21,600 vph;
zero-reset mechanism, constant force escapement
(remontoir); 42-hour power reserve
Functions: off-center hours and minutes, large seconds
(jumping); winding reminder
Case: white gold, ø 39.9 mm, height 10.6 mm; sapphire
crystal; transparent case back; water-resistant to 3 atm
Band: reptile skin, buckle
Price: $97,800

Richard Lange Minute Repeater

Reference number: 606.079
Movement: hand-wound, Lange caliber L122.1;
ø 30 mm, height 5.4 mm; 40 jewels; 21,600 vph;
4 screw-mounted gold chatons, hand-engraved balance
cock, parts finished and assembled by hand; 72-hour
power reserve
Functions: hours, minutes, subsidiary seconds; minute
Repeater
Case: platinum, ø 39 mm, height 9.7 mm; sapphire
crystal; transparent case back; water-resistant to 2 atm
Band: reptile skin, folding clasp
Price: $400,000; limited to 50 pieces (boutique
edition)

Caliber L155.1 Datomatic

Automatic; swan-neck fine adjustment, second-stop system, oscillating mass in platinum; single mainspring barrel, 50-hour power reserve
Functions: hours, minutes, subsidiary seconds; date and weekday
Diameter: 32.9 mm
Height: 6.2 mm
Jewels: 31, including 1 in screw-mounted gold chatons
Balance: glucydur with regulating screws
Frequency: 28,800 vph
Hairspring: in-house manufacture
Remarks: parts hand-finished and assembled; 312 parts

Caliber L156.1 Datomatic

Automatic; swan-neck fine adjustment, second-stop system, oscillating mass in platinum; single mainspring barrel, 50-hour power reserve
Functions: hours, minutes, subsidiary seconds; chronograph (fast rotation reset in force flow); date and weekday
Diameter: 34.9 mm
Height: 8.4 mm
Jewels: 52, including 4 in screw-mounted gold chatons
Balance: glucydur with regulating screws
Frequency: 28,800 vph
Hairspring: in-house manufacture
Remarks: parts hand-finished and assembled; 516 parts

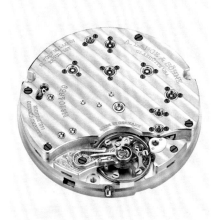

Caliber L121.1

Hand-wound; second-stop system, 8 screw-mounted gold chatons, swan-neck fine adjustment; double mainspring barrel, 72-hour power reserve
Functions: hours, minutes, subsidiary seconds; power reserve indicator; large date
Diameter: 30.6 mm
Height: 5.7 mm
Jewels: 43
Balance: glucydur with eccentric adjustment cams
Frequency: 21,600 vph
Hairspring: in-house manufacture
Shock protection: Kif
Remarks: mainplate and bridges of untreated German silver, largely decorated and assembled by hand, hand-engraved balance cock; 368 parts

Caliber L141.1

Hand-wound; second-stop system, 3 screw-mounted gold chatons, swan-neck fine adjustment;
single mainspring barrel, 72-hour power reserve
Functions: hours, minutes, subsidiary seconds; second time zone, dual day/night indicator, power reserve indicator, daylight savings; large date
Diameter: 34.1 mm
Height: 6.7 mm
Jewels: 38
Balance: glucydur with eccentric adjustment cams
Frequency: 21,600 vph
Hairspring: in-house manufacture
Shock protection: Kif
Remarks: mainplate and bridges of untreated German silver, hand-engraved balance cock

Caliber L021.3

Automatic; unidirectional gold rotor with platinum oscillating mass; single mainspring barrel, 50-hour power reserve
Functions: hours, minutes, subsidiary seconds; day/night indicator; perpetual calendar with large date, weekday, month, moon phase, leap year
Diameter: 35.8 mm
Height: 8.8 mm
Jewels: 63, including 5 in screw-mounted gold chatons
Balance: glucydur with eccentric adjustment cams
Frequency: 21,600 vph
Hairspring: in-house manufacture
Remarks: hand-engraved and -decorated, hand-engraved balance cock; 621 parts

Caliber L951.6

Hand-wound; second-stop system, jumping minute totalizer; single mainspring barrel, 60-hour power reserve
Functions: hours, minutes, subsidiary seconds; power reserve indicator; flyback chronograph; large date
Diameter: 30.6 mm
Height: 7.9 mm
Jewels: 46
Balance: glucydur screw balance
Frequency: 18,000 vph
Hairspring: in-house manufacture
Shock protection: Incabloc
Remarks: untreated German-silver three-quarter plate, mostly hand-engraved and -decorated according to top quality criteria, hand-engraved balance cock; 451 parts

ALEXANDER SHOROKHOFF

The goal for the watch connoisseur may be realizing one's own ideas for timepieces. In the first stages of his life, Alexander Shorokhoff, born in Moscow in 1960, was an engineer and then an architect with his own construction company. This turned out to be an excellent platform to begin expanding into the field of fine timepieces. In 1992, shortly after the break-up of the Soviet Union, Shorokhoff founded a distribution company in Germany to market Russia's own Poljot watches. This gave him the insight and practice needed to launch phase two of his plan: establishing his own manufacturing facilities for an independent watch brand under his own name.

At Shorokhoff Watches, three main creative lines are bundled under the general concept "Art on the Wrist": Heritage, Avantgarde, and Vintage. The three families share a design with a distinctly artistic orientation. They all focus on technical quality, sophisticated hand-engraving, and culture. "We consider watches not only as timekeepers, but also as works of art," says Alexander Shorokhoff. It's a statement that is clearly expressed by the product. The brand is at home in the world of international and Russian art and culture (models named Dostoevsky, Leo Tolstoy, and Peter Tchaikovsky, for example). Each dial is designed down to the smallest detail. The engraving and finishing of the movements are unique as well. These timepieces are bold, innovative, and visually striking, which explains numerous and illustrious design awards.

The movements are mostly Swiss-made, with some Russian movements thrown in. They are taken apart in Alzenau, reworked, decorated, and then reassembled with great care, which is why the brand has stamped each watch with "Handmade in Germany." Some of the modules used in these timepieces were developed by the company itself. Before a watch leaves the manufacture, it is subjected to strict quality control. The timepiece's functionality must be given the cleanest bill of health before it can be sent out to jewelers around the world.

ALEXANDER SHOROKHOFF UHRENMANUFAKTUR
Hanauer Strasse 25
63755 Alzenau
Germany

TEL.:
+49-6023-919-93

E-MAIL:
info@alexander-shorokhoff.de

WEBSITE:
www.alexander-shorokhoff.de

FOUNDED:
2003

NUMBER OF EMPLOYEES:
17

ANNUAL PRODUCTION:
approx. 1,500-2,000 watches

DISTRIBUTOR:
About Time Luxury Group
210 Bellevue Avenue
Newport, RI 02840
401-846-0598

**MOST IMPORTANT COLLECTIONS/
PRICE RANGE**
Heritage / starting at approx. $4,500; Avantgarde / starting at approx. $1,500; Vintage / starting at approx. $800

Avantgarde Full Calendar "Cadamomo"

Reference number: AS.VK-CDMM2
Movement: automatic, Dubois Dépraz caliber 9000; ø 28 mm, height 5.2 mm; 25 jewels; 28,800 vph; hand-engraved oscillating mass, blued screws; 42-hour power reserve
Functions: hours, minutes, sweep seconds; full calendar with date, weekday, month, moon phase
Case: stainless steel, ø 43.5 mm, height 11.55 mm; sapphire crystal; transparent case back; water-resistant to 5 atm
Band: calfskin, pin buckle
Price: $4,200; limited to 50 pieces

Avantgarde "Wintergenta"

Reference number: AS.LA-WTG
Movement: automatic, La Joux-Perret caliber G 100; ø 25.6 mm, height 4.45 mm; 24 jewels; 28,800 vph; 68-hour power reserve
Functions: hours, minutes, sweep seconds; date
Case: silver, ø 39 mm, height 10.6 mm; sapphire crystal; transparent case back; water-resistant to 3 atm
Band: ray leather, pin buckle
Remarks: hand-engraved case
Price: $5,600; limited to 50 pieces

Avantgarde "Home"

Reference number: AS.KD02-HOME
Movement: automatic, ETA caliber 2892-A2; ø 25.6 mm, height 3.6 mm; 21 jewels; 28,800 vph; hand-engraved and decorated rotor, blued screws; 47-hour power reserve
Functions: hours, minutes, sweep seconds; date
Case: stainless steel with black PVD, 41 mm x 41 mm, height 9 mm; sapphire crystal; transparent case back; water-resistant to 3 atm
Band: calfskin (bicolor), pin buckle
Price: $4,450; limited to 10 pieces

Avantgarde "Swan Lake AVG"

Reference number: AS.PT-SL5
Movement: hand-wound, caliber 2612.AS (Poljot 2612/AS1475 base); ø 26 mm, height 5.8 mm; 18 jewels; 18,000 vph; hand-engraved and decorated; 38-hour power reserve
Functions: hours, minutes, sweep seconds; alarm
Case: stainless steel, ø 40 mm, height 11.5 mm; sapphire crystal; transparent case back; water-resistant to 3 atm
Band: reptile skin, pin buckle
Remarks: hinged double case
Price: $3,500; limited to 30 pieces

Avantgarde "Avantgarde 08"

Reference number: AS.AVG08.2
Movement: hand-wound, caliber 2614.AS; ø 26 mm, height 4.3 mm; 17 jewels; 21,600 vph; hand-engraved and decorated; 42-hour power reserve
Functions: hours, minutes, sweep seconds
Case: stainless steel, ø 43.5 mm, height 11.5 mm; sapphire crystal; transparent case back; water-resistant to 5 atm
Band: calfskin, pin buckle
Remarks: limited to 50 pieces
Price: $1,800

Avantgarde Shar

Reference number: AS.SH01-5
Movement: automatic, caliber 2671.AS (ETA 2671 base); ø 17.5 mm, height 4.8 mm; 25 jewels; 28,800 vph; hand-engraved oscillating mass, blued screws; 42-hour reserve
Functions: hours, minutes, sweep seconds; date
Case: stainless steel, ø 25 mm, height 20 mm; sapphire crystal; water-resistant to 3 atm
Band: reptile skin, pin buckle
Remarks: malachite dial; sapphire crystal shaped like a hemisphere; limited to 30 pieces
Price: $2,100

Avantgarde Full Calendar "Merkur"

Reference number: AS.VK-MKR2
Movement: automatic, Dubois Dépraz caliber 9000; ø 28 mm, height 5.2 mm; 25 jewels; 28,800 vph; hand-engraved oscillating mass, blued screws; 42-hour power reserve
Functions: hours, minutes, sweep seconds; full calendar with date, weekday, month, moon phase
Case: stainless steel, ø 43.5 mm, height 11.55 mm; sapphire crystal; transparent case back; water-resistant to 5 atm
Band: calfskin, pin buckle
Price: $4,200; limited to 31 pieces

Avantgarde "Four Seasons"

Reference number: AS.APV-4S
Movement: automatic, ETA caliber 2000-1; ø 20 mm, height 3.6 mm; 20 jewels; 28,800 vph; hand-engraved oscillating mass, blued screws; 40-hour power reserve
Functions: hours, minutes, sweep seconds
Case: stainless steel, 36 mm x 36 mm, height 8.55 mm; sapphire crystal; transparent case back; water-resistant to 3 atm
Band: ostrich leather, pin buckle
Price: $2,880; limited to 30 pieces

Avantgarde "Black Cat"

Reference number: AS.APV-BCH
Movement: automatic, caliber 2009.AS; ø 20.5 mm, height 2.9 mm; 21 jewels; 21,600 vph; hand-engraved and decorated, blued screws; 37-hour power reserve
Functions: hours, minutes, sweep seconds
Case: stainless steel, 36 x 36 mm, height 8.55 mm; sapphire crystal; transparent case back; water-resistant to 3 atm
Band: ostrich leather, pin buckle
Price: $2,900; limited to 19 pieces

ALPINA

The origins of the Alpina brand go back to 1883, when a confederation of watchmakers known as the Alpina Union Horlogère SA, founded by one Gottlieb Hauser, decided to make watches for mountaineers, a logical mission in a country like Switzerland. The group expanded quickly, and by 1901 had renamed itself Alpina and created the triangular logo that expressed its attachment to mountains. At one point, it even had a factory in Glashütte. For a while in the 1930s, it even merged with Gruen, one of the most important watch companies in the United States at the time.

The genuine toughness of these watches attracted the interest of the military aand even the budding air forces. The company produced two icons in 1933 and 1938 respectively. The first was the Block Uhr, which had a crown close to the winding stem to prevent dust from entering the case. The second was the Alpina 4, a sports watch that was built with four key properties: impact-resistant, non-magnetic, water-resistant, and made of stainless steel.

Today, Geneva-based Alpina is no longer associated with that watchmaker cooperative of yore. It is a sister brand to Frederique Constant and is located in the watchmaking suburb of Geneva, Plan-les-Ouates. But the reputation as a manufacturer of tough, can-do sports watches that could stand a bit of battery without losing accuracy and reliability in extreme environments has remained. In keeping with its past codes, the company has divided its portfolio into three areas, namely, air (Startimer collection), sea (Seastrong collection) and Earth (Alpiner collection). These were joined in 2023 by the Heritage collection, which pays tribute to the brand's legacy watches. These timepieces are popular for their value, refined finishings, and affordability.

Alpina has also built up robust partnerships reflecting its enduring commitment to the mountain environment – a constant source of inspiration – as well as a team of athletes and other friends of the brand.

ALPINA WATCH INTERNATIONAL SA
Route de la Galaise, 8
CH-1228 Plan-les-Ouates, Geneva
Switzerland

TEL.:
+41-0-22-860-87-40

E-MAIL:
info@alpina-watches.com

WEBSITE:
us.alpinawatches.com

FOUNDED:
1883

NUMBER OF EMPLOYEES:
100

U.S. SUBSIDIARY:
Alpina Frederique Constant USA
350 5th Avenue, 29th Floor
New York, NY 10118
310-532-8463
customercare@alpinawatches.com

MOST IMPORTANT COLLECTIONS/PRICE RANGE:
Alpiner / from approx. $1,295 to $3,295;
Seastrong / from approx. $1,895 to $2,695;
Startimer / from approx. $995 to $1,295

Seastrong Diver Extreme Automatic
Reference number: AL-525BO3VE6
Movement: automatic, caliber AL-525 (Sellita SW200-1 base); ø 25.6 mm, height 4.6 mm; 26 jewels; 28,800 vph; 38-hour power reserve
Functions: hours, minutes, sweep seconds; date
Case: stainless steel, ø 40.5 mm, height 12.65 mm; unidirectional bezel with ceramic insert, with 0-60 scale; sapphire crystal; screw-down crown; water-resistant to 30 atm
Band: rubber, folding clasp
Price: $2,295
Variations: with blue strap and index ring; with stainless steel bracelet

Seastrong Diver Extreme Automatic GMT
Reference number: AL-560LG3VE6
Movement: automatic, caliber AL-560 (Sellita SW330 base); ø 25.6 mm, height 3.6 mm; 25 jewels; 28,800 vph; 50-hour power reserve
Functions: hours, minutes, sweep seconds; additional 24-hour display (second time zone); date
Case: stainless steel, ø 40.5 mm, height 12.8 mm; bidirectional bezel with ceramic insert with 0-24 scale; sapphire crystal; screw-down crown; water-resistant to 30 atm
Band: rubber, folding clasp
Price: $2,695
Variations: with black dial

Alpiner Extreme Quartz
Reference number: AL-220BG2AE6B
Movement: quartz
Functions: hours, minutes, sweep seconds; date
Case: stainless steel, ø 35.2 mm, height 8.35 mm; sapphire crystal; water-resistant to 10 atm
Band: stainless steel, folding clasp
Price: $1,295
Variations: various straps and dials

ANGELUS

The watch landscape in Switzerland has always been rich in small, vital brands. Many are no longer active, but their names still make for weepy eyes with connoisseurs and collectors. And every now and then, an older company is revived with varying degrees of success. It its day, Angelus, founded by Gustave and Albert Stolz in Le Locle in 1891, quickly forged a reputation for complicated watches, notably repeaters and chronographs. The brothers, Catholics, named the brand after the first word of a standard Catholic prayer and the midday church bells.

One of the brand's claims to fame was a two-handed chronograph, which became a hit in the thirties, culminating in a contract with the Hungarian air force in 1940. The company then built a chronograph with a date, and later one of the first digital dates. Meanwhile, it was creating excellent movements, one of which drove Panerai's Mare Nostrum in the fifties. Among its most iconic models was the waterproof repeater/alarm called the Tinkler, and, in the seventies, a five-minute repeater, which never really got off the ground due to the quartz crisis, which brought Angelus to its knees...

In 2011, La Joux-Perret, a company known for movements and modules and which was already behind Arnold & Son, relaunched the brand and returned to its chronographic roots. One example is the "Instrument de Vitesse," which looks like a retro three-hand watch. Only the pusher embedded in the crown and the tachymeter scale printed on the outer edge of the dial reveal the chronograph function. Here is the catch: the lone second hand in the middle allows measurements of a maximum of one minute, as there is no totalizer. This is sufficient for short sprints or speed measurements using markers on the highway. True connoisseurs will appreciate the classic look and delight in the beguiling architecture of the hand-wound A-5000 movement, the structure of which can be viewed through the glass back.

ANGELUS
Manufacture La Joux-Perret SA
Boulevard des Eplatures 38
2300 La Chaux-de-Fonds
Switzerland

TEL:
+41-32-967-97-97

E-MAIL:
info@angelus-watches.com

WEBSITE:
www.angelus-watches.com

FOUNDED:
1891; relaunched 2011

NUMBER OF EMPLOYEES:
about 100, including at the La Joux-Perret manufacture

DISTRIBUTOR:
Angelus USA
510 West 6th Street, Suite 309
Los Angeles, CA 90014
213-622-1133
info@arnoldandsonusa.com

**MOST IMPORTANT COLLECTIONS/
PRICE RANGE**
U23 / U30 / U41 / U50 / U51 / U53 / La Fabrique
$32,000; various tourbillons / $28,000 to $110,000

Chronodate Titanium
Reference number: 0CDYF.F01A.M009T
Movement: automatic, A 500 caliber (La Joux-Perret base); ø 30 mm, height 7.9 mm; 26 jewels; 28,800 vph; column wheel control of chronograph functions; tungsten and red gold rotor; 60-hour power reserve
Functions: hours, minutes, subsidiary seconds; chronograph; date
Case: titanium monobloc, ø 42.5 mm, height 14.25 mm; sapphire crystal; carbon composite pushers and case back; water-resistant to 3 atm
Band: titanium, double folding clasp
Price: $25,200
Variations: with black rubber strap ($23,100)

Chronographe Médical
Reference number: 0CHAS.A01A.V010S
Movement: hand-wound, Angelus caliber A-500 (based on La Joux Perret); ø 29.40 mm, height 4.20 mm; 23 jewels; 21,600 vph; column wheel control of monopusher chronograph; black DLC- coated, snailed, and beveled mainplate and bridges; 42-hour power reserve
Functions: hours, minutes, subsidiary seconds; chronograph; pulsometer; asthmometer
Case: titanium, ø 39 mm, height 9.22 mm; sapphire crystal; transparent case back; water-resistant to 30 atm
Band: calfskin, pin buckle
Remarks: collaboration with Massena LAB
Price: $19,900; limited to 99 pieces

Instrument de Vitesse
Reference number: 0CHBS.B01A.V010S
Movement: hand-wound, Angelus caliber A5000 (La Joux-Perret base); ø 24 mm, height 4.2 mm; 23 jewels; 21,600 vph; column wheel control of monopusher chronograph (only the second hand); 42-hour power reserve
Functions: hours, minutes; chronograph
Case: stainless steel, ø 39 mm, height 9.27 mm; sapphire crystal; transparent case back; water-resistant to 3 atm
Band: calfskin, pin buckle
Price: $17,300
Variations: with ivory-colored dial, limited to 25 editions

ARISTO

"If you lie down with dogs,..." goes the old saying. And if you work closely with watchmakers...you may catch their more beneficial bug and become one yourself. That at any rate is what happened to the watch case and metal bracelet manufacturer Vollmer, Ltd., established in Pforzheim, Germany, by Ernst Vollmer in 1922. Is it any wonder, then, that the third-generation president Hansjörg Vollmer decided he was interested in producing watches as well?

Vollmer, who studied business in Stuttgart, had the experience but also the connections with manufacturers in Switzerland. He speaks French fluently, another asset. He acquired Aristo and launched a series of pilot watches in 1998 housed in sturdy titanium cases with bold onion crowns and secured with Vollmer's own light and comfortable titanium bracelets. Bit by bit, thanks to affordable prices and no-nonsense design—reviving some classic dials from World War II—Vollmer's watches caught hold. The collection grew with limited editions and a few chronographs.

In 2005, Vollmer GmbH and Aristo Watches consolidated for a bigger impact. Besides their own lines, they produce quartz watches, automatics, and chronographs under various names. The Aristo brand has been trademarked worldwide and is sold mainly in Europe, North America, and Asia. The collection is divided up into Classic, Design, and Sports with the mechanical segment further split based on the elements Land, Water, and Air. The classic pilot's watches are still the mainstay of the brand, whereby anyone seeking a more upscale watch will find satisfaction with the "Erbprinz" series, named after the street where the company also has a workshop for manufacturing metal bracelets. Finally, Aristo has a special section devoted to historical movements. In 2024, the company launched a limited edition of watches running on Swiss Record movements from the 1970s.

ARISTO VOLLMER GMBH
Erbprinzenstr. 36
D-75175 Pforzheim
Germany

TEL.:
+49-7231-17031

FAX:
+49-7231-17033

E-MAIL:
info@aristo-vollmer.de

WEBSITE:
www.aristo-vollmer.de

FOUNDED:
1907/1998

NUMBER OF EMPLOYEES:
12

ANNUAL PRODUCTION:
4,000 watches and 4,000 bracelets

DISTRIBUTION:
Retail

U.S. DISTRIBUTOR:
Long Island Watch, Marc Frankel
273 Walt Whitman Road, Suite 217
Huntington Station, NY 11746
631-470-0762
888-673-1129 (fax)
www.longislandwatch.com

MOST IMPORTANT COLLECTIONS/PRICE RANGE:
Aristo watches / starting at $400; Erbprinz watches / $1000

Flieger Chrono Retro Design
Reference number: 3H243-VL
Movement: automatic, Sellita caliber SW-500; ø 30 mm, height 7.9 mm; 25 jewels; 28,800 vph; 48-hour power reserve
Functions: hours, minutes, subsidiary seconds (stop-seconds); chronograph; day, date (quick correction)
Case: stainless steel, ø 40.5 mm, height 14 mm; unidirectional bezel; sapphire crystal; transparent case back; water-resistant to 5 atm
Band: calfskin, pin buckle
Remarks: NOS case from the Swiss company BWC (Buttes Watch Co.)
Price: $1,390

U-Boot Watch
Reference number: 3H17M
Movement: automatic, Sellita SW200 caliber; ø 25.6 mm, height 4.6 mm; 26 jewels; 28,800 vph; 38-hour power reserve
Functions: hours, minutes, sweep seconds; date
Case: stainless steel, ø 38.5 mm, height 10 mm; mineral glass; screw-down crown; water-resistant to 10 atm
Band: milanaise mesh, folding clasp
Remarks: full-lume dial
Price: $625
Variations: with textile strap ($565)

Record Automatic
Reference number: 98101Rec-1
Movement: automatic, Record 1959 caliber; ø 25.6 mm, height 6 mm; 17 jewels; 19,800 vph; 40-hour power reserve
Functions: hours, minutes, sweep seconds
Case: stainless steel, ø 38.5 mm, height 10 mm; sapphire crystal; transparent case back; water-resistant to 5 atm
Band: calfskin, folding clasp
Remarks: original Swiss caliber from the early 1970s made by Record Watch, Geneva
Price: $685: limited to 100 pieces
Variations: with milanaise band ($725)

ARMIN STROM

For more than thirty years, Armin Strom's name was associated mainly with the art of skeletonizing. But this "grandmaster of skeletonizers" then decided to entrust his life's work to the next generation, which turned out to be the Swiss industrialist and art patron Willy Michel.

Michel had the wherewithal to expand the one-man show into a full-blown *manufacture* able to conceive, design, and produce its own mechanical movements. The endeavor attracted Claude Geisler, a very skilled designer, and Michel's own son, Serge, who became business manager. When this triumvirate joined forces, it was able to come up with a technically fascinating movement at the quaint little *manufacture* in the Biel suburb of Bözingen within a brief period.

The new movement went on to grow into a family of ten, which forms the backbone of a new collection, including a tourbillon with microrotor—no mean feat for a small firm. The ARF15 caliber of the Mirrored Force Resonance, for example, features two balance wheels placed close enough to influence each other (resonance) and give the movement greater stability. The two oscillating systems are coupled via a spiral spring with two counter-rotating coils, which was developed completely in-house. The company has innovated in many other directions, notably, in its System 78 line with a clever stop-work mechanism for an automatic movement, and development of a motor barrel, whereby the arbor drives the movement.

This essential portfolio has given the *manufacture* the industrial autonomy to implement its projects quickly and independently. Armin Strom has additionally created an online configurator (on its homepage) giving fans and collectors the opportunity to personalize their watches. All components can be selected individually and combined, from the dial, hands, and finishing to the straps. The finished product can be picked up at a local dealership or at the manufacturer in Biel/Bienne, including a tour of the place.

ARMIN STROM AG
Bözingenstrasse 46
CH-2502 Biel/Bienne
Switzerland

TEL.:
+41-32-343-3344

E-MAIL:
info@arminstrom.com

WEBSITE:
www.arminstrom.com

FOUNDED:
2006 (first company 1967)

NUMBER OF EMPLOYEES:
22

ANNUAL PRODUCTION:
approx. 1000 watches

U.S. REPRESENTATIVE:
Jean-Marc Bories
Head of North America
929-353-5395
Jean-marc@arminstrom.com

MOST IMPORTANT COLLECTIONS/ PRICE RANGE:
Masterpiece Collection, Resonance Collection, Skeleton Collection, System 78 Collection / $9,900 to $100,000 plus

Dual Time GMT Resonance

Reference number: WG24-DT.90
Movement: hand-wound, caliber ARF22; ø 34.15 mm, height 4.92 mm; 70 jewels; 25,200 vph; two independent regulation systems, connected by a resonance clutch spring that stabilize each other mutually; 2 mainsprings; hand-decorated mainplate and bridges; 42-hour power reserve
Functions: hours, minutes (double); additional 24-hour display (second time zone), power reserve indicator (double)
Case: white gold, ø 39 mm, height 9.05 mm; sapphire crystal; transparent case back; water-resistant to 5 atm
Band: reptile skin, double folding clasp
Remarks: comes with extra reptile skin strap
Price: $120,700; limited to 25 pieces

One Week Manufacture Edition

Reference number: ST23-OW.ME
Movement: hand-wound, Armin Strom caliber ARM21; ø 36.6 mm, height 6 mm; 35 jewels; 25,200 vph; 2 mainsprings, balance wheel with variable inertia; mainplate with anthracite PVD; finely finished movement; 168-hour power reserve
Functions: hours, minutes, subsidiary seconds
Case: stainless steel, ø 41 mm, height 10.6 mm; sapphire crystal; transparent case back; water-resistant to 10 atm
Band: stainless steel, double folding clasp
Price: $33,600; limited to 100 pieces

Tribute 1 Fumé Ocean

Reference number: ST23-TRI.75.CS.M.35.FC
Movement: hand-wound, Armin Strom caliber AMW21; ø 33.5 mm, height 4.2 mm; 21 jewels; 25,200 vph; balance wheel with variable inertia, finely finished movement; 100-hour power reserve
Functions: hours, minutes, sweep seconds
Case: stainless steel, ø 38 mm, height 9.38 mm; sapphire crystal; transparent case back; water-resistant to 5 atm
Band: Alcantara leather, double folding clasp
Remarks: hand-guilloché dial
Price: $20,800

Gravity Equal Force Ultimate Sapphire Purple

Reference number: ST24-GEF.SA.AC.M.A7.FC
Movement: automatic, Armin Strom caliber ASB19; ø 35.52 mm, height 11.67 mm; 28 jewels; 25,200 vph; micro-rotor; spring barrel with Maltese cross stop-work for constant and limited force; finely finished movement; 72-hour power reserve
Functions: hours and minutes (off-center), subsidiary seconds; power reserve indicator
Case: stainless steel, ø 41 mm, height 12.65 mm; sapphire crystal; transparent case back; water-resistant to 3 atm
Band: textile, double folding clasp
Price: $28,900

Mirrored Force Resonance Manufacture Edition Green

Reference number: ST22-RF.20
Movement: hand-wound, caliber ARF21; ø 37.2 mm, height 6.7 mm; 39 jewels; 25,200 vph; two independent regulating mechanisms connected by a resonance clutch spring that stabilize each other mutually; finely finished movement; 48-hour power reserve
Functions: hours and minutes (off-center), two subsidiary seconds
Case: stainless steel, ø 43 mm, height 11.55 mm; sapphire crystal; transparent case back; water-resistant to 3 atm
Band: Alcantara leather, double folding clasp
Price: $63,000; limited to 50 pieces

Tribute 1 Rose Gold

Reference number: RG21-TRI.70
Movement: hand-wound, Armin Strom caliber AMW21; ø 33.5 mm, height 4.2 mm; 21 jewels; 25,200 vph; balance wheel with variable inertia, finely finished movement; 100-hour power reserve
Functions: hours, minutes, sweep seconds
Case: stainless steel, ø 38 mm, height 9.38 mm; sapphire crystal; transparent case back; water-resistant to 5 atm
Band: reptile skin, double folding clasp
Remarks: limited to 100 pieces
Price: $23,900

Caliber ARM21

Hand-wound; two spring barrels, 168-hour power reserve
Functions: hours, minutes, subsidiary seconds
Diameter: 36.6 mm
Height: 6 mm
Jewels: 35
Balance: with variable inertia
Frequency: 25,200 vph
Hairspring: flat hairspring
Remarks: mainplate with blue PVD, finely finished movement; 194 parts

Caliber ARF22

Hand-wound; two spring barrels, 42-hour power reserve
Functions: hours, minutes (double); additional 24-hour display (second time zone), power reserve indicator (double)
Diameter: 34.15 mm
Height: 4.92 mm
Jewels: 70
Balance: two independent regulating systems connected by a resonance clutch spring
Frequency: 25,200 vph
Remarks: hand-decorated mainplate and bridges

Caliber AMW21

Hand-wound; single spring barrel; 100-hour power reserve
Functions: hours, minutes, sweep seconds
Diameter: 33.5 mm
Height: 4.2 mm
Jewels: 21
Balance: with variable inertia
Frequency: 25,200 vph
Hairspring: flat spring
Shock protection: Incabloc
Remarks: rose gold-plated bridges, finely finished movement; 135 parts

ARNOLD & SON

John Arnold holds a special place among the British watchmakers of the eighteenth and nineteenth centuries because he was the first to organize the production of his chronometers along industrial lines. He developed his own standards and employed numerous watchmakers. During his lifetime, he is said to have manufactured around 5,000 marine chronometers, which he sold at reasonable prices to the Royal Navy and the West Indies merchant fleet. Arnold chronometers were packed in the trunks of some of the greatest explorers, from John Franklin and Ernest Shackleton to Captain James Cook and Dr. David Livingstone.

As Arnold & Son was once synonymous with precision timekeeping on the high seas, it stands to reason, then, that the modern brand should also focus its design policies on the interplay of time and geography as well as the basic functions of navigation. Independence from The British Masters Group has meant that the venerable English chronometer brand has been reorienting itself, setting its sights on classic, elegant watchmaking. With the expertise of watch manufacturer La Joux-Perret behind it (and the expertise housed in the building behind the complex on the main road between La Chaux-de-Fonds and Le Locle), the brand has been able to implement several new ideas.

Keeping it modern is, perhaps, the biggest challenge for any brand, and here Arnold shows remarkable skill in combining three aspects: astronomy, chronometry, and universal time. Like a kind of echo of John Arnold's inventions and interests, these three pillars form the foundation upon which the collections are based. The Globetrotter has a bold split bridge over the dial, for example. The Luna Magna offers a sculptural moon that really resembles what we see in the night sky. And the Longitude's simplicity is a direct connection to Arnold's glorious past on the seas.

More subtle, perhaps, for the connoisseurs of Arnold & Son's watches: the movements have been reworked to fit into slightly smaller cases, which is entirely within the trend of the past few years.

ARNOLD & SON
38, boulevard des Eplatures
CH-2300 La Chaux-de-Fonds
Switzerland

TEL.:
+41-32-967-9797

E-MAIL:
info@arnoldandson.com

WEBSITE:
www.arnoldandson.com

FOUNDED:
1995

NUMBER OF EMPLOYEES:
approx. 30

U.S. DISTRIBUTOR:
Arnold & Son USA
510 West 6th Street, Suite 309
Los Angeles, CA 90014
213-622-1133

**MOST IMPORTANT COLLECTIONS/
PRICE RANGE:**
Eight-Day / Globetrotter / Longitude / Nebula /
TB88, TBR, TE8 (Tourbillon), Time Pyramid, UTTE /
from approx. $10,000 to $325,000

Luna Magna
Reference number: 1LMAR.A02A.C153A
Movement: hand-wound, Arnold & Son caliber 1021 (La Joux-Perret base); ø 37.6 mm, height 4.75 mm; 35 jewels; 21,600 vph; astronomically precise 122-year moon phase; 90-hour power reserve
Functions: hours, minutes; moon phase
Case: red gold, ø 44 mm, height 15.9 mm; sapphire crystal; transparent case back; water-resistant to 3 atm
Band: reptile skin, pin buckle
Remarks: sculptural moon (12 mm diameter), made of aventurine and marble; limited to 28 editions
Price: $47,800

Longitude
Reference number: 1LTAT.J01A.N001U
Movement: automatic, Arnold & Son caliber 6302 (La Joux-Perret base); ø 33 mm, height 6.65 mm; 36 jewels; 28,800 vph; COSC-certified chronometer; 60-hour power reserve
Functions: hours, minutes, subsidiary seconds; power reserve indicator
Case: titanium, ø 42.5 mm, height 12.25 mm; sapphire crystal; transparent case back; water-resistant to 10 atm
Band: titanium, folding clasp
Remarks: limited to 88 editions
Price: $23,900
Variations: ocean blue or fern-green dial, unlimited

Globetrotter Platinum
Reference number: 1WTAX.U02C.C183C
Movement: hand-wound, Arnold & Son caliber 6022 (La Joux-Perret base); ø 39 mm, height 6.55 mm; 29 jewels; 28,800 vph; astronomically precise 122-year moon phase; 45-hour power reserve
Functions: hours, minutes; world time display (second time zone)
Case: platinum, ø 45 mm, height 13 mm; sapphire crystal; transparent case back; water-resistant to 3 atm
Band: reptile skin, platinum and titanium folding clasp
Remarks: disc hands and world map under a white-gold vaulted bridge; limited to 28 editions
Price: $67,400

ARTYA

The business gurus like to use or create buzzwords for their processes like "agility," and "disruptive," and even "innovative," to describe more of the same with a few small changes. . . . In watchmaking, the approach often involves small engineering advances and a noisy campaign. Yvan Arpa, founder of ArtyA watches, does it differently.

This refreshingly candid personality who spent his *Wanderjahre* crossing Papua New Guinea on foot and practicing Thai boxing in its native land, lives, breathes, and garrulously posts his lived horology online, be it the diving trip to test his divers' watches, or some trek up a mountain.

After various trials and tribulations in the industry, Arpa founded ArtyA, where he could get his "monster" off the slab as it were, with a divine spark. "I had worked with water, rust, dust, and other elements, and then I really caught fire," says Arpa. Indeed, among his first creations were steel cases struck by artificial lightning from a Tesla generator.

One of Arpa's not-so-secret weapons in the fight for market share is his artist wife, Dominique Arpa-Cirpka, who delivers dreamier dials that carefully mix textures and pigments or use real butterfly wings and collages of earth, shells, pigments, or fish scales. And now one of his sons, Jérémie, has joined the team by designing a very "wavy" sapphire crystal case.

Artya's watches hit nerves and draw a gamut of emotional responses. His dials shake up the owner and are often unique in the real sense of the word. No two are alike.

Thinking outside of the box is not enough for Arpa. He thinks out of the dial. He will personally go and test watches like the Depth Gauge, whose arched colored bands on the dial disappear as the watch reaches depths at which certain color frequencies fail. He continues to explore artificial sapphire that changes color. The recent Tiny Purity Tourbillon took a full 7 mm off compared to its bigger sister (it's *la montre* in French) thanks to some serious reorganizing of the movement that included keeping the double barrel for the full 72-hour power reserve.

LUXURY ARTPIECES ARTYA SA
Route de Gy, 27
1252 Meinier
Switzerland

TEL.:
+41-22-752-4940

WEBSITE:
www.artya.com

FOUNDED:
2010

NUMBER OF EMPLOYEES:
12

U.S. DISTRIBUTOR:
BeauGeste Luxury Brands
www.beaugesteluxury.com

MOST IMPORTANT COLLECTIONS/PRICE RANGE:
Purity, Gears, Aqua, Art (and some exceptional pieces) / $3,800 to $190,000; more for individual complications

Purity Central Tourbillon (Red)

Movement: hand-wound, ArtyA exclusive tourbillon; ø 30.4 mm, height 9.35 mm; 28,800 vph; 36 jewels; 2 parallel-mounted spring barrels; 1-minute, 20-millimeter central flying tourbillon; fully skeletonized movement; hand-finished parts; 60-hour power reserve
Functions: hours, minutes, seconds on tourbillon cage
Case: sapphire crystal; ø 43 mm, height 18 mm; screwed-down transparent case back; water-resistant to 3 atm
Band: calfskin, pin buckle
Remarks: red sapphire crystal dial
Price: $150,000; unique piece

Curvy Purity Tourbillon NanoSaphir Emerald

Movement: hand-wound, ArtyA exclusive tourbillon; ø 35 mm, height 10 mm; 28,800 vph; 17 jewels; 2 parallel-mounted spring barrels; 1-minute, 18-millimeter flying tourbillon; fully skeletonized movement; hand-finished parts; 72-hour power reserve
Functions: hours, minutes, seconds on tourbillon cage
Case: green NanoSaphir; 43 x 38.5 mm, height 12 mm; screwed-down transparent case back; water-resistant to 3 atm
Band: calfskin, pin buckle
Price: $175,000; limited to 13 pieces

Purity "Stairway To Heaven" HMS Wavy

Movement: hand-wound, ArtyA exclusive tourbillon; ø 35 mm, height 10 mm; 28,800 vph; 17 jewels; fully skeletonized movement; 2 parallel-mounted spring barrels, with special design; centrally positioned, suspended screw balance; hand-finished parts; 72-hour power reserve
Functions: hours (engraved on top crystal), minutes, sweep seconds
Case: sapphire crystal; ø 40 mm, height 13 mm; wavy sapphire crystal dome; screwed-down transparent case back; water-resistant to 3 atm
Band: calfskin, pin buckle
Price: $49,700; limited to 13 pieces

Green Smoke Steel

Movement: automatic, La Joux-Perret G100 modified by ArtyA; ø 25.60 mm, height 4.45 mm; 24 jewels; 28,800 vph; with côtes de Genève; 68-hour power reserve
Functions: hours, minutes, sweep seconds; date
Case: stainless steel, ø 43 mm, height 14 mm; unidirectional rotating bezel with ceramic insert; transparent case back; water-resistant to 30 atm
Band: rubber, pin buckle
Price: $9,000; limited to 99 pieces

Steel Depth Gauge

Movement: automatic, La Joux-Perret G100 modified by ArtyA; ø 25.60 mm, height 4.45 mm; 24 jewels; 28,800 vph; with côtes de Genève; 68-hour power reserve
Functions: hours, minutes, sweep seconds; date
Case: stainless steel, ø 43 mm, height 14 mm; unidirectional rotating bezel in steel with ceramic insert; transparent case back; water-resistant to 30 atm
Band: rubber, pin buckle
Remarks: depth gauge on dial with colored arches that disappear one by one the deeper the diver goes due to light wavelengths no longer reaching the dial
Price: $9,000; limited to 99 pieces

Butterfly Pink Saphir

Movement: automatic, La Joux-Perret G100 modified by ArtyA; ø 25.60 mm, height 4.45 mm; 24 jewels; 28,800 vph; with côtes de Genève; 68-hour power reserve
Functions: hours, minutes, sweep seconds
Case: sapphire, ø 39 mm, height 12 mm; transparent case back; water-resistant to 3 atm
Band: calfskin, pin buckle
Remarks: real butterfly wings on the dial
Price: $29,900; unique piece

Large Orange Diver Carbon

Movement: automatic, exclusive ArtyOn caliber; ø 25.6 mm, height 3.6 mm; 28,800 vph; 25 jewels; COSC-certified movement; 42-hour power reserve
Functions: hours, minutes, seconds; date
Case: forged carbon, ø 43 mm, height 14 mm; engraved and screwed-down transparent case back; water-resistant to 30 atm
Band: rubber, pin buckle
Remarks: forged-carbon dial
Price: $11,900; unique piece

Butterfly Farfalla

Movement: automatic, exclusive ArtyOn caliber; ø 25.6 mm, height 3.6 mm; 28,800 vph; 25 jewels; skeletonized movement; COSC-certified movement; 42-hour power reserve
Functions: hours, minutes, sweep seconds
Case: stainless steel with carbon inserts in the barrel, ø 40 mm, height 10.8 mm; engraved and screwed-down transparent case back; water-resistant to 5 atm
Band: rubber, pin buckle
Remarks: real butterfly wings on the dial
Price: $11,900; unique piece

Butterfly Delicacy Set

Movement: automatic, exclusive ArtyOn caliber; ø 25.6 mm, height 3.6 mm; 28,800 vph; 25 jewels; COSC-certified movement; 42-hour power reserve
Functions: hours, minutes, sweep seconds
Case: stainless steel set with 256 diamonds, ø 40 mm, height 10.8 mm; engraved and screwed-down transparent case back; water-resistant to 10 atm
Band: reptile skin, pin buckle
Remarks: real butterfly wings on the dial
Price: $25,000; unique piece

AUDEMARS PIGUET

Jules-Louis Audemars (b. 1851) and Edward-Auguste Piguet (b. 1853) knew they would follow in the footsteps of their fathers and grandfathers and become watchmakers. They were members of the same sports association, sang in the same choir, attended the same vocational school—and both became outstandingly talented watchmakers. The *manufacture*, founded over 140 years ago by these two, is still in family hands, and it has become one of the leading names in the industry.

In the history of watchmaking, only a handful of watches have really achieved cult status. One of them is the Royal Oak, which truly disrupted the idea that the quartz watch was the end-all in horology. Audemars Piguet contacted the designer Gérald Genta to create a watch for a new generation of customers, a sportive luxury timepiece with a modern look, which could be worn every day. The result was a luxurious watch of stainless steel. The octagonal bezel held down with boldly "industrial" hexagonal bolts onto a 39-millimeter case was provocatively big and was nicknamed "Jumbo." It ran on what was then the thinnest automatic movement, a slice 3.05 millimeters high. This iconic piece is still delivering.

The second key to the brand's enduring success was no doubt the acquisition of the atelier Renaud et Papi in 1992. APRP, as it is known, specializes in creating and executing complex complications, a skill it lets other brands share in as well.

The "Code 11.59," with its round bezel and case and octagonal barrel, has evolved since its launch in 2019. The Code 11.59 Universelle is the most complicated watch ever made by AP, with 40 functions, including 23 complications. A masterpiece of ergonomics and design, it took seven years to develop. The collection celebrated its fifth anniversary in 2024 (a sign of staying power) with a host of new models in 38 and 41 mm in rose and white gold, including models with diamonds and sapphires. AP, as it is known, is showing its tried-and-true combination of design diversity and watchmaking expertise. A special model was added to the Royal Oak Concept: the limited edition Royal Oak Concept Flying Tourbillon, designed in collaboration with fashion designer Tamara Ralph, celebrating the natural synergies between *haute horlogerie* and *haute couture*.

MANUFACTURE D'HORLOGERIE
Audemars Piguet
Route de France 16
CH- 1348 Le Brassus
Switzerland

TEL.:
+41-21-642-3900

E-MAIL:
info@audemarspiguet.com

WEBSITE:
www.audemarspiguet.com

FOUNDED:
1875

NUMBER OF EMPLOYEES:
approx. 1,300

ANNUAL PRODUCTION:
50,000 watches

U.S. DISTRIBUTOR:
Audemars Piguet (North America) Inc.
Service Center of the Americas
3040 Gulf to Bay Boulevard
Clearwater, FL 33759

MOST IMPORTANT COLLECTIONS/PRICE RANGE:
CODE 11.59 / from approx. $26,000; Millenary / from approx. $28,400; Royal Oak / from approx. $17,800; special concept watches
Note: Some prices given in Swiss francs (CHF) with a daily exchange in dollars

[Re]Master Automatic
Reference number: 15240SG.OO.A347CR.01
Movement: automatic, AP caliber 7129; ø 29.6 mm, height 2.8 mm; 31 jewels; 28,800 vph; skeletonized Rotor in rose gold ("Sandgold"), finely finished movement; 52-hour power reserve
Functions: hours, minutes
Case: rose gold ("Sandgold"), ø 41 mm, height 9.7 mm; sapphire crystal; transparent case back; water-resistant to 3 atm
Band: reptile skin, pin buckle
Remarks: limited to 250 pieces
Price: $47,200

Royal Oak Flying Tourbillon Automatic Squelette
Reference number: 26735SG.OO.1320SG.01
Movement: automatic, AP caliber 2972; ø 31.5 mm, height 6.2 mm; 27 jewels; 21,600 vph; flying 1-minute tourbillon; fully skeletonized and finely finished movement; 65-hour power reserve
Functions: hours, minutes
Case: rose gold ("Sandgold"), ø 41 mm, height 10.6 mm; bezel screwed to case with 8 white-gold screws; sapphire crystal; transparent case back; water-resistant to 5 atm
Band: rose gold ("Sandgold"), folding clasp
Price: CHF 250,000 ($292,000)

Royal Oak Perpetual Calendar "John Mayer"
Reference number: 26574BC.OO.1220BC.02
Movement: automatic, AP caliber 5134; ø 29 mm, height 4.5 mm; 38 jewels; 19,800 vph; skeletonized rose-gold rotor, finely finished movement; 40-hour power reserve
Functions: hours, minutes; perpetual calendar with date, weekday, calendar week, month, moon phase, leap year
Case: white gold, ø 41 mm, height 9.5 mm; bezel screwed to case with 8 white-gold screws; sapphire crystal; transparent case back
Band: white gold, folding clasp
Remarks: designed in collaboration with US singer John Mayer; limited to 200 pieces
Price: $180,700

Royal Oak Offshore Automatic
Reference number: 15605SK.OO.A350CA.01
Movement: automatic, AP caliber 4302; ø 32 mm, height 4.9 mm; 32 jewels; 28,800 vph; gold rotor, finely finished movement; 70-hour power reserve
Functions: hours, minutes, sweep seconds; date
Case: stainless steel, ø 43 mm, height 14.4 mm; bezel screwed to case with 8 white-gold screws, with rubber layer; sapphire crystal; transparent case back; screw-down crown; water-resistant to 10 atm
Band: rubber, pin buckle
Remarks: comes with extra black rubber strap
Price: $27,400

Royal Oak Offshore Chronograph
Reference number: 26420ST.OO.A828CR.01
Movement: automatic, AP caliber 4401; ø 32 mm, height 6.8 mm; 40 jewels; 28,800 vph; movement entirely decorated by hand; 70-hour power reserve
Functions: hours, minutes, subsidiary seconds; flyback chronograph; date
Case: stainless steel, ø 43 mm, height 14.4 mm; bezel screwed to case with 8 white-gold screws; sapphire crystal; ceramic crown and pusher in ceramic; water-resistant to 10 atm
Band: reptile skin, pin buckle
Remarks: comes with extra rubber strap
Price: $41,600

Royal Oak Offshore Flying Tourbillon Chronograph Automatic
Reference number: 26622CE.OO.D002CA.02
Movement: automatic, AP caliber 2967; ø 33.6 mm, height 8.4 mm; 40 jewels; 21,600 vph; flying 1-minute tourbillon; 65-hour power reserve
Functions: hours, minutes; flyback chronograph
Case: ceramic with rose-gold elements, ø 43 mm, height 15.5 mm; bezel screwed to case with 8 white-gold screws; sapphire crystal; transparent case back; screw-down crown; water-resistant to 10 atm
Band: rubber, folding clasp
Remarks: skeletonized dial; comes with additional reptile skin strap
Price: CHF 305,000 (around $350,000)

CODE 11.59 Chronograph
Reference number: 26393NR.OO.A002KB.02
Movement: automatic, AP caliber 4401; ø 32 mm, height 6.8 mm; 40 jewels; 28,800 vph; skeletonized gold rotor, finely finished movement; 70-hour power reserve
Functions: hours, minutes, subsidiary seconds; flyback chronograph; date
Case: ceramic, ø 41 mm, height 12.6 mm; bezel, lugs and back in rose gold; sapphire crystal; transparent case back; water-resistant to 3 atm
Band: textile with rubber coating, pin buckle
Price: $49,700
Variations: various cases, straps, and dials

CODE 11.59 Automatic
Reference number: 15210OR.OO.A056KB.01
Movement: automatic, AP caliber 4302; ø 32 mm, height 4.9 mm; 32 jewels; 28,800 vph; gold rotor, finely finished movement; 70-hour power reserve
Functions: hours, minutes, sweep seconds; date
Case: rose gold, ø 41 mm, height 10.7 mm; sapphire crystal; transparent case back; water-resistant to 3 atm
Band: textile with rubber coating, pin buckle
Price: $35,400
Variations: various cases, straps, and dials

CODE 11.59 Automatic
Reference number: 77410OR.OO.A342CR.01
Movement: automatic, AP caliber 5900; ø 26.2 mm, height 3.9 mm; 29 jewels; 28,800 vph; gold rotor, finely finished movement; 60-hour power reserve
Functions: hours, minutes, sweep seconds; date
Case: rose gold, ø 38 mm, height 9.6 mm; sapphire crystal; transparent case back; water-resistant to 3 atm
Band: reptile skin, pin buckle
Price: $34,200
Variations: various cases, straps, and dials

Royal Oak Flying Tourbillon Automatic Extra-Thin (RD#3)

Reference number: 26660ST.OO.1356ST.02
Movement: automatic, AP caliber 2968; ø 29.6 mm, height 3.4 mm; 33 jewels; 21,600 vph; flying 1-minute tourbillon; skeletonized rotor; 50-hour power reserve
Functions: hours, minutes, tourbillon seconds
Case: stainless steel, ø 37 mm, height 8.1 mm; bezel screwed to case with 8 white-gold screws; sapphire crystal; transparent case back; water-resistant to 5 atm
Band: stainless steel, folding clasp
Price: CHF 165,400 (about $192,000)

Royal Oak Double Balance Wheel Openworked

Reference number: 15407ST.OO.1220ST.02
Movement: automatic, AP caliber 3132; ø 26.6 mm, height 4.4 mm; 38 jewels; 21,600 vph; double balance, skeletonized movement and rotor in rose gold; 45-hour power reserve
Functions: hours, minutes, sweep seconds
Case: stainless steel, ø 41 mm, height 9.9 mm; sapphire crystal; transparent case back; screw-down crown; water-resistant to 5 atm
Band: stainless steel, folding clasp
Price: $76,400

Royal Oak Concept Flying Tourbillon "Tamara Ralph"

Reference number: 26630OR.GG.D626CR.01
Movement: hand-wound, AP caliber 2964; ø 29.5 mm, height 4.8 mm; 17 jewels; 21,600 vph; flying 1-minute tourbillon; 72-hour power reserve
Functions: hours, minutes
Case: rose gold, ø 38.5 mm, height 11.9 mm; bezel screwed to case with 8 white-gold screws; sapphire crystal; transparent case back; crown with sapphire cabochon
Band: reptile skin, pin buckle
Remarks: multilevel rose-gold dial; comes with extra reptile skin strap; developed in collaboration with fashion designer Tamara Ralph; limited to 102 pieces
Price: CHF 177,000 (around $205,000)

Royal Oak Automatic

Reference number: 15551OR.ZS.D344CR.01
Movement: automatic, AP caliber 5900; ø 26.2 mm, height 3.9 mm; 29 jewels; 28,800 vph; finely finished movement; 60-hour power reserve
Functions: hours, minutes, sweep seconds; date
Case: rose gold, set with 82 diamonds, lugs set with 40 diamonds, ø 37 mm, height 9 mm; bezel screwed to case with 8 white-gold screws, set with 40 sapphires; sapphire crystal; transparent case back; water-resistant to 5 atm
Band: reptile skin, folding clasp set with 42 diamonds
Price: $67,900

Royal Oak Frosted Gold Automatic

Reference number: 77450BA.GG.1361BA.01
Movement: automatic, AP caliber 5800; ø 23.9 mm, height 4 mm; 28 jewels; 28,800 vph; finely finished movement; 50-hour power reserve
Functions: hours, minutes, sweep seconds; date
Case: yellow gold, with a structured surface, ø 34 mm, height 8.8 mm; bezel screwed to case with 8 white-gold screws; sapphire crystal; transparent case back; water-resistant to 5 atm
Band: yellow gold, folding clasp
Remarks: microstructured yellow-gold dial ("Crystal Sand")
Price: $62,100

Royal Oak Mini Frosted Gold

Reference number: 67630OR.GG.1312OR.01
Movement: quartz, AP caliber 2730
Functions: hours, minutes
Case: rose gold, with a structured surface, ø 23 mm, height 6.6 mm; bezel screwed to case with 8 white-gold screws; sapphire crystal; water-resistant to 5 atm
Band: rose gold, folding clasp
Remarks: microstructured rose-gold dial
Price: $34,400

Caliber 5800

Automatic; skeletonized gold rotor; single mainspring
barrel, 50-hour power reserve
Functions: hours, minutes, sweep seconds; date
Diameter: 23.3 mm
Height: 3.9 mm
Jewels: 28
Balance: with variable inertia
Frequency: 28,800 vph
Remarks: polished and beveled steel parts, perlage on
mainplate, côtes de Genève on bridges; 189 parts

Caliber 7129

Automatic; fully skeletonized movement, skeletonized
rotor in rose gold ("Sandgold"); single mainspring
barrel, 52-hour power reserve
Functions: hours, minutes
Diameter: 29.6 mm
Height: 2.8 mm
Jewels: 31
Frequency: 28,800 vph
Shock protection: Kif
Remarks: finely finished movement; 211 parts

Caliber 5134

Automatic; single mainspring barrel, 40-hour power
reserve
Functions: hours, minutes; perpetual calendar with
date, weekday, calendar week, month, moon phase,
leap year
Diameter: 29 mm
Height: 4.5 mm
Jewels: 38
Balance: with adjustable inertia
Frequency: 19,800 vph
Hairspring: flat hairspring
Remarks: finely-finished by hand; gold rotor; 374 parts

Caliber 2964

Hand-wound; flying 1-minute tourbillon; single
mainspring barrel, 72-hour power reserve
Functions: hours, minutes
Diameter: 29.5 mm
Height: 4.8 mm
Jewels: 17
Frequency: 21,600 vph
Remarks: 207 parts

Caliber 4401

Automatic; column-wheel control of chronograph
functions; skeletonized gold rotor; single mainspring
barrel, 70-hour power reserve
Functions: hours, minutes, subsidiary seconds; flyback
chronograph; date
Diameter: 32 mm
Height: 6.8 mm
Jewels: 40
Balance: with variable inertia
Frequency: 28,800 vph
Remarks: polished and beveled steel parts, perlage on
mainplate, côtes de Genève on bridges; 367 parts

Caliber 2972

Automatic; flying 1-minute tourbillon; skeletonized er
rotor; single mainspring barrel, 65-hour power reserve
Functions: hours, minutes
Diameter: 31.5 mm
Height: 6.24 mm
Jewels: 27
Frequency: 21,600 vph
Remarks: 271 parts

AZIMUTH

Creativity can take on all forms and accept all forms. This appears to be the philosophy behind Azimuth, an independent watch brand that has sprouted an eclectic and surprising bouquet of watch designs. For the company, the path is by no means well-beaten: like them or not, Azimuth always guarantees a raised eyebrow with its avant-garde designs. If the word iconic means "instantly identifiable," then it does apply to models like the Mr. Roboto, the Spaceship series, and the automobile series. In fact, these almost enjoy cult status.

Toys, cars, the ephemera of a teenager, science fiction are all inspirations for Chris Long, founder and CEO of the company. The Land Cruiser carries the DNA of its predecessor, the SP-1 Landship, created in 2010, which was inspired by the World War I military tank. Time is told by the domed wandering hour at the 12 o'clock position and the slanted retrograde minute aperture at the 6 o'clock position. The Land Cruiser is sleek, with chiseled sides and smooth curves reminiscent of the Stealth Bomber. It even features the afterburner, namely the winding crown at 12 o'clock.

The company has been updating its portfolio of late. The year 2024 produced a new Back in Time Series 2 (BIT S2), a timepiece that started its career at Baselworld 2009 and was a world premiere. As the name suggests, time turns counterclockwise for this one-hander. It made a hit back then and has gathered a dedicated following. The case and crown have been modernized and the writing now appears mirrored. And a new three-hander, the Micromatic Wood Dragon, has been added to the collections, this one running on a vintage Universal movement.

As for the Mr. Roboto, it now has a "new armour," a special crystallized titanium case that gives it a raw industrial machine look. Mr. Roboto's eyes have been enlarged with super-domed sapphire crystals, ensuring visibility from all sides. The complex CNC operation and post treatment process to create the titanium crystalized effect makes this model by far the most complex Mr. Roboto ever created.

AZIMUTH WATCH CO. SÀRL
Rue des Draizes n° 5
CH-2000 Neuchâtel
Switzerland

TEL.:
+41-79-765-1466

E-MAIL:
gpi@azimuthwatch.com
chrislong@azimuthwatch.com

WEBSITE:
www.azimuthwatch.com

FOUNDED:
2003

NUMBER OF EMPLOYEES:
4

U.S. DISTRIBUTOR:
About Time Luxury Group
210 Bellevue Avenue
Newport RI 02840
401-952-4684

MOST IMPORTANT COLLECTIONS/PRICE RANGE:
SP-1 / Mr. Roboto / Back in Time / Micromatic from
$2,600

SP-1 Mr. Roboto Titanium

Reference number: SP.TI.MRT.L001
Movement: automatic, in-house modified ETA caliber 2836-2; ø 32.5 mm, height 6.7 mm; 28,800 vph; 36-hour power reserve
Functions: regulator hours, retrograde minutes; world time
Case: crystalized titanium, 43 mm x 50 mm; sapphire crystal, water-resistant to 3 atm
Band: rubber strap, pin buckle
Price: $10,450

SP-1 Mr. Roboto Sapphire

Reference number: SP.TI.MRS.L003
Movement: automatic, in-house modified ETA caliber 2836-2; ø 32.5 mm, height 6.7 mm; 28,800 vph; 36-hour power reserve
Functions: regulator hours, retrograde minutes; world time display
Case: sapphire crystal, 43 mm x 50 mm; water-resistant to 3 atm
Band: textile, bronze pin buckle
Remarks: 20th anniversary collection for 2023; Damascus steel dial
Price: $23,000; limited to 20 pieces

SP-1 Mr. Roboto Bronzo Artist Series

Reference number: SP.BR.MRB.L002
Movement: automatic, in-house modified ETA caliber 2836-2; ø 32.5 mm, height 6.7 mm; 28,800 vph; 36-hour power reserve
Functions: regulator hours, retrograde minutes; world time display
Case: bronze, 43 mm x 50 mm; water-resistant to 3 atm
Band: calfskin, bronze pin buckle
Remarks: individually hand-engraved bezel with a unique motif
Price: $10,450; unique piece

SP-1 Mr. Roboto R2

Reference number: SP.SS.ROT.N001
Movement: automatic, in-house modified ETA caliber 2836-2; ø 32.5 mm, height 6.7 mm; 28,800 vph; 36-hour power reserve
Functions: regulator hours, retrograde minutes; world time display
Case: stainless steel, 47 mm x 55 mm; sapphire crystal; water-resistant to 3 atm
Band: calf strap, folding clasp
Price: $6,600
Variations: mid-case in titanium with blue PVD

SP-1 Land Cruiser

Reference number: SP.SS.LC.L001
Movement: automatic, in-house modified Sellita caliber SW200-1; ø 32.5 mm, height 6.7 mm; 28,800 vph; 36-hour power reserve
Functions: regulator hours, retrograde minutes
Case: stainless steel, 50 mm x 45 mm; water-resistant to 3 atm
Band: rubber strap, folding clasp
Price: $7,500; limited to 100 pieces

SP-1 Gran Turismo

Reference number: SP.SS.GT.N001
Movement: automatic, ETA caliber 2671; ø 17.2 mm, height 4.8 mm; 28,800 vph; 38-hour power reserve
Functions: hours, minutes, seconds
Case: stainless steel, 50 mm x 45 mm; water-resistant to 3 atm
Band: calf strap, folding clasp
Price: $5,500; limited to 150 pieces
Variations: top case in black, gold or camo design with PVD

SP-1 Spaceship Predator PVD Lava OverLand

Reference number: SP.TI.PR.N003
Movement: manual winding, ETA caliber 6497-1; ø 36.6 mm, height 4.5 mm; 18,800 vph; micro-sandblasted finishing with blued screws; 40-hour power reserve
Functions: jumping hours, minutes
Case: titanium with PVD treatment and stainless steel, ø 44 mm, domed sapphire crystal; water-resistant to 3 atm
Band: rubber strap, folding clasp
Price: $5,800

Azimuth Wood Dragon

Reference number: RN.UG.SS.S201
Movement: automatic, vintage Universal Genève caliber; ø 27 mm, height 3.9 mm; 21,600 vph; micro-rotor; côtes de Genève; 38-hour power reserve
Functions: hours, minutes, sweep seconds
Case: stainless steel, ø 41.30 mm, height 11.15 mm; sapphire crystal; water-resistant to 3 atm
Band: calf strap, folding clasp
Remarks: 1960s Universal Genève caliber; malachite stone dial
Price: $3,050; limited to 50 pieces
Variations: various dial colours and straps combination

Azimuth Back-In-Time Series 2

Reference number: RN.BT.SS.S201
Movement: automatic, SW200-1 in-house modified; ø 32.9 mm, height 4.5 mm; 28,800 vph, power reserve 38 hours
Functions: single minute hand in counterclockwise motion
Case: stainless steel, ø 41.30 mm, height 13.35 mm; sapphire crystal; water-resistant to 3 atm
Band: calf strap, folding clasp
Price: $2,850
Variations: various dial colours and straps combination

BALL WATCH CO.

Ball Watch Co. collections trace back to the company's origins and evoke the glorious age when trains blowing smoke and steam crisscrossed America. The General Railroads Timepiece Standards back then included such norms as regulation in at least five positions, precision to within thirty seconds per week, Breguet hairsprings, and so on. One of the chief players in developing the standards was Webster Clay Ball, a farm boy-turned-watchmaker from Fredericktown, Ohio. He decided to leave the homestead and apprentice as a watchmaker.

Ball worked as a sales representative for Dueber watch cases and finally opened the Webb C. Ball Company in Cleveland. In 1891, he added the position of chief inspector of the Lake Shore Lines to his CV. His defining moment came when a hogshead's watch stopped for a few minutes on April 18 that year, resulting in a crash between a fast mail train and the Toledo Express near Kipton, Ohio.

The Lake Shore and Michigan Southern Railroad appointed Ball to investigate the tragedy, which killed nine people. After a two-year investigation, Ball decided to establish quality benchmarks for watch manufacturing that included antimagnetic technology. He also set up a standardized timekeeping tool that gave rise to an expression in the American vernacular, to be "on the Ball." It also inspired the future Swiss Society of Chronometry (COSC), which governs the highest watch timing certification standards today.

Sticking to its origins, Ball still produces tool-like watches, including divers, although now the manufacturing is done in Switzerland. These rugged, durable watches aim to be "accurate in adverse conditions," so says the company tagline—and at a very decent price. Since functionality is a top priority, Ball has developed several mechanisms like the patented SpringLOCK anti-shock system that prevents the balance spring from unfurling when jostled. Ball has also developed special oils for cold temperatures, and it is one of few brands to use tritium gas tubes to light up dials, hands, and markers. For those who need to read the time accurately in dark places—divers, pilots, commandos, hunters, etc.—this is essential.

BALL WATCH COMPANY SA
Rue du Châtelot 21
CH-2300 La Chaux-de-Fonds
Switzerland

TEL.:
+41-32-724-53-00

E-MAIL:
info@ballwatch.ch

WEBSITE:
www.ballwatch.ch

FOUNDED:
1891

U.S. DISTRIBUTION:
888-660-0691

MOST IMPORTANT COLLECTIONS/PRICE RANGE:
Engineer, Fireman, Trainmaster / $1,200 to $6,300

Engineer Hydrocarbon AeroGMT II Meteorite

Reference number: DG2018C-S20C-MSL
Movement: automatic, Ball caliber RR1201-C; ø 25.6 mm, height 4.1mm; 21 jewels; 28,800 vph; COSC-certified chronometer; 42-hour power reserve
Functions: hours, minutes, sweep seconds; date; three time zone indication
Case: stainless steel, ø 42 mm, height 13.85 mm; sapphire bidirectional bezel with micro gas tubes; dome-shaped anti-reflective sapphire crystal; crown protection system; water-resistant to 10 atm
Band: stainless steel, folding clasp and extension
Remarks: micro gas tube illumination; shock-resistant; anti-magnetic
Price: $4,499
Variations: rubber strap; comes in smaller size, ø 40 mm, height 14.5 mm

Engineer Hydrocarbon EOD

Reference number: DM3200A-S1C-BK
Movement: automatic, Ball caliber RR1101-CSL; ø 25.6 mm, height 3.6 mm; 25 jewels; 28,800 vph; COSC-certified chronometer; SpringLOCK antishock system; SpringSEAL patented regulator anti-shock system; special movement oil to endure -45°C to 80°C / -49°F to 176°F; 42-hour power reserve
Functions: hours, minutes, sweep seconds; magnified date
Case: titanium, ø 42 mm, height 13.7 mm; stainless steel unidirectional bezel with micro gas tube inset; Mu-metal shield; sapphire crystal; special screwed-in crown protection cap; push-in crown; water-resistant to 30 atm; patented shock absorption ring
Band: titanium and stainless steel, folding clasp with extension link
Remarks: micro gas tube illumination; shock-resistant; anti-magnetic
Price: $3,349
Variations: ceramic bezel

Engineer Hydrocarbon NEDU

Reference number: DC3226A-S3C-BE
Movement: automatic, Ball caliber RR1402-C; ø 30 mm, height 7.9 mm; 25 jewels; 28,800 vph; COSC-certified chronometer; 48-hour power reserve
Functions: hours, minutes, subsidiary seconds; day, date; 12-hour chronograph operable underwater
Case: stainless steel, ø 42 mm, height 17.3 mm; patented helium system; ceramic unidirectional bezel; sapphire crystal; crown protection system; water-resistant to 60 atm
Band: titanium and stainless steel, folding clasp with extension link
Remarks: micro gas tube illumination; shock-resistant; anti-magnetic
Price: $4,849
Variations: black dial; rubber strap

Engineer Master II Diver Chronometer

Reference number: DM2280A-S1C-BKR
Movement: automatic, Ball caliber RRM7337-C; ø 25.6 mm, height 3.6 mm; 25 jewels; 28,800 vph; COSC-certified chronometer; 42-hour power reserve
Functions: hours, minutes, sweep seconds; magnified date
Case: stainless steel, ø 42 mm, height 13.5 mm; inner bezel with micro gas tube illumination; Mu-metal shield; sapphire crystal; screwed-in crown; water-resistant to 30 atm
Band: stainless steel, folding clasp
Remarks: micro gas tube illumination; shock-resistant; anti-magnetic
Price: $2,599
Variations: blue dial; standard tubes colors; rubber strap

Engineer III Endurance 1917 GMT

Reference number: GM9100C-S2C-IBER
Movement: automatic, Ball caliber RRM7337-C; ø 26.2 mm, height 4.5 mm; 25 jewels; 28,800 vph; COSC-certified chronometer; Amortiser anti-shock system; special movement oil to endure -45°C / -49°F; 42-hour power reserve
Functions: hours, minutes, sweep second; magnified date; quick-set local 12-hour hand; second time zone indication
Case: stainless steel, ø 41 mm, height 13.15 mm; Mu-metal shield; sapphire crystal; screwed-in crown; water-resistant to 10 atm
Band: stainless steel, folding clasp
Remarks: micro gas tube illumination; shock-resistant; anti-magnetic
Price: $3,199
Variations: grey dial; blue dial; standard tubes colors

Engineer III Marvelight Chronometer Meteorite

Reference number: NM9026C-S46C-MSLR
Movement: automatic, Ball caliber RR1103-C; ø 25.6 mm, height 4.6 mm; 25 or 26 jewels; 28,800 vph; anti-magnetic Mu-metal shield; COSC-certified chronometer; Amortiser anti-shock system; 38-hour power reserve
Functions: hours, minutes, sweep seconds; magnified date
Case: stainless steel, ø 40 mm, height 12.45 mm; bidirectional bezel; stainless steel; screw-down crown; transparent case back; water-resistant to 20 atm
Band: stainless-steel, folding clasp
Remarks: micro gas tube illumination; shock-resistant; anti-magnetic
Price: $2,749

Engineer III Marvelight Chronometer (36mm)

Reference number: NL9616C-S1C-PK
Movement: automatic, Ball caliber RR1101-C; ø 25.6 mm, height 3.6 mm; 25 jewels; 28,800 vph; COSC-certified chronometer; Amortiser anti-shock system; 42-hour power reserve
Functions: hours, minutes, sweep seconds; magnified date
Case: stainless steel, ø 36 mm, height 11.5 mm; Mu-metal shield; sapphire crystal; screw-in crown; water-resistant to 10 atm
Band: stainless steel, folding clasp
Remarks: micro gas tube illumination; shock-resistant; anti-magnetic
Price: $2,899
Variations: black dial; ice blue dial; green dial; rainbow tubes colors

Engineer III Marvelight Chronometer Day/Date

Reference number: NM9036C-S1C-IBE
Movement: automatic, Ball caliber RR1102-C; ø 25.6 mm, height 5.05 mm; 25 or 26 jewels; 28,800 vph; COSC-certified chronometer; Amortiser anti-shock system; 38-hour power reserve
Functions: hours, minutes, sweep seconds; day, magnified date
Case: stainless steel, ø 40 mm, height 13 mm; Mu-metal shield; sapphire crystal; screwed-in crown; water-resistant to 10 atm
Band: stainless steel, folding buckle
Remarks: micro gas tube illumination; shock-resistant; anti-magnetic
Price: $2,599
Variations: black dial; blue dial; green dial; grey dial; rainbow tubes colors

Engineer M Skindiver III Beyond

Reference number: DD3100A-S2C-BE
Movement: automatic, Ball caliber RRM7309-C; ø 34.24 mm, height 5.16 mm; 25 jewels; 28,800 vph; COSC-certified chronometer; Amortiser anti-shock system; 80-hour power reserve
Functions: hours, minutes, sweep seconds; magnified date
Case: stainless steel, ø 41.5 mm, height 13.8 mm; sapphire unidirectional bezel; sapphire crystal; screwed-in crown; water-resistant to 30 atm
Band: stainless steel, folding clasp
Remarks: micro gas tube illumination; shock-resistant; anti-magnetic
Price: $3,699

Roadmaster M Model A

Reference number: DA9100C-S1-BKR
Movement: automatic, Ball caliber RRM7379;
ø 30.4 mm, height 7.6 mm; 31 jewels; 28,800 vph;
40-hour power reserve
Functions: hours, minutes, sweep seconds; magnified
date; AlarmMATIC 12-hour automatic mechanical alarm;
triple time zone
Case: titanium, ø 41 mm, height 15.2 mm; bidirectional
bezel; sapphire crystal; screw-down crown; transparent
case back; water-resistant to 10 atm
Band: stainless-steel, folding clasp
Remarks: micro gas tube illumination; shock-resistant;
anti-magnetic
Price: $6,299

Roadmaster Marine GMT

Reference number: DG3000A-S4C-BK
Movement: automatic, Ball caliber RR1203-C;
ø 31.4 mm, height 5.75 mm; 25 or 26 jewels; 28,800 vph;
COSC-certified chronometer; 38-hour power reserve
Functions: hours, minutes, sweep seconds; day and
date, three time zone indication
Case: titanium, ø 40 mm, height 14 mm; bidirectional
bezel; sapphire crystal; screwed-in crown; transparent
case back; water-resistant to 20 atm
Band: titanium and stainless-steel, folding clasp
Remarks: micro gas tube illumination; shock-resistant;
anti-magnetic
Price: $3,249

Roadmaster Perseverer

Reference number: NM9050C-S1-IBE
Movement: automatic, Ball caliber RR1103; ø 25.6 mm,
height 4.6 mm; 25 or 26 jewels; 28,800 vph; 38-hour
power reserve
Functions: hours, minutes, sweep seconds; magnified
date
Case: stainless steel, ø 40 mm, height 12 mm;
bidirectional bezel; sapphire crystal; screwed-down
crown; transparent case back; water-resistant to 10 atm
Band: stainless steel bracelet with folding clasp
Remarks: micro gas tube illumination; shock-resistant;
anti-magnetic
Price: $1,849
Variation: with black dial

Roadmaster Rescue Chronograph

Reference number: DC3030C-S-BK
Movement: automatic, Ball caliber RR1402; ø 30 mm,
height 7.9 mm; 25 or 26 jewels; 28,800 vph; special
movement oil to endure -45°C / -49°F; 48-hour power
reserve
Functions: hours, minutes, subsidiary seconds; day and
date; chronograph; pulsometer
Case: titanium, ø 41 mm, height 14.8 mm; unidirectional
ceramic bezel; sapphire crystal; screw-down crown;
transparent case back; water-resistant to 10 atm
Band: titanium and stainless steel, folding clasp
Remarks: micro gas tube illumination; shock-resistant;
anti-magnetic
Price: $3,749
Variation: with blue, green, or white dial

Trainmaster Eternity

Reference number: NM2080D-S2J-IBE
Movement: automatic, Ball caliber RR1102; ø 25.6 mm,
height 5.05 mm; 25 or 26 jewels; 28,800 vph; 38-hour
power reserve
Functions: hours, minutes, sweep seconds; day and
date
Case: stainless steel, ø 39.5 mm, height 11.8 mm;
sapphire crystal; transparent case back; screw-in crown;
water-resistant to 3 atm
Band: stainless steel, folding buckle
Remarks: micro gas tube illumination; shock-resistant;
anti-magnetic
Price: $2,099
Variations: black dial; silver dial; reptile skin

Fireman Victory

Reference number: NM2098C-S5J-SL
Movement: automatic, Ball caliber RR1103; ø 25.6 mm,
height 4.6 mm; 25 or 26 jewels; 28,800 vph; 38-hour
power reserve
Functions: hours, minutes, sweep seconds; date
Case: stainless steel, ø 40 mm, height 11.3 mm;
sapphire crystal; screw-in crowns; water-resistant to
10 atm
Band: stainless steel, folding buckle
Remarks: micro gas tube illumination; shock-resistant;
anti-magnetic
Price: $1,499
Variations: black dial; blue dial; calf leather

BALTIC WATCHES

In 2005, Etienne Malec found a treasure: a suitcase once belonging to his photographer father, who had died when he was just a boy and who had been an avid watch collector. Inside, he found a diary filled with notes on purchases, trades, and sales of various watches. The discovery ignited Malec's fascination with horology and set him on a very unexpected path.

Armed with an MBA, Etienne Malec founded Baltic Watches in 2016 using Kickstarter. The name is a tribute to his father, who came from northeastern Poland, a region with a rich history and culture and a stunning landscape that includes a coastline on the Baltic Sea. Another acknowledgement of his father's collection and heritage is a vintage spirit that governs many of the brand's models without being overwhelming.

This aesthetic mission means that the collections often have modern touches, like the off-center subsidiary seconds dial on the MR series, which has a diameter of 36 millimeters. The Prismic series, for its part, features a combination of guilloché and a sandy surface on the dial.

Malec's idea, when founding his brand, was to make affordable timepieces, which is one reason why they distributed by direct sales. They are equipped with Miyota and Sea-Gull movements, which have improved their quality over the past decade and are becoming competitive. Parts are made in Hong Kong, and all assembly and adjustments are done in Besançon, France, which is a hub of watchmaking in the country and has the expertise. Accessories, like bracelets and straps of rubber, Perlon, and leather, or rolls for traveling are made in Italy.

Among Baltic's other collections are the Aquascaphe diving watches, which have full functionality for underwater exploration (water resistant to 20 atm) and a very retro look reminiscent of 1950s dive watches. Chronographs, which are always popular, are also part of the portfolio, including the "panda" Tricompax and the Bicompax, which has a typical stepped case from the 1940s. And for its part, the Hermétique Tourer collection is dressy-sportive type with rich colors that seem chosen to fit any sartorial fashion, including beach garb.

BALTIC WATCHES
29, rue du Château Landon
F-75010 Paris
France

TEL.:
+33-1-40-16-07-17

E-MAIL:
support@baltic-watches.com

WEBSITE:
www.baltic-watches.com

FOUNDED:
2016

DISTRIBUTION:
Direct sales

MOST IMPORTANT COLLECTIONS/PRICE RANGE:
Aquascaphe, Bicompax, Hermétique, HMS,
Tricompax / $500 to $1000

Aquascaphe Titanium Blue
Movement: hand-wound, Miyota caliber 9039;
ø 26 mm, height 5.64 mm; 24 jewels; 28,800 vph;
42-hour power reserve
Functions: hours, minutes, sweep seconds
Case: titanium, ø 41 mm, height 13.6 mm; unidirectional
ceramic bezel; screw-down crown; sapphire crystal;
transparent case back; water-resistant to 30 atm
Band: rubber (FKM), folding clasp
Price: $710; limited to 300 numbered pieces
Variations: with black dial

Bicompax 3 Blue Gilt
Movement: hand-wound, Seagull caliber ST1901;
ø 31 mm, height 5.85 mm; 23 jewels; 21,600 vph;
column wheel control chronograph; 42-hour power
reserve
Functions: hours, minutes, subsidiary seconds;
chronograph with 30-minute totalizer; date
Case: stainless steel, ø 36.5 mm, height 13 mm;
sapphire crystal; transparent case back; water-resistant
to 5 atm
Band: stainless steel, folding clasp
Price: $540
Variations: comes with silver, blue, and salmon dials

Hermétique Tourer – Brown
Movement: hand-wound, Miyota caliber 9039;
ø 26 mm, height 5.64 mm; 24 jewels; 28,800 vph;
42-hour power reserve
Functions: hours, minutes, sweep seconds
Case: stainless steel, ø 37 mm, height 10.8 mm;
sapphire crystal; transparent case back; water-resistant
to 5 atm
Band: rubber (FKM), folding clasp
Price: $550
Variations: with beige, blue, or green dial; various strap
colors; stainless-steel beads-of-rice or link bracelet
($615)

BAUME & MERCIER

Baume & Mercier, a company founded in 1830, has staked a claim on the market by its ability to keep a finger on the pulse of stylish, urban fashionistas, who are looking for affordable yet remarkable timepieces. Since the early 2000s, it has created a number of noteworthy—and often copied—classics, like the Riviera and the Catwalk.

Joining the Richemont Group has boosted the brand's technical value. In 2018, after four years of development with ValFleurier, the Group's movement manufacturer, and the RIMS research and innovation team, Baume & Mercier released its first in-house *manufacture* movement, the Baumatic Caliber BM12-1975A. In 2020, it added two new complications to the in-house caliber. Models using the caliber boast a five-day power reserve and accuracy of just –4/+6 seconds per day and anti-magnetism that is about twenty-five times higher than the current ISO norm.

The new BM14.1975 AC1/AC2 caliber is used in four of the Clifton models and drives a moon phase plus, in two models, a weekday and date display. To make way for the subsidiary dials and apertures, the crosshairs that "ordered" the dial of the simpler three-handers were removed.

The Hampton line now also includes a series of watches whose rectangular shape recalls Art Deco predecessors. Most recently, the company rebooted the Riviera collection, which celebrated its fiftieth anniversary in 2023 and has been a perennial favorite for the whole half-century. The Riviera of 2024 comes in a range of colors, notably elegant darker hues, and different sizes (42 mm, 39 mm, 36 mm, and 32 mm). The larger models are equipped with the in-house Baumatic movement caliber, which was created exclusively for Baume & Mercier by the Richemont Group and boasts a 120-hour power reserve. The high-performance movement boasts a power reserve of 120 hours with magnetic field protection. Best of all, it can be admired through a dial made of tinted sapphire glass that allows a view of the mechanics.

BAUME & MERCIER
Rue André de Garrini 4
CH-1217 Meyrin
Switzerland

TEL.:
+41-022-580-2948

WEBSITE:
www.baume-et-mercier.com

FOUNDED:
1830

ANNUAL PRODUCTION:
100,000 (estimated)

U.S. DISTRIBUTOR:
Baume & Mercier
Richemont North America
New York, NY 10022
800-637-2437

MOST IMPORTANT COLLECTIONS/ PRICE RANGE:
Clifton (men) / $3,250 o $26,800; Riviera (men and women) / $1,900 to $6,400 / Classima (men and women) / $1,050 to $4,700; Hampton (men and women) / $1,600 to $4,450

Riviera Baumatic

Reference number: M0A10769
Movement: automatic, caliber Baumatic BM13.1975A; ø 28.2 mm, height 4.2 mm; 21 jewels; 28,800 vph; silicon anchor and escape wheel; balance wheel with variable inertia; skeletonized rotor; 120-hour power reserve
Functions: hours, minutes, sweep seconds; date
Case: stainless steel with blue PVD, ø 39 mm, height 10.31 mm; sand-blasted titanium bezel screwed to case with 4 screws; sapphire crystal; transparent case back; water-resistant to 10 atm
Band: rubber, triple folding clasp
Remarks: transparent dial
Price: $4,500

Riviera Baumatic Tideograph

Reference number: M0A10761
Movement: automatic, caliber Baumatic BM13.1975AC3; ø 28.2 mm, height 5.8 mm; 21 jewels; 28,800 vph; silicon anchor and escape wheel; balance wheel with variable inertia; skeletonized rotor; 120-hour power reserve
Functions: hours, minutes, sweep seconds; tidal indicator
Case: stainless steel, ø 43 mm, height 12.34 mm; bezel screwed to case with 4 screws; sapphire crystal; transparent case back; water-resistant to 10 atm
Band: rubber, triple folding clasp
Price: $5,350; limited to 500 pieces

Riviera Baumatic

Reference number: M0A10770
Movement: automatic, caliber Baumatic BM13.1975A; ø 28.2 mm, height 4.2 mm; 21 jewels; 28,800 vph; silicon anchor and escape wheel; balance wheel with variable inertia; skeletonized rotor; 120-hour power reserve
Functions: hours, minutes, sweep seconds; date
Case: stainless steel, ø 39 mm, height 10.31 mm; bezel screwed to case with 4 screws; sapphire crystal; transparent case back; water-resistant to 10 atm
Band: stainless steel, triple folding clasp
Remarks: transparent dial
Price: $3,900

Riviera

Reference number: M0A10764
Movement: automatic, Sellita caliber SW200-1;
ø 25.2 mm, height 4.6 mm; 26 jewels; 28,800 vph;
38-hour power reserve
Functions: hours, minutes, sweep seconds; date
Case: stainless steel, ø 33 mm, height 9.6 mm; bezel
screwed to case with 4 screws; sapphire crystal;
transparent case back; water-resistant to 5 atm
Band: stainless steel, triple folding clasp
Price: $2,900

Riviera Baumatic

Reference number: M0A10787
Movement: automatic, caliber Baumatic BM13.1975A;
ø 28.2 mm, height 4.2 mm; 21 jewels; 28,800 vph;
silicon anchor and escape wheel; balance wheel with
variable inertia; skeletonized rotor; 120-hour power
reserve
Functions: hours, minutes, sweep seconds; date
Case: rose gold, ø 39 mm, height 10.31 mm; bezel
screwed to case with 4 screws; sapphire crystal;
transparent case back; water-resistant to 5 atm
Band: reptile skin, triple folding clasp
Remarks: transparent dial
Price: $20,500

Riviera Skeleton

Reference number: M0A10721
Movement: automatic, Sellita caliber
SW200 skeletonized; ø 25.2 mm, height 4.6 mm;
27 jewels; 28,800 vph; 38-hour power reserve
Functions: hours, minutes
Case: stainless steel, ø 42 mm, height 11.11 mm; bezel
screwed to case with 4 screws; sapphire crystal;
transparent case back; water-resistant to 5 atm
Band: rubber, triple folding clasp
Remarks: skeletonized dial
Price: $4,500

Riviera Perpetual Calendar

Reference number: M0A10786
Movement: automatic, caliber Baumatic
BM13.1975AC2 with Dubois Dépraz 55102 module;
ø 28.2 mm, height 5.8 mm; 21 jewels; 28,800 vph;
silicon anchor and escape wheel; balance wheel with
variable inertia; skeletonized rotor; 120-hour power
reserve
Functions: hours, minutes, sweep seconds; perpetual
calendar with date, weekday, month, moon phase, leap
year
Case: stainless steel, ø 40 mm, height 11.8 mm; bezel
screwed to case with 4 screws; sapphire crystal;
transparent case back; water-resistant to 5 atm
Band: stainless steel, triple folding clasp
Remarks: limited to 50 pieces
Price: $21,000;

Clifton Baumatic

Reference number: M0A10756
Movement: automatic, caliber Baumatic BM14-
1975AC1; ø 28.2 mm, height 4.2 mm; 21 jewels;
28,800 vph; silicon anchor and escape wheel; balance
wheel with variable inertia; skeletonized rotor; 120-hour
power reserve
Functions: hours, minutes, sweep seconds; date, moon
phase
Case: stainless steel, ø 39 mm, height 12.25 mm;
sapphire crystal; transparent case back; water-resistant
to 5 atm
Band: reptile skin, triple folding clasp
Price: $4,900

Hampton

Reference number: M0A10751
Movement: quartz
Functions: hours, minutes
Case: stainless steel, 22.2 mm x 34.9 mm, height
6.92 mm; sapphire crystal; crown cabochon; water-
resistant to 5 atm
Band: stainless steel with rose gold PVD-coated middle
links, double folding clasp
Price: $3,400

BELL & ROSS

If there is such a class as "military chic," Bell & Ross is undoubtedly one of the leaders. The Paris-headquartered brand develops, manufactures, assembles, and regulates its timepieces in a modern factory in La Chaux-de-Fonds in the Jura mountains of Switzerland. The early models had a certain stringency that one might associate with soldierly life, but in the past years, working with outside specialists, the company has ventured into even more complicated watches such as tourbillons and wristwatches with uncommon shapes. This kind of ambitious innovation has only been possible since perfume and fashion specialist Chanel—which also maintains a successful watch line in its own right—became a significant Bell & Ross shareholder and brought the watchmaker access to the production facilities where designer Bruno Belamich and team can create more complicated, more interesting designs for their aesthetically unusual "instrument" watches.

What sets Bell & Ross timepieces apart from those of other, more traditional professional luxury makers is their special, roguish look: a delicate balance between striking, martial, and poetic—think Lawrence of Arabia, the gallivanting warrior. And it is this beauty for the eye to behold that makes the company's wares popular with style-conscious "civilians" as well as with the pilots, divers, astronauts, sappers, and other hard-riding professionals drawn to Bell & Ross timepieces for their superior functionality. The plane-cockpit gauge look is especially strong in recent models, like the Radiocompass and the one paying tribute to France's air ace troop, Patrouille de France. The latest line, the BR-05, forms a bridge between the square instrument watches and the round vintage ones. And it's not only about the geometrical patterns, but rather about aesthetics.

BELL & ROSS LTD.
8 rue Copernic
F-75116 Paris
France

TEL.:
+33-1-73-73-93-00

E-MAIL:
sav@bellross.com

WEBSITE:
www.bellross.com

FOUNDED:
1992

U.S. DISTRIBUTOR:
Bell & Ross, Inc.
605 Lincoln Road, Suite 300
Miami Beach, FL 33139
888-307-7887
information@bellross.com
www.bellross.com

MOST IMPORTANT COLLECTIONS/ PRICE RANGE:
Instrument BR-X1, BR 01, BR 03, and BR 05 / approx. $3,100 to $450,000

BR 03 Cyber Ceramic
Reference number: BR03-CYBER-CE
Movement: automatic, caliber BR-CAL.383; ø 25.6 mm; height 7.8 mm; 25 jewels; 28,800 vph; fully skeletonized mainplate and bridges, with black coating; 48-hour power reserve
Functions: hours, minutes
Case: ceramic, 42 mm x 43.7 mm, height 10.8 mm; sapphire crystal; transparent case back; screw-down crown; water-resistant to 5 atm
Band: rubber, pin buckle
Remarks: skeletonized dial
Price: $13,400; limited to 500 pieces

BR 05 Black Ceramic
Reference number: BR05A-BL-CE
Movement: automatic, caliber BR-CAL.321-1 (Sellita SW300-1 base); ø 25.6 mm, height 3.6 mm; 21 jewels; 28,800 vph; 54-hour power reserve
Functions: hours, minutes, sweep seconds; date
Case: ceramic, 41 mm x 41 mm, height 11.2 mm; bezel screwed to monocoque with 4 screws; sapphire crystal; transparent case back; screw-down crown; water-resistant to 10 atm
Band: ceramic, folding clasp
Price: $7,500
Variations: with rubber strap

BR 05 Skeleton Black Lum Ceramic
Reference number: BR05A-BLM-SKCE
Movement: automatic, caliber BR-CAL.322-1 (Sellita SW300-1 base); ø 25.6 mm, height 3.6 mm; 21 jewels; 28,800 vph; 54-hour power reserve
Functions: hours, minutes, sweep seconds
Case: ceramic, 41 mm x 41 mm, height 11.2 mm; bezel screwed to monocoque with 4 screws; sapphire crystal; transparent case back; screw-down crown; water-resistant to 10 atm
Band: ceramic, folding clasp
Remarks: skeletonized dial with luminous indexes
Price: $9,400; limited to 500 pieces

BR-X5 Black Titanium

Reference number: BRX5R-BL-TI
Movement: automatic, caliber BR-CAL.323; ø 31 mm; height 6.52 mm; 28 jewels; 28,800 vph; 70-hour power reserve
Functions: hours, minutes, sweep seconds; power reserve indicator; date
Case: stainless steel, 41 mm x 41 mm, height 12.8 mm; bezel screwed to monocoque with 4 screws; sapphire crystal; transparent case back; screw-down crown; water-resistant to 10 atm
Band: titanium, folding clasp
Remarks: iridescent green to purple dial
Price: $8,400
Variations: with rubber strap ($7,900); also as Black Titanium ($9,900)

BR 05 Chrono Grey Steel & Gold

Reference number: BR05C-RTH-STPG
Movement: automatic, caliber BR-CAL.326 (Sellita SW510-1 base); ø 30 mm, height 7.9 mm; 25 jewels; 28,800 vph; 60-hour power reserve
Functions: hours, minutes, subsidiary seconds; chronograph; date
Case: stainless steel, 42 mm x 42 mm, height 14.25 mm; rose-gold bezel screwed to monocoque with 4 screws; sapphire crystal; transparent case back; screw-down crown; water-resistant to 10 atm
Band: stainless steel with rose-gold middle links, folding clasp
Price: $14,100
Variations: with rubber strap

BR 03 Diver Full Lum

Reference number: BR03A-D-LM-CE/SRB
Movement: automatic, caliber BR-CAL.302-1 (Sellita SW300-1 base); ø 25.6 mm, height 3.6 mm; 25 jewels; 28,800 vph; 54-hour power reserve
Functions: hours, minutes, sweep seconds; date
Case: ceramic, 42 x 42 mm, height 12.05 mm; unidirectional bezel, with 0-60 scale; sapphire crystal; screw-down crown; water-resistant to 30 atm
Band: rubber, pin buckle
Remarks: comes with extra textile strap
Price: $5,400
Variations: in stainless steel

BR 03 Diver

Reference number: BR03A-D-BL-ST/SRB
Movement: automatic, caliber BR-CAL.302-1 (Sellita SW300-1 base); ø 25.6 mm, height 3.6 mm; 25 jewels; 28,800 vph; 54-hour power reserve
Functions: hours, minutes, sweep seconds; date
Case: stainless steel, 42 mm x 42 mm, height 12.05 mm; unidirectional bezel with ceramic insert, with 0-60 scale; sapphire crystal; screw-down crown; water-resistant to 30 atm
Band: rubber, pin buckle
Remarks: comes with extra textile strap
Price: $4,400
Variations: with white dial; in ceramic or steel

BR-03 Horizon

Reference number: BR03A-HRZ-CE/SRB
Movement: automatic, caliber BR-CAL.327 (Sellita SW300-1 base); ø 25.6 mm, height 3.6 mm; 21 jewels; 28,800 vph; 54-hour power reserve
Functions: hours, minutes, sweep seconds
Case: ceramic, 41 mm x 41 mm, height 10.6 mm; bezel screwed to monocoque with 4 screws, crown-activated scale ring with 0-60 scale to adjust horizon line; sapphire crystal; water-resistant to 10 atm
Band: rubber, pin buckle
Remarks: comes with extra textile strap in orange
Price: $4,500; limited to 999 pieces

BR-X5 Racing

Reference number: BRX5R-RAC-TI
Movement: automatic, caliber BR-CAL.323; ø 31 mm; 6.52 mm thick; 28 jewels; 28,800 vph; 70-hour power reserve
Functions: hours, minutes, sweep seconds; power reserve indicator; date
Case: titanium, 41 mm x 41 mm, height 12.8 mm; bezel with carbon fiber insert, screwed to the monocoque with 4 screws; sapphire crystal; transparent case back; screw-down crown; water-resistant to 10 atm
Band: titanium, folding clasp
Price: $11,800; limited to 500 pieces
Variations: with rubber strap

BLANCPAIN

Blancpain, launched in 1735, is Switzerland's oldest watch brand, and it can proudly say that it never produced a quartz watch. In the 1970s, it was part of the famous conglomerate Société Suisse pour l'Industrie Horlogère (SSIH), but after the "Quartz Crisis" destroyed the industry, the name was sold off to Jacques Piguet and Jean-Claude Biver. The company moved to the Frédéric Piguet watch factory in Le Brassus, where it produced mechanical watches, notably one with six great complications, which sold for 1 million Swiss francs, an eye-catching sum of money. Thus, Blancpain became largely responsible for the renaissance of the mechanical wristwatch in Switzerland and worldwide.

This success caught the attention of the Swatch Group—known at that time as SMH. In 1992, it swooped in and purchased both companies to add to its portfolio. Movement fabrication and watch production were melded to form the Blancpain Manufacture in mid-2010.

But being quartz-less does not mean being old-fashioned. Over the past several years, Blancpain president Marc A. Hayek has put a great deal of energy into developing the company's technical originality. In terms of complications, Blancpain watches have always been in a class of their own. The product families were all consolidated into four families: the Villeret; the legendary Fifty Fathoms diver's watches; Ladybird, a graceful series for women; and Métier's d'art, a collection of unique pieces that express the brand's artistic and watchmaking prowess.

In 2023, the Fifty Fathoms celebrated its seventieth anniversary, accounting for a wave of iterations of this classic diver's watch. The series of models in restrained 42-millimeter stainless-steel cases was followed by the Fifty Fathoms Tech Gombessa. This titanium watch, developed for rebreathing divers, has a three-hour hand with a correspondingly marked rotating bezel. Three hours is considered a possible dive time with new technology, in which the exhaled air is partially recycled and enriched with fresh oxygen.

Having "encroached" into the world of divers, Blancpain has also made preservation of the seas and marine life one of its commitments to sustainability.

BLANCPAIN SA
Le Rocher 12
CH-1348 Le Brassus
Switzerland

TEL.:
+41-21-796-3636

WEBSITE:
www.blancpain.com

FOUNDED:
1735

U.S. DISTRIBUTOR:
Blancpain
The Swatch Group (U.S.), Inc.
1200 Harbor Boulevard
Weehawken, NJ 07086
201-271-4680

MOST IMPORTANT COLLECTIONS/PRICE RANGE:
Villeret, Fifty Fathoms, Ladybird, Air Command, Métiers d'Art / $9,800 to $420,000

Fifty Fathoms Automatique

Reference number: 5010-12B40-064B
Movement: automatic, Blancpain caliber 1315; ø 30.6 mm, height 5.65 mm; 35 jewels; 28,800 vph; silicon hairspring; 120-hour power reserve
Functions: hours, minutes, sweep seconds; date
Case: titanium, ø 42.3 mm, height 14.3 mm; unidirectional bezel with sapphire crystal insert with 0-60 scale; sapphire crystal; transparent case back; screw-down crown; water-resistant to 30 atm
Band: textile, folding clasp
Price: $18,400
Variations: various straps and dials

Fifty Fathoms Automatique

Reference number: 5010-36B40-052B
Movement: automatic, Blancpain caliber 1315; ø 30.6 mm, height 5.65 mm; 35 jewels; 28,800 vph; silicon hairspring; 120-hour power reserve
Functions: hours, minutes, sweep seconds; date
Case: red gold, ø 42.3 mm, height 14.3 mm; unidirectional bezel with sapphire crystal insert with 0-60 scale; sapphire crystal; transparent case back; screw-down crown; water-resistant to 30 atm
Band: textile, folding clasp
Price: $34,300

Fifty Fathoms Automatique

Reference number: 5010-12B30-98S
Movement: automatic, Blancpain caliber 1315; ø 30.6 mm, height 5.65 mm; 35 jewels; 28,800 vph; silicon hairspring; 120-hour power reserve
Functions: hours, minutes, sweep seconds; date
Case: titanium, ø 42.3 mm, height 14.3 mm; unidirectional bezel with sapphire crystal insert with 0-60 scale; sapphire crystal; transparent case back; screw-down crown; water-resistant to 30 atm
Band: titanium, folding clasp
Price: $19,300
Variations: with sailcloth strap with rubber lining ($18,400)

Fifty Fathoms 70th Anniversary "Act 3"

Reference number: 5901-5630-NANA
Movement: automatic, Blancpain caliber 1154.P2; ø 27.4 mm, height 3.55 mm; 28 jewels; 28,800 vph; silicon hairspring; 100-hour power reserve
Functions: hours, minutes, sweep seconds; moisture indicator
Case: bronze gold, ø 41.3 mm, height 13.3 mm; unidirectional bezel with ceramic insert with 0-60 scale; sapphire crystal; transparent case back; screw-down crown; water-resistant to 30 atm
Band: textile, pin buckle
Price: $32,700; limited to 555 pieces

Fifty Fathoms 70th Anniversary "Act 2" Tech Gombessa

Reference number: 5019-12B30-64A
Movement: automatic, Blancpain caliber 13P8; ø 30.6 mm, height 5.65 mm; 35 jewels; 28,800 vph; silicon hairspring; 120-hour power reserve
Functions: hours, minutes, sweep seconds; dive time indicator (3 hours)
Case: titanium, ø 47 mm, height 14.81 mm; unidirectional bezel with ceramic insert, with 3-hour scale; sapphire crystal; transparent case back; screw-down crown, helium valve; water-resistant to 30 atm
Band: rubber, pin buckle
Price: $28,000

Fifty Fathoms Bathyscaphe Quantième Complet Phases de Lune

Reference number: 5054-3640-O52A
Movement: automatic, Blancpain caliber 6654.P; ø 32 mm, height 5.48 mm; 28 jewels; 28,800 vph; 2 mainsprings, 72-hour power reserve
Functions: hours, minutes, sweep seconds; full calendar with date, weekday, month, moon phase
Case: red gold, ø 43 mm, height 13.3 mm; unidirectional bezel with ceramic insert with 0-60 scale; sapphire crystal; transparent case back; screw-down crown; water-resistant to 30 atm
Band: textile, pin buckle
Price: $32,000

Fifty Fathoms Bathyscaphe Titan

Reference number: 5000-1210-G52A
Movement: automatic, Blancpain caliber 1315; ø 30.6 mm, height 5.65 mm; 35 jewels; 28,800 vph; silicon hairspring; 120-hour power reserve
Functions: hours, minutes, sweep seconds; date
Case: titanium, ø 43 mm, height 13.45 mm; unidirectional bezel with ceramic insert with 0-60 scale; sapphire crystal; transparent case back; screw-down crown; water-resistant to 30 atm
Band: textile, pin buckle
Price: $12,400

Air Command

Reference number: AC02-36B40-63B
Movement: automatic, Blancpain caliber F388B; ø 31.8 mm, height 6.65 mm; 35 jewels; 28,800 vph; 50-hour power reserve
Functions: hours, minutes; flyback chronograph
Case: red gold, ø 42.5 mm, height 13.77 mm; bidirectional bezel with ceramic insert with 0-60 scale; sapphire crystal; transparent case back; water-resistant to 3 atm
Band: calfskin, folding clasp
Price: $33,000
Variations: in titanium ($20,500)

Villeret Quantième Perpétuel

Reference number: 6656-3653-55B
Movement: automatic, Blancpain caliber 5954; ø 32 mm, height 4.97 mm; 32 jewels; 28,800 vph; 72-hour power reserve
Functions: hours, minutes, sweep seconds; perpetual calendar with date, weekday, month, moon phase, leap year
Case: red gold, ø 40.3 mm, height 10.8 mm; sapphire crystal; transparent case back; water-resistant to 3 atm
Band: reptile skin, folding clasp
Price: $50,600

L-Evolution Big Date 8 Days

Reference number: 8850-11B34-53B
Movement: hand-wound, Blancpain caliber 6938; ø 32 mm, height 7.85 mm; 43 jewels; 21,600 vph; high-density gold rotor; 3 mainsprings, 192-hour power reserve
Functions: hours, minutes, sweep seconds; large date
Case: stainless steel, ø 43.5 mm, height 15.55 mm; sapphire crystal; transparent case back; water-resistant to 10 atm
Band: reptile skin, folding clasp
Remarks: multilevel dial with côtes de Genève decoraton
Price: $21,400
Variations: rose-gold case ($37,700); with hand-wound movement

Villeret Tourbillon Volant Une Minute 12 Jours

Reference number: 66240-3431-55B
Movement: automatic, Blancpain caliber 242; ø 30.6 mm, height 6.1 mm; 43 jewels; 28,800 vph; flying 1-minute tourbillon; 288-hour power reserve
Functions: hours, minutes; power reserve indicator (on the rear)
Case: platinum, ø 42 mm, height 11.65 mm; sapphire crystal; transparent case back; water-resistant to 3 atm
Band: reptile skin, folding clasp
Remarks: enamel dial
Price: $155,400; limited to 188 pieces
Variations: in red gold ($133,100)

Villeret Complete Calendar GMT

Reference number: 6676-1127-55B
Movement: automatic, Blancpain caliber 67A5.4; ø 27 mm, height 6 mm; 28 jewels; 28,800 vph; 2 mainsprings, 72-hour power reserve
Functions: hours, minutes; additional 24-hour display (second time zone); full calendar with date, weekday, month, moon phase
Case: stainless steel, ø 40.5 mm, height 11.8 mm; sapphire crystal; transparent case back; water-resistant to 3 atm
Band: reptile skin, folding clasp
Price: $17,200

Villeret Ultra Thin

Reference number: 6605-1127-55B
Movement: hand-wound, Blancpain caliber 11A4B; ø 27.4 mm, height 2.8 mm; 21 jewels; 21,600 vph; 100-hour power reserve
Functions: hours, minutes; power reserve indicator (on the rear)
Case: stainless steel, ø 39.7 mm, height 7.45 mm; sapphire crystal; transparent case back; water-resistant to 3 atm
Band: reptile skin, folding clasp
Price: $10,700

Ladybird Colors Phases de Lune

Reference number: 3662-2954-55B
Movement: automatic, Blancpain caliber 1163L; ø 26.2 mm, height 4.58 mm; 30 jewels; 28,800 vph; 100-hour power reserve
Functions: hours, minutes, subsidiary seconds; moon phase
Case: red gold, ø 34.9 mm, height 10.43 mm; bezel and lugs set with diamonds; sapphire crystal; transparent case back; water-resistant to 3 atm
Band: reptile skin, folding clasp
Remarks: mother-of-pearl dial set with diamonds
Price: $34,800

Ladybird Colors

Reference number: 3661A-1954-95A
Movement: automatic, Blancpain caliber 1163; ø 26.2 mm, height 3.25 mm; 30 jewels; 28,800 vph; silicon hairspring, 100-hour power reserve
Functions: hours, minutes, subsidiary seconds
Case: white gold, ø 34.9 mm, height 9.2 mm; bezel and lugs set with 59 diamonds; sapphire crystal; transparent case back; water-resistant to 3 atm
Band: reptile skin, pin buckle
Remarks: mother-of-pearl dial set with diamonds
Price: $34,500

BOTTA

The old exhortation "Keep it simple!" has found favor in many brands of watches. The Bauhaus movement in Germany and the parallel *neue Sachlichkeit* (New Objectivity) movement in art both codified many of the aesthetic elements that make up a simple, pleasing, and functional timepiece. Wristwatches from Botta meet the criteria for basic design and avoid the crime of ornamentation, to paraphrase the Viennese architect Alfred Loos.

The company's seven collections embody different time concepts all expressed with minimal means. The spectrum of the traditional brand from the Taunus region near Frankfurt ranges from original one-hand watches to sun-synchronized twenty-four-hour watches.

The design of the watches is just as individual as their themes. Each concept has its own message. The common theme of all Botta watches is total clarity and logic, making the reading of time easy and fast for the wearer. From the watch case to the smallest scale, every detail is implemented with impressive perfection.

Klaus Botta is a graduate of the renowned Offenbach University of Art and Design (HfG). His work has won over sixty national and international design awards.

Watches, however, were not his only ambit at the start. Rather he worked with cars, hi-fi equipment, and other products. In the mid-1980s, he designed a one-hand watch, which later became a trailblazer for such timepieces, one example being those manufactured by the company MeisterSinger.

Simplicity has a way of always being timeless, and it was Botta's goal when he founded his company. Botta's watches not only stand out clearly from more conventional timepieces but also enable the wearer to consciously deal with that very special "resource": time. The key to this success, however, is the overall attention paid to first-class materials and components used in production. All Botta watches are now made from trititanium, a special alloy used in aerospace, for example. Furthermore, they run on robust ETA or Sellita calibers.

BOTTA DESIGN
Klosterstrasse 15a
D-61462 Königstein im Taunus
Germany

TEL.:
+49-6174-96 -11-88

EMAIL:
info@botta-design.de

WEBSITE:
www.botta-design.de

FOUNDED:
1986

NUMBER OF EMPLOYEES:
8

U. S. DISTRIBUTION:
Retail, online direct sales

MOST IMPORTANT COLLECTIONS:
UNO, UNO 24, TRES, TRES 24

Clavius Cumulus Automatic

Movement: automatic, Sellita caliber SW200-1; ø 25.6 mm, height 4.6 mm; 26 jewels; 28,800 vph; 38-hour power reserve
Functions: hours, minutes, sweep seconds
Case: titanium, ø 44 mm, height 9.5 mm; sapphire crystal; transparent case back; water-resistant to 5 atm
Band: stainless steel milanaise mesh, folding clasp
Remarks: the second hand flashes every second through slits in the dial
Price: $2,250; limited to 20 pieces
Variants: with calfskin strap ($2,150); with stainless steel bracelet as "Black Edition" ($2,200)

UNO 24 Edition 15 Automatic

Movement: automatic, ETA caliber 2893-2; ø 25.6 mm, height 4.1 mm; 21 jewels; 28,800 vph; 50-hour power reserve
Functions: 24 hours (each graduation mark stands for 10 minutes); date
Case: titanium, ø 40 mm, height 9.5 mm; sapphire crystal; transparent case back; water-resistant to 5 atm
Band: calfskin, pin buckle
Price: $2,350
Variations: with stainless steel bracelet ($2,400); with stainless steel milanaise mesh as "Black Edition" ($2,630)

MONDO GMT Automatic 45 mm "Black Edition"

Movement: automatic, ETA caliber 2893-2; ø 25.6 mm, height 4.1 mm; 21 jewels; 28,800 vph; 50-hour power reserve
Functions: hours, minutes, sweep seconds (small C-hand in the center); additional 24-hour display (second time zone); date
Case: titanium, ø 45 mm, height 9.5 mm; sapphire crystal; transparent case back; water-resistant to 5 atm
Band: saddle leather, pin buckle
Price: $2,390
Variants: with calfskin strap ($2,350)

BOVET

If any brand can claim real connections to China, it is Bovet, founded by Swiss businessman Edouard Bovet. Bovet emigrated to Canton, China, in 1818 and sold four watches of his own design there. On his return to Switzerland in 1822, he set up a company for shipping his Fleurier-made watches to China. The company, pronounced "Bo Wei" in Mandarin, became a synonym for "watch" in Asia and at one point had offices in Canton. For more than eighty years, Bovet and his successors supplied the Chinese ruling class with valuable timepieces.

In 2001, the brand was bought by entrepreneur Pascal Raffy. He ensured the company's industrial independence by acquiring several other companies as well, notably the high-end watchmaker Swiss Time Technology (STT) in Tramelan, which he renamed Dimier 1738. In addition to creating its own line of watches, this *manufacture* produces complex technical components such as tourbillons for Bovet watches. Assembly of Bovet creations takes place at the headquarters in the thirteenth-century Castle of Môtiers in Val-de-Travers not far from Fleurier.

These high-end timekeepers, with appeal to men and women, do have several distinctive features. The first is intricate dial work, featuring not only complex architecture, but also intricate guilloché patterns and very fine enameling techniques. Bovet has collaborated with car manufacturers like Pininfarina and Rolls-Royce, for which it manufactured a bespoke dashboard clock that can be used as a table clock or wristwatch thanks to the Amadéo conversion system. This allows the wristbands to be easily attached or removed from the watch. Some models convert to table clocks, and the Amadeo Fleurier Miss Audrey series can even be worn on a necklace.

Bovet always pushes the envelope, and it has earned them several "Oscars" at the Grand Prix d'Horlogerie in Geneva. One such winner, the Astérium, shows the sky as seen from the Earth, and gives the sun time (equation complication), plus a complete calendar with astrological signs on the back. And the 2024 Recital 28 Prowess 1 features a genuine first in terms of complications, a world timer mechanism on twenty-four cylinders that can be corrected for Daylight Savings Time in the USA and Europe.

BOVET FLEURIER S.A.
Le Château, CP20
CH-2112 Môtiers
Switzerland

TEL.:
+41-32-862-0808

E-MAIL:
info@bovet.com

WEBSITE:
www.bovet.com

FOUNDED:
1822

ANNUAL PRODUCTION:
around 1,000 timepieces

U.S. DISTRIBUTOR:
Bovet LLC North America
305-974-4826

MOST IMPORTANT COLLECTIONS/PRICE RANGE:
Dimier, Fleurier, Pininfarina / $18,500 to $1,000,000

Recital 21

Movement: hand-wound, caliber 13DM05-QP; ø 30.44 mm (36 mm with module), height 6.75 mm; 37 jewels; 21,600 vph; 5-day power reserve
Functions: hours, minutes, subsidiary coaxial seconds; day, retrograde date, month, leap year; power reserve indicator
Case : polished titanium, ø 44.4, height 10.25 to 15.4 mm; crown set with sapphire cabochon; water-resistant to 3 atm;
Band: reptile skin, pin buckle
Remarks: slant-top case; transparent, tinged sapphire dial
Price: $110,000; limited to 60 pieces
Variations: smoked or blue dial

Pininfarina Aperto 1

Movement: hand-wound, caliber 15BMPF09-OW; ø 34 mm, height 5.8 mm; 38 jewels; 21,600 vph; fully skeletonized; finely finished movement, PVD or CVD coated bridges; 7-day power reserve
Functions: hours, minutes, subsidiary seconds; power reserve indicator
Case: polished titanium, ø 42, height 10.95 mm; crown set with sapphire cabochon; water-resistant to 3 atm
Band: rubber, folding clasp
Remarks: latest model in the collaboration with Pininfarina
Price: $57,000; limited to 60 pieces
Variations: with blue bridges

19Thirty OWO

Movement: hand-wound, caliber 15BMPF09-OW; ø 34 mm, height 5.8 mm; 38 jewels; 21,600 vph; fully skeletonized; finely finished movement, PVD or CVD coated bridges; 7-day power reserve
Functions: hours, minutes, subsidiary seconds; power reserve indicator
Case: polished titanium, ø 42 mm, height 9.05 mm; crown set with sapphire cabochon; transparent case back; water-resistant to 3 atm;
Band: reptile skin, folding clasp
Remarks: inspired by the Rose Ceiling of the Old War Office in London
Price: $45,000; limited to 10 pieces
Variations: smoked or blue dial

Recital 28 Prowess 1

Movement: hand-wound, caliber R28-70-00X; ø 38 mm, height 13.3 mm; 51 jewels; 18,000 vph; double-sided 1-minute tourbillon; finely finished, hand-engraving, côtes de Genève, and perlage, 10-day power reserve
Functions: hours, minutes, seconds on tourbillon; full calendar, including leap year; world timer on rollers with adjustment for daylight saving time in different parts of the globe
Case: titanium, ø 46.3 mm, height 17.85 mm; crown set with sapphire cabochon; transparent case back; water-resistant to 3 atm
Band: reptile skin, folding clasp
Remarks: slant-top case
Price: $720,000; limited to 60 pieces in all, 8 per year
Variations: case in red gold, platinum

Récital Asterium (front)

Reference number: R20N005/1/PU
Movement: hand-wound, Bovet caliber 17DM02-SKY; ø 38 mm, height 12.45 mm; 18,000 vph; double-side flying tourbillon; fully skeletonized movement; 10-day power reserve
Functions (front): hours, minutes (retrograde at 3 o'clock), seconds; day/night display; calendar with day, date, month; double hemispheric moon phase; equation of time (at 9 o'clock); power reserve indicator (at 3 o'clock)
Remarks: the Asterium represents the sky seen from the earth; sidereal year shown, with 365 days, 6 hours, 9 minutes

Récital Asterium (back)

Functions (back): single hand traveling 365.25 days (thanks to the equation of time) for the calendar with date (on bezel and gradated track) and months; astrological signs, four seasons indication, solstices and equinoxes
Case: red gold, with white gold sections, reversed hand fitting, ø 46 mm, height 18.30 mm; sapphire crystal on both sides
Band: leather, pin buckle
Remarks: easy setting of the annual calendar and all other functions with the crown; slant-top case
Price: $350,000; unique piece

Recital 12

Movement: hand-wound, caliber 13BMDR12C2; ø 31 mm, height 4 mm; 45 jewels; 21,600 vph; openworked dial; finely finished movement; 7-day power reserve
Functions: hours, minutes, subsidiary seconds; power reserve indicator
Case: polished titanium, ø 40 mm, height 9.08 mm; crown set with sapphire cabochon; transparent case back; water-resistant to 3 atm;
Band: titanium, folding clasp
Remarks: dial with guilloché, blued hands
Price: $35,000
Variations: with turquoise or green dial

Virtuoso XI

Movement: hand-wound, caliber 17BM03-GD; ø 38 mm, height 6.7 mm; 36 jewels; 18,000 vph, 1-minute flying tourbillon; 10-day power reserve
Functions: hours, minutes, subsidiary seconds
Case: white gold, engraved and bezel set with 60 baguette-cut diamonds, ø 44 mm; water-resistant to 3 atm
Band: reptile skin, pin buckle
Remarks: slant-top case; all plates and bridges hand-engraved in Fleurisanne style on both sides, fully skeletonized movement
Price: $400,000
Variations: comes without diamonds nor engraving on the case

Virtuoso VIII Chapter 2

Movement: hand-wound, Bovet caliber 17BM03-GD; ø 38 mm, height 6.7 mm; 18,000 vph; with côtes de Genève; 1-minute double-faced flying tourbillon; decorate with blackened Côtes de Genève; 10-day power reserve
Functions: hours, minutes, seconds on tourbillon cage; power reserve indicator; big date
Case: red gold, ø 44 mm, height 13.45 mm; transparent case back; water-resistant to 3 atm
Band: reptile skin, buckle
Price: on request; limited to 8 pieces each
Variations: dials with green, blue, yellow, pink and salmon Super-LumiNova; titanium case, and guilloché dial

BREGUET

Abraham-Louis Breguet (1747–1823), who hailed from Switzerland, brought his craft to Paris in the *Sturm und Drang* atmosphere of the late eighteenth century. It was fertile ground for one of the most inventive watchmakers in the history of horology, and his products soon found favor with the highest levels of society.

Little has changed two centuries later. After a few years of drifting, in 1999 the brand carrying this illustrious name became the prize possession of the Swatch Group and came under the personal management of Nicolas G. Hayek, CEO. Hayek worked assiduously to restore the brand's roots, going as far as rebuilding the legendary Marie Antoinette pocket watch and contributing to the restoration of the Petit Trianon at Versailles.

Breguet is a full-fledged *manufacture*, and this has allowed it to forge ahead uncompromisingly with upscale watches and even jewelry. In modern facilities on the shores of Lake Joux, traditional craftsmanship still plays a significant role in the production of its fine watches, but at the same time, Breguet is one of the few brands to work with modern materials for its movements. After years focusing on the Reine de Naples, Tradition, Classique, and Marine collections, Breguet decided to spotlight pilot chronographs. In the post-war period, the company supplied the French Air Force with the standard pilot's chronograph in addition to on-board watches. Now, the model family has been supplemented by two new models in a historicized look, equipped with a brand new chronograph movement with automatic winding.

The two new watches are stylish interpretations of Breguet's Type XX line, which has indeed been delighting watch lovers for seventy years now: a "military" bicompax version with horizontally arranged small seconds and half-hour subdials, and a "civilian" tricompax version with three totalizers, including a 15-minute counter (a reminder of the days when you needed to track minutes for long-distance calls). A closer look at the model designations reveals that the "military" chronograph (reference 2057) is called "Type 20," written in Arabic numerals as in the original series from the fifties. The "civilian" version (reference 2067) is designated "Type XX," with Roman numerals.

MONTRES BREGUET SA
CH-1344 L'Abbaye
Switzerland

TEL.:
+41-21-841-9090

WEBSITE:
www.breguet.com

FOUNDED:
1775 (Swatch Group since 1999)

NUMBER OF EMPLOYEES:
1,000

U.S. DISTRIBUTOR:
Breguet
The Swatch Group (U.S.), Inc.
1200 Harbor Boulevard, 7th Floor
Weehawken, NJ 07086
201-271-1400

MOST IMPORTANT COLLECTIONS:
Classique, Tradition, Héritage, Marine, Reine de Naples, Type XX, Type XXI, Type XXII

Classique Double Tourbillon "Quai De l'Horloge"

Reference number: 5345BR 1S 5XU
Movement: hand-wound, Breguet caliber 588N; ø 35.5 mm; 81 jewels; 18,000 vph; two independent tourbillons, affixed to a central disc by a bridge, which complete one rotation in 12 hours; 2 mainsprings; Breguet hairspring; skeletonized movement; 50-hour power reserve
Functions: hours, minutes
Case: rose gold, ø 46 mm, height 16.8 mm; sapphire crystal; transparent case back
Band: rubber, triple folding clasp
Remarks: guilloché dial
Price: $789,000
Variations: in platinum

Type XX Flyback Chronograph

Reference number: 2067ST 92 3WU
Movement: automatic, Breguet caliber 728; ø 32.7 mm; 39 jewels; 28,800 vph; silicon Breguet hairspring and escapement; gold oscillating mass; 60-hour power reserve
Functions: hours, minutes, subsidiary seconds; flyback chronograph; date
Case: stainless steel, ø 42 mm, height 14,1 mm; bidirectional bezel, with 0-12 scale; sapphire crystal; transparent case back; water-resistant to 10 atm
Band: textile, pin buckle
Remarks: comes with extra calfskin strap
Price: $19,100

Type 20 Flyback Chronograph

Reference number: 2057ST 92 SW0
Movement: automatic, Breguet caliber 7281; ø 32.7 mm; 34 jewels; 28,800 vph; silicon Breguet hairspring and escapement; gold oscillating mass; 60-hour power reserve
Functions: hours, minutes, subsidiary seconds; flyback chronograph; date
Case: stainless steel, ø 42 mm, height 14.1 mm; bidirectional bezel with reference markers; sapphire crystal; transparent case back; water-resistant to 10 atm
Band: stainless steel, folding clasp
Remarks: comes with extra textile strap
Price: $22,300

Marine Tourbillon

Reference number: 5577PT Y2 5WV
Movement: automatic, Breguet caliber 581; ø 36 mm;
33 jewels; 28,800 vph;1-minute tourbillon; silicon pallet
lever and hairspring; 80-hour power reserve
Functions: hours, minutes, subsidiary seconds (on the
tourbillon cage)
Case: platinum, ø 42.5 mm, height 9.35 mm; sapphire
crystal; transparent case back; water-resistant to
10 atm
Band: rubber, folding clasp
Price: $185,800
Variations: various straps

Marine Chronograph

Reference number: 5527BB Y2 5WV
Movement: automatic, Breguet caliber 582QA;
ø 32.7 mm; height 6.5 mm, 28 jewels; 28,800 vph;
silicon pallet lever and hairspring; 48-hour power
reserve
Functions: hours, minutes, subsidiary seconds;
chronograph; date
Case: white gold, ø 42.3 mm, height 14 mm; bezel set
with 90 diamonds; sapphire crystal; transparent case
back; screw-down crown; water-resistant to 10 atm
Band: rubber, folding clasp
Remarks: dial set with 8 baguette-diamonds
Price: $39,700
Variations: with reptile skin strap

Marine Date

Reference number: 5517TI G2 TZ0
Movement: automatic, Breguet caliber 777A;
ø 33.8 mm; 26 jewels; 28,800 vph; silicon pallet lever
and hairspring; 55-hour power reserve
Functions: hours, minutes, sweep seconds; date
Case: titanium, ø 40 mm, height 11.5 mm; sapphire
crystal; transparent case back
Band: titanium, folding clasp
Price: $22,300
Variations: with reptile skin or rubber strap

Tradition Quantième Rétrograde

Reference number: 7597BB GY 9WU
Movement: automatic, Breguet caliber 505 Q; ø 33 mm;
38 jewels; 21,600 vph; silicon Breguet hairspring and
pallet fork; 50-hour power reserve
Functions: hours and minutes (off-center); date
(retrograde)
Case: white gold, ø 40 mm, height 12,1 mm; sapphire
crystal; transparent case back; water-resistant to 3 atm
Band: reptile skin, folding clasp
Remarks: blued-gold dial with hand-guilloché
Price: $45,300
Variations: in rose gold, without blued-gold dial
($44,400)

Tradition Grande Complication Fusée

Reference number: 7047PT 1Y 9ZU
Movement: hand-wound, Breguet caliber 569;
ø 35.7 mm, height 10.82 mm; 43 jewels; 18,000 vph;
silicon Breguet hairspring, torque regulation by fusée
and chain, 1-minute tourbillon; 50-hour power reserve
Functions: hours, minutes; power reserve indicator
Case: platinum, ø 41 mm, height 15.95 mm; sapphire
crystal; transparent case back; water-resistant to 3 atm
Band: reptile skin, folding clasp
Price: $222,200
Variations: in rose gold ($206,100)

Classique Tourbillon Extra-Plat 5367

Reference number: 5367BR 299 WU
Movement: automatic, Breguet caliber 581; ø 36 mm;
33 jewels; 28,800 vph;1-minute tourbillon; silicon
anchor and hairspring; 80-hour power reserve
Functions: hours, minutes, subsidiary seconds (on the
tourbillon cage)
Case: rose gold, ø 41 mm, height 7.45 mm; sapphire
crystal; transparent case back; water-resistant to 3 atm
Band: reptile skin, triple folding clasp
Remarks: enamel dial
Price: $173,300
Variations: in platinum ($190,300)

Classique Quantième Perpétuel

Reference number: 7327BR 11 9VU
Movement: automatic, Breguet caliber 502.3.P;
ø 27.1 mm, height 4.5 mm; 35 jewels; 21,600 vph; silicon
Breguet hairspring and escapement; gold oscillating
mass; 45-hour power reserve
Functions: hours, minutes; perpetual calendar with
date, weekday, month (retrograde), moon phase and
leap year
Case: rose gold, ø 39 mm, height 9.13 mm; sapphire
crystal; transparent case back; water-resistant to 3 atm
Band: reptile skin, folding clasp
Remarks: hand-guilloché on gold dial
Price: $89,300
Variations: in white gold

Classique

Reference number: 7147BB 299 WU
Movement: automatic, Breguet caliber 502.3SD;
ø 24.9 mm, height 2.4 mm; 35 jewels; 21,600 vph;
silicon anchor and hairspring; 45-hour power reserve
Functions: hours, minutes, subsidiary seconds
Case: white gold, ø 40 mm, height 6.1 mm; sapphire
crystal; transparent case back; water-resistant to 3 atm
Band: reptile skin, pin buckle
Remarks: enamel dial
Price: $25,300
Variations: in rose gold

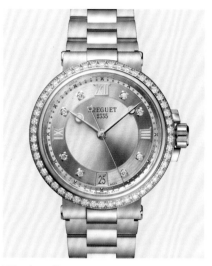

Marine Dame

Reference number: 9518ST 1D S80 D001
Movement: automatic, Breguet caliber 591A;
ø 25.6 mm; 25 jewels; 28,800 vph; silicon Breguet
hairspring and escapement, gold oscillating mass set
with 31 diamonds; 38-hour power reserve
Functions: hours, minutes, sweep seconds; date
Case: stainless steel, ø 38.8 mm, height 9.89 mm; bezel
set with 50 diamonds; sapphire crystal; transparent
case back; water-resistant to 5 atm
Band: stainless steel, folding clasp
Remarks: dial set with 8 diamonds
Price: $28,680
Variations: reptile skin or rubber strap; in white gold;
in rose gold

Reine de Naples

Reference number: 8918BB 5D 964D0
Movement: automatic, Breguet caliber 537/3;
ø 19.7 mm, height 3.9 mm; 26 jewels; 21,600 vph; silicon
Breguet hairspring and escapement; 45-hour power
reserve
Functions: hours, minutes
Case: white gold, 28.45 mm x 36.5 mm, height
10.05 mm; bezel and flange set with 117 diamonds;
sapphire crystal; transparent case back; crown with
diamond; water-resistant to 3 atm
Band: reptile skin, folding clasp set with 26 diamonds
Remarks: mother-of-pearl dial with drop-shaped
diamonds and a central diamond pavé
Price: $49,700
Variations: various cases, straps, and dials

Reine de Naples

Reference number: 8928BR 5W 944 DD0D 3L
Movement: automatic, Breguet caliber 586/1;
ø 19.7 mm; height 3.9 mm, 29 jewels; 21,600 vph; silicon
hairspring and pallet horns; 38-hour power reserve
Functions: hours, minutes
Case: rose gold, 24.95 mm x 33 mm, height 10.05 mm;
bezel, flange, and lugs set with 139 diamonds; sapphire
crystal; transparent case back; crown with diamond
cabochon; water-resistant to 3 atm
Band: reptile skin, folding clasp set with 26 diamonds
Remarks: mother-of-pearl dial
Price: $42,600
Variations: in white gold ($43,900)

Reine de Naples

Reference number: 8908BR 5T 964 D00D 3L
Movement: automatic, Breguet caliber 537 DRL1;
ø 19.7 mm; 22 jewels; 25,200 vph; silicon Breguet
balance wheel, escapement, and hairspring; 40-hour
power reserve
Functions: hours, minutes, subsidiary seconds; power
reserve indicator; moon phase
Case: rose gold, 28.48 mm x 36.5 mm, height 10.05 mm;
bezel and dial set with 128 diamonds; sapphire crystal;
transparent case back; crown with sapphire cabochon
Band: reptile skin, folding clasp set with diamonds
Remarks: mother-of-pearl dial
Price: $43,900
Variations: various cases, straps, and dials

BREITLING

When Léon Breitling opened his workshop in St. Imier in the Jura Mountains in 1884, he set a course focusing consistently on instrument watches with a distinctive design. High quality standards and the rise of aviation completed the picture.

Today, Breitling's relationship with air sports and commercial and military aviation is clear from its brand identity. The unveiling of its own modern chronograph movement at Basel in 2009 was a major milestone in the company's history and also a return to its roots. The new design was to be "100 percent Breitling" and industrially produced in large numbers at a reasonable cost. Although Breitling's operations in Grenchen and in La Chaux-de-Fonds both boast state-of-the-art equipment, the contract for the new chronograph was awarded to a small team in Geneva. In 2006, the brand-new Caliber B01 made the COSC grade and has enjoyed great popularity ever since. For the team of designers, the innovative centering system on the reset mechanism that requires no manual adjustment was one of the great achievements.

Under CEO Georges Kern, Breitling expanded beyond the pilot watch niche and tapped markets in the Far East. The new collections were streamlined and given more defined profiles, a recipe Kern brought in from his IWC days. The winged logo was replaced mostly with a coquettish "B."

The brand has also introduced a new hypoallergenic material called Breitlight and is boldly using bright colors, like bright red straps. But of course, the models of the past still have top billing. For its seventieth birthday in 2022, the Navitimer was equipped with the in-house Caliber B01, housed in an entirely redesigned case. Because the slide rule function was indispensable, water resistance remained a modest 3 atmospheres (30 meters/100 feet).

Recently, the collection went all out to expand its popular lines, with new models for the Chronomat family, like the Chronomat GMT and the Super Chronomat 38. The Superocean, Top Time, and Premier collections have also been expanded. In 2024, to mark the brand's 140th anniversary, Breitling launched the iconic pilot's chronograph, the Navitimer, with slide rule bezel in a 43-millimeter case. Regardless of the spread of electronic instruments for the wrist, the fan club seems to be growing.

BREITLING
Léon Breitling-Strasse 2
2540 Grenchen
Switzerland

TEL.:
+41-32-654-5454

E-MAIL:
info.US@Breitling.com

WEBSITE:
www.breitling.com

FOUNDED:
1884

ANNUAL PRODUCTION:
700,000 (estimated)

U.S. DISTRIBUTOR:
Breitling U.S.A. Inc.
206 Danbury Road
Wilton, CT 06897
203-762-1180
www.breitling.com

MOST IMPORTANT COLLECTIONS:
Navitimer, Avenger, Premier, Chronomat, Top Time, Superocean Heritage, Superocean, Professional, Classic Avi

Navitimer B01 Chronograph 43

Reference number: AB0138241C1P1
Movement: automatic, Breitling caliber B01; ø 30 mm, height 7.2 mm; 47 jewels; 28,800 vph; column-wheel control of chronograph functions; COSC-certified chronometer; 70-hour power reserve
Functions: hours, minutes, subsidiary seconds; chronograph; date
Case: stainless steel, ø 43 mm, height 13.6 mm; bidirectional bezel, with integrated slide rule and tachymeter scale; sapphire crystal; transparent case back; water-resistant to 3 atm
Band: reptile skin, folding clasp
Price: $9,550
Variations: various cases, straps, and dials

Navitimer Automatic 41

Reference number: A17329161C1A1
Movement: automatic, Breitling caliber 17 (Sellita SW200-1 base); ø 25.6 mm, height 4.6 mm; 26 jewels; 28,800 vph; 38-hour power reserve; COSC-certified chronometer
Functions: hours, minutes, sweep seconds
Case: stainless steel, ø 41 mm, height 11.6 mm; bidirectional bezel, with integrated slide rule and tachymeter scale; sapphire crystal; water-resistant to 3 atm
Band: stainless steel, folding clasp
Price: $5,600
Variations: various cases, straps, and dials

Navitimer Automatic GMT 41

Reference number: A32310211G1P1
Movement: automatic, Breitling caliber 32 (Sellita SW330-2 base); ø 25.6 mm, height 4.1 mm; 21 jewels; 28,800 vph; 42-hour power reserve
Functions: hours, minutes, sweep seconds; additional 24-hour display (second time zone); date
Case: stainless steel, ø 41 mm, height 11.6 mm; bidirectional bezel, with integrated slide rule and tachymeter scale; sapphire crystal; water-resistant to 3 atm
Band: reptile skin, pin buckle
Price: $5,850
Variations: various cases, straps, and dials

Avenger B01 Chronograph 44

Reference number: AB0147101L1X1
Movement: automatic, Breitling caliber B01; ø 30 mm, height 7.2 mm; 45 jewels; 28,800 vph; column wheel control of chronograph functions; COSC-certified chronometer; 70-hour power reserve
Functions: hours, minutes, subsidiary seconds; chronograph; date
Case: stainless steel, ø 44 mm, height 15.2 mm; unidirectional bezel, with 0-60 scale; sapphire crystal; screw-down crown; water-resistant to 30 atm
Band: calfskin, folding clasp
Price: $8,250
Variations: various cases, straps, and dials

Avenger B01 Chronograph 44 Night Mission

Reference number: SB0147101B1X1
Movement: automatic, Breitling caliber B01; ø 30 mm, height 7.2 mm; 45 jewels; 28,800 vph; column wheel control of chronograph functions; COSC-certified chronometer; 70-hour power reserve
Functions: hours, minutes, subsidiary seconds; chronograph; date
Case: ceramic, ø 44 mm, height 15.2 mm; unidirectional bezel, with 0-60 scale; sapphire crystal; screw-down crown; water-resistant to 30 atm
Band: calfskin, folding clasp
Price: $9,850
Variations: various cases, straps, and dials

Avenger Automatic 42

Reference number: A17328101C1A1
Movement: automatic, Breitling caliber 17 (Sellita SW200-1 base); ø 25.6 mm, height 4.6 mm; 25 jewels; 28,800 vph; COSC-certified chronometer; 38-hour power reserve
Functions: hours, minutes, sweep seconds; date
Case: stainless steel, ø 42 mm, height 12.1 mm; unidirectional bezel, with 0-60 scale; sapphire crystal; screw-down crown; water-resistant to 30 atm
Band: stainless steel, folding clasp
Price: $5,050
Variations: various cases, straps, and dials

Chronomat Automatic GMT 40

Reference number: A32398101L1A1
Movement: automatic, Breitling caliber 32 (Sellita SW330-2 base); ø 25.6 mm, height 4.1 mm; 21 jewels; 28,800 vph; 42-hour power reserve
Functions: hours, minutes, sweep seconds; additional 24-hour display (second time zone); date
Case: stainless steel, ø 40 mm, height 11.77 mm; unidirectional bezel, with 0-60 scale; sapphire crystal; screw-down crown; water-resistant to 20 atm
Band: stainless steel, folding clasp
Price: $6,150

Super Chronomat B01 42

Reference number: AB0134101C1A1
Movement: automatic, Breitling caliber B01; ø 30 mm, height 7.2 mm; 47 jewels; 28,800 vph; column wheel control of chronograph functions; COSC-certified chronometer; 70-hour power reserve
Functions: hours, minutes, subsidiary seconds; chronograph; date
Case: stainless steel, ø 42 mm, height 15.1 mm; unidirectional bezel, with 0-60 scale; transparent case back; screw-down crown; water-resistant to 20 atm
Band: stainless steel, folding clasp
Price: $8,950

Superocean Automatic 44

Reference number: A17376211C1S1
Movement: automatic, Breitling caliber 17 (Sellita SW200-1 base); ø 25.6 mm, height 4.6 mm; 26 jewels; 28,800 vph; COSC-certified chronometer; 38-hour power reserve
Functions: hours, minutes, sweep seconds
Case: stainless steel, ø 44 mm, height 12.6 mm; unidirectional bezel, with 0-60 scale; sapphire crystal; water-resistant to 30 atm
Band: rubber, folding clasp
Price: $5,250
Variations: various cases, dials, and straps

Superocean Heritage B20 Automatic 46

Reference number: AB2020121L1S1
Movement: automatic, Breitling caliber B20 (Tudor MT 5612 base); ø 31.8 mm, height 6.5 mm; 26 jewels; 28,800 vph; COSC-certified chronometer; 70-hour power reserve
Functions: hours, minutes, sweep seconds; date
Case: stainless steel, ø 46 mm, height 14.9 mm; unidirectional bezel set with ceramic insert; sapphire crystal; screw-down crown; water-resistant to 20 atm
Band: rubber, folding clasp
Price: $5,500
Variations: various cases, straps, and dials

Super Chronomat Automatic 38

Reference number: U17356531L1U1
Movement: automatic, Breitling caliber 17 (Sellita SW200-1 base); ø 25.6 mm, height 4.6 mm; 25 jewels; 28,800 vph; COSC-certified chronometer; 38-hour power reserve
Functions: hours, minutes, sweep seconds; date
Case: stainless steel, ø 38 mm, height 11.8 mm; bezel in red gold, set with 32 diamonds; sapphire crystal; water-resistant to 10 atm
Band: stainless steel with red-gold elements, folding clasp
Price: $14,600

Navitimer Automatic 36

Reference number: A17327381B1P1
Movement: automatic, Breitling caliber 17 (Sellita SW200-1 base); ø 25.6 mm, height 4.6 mm; 26 jewels; 28,800 vph; COSC-certified chronometer; 38-hour power reserve
Functions: hours, minutes, sweep seconds
Case: stainless steel, ø 36 mm, height 11.4 mm; bidirectional bezel, with integrated slide rule and tachymeter scale; sapphire crystal; water-resistant to 3 atm
Band: reptile skin, folding clasp
Price: $5,150

Caliber B01

Automatic; column-wheel control of the chronograph functions; vertical clutch; single mainspring barrel, 70-hour power reserve; COSC-certified chronometer
Functions: hours, minutes, subsidiary seconds; chronograph; date
Diameter: 30 mm
Height: 7.2 mm
Jewels: 47
Balance: glucydur
Frequency: 28,800 vph
Remarks: 346 parts

Caliber B04

Automatic; column-wheel control of the chronograph functions; vertical clutch; single mainspring barrel, 70-hour power reserve; COSC-certified chronometer
Functions: hours, minutes, subsidiary seconds; additional 24-hour display (second time zone); chronograph; date
Diameter: 30 mm
Height: 7.4 mm
Jewels: 47
Balance: glucydur
Frequency: 28,800 vph

Caliber B05

Automatic; column-wheel control of the chronograph functions; vertical clutch; time zone disk connected to hands-driving mechanism by planetary transmission; single mainspring barrel, 70-hour power reserve; COSC-certified chronometer
Functions: hours, minutes, subsidiary seconds; world time display (crown-activated second time zone); chronograph; date
Diameter: 30 mm
Height: 8.1 mm
Jewels: 56
Balance: glucydur
Frequency: 28,800 vph

BREMONT

Bremont watches have adventure in their DNA, as it were, but adventure with a bit of Anglo-Saxon understatement. They have been worn by a number of people who have exhibited their taste for derring-do, like polar explorer Ben Saunders or Levison Wood, who was the first person to walk the length of the Nile. And it's hardly any wonder, since the brand is the brainchild of brothers Nick and Giles English, themselves dyed-in-the-wool pilots and restorers of vintage airplanes. The brand name has a wild story as well: to avoid a storm, the brothers were forced to land their vintage biplane in a field in southern France. The farmer, a former World War II pilot, was more than happy to put them up for the night. His name: Antoine Bremont.

These British-made timepieces hit the market in 2007 and hit a nerve in those seeking a watch that tells the time and expresses some smoldering attraction to danger, perhaps. They use sturdy, COSC- or ISO-3159-certified automatic movements, extensively modified; hardened steel; a patented shock-absorbing system; and a rotor whose design recalls a flight of planes. The brand has steadily increased its production and programmatic scope. Bremont has sought its inspiration from such British icons as the Spitfire, Bletchley Park (where the German codes were broken during World War II), Jaguar sports cars, or even Boeing. Water sport is another area Bremont has explored, with models inspired by the legendary J-Class yachts, like the ladies' model AC I 32, and a special set devoted to the America's Cup.

Of the new releases by Bremont in 2024, the Supermarine 300m GMT diver's watches do stand out. They come in a very classic 40-millimeter case made of 904L stainless steel, which is chemically more resistant (austenitic) to an aggressive environment, so is ideal for salt water. The Terra Nova models use the same steel, and with their large, Super-LumiNova hands and numerals, are designed as companions for the adventure-seekers.

BREMONT WATCH COMPANY
P.O. Box 4741
Henley-on-Thames
RG9 9BZ Oxfordshire
United Kingdom

TEL.:
+44-800-817-4281

E-MAIL:
info@bremont.com

WEBSITE:
www.bremont.com

FOUNDED:
2002

NUMBER OF EMPLOYEES:
100

ANNUAL PRODUCTION:
several thousand watches

U.S. DISTRIBUTOR:
Michael.Pearson@bremont.com
Anthony.kozlowsky@bremont.com
Bremont Inc.
501 Madison Avenue
New York, NY 10022
855-273-6668

MOST IMPORTANT COLLECTIONS/PRICE RANGE:
ALT1, Armed Forces collection, Bremont Boeing, Bremont Jaguar, MB, SOLO, Supermarine, U-2, and limited editions / $3,600 to $42,500

Terra Nova 40.5 Turning Bezel

Reference number: TN40-PWR-SS-BL-B
Movement: automatic, caliber BE-79AL (Sellita SW279 base); ø 25.6 mm, height 4.2 mm; 31 jewels; 28,800 vph; 38-hour power reserve
Functions: hours, minutes, subsidiary seconds; power reserve indicator; date
Case: stainless steel, ø 40.5 mm, height 12 mm; bidirectional bezel with cardinal points; sapphire crystal; water-resistant to 10 atm
Band: stainless steel, double folding clasp
Price: $4,500
Variations: with black textile strap ($4,150); with brown calfskin strap ($4,150)

Terra Nova 42.5 Chronograph

Reference number: TN42-CHR-SS-BK-L-S
Movement: automatic, caliber BE-50AV (Sellita SW510Bha base); ø 30 mm, height 7.9 mm; 27 jewels; 28,800 vph; 56-hour power reserve
Functions: hours, minutes, subsidiary seconds; chronograph; date
Case: stainless steel, ø 42.5 mm, height 14.8 mm; bidirectional stainless steel compass bezel with ceramic insert; sapphire crystal; water-resistant to 10 atm
Band: calfskin, pin buckle
Price: $5,700
Variations: with black textile strap ($5,700); with stainless steel bracelet ($5,950)

Supermarine 300M

Reference number: SM40-ND-SS-BL-R-S
Movement: automatic, caliber BE-92AO (Sellita SW300-1b base); ø 25.6 mm, height 3.6 mm; 25 jewels; 28,800 vph; 50-hour power reserve
Functions: hours, minutes, sweep seconds
Case: stainless steel, ø 40 mm, height 12 mm; unidirectional aluminum bezel with 0-60 scale; sapphire crystal; screw-down crown; water-resistant to 30 atm
Band: rubber, pin buckle
Price: $3,550
Variations: with stainless steel bracelet ($3,850); with brown calfskin strap ($3,550)

B.R.M. CHRONOGRAPHES

Glance at a B.R.M. and you can tell almost immediately that it was designed by a Frenchman. It's not the car theme either. When it comes to design, France has long been a nation of dreamers. Think of the Citroën DS, or even the 2CV. But design means nothing if the implementation is shoddy.

For Bernard Richards, the true sign of luxury lies in "technical skills and perfection in all stages of manufacture." The exterior of the product is of course crucial, but all of B.R.M.'s major operations for making a wristwatch—such as encasing, assembling, setting, and polishing—are performed by hand in his little garage-like factory located outside Paris in Magny-en-Vexin.

B.R.M. is devoted to the ultra-mechanical look combined with materials that derive from various industries, notably automotive. His inspiration at the start came from the 1940s, the age of axle grease, pinups, real pilots, and a can-do attitude. The design: three dimensions visible to the naked eye, big mechanical landscapes. The inside: custom-designed components, fitting perfectly into Richards's engineering ideal. Gradually, though, Richards has been modernizing.

B.R.M.'s unusual timepieces have mainly been based on the tried and trusted ETA movements. But Richards has set lofty goals for himself and his out-of-the-box venture, for he intends to set up a true *manufacture* in his French factory. His Birotor model is thus outfitted with the Precitime, a caliber conceived and manufactured on French soil. The movement features B.R.M.'s shock absorbers mounted on the conical springs of its so-called Isolastic system, and they frequently appear on the watches' dials. Plates and bridges are crafted of ARCAP, rotors are made of Fortal HR—an aluminum alloy harder than some steels—and tantalum. The twin rotors of the Precitime, found at 12 and 6 o'clock, are mounted on double rows of ceramic bearings that require no lubrication.

Richards recently started a sailing-oriented collection, with the names of winds on the four compass points of a watch. And the Free Floating collection experiments with a trapezoidal case and an entirely "strung-up" movement inside. B.R.M. was an early adopter of personalization methods. The company has an online configurator that gives potential customers a free hand in choosing color combinations and straps.

B.R.M. CHRONOGRAPHES
(Bernard Richards Manufacture)
2 Impasse de L'Aubette
ZA des Aulnaies
F-95420 Magny-en-Vexin
France

TEL.:
+33-1-61-02-00-25

FAX:
+33-1-61-02-00-14

WEBSITE:
www.brm-chronographes.com

FOUNDED:
2003

NUMBER OF EMPLOYEES:
20

ANNUAL PRODUCTION:
approx. 2,000 pieces

U.S. DISTRIBUTOR:
B.R.M Manufacture North America
25 Highland Park Village, Suite 100-777
Dallas, TX 75205
214-231-0144
usa@brm-manufacture.com

PRICE RANGE:
$3,000 to $150,000

V7-38 Touring

Movement: automatic, ETA caliber 2824/2; ø 25.6 mm, height 4.60 mm; 25 jewels; 28,800 vph; open-worked dial with tachymeter scale; 38-hour power reserve
Functions: hours, minutes, sweep hacking seconds; date
Case: stainless steel with black PVD, ø 38 mm, height 10.7 mm; stainless steel; crystal sapphire; transparent case back; screw-down crown; water-resistant to 10 atm
Band: Alcantara, pin buckle
Price: $5,900
Variations: comes in 44-mm version; different colors on request

V6-44-SA Cercolor

Movement: automatic, ETA caliber 2824/2; ø 25.6 mm, height 4.60 mm; 25 jewels; 28,800 vph; carbon-fiber dial with visible shock absorbers; 38-hour power reserve
Functions: hours, minutes, sweep hacking seconds; date
Case: titanium with red ceramic coating, ø 44 mm, height 11 mm; sapphire crystal; screw-down crown; antireflective on both sides; transparent case back; water-resistant to 10 atm
Band: rubber, pin buckle
Price: $5,910
Variations: case available in orange or blue

FF39-40 Light Bronze

Movement: automatic, B.R.M. Precitime in-house development; ø 25.6 mm, height 4.6 mm; 25 jewels; 28,800 vph; fully skeletonized movement; anodized Fortal (aluminum alloy) balance and rotor; Fortal casing ring mounted on shock absorbers; 38-hour power reserve
Functions: hours, minutes, stop sweep seconds
Case: titanium with colored ceramic treatment, trapezoidal form, 40 mm x 39 mm, height 11.2 mm; bronze bezel and case back; sapphire crystal; transparent case back; water-resistant to 3 atm
Band: Alcantara, pin buckle
Remarks: the movement "floats" inside the case thanks to 5 silent blocs and two nitrile belts; carbon struts prevent lateral displacement
Price: $13,700
Variations: several variations available

BULGARI

Although Bulgari is one of the largest jewelry manufacturers in the world, watches have always played an important role for the brand. The purchase of Daniel Roth and Gérald Genta in the Vallée de Joux opened new perspectives for its timepieces, thanks to specialized production facilities and the watchmaking talent in the Vallée de Joux—especially where complicated timepieces are concerned. In March 2011, luxury goods giant Louis Vuitton Moët Hennessy (LVMH) secured all the Bulgari family shares in exchange for 16.5 million LVMH shares and a say in the group's future. The financial backing of the mega-group boosted the company's strategy to become fully independent.

Under the bold leadership of Guido Terrini, the watch division continued pushing the envelope with a series of increasingly thin and complicated automatics. After the tourbillon in 2014 came a minute repeater in 2016, which is 3.12 millimeters high and whose dial features slotted indices for better sound transmission. It was followed by the 5.15-millimeter-high Octo Finissimo Automatic run on the Caliber BVL 138. The Chronograph GMT (2019) was another record in streamlining. It is 6.9 millimeters high and runs on the BVL 318, featuring a hubless peripheral rotor and an hour hand that can be quickly and easily clicked through the time zones.

The sixth world record came in 2020 with the Octo Finissimo Tourbillon Chronograph Skeleton Automatic, which combines the essential complications of modern watchmaking in the thinnest possible case. And in November 2021, Bulgari picked up the coveted Aiguille d'Or of the Grand Prix d'Horlogerie de Genève (GPHG) for the Octo Finissimo Perpetual Calendar, which measures 5.8 millimeters. The Octo Finissimo Ultra held the record for thinnest mechanical watch, with a total height of 1.8 millimeters. But it was beaten by five hundredths of a millimeter after just a few months. So the battle was on again. They set to work and the Octo Finissimo Ultra Mk II presented at Watches and Wonders 2024. They shaved a full tenth of a millimeter off the octagonal tungsten carbide case and fitted a new wafer-thin sapphire crystal to reduce the overall height of the watch to a record 1.7 millimeters.

BULGARI HORLOGERIE SA
rue de Monruz 34
CH-2000 Neuchâtel
Switzerland

TEL.:
+41-32-722-7878

E-MAIL:
info@bulgari.com

WEBSITE:
www.bulgari.com

FOUNDED:
1884 (Bulgari Horlogerie was founded in the early 1980s as Bulgari Time)

U.S. DISTRIBUTOR:
Bulgari Corporation of America
555 Madison Avenue
New York, NY 10022
212-315-9700

MOST IMPORTANT COLLECTIONS/PRICE RANGE:
Bulgari-Bulgari / from approx. $4,700 to $30,300; Diagono / from approx. $3,200; Octo Roma or Finissimo / from approx. $7,700 to $690,000 and above; Daniel Roth and Gérald Genta collections

Octo Finissimo Automatic

Reference number: 102713
Movement: automatic, Bulgari caliber BVL 138 Finissimo; ø 36 mm, height 2.23 mm; 23 jewels; 21,600 vph; platinum micro-rotor; finely finished with côtes de Genève; 60-hour power reserve
Functions: hours, minutes, subsidiary seconds
Case: titanium, ø 40 mm, height 6.9 mm; sapphire crystal; transparent case back; screw-down crown; water-resistant to 10 atm
Band: titanium, folding clasp
Price: $18,800

Octo Finissimo Automatic

Reference number: 103856
Movement: automatic, Bulgari caliber BVL 138 Finissimo; ø 36 mm, height 2.23 mm; 23 jewels; 21,600 vph; platinum micro-rotor; finely finished with côtes de Genève; 60-hour power reserve
Functions: hours, minutes, subsidiary seconds
Case: stainless steel, ø 40 mm, height 6.9 mm; sapphire crystal; transparent case back; screw-down crown; water-resistant to 10 atm
Band: stainless steel, folding clasp
Price: $13,500

Octo Finissimo Automatic

Reference number: 103812
Movement: automatic, Bulgari caliber BVL 138 Finissimo; ø 36 mm, height 2.23 mm; 23 jewels; 21,600 vph; platinum micro-rotor; finely finished with côtes de Genève; 60-hour power reserve
Functions: hours, minutes, subsidiary seconds
Case: yellow gold, ø 40 mm, height 6.9 mm; sapphire crystal; transparent case back; screw-down crown; water-resistant to 10 atm
Band: yellow gold, folding clasp
Price: $45,500

Octo Finissimo Automatic

Reference number: 103286
Movement: automatic, Bulgari caliber BVL
138 Finissimo; ø 36 mm, height 2.23 mm; 23 jewels;
21,600 vph; platinum micro-rotor; finely finished with
côtes de Genève; 60-hour power reserve
Functions: hours, minutes, subsidiary seconds
Case: rose gold, ø 40 mm, height 6.4 mm; sapphire
crystal; transparent case back; screw-down crown;
water-resistant to 10 atm
Band: reptile skin, pin buckle
Price: $26,800

Octo Finissimo Tourbillon Skeleton

Reference number: 103981
Movement: hand-wound, Bulgari caliber BVL 268SK;
ø 36 mm, height 1.95 mm; 24 jewels; 21,600 vph; flying
1-minute tourbillon; skeletonized movement; 52-hour
power reserve
Functions: hours, minutes
Case: rose gold, ø 40 mm, height 4.85 mm; sapphire
crystal; transparent case back; water-resistant to 3 atm
Band: reptile skin, pin buckle
Price: on request

Octo Finissimo Skeleton 8 Days

Reference number: 103667
Movement: hand-wound, Bulgari caliber BVL 199 SK;
ø 33.9 mm, height 2.5 mm; 33 jewels; 21,600 vph;
skeletonized movement; 192-hour power reserve
Functions: hours, minutes, subsidiary seconds; power
reserve indicator
Case: rose gold, ø 40 mm, height 5.95 mm; sapphire
crystal; water-resistant to 3 atm
Band: reptile skin, pin buckle
Remarks: skeletonized dial
Price: $39,200

Octo Finissimo Sketch

Reference number: 104163
Movement: automatic, Bulgari caliber BVL
138 Finissimo; ø 36 mm, height 2.23 mm; 23 jewels;
21,600 vph; platinum micro-rotor; finely finished with
côtes de Genève; 60-hour power reserve
Functions: hours, minutes, subsidiary seconds
Case: stainless steel, ø 40 mm, height 6.4 mm; sapphire
crystal; transparent case back; screw-down crown;
water-resistant to 10 atm
Band: stainless steel, folding clasp
Remarks: dial with sketch of the movement
Price: $16,200; limited to 280 pieces

Bulgari Bulgari

Reference number: 103968
Movement: automatic, Bulgari caliber BVL 191;
ø 26.2 mm, height 3.8 mm; 26 jewels; 28,800 vph; with
côtes de Genève; 42-hour power reserve
Functions: hours, minutes, sweep seconds; date
Case: rose gold, ø 38 mm, height 8.7 mm; sapphire
crystal; water-resistant to 5 atm
Band: reptile skin, pin buckle
Price: $13,200

Bulgari Bulgari

Reference number: 103897
Movement: quartz
Functions: hours, minutes
Case: yellow gold, ø 26 mm, height 7 mm; sapphire
crystal; water-resistant to 3 atm
Band: reptile skin, pin buckle
Price: $8,250

BULGARI

Octo Roma Precious Naturalia
Reference number: 103675
Movement: hand-wound, Bulgari caliber BVL 206; ø 34 mm, height 5 mm; 21,600 vph; flying 1-minute tourbillon; skeletonized movement, bridges with brown DLC; 64-hour power reserve
Functions: hours, minutes
Case: rose gold, ø 44 mm, height 11.35 mm; sapphire crystal; water-resistant to 5 atm
Band: reptile skin, folding clasp
Price: $167,070

Octo Roma Tourbillon Sapphire Carbon
Reference number: 103316
Movement: hand-wound, Bulgari caliber BVL 206; ø 34 mm, height 5 mm; 21,600 vph; flying 1-minute tourbillon; skeletonized movement, 11 bridges as hour markers with green DLC; 64-hour power reserve
Functions: hours, minutes
Case: carbon fiber with sapphire crystal barrel, ø 44 mm, height 11.02 mm; sapphire crystal; transparent case back; crown in titanium; water-resistant to 5 atm
Band: reptile skin with rubber coating, folding clasp
Price: on request

Octo Roma Chronograph
Reference number: 103829
Movement: automatic, Bulgari caliber BVL 399 (Bulgari BVL 191 base with Dubois Dépraz module); 28,800 vph; 48-hour power reserve
Functions: hours, minutes, subsidiary seconds; chronograph; date
Case: stainless steel, ø 42 mm, height 12.4 mm; sapphire crystal; water-resistant to 10 atm
Band: stainless steel, folding clasp
Price: $9,150

Aluminum Smeraldo Chronograph
Reference number: 104076
Movement: automatic, ETA caliber 2894; ø 28.6 mm, height 6.1 mm; 37 jewels; 28,800 vph; 42-hour power reserve
Functions: hours, minutes, subsidiary seconds; chronograph; date
Case: aluminum, ø 40 mm, height 11.1 mm; bezel in titanium with rubber coating; sapphire crystal; water-resistant to 10 atm
Band: rubber, pin buckle
Price: $5,000; limited to 1000 pieces

Aluminum GMT
Reference number: 103554
Movement: automatic, Bulgari caliber B192 (ETA 2893-2 base); ø 25.6 mm, height 4.1 mm; 21 jewels; 28,800 vph; 50-hour power reserve
Functions: hours, minutes, sweep seconds; additional 24-hour display (second time zone); date
Case: aluminum, ø 40 mm, height 9.4 mm; bezel in titanium with rubber coating; sapphire crystal; water-resistant to 10 atm
Band: rubber, pin buckle
Price: $3,700
Variations: various straps and dials

Aluminium
Reference number: 103382
Movement: automatic, ETA caliber 2892-A2; ø 25.6 mm, height 3.6 mm; 21 jewels; 28,800 vph; 42-hour power reserve
Functions: hours, minutes, sweep seconds; date
Case: aluminum, ø 40 mm, height 9.4 mm; bezel in titanium with rubber coating; sapphire crystal; water-resistant to 10 atm
Band: rubber, pin buckle
Price: $3,150
Variations: with black dial

Serpenti Tubogas Infiniti

Reference number: 103924
Movement: quartz
Functions: hours, minutes
Case: rose gold, ø 35 mm; bezel set with diamonds; sapphire crystal; crown with rubellite cabochon
Band: rose gold (Tubogas clasp), set with diamonds
Remarks: dial set with diamonds (full pavé)
Price: $67,000

Serpenti Tubogas

Reference number: 103434
Movement: quartz
Functions: hours, minutes
Case: stainless steel, ø 35 mm; bezel set with diamonds; sapphire crystal; crown with rubellite cabochon
Band: stainless steel (Tubogas clasp)
Price: $9,900

Serpenti Tubogas

Reference number: 101815
Movement: quartz
Functions: hours, minutes
Case: rose gold, ø 35 mm; bezel set with diamonds; sapphire crystal; crown with rubellite cabochon
Band: rose gold (Tubogas clasp)
Price: $31,700

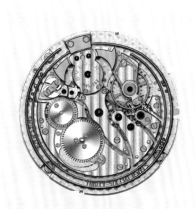

Caliber BVL 362

Hand-wound; single mainspring barrel, 42-hour power reserve
Functions: hours, minutes, subsidiary seconds; minute repeater
Diameter: 28.5 mm
Jewels: 36
Height: 3.12 mm
Frequency: 21,600 vph
Hairspring: flat hairspring
Remarks: hand-decorated, côtes de Genève; 362 parts

Caliber BVL 305

Automatic; platinum micro-rotor; single flying mainspring barrel, 60-hour power reserve
Functions: hours, minutes; perpetual calendar with date (retrograde), weekday, month, leap year display (retrograde)
Diameter: 36 mm
Height: 2.75 mm
Jewels: 30
Balance: glucydur
Frequency: 21,600 vph
Hairspring: flat hairspring with index fine adjustment
Shock protection: Incabloc
Remarks: finely finished with côtes de Genève; currently the thinnest perpetual calendar

Caliber BVL 138 "Finissimo"

Automatic; flying platinum micro-rotor; single flying mainspring barrel, 60-hour power reserve
Functions: hours, minutes, subsidiary seconds; date
Diameter: 36 mm
Height: 2.23 mm
Jewels: 23
Balance: glucydur
Frequency: 21,600 vph
Hairspring: flat hairspring with index fine adjustment
Shock protection: Incabloc
Remarks: finely finished with côtes de Genève

CARL SUCHY & SÖHNE

Reviving an old and venerable brand of anything can be a risky enterprise. Carl Suchy & Söhne, founded in 1822, was a clock and pocket-watch maker with a presence in Vienna and Prague and workshops in La Chaux-de-Fonds. The products were the ultimate in fashion at the time, made in the somewhat restrained, bourgeois Biedermeier style, which found favor well beyond Vienna's borders.

In 2016, a Viennese businessman with experience in "curating art" decided it was time for Vienna to have a watch brand again. The new Carl Suchy, however, would be an ode to this city, which was at the center of a huge empire.

The story begins with a modern timepiece reflecting the streamlined aesthetic concepts of architect Alfred Loos, whose main idea was encapsulated in a 1910 essay entitled "Ornament and Crime," in which he formulated his basic tenet: "Cultural evolution is equivalent to the removal of ornament from articles in daily use."

The Waltz N°1 was designed in a dialogue between CEO Robert Punkenhofer and a young graduate from the ECAL in Lausanne, Miloš Ristin, with the final product supervised by Swiss watchmaker Marc Jenni. A calm, thin model, it features a simple geometrical pattern with perpendicular guilloché on one half and a vertical guilloché on the other. At 6 o'clock, a small seconds disk turns, breaking up the pattern, but "clicking in place" twice each minute, sort of like a waltzing couple. The model was skeletonized for the second version, giving the dial face a peculiar look, as if the movement, a Vaucher 5401/180, was covered by a shutter.

In the meantime, the brand has come up with three distinct styles: Day, Night, and Danube, meaning white, black, and blue dials.

After devoting time and energy to a table clock, Carl Suchy & Söhne released a second collection, the Belvedere, a homage to the eponymous palace in Vienna, which appears as an engraving on the gold-plated rotor. The watch runs on a Dubois Dépraz movement. The hands are like spires with a porthole attic window. They point to indices that are clearly inspired by the great arched entrance of Belvedere Palace in Vienna.

CARL SUCHY & SÖHNE
Prinz-Eugen-Strasse 48/Top 3
A-1010 Wien
Austria

TEL.:
+43-660-75-24-331

E-MAIL:
office@carlsuchy.com

WEBSITE:
www.carlsuchy.com

FOUNDED:
1822/2017

DISTRIBUTION:
Retail

MOST IMPORTANT COLLECTIONS:
Waltz N°1, Waltz N°1 Skeleton, Belvedere

Waltz N°1 Moll
Reference number: W1M.01.001
Movement: automatic, Vaucher caliber VMF 5401; ø 30 mm, height 2.6 mm; 29 jewels; 21,600 vph; micro-rotor; finely finished movement; 48-hour power reserve
Functions: hours, minutes, subsidiary seconds (as a rotating disc)
Case: stainless steel, ø 41.5 mm, height 9.3 mm; bezel with black ADLC; sapphire crystal; transparent case back; water-resistant to 3 atm
Band: reptile skin, double folding clasp
Remarks: dial horizontal and vertical guilloché pattern; black seconds disc; limited to 10 pieces
Price: $17,015

Belvedere Titanium
Reference number: BT.01.001
Movement: automatic, caliber CSS201 (Dubois Dépraz DD90010 base); ø 25.6 mm, height 3.8 mm; 21 jewels; 28,800 vph; gold-plated oscillating mass with micro-engraving of Belvedere Palace; 42-hour power reserve
Functions: hours, minutes, sweep seconds; date aperture on a rotating disc
Case: titanium, ø 40.8 mm, height 12.2 mm; sapphire crystal; transparent case back; water-resistant to 3 atm
Band: rubber, folding clasp
Price: $8,670

Belvedere Midnight
Reference number: B.02.002
Movement: automatic, caliber CSS201 (Dubois Dépraz DD90010 base); ø 25.6 mm, height 3.8 mm; 21 jewels; 28,800 vph; gold-plated oscillating mass with micro-engraving of Belvedere Palace; 42-hour power reserve
Functions: hours, minutes, sweep seconds; date aperture on a rotating disc
Case: stainless steel with black DLC, ø 40.8 mm, height 12.2 mm; sapphire crystal; transparent case back; water-resistant to 3 atm
Band: rubber, folding clasp
Price: $10,870

CARTIER

Cartier, founded as a maker of jewels in 1847, is today one of the main drivers of the Richemont Group, which it joined in 2012. It took a while for the company to find its footing and convince the market of its seriousness and potential in the watch industry. It was thanks to Carole Forestier-Kasapi—now at TAG Heuer—head of the watchmaking division that Cartier really made a splash and verticalized its production. It produced a host of outstanding calibers, beginning with the 1904 MC, a reference to the year in which Louis Cartier developed the first wristwatch made for men—a pilot's watch custom designed for his friend and early pioneer of aviation, Alberto Santos-Dumont. The automatic movement is powered by twin barrels and is available for chronographs or diver's watches. It is also now just one of a family of outstanding calibers that continue to push Cartier to the top rung of *haute horlogerie*.

In a period that values vintage, the Cartier brand has an advantage. More than a century of watchmaking has provided it with a steady stream of models to revive and modernize. The Pasha, Santos, Tank, Rotonde, Drive, and Calibre de Cartier are among the best-known and most successful watches in the world. And there is the series of "mystérieuse" watches, which in fine watchmaking stands for the invisible drive of an indicator or function.

Skeletonization has been on the menu recently, which is not surprising, since Cartier pushed the trend in 2009 already with the Santos. They released a new version of the Santos-Dumont with a newly developed movement that provides some animation on the dial: the micro-rotor of the automatic caliber 9629 MC bears a miniature of the Demoiselle (damselfly) airplanes designed by pilot Alberto Santos-Dumont, for whom Cartier once developed the watch. The highlight of these new versions is a model with skeletonized movement and 24-hour display.

The brand's creativity was on full display at Watches and Wonders 2024. Once again, the company presented numerous innovations, particularly for lovers of fine mechanics and for what's known as "ladies' watches." The Cartier Privé line in recent years has become the home to limited reissues of classics. The collection has now been expanded to include the Tortue model as a single-button chronograph. This complication was already built by Cartier in 1928, also in the Tortue line with its tonneau-shaped case. Now the *Monopoussoir*, or monopusher, in which the chronograph function is controlled by a column wheel, is back with the hand-wound caliber 1928 MC. The crown, with integrated chronograph pusher, is a charming detail: as is typical of Cartier, it features a cabochon, either a red ruby or a blue sapphire, depending on the case material.

CARTIER
1201 Geneva
Switzerland

E-MAIL:
contact.na@cartier.com

WEBSITE:
https://www.cartier.com

FOUNDED:
1847

NUMBER OF EMPLOYEES:
approx. 1,300 (watch manufacturing)

U.S. DISTRIBUTOR:
Cartier North America
645 Fifth Avenue
New York, NY 10022
1-800-CARTIER
www.cartier.us

MOST IMPORTANT COLLECTIONS:
Santos de Cartier, Panthère de Cartier, Baignoire, Tank, Ballon Bleu de Cartier, Drive de Cartier, Calibre de Cartier, Clé de Cartier, Ronde de Cartier, Pasha de Cartier, Mystérieuse

Santos de Cartier

Reference number: WSSA0064
Movement: automatic, Cartier caliber 1847 MC; ø 25.6 mm, height 3.77 mm; 23 jewels; 28,800 vph; 40-hour power reserve
Functions: hours, minutes, sweep seconds
Case: stainless steel, 39.8 mm x 47.5 mm, height 9.38 mm; sapphire crystal; crown with spinel cabochon; water-resistant to 10 atm
Band: stainless steel, double folding clasp
Remarks: comes with extra reptile-skin strap with QuickSwitch rapid change system
Price: $7,750

Santos de Cartier Dual Time

Reference number: WSSA0076
Movement: automatic, Cartier-modified Sellita SW330-2; ø 25.6 mm, height 3.77 mm; 23 jewels; 28,800 vph; 40-hour power reserve
Functions: hours, minutes, sweep seconds; additional 12-hour display, day/night indicator; date
Case: stainless steel, 40.2 mm x 47.5 mm, height 10.1 mm; sapphire crystal; crown with spinel cabochon; water-resistant to 10 atm
Band: stainless steel, double folding clasp
Remarks: comes with extra reptile-skin strap with QuickSwitch rapid change system
Price: $9,150

Santos Dumont

Reference number: WGSA0096
Movement: hand-wound, Cartier caliber 430 MC; ø 20.55 mm, height 2.1 mm; 18 jewels; 21,600 vph; 38-hour power reserve
Functions: hours, minutes
Case: platinum with green lacquer, 31.4 mm x 43.5 mm, height 7.3 mm; sapphire crystal; crown with ruby cabochon; water-resistant to 3 atm
Band: reptile skin, pin buckle
Price: $21,500; limited to 200 pieces

Santos Dumont

Reference number: WGSA0098
Movement: hand-wound, Cartier caliber 430 MC;
ø 20.55 mm, height 2.1 mm; 18 jewels; 21,600 vph;
38-hour power reserve
Functions: hours, minutes
Case: rose gold with dark-blue lacquer, 31.4 mm x
43.5 mm, height 7.3 mm; sapphire crystal; crown with
sapphire cabochon; water-resistant to 3 atm
Band: reptile skin, pin buckle
Price: $15,600

Santos de Cartier

Reference number: WGSA0095
Movement: automatic, Cartier caliber 1847 MC;
ø 25.6 mm, height 3.77 mm; 23 jewels; 28,800 vph;
40-hour power reserve
Functions: hours, minutes, sweep seconds; date
Case: yellow gold, 39.8 mm x 47.5 mm, height 9.38 mm;
sapphire crystal; crown with spinel cabochon; water-
resistant to 10 atm
Band: yellow gold, double folding clasp
Remarks: comes with extra reptile-skin strap and
QuickSwitch rapid change system
Price: $36,600

Santos de Cartier

Reference number: W2SA0030
Movement: automatic, Cartier caliber 1847 MC;
ø 25.6 mm, height 3.77 mm; 23 jewels; 28,800 vph;
40-hour power reserve
Functions: hours, minutes, sweep seconds; date
Case: stainless steel, 39.8 mm x 47.5 mm, height
9.38 mm; bezel in yellow gold; sapphire crystal; crown
with spinel cabochon; water-resistant to 10 atm
Band: stainless steel, double folding clasp
Remarks: comes with extra reptile-skin strap and with
QuickSwitch rapid-changing system
Price: $11,700

Santos de Cartier Skeleton

Reference number: WHSA0042
Movement: hand-wound, Cartier caliber 9612 MC;
28.6 x 28.6 mm, height 3.97 mm; 20 jewels; 28,800 vph;
skeletonized movement with integrated Roman hour
numerals; 2 mainsprings, 72-hour power reserve
Functions: hours, minutes
Case: yellow gold, ø 39.8 mm, height 9.08 mm; sapphire
crystal; transparent case back; crown with sapphire
cabochon; water-resistant to 10 atm
Band: yellow gold, double folding clasp
Remarks: comes with extra stainless-steel bracelet with
QuickSwitch rapid-changing system
Price: $70,000

Santos de Cartier Skeleton

Reference number: WHSA0009
Movement: hand-wound, Cartier caliber 9612 MC;
28.6 mm x 28.6 mm, height 3.97 mm; 20 jewels;
28,800 vph; skeletonized movement with integrated
Roman hour numerals; 2 mainsprings; 72-hour power
reserve
Functions: hours, minutes
Case: stainless steel with black DLC, ø 39.8 mm, height
9.08 mm; sapphire crystal; transparent case back;
crown with spinel cabochon; water-resistant to 10 atm
Band: reptile skin, double folding clasp
Remarks: comes with extra stainless steel-bracelet with
QuickSwitch rapid change system
Price: $30,400

Tank Américaine

Reference number: WGTA0300
Movement: automatic, Cartier caliber 1899 MC; 9 mm x
9 mm, height 3.63 mm; 24 jewels; 28,800 vph; 40-hour
power reserve
Functions: hours, minutes
Case: yellow gold, 24.4 mm x 44.4 mm, height 8.6 mm;
sapphire crystal; crown with sapphire cabochon; water-
resistant to 3 atm
Band: reptile skin, folding clasp
Price: $16,800

Tank Américaine

Reference number: WGTA0297
Movement: automatic, Cartier caliber 1899 MC; 9 x 9 mm, height 3.63 mm; 24 jewels; 28,800 vph; 40-hour power reserve
Functions: hours, minutes
Case: platinum, 24.4 mm x 44.4 mm, height 8.6 mm; sapphire crystal; crown with ruby cabochon; water-resistant to 3 atm
Band: reptile skin, folding clasp
Price: $24,100

Ballon Bleu de Cartier

Reference number: W2BB0039
Movement: automatic, Cartier caliber 1847 MC; ø 25.6 mm, height 3.77 mm; 23 jewels; 28,800 vph; 40-hour power reserve
Functions: hours, minutes, sweep seconds; date
Case: stainless steel, ø 42 mm, height 13 mm; bezel in yellow gold; sapphire crystal; crown in yellow gold with spinel cabochon; water-resistant to 3 atm
Band: stainless steel with yellow-gold center links, folding clasp
Price: $12,100

Ballon Bleu de Cartier

Reference number: WSBB0071
Movement: automatic, Cartier caliber 1847 MC; ø 25.6 mm, height 3.77 mm; 23 jewels; 28,800 vph; 40-hour power reserve
Functions: hours, minutes, sweep seconds; date
Case: stainless steel, ø 40 mm, height 12.4 mm; sapphire crystal; crown with spinel cabochon; water-resistant to 3 atm
Band: stainless steel, folding clasp
Price: $7,000

Pasha de Cartier Chronograph

Reference number: CRWSPA0046
Movement: automatic, Cartier caliber 1904-CH3; ø 25.58 mm, height 5.72 mm; 37 jewels; 28,800 vph; 47-hour power reserve
Functions: hours, minutes, subsidiary seconds; chronograph; date
Case: stainless steel, ø 41 mm, height 12 mm; unidirectional bezel, with 0-60 scale; sapphire crystal; crown and pushers with screw-down cap and spinel cabochons; water-resistant to 10 atm
Band: reptile skin, pin buckle
Remarks: comes with extra stainless-steel bracelet
Price: $10,400

Pasha de Cartier Skeleton

Reference number: WHPA0007
Movement: automatic, Cartier caliber 9624 MC; ø 31.63 mm, height 5.66 mm; 23 jewels; 28,800 vph; skeletonized movement, bridges with grey lacquer; 48-hour power reserve
Functions: hours, minutes
Case: stainless steel, ø 41 mm, height 10.45 mm; sapphire crystal; transparent case back; crown with a screw-down crown and sapphire cabochon; water-resistant to 3 atm
Band: stainless steel, folding clasp
Remarks: comes with extra reptile-skin strap
Price: $29,000

Privé Tortue Chronographe Monopoussoir

Reference number: WHTO0008
Movement: hand-wound, Cartier caliber 1928 MC; ø 27.6 mm, height 4.32 mm; 24 jewels; 28,800 vph; monopusher control of chronograph functions; 44-hour power reserve
Functions: hours, minutes, subsidiary seconds; chronograph
Case: platinum, ø 43.7 mm, height 10.2 mm; sapphire crystal; crown with ruby cabochon; water-resistant to 3 atm
Band: reptile skin, pin buckle
Price: $59,000; limited to 200 pieces

CHANEL

After putting the occasional jewelry watch onto the market, family-owned Chanel decided to launch its own horology division in 1987, a move that gave the brand instant access to the world of watchmaking art. While the brand's first collections were directed exclusively at its female clientele, it was actually with the rather simple and masculine J12 that Chanel finally achieved a breakthrough. That was in 1999, over twenty years ago. The brand's artistic director at the time was still Jacques Hélleu. The J12 collection showpiece, the Rétrograde Mystérieuse, was a stroke of genius—courtesy of the innovative think tank Renaud et Papi. Its sleek ceramic case and complex mechanics instantly propelled Chanel into the world of *haute horlogerie*.

It was Arnaud Chastaingt, formerly at Cartier, who actually designed the iconic J12. It still comes in a shiny ceramic case. As part of a rejuvenation move, a new caliber was added to the roster. It was built by Kenissi, a joint venture Chanel shares with Tudor and Breitling. It no longer uses a silicon hairspring and has returned to the soft iron cage to protect from magnetic fields.

In 2024, the French fashion brand surprised its customers with a tribute to founder Coco Chanel and a paean to *haute couture*. At the Watches fair in Geneva, Chanel unveiled an entire collection of wristwatches with characteristic couture decorations and, at times, some lovingly crafted allusions to the history of the house.

CHANEL
135, avenue Charles de Gaulle
F-92521 Neuilly-sur-Seine Cedex
France

TEL.:
+33-1-41-92-08-33

WEBSITE:
www.chanel.com

FOUNDED:
1914

DISTRIBUTION:
retail and 200 Chanel boutiques worldwide

U.S. DISTRIBUTOR:
Chanel Fine Jewelry and Watches
600 Madison Avenue, 19th Floor
New York, NY 10022
212-715-4741
www.chanel.com

MOST IMPORTANT COLLECTIONS:
J12, Première, Boy.Friend, Monsieur de Chanel

J12 Couture Workshop Automaton Caliber 6 Watch

Reference number: H9869
Movement: hand-wound, Chanel caliber 6; ø 28.4 mm, height 7.7 mm; 54 jewels; 28,800 vph; balance wheel with variable inertia; 2 mainsprings, 70-hour power reserve
Functions: hours, minutes; automaton (pusher-activated figure of Coco Chanel)
Case: ceramic, ø 38 mm; blackened stainless-steel bezel set with 48 baguette diamonds; sapphire crystal; transparent case back; crown in stainless steel with diamond cabochon; water-resistant to 5 atm
Band: ceramic, triple folding clasp (in stainless steel)
Price: on request; limited to 100 pieces

J12 Diamond Tourbillon Caliber 5 Watch

Reference number: H9961
Movement: hand-wound, Chanel caliber 5; ø 28.4 mm, height 6.25 mm; 29 jewels; 28,800 vph; flying 1-minute tourbillon with large diamond capstone; 42-hour power reserve
Functions: hours and minutes (off-center)
Case: ceramic, ø 38 mm; blackened stainless-steel bezel with ceramic insert; sapphire crystal; transparent case back; blackened stainless-steel crown with ceramic cabochon; water-resistant to 5 atm
Band: ceramic, triple folding clasp
Remarks: skeletonized dial
Price: $108,100
Variations: in white ceramic

Monsieur de Chanel Superleggera Edition Intense Black

Reference number: H9870
Movement: hand-wound, Chanel caliber I; ø 32.6 mm, height 5.5 mm; 30 jewels; 28,800 vph; 2 mainsprings; mainplate and bridges skeletonized and blackened; 72-hour power reserve
Functions: hours (digital, jumping), minutes (retrograde), subsidiary seconds
Case: ceramic, ø 42 mm, height 12 mm; sapphire crystal; transparent case back; water-resistant to 3 atm
Band: textile with calfskin lining, folding clasp
Remarks: guilloché dial
Price: $45,600; limited to 100 pieces

CHOPARD

The Chopard *manufacture* was founded by Louis-Ulysse Chopard in 1860 in the tiny village of Sonvillier in the Jura mountains of Switzerland. In 1963, it was purchased by Karl Scheufele, a goldsmith from Pforzheim, Germany, and revived as a producer of fine watches and jewelry.

The past seventeen years have seen a breathtaking development, when Karl Scheufele's son, Karl-Friedrich, and his sister, Caroline, decided to create watches with in-house movements, thus restoring the old business launched by Louis-Ulysse back in the nineteenth century.

In 1996, out of nowhere, Chopard opened up its watchmaking *manufacture* in the sleepy town of Fleurier in the Val-de-Travers, which had not yet experienced the revival of the mechanical watch. Focus on vertical integration drove the opening of a second building, Fleurier Ebauches SA, a hub of caliber kits, including the L.U.C series. Chopard now has a line-up of eleven calibers, ranging from simple three-hander automatics to a tourbillon; a perpetual calendar; chronographs; an ultra-high-frequency chronometer; and a minute repeater, now with sapphire chimes that produce a very clear sound.

The sportive bestseller at the Geneva-based company is the Alpine Eagle series. It was unmistakably inspired by the Chopard classic of the 1980s, the St. Moritz. In keeping with the times, the new model has been given a modern facelift, and the inner workings have also been updated. In 2023, Chopard presented the 41 XPS, a version with small seconds and a particularly thin movement, the L.U.C 96.40-L caliber, which measures just 3.3 millimeters. The sporty, casual style with subtle references to a vintage model was expanded in 2024 to include a flyback chronograph in titanium. In harmony with the industry's attempts to be sustainable, the Alpine Eagle collection uses the Chopard-exclusive "Lucent" steel alloy with a bright shimmer.

CHOPARD & CIE. SA
8, rue de Veyrot
CH-1217 Meyrin (Geneva)
Switzerland

TEL.:
+41-22-719-3131

E-MAIL:
info@chopard.ch

WEBSITE:
www.chopard.ch

FOUNDED:
1860

DISTRIBUTION:
149 boutiques

U.S. DISTRIBUTOR:
Chopard USA
75 Valencia Ave, Suite 1200
Coral Gables, FL 33134
1-800-CHOPARD
www.chopard.com/en-us

MOST IMPORTANT COLLECTIONS/PRICE RANGE:
L.U.C / from $8,110; Happy Sport / from $4,420; Imperiale / from $5,780; Classic Racing / from $5,910; Alpine Eagle / from $9,810

Mille Miglia Classic Chronograph
Reference number: 168619-3001
Movement: automatic, ETA caliber A32.211; ø 28.6 mm, height 6.1 mm; 37 jewels; 28,800 vph; 54-hour power reserve; COSC-certified chronometer
Functions: hours, minutes, subsidiary seconds; chronograph; date
Case: stainless steel, ø 40.5 mm, height 12.9 mm; sapphire crystal; transparent case back; screw-down crown; water-resistant to 5 atm
Band: rubber, pin buckle
Price: $9,140

Mille Miglia Classic Chronograph
Reference number: 168619-4001
Movement: automatic, ETA caliber A32.211; ø 28.6 mm, height 6.1 mm; 37 jewels; 28,800 vph; 54-hour power reserve; COSC-certified chronometer
Functions: hours, minutes, subsidiary seconds; chronograph; date
Case: stainless steel, ø 40.5 mm, height 12.9 mm; bezel, yellow-gold crown and pushers; sapphire crystal; transparent case back; water-resistant to 5 atm
Band: calfskin, pin buckle
Price: $11,100

Mille Miglia Classic Chronograph
Reference number: 168619-3004
Movement: automatic, ETA caliber A32.211; ø 28.6 mm, height 6.1 mm; 37 jewels; 28,800 vph; 54-hour power reserve; COSC-certified chronometer
Functions: hours, minutes, subsidiary seconds; chronograph; date
Case: stainless steel, ø 40.5 mm, height 12.9 mm; sapphire crystal; transparent case back; screw-down crown; water-resistant to 5 atm
Band: calfskin, pin buckle
Price: $9,350

MilleMigliaClassicChronograph

Reference number: 168619-3005
Movement: automatic, ETA caliber A32.211; ø 28.6 mm, height 6.1 mm; 37 jewels; 28,800 vph; 54-hour power reserve; COSC-certified chronometer
Functions: hours, minutes, subsidiary seconds; chronograph; date
Case: stainless steel, ø 40.5 mm, height 12.9 mm; sapphire crystal; transparent case back; screw-down crown; water-resistant to 5 atm
Band: calfskin, pin buckle
Price: $9,350

MilleMigliaClassicChronograph Jacky Ickx Edition

Reference number: 168619-3006
Movement: automatic, ETA caliber A32.211; ø 28.6 mm, height 6.1 mm; 37 jewels; 28,800 vph; 54-hour power reserve; COSC-certified chronometer
Functions: hours, minutes, subsidiary seconds; chronograph; date
Case: stainless steel, ø 40.5 mm, height 12.9 mm; sapphire crystal; transparent case back; screw-down crown; water-resistant to 5 atm
Band: rubber, pin buckle
Remarks: special edition in honor of the Belgian racing driver Jacky Ickx
Price: $10,300; limited to 250 pieces

Alpine Eagle XL Chrono

Reference number: 295393-5002
Movement: automatic, Chopard caliber 03.05-C; ø 28.8 mm, height 7.6 mm; 45 jewels; 28,800 vph; 60-hour power reserve; COSC-certified chronometer
Functions: hours, minutes, subsidiary seconds; flyback chronograph; date
Case: rose gold, ø 44 mm, height 13.15 mm; bezel mounted to case with 8 screws; sapphire crystal; transparent case back; screw-down crown; water-resistant to 10 atm
Band: rose gold, folding clasp
Price: $73,400
Variations: various cases, straps, and dials

Alpine Eagle Chronograph

Reference number: 298609-3001
Movement: automatic, Chopard caliber 03.05-C; ø 28.8 mm, height 7.6 mm; 45 jewels; 28,800 vph; 60-hour power reserve; COSC-certified chronometer
Functions: hours, minutes, subsidiary seconds; flyback chronograph; date
Case: stainless steel, ø 44 mm, height 13.15 mm; bezel mounted to case with 8 screws; sapphire crystal; transparent case back; water-resistant to 10 atm
Band: stainless steel, folding clasp
Price: $21,600
Variations: various cases, straps, and dials

Alpine Eagle Chronograph

Reference number: 295387-9001
Movement: automatic, Chopard caliber 03.05-C; ø 28.8 mm, height 7.6 mm; 45 jewels; 28,800 vph; 60-hour power reserve; COSC-certified chronometer
Functions: hours, minutes, subsidiary seconds; flyback chronograph; date
Case: titanium and rose gold, ø 44 mm, height 13.15 mm; bezel mounted to case with 8 screws; sapphire crystal; transparent case back; screw-down crown; water-resistant to 10 atm
Band: calfskin, folding clasp
Price: $39,300
Variations: various cases, straps, and dials

Alpine Eagle Chronograph

Reference number: 298609-3008
Movement: automatic, Chopard caliber 03.05-C; ø 28.8 mm, height 7.6 mm; 45 jewels; 28,800 vph; 60-hour power reserve; COSC-certified chronometer
Functions: hours, minutes, subsidiary seconds; flyback chronograph; date
Case: titanium, ø 44 mm, height 13.15 mm; bezel mounted to case with 8 screws; sapphire crystal; transparent case back; water-resistant to 10 atm
Band: rubber, pin buckle
Remarks: exclusively available in Chopard boutiques
Price: $25,000

Alpine Eagle Large Tourbillon

Reference number: 298616-3001
Movement: automatic, L.U.C caliber 96.24-L; ø 27.4 mm,
height 3.3 mm; 25 jewels; 25.200 A/h; flying 1-minute
tourbillon, 2 mainsprings, micro-rotor; 65-hour power
reserve; Geneva Seal, COSC-certified chronometer
Functions: hours, minutes, subsidiary seconds (on the
tourbillon cage)
Case: stainless steel, ø 41 mm, height 8.03 mm; bezel
mounted to case with 8 screws; sapphire crystal;
transparent case back; water-resistant to 10 atm
Band: stainless steel, folding clasp
Price: on request

Alpine Eagle Large

Reference number: 298600-3001
Movement: automatic, Chopard caliber 01.01-C;
ø 28.8 mm, height 4.95 mm; 31 jewels; 28,800 vph;
60-hour power reserve; COSC-certified chronometer
Functions: hours, minutes, sweep seconds; date
Case: stainless steel, ø 41 mm, height 9.7 mm; bezel
mounted to case with 8 screws; sapphire crystal;
transparent case back; water-resistant to 10 atm
Band: stainless steel, folding clasp
Price: $14,800
Variations: various dial colors

Alpine Eagle Large

Reference number: 298600-3002
Movement: automatic, Chopard caliber 01.01-C;
ø 28.8 mm, height 4.95 mm; 31 jewels; 28,800 vph;
60-hour power reserve; COSC-certified chronometer
Functions: hours, minutes, sweep seconds; date
Case: stainless steel, ø 41 mm, height 9.7 mm; bezel
mounted to case with 8 screws; sapphire crystal;
transparent case back; water-resistant to 10 atm
Band: stainless steel, folding clasp
Price: $14,800
Variations: with rose-gold bezel; various dial colors

Alpine Eagle Large

Reference number: 295363-5001
Movement: automatic, Chopard caliber 01.01-C;
ø 28.8 mm, height 4.95 mm; 31 jewels; 28,800 vph;
60-hour power reserve; COSC-certified chronometer
Functions: hours, minutes, sweep seconds; date
Case: rose gold, ø 41 mm, height 9.7 mm; bezel
mounted to case with 8 screws; sapphire crystal;
transparent case back; water-resistant to 10 atm
Band: rose gold, folding clasp
Price: $54,700
Variations: in stainless steel ($14,800)

Alpine Eagle 41 XPS

Reference number: 298623-3001
Movement: automatic, L.U.C caliber 96.40-L;
ø 27.4 mm, height 3.3 mm; 29 jewels; 28,800 vph;
2 mainsprings, hairspring with Phillips end curve, gold
oscillating mass; 65-hour power reserve; Geneva Seal,
COSC-certified chronometer
Functions: hours, minutes, subsidiary seconds
Case: stainless steel, ø 41 mm, height 8.03 mm;
sapphire crystal; transparent case back; screw-down
crown; water-resistant to 10 atm
Band: stainless steel, folding clasp
Remarks: "Lucent steel" is an alloy using recycled steel
with an especially bright sheen
Price: $24,300

Alpine Eagle 41 XP TT

Reference number: 298630-3001
Movement: automatic, L.U.C caliber 96.17-S; ø 27.4 mm,
height 3.3 mm; 29 jewels; 28,800 vph; 2 mainsprings;
yellow-gold micro-rotor; skeletonized mainplate;
65-hour power reserve; Geneva Seal
Functions: hours, minutes
Case: titanium, ø 41 mm, height 8 mm; sapphire crystal;
transparent case back; water-resistant to 10 atm
Band: titanium, triple folding clasp
Price: $26,500

L.U.C Quattro Spirit 25

Reference number: 161977-1001
Movement: hand-wound, L.U.C caliber 98.06-L;
ø 28.6 mm, height 4.85 mm; 42 jewels; 28,800 vph;
4 mainsprings, hairspring with Phillips end curve; 192-hour power reserve; Geneva Seal
Functions: hours (digital, jumping), minutes; power reserve indicator (on the rear)
Case: white gold, ø 40 mm, height 10.3 mm; sapphire crystal; transparent case back
Band: reptile skin, pin buckle
Remarks: enamel dial; case of certified Fairmined gold; limited to 100 pieces
Price: $50,200

L.U.C Qualité Fleurier

Reference number: 168631-3001
Movement: automatic, L.U.C caliber 96.09-L;
ø 27.4 mm, height 3.3 mm; 29 jewels; 28,800 vph;
2 mainsprings, hairspring with Phillips end curve, micro-rotor; 65-hour power reserve; Geneva Seal, COSC-certified chronometer, Qualité Fleurier
Functions: hours, minutes, subsidiary seconds
Case: stainless steel, ø 39 mm, height 8.92 mm; sapphire crystal; transparent case back; water-resistant to 3 atm
Band: calfskin, pin buckle
Price: $20,300

L.U.C Full Strike Tourbillon

Reference number: 161987-5001
Movement: hand-wound, L.U.C caliber 08.01-L;
ø 37.2 mm, height 7.97 mm; 63 jewels; 28,800 vph;
1-minute tourbillon; sapphire crystal chimes; 60-hour power reserve; Geneva Seal, COSC-certified chronometer
Functions: hours, minutes, subsidiary seconds (on the tourbillon cage); power reserve indicator, minute repeater
Case: rose gold, ø 42.5 mm, height 12.58 mm; sapphire crystal; transparent case back
Band: reptile skin, folding clasp
Price: on request; limited to 20 pieces

L.U.C XPS Tourbillon Volant

Reference number: 161978-5001
Movement: automatic, L.U.C caliber 96.24-L; ø 27.4 mm, height 3.3 mm; 25 jewels; 25,200 vph; flying 1-minute tourbillon, 2 mainsprings, micro-rotor; 65-hour power reserve; Geneva Seal, COSC-certified chronometer
Functions: hours, minutes
Case: rose gold, ø 40 mm, height 7.2 mm; sapphire crystal; transparent case back; water-resistant to 3 atm
Band: reptile skin, pin buckle
Remarks: case of certified Fairmined gold; hand guilloché on rose-gold dial
Price: on request; limited to 50 pieces

L.U.C Perpetual Twin

Reference number: 168561-3003
Movement: automatic, L.U.C caliber 96.22-L; ø 33 mm, height 6 mm; 29 jewels; 28,800 vph; 2 mainsprings, micro-rotor in gold with heavy metal oscillating mass; with côtes de Genève; 65-hour power reserve; COSC-certified chronometer
Functions: hours, minutes, subsidiary seconds; perpetual calendar with large date, weekday, month, leap year
Case: stainless steel, ø 43 mm, height 11.47 mm; sapphire crystal; transparent case back; water-resistant to 3 atm
Band: calfskin, pin buckle
Price: $27,800

Alpine Eagle Large

Reference number: 295363-5013
Movement: automatic, Chopard caliber 01.01-C;
ø 28.8 mm, height 4.95 mm; 31 jewels; 28,800 vph;
60-hour power reserve; COSC-certified chronometer
Functions: hours, minutes, sweep seconds
Case: rose gold, ø 41 mm, height 9.7 mm; bezel mounted to case with 8 screws, set with baguette-cut diamonds; sapphire crystal; transparent case back; water-resistant to 10 atm
Band: rose gold, folding clasp
Price: $78,600

Caliber L.U.C 96.24-L

Automatic; flying 1-minute tourbillon; gold micro-rotor; 2 mainspring barrels, 65-hour power reserve; Geneva Seal, COSC-certified chronometer

Functions: hours, minutes
Diameter: 27.4 mm
Height: 3.3 mm
Jewels: 25
Balance: glucydur
Frequency: 25,200 vph
Hairspring: flat hairspring, Nivarox 1
Remarks: 190 parts

Caliber L.U.C 01.01-C

Automatic; single mainspring barrel, 60-hour power reserve; COSC-certified chronometer

Functions: hours, minutes, sweep seconds; date
Diameter: 28.8 mm
Height: 4.95 mm
Jewels: 31
Balance: glucydur
Frequency: 28,800 vph
Hairspring: flat hairspring, Nivarox
Remarks: 207 parts

Caliber L.U.C 03.05-C

Automatic; column-wheel control of chronograph functions, vertical clutch; single spring barrel, 60-hour power reserve; COSC-certified chronometer

Functions: hours, minutes, subsidiary seconds; flyback chronograph; date
Diameter: 28.8 mm
Height: 7.6 mm
Jewels: 45
Balance: glucydur
Frequency: 28,800 vph
Hairspring: flat hairspring
Remarks: slotted bridges; skeletonized rose-gold winding rotor

Caliber L.U.C 08.01-L

Hand-wound; sapphire crystal chimes for the repeater mechanism; single spring barrel, 60-hour power reserve; Geneva Seal, COSC-certified chronometer

Functions: hours, minutes, subsidiary seconds; power-reserve indicator, minute repeater
Diameter: 37.2 mm
Height: 7.97 mm
Jewels: 63
Frequency: 28,800 vph
Hairspring: hairspring with Phillips end curve
Remarks: German-silver mainplate and balance cock; 533 parts

Caliber L.U.C 96.09-L

Automatic; gold micro-rotor; double spring barrel, 65-hour power reserve; COSC-certified chronometer

Functions: hours, minutes, subsidiary seconds
Diameter: 27.4 mm
Height: 3.3 mm
Jewels: 29
Balance: glucydur
Frequency: 28,800 vph
Hairspring: flat hairspring, Nivarox 1
Remarks: finely hand-decorated movement

Caliber L.U.C 98.06-L

Hand-wound; swan-neck fine adjustment; four spring barrels, arranged serially in pairs, 192-hour power reserve; Geneva Seal

Functions: hours (digital, jumping), minutes; power reserve indicator (on the movement side)
Diameter: 28.6 mm
Height: 4.85 mm
Jewels: 42
Frequency: 28,800 vph
Hairspring: Breguet hairspring with Phillips end curve
Remarks: 240 parts

CHRONOSWISS

Chronoswiss celebrated its fortieth anniversary in 2023, but the festivities were dampened by the death of the brand's founder, Gerd-Rüdiger Lang. He loved to joke about having "the only Swiss watch factory in Germany," as the brand used Swiss technology with concepts and designs "made in Germany," in Karlsfeld, near Munich, to be precise.

Lang was a pioneer who created regulator watches in the 1980s, an idea that found many fans of new ways to tell the time. Whether in a rectangular or round case, with a tourbillon or without, the off-center dial became the absolute identity of Chronoswiss watches and remains so to this day.

Chronoswiss has always been a little on the edge of the industry in terms of style and technical developments. It created the enduring *manufacture* caliber C.122—based on an old Enicar automatic movement with a patented rattrapante mechanism—and its Chronoscope chronograph has earned a solid reputation for technical prowess. The Pacific and Sirius models, additions to the classic collection, point the company in a new stylistic direction designed to help win new buyers and the attention of the international market.

In March 2012, a Swiss couple, Oliver and Eva Ebstein, purchased Chronoswiss and moved the company headquarters to Lucerne, Switzerland. They decided to remain faithful to the brand's codes. In-house calibers beat inside, and the design became edgier, with daring skeletonizing feats and bold colors. The new tagline, "Modern Mechanical," suggests the brand's direction. The geometrically cut bridges and deep black of the case and parts further underline the contemporary design.

The fortieth anniversary was still celebrated with another re-designing of the Delphis, with jumping hour and retrograde minute. The dial of the Delphis Oracle is in "curved-hand guilloché" with Grand Feu enamel lines curving mellifluously under the hands of the minute and small seconds. The movement that powers this timepiece was developed by La Joux-Perret in exclusivity. And for the 2024 season, the brand decided to flagship a new Delphis named "Sapphire." It's a kind of summation of over 40 years of the brand's watchmaking tradition with modern avant-garde design, with a regal aura, thanks to the striking sapphire blue color.

CHRONOSWISS AG
Löwenstrasse 16b
CH-6004 Lucerne
Switzerland

TEL.:
+41-41-552-21-80

E-MAIL:
luzern@chronoswiss.com

WEBSITE:
www.chronoswiss.com

FOUNDED:
1983

NUMBER OF EMPLOYEES:
approx. 20

ANNUAL PRODUCTION:
About 3,000 wristwatches

U.S. DISTRIBUTOR:
Chronoswiss US Service Office
Shami Fine Watchmaking
372 Fairfield Rd
Fairfield, NJ 07004
973-785-0004

MOST IMPORTANT COLLECTIONS/PRICE RANGE:
Approx. 30 models including, Space Timer, Flying Regulator, Open Gear ReSec, Lunar Chronograph, Opus Chronograph, SkelTec, Sirius Artist, (no current collection) / approx. $5,800 to $47,000

Delphis Venture
Reference number: CH-1423.1-BKBL
Movement: automatic, Chronoswiss caliber C.6004; ø 33 mm; 37 jewels; 28,800 vph; finely finished movement; 55-hour power reserve
Functions: hours (digital, jumping), minutes (retrograde), subsidiary seconds
Case: stainless steel, ø 42 mm, height 14.5 mm; sapphire crystal; transparent case back; water-resistant to 10 atm
Band: rubber, folding clasp
Remarks: hand guilloché on dial
Price: $17,400; limited to 50 pieces

Space Timer Black Hole
Reference number: CH-9345M.2-GRBK
Movement: automatic, Chronoswiss caliber C.308; ø 32.8 mm; 33 jewels; 28,800 vph; hands mechanism (transmission wheel) visible on dial side; finely finished movement; 42-hour power reserve
Functions: hours (off-center), minutes, sweep seconds; date
Case: stainless steel with black DLC, ø 44 mm, height 15.2 mm; sapphire crystal; transparent case back; water-resistant to 10 atm
Band: calf skin, folding clasp
Price: $20,600; limited to 50 pieces

Strike Two H2O
Reference number: CH-5023-BLSI
Movement: automatic, Chronoswiss caliber C.6000; ø 33 mm; 25 jewels; 28,800 vph; skeletonized tungsten rotor; finely finished movement; 55-hour power reserve
Functions: hours (off-center), minutes, subsidiary seconds
Case: stainless steel, ø 40 mm, height 12.7 mm; sapphire crystal; transparent case back; water-resistant to 3 atm
Band: calfskin, folding clasp
Price: $10,800; limited to 100 pieces
Variations: with rubber strap

ReSec Green Monster Manufacture

Reference number: CH-6923T.1-GRBL
Movement: automatic, Chronoswiss caliber C.6005; ø 33 mm; 31 jewels; 28,800 vph; hands mechanism (transmission wheel) visible on dial side; skeletonized tungsten rotor; finely finished movement; 55-hour power reserve
Functions: hours (off-center), minutes, subsidiary seconds (retrograde)
Case: titanium, ø 42 mm, height 14.2 mm; sapphire crystal; transparent case back; water-resistant to 10 atm
Band: rubber, folding clasp
Price: $15,800; limited to 100 pieces
Variations: with blue strap and dial

Flying Regulator Night and Day

Reference number: CH-8763.1-BLSI2
Movement: automatic, Chronoswiss caliber C.296; ø 26.2 mm, height 4,35 mm; 27 jewels; 28,800 vph; skeletonized rotor; finely finished movement; 42-hour power reserve
Functions: hours (off-center), minutes, subsidiary seconds; day/night indicator; date
Case: stainless steel, ø 41 mm, height 13.85 mm; sapphire crystal; transparent case back; water-resistant to 10 atm
Band: bamboo, folding clasp
Remarks: hand guilloché on dial; as "Whiteout" model with white dial
Price: $11,700; limited to 50 pieces

Strike Two Golden Gear

Reference number: CH-5023-ANGO
Movement: automatic, Chronoswiss caliber C.6000; ø 33 mm; 25 jewels; 28,800 vph; skeletonized tungsten rotor; finely finished movement; 55-hour power reserve
Functions: hours (off-center), minutes, subsidiary seconds
Case: stainless steel, ø 40 mm, height 12.7 mm; sapphire crystal; transparent case back; water-resistant to 3 atm
Band: calfskin, folding clasp
Price: $10,800
Variations: with rubber strap

Opus Chronograph Titanium

Reference number: CH-7543T.1S-DGR
Movement: automatic, Chronoswiss caliber C.741 S (Valjoux 7750 base); ø 30 mm, height 7.9 mm; 25 jewels; 28,800 vph; fully skeletonized movement and with decorative ribbing, skeletonized rotor; 46-hour power reserve
Functions: hours, minutes, sweep seconds; chronograph; date
Case: titanium, ø 41 mm, height 14.8 mm; sapphire crystal; transparent case back; water-resistant to 10 atm
Band: textile, folding clasp
Remarks: skeletonized dial
Price: $15,300

ReSec Helium Manufacture

Reference number: CH-6923TM.1-ORBL
Movement: automatic, Chronoswiss caliber C.6005; ø 33 mm; 31 jewels; 28,800 vph; hands mechanism (transmission wheel) visible on dial side; skeletonized tungsten rotor; finely finished movement; 55-hour power reserve
Functions: hours (off-center), minutes, subsidiary seconds (retrograde)
Case: titanium, ø 42 mm, height 14.2 mm; sapphire crystal; transparent case back; water-resistant to 10 atm
Band: rubber, folding clasp
Price: $15,300; limited to 100 pieces
Variations: with black or red dial and strap

Lunar Chronograph

Reference number: CH-7541LR
Movement: automatic, Chronoswiss caliber C.755 (Valjoux 7750 base); ø 30 mm, height 7.9 mm; 25 jewels; 28,800 vph; côtes de Genève, perlage on movement, skeletonized rotor; finely finished movement; 46-hour power reserve
Functions: hours, minutes, subsidiary seconds; chronograph; date, moon phase
Case: red gold, ø 41 mm, height 14.8 mm; sapphire crystal; transparent case back; water-resistant to 3 atm
Band: reptile skin, folding clasp
Price: $24,800

CIGA DESIGN

Jianmin Zhang is considered one of China's top industrial designers. He built a reputation for creating guidance systems for large architectural projects, like the Shanghai Expo and the Beijing Olympics. In 2016, he turned to watchmaking and founded CIGA Design (from a Chinese word meaning "amazing"). His mission was to make high-quality, eye-catching watches at an affordable price for the young generation. China's industrial machine made this possible. So, CIGA began manufacturing a range of watches, from sleek Bauhaus-inspired one-handers to edgily futuristic and minimalist pieces.

Jianmin Zhang is keenly aware of the new "national trend" (*guochao*), with consumers seeking Chinese-themed products, though not necessarily made in China. On the other hand, he somehow bridges east and west. Several models won awards in Europe, but in 2021, the Blue Planet clinched the Challenge Prize at the Grand Prix d'Horlogerie in Geneva. The watch features a detailed view of Earth from the sky, with engraved silver land masses. The time-telling mechanism uses a patented system referred to as non-synchronous follower technology, allowing for a stationary hour ring and a rotating minute ring that coordinates with a rotating hand. On the Blue Planet, the reference to China was a compass, which was a Chinese invention.

Naturally, CIGA Design watches are steeped in the spiritual/intellectual concepts of Daoism. The frequent pairing of a square and circle, for example, expresses the symbiotic duality of Earth (square) and Sky (circle), one of the founding principles of Daoism. This design element is found in the mysterious Tourbillon Chinese Zodiac The Year Of Dragon, whose hour and minute hands, highlighted with three and four diamonds respectively, move across a "Super Black" dial, with the tourbillon gently revolving at 6 o'clock in a dragon-shaped cage. The Year of the Snake, launched in 2024 to celebrate the astrological animal of 2025 uses the Blue Planet movement to drive a gold snake around the hour ring. Finally, the Mount Everest Central Tourbillon is a tribute to human achievement—and the brand's own success in some ways—that turns two ice axes into an hour and minute hand, the latter sporting the four first flags to be planted atop the Everest.

CIGA DESIGN
43F, Block A, Tanglang Square Office Bldg
Liuxian Blvd, Nanshan District
Shenzhen, Guangdong 518000
China

TEL.:
+86-755-827-951-80

E-MAIL:
waterman@cigadesign.com

WEBSITE:
www.cigadesign.com

FOUNDED:
2016

NUMBER OF EMPLOYEES:
109

DISTRIBUTION:
Online sales
www.cigadesign.com

MOST IMPORTANT COLLECTIONS:
Chinese Astrology watches, Blue Planet, Magician, Edge, Zen, Denmark Rose

Year Of The Snake

Movement: automatic, customized CIGA Design caliber; ø 26 mm; 26 jewels; 21,600 vph; 41-hour power reserve
Functions: hours, minutes
Case: black jadeite; ø 46 mm, height 15 mm; sapphire crystal; water-resistant to 3 atm
Band: rubber; pin buckle
Remarks: sculptural gold-plated snake's head points to the fixed hour ring, while the tail points to the rotating minute ring
Price: $3,299; limited to 365 pieces

Central Tourbillon Mount Everest Homage

Movement: automatic, CD-05 caliber, in-house customized movement; ø 35.6 mm; 33 jewels; 21,600 vph; 120-hour power reserve
Functions: hours (part of the bezel), minutes
Case: titanium alloy, 46 mm, height 13 mm; lugless case; sapphire crystal; water-resistant to 3 atm
Band: rubber, pin buckle
Remarks: dial made of rock hand-selected from Mount Everest; minute hands with flags of four nations
Price: $3,999

Tourbillon Chinese Zodiac The Year Of Dragon

Movement: hand-wound, CD-06; ø 33 mm; 19 jewels; 21,600 vph; 1-minute tourbillon with dragon-shaped cage; 40-hour power reserve
Functions: hours, minutes, subsidiary seconds
Case: black agate, 45 mm, height 13.7 mm; sapphire crystal; sterling silver case back with personalization option; water-resistant to 3 atm
Band: reptile skin, folding clasp
Remarks: dial in special Super Black with 3 diamonds on the hour hand, 4 on the minute hand; can be personalized on the back on request
Price: $3,299; limited edition to 365 pieces

CIRCULA

Germany has two hubs of watchmaking, each with their own style. Glashütte in the east near Dresden is well known. Somewhat less famous is Pforzheim on the edge of the Black Forest, where the cuckoo clock originated. The small industrial city was heavily bombed during World War II. During the reconstruction phase, one Heinz Huber decided that he would expand his jewelry and watch wholesale business to watchmaking. The brand Circula was born in 1955, the name a reference to the rotating wheels and all round elements in watches.

It was his grandson, Cornelius Huber, who redirected the brand in 2018, continuing the original mission of making precision timepieces with a modern and—for German aesthetics, not unusual—minimalist look. Being a small company gives them a certain agility, so for a personalized experience, Circula regularly offers its customers the opportunity to participate in the watch design process.

The company's collections are designed along two main planks. On the one hand, models from earlier catalogs serve as inspiration, such as the AquaSport II and AquaSport GMT, patterned after the Circula divers from the 1970s. They come in a compressor titanium case and are water-resistant to 20 atm, while the DiveSport is water-resistant to 50 atm.

The other aesthetic line goes back to the classics of the 1950s, whose unadorned designs have been updated without interfering too much with the discreetness of the original. The ProTrail Sand presented here is a good example: a simple three-hand watch with a night-time hour track on the dial in a toned-down sandy yellow.

Thanks to its strategy of affordability combined with quality and minimalist designs that ensure timelessness, Circula has managed to establish a reputation of producing watches that can attract the seasoned collector or the budding one likewise.

The watches are generally run on mechanical movements by Sellita from Switzerland in *élaboré* or *top* versions. The rate is checked and readjusted if necessary before each case is closed to ensure a high level of precision.

CIRCULA WATCHES
Inh. Cornelius Huber e.K.
Poststr. 38
75210 Keltern
Germany

TEL.:
+49 7236 70 90 864

E-MAIL:
hello@circulawatches.com

WEBSITE:
www.circulawatches.com

FOUNDED:
1955

U. S. DISTRIBUTION:
Island Watch
215 Central Ave
Suite C
Farmingdale, NY 11735
(for mail only)
sales@longislandwatch.com
www.longislandwatch.com

MOST IMPORTANT COLLECTIONS:
AquaSport, DiveSport, SuperSport, ProTrail, ProFlight

ProTrail Sand

Reference: PE-SS-DD
Movement: automatic, Sellita caliber SW200-1; ø 25.6 mm, height 4.6 mm; 26 jewels; 28,800 vph; antimagnetic to 80,000 A/m in soft iron cage; 41-hour power reserve
Functions: hours, minutes, sweep seconds
Case: stainless steel, ø 40 mm, height 12 mm; sapphire crystal; screw-down crown; water-resistant to 15 atm
Strap: textile (nylon canvas), pin buckle
Price: $989
Variants: in green, black, gray or brown; with stainless steel bracelet ($1,169)

DiveSport Titanium Petrol

Reference: DE-TR-PP-TH-T
Movement: automatic, Sellita caliber SW200-1; ø 25.6 mm, height 4.6 mm; 26 jewels; 28,800 vph; 41-hour power reserve
Functions: hours, minutes, sweep seconds; date
Case: titanium, ø 42 mm, height 14.1 mm; unidirectional bezel, with 0-60 scale; sapphire crystal; screw-down crown; water-resistant to 50 atm
Band: titanium, double folding clasp
Price: $1,299
Variants: in black, gray or yellow; with rubber strap ($1,079)

ProFlight

Reference: PFE-SS-BB
Movement: automatic, Sellita caliber SW200-1; ø 25.6 mm, height 4.6 mm; 26 jewels; 28,800 vph; antimagnetic to 80,000 A/m in soft iron cage; 41-hour power reserve
Functions: hours, minutes, sweep seconds
Case: stainless steel, ø 40 mm, height 12 mm; sapphire crystal; screw-down crown; water-resistant to 15 atm
Strap: textile (nylon canvas), pin buckle
Price: $1,029
Variations: with gray dial; with stainless steel bracelet ($1,199)

CITIZEN

Citizen is an internationally active company with a broad range of watch manufacturing activities. The Shokosha Watch Research Institute, which later became the Citizen Watch Co., was founded in 1918. In 1924, the institute's industrial production history began with a pocket watch that was affordable for everyone, and it was ultimately Tokyo's mayor at the time, Shinpei Goto, who suggested the name Citizen for this "citizen-orientated" timepiece.

Today, Citizen Watch is one of the world's largest watchmaking manufacturers with a vertical production process that extends from the development and manufacture of the individual components of a watch through to final assembly. The focus of production may be on quartz-controlled watches with intelligent energy generation (e.g., solar cells), but the mechanical watch segment has not been neglected over the past decades.

A part of the brand's global reputation is based on its ability to produce affordable diving and everyday watches. It is now also aiming for the higher-priced segment of manufacture watches. Unbeknownst to many, the very Swiss La Joux-Perret manufacture in La Chaux-de-Fonds, Switzerland, has actually been part of the Citizen Group for almost ten years. The acquisition was prescient, since the key to contemporary mechanical technology usually passes by a solid "motorist." This is also where the caliber 200 automatic movement was developed, with which the model named The Citizen aims to herald the brand's entrée into the higher market segments.

Anniversaries are always a great occasion to make big moves. Citizen celebrated its 100th anniversary in 2024 with numerous limited editions that look to both the mechanical past and the future. From the reissue of the first pocket watch in a titanium case (100 pieces worldwide) to a satellite-controlled high-tech model, there is something for every customer.

CITIZEN WATCH CO. LTD.
Nishitokyo, Prefecture, Tokyo
Japan

WEBSITES:
www.citizen.co.jp
www.citizenwatch.com

FOUNDED:
1924 (1918)

NUMBER OF EMPLOYEES:
About 15,500

U.S. SUBSIDIARY:
Citizen Service Headquarters
1000 West 190th Street
Torrance, CA 90502-1040
310-532-8463
800-321-1023
customerservice_us@citizenwatch.com

MOST IMPORTANT COLLECTIONS/PRICE
Series8, Super Titanium, The Citizen, Tsuki-yomi A-T,
Tsuyosa / $450 to $8,400

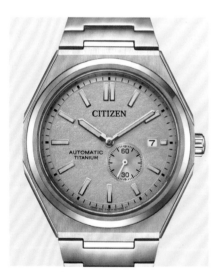

Super Titanium Subsidiary Seconds

Reference number: NJ0180-80M
Movement: automatic, Citizen caliber 8213; ø 25.6 mm, height 5.2 mm; 21 jewels; 21,600 vph; 40-hour power reserve
Functions: hours, minutes, subsidiary seconds; date
Case: titanium (Duratect surface-hardening), ø 40.5 mm, height 11.05 mm; sapphire crystal; transparent case back; water-resistant to 10 atm
Band: titanium, folding clasp
Price: $650
Variations: with white, blue or green dial

The Citizen

Reference number: NC1000-51E
Movement: automatic, Citizen caliber 0210; ø 25.6 mm, height 3.8 mm; 26 jewels; 28,800 vph; manufacture caliber developed in collaboration with La Joux-Perret, Switzerland; regulated to chronometer value; 60-hour power reserve
Functions: hours, minutes, subsidiary seconds; date
Case: stainless steel, ø 40 mm, height 11.2 mm; sapphire crystal; transparent case back; water-resistant to 10 atm
Band: stainless steel, folding clasp
Price: $8,400
Variations: with silver white dial

Tsuyosa Automatic

Reference number: NJ0151-88M
Movement: automatic, Citizen caliber 8210; ø 25.6 mm, height 5.2 mm; 21 jewels; 21,600 vph; 45-hour power reserve
Functions: hours, minutes, sweep seconds; date
Case: stainless steel, ø 40 mm, height 11.7 mm; sapphire crystal; transparent case back; water-resistant to 5 atm
Band: stainless steel, folding clasp
Price: $450

CLAUDE MEYLAN

The Swiss brand Claude Meylan, located in L'Abbaye near Joux Lake in the heart of watch country, specializes in skeletonization, which is the art of removing as much material as possible from bridges, plates, the dial, even the hands. It transforms a watch, making it transparent and allowing a view of the movement. Further, it allows for imaginative designs using what's left of the material.

Skeletonization has become popular in recent years, but it's not as simple as it might sound. As the various metal components are hollowed out and properly finished with chamfering and sanding, the tensions within the material change. This can then have a deleterious effect on the functioning of the mechanism, since the bridges and plates are in fact used to hold and stabilize the movement.

In 1988, Claude Meylan founded his company. It was taken over soon after by another watchmaker, Henri Berney, who kept up the old tradition. In 2011, the next CEO, Philippe Belais, a man with long experience in the industry, took charge. He also heads Vaudaux, a maker of high-end boxes and cases in Geneva.

Claude Meylan's products, which show many different aspects of the art of skeletonization, live up to the brand's tagline: "Sculptors of time." The company has five main collections, all relating in some way to the region: Lac, for Joux Lake; l'Abbaye, the village where the company has its headquarters; Légendes, exploring local tales; Lionne, the tiny, 1,800-foot-long river with a big name (Lioness, because it sometimes turns into a raging torrent) that flows by the workshops; and, finally, Tortue, whose tonneau case is reminiscent of a turtle. Lately, the Lionne line has been evolving, with a smaller version to attract female watch fans, and the *sur-mesure* (bespoke) version that lets buyers have initials placed on the watch dial. The Lionne Ondine is a ladies' watch released in 2024. It features a special bracelet made of rings filled with mother-of-pearl. It, too, mirrors that short river, but when it is lingering poetically toward the Lac de Joux. The ladies' Tortue was born in the mind of the company's communication officer, Pia de Chefdebien, who was asked to dream up her own mechanical watch.

CLAUDE MEYLAN
Route de l'Hôtel de Ville 2
CH-1344 L'Abbaye
Switzerland

TEL.:
+41-21-841-14-57

E-MAIL:
info@claudemeylan.ch

WEBSITE:
www.claudemeylan.ch

FOUNDED:
originally mid-18th century; revived in mid-20th century and purchased in 2011

NUMBER OF EMPLOYEES:
7

ANNUAL PRODUCTION:
approx. 2,500 pieces

MOST IMPORTANT COLLECTIONS/PRICE RANGE:
Tortue, Lac, Lionne, Abbaye / $4,500 to $6,850; Légendes series / up to $33,000

Lionne sure-mesure Initiales

Reference number: 6040-PI
Movement: hand-wound, Peseux 7040; ø 23.30 mm, height 3.10 mm; 17 jewels; 21,600 vph; skeletonized movement; 44-hour power reserve
Functions: hours, minutes
Case: yellow gold-plated stainless steel, ø 35 mm, height 11 mm; sapphire crystal; transparent case back; water-resistant to 3 atm
Band: leather, pin buckle
Remarks: personalization with initials on the dial
Price: $3,400

Lionne Ondine

Reference number: 6060-PNA
Movement: hand-wound, Peseux 7001; ø 23 mm, height 2.50 mm; 17 jewels; 21,600 vph; skeletonized movement; 42-hour power reserve
Functions: hours, minutes
Case: stainless steel with rose-gold plating, ø 35 mm, height 8 mm; sapphire crystal; transparent case back; water-resistant to 3 atm
Band: gold-plated steel, clasp
Remarks: mother-of-pearl-filled bracelet links
Price: $7,700
Variations: silver plating

Tortue Petite Fleur

Reference number: 6080-DIA
Movement: automatic, caliber 7.75CM17; ø 26.5 mm, height 5 mm; 25 jewels; 28,800 vph; micro-rotor with 68 pavé diamonds; 38-hour power reserve
Functions: hours, minutes, seconds
Case: stainless steel, 31 mm x 31 mm, height 11 mm; sapphire crystal; transparent case back; water-resistant to 3 atm
Band: technical satin, buckle
Price: $7,700

COLORADO WATCH COMPANY

In the mid-nineteenth century, the United States of America became a big player in the watch industry. The main reason was the development of new industrial processes that allowed a company to make watches with interchangeable parts and thus to mass-produce a quality product. For a variety of reasons, the system ran out of steam and by the mid twentieth century, the U.S. market was flooded with excellent Swiss movements that allowed brands to make watches with considerable ease. For R. T. Custer, who built up the Vortic brand from scratch over the past decade using discarded movements from old American pocket watches, the idea of making a very American watch became a goal.

The mission of his newly founded Colorado Watch Company is to make "the most American watch at scale" by leveraging the infrastructure of the Vortic brand to make modern, automatic watches in the USA. This involves above all "educating the customer on the definition of American-made and how it's drastically different than Swiss-made."

To achieve its goals, Colorado Watch Co. has decided to be extremely transparent. The young company will be displaying information about every single component on its website so that anyone considering a purchase can see exactly what's inside. For example, the Americhron calibers are by the Arizona-based FTS company. For the sapphire crystals, Custer found a small company in New Hampshire.

Currently the two models available are military style. The GCT (which stands for Greenwich Civil Time, used by the American military until the 1950s) features a standard 12-hour track with an additional 24-hour track. Accentuating the vintage look is the radium-colored luminescent material. The Field Watch takes its name from the timepieces issued by the British army during World War II. Both watches are 85% American made, meaning that 85% of the cost to build the watch stays within the United States. It's already a high percentage, considering that the Swiss have a 60% limit, but Custer is planning to continuously improve that number in the future until it reaches the one-hundred mark.

COLORADO WATCH COMPANY
324 Jefferson St
Fort Collins, CO 80524
USA

TEL.:
855-285-7884

E-MAIL:
info@coloradowatchcompany.com

WEBSITE:
www.coloradowatchcompany.com

FOUNDED:
2023

NUMBER OF EMPLOYEES:
2

DISTRIBUTION:
Contact the company directly

MOST IMPORTANT COLLECTIONS/PRICE RANGE:
Field Watch / $1,395; the GCT / $1,895

"The GCT" Batch 1

Movement: automatic, FTS Manufacturing Americhron; ø 26.4 mm, height 5.1 mm; 22 jewels; 28,800 vph; gunmetal movement with custom Colorado rotor; 36-hour power reserve
Functions: hours, minutes, sweep seconds (hacking)
Case: stainless steel with black DLC, ø 42 mm, height 13 mm; sapphire crystal; stainless steel crown with black DLC; transparent case back; water-resistant to 15 atm
Band: cordura, pin buckle
Price: $1,895

"Field Watch" Batch 1

Movement: automatic, FTS Manufacturing Americhron; ø 26.4 mm, height 5.1 mm; 22 jewels; 28,800 vph; gunmetal movement with custom Colorado rotor; 36-hour power reserve
Functions: hours, minutes, sweep seconds (hacking)
Case: stainless steel, ø 40 mm, height 10.5 mm; sapphire crystal; transparent case back; water-resistant to 10 atm
Band: cordura, pin buckle
Price: $1,395

"FieldWatch"Batch2-ClassicDial and DLC Case

Movement: automatic, FTS Manufacturing Americhron; ø 26.4 mm, height 5.1 mm; 22 jewels; 28,800 vph; gunmetal movement with custom Colorado rotor; 36-hour power reserve
Functions: hours, minutes, sweep seconds (hacking)
Case: stainless steel with black DLC, ø 40 mm, height 10.5 mm; sapphire crystal; stainless steel crown with black DLC; transparent case back; water-resistant to 10 atm
Band: cordura, pin buckle
Price: $1,395

CORUM

Founded in 1955, Switzerland's youngest luxury watch brand, Corum, celebrated sixty years of unusual—and sometimes outlandish—case and dial designs in 2015. The brand has had quite a busy history but still by and large remains true to the collections launched by founders Gaston Ries and his nephew René Bannwart: the Admiral's Cup, Bridges, and Heritage. Among Corum's most iconic pieces is the legendary Golden Bridge baguette, or stick, movement, which has received a complete makeover in recent years with the use of modern materials and complicated mechanisms. It is built around the idea of concentrating all parts along a straight axis in the middle of a rectangular dial. The development of these extraordinary movements required great watchmaking craftsmanship.

The Bridges collection has always been an eye-catcher. It was originally the brainchild of the great watchmaker Vincent Calabrese, though these types of movements trace back further in time. Its introduction was a milestone in watchmaking history. And the Golden Bridge recently acquired a new highlight in the Golden Bridge Avant-Garde, with all components appearing to float in thin air, with six black indices framing the movement, themselves surrounded by a dangerous-looking black frame. It's very sleek and modern. But Corum also has more classical watches, like the sporty Admiral's Cup collection, which is divided into the staid Legend and the more athletic AC-One 45.

In 2013, the Chinese Citychamp Group became a shareholder and added much needed development cash and an extensive distribution network in Hong Kong and China. The Group has since also acquired the Rotary and Eterna brands, thus creating a strong manufacturing pool in Switzerland. Corum's vision is expressed in its logo: a key facing the sky, which symbolizes both the mysteries to be discovered as well as openness to the new. For a more popular experience of watch-wearing, the company revived the remarkable Bubble, which earned its moniker from the domed shape of the crystal, allowing room for all sorts of dial decoration.

MONTRES CORUM SÀRL
Rue du Petit-Château 1
Case postale 374
CH-2301 La Chaux-de-Fonds
Switzerland

TEL.:
+41-32-967-0670

E-MAIL:
info@corum.ch

WEBSITE:
www.corum-watches.com

FOUNDED:
1955

NUMBER OF EMPLOYEES:
50 worldwide

ANNUAL PRODUCTION:
5,000 watches

U.S. DISTRIBUTOR:
Montres Corum USA
CWJ BRANDS
1551 Sawgrass Corporate Parkway, Suite 109
Sunrise, FL 33323
954-279-1220
www.corum.ch

MOST IMPORTANT COLLECTIONS/PRICE RANGE:
Admiral's Cup, Golden Bridge, Lab, Bubble, Coin, Heritage, Romvlvs and Artisan /
$4,400 to over $1,000,000

Admiral 38 Automatic

Reference number: A082/04472
Movement: automatic, caliber CO 082; ø 25.6 mm, height 3.6 mm; 25 jewels; 28,800 vph; 42-hour power reserve
Functions: hours, minutes, sweep seconds; date
Case: rose gold, ø 38 mm, height 8.95 mm; bezel set with 72 diamonds; sapphire crystal; transparent case back; water-resistant to 10 atm
Band: rubber, triple folding clasp
Remarks: malachite-dial
Price: $29,900
Variations: various cases, straps, and dials

Admiral 42 Automatic

Reference number: A395/04480
Movement: automatic, caliber CO 395; ø 25.6 mm, height 4.35 mm; 27 jewels; 28,800 vph; 42-hour power reserve
Functions: hours, minutes, subsidiary seconds; date
Case: stainless steel, ø 42 mm, height 10.3 mm; sapphire crystal; transparent case back; water-resistant to 10 atm
Band: stainless steel, triple folding clasp
Remarks: meteorite dial
Price: $8,700
Variations: various cases, straps, and dials

Golden Bridge Classic

Reference number: B113/02890
Movement: hand-wound, caliber CO 113; 11 mm x 33 mm, height 3 mm; 19 jewels; 28,800 vph; baguette movement, bridges and hand-engraved gold mainplate; 40-hour power reserve
Functions: hours, minutes
Case: rose gold, 34 mm x 51 mm, height 10.9 mm; sapphire crystal; transparent case back; water-resistant to 3 atm
Band: reptile skin, triple folding clasp
Price: $47,700

CUERVO Y SOBRINOS

Many brands have been going vintage to surf a wave of nostalgia in an age of techno-frigidity. Cuervo y Sobrinos, however, has vintage, nostalgia, romance, and a touch of derring-do as a genome set. The brand originated with Ramón Fernandos Cuervo, who emigrated from Spain to Cuba in 1862 and opened a jewelry business. Twenty years later, he recruited his sister's sons to help out with the booming business (that would be his nephews, the *sobrinos* of the brand name). Don Ramón died in 1907, but the company continued to expand, adding wrist-watches made in La Chaux-de-Fonds.

The advent of Communist rule on the island ended the streak of successes. But in 2002, an Italian watch enthusiast, Marzio Villa, resuscitated the brand. The tagline "Latin heritage, Swiss manufacture" says it all. The purchase was well-advised, because vintage, even in an updated form, will always find a fan, and Cuba is filled with iconic images from its past.

The many collections produced by Cuervo y Sobrinos epitomize—or even romanticize—the island's heyday. In these pieces is the faded elegance of the age of steamships and the nostalgia for a past time, mostly the 1930s to the 1950s, when the world's troubles could be ignored by those with enough wherewithal to travel to the island, walk down shop-lined streets with a good cigar, and then lose some cash in the casinos. The lines are elegant and sober, or blatantly vintage with fissured dial effect (like the Historiador collection), or radiate the ease of those who still have time on their hands, as it were. The color codes recall Cuba's famous products: tobacco, coffee, salmon. In fact, when you purchase a Cuervo y Sobrinos watch, it comes in a humidor. Lately, the brand has focused on these decades of slightly decadent life on the island with a range of models in the Robusto line.

While some collections, like the Buceador, have some more modern models, the Espléndidos and Prominente collections are the ones that really epitomize the brand's DNA, with at times overly long, languorous, elegant, rectangular, thin cases and colors named "rhum," "salmon," or "tobacco."

CYS SA
Via Carlo Maderno 54
CH-6825
Switzerland

TEL.:
+41 21-552-18-82

E-MAIL:
contact@cuervoysobrinos.com

WEBSITE:
www.cuervoysobrinos.com

FOUNDED:
1882

ANNUAL PRODUCTION:
3,500 watches

DISTRIBUTOR:
Provenance Gems LLC
ines@provenancegems.com
800-305-3869

MOST IMPORTANT COLLECTIONS/PRICE RANGE:
Esplendidos, Historiador, Pirata, Prominente, Robusto, Vuelo/ $2,000 to $20,000

Robusto 1935

Reference number: 3161B.1HAB
Movement: automatic, CYS 8130 caliber (Soprod Newton base); ø 26 mm, height 4.6 mm; 23 jewels, 28,800 vph, blued oscillating weight with logo; 44-hour power reserve
Functions: hours, minutes, sweep seconds; date
Case: stainless steel, ø 40 mm, height 11.85 mm; sapphire crystal; transparent case back; screw-down crown; water-resistant to 10 atm
Band: stainless steel, folding clasp
Price: $3,100; limited to 882 pieces
Variations: various dials; silver, blue, and green

Robusto "Pedro Murias"

Reference number: 3162.1PM
Movement: automatic, CYS 8130 caliber (Sellita SW 261); ø 25.6 mm, height 5.6 mm; 31 jewels, 28,800 vph, blued oscillating weight with logo; 38-hour power reserve
Functions: hours, minutes, subsidiary seconds
Case: stainless steel, ø 40 mm, height 11.85 mm; sapphire crystal; screw-down crown; water-resistant to 5 atm
Band: calfskin, pin buckle
Remarks: homage to Pedro Murias, case back engraved with Murias's tobacco factory
Price: $3,100; limited to 100 pieces
Variations: various dials; silver, blue, and green,

Robusto Sans Souci

Reference number: 3162.1N
Movement: automatic, CYS 8130 caliber (Sellita SW 261); ø 25.6 mm, height 5.6 mm; 31 jewels, 28,800 vph, blued oscillating weight with logo; 38-hour power reserve
Functions: hours, minutes, subsidiary seconds
Case: stainless steel, ø 40 mm, height 11.85 mm; sapphire crystal; transparent case back; screw-down crown; water-resistant to 5 atm
Band: calfskin, pin buckle
Price: $2,750

Historiador Tradición "San Rafael"

Reference number: 3102.1ASV
Movement: automatic, CYS 5203 (Sellita SW 240-1 base); ø 29 mm, height: 5.05 mm, 26 jewels, 28,800 vph, finished oscillating weight with engraving; 68-hour power reserve
Functions: hours, minutes, sweep seconds; day, date
Case: stainless steel, ø 40 mm, height 10.7 mm; sapphire crystal; water-resistant to 5 atm
Band: reptile skin, folding clasp
Remarks: dial with traditional "frappage" motif; case back features engraving of former Cuervo y Sobrinos boutique on San Rafael Street in Havana, Cuba
Price: $3,250; limited to 188 pieces
Variations: with champagne or white dial

Historiador Flameante

Reference number: 3130.1FB
Movement: automatic, CYS 2052 caliber (ETA 7001 base); ø 23.3 mm, height: 2.5 mm, 17 jewels, 21,600 vph, oscillating weight with côtes de Genève slate-colored treatment; 42-hour power reserve
Functions: hours, minutes, subsidiary seconds
Case: stainless steel, ø 40 mm, height 6.2 mm; sapphire crystal; transparent case back; water-resistant to 3 atm
Band: reptile skin, folding clasp
Remarks: "flaming" design on the dial
Price: $3,840

Historiador Nino Farina II

Reference number: 3144.1NF
Movement: automatic, CYS 8129 caliber (ETA 2894 base); ø 28 mm, height 6.1 mm, 37 jewels, 28,800 vph, oscillating weight with côtes de Genève; 42-hour power reserve
Functions: hours, minutes, subsidiary seconds; chronograph with tachymeter scale; date
Case: stainless steel, ø 40 mm, height 12.45 mm; sapphire crystal; transparent case back overlayed with race car driver Nino Farina signature; water-resistant to 5 atm
Band: calfskin, folding clasp
Price: $4,800

Vuelo Emilio Carranza Bicompax

Reference number: 3202.1CN.Bl
Movement: automatic, CYS 5160 (Sellita SW 295 base); ø 25.6 mm, height: 5.6 mm, 31 jewels, 28,800 vph, finished oscillating weight with applied logo; 38-hour power reserve
Functions: hours, minutes, subsidiary seconds; date
Case: stainless steel, ø 44 mm, height 11.6 mm; sapphire crystal; screw-down case back; water-resistant to 3 atm
Band: leather, folding clasp
Remarks: engraving on back homage to pioneering Mexican pilot Emilio Carranza (1905-1928)
Price: $4,120

Prominente Icónico Doble Tiempo

Reference number: 1112.1NM
Movement: automatic, caliber CYS 5024 (ETA 2671 base modified in-house); ø 17.2 mm, height 4.80 and 4.8 mm; 25 jewels; 28,800 vph; rotor with fan decoration and CyS engraving; 44-hour power reserve
Functions: hours, minutes; 2nd 24-hour display; 12-hour display (2nd time zone)
Case: stainless steel, 52 mm x 30.5 mm, height 9.5 mm; sapphire crystal; double transparent case backs affixed with 6 screws; water-resistant to 3 atm
Band: reptile skin, folding clasp
Remarks: black guilloché dial
Price: $5,050
Variations: rhum, tobacco, salmon guilloché dials

Prominente Clásico

1015.1RB
Reference number: 1015.1RB
Movement: automatic, CYS 5103 caliber (Soprod M100 base); ø 25.6 mm, height 3.6 mm; 25 jewels; 28,800 vph; oscillating weight with CyS logo; 42-hour power reserve
Functions: hours, minutes, sweep seconds; date
Case: stainless steel, ø 43 mm x 32 mm, height 8.6 mm; sapphire crystal; transparent case back; water-resistant to 3 atm
Band: reptile skin, folding clasp
Price: $3,550

CURTIS AUSTRALIA

Watches made by an independent often have a special aura. It is rarely the engine running the models, because these creators have to rely on off-the-shelf calibers that are robust, accurate, and may just need some tweaking and perhaps decoration. What catches the eye of the beholder are the visuals, naturally. And that unique look is made up of myriad signals that combine the skill of the craftsperson doing the finishing and his or her environmental surroundings.

Glenn Curtis grew up in the nature of Gippsland, Australia, a region in the southeast of the country embraced by the Australian Alps in the north and the sea in the south. He is also the offspring of a family-run business going back to the 1890s. For the past sixty years or so, he has been assiduously crafting writing implements and jewelry. He added watches when he inherited his watchmaking grandfather's tools.

Curtis Australia's creations owe their aesthetic pedigree to Art Deco, with an added tribute to local nature, with its lakes, mellifluous sand beaches, and a notorious diversity of flora and fauna. Curtis uses his craftmanship to incorporate all these elements into his products, including the watches, of which he makes about 200 per year. "A watch isn't just a tool to mark time," he pointed out, "it's a companion that holds memories, milestones, and meaning."

Curtis has three men's collections. They all run on a reliable Sellita 300 family movement, but each collection has a distinctive look and feel. The Motima line (the name is a combination of motion + time) is a timepiece for daily wear. Its main features are a hand-carved coin bezel on and round (RT) or octagonal (XT) base and a complex dial featuring a sun-brushed center and a grained circle. The Myst and Alpha collections boast richly engraved cases with flowing lines and enough space for jewelry. The watches can be personalized on demand.

Noteworthy—and a rare touch in the watch world—is Glenn Curtis's choice of 9-carat gold for some models, an alloy that is durable thanks to an approximately 60 percent admixture of copper, silver, and nickel. The advantage is a material that looks like full gold but is more affordable.

CURTIS AUSTRALIA
129 Macleod Street
Bairnsdale, Victoria
Australia 3875

TEL.:
+61-35-152-1089

EMAIL:
replyto@curtisaustralia.com

WEBSITE:
www.curtisaustralia.com

FOUNDED:
1890

ANNUAL PRODUCTION:
less than 200 watches

DISTRIBUTION:
Contact Curtis Australia

MOST IMPORTANT COLLECTIONS/PRICE RANGE:
Motima, Myst, Alpha, range of ladies' watches (Colours, Floriale, Fortuna, Grace, Monroe, Myst, Sophia) / $6,800 to $84,000

Motima XT Perpetual

Movement: automatic, Sellita SW 300-1 caliber; ø 25.6mm, height 3.6 mm; 25 jewels; 28,800 vph; custom-engraved rotor; 42-hour power reserve
Functions: hours, minutes, sweep seconds; date
Case: yellow gold, ø 46 mm, height 11 mm; with fluted (coin) bezel; sapphire crystal with gem set transparent case back; screw-down crown; water-resistant to 5 atm
Band: stainless steel and gold, folding clasp
Remarks: single diamond at 12 o'clock
Price: $14,800
Variations: various dial colors (burgundy, midnight blue, black, champagne, white); 18ct gold case

Myst Diamond

Movement: automatic, Sellita SW 300-1 caliber; ø 25.6mm, height 3.6 mm; 25 jewels; 28,800 vph; custom-engraved rotor; 42-hour power reserve
Functions: hours, minutes, sweep seconds
Case: yellow gold set with 54 brilliant-cut diamonds; 46 mm x 38 mm, height 7.5 mm; sapphire crystal; gold case back; screw-down crown; water-resistant to 5 atm
Band: calfskin, folding clasp
Price: $18,800
Variations: dials in black guilloché, antique white; 18ct gold case, gold bracelet (up to $48,000)

Alpha Rose Gold

Movement: automatic, Sellita SW 300-1 caliber; ø 25.6mm, height 3.6 mm; 25 jewels; 28,800 vph; custom-engraved rotor; 42-hour power reserve
Functions: hours, minutes, sweep seconds
Case: rose gold; 46 mm x 38 mm, height 8.8 mm; sapphire crystal; gold case back; screw-down crown; water-resistant to 5 atm
Band: calfskin, folding clasp
Price: $14,800
Variations: dials in black guilloché, antique white; 18ct gold case, gold bracelet (up to $44,800)

CZAPEK & CIE.

Born in Bohemia (Czech Republic today) in 1811, watchmaker Frantiszek Czapek fought in the failed Polish insurrection of 1832 against Russia and then fled to Geneva. In 1839, he joined another Pole, Antoine de Patek, in a business venture. When the contract expired in 1845, Patek decided on a partnership with Jean Philippe, inventor of the keyless watch. Czapek went on to become purveyor of watches to Emperor Napoleon III and author of a book on watches. Then he vanished without a trace sometime in the late 1860s.

His "resurrection" is due to entrepreneur, art specialist, and occasional watch collector Harry Guhl, who registered the name and set up a management team that included Xavier de Roquemaurel and Sébastien Follonier. They chose Czapek's model No. 3430 as a model upon which to build up a new brand. It is an intriguing piece with elongated Roman numerals, elegant fleur-de-lis hands, and two oddly placed subdials at 7:30 and 4:30, one for small seconds, the other featuring a clever double hand for the seven-day power reserve and days of the week.

The team's claim to fame is collaborating with friends of the brand to create new models, which are always implemented by outstanding Swiss suppliers like Donzé for the Grand Feu dials with the secret signature, and Aurélien Bouchet for the fine fleur-de-lys hands.

Over the years, Czapek has gradually diversified, producing classically stylish watches, like the Place Vendôme and the Faubourg de Cracovie. Recently, the company has even moved into some serious complications, with a split-seconds chronograph coupled with some impressive skeletonizing to show off, legitimately, the mechanism on the dial side. In 2024, the company collaborated with watchmaker Bernhard Lederer, a friend of de Roquemaurel, to create a special version of the Place Vendôme with two counter-rotating balances driven by a single differential for greater precision.

CZAPEK & CIE
18 Rue de la Corraterie
CH-1204 Geneva
Switzerland

TEL.:
+41-22-557-41-41

E-MAIL:
info@czapek.com

WEBSITE:
www.czapek.com

FOUNDED:
2012

U.S. DISTRIBUTOR:
Horology Works
11 Flagg Road
West Hartford, CT 06117
860-986-9676
info@horologyworks.com

MOST IMPORTANT COLLECTIONS/PRICE RANGE:
Antarctique, Quai des Bergues men's and ladies' watches, Place Vendôme, Faubourg de Cracovie / $12,000 to $226,000

Antarctique Purple Storm

Movement: automatic, Czapek caliber SXH5; ø 30 mm, height 4.2 mm; 28 jewels; 28,800 vph; micro-rotor of recycled platinum, balance wheel with variable inertia; finely finished movement; 60-hour power reserve
Functions: hours, minutes, sweep seconds
Case: stainless steel, ø 40.5 mm, height 10.6 mm; screw-down crown; sapphire crystal; transparent case back; water-resistant to 12 atm
Band: stainless steel, folding clasp with micro-adjustment system
Remarks: unique dials with hand-applied varnish
Price: $29,500; limited to 18 pieces
Variations: comes with extra strap in purple leather

Place Vendôme – Complicité Stardust Cobalt

Movement: automatic, caliber 8, c; ø 30 mm, height 4.2 mm; 28 jewels; 28,800 vph; 2 balance wheels with variable inertia oscillating in opposite directions; finely finished movement with; 60-hour power reserve
Functions: hours, minutes, sweep seconds; power reserve indicator
Case: white gold, ø 41.8 mm, height 14.8 mm; screw-down crown; sapphire crystal; transparent case back; water-resistant to 12 atm
Band: reptile skin, folding clasp with micro-adjustment system
Remarks: openworked dial with the escapements on the dial side
Price: $100,000
Variations: comes with extra strap in purple leather

Antarctique Polar Sky

Movement: automatic, Czapek caliber SXH5; ø 30 mm, height 4.2 mm; 28 jewels; 28,800 vph; micro-rotor of recycled platinum, balance wheel with variable inertia; finely finished movement; 60-hour power reserve
Functions: hours, minutes, sweep seconds
Case: stainless steel, ø 40.5 mm, height 10.6 mm; screw-down crown; sapphire crystal; transparent case back; water-resistant to 12 atm
Band: stainless steel, folding clasp with micro-adjustment system
Remarks: aventurine dial
Price: $39,500; limited to 99 pieces

DAMASKO

When it comes to sheer toughness, Damasko has built up quite a track record ever since its founding in 1994, in Germany. But it's not visible at first glance. These unadorned watches with clean, sharp lines are almost archetypical watches. They are robust, indestructible even, and will not need much servicing.

The company's claim to fame lies in its choice of materials, such as polycrystalline silicon hairsprings and components made of a special ice-hardened steel. This special patent involves adding nitrogen and carbon to the molten stainless steel and then cooling it quickly. The resulting material, which has been used in machines like the space shuttle, is extremely hard and does not corrode easily, so these are watches that will keep their look for a long time.

In fact, the research done by this small brand, located near Regensburg in southern Germany, has generated over one hundred patents for the brand, as well as registered samples and designs. The "German" look means well-groomed dials and an immediate view of the time, thanks to contrasting hues.

These watches boast outstanding technical quality, which combines with a very clear stylistic concept. The collection ranges from very classical-functional pilot watches to a line of timeless sportive chronographs, and some very elegant watches for daily use. The latest models in the Damasko watch collection are the DC76/2 and DC86/2 chronographs with manufacture movement C51-6 and the DK36 as a three-hand watch with manufacture caliber A26-3. An innovative feature is the chronograph with a sweep minute totalizer.

Many of the models run on ETA movements, but Damasko also assembles its own caliber, the A35, which allows for a manufacturing depth of ninety percent. Parts made in the small factory include plates, bridges, pinions, balance, spring barrel, and rotors. Despite this, Damasko watches manage to stay in the affordable range.

DAMASKO GMBH
Unterheising 17c
93092 Barbing
Germany

TEL.:
+49-9401-80481

E-MAIL:
sales@damasko-watches.com

WEBSITE:
www.damasko-watches.com

FOUNDED:
1994

NUMBER OF EMPLOYEES:
30

DISTRIBUTION:
U.S. Sales
Island Watch
273 Walt Whitman Road, Suite 217
11746 Huntington Station, NY
631-470-0762
sales@longislandwatch.com

PRICE RANGE:
$1,000 to $5,000

DK 20

Movement: automatic, Damasko caliber A26-1; ø 25.6 mm, height 4.6 mm; 20 jewels; 28,800 vph; DIN standard shock protection and anti-magnetism; 42-hour power reserve
Functions: hours, minutes, sweep seconds
Case: stainless steel (submarine steel), ø 39 mm, height 9.95 mm; sapphire crystal; transparent case back; screw-down crown; water-resistant to 20 atm
Band: rubber with calfskin overlay, pin buckle
Price: $1,568

DK 22

Movement: automatic, Damasko caliber A26-2; ø 25.6 mm, height 4.6 mm; 20 jewels; 28,800 vph; DIN standard shock protection and anti-magnetism; 42-hour power reserve
Functions: hours, minutes, sweep seconds; date
Case: stainless steel (submarine steel), ø 39 mm, height 9.95 mm; sapphire crystal; transparent case back; screw-down crown; water-resistant to 20 atm
Band: calfskin, pin buckle
Price: $1,706

DK 30/2 Olive

Movement: automatic, Damasko caliber A26-1; ø 25.6 mm, height 4.6 mm; 20 jewels; 28,800 vph; DIN standard shock protection and anti-magnetism; 42-hour power reserve
Functions: hours, minutes, sweep seconds
Case: stainless steel (submarine steel), ø 39 mm, height 9.95 mm; sapphire crystal; transparent case back; screw-down crown; water-resistant to 20 atm
Band: stainless steel (submarine steel), folding clasp
Price: $1,617

DK 32/2

Movement: automatic, Damasko caliber A26-2; ø 25.6 mm, height 4.6 mm; 20 jewels; 28,800 vph; DIN standard shock protection and anti-magnetism; 42-hour power reserve
Functions: hours, minutes, sweep seconds; date
Case: stainless steel (submarine steel), ø 39 mm, height 9.95 mm; sapphire crystal; transparent case back; screw-down crown; water-resistant to 20 atm
Band: calfskin, pin buckle
Price: $1,737

DK 36 Olive

Movement: automatic, Damasko caliber A26-3; ø 25.6 mm, height 5.05 mm; 20 jewels; 28,800 vph; DIN standard shock protection and anti-magnetism; 42-hour power reserve
Functions: hours, minutes, sweep seconds; date and weekday
Case: ice-hardened stainless steel, ø 40 mm, height 12.3 mm; sapphire crystal; screw-down crown; water-resistant to 10 atm
Band: calfskin, pin buckle
Price: $1,737

DK 37

Movement: automatic, Damasko caliber A26-3; ø 25.6 mm, height 5.05 mm; 20 jewels; 28,800 vph; DIN standard shock protection and anti-magnetism; 42-hour power reserve
Functions: hours, minutes, sweep seconds; date and weekday
Case: ice-hardened stainless steel, ø 40 mm, height 12.3 mm; sapphire crystal; screw-down crown; water-resistant to 10 atm
Band: stainless steel, folding clasp
Price: $2,361

DC 86/2

Movement: automatic, Damasko caliber C51-6; ø 30.4 mm, height 7.9 mm; 27 jewels; 28,800 vph; sweep minute and seconds chrono counters; DIN standard shock protection and anti-magnetism; 50-hour power reserve
Functions: hours, minutes, subsidiary seconds; additional 24-hour display; chronograph; date
Case: ice-hardened stainless steel, ø 42 mm, height 14.4 mm; bidirectional bezel with 0-12 scale; sapphire crystal; screw-down crown; water-resistant to 10 atm
Band: stainless steel, folding clasp
Price: $3,786

DC 96

Movement: automatic, Damasko caliber C51-6; ø 30.4 mm, height 7.9 mm; 27 jewels; 28,800 vph; sweep minute and seconds chrono counters; DIN standard shock protection and anti-magnetism; 50-hour power reserve
Functions: hours, minutes, subsidiary seconds; additional 24-hour display; chronograph; date
Case: stainless steel (austenite or instrument steel), ø 41 mm, height 14.6 mm; bidirectional bezel with 0-12 scale; sapphire crystal; screw-down crown; water-resistant to 10 atm
Band: calfskin, pin buckle
Price: $4,098

DSub 10

Movement: automatic, Damasko caliber A26-2; ø 25.6 mm, height 4.6 mm; 20 jewels; 28,800 vph; DIN standard shock protection and anti-magnetism; 42-hour power reserve
Functions: hours, minutes, sweep seconds; date
Case: stainless steel (submarine steel), ø 42 mm, height 12.6 mm; unidirectional bezel, with 0-60 scale; sapphire crystal; screw-down crown; water-resistant to 30 atm
Band: rubber, folding clasp
Price: $2,219

DAVOSA

One of the more important brands occupying the lower segment of the market is Davosa, which manufactures a wide range of watches with all the complications one might want but in an affordable segment: pilot watches, quality divers (with helium valve), dress watches, and ladies' watches. The brand has even come out with an apnea training watch that can be removed from its case and stood upright. These timepieces use solid Swiss movements (Sellita and ETA), which are occasionally modified to fit the watches' specific designs. Among these dressy-in-a-sporty-sort-of-way timepieces, one finds a limited-edition automatic chronograph with a moon phase, at under $2,400.

To create a broad portfolio requires experience, and that is something Davosa has in spades. The company was founded in 1891, when farmer Abel Frédéric Hasler from Tramelan, in Switzerland's Jura mountains, spent the winter months making silver pocket watch cases. The following generation of Haslers took up the flame. However, playing the role of unassuming private-label watchmakers, they remained in the background and let their customers in Europe and the United States run away with the show. It wasn't until after World War II that brothers Paul and David Hasler dared produce their own timepieces.

The long experience with watchmaking and watches culminated in 1987 with the brothers developing their own line of watches under the brand name Davosa. The Haslers then signed a partnership with the German distributor Bohle. In Germany, mechanical watches were experiencing a new boom, so the brand was able to evolve quickly. In 2000, Corinna Bohle took over as manager of strategic development. Davosa now reaches well beyond Switzerland's borders and has become an integral part of the world of mechanical watches. It has streamlined its offering, which is now divided into three families: diving, performance, and pilot.

DAVOSA SWISS BOHLE GMBH
Bunsenstrasse 1a
32052 Herford
Germany

TEL.:
+49 (0)5221-9942400

E-MAIL:
info@davosa.com

WEBSITE:
www.davosa.com

FOUNDED:
1881

U.S. DISTRIBUTOR:
Gyrax LTD - Davosa U.S.A,
200 S. Biscayne Blvd
Miami, FL 33131
877-DAVOSA1
info@davosa-usa.com
www.davosa-usa.com

MOST IMPORTANT COLLECTIONS/PRICE RANGE:
Apnea Diver, Argonautic, Classic, Gentleman, Military, Newton, Pilot, Ternos / $800 to $2,600

Newton Pilot Rally Chronograph Limited Edition

Reference number: 161.536.45
Movement: automatic, Davosa caliber DAV3052 (Sellita SW510 base); ø 30 mm, height 7.9 mm; 27 jewels; 28,800 vph; 62-hour power reserve
Functions: hours, minutes, subsidiary seconds; chronograph; date
Case: stainless steel, ø 42 mm, height 15.5 mm; sapphire crystal; transparent case back; water-resistant to 7 atm
Band: calfskin, pin buckle
Remarks: limited to 300 editions
Price: $2,495
Variations: various colors and strap variations

Evo 1908 Automatic

Reference number: 161.575.44
Movement: automatic, Davosa caliber DAV3020 (Sellita SW260 base); ø 25.6 mm, height 5.6 mm; 31 jewels; 28,800 vph; 41-hour power reserve
Functions: hours, minutes, subsidiary seconds; date
Case: stainless steel, ø 42 mm, height 12 mm; sapphire crystal; transparent case back; water-resistant to 5 atm
Band: calfskin, pin buckle
Price: $995

Ternos Professional 68H Automatic

Reference number: 161.538.50
Movement: automatic, Davosa caliber DAV3121 (La Joux-Perret G100 base); ø 25.6 mm, height 4.45 mm; 24 jewels; 28,800 vph; 68-hour power reserve
Functions: hours, minutes, sweep seconds; date
Case: stainless steel, ø 42 mm, height 12.8 mm; unidirectional bezel with ceramic insert, with 0-60 scale; sapphire crystal; screw-down crown, helium valve; water-resistant to 30 atm
Band: stainless steel, folding clasp, with safety lock, with extension link
Price: $1,395
Variations: different colors

Ternos Medium California Automatic

Reference number: 166.199.60
Movement: automatic, Davosa caliber DAV3021 (Sellita SW200-1 base); ø 25.6 mm, height 4.6 mm; 26 jewels; 28,800 vph; 41-hour power reserve
Functions: hours, minutes, sweep seconds; date
Case: stainless steel, ø 36.5 mm, height 11.8 mm; unidirectional bezel, with 0-60 scale; sapphire crystal; screw-down crown; water-resistant to 20 atm
Band: stainless steel, folding clasp, with safety lock
Price: $995
Variations: various colors and strap variations

Newton Pilot Speedometer Automatic

Reference number: 161.587.20
Movement: automatic, Davosa caliber DAV3023 (Sellita SW240-1 base); ø 29 mm, height 5.05 mm; 25 jewels; 28,800 vph; 41-hour power reserve
Functions: hours (digital, sliding, in aperture), minutes, sweep seconds (disc)
Case: stainless steel, ø 44 mm, height 12.8 mm; sapphire crystal; transparent case back; water-resistant to 5 atm
Band: stainless steel, folding clasp
Price: $1,100
Variations: various colors and strap variations

Argonautic Lumis Automatic

Reference number: 161.529.10
Movement: automatic, Davosa caliber DAV3021 (Sellita SW200-1 base); ø 25.6 mm, height 4.6 mm; 26 jewels; 28,800 vph; 41-hour power reserve
Functions: hours, minutes, sweep seconds; date
Case: stainless steel, ø 43 mm, height 13.5 mm; unidirectional bezel, with 0-60 scale; sapphire crystal; screw-down crown, helium valve; water-resistant to 30 atm
Band: stainless steel, folding clasp, with safety lock, with extension link
Remarks: self-lighting tritium gas light source on indexes and hands
Price: $1,150
Variations: various colors and strap variations

Argonautic 39 Automatic

Reference number: 161.533.40
Movement: automatic, Davosa caliber DAV3021 (Sellita SW200-1 base); ø 25.6 mm, height 4.6 mm; 26 jewels; 28,800 vph; 41-hour power reserve
Functions: hours, minutes, sweep seconds; date
Case: stainless steel, ø 39 mm, height 12.4 mm; unidirectional bezel with yellow-gold PVD and ceramic insert, with 0-60 scale; sapphire crystal; screw-down crown; water-resistant to 20 atm
Band: stainless steel with yellow-gold PVD coated middle links, folding clasp, with safety lock, with extension link
Price: $1,100
Variations: different colors

Ternos Professional Nebulous Automatic

Reference number: 161.535.10
Movement: automatic, Davosa caliber DAV3021 (Sellita SW200-1 base); ø 25.6 mm, height 4.6 mm; 26 jewels; 28,800 vph; 41-hour power reserve
Functions: hours, minutes, sweep seconds; date
Case: stainless steel, ø 42 mm, height 14.6 mm; unidirectional bezel with ceramic insert, with 0-60 scale; sapphire crystal; screw-down crown, helium valve; water-resistant to 50 atm
Band: stainless steel, folding clasp, with safety lock
Price: $1,195

Argonautic 43 Automatic

Reference number: 161.528.70
Movement: automatic, Davosa caliber DAV3021 (Sellita SW200-1 base); ø 25.6 mm, height 4.6 mm; 26 jewels; 28,800 vph; 41-hour power reserve
Functions: hours, minutes, sweep seconds; date
Case: stainless steel, ø 43 mm, height 13.5 mm; unidirectional bezel with ceramic insert, with 0-60 scale; sapphire crystal; screw-down crown, helium valve; water-resistant to 30 atm
Band: stainless steel, folding clasp, with safety lock, with extension link
Price: $1,050
Variations: various colors and strap variations

DE BETHUNE

De Bethune was named after an eighteenth-century French navy captain from an old aristocratic family, the Chevalier De Béthune, who did extensive research into watch and clockmaking and whose name is associated with a particularly clever escapement. Similarly, Denis Flageollet had had many years of experience in the research, conception, and implementation of prestigious timepieces. So he and David Zanetta, a well-known consultant for a number of high-end watch brands, founded their own company in 2002 in what used to be the village pub and turned it into a stunning factory. The modern CNC machinery, combined with an outstanding team of watchmakers and research and development specialists allowed the company to rapidly produce prototypes and make small movement series with great dispatch. The little factory even made its own cases, dials, and hands. This all cost money, so in 2021, they agreed to the Watchbox trading platform becoming a majority owner.

De Bethune watches are aesthetically compelling, thanks to the use of simple color schemes, mirror-polished titanium, and discreet microlight engraving. The "delta" on many of the dials is natural decoration, explains Flageollet: "The triangle is essential to holding the gearwheel pivots, so why not turn them into a natural ogival arch?" This cool-modern visual is contrasted with certain classic elements that soften the brand's sharpness. These two aspects were brought together in a single two-sided watch released in early 2021, the Kind of Two.

Engineering innovations are also a De Bethune specialty. Among others, the company developed a manually wound caliber with a power reserve of up to eight days, a self-regulating double barrel, a balance wheel in titanium and platinum that allows for an ideal inertia/mass ratio, a balance spring with a patented De Bethune end curve, and a triple "parachute" shock-absorbing system. It also boasts the lightest and one of the fastest silicon/titanium tourbillons on the market, now appearing in the Steel Wheels line. 2024 also saw the appearance of rare materials: a zirconium Aérolite with a meteorite dial and a rose-gold Starry Varius.

DE BETHUNE SA
Chemin des Grangettes 19
CH-1454 L'Auberson
Switzerland

TEL.:
+41-22-310-22-71

E-MAIL:
geneva@debethune.com

WEBSITE:
www.debethune.ch

FOUNDED:
2002

NUMBER OF EMPLOYEES:
40

ANNUAL PRODUCTION:
200

DISTRIBUTION:
For all inquiries from the U.S., please contact the company directly.

DB28 XS Aérolite

Reference number: DB28xsZM
Movement: hand-wound, De Bethune caliber DB2005; ø 30 mm; 27 jewels; 28,800 vph; self-regulating double spring barrel, titanium balance, silicon escape wheel, optimized for temperature fluctuations and air penetration; finely finished movement with "côtes de Bethune"; 6-day power reserve
Functions: hours, minutes
Case: zirconium with matte covering, ø 38.7 mm, height 7.4 mm; sapphire crystal; transparent case back; water-resistant to 3 atm
Band: reptile skin, pin buckle
Remarks: dial crafted from the Muonionalusta meteorite with thermal oxidation coloring and "arbitrary" guilloché, with grey-gold stars
Price: $120,000

DB28 XP Steel Wheels Tourbillon

Reference number: DB28XPSWT
Movement: hand-wound, De Bethune caliber DB2009v6; ø 30 mm; 40 jewels; 36,000 vph; self-regulating double-spring barrel, titanium balance and tourbillon, balance spring with De Bethune flat terminal, silicon escape wheel, optimized for temperature fluctuations and air penetration; finely finished parts; 120-hour power reserve
Functions: hours, minutes, 30-seconds on tourbillon cage; linear power reserve on the rear
Case: polished titanium, ø 43 mm, height 9.1 mm; sapphire crystal; transparent case back; water-resistant to 3 atm
Band: reptile skin (extra supple), pin buckle
Remarks: côtes de Genève on the dial, côtes de Bethune on case back
Price: $228,000; limited to 20 pieces

DB25GMT Starry Varius

Reference number: DB25VGR
Movement: hand-wound, De Bethune caliber DB2507; ø 30 mm; height 5.19 mm; 40 jewels; 28,800 vph; titanium balance wheel with white-gold inserts, silicon escape wheel, optimized for temperature fluctuations and air penetration; 60-hour power reserve
Functions: hours, minutes, second time zone (GMT), world time, day/night indicator, jumping date
Case: rose gold, ø 42 mm, height 11.8 mm; sapphire crystal; transparent case back; water-resistant to 3 atm
Band: reptile skin (extra-supple), pin buckle
Price: $122,000

DEEP BLUE

As far as anyone can tell, the fish do not care what you are wearing on your wrist. For the diver, it has to be accurate, genuinely water-resistant, and readable in less-than-ideal conditions. Those are the basics—or should be—of any real diver's watch. The rest is in the eye of the beholder. And it seems that New York–based Deep Blue does not wander too far off home plate, as it were. The company was founded with the idea of providing divers with an array of tough watches that do the job and have the look and feel of a professional-quality diver's watch at a fraction of what you might expect to pay.

Little did they know in 2007 that Deep Blue watches would achieve cult status among divers. Deep Blue watches are accurate, robust, and ready for life in the open and underwater. There's no need to hide them in a safe, and getting banged up a little does them no harm—it's called patina, and it gives these timepieces the look and feel of a real tool watch... which is what they are.

The collection includes all sorts of models for every type of diving. The power is supplied by an array of ETA, Sellita, Miyota, and Seiko/Time calibers, and occasionally quartz movements. Some have special features like ceramic bezels; some are water-resistant to as much as 3,000 meters, like the Depthmaster, whose dimensions (ø 49 mm, height 19.5) and weight (300 g) will certainly contribute to the speed of the diver's descent. Lots of care has been given to lighting the dial, with generous application of Super-LumiNova and the occasional use of autoluminescent tritium tubes, which may well attract some interesting fish.

DEEP BLUE WATCHES
1716 Coney Island Avenue
Suite 3r
Brooklyn, NY 11230

TEL.:
718-484-7717

WEBSITE:
www.deepbluewatches.com

E-MAIL:
info@deepbluewatches.com

FOUNDED:
2007

NUMBER OF EMPLOYEES:
70

ANNUAL OUTPUT:
n/a

DISTRIBUTION:
Retail and online

MOST IMPORTANT COLLECTIONS/PRICE RANGE:
Master 1000, Diver 1000, Defender / $300 to 500; Pro Sea Diver / $500 to 900; Daynight / $600 to 1,000; Alpha, Marine, Ocean $700 to 1,500; Blue Water $600 to 1,400

Deep Star 1000 Vintage Swiss Automatic

Reference number: DSTAREXPEDBLKWHITEBRC
Movement: automatic, Sellita caliber SW-200-01; ø 25.6 mm, height 4.6 mm; 26 jewels; 28,800 vph; 38-hour power reserve
Functions: hours, minutes, sweep seconds; date
Case: stainless steel, ø 45 mm, height 15 mm; unidirectional ceramic bezel with 120 clicks; screw-down crown; helium release valve; transparent case back; sapphire crystal; water-resistant to 33 atm
Band: stainless steel mesh, folding clasp with extension
Remarks: tritium gas-filled tube illumination on hands and hour markers
Price: $799
Variations: silicon or rubber strap

Daynight Alpha Marine 500 Tritium T-100 Swiss Automatic

Reference number: AM500TRITWHITBLUE
Movement: automatic, Sellita caliber SW-200-1; ø 25.6 mm, height 4.6 mm; 26 jewels; 28,800 vph; 38-hour power reserve
Functions: hours, minutes, sweep seconds; date
Case: stainless steel, ø 45 mm, height 15 mm; unidirectional ceramic bezel with 0-60 scale and 120 clicks; screw-down crown and case back; transparent case back; helium release valve; sapphire crystal; water-resistant to 33 atm
Band: stainless steel, folding clasp with extension
Remarks: tritium gas-filled tube illumination on hands and hour markers; full-lume blue dial
Price: $1,299
Variations: green lume dial; leather strap ($1,149)

Daynight Scuba 500 Tritium T-100 Swiss Automatic

Reference number: DNSCUBASW200BLACK
Movement: automatic, Sellita SW-200-1; ø 25.6 mm, height 4.6 mm; 26 jewels; 28,800 vph
Functions: hours, minutes, sweep seconds; 2nd time zone; date
Case: stainless steel, ø 45 mm, height 15 mm; unidirectional bezel with ceramic insert and 0-60 scale; transparent case back; sapphire crystal; water-resistant to 50 atm
Band: stainless steel, folding clasp with extension
Remarks: tritium gas-filled tube illumination on hands and hour markers
Price: $1,299
Variations: with rubber strap ($1,149)

DELMA

Industries all have their major players and their minor ones. The major brands attract the attention thanks, oftentimes, to lots of clamorous advertising plus name recognition. In the watch business, as in many others, there are smaller, less noisy brands that also produce quality watches.

Delma began as one of four brands produced by a company founded in 1924 by two brothers, Albert and Adolf Gilomen. For several decades, they manufactured many different models, from classic pocket watches and dress watches to a fine chronograph in 1946 marketed under the name Midland, which made a bit of a splash.

In 1966, the brand was sold to Ulrich Wüthrich. He decided to use a single name, Delma, and focus production on diver's watches, without, however, losing the customers in search of a nice watch that could be used every day. In 1969, they came out with the Periscope, an automatic diver's able to go down to 50 atm (500 meters). It established a new style for the brand, one it has remained faithful to ever since. A few years later, Delma released the Shell Star, a professional diver's watch.

Today, the company is run by Wüthrich's son-in-law, Fred Leibundgut and his son Andreas. The brand produces casual watches, but its claim to fame is still its diver's models. As with many brands, Delma is reviving and modernizing many of its older models, like the Periscope and the Shell Star, which features a special table to help divers optimize their gas mixtures in dives up to 70 atm. The Blue Shark, launched originally in 2011, has been plumbing ever deeper depths (without a diver) and on the way proving the company's ability to compete with the best. In 2023, the Blue Shark IV reached a water resistance of 500 atm. Surface water sports are part of the program, too, with the recent Oceanmaster Oliver Heer Ocean Racing that includes a nautical bezel, tactical planner, and points of sail indicators that enable the skipper to time and position the crossing of the starting line.

Finally, for its 100th anniversary, Delma raised a few eyebrows with a very modern, tonneau-shaped tourbillon with subsidiary seconds on the cage. It could be a signal for further modernization in the aesthetics of this classic Swiss brand.

DELMA WATCH LIMITED
Solothurnstrasse 47
2543 Lengnau
Switzerland

TEL.:
+41-32-654-22-11

E-MAIL:
info@delma.ch

WEBSITE:
www.delma.ch

FOUNDED:
1924

NUMBER OF EMPLOYEES:
15

ANNUAL PRODUCTION:
25,000 watches

DISTRIBUTION:
Contact headquarters in Switzerland

MOST IMPORTANT COLLECTIONS/PRICE RANGE:
Aero, Racing, Diver, Dress, and Elegance collections / up to $4,000

Oceanmaster Oliver Heer Ocean Racing

Reference number: 41701.670.6.818
Movement: automatic, Sellita SW-200-1; ø 25.6 mm, height 4.6 mm; 26 jewels; 28,800 vph; decorated rotor; 41-hour power reserve
Functions: hours, minutes, sweep seconds; date
Case: stainless steel, ø 44 mm, height 13.8 mm; sapphire crystal; unidirectional nautical bezel; helium valve; screw-in crown and case back; water-resistant to 50 atm
Band: stainless steel, deployant clasp with pushers
Price: $1,650; limited to 200 pieces
Variations: comes in a quartz version ($650)

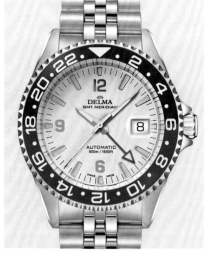

Santiago GMT Meridian Automatic

Reference number: 41702.756.6P014
Movement: automatic, Sellita SW-330-2; ø 25.6 mm, height 4.6 mm; 25 jewels; 28,800 vph; decorated rotor; 56-hour power reserve
Functions: hours, minutes, seconds; 2nd time zone on the bezel; date
Case: stainless steel, ø 43 mm, height 13.3 mm; sapphire crystal; unidirectional bezel with anodized aluminum with 0-24 scale; helium valve; screw-down crown; transparent case back (mineral glass); water-resistant to 50 atm
Band: stainless steel, folding clasp with safety lock
Price: $1,850; limited to 999 pieces

Blue Shark IV

Reference number: 41701.760.6034
Movement: automatic, Sellita SW-200-1; ø 25.6 mm, height 4.6 mm; 25 jewels; 28,800 vph; decorated rotor; 38-hour power reserve
Functions: hours, minutes, sweep seconds; date
Case: stainless steel black DLC, ø 47 mm, height 18.5 mm; sapphire crystal; unidirectional bezel with DLC; helium valve; screw-in crown and case back; water-resistant to 500 atm
Band: stainless steel black DLC, folding clasp with safety lock
Price: $2,800; limited to 999 pieces per case type
Variations: various cases and color combinations

Klondike Chronotec

Reference number: 41601.660.6.031
Movement: automatic, Valjoux 7750; ø 30 mm, height 7.9 mm; 29 jewels; 28,800 vph; custom rotor; 48-hour power reserve
Functions: hours, minutes, subsidiary seconds; chronograph; day, date; tachymeter
Case: stainless steel, ø 44 mm at bezel, height 14.8 mm; screw-down crown; sapphire crystal; transparent case back with mineral glass; water-resistant to 20 atm
Band: calfskin, pin buckle
Price: $3,575
Variations: white dial, different case colors; stainless steel bracelet (available in bicolor version) and folding clasp ($3,825)

Continental Pulsometer

Reference number: 41701.702.6.039
Movement: automatic, Sellita caliber SW510; ø 30 mm, height 7.9 mm; 27 jewels; 28,800 vph; 48-hour power reserve
Functions: hours, minutes, subsidiary seconds; bicompax chronograph; date
Case: stainless steel, ø 42 mm at bezel, height 15.2 mm; screw-in crown; sapphire crystal; transparent case back with mineral glass; water-resistant to 10 atm
Band: calfskin, folding clasp
Remarks: dial with pulsometer, tachymeter, and telemeter for measuring heart rate, speed, and distance
Price: $2,800
Variations: with black, blue, green; yellow gold bezel and bicolor bracelet ($2,950)

Heritage Chronograph LE

Reference number: 42601.730.6.062
Movement: automatic, Valjoux 7750; ø 30 mm, height 7.9 mm; 25 jewels; 28,800 vph; custom rotor ; 48-hour power reserve
Functions: hours, minutes, subsidiary seconds; day, date; tricompax chronograph with tachymeter scale
Case: stainless steel, ø 43 mm, height 15.7 mm; sapphire crystal; water-resistant to 10 atm
Band: calfskin, folding clasp with pushers
Price: $3,100

Classic

Reference number: 41603.722.6.041
Movement: automatic, Sellita caliber SW200-1; ø 25.6 mm, height 4.6 mm; 26 jewels; 28,800 vph; custom Delma rotor; 41-hour power reserve
Functions: hours, minutes, sweep seconds; date
Case: stainless steel, ø 40 mm, height 11.5 mm; sapphire crystal; transparent case back (mineral crystal); water-resistant to 5 atm
Band: calfskin, pin buckle
Remarks: sun-brushed dial
Price: $1,000
Variations: various dial colors

1924 Tourbillon

Reference number: 41701.770.6.031
Movement: hand-wound, Delma caliber DT100.01; ø 31.8 mm, height 6.5 mm; 19 jewels; 21,600 vph; 105-hour power reserve
Functions: hours, minutes, tourbillon with subsidiary seconds
Case: stainless steel, ø 41 mm, height 14 mm; sapphire crystal; screw-down crown and case back; water-resistant to 20 atm
Band: stainless steel, folding clasp with pushers
Price: $13,900; limited to 200 pieces

Midland Automatic

Reference number: 41701.740.6.181
Movement: automatic, Sellita caliber SW 200-1; ø 25.6 mm, height 4.6 mm; 26 jewels; 28,800 vph; decorated rotor; 41-hour power reserve
Functions: hours, minutes, sweep seconds; date
Case: stainless steel, ø 40.5 mm, height 10.8 mm; sapphire crystal; water-resistant to 10 atm
Band: stainless steel, deployant clasp with pushers
Price: $1,350

DETROIT WATCH COMPANY

Patrick Ayoub and Amy Ayoub launched Detroit Watch Company in 2013 with the first and only mechanical timepieces designed and assembled in Detroit, Michigan. Patrick, a car designer, and Amy, an interior designer, share a passion for original design and timepieces and have worked hard to develop their brand, which draws inspiration from, and celebrates, the city of "Détroit."

Detroit means a lot of things to different people. Because the history of the people and places have shaped the city, Detroit's stories are also part of the Detroit Watch Company's collective story. The 1701, for instance, commemorates Antoine de la Mothe Cadillac, Knight of St. Louis, who, with his company of colonists, arrived at Détroit on July 24, 1701. On that day, under the patronage of Louis XIV and protected by the flag of France, the city, then called Fort Pontchartrain, was founded. These watches, while modern and chic, do recall the fairly clear-cut lines of an old church clock (*horloge*).

People phoning Detroit will understand why the company came out with a watch named 313. It's the area code of the city that brought not only cars, but also Motown (*motor* + *town*) music to the world. Needless to say, the dial looks like an old-fashioned phone dial. And where did Detroit's cars ride and race informally? On Woodward Avenue, the first mile of concrete highway in the USA, where carriages once rolled. It's the name for a collection of sporty chronographs. Finally, the city supplied the war effort against the Axis with many vital vehicles, including the B-24 Liberator bomber. No wonder the brand's line of watches includes an aviator collection.

The Detroit Watch Company timepieces are classically designed and hand-assembled in-house and may be purchased directly through the Detroit Watch Company website. The company also offers a wide range of straps and has a transparent and affordable servicing program.

DETROIT WATCH COMPANY, LLC
P.O. Box 1328
Birmingham, MI 48012
USA

TEL:
248-321-5601

E-MAIL:
dwc@detroitwatchco.com

WEBSITE:
detroitwatchco.com

FOUNDED:
2013

NUMBER OF EMPLOYEES:
2

ANNUAL PRODUCTION:
400 watches

DISTRIBUTION:
direct sales only

MOST IMPORTANT COLLECTIONS/PRICE RANGE:
M1 Woodward classic, 1701 Pontchartrain GMT, 1701 Louis XIV / $1,100 to $2,950

M1 1805 Edition

Reference number: DWC M1W-EXH
Movement: automatic, Sellita caliber SW 510b; ø 30 mm, height 7.9 mm; 25 jewels; 28,800 vph; custom M1 rotor; 62-hour power reserve
Functions: hours, minutes, subsidiary seconds; chronograph with tachymeter scale
Case: stainless steel, ø 42 mm, height 14.4 mm; screw down-crown, transparent case back, sapphire crystal; water-resistant to 5 atm
Band: calfskin; folding clasp
Price: $2,375
Variations: comes with stainless-steel bracelet; second iteration with hand-wound Sellita caliber

M1 Woodward Classic

Movement: automatic, Sellita caliber SW 510b; ø 30 mm, height 7.9 mm; 25 jewels; 28,800 vph; custom M1 rotor; 48-hour power reserve
Functions: hours, minutes, subsidiary seconds; chronograph with tachymeter scale
Case: stainless steel, ø 42 mm, height 14.5 mm; sapphire crystal; transparent case back, screw-down crown; water-resistant to 5 atm
Band: calf leather, folding clasp
Price: $2,375
Variations: various straps

Aviator Power Reserve

Reference number: DWC-A-PW
Movement: automatic (or manual winding), Sellita SW279-1; ø 25.6, height 5.6 mm, 26 jewels (manual winding: height 4.35 mm, 24 jewels); 28,800 vph; decorated movement with blued screws, perlage, côtes de Genève; 38-hour power reserve
Functions: hours, minutes, subsidiary seconds; power reserve indicator; date with quick corrector
Case: stainless steel, ø 42 mm, height 9.7 mm; sapphire crystal, transparent case back, screw-in crown; water-resistant to 5 atm
Band: calf leather, buckle
Price: $1,550
Variations: graphite dial, green dial

1701 Pontchartrain GMT – Great Lakes Edition

Reference number: DWC-1701GMTGLE-S1
Movement: automatic, ETA caliber 2893-2; ø 26.6 mm, height 4.1 mm; 21 jewels; 28,800 vph; 42-hour power reserve
Functions: hours, minutes, sweep seconds; second time zone, date
Case: stainless steel, ø 43 mm, height 13 mm; sapphire crystal, unidirectional bezel, screw-down crown; helium valve; water resistant to 300 atm
Band: stainless steel, buckle
Price: $1,750; limited to 150 numbered pieces
Variations: with blue or black dial and bezel

1701 Pontchartrain GMT Dual Timezone

Reference number: DWC-A-PW
Movement: automatic, ETA caliber 2893-2; ø 26.6 mm, height 4.1 mm; 21 jewels; 28,800 vph; 42-hour power reserve
Functions: hours, minutes, sweep seconds; 2nd time zone (24-hour scale); date with quick corrector
Case: stainless steel, ø 42 mm, height 11.5 mm; sapphire crystal, transparent case back, screw-in crown; water-resistant to 5 atm
Band: calf leather, folding clasp
Price: $1,695
Variations: with white dial; with full case back ($1,595)

1701 Pontchartrain Power Reserve

Reference number: DWC-1701-PW
Movement: automatic, Sellita SW279-1; ø 25.6, height 5.6 mm, 26 jewels; 28,800 vph; decorated movement with blued screws, perlage, côtes de Genève; 38-hour power reserve
Functions: hours, minutes, subsidiary seconds; power reserve indicator; date with quick corrector
Case: stainless steel, ø 42 mm, height 9.7; mm; sapphire crystal, transparent case back, screw-in crown; water-resistant to 5 atm
Band: calf leather, buckle
Price: $1,550

Pontchartrain Watch Co. 1st Edition

Movement: automatic, caliber ETA 2892-A2, ø 25.6 mm, height 3.6 mm; 28,800 vph, decorated movement with blued screws, perlage, côtes de Genève; 42-hour power reserve
Functions: hours, minutes, sweep seconds
Case: stainless steel, ø 42 mm, height 9.7 mm; sapphire crystal, transparent case back, screw-down crown; water-resistant to 5 atm
Band: calf leather, pin buckle
Price: $1,495
Variations: with stainless steel bracelet and folding clasp; black dial

1701 Louis XIV

Reference number: DWC-1701-XIV
Movement: automatic, Sellita caliber SW280-1; ø 25.6 mm, height 5.4 mm; 26 jewels; 28,800 vph; finely finished movement with perlage and côtes de Genève; blued screws; DWC custom rotor; 38-hour power reserve
Functions: hours, minutes, sweep seconds; moon phase; date
Case: stainless steel, ø 39 mm, height 11 mm; transparent case back; screw-down crown; water-resistant to 5 atm
Band: calfskin, pin buckle
Price: $1,550
Variations: with hand-wound caliber

1701 Moonphase Chronograph

Reference number: PCT-Moon-Chrono
Movement: automatic, ETA caliber 7751; ø 30 mm, height 7.9 mm; 25 jewels; 28,800 vph; 48-hour power reserve
Functions: hours, minutes, subsidiary seconds; chronograph; date, day, month; moon phase
Case: stainless steel, ø 42 mm, height 14.5 mm, sapphire crystal with anti-reflective coating, screw-down transparent case back with engraving; water resistant to 5 atm
Band: calfskin, pin buckle
Price: $2,950

DLOKE

Founder and creator of DLoke watches, Donald R. Loke has a diverse and rich track record within the luxury watch industry. He's been a distributor, designer, service center manager (notably for the very complex Louis Moinet timepieces), and a restoration expert sought out by owners of some of the most complicated watches ever to be created. His training began at the Bowman Technical School where he earned both his Master Watchmaker and Clockmaker degrees, followed by training at the Centre De Perfectionnement Horloger (WOSTEP) in Neuchâtel, Switzerland, where he achieved perfect scores in both the technical and practical exams. A friend and fan of the late George Daniels, he's also a talented designer and engineer who decided to create his own complex dual-direct chronometer escapement. As if the mastery of the mystic arts of high watchmaking were not enough. As for the design, it is informed by a balanced and thoughtful approach and guided by adherence to traditional watchmaking canons. Loke has, after all, even designed watches for a well-known Swiss luxury brand.

DLoke currently has one watch in several iterations. But each model requires careful examination, as he applies many classical techniques to aesthetics. Rather than attack the senses with overwhelming displays of color and complication, radical shapes, or exotic materials, his method highlights how the devil really is in the details. Dials crafted in glowing white or deep blue Grand Feu enamel are the simple, but elegant backdrop hosting the composed set of subdials, while asymmetrical hands merge with the applied markers to form a complete arrow as they cross one another. Even the case is an essay in less being more. While the dual crowns that oppose each other on the horizontal axis are quite visible, you'll have to look closely to note the presence of the integrated plungers that control the chronograph function.

Inside the Grade 5 titanium case beats a "quality one" grade customized Concepto 8100 chronometer/chronograph movement visible through the sapphire back. Each watch is hand-built to order by the master himself in very limited quantities.

DLOKE
124 Bennets Farm Rd.
Ridgefield, CT 06877
USA

TEL:
203-570-8463

EMAIL:
Lok.dr@gmail.com

WEBSITE:
www.drlokewatches.com

FOUNDED:
2015

NUMBER OF EMPLOYEES:
3

ANNUAL PRODUCTION:
75

MOST IMPORTANT COLLECTION/PRICE:
Dress Chronograph / $8,950

Dress Chronograph
Reference number: DRL DC WB
Movement: automatic, Concepto 8100 Quality No. 1 caliber; ø26 mm, height 7.9 mm; 25 jewels; 28,800 vph; rotor decorated with côtes de Genève; chronometer rated; 42-hour power reserve
Functions: hours, minutes; sweep chronograph, rotating inner bezel
Case: titanium; ø 43 mm, height 12.5 mm; sapphire crystal; transparent case back; water-resistant to 5 atm
Band: reptile skin, pin buckle
Price: $8,950

Dress Chronograph
Reference number: DRL DC WW
Movement: automatic, Concepto 8100 Quality No. 1 caliber; ø26 mm, height 7.9 mm; 25 jewels; 28,800 vph; rotor decorated with côtes de Genève; chronometer rated; 42-hour power reserve
Functions: hours, minutes; sweep chronograph, rotating inner bezel
Case: titanium; ø 43 mm, height 12.5 mm; sapphire crystal; transparent case back; water-resistant to 5 atm
Band: reptile skin, pin buckle
Price: $8,950

Dress Chronograph
Reference number: DRL DC BW
Movement: automatic, Concepto 8100 Quality No. 1 caliber; ø26 mm, height 7.9 mm; 25 jewels; 28,800 vph; rotor decorated with côtes de Genève; chronometer rated; 42-hour power reserve
Functions: hours, minutes; sweep chronograph, rotating inner bezel
Case: titanium; ø 43 mm, height 12.5 mm; sapphire crystal; transparent case back; water-resistant to 5 atm
Band: reptile skin, pin buckle
Price: $8,950

DOXA

Watch aficionados who have visited the world-famous museum in Le Locle will know that the little castle in which it is housed once belonged to Georges Ducommun, the founder of Doxa. The *manufacture* was launched as a backyard operation in 1889 and originally produced pocket watches. Quality products and good salesmanship quickly put Doxa on the map, but the company's real game changer came in 1967 with the uncompromising SUB 300, a heavy, bold diver's watch. It featured a unidirectional bezel with the official U.S. dive table engraved on it. The bright orange dial might seem quite ostentatious, but, in fact, it offers the best legibility under water. It also marked the beginning of a trend for colorful dials.

The popularity of Doxa watches was boosted early on by the commercialization of diving in the 1970s. Thriller writer Clive Cussler, chairman and founder of the National Underwater and Marine Agency (NUMA), even chose a Doxa as gear for his action hero Dirk Pitt.

The enduring vintage trend has shaped the recent development of the brand. Focus is on fewer lines with greater variations, with almost every model coming in different colors besides the striking orange: brilliant white, dreamy turquoise, bright yellow, and more.

Doxa has maintained its diving profile and, mostly, the cushion case and avoided too many fancy complications. The watches are usually three-handers with a date. The SUB 200 C-Graph is an automatic chronograph, however, which comes in various colors and a "beads of rice" rubber strap. The SUB 300 Professional is another genuine diver's that also comes in various colors. The SUB 300 Carbon Aqua Lung US Divers is, as the name says, made of a modern material. It's a revived and improved watch created in a collaboration with Aqua Lung, the company that essentially launched scuba diving with the creation of a demand regulator in 1943. In 2023, it received a companion, the β (beta) Sharkhunter, a dark ceramic, elegant, diver's watch conceived for a night out or a day under water. The carbon case is light and robust and a good background for the no-decompression dive table—devised originally by the U.S. Navy—made up of an orange depth scale on the outer bezel and an inner scale for the dive timing.

MONTRES DOXA SA
Rue de Zurich 23A
P.O. Box 6031
2500 Bienne 6,
Switzerland

TEL.:
+41-32-344-42-72

E-MAIL:
contact@doxawatches.com

WEBSITE:
doxawatches.com

FOUNDED:
1889

NUMBER OF EMPLOYEES:
40

DISTRIBUTION:
DOXA USA
520-369-2872
usa@doxawatches.com

MOST IMPORTANT COLLECTION/PRICE RANGE:
DOXA SUB dive watch collection / $950 to $4,900

SUB 300T Clive Cussler

Reference number: 840.80.031.15
Movement: automatic, Sellita caliber SW200-1; ø 25.6 mm, height 4.6 mm; 26 jewels; 28,800 vph; 38-hour power reserve
Functions: hours, minutes, sweep seconds; date
Case: stainless steel, ø 42.5 mm, height 13.65 mm; unidirectional bezel with 0-60 scale and decompression times; sapphire crystal; screw-in crown, automatic helium valve; water-resistant to 30 atm
Band: stainless steel, folding clasp
Remarks: special edition paying tribute to novelist Clive Cussler, whose hero, Dirk Pitt, wore a Doxa; comes with additional NATO strap
Price: $2,790

Sub 200T Sea Emerald

Reference number: 804.10.131S.26
Movement: automatic, Sellita caliber SW200; ø 25.6 mm, height 4.6 mm; 25 jewels; 28,800 vph; 38-hour power reserve
Functions: hours, minutes, sweep seconds; date
Case: stainless steel, ø 39 mm, height 10.7 mm; unidirectional bezel with 0-60 scale and decompression times; sapphire crystal; screw-in crown; water-resistant to 20 atm
Band: FKM rubber, folding clasp with extension link
Price: $1,550
Variations: with stainless steel bracelet ($1,590)

SUB 300 Professional

Reference number: 821.10.351.10
Movement: automatic, Sellita caliber SW 200-1; ø 25.6 mm, height 4.6 mm; 26 jewels; 28,800 vph; 42-hour power reserve; COSC-certified chronometer
Functions: hours, minutes, sweep seconds; date
Case: stainless steel, ø 42.5 mm, height 13.4 mm; unidirectional bezel with 0-60 scale and decompression times; sapphire crystal; screw-in crown; water-resistant to 30 atm
Band: stainless steel bracelet, folding clasp with wetsuit extension
Price: $2,590
Variations: FKM rubber strap, folding clasp with ratcheting wetsuit extension ($2,550); various dial colors

EBERHARD & CO.

Chronographs weren't always the main focus of the Eberhard & Co. brand. In 1887, Georges-Emile Eberhard rented a workshop in La Chaux-de-Fonds to produce a small series of pocket watches, but it was the unstoppable advancement of the automotive industry that gave the young company its inevitable direction. By the 1920s, Eberhard was producing timekeepers for the first auto races. In Italy, Eberhard & Co. functioned well into the 1930s as the official timekeeper for all important events relating to motor sports. And the Italian air force later commissioned some split-second chronographs from the company, one of which went for 56,000 euros at auction.

Eberhard & Co. is still doing well, thanks to the late Massimo Monti. In the 1990s, he associated the brand with legendary racer Tazio Nuvolari. The company dedicated a chronograph collection to Nuvolari and sponsored the annual Gran Premio Nuvolari vintage car rally in his hometown of Mantua.

With the launch of its four-counter chronograph, this most Italian of Swiss watchmakers underscored its expertise and ambitions where short time/sports time measurement is concerned. Indeed, Eberhard & Co.'s Chrono 4 chronograph, featuring four little counters all in a row, has brought new life to the chronograph in general. CEO Mario Peserico has continued to develop it, putting out versions with new colors and slightly altered looks.

The brand is pure vintage, so it will come as no surprise that it regularly reissues and updates some of its older, popular models, with great skill. The Chronographe 1887 is an example. It is available as both a classic hand-wound and automatic version and runs on a modified Sellita caliber. Another model based on a vintage Eberhard is called the Scientigraf, which was first issued in 1961.

EBERHARD & CO.
73, Ave. Léopold-Robert
CH-2300 La Chaux-de-Fonds
Switzerland

TEL.:
+41-32-342-5141

E-MAIL:
info@eberhard1887.com

WEBSITE:
www.eberhard1887.com

FOUNDED:
1887

DISTRIBUTION:
Contact main office for information
Astor Time Ltd
Riva Paradiso 12
6900 Lugano Paradiso
+41-91-993-2601
info@eberhard1887.com

MOST IMPORTANT COLLECTIONS:
Chrono 4, 8 Jours, Tazio Nuvolari, Extra-fort, Gilda, Scafograf, Scientigraph

Chronographe 1887 Édition Limitée

Reference number: 31081.01
Movement: hand-wound, Eberhard caliber EB 280 (Sellita AMT 5100 base); ø 30 mm, height 7 mm; 23 jewels; 28,800 vph; column wheel control of chronograph functions; 58-hour power reserve
Functions: hours, minutes, subsidiary seconds; flyback chronograph
Case: stainless steel, ø 41.5 mm, height 13.9 mm; sapphire crystal; transparent case back; water-resistant to 5 atm
Band: reptile skin, pin buckle
Remarks: limited to 250 pieces
Price: $8,740; limited to 250 pieces
Variations: with black dial

Chronographe 1887 Automatique

Reference number: 31082.03
Movement: automatic, Eberhard caliber EB 380 (Sellita AMT 5100 base); ø 30 mm, height 7.9 mm; 23 jewels; 28,800 vph; column wheel control of chronograph functions; 55-hour power reserve
Functions: hours, minutes, subsidiary seconds; flyback chronograph
Case: stainless steel, ø 41.5 mm, height 14.4 mm; sapphire crystal; transparent case back; water-resistant to 5 atm
Band: reptile skin, pin buckle
Price: $6,500

Chronographe 1887 Automatique

Reference number: 31082.06
Movement: automatic, Eberhard caliber EB 380 (Sellita AMT 5100 base); ø 30 mm, height 7.9 mm; 23 jewels; 28,800 vph; column wheel control of chronograph functions; 55-hour power reserve
Functions: hours, minutes, subsidiary seconds; flyback chronograph
Case: stainless steel, ø 41.5 mm, height 14.4 mm; sapphire crystal; transparent case back; water-resistant to 5 atm
Band: reptile skin, pin buckle
Price: $6,500

Tazio Nuvolari

Reference number: 31075.02
Movement: automatic, Eberhard-modified ETA caliber 7750; ø 30 mm, height 7.9 mm; 25 jewels; 28,800 vph; 42-hour power reserve
Functions: hours, minutes; chronograph with minute and hour totalizer
Case: stainless steel, ø 41 mm, height 13.2 mm; bezel with perlage finishing and tachymeter scale; screw-down crown; water-resistant to 5 atm
Band: calfskin, pin buckle
Price: $4,510

Traversetolo

Reference number: 21116.22
Movement: hand-wound, ETA caliber 6498-1; ø 36.6 mm, height 4.5 mm; 17 jewels; 21,600 vph; 38-hour power reserve
Functions: hours, minutes, subsidiary seconds
Case: stainless steel, ø 43 mm, height 10.7 mm; sapphire crystal; water-resistant to 5 atm
Band: calfskin, pin buckle
Price: $2,820
Variations: with stainless steel bracelet ($2,950)

Scientigraf Chrono

Reference number: 31077.02
Movement: automatic, ETA caliber 2894-2; ø 28.6 mm, height 6.1 mm; 37 jewels; 28,800 vph; 42-hour power reserve
Functions: hours, minutes, subsidiary seconds; chronograph
Case: stainless steel, ø 41 mm, height 13.55 mm; sapphire crystal; screw-down crown; water-resistant to 5 atm
Band: stainless steel, folding clasp
Price: $5,510

Extra-fort Édition Vitré

Reference number: 31952.7
Movement: automatic, ETA caliber 7750; ø 30 mm, height 7.9 mm; 25 jewels; 28,800 vph; finely finished movement; 42-hour power reserve
Functions: hours, minutes, subsidiary seconds; chronograph; date
Case: stainless steel, ø 39 mm, height 14.12 mm; sapphire crystal; transparent case back; screw-down crown; water-resistant to 5 atm
Band: reptile skin, pin buckle
Price: $4,390
Variations: with light-blue dial

Extra-fortRoueàColonnesRetour en Vol

Reference number: 31957.05
Movement: automatic, AMT5100 caliber; ø 30 mm, height 7 mm; 23 jewels; 28,800 vph; blued column wheel for chronograph with flyback function; 63-hour power reserve
Functions: hours, minutes, subsidiary seconds; chronograph; date
Case: stainless steel, ø 41 mm, height 14.2 mm; sapphire crystal; screw-down crown; water-resistant to 5 atm
Band: reptile skin, folding clasp
Price: $6,500

Scafograf 300 MCMLIX

Reference number: 41034V
Movement: automatic, Sellita caliber SW200-1; ø 25.6 mm, height 4.6 mm; 26 jewels; 28,800 vph; 38-hour power reserve
Functions: hours, minutes, sweep seconds; date
Case: stainless steel, ø 43 mm, height 12.6 mm; unidirectional bezel with ceramic insert with 0-60 scale; sapphire crystal; screw-down crown, helium valve; water-resistant to 30 atm
Band: stainless steel, folding clasp
Remarks: the diver's watch is based on a 1959 model
Price: $3,010
Variations: with calfskin strap ($2,900)

EDOUARD KOEHN

Well before Germany became a Federal Republic, it was a large collection of states, small and large, run by a potpourri of nobles and high clergymen. One particularly wealthy state was the Grand Duchy of Saxe-Weimar-Eisenach, today in the German state of Thuringia. As with all courts, it gave out royal warrants to suppliers of outstanding goods and services. Among these warrants was one for the clockmaker Karl Köhn. In 1859, his son, Edouard Koehn—he later Gallicized his name—set off to Geneva to learn watchmaking with the top school. In 1861, he joined Patek Philippe, and was soon promoting that brand as far away as the USA. He also made partner.

Koehn was an outstanding salesman and a fine watchmaker, notably of thin pocket watches. He even patented an improvement on a Breguet retrograde system. In 1891, he purchased the company of the Swedish watchmaker Henri-Robert Ekegren and started producing highly complicated pocket watches on his own.

The company went dormant in the 1930s. It was revived recently and has already made its mark with rather bold collections. One, the Tempus, features a high-tech brushed ceramic bezel. It comes as a sportive tricompax chronograph or in a slightly more sedentary skeleton-ized version with an elegant clous-de-Paris dial. The Tempus II is a bicompax chrono activated with a single pusher. As for the Tempus III, it is in lighter titanium and has a diameter of 41 millimeters.

The World Heritage collection is for travelers, with a central 24-hour, 24-city function surrounded by a pretty wave guilloché. Travelers will appreciate the alarm function, always handy when taking power naps on the road. The latest collection is the Legacy Rattrapante, a split-seconds chronograph that reproduces an original Koehn pocket watch in a comfortably dimensioned 40-millimeter case. The mechanisms driving the Edouard Koehn watches are the product of a collaboration with Concepto in La Chaux-de-Fonds, Switzerland.

EDOUARD KOEHN
Company representation
Edouard Koehn Master Watchmaker Sàrl
Rue des 22-Cantons 36
2300 La Chaux-de-Fonds
Switzerland

TEL.:
+41 (0)79-137-60-29

WEBSITE:
www.edouardkoehn.com

FOUNDED:
2018

US DISTRIBUTION:
Totally Worth It Inc.
76 Division Ave
Summit, NJ 07901
USA
+1-724-263-2286
info@totallyworthit.com

ANNUAL PRODUCTION:
approx. 300 pieces

MOST IMPORTANT COLLECTIONS/PRICE RANGE:
World Heritage ($9,950), Tempus I ($7,950), Tempus II ($9,950), Tempus III ($8,950), Legacy Rattrapante ($16,800)

Legacy Rattrapante

Reference number: EK-CHR11SS-SL-WEEL-ASBK
Movement: automatic, caliber EK-MVT-CHR03 (modified Concepto base); ø 30.4 mm, height 8.4 mm; 31 jewels; 28,800 vph; oscillating mass with côtes de Genève; 48-hour power reserve
Functions: hours, minutes, subsidiary second; split-seconds chronograph with 60-minute totalizer at 12 o'clock
Case: stainless steel, ø 40 mm, height 13 mm (without sapphire crystal); sapphire; transparent case back; water resistant to 5 atm
Remarks: Grand Feu enamel dial
Band: reptile skin, folding clasp
Price: $16,800; limited to 50 pieces
Variations: in rose-gold case (price on request); limited to 25 editions

Tempus III Sand Skeleton

Reference number: EK-CHR10SRIB
Movement: automatic, caliber EK-MVT-CHR01 (modified Concepto base); ø 30.4 mm, height 8.4 mm; 27 jewels; 28,800 vph; semi skeleton; 48-hour power reserve
Functions: hours, minutes, subsidiary seconds; chronograph
Case: titanium, ø 43 mm, height 15 mm; ceramic bezel; sapphire crystal; transparent case back; water-resistant to 10 atm
Band: rubber, pin buckle
Remarks: skeleton dial
Price: $8,950
Variation: comes in different colors with skeleton or guilloché dial

World Heritage Green

Reference number: EK-WTA05IBASBK
Movement: automatic, caliber EK-MVT-WTA01 (modified Concepto base); ø 30.40 mm, height 7.6 mm; 31 jewels; 28,800 vph; double barrel for time and alarm mechanism; 48-hour power reserve
Functions: hours, minutes, sweep seconds, 24-hour display (world time, with 24 reference cities); day/night indicator; alarm (around 12 seconds)
Case: titanium, ø 42 mm, height 14.5 mm; sapphire; transparent case back; water resistant to 50 meters
Remarks: wave-pattern guilloché on the dial
Band: reptile skin, folding clasp
Price: $9,950
Variations: comes with different color dials

ELKA WATCH

The old saying "Many are called, few are chosen" could be the motto for any start-up watch brand facing off high start-up costs, stiff competition, and a market that is very fickle on the buyer side. It is not enough to look for a niche to fill—you need to get into the fray with confidence and long-term planning.

The story of Elka, however, has an almost mystical aspect. Founder Hakim El Kadiri was born in Casablanca, Morocco. His mother, a photographer, was Swiss, and his father, a forest and water engineer, was Moroccan. The family moved to Neuchâtel, a hub of Swiss watchmaking, where young Hakim studied precision engineering and ultimately went to work for a major player as a designer. But he had other ideas. "I dreamt of developing my own brand, which I wanted above all to have a story, truth and credibility," he says. "I was particularly inspired by the products and aesthetics of the 60s." Besides a clear idea, he had the technical knowledge to ensure affordable quality, and he had name: Elka (an old nickname derived from his surname, El Kadiri).

Then he discovered that there already had been a brand named Elka in the early 70s founded by a Dutchman named Eduard Louis Kiek. It had worked closely with other big names in the business, including Ulysse Nardin, Heuer, Rolex, and Minerva. The Fates, he felt, were favorable, and in 2022, El Kadiri launched "his" Elka.

Currently, there are three main collections plus some special editions, all run on the "you-can't-go-wrong" La Joux-Perret G100 caliber. The X series is inspired from an airplane gauge (and a Heuer dial). It comes in various vintage-ish colored dials, from black to gradated brown hues. The D series is a minimalistic dress watch with sun-brushed dial and slim hands and markers, which will be complemented in 2025 with two limited editions in green and burgundy. The Arinis model, named for a prehistoric village that once stood on the banks of Lake Neuchâtel, is a solid diver's watch. As a "local hero," it is tested in the neighboring lake.

ELKA WATCH CO. SARL
Rue du Musée 4,
CH-2000 Neuchâtel
Switzerland

TEL.:
+41-79-500-9113

E-MAIL:
info@elkawatch.com

WEBSITE:
www.elkawatch.com

FOUNDED:
2022

NUMBER OF EMPLOYEES:
1

ANNUAL PRODUCTION:
230 watches

DISTRIBUTION:
direct sales only, with retailers in Switzerland, Austria, Netherlands, Germany, UK, Canada, France, USA

MOST IMPORTANT COLLECTIONS/PRICE RANGE:
X, S, D series, Arinis, special editions / $1,760 to $2,300

Arinis

Reference number: AF01-1201
Movement: automatic, La Joux-Perret G100; ø 25.60 mm, height 4.45 mm; 24 jewels; 28,800 vph; 68-hour power reserve
Functions: hours, minutes, sweep seconds; date or not
Case: stainless steel, ø 41 mm, height 11.85 mm; unidirectional rotating bezel with ceramic insert with Super-LumiNova; "chevé" sapphire crystal; stamped case back with 3 fishes resembling ancient artefacts; water-resistant to 20 atm
Band: rubber (FKM), pin buckle
Remarks: Arinis is the prehistoric name of St. Blaise, the stamped case back with 3 fishes resembling ancient artefacts
Price: $2,030
Variations: blue or black dials colors; with stainless steel rice-grain bracelet ($2,070), NATO strap ($1,960)

X Series

Reference number: X02w-0901
Movement: automatic, La Joux-Perret G100; ø 25.60 mm, height 4.45 mm; 24 jewels; 28,800 vph; with côtes de Genève; 68-hour power reserve
Functions: hours, minutes, sweep seconds, date
Case: stainless steel, ø 40.8 mm, height 11.85 mm; unidirectional rotating bezel with ceramic insert with Super-LumiNova; "chevé" sapphire crystal; screw-down case back; water-resistant to 3 atm
Band: 0901 is a Nylon Nato strap, pin buckle
Remarks: leaf hands with old-radium Super-LumiNova
Price: $1,820
Variations: various dial colors; comes with date at 3 o'clock ($1,760)

S Series

Reference number: S01-0811
Movement: automatic, La Joux-Perret G100; ø 25.60 mm, height 4.45 mm; 25 jewels; 28,800 vph; with côtes de Genève; grey NAC coating on bridges; the rhodium-plated gold oscillator; COSC-certified; 68-hour power reserve
Functions: hours, minutes, sweep seconds
Case: stainless steel, ø 40.8 mm, height 10.8 mm; "chevé" sapphire crystal; water-resistant to 20 atm
Band: calfskin, pin buckle
Remarks: sun-brushed gradated dial
Price: $1,820; limited to 25 pieces

ERNST BENZ

"Precision instruments for timekeeping" was the guiding principle under which Ernst Benz, a Swiss inventor and precision engineer, embarked on his watchmaking journey. Benz first made his mark through his Benz Micro factory, which produced high-performance timepiece and industrial jewels for leading watch movement manufacturers, alongside his renowned Benz Micro turntable styluses. Being a passionate aviator, he applied his expertise to developing aircraft instruments, including altimeters, military timing devices, and the iconic Benz Micro aircraft gauge. This essential tool became standard in many small aircraft. Since a robust, highly legible, and precise wristwatch was needed in the cockpit, he created the first Great Circle ChronoScope, an oversized, vintage-inspired dial design with the famous Valjoux 7750 inside.

The brand's trajectory took a significant turn in 2002 with the introduction of what would become one of its signature models, the ChronoLunar, developed in collaboration with an experienced watchmaker, Leonid Khankin, who expanded the brand both geographically and creatively. Soon it had developed quite a reputation thanks to a wider portfolio that included several collaborations. The ChronoScope, ChronoLunar, and ChronoSport collections evolved with new variations, while entirely new models, such as the ChronoFlite GMT, WorldTimer, and ChronoDiver, were introduced—each drawing inspiration from Benz's original aviation instruments.

Recognizing the diverse preferences of collectors and enthusiasts, the brand also expanded its offerings beyond the original 47mm case, now presenting its timepieces in 44, 40, and 36 millimeter sizes. These have found favor especially in recent years, when watch diameters have been trending downward.

The Ernst Benz brand has walked that fine line between the retro look and being modern. Particularly noticeable are the stark colors used, which are especially noticeable on the large models. The look was changed slightly for the Instrument and Officer series, an extensive range of bespoke and limited editions, and collaborations with renowned figures, organizations, and athletes. Most recently, Ernst Benz has ventured into the world of motorsports, with new collections inspired by its various partnerships.

ERNST BENZ
7 Route de Crassier
CH-1262 Eysins
Switzerland

E-MAIL:
info@ernstbenz.com

WEBSITE:
www.ernstbenz.com

FOUNDED:
early 1960s

U.S. DISTRIBUTOR:
Ernst Benz North America
177 S Old Woodward
Birmingham, MI 48009
248-203-2323

MOST IMPORTANT COLLECTIONS:
ChronoLunar, ChronoScope, ChronoSport, ChronoDiver, ChronoFlite

ChronoScope Traditional
Reference number: GC10117
Movement: automatic, Valjoux caliber 7750; ø 30 mm, height 7.9 mm; 25 jewels; 28,800 vph; 48-hour power reserve
Functions: hours, minutes, subsidiary seconds; day, date; chronograph with hours, minutes, sweep seconds
Case: stainless steel, ø 47 mm, height 16 mm; sapphire crystal; screw-down transparent case back; double O-ring sealed crown; water-resistant to 5 atm
Band: reptile skin, pin buckle
Price: $5,375

ChronoScope Traditional DLC
Reference number: GC10119-DLC
Movement: automatic, Valjoux caliber 7750; ø 30 mm, height 7.9 mm; 25 jewels; 28,800vph; 48-hour power reserve
Functions: hours, minutes, subsidiary seconds; day, date; chronograph with hours, minutes, sweep seconds
Case: stainless steel with black DLC, ø 47 mm, height 16 mm; sapphire crystal; screw-down transparent case back; double O-ring sealed crown; water-resistant to 5 atm
Band: reptile skin, buckle
Price: $6,225
Variations: 44 millimeters ($5,625)

ChronoLunar Traditional
Reference number: GC10312
Movement: automatic, Valjoux caliber 7751; ø 30 mm, height 7.9 mm; 25 jewels; 28,800vph; 48-hour power reserve
Functions: hours, minutes, subsidiary seconds; day, date, month, moon phase; 24-hour display; chronograph with hours, minutes, sweep seconds
Case: stainless steel, ø 47 mm, height 16 mm; sapphire crystal; screw-down transparent case back; double O-ring sealed crown; water-resistant to 5 atm
Band: reptile skin, buckle
Price: $7,225

ChronoLunar Officer

Reference number: GC10381
Movement: automatic, Valjoux caliber 7751; ø 30 mm, height 7.9 mm; 25 jewels; 28,800 vph; 48-hour power reserve
Functions: hours, minutes, subsidiary seconds; day, date, month, moon phase; 24-hour display; chronograph with hours, minutes, sweep seconds
Case: stainless steel, ø 47 mm, height 16 mm; sapphire crystal; screw-down transparent case back; double O-ring sealed crown; water-resistant to 5 atm
Band: reptile skin, buckle
Price: $7,625

ChronoLunar Officer

Reference number: GC10384
Movement: automatic, Valjoux caliber 7751; ø 30 mm, height 7.9 mm; 25 jewels; 28,800 vph; 48-hour power reserve
Functions: hours, minutes, subsidiary seconds; day, date, month, moon phase; 24-hour display; chronograph with hours, minutes, sweep seconds
Case: stainless steel, ø 47 mm, height 16 mm; sapphire crystal; screw-down transparent case back; double O-ring sealed crown; water-resistant to 5 atm
Band: reptile skin
Price: $7,625

ChronoLunar Officer

Reference number: GC10385
Movement: automatic, Valjoux caliber 7751; ø 30 mm, height 7.9 mm; 25 jewels; 28,800 vph; 48-hour power reserve
Functions: hours, minutes, subsidiary seconds; day, date, month, moon phase; 24-hour display; chronograph with hours, minutes, sweep seconds
Case: stainless steel, ø 47 mm, height 16 mm; sapphire crystal; screwed-down transparent case back; double O-ring sealed crown; water-resistant to 5 atm
Band: reptile skin, buckle
Price: $7,625

ChronoLunar Officer

Reference number: GC10386
Movement: automatic, Valjoux caliber 7751; ø 30 mm, height 7.9 mm; 25 jewels; 28,800 vph; 48-hour power reserve
Functions: hours, minutes, subsidiary seconds; day, date, month, moon phase; 24-hour display; chronograph with hours, minutes, sweep seconds
Case: stainless steel, ø 47 mm, height 16 mm; sapphire crystal; screwed-down transparent case back; double O-ring sealed crown; water-resistant to 5 atm
Band: reptile skin, buckle
Price: $7,625

ChronoDiver Instrument

Reference number: GC10721
Movement: automatic, Valjoux caliber 7750; ø 30 mm, height 7.9 mm; 25 jewels; 28,800 vph; 48-hour power reserve
Functions: hours, minutes, subsidiary seconds; day, date; chronograph with hours, minutes, sweep seconds
Case: stainless steel, ø 47 mm, height 16 mm; unidirectional bezel with 0-60 scale; sapphire crystal; screw-down transparent case back; screw-down crown; water-resistant to 20 atm
Band: reptile skin, buckle
Price: $5,825

ChronoFlite World Timer

Reference number: GC10851_GENEVE
Movement: automatic, ETA caliber 2893-2A; ø 25.6 mm, height 4.1 mm; 21 jewels; 28,800 vph; 42-hour power reserve
Functions: hours, minutes, sweep seconds; world time; 2nd time zone; date
Case: stainless steel, ø 47 mm, height 14 mm; sapphire crystal; screw-down transparent case back; double O-ring sealed crown; water-resistant to 5 atm
Band: reptile skin, buckle
Price: $5,575

FERDINAND BERTHOUD

The old saying "nomen est omen" could be the slogan for many brands in the watch industry, whose strategy and style is all in the name they choose. Karl-Friedrich Scheufele, himself vice president of a brand named after a Swiss watchmaker, Louis-Ulysse Chopard, stumbled upon another historical personality when he founded his manufactory in the Jura in 1996. Ferdinand Berthoud. Berthoud (1727-1807) was one of the most important watchmakers of his era, a contemporary of Abraham-Louis Breguet and Thomas Mudge, a master watchmaker at the French court and supplier to the Royal Navy. He was also the author of numerous books and writings on the theory of watchmaking. Finally, he was not French, but Swiss, born in Val-de-Travers near Fleurier.

Reviving that eighteenth-century DNA seemed worthwhile. In 2015, the first Berthoud watch of the modern era was presented in Paris, a chronometer, of course. The movement of the FB 1 was equipped with a constant force mechanism using a traditional chain and fusee. It also features an unusual power reserve display (53 hours) and a rather large tourbillon under a filigree one-armed cock.

The FB 1R model presented in 2016 had a special regulator dial with a discreet time display, and the FB 1L iteration that followed a little later shows the moon phase and moon age in an unconventional manner. In 2020, Ferdinand Berthoud launched a completely new collection with the FB 2RE, which is conspicuously inspired by Berthoud's marine chronometer No. 6 and has a sophisticated mechanism chain and fusee constant force escapement (*remontoir d'égalité*) and a jumping seconds.

The FB 3 chronometer was unveiled in 2022. Powered by a mechanical movement with a cylindrical balance-spring, it is the only timepiece of its kind to be awarded a COSC chronometer certificate. The elegance of its 42 mm case, inspired by nineteenth-century pocket watches, reveals the movement and provides a stage for the regulating organ.

Only a few dozen of these exquisite timepieces are produced each year. They are all developed, manufactured, decorated, adjusted, and tested by hand in the workshops of Chronométrie Ferdinand Berthoud in Fleurier (Switzerland).

CHRONOMÉTRIE FERDINAND BERTHOUD SA
20, rue des Moulins
CH-2114 Fleurier
Switzerland

E-MAIL:
contact@ferdinandberthoud.ch

WEBSITE:
www.ferdinandberthoud.ch

FOUNDED:
2013

DISTRIBUTOR:
Cellini Jewelers
430 Park Avenue at 56th Street
New-York 10022
212-888-0505
www.cellinijewelers.com

COLLECTIONS / PRICE RANGE:
Exclusively built chronometers/$150,000 to $260,000

Chronomètre FB 3

Reference number: FB 3SPC.1-1
Movement: hand-wound, Ferdinand Berthoud caliber FB-SPC; ø 34 mm, height 6.84 mm; 47 jewels; 21,600 vph; balance wheel with variable inertia with 4 regulating screws and 8 weighted screws; COSC-certified chronometer; 72-hour power reserve
Functions: hours, minutes, subsidiary seconds; power reserve indicator
Case: white gold, ø 42.3 mm, height 9.43 mm; sapphire crystal; transparent case back; water-resistant to 3 atm
Band: reptile skin, pin buckle
Price: on request

Chronomètre FB RES

Reference number: FB 1RES.4
Movement: hand-wound, caliber FB-RES.FC; ø 37.3 mm, height 9.37 mm; 58 jewels; 18,000 vph; fusee-and-chain constant force with a one-second "remontoir d'égalité," flying spring barrel; COSC-certified chronometer; 50-hour power reserve
Functions: hours, minutes, sweep seconds (jumping); power reserve indicator
Case: titanium (ceramic-coated, side crystal), ø 44 mm, height 14.26 mm; sapphire crystal; transparent case back; water-resistant to 3 atm
Band: reptile skin, folding clasp
Remarks: openworked dial
Price: on request
Variations: various case types

Chronomètre FB RES

Reference number: FB 2RES6-2
Movement: hand-wound, caliber FB-RES.FC; ø 37.3 mm, height 9.37 mm; 58 jewels; 18,000 vph; fusee-and-chain constant force with a one-second "remontoir d'égalité," flying spring barrel; COSC-certified chronometer; 50-hour power reserve
Functions: hours, minutes, sweep seconds (jumping); power reserve indicator
Case: stainless steel, sapphire portholes on case barrel, ø 44 mm, height 14.3 mm; sapphire crystal; transparent case back; water-resistant to 3 atm
Band: reptile skin, folding clasp
Remarks: openworked dial
Price: on request
Variations: various case types

F.P.JOURNE

In the pantheon of exceptional watchmakers, François-Paul Journe holds a special place. Born in Marseilles, he decided early on to attend a watchmaking school in Paris and then went to work for his uncle. By the age of twenty, he had made his first tourbillon and was soon producing watches for very high-flying connoisseurs of the art.

He moved to Switzerland and continued cultivating his rarified clientele while at the same time developing the most creative and complicated timekeepers for other brands. Then he took the plunge and founded his own brand in the heart of Geneva. These timepieces he conceived and produced basically single-handedly and certainly single-mindedly, hence his tagline *invenit et fecit*, invented and made. They are of such extreme complexity that it is no wonder they leave his workshop in relatively small quantities. Journe has won numerous top awards, some several times over. He particularly values the Prix de la Fondation de la Vocation Bleustein-Blanchet, since it came from his peers.

The family of Journe watches is divided into several collections: the automatic Octa collection, with classic complications based on a very powerful caliber, the 1300.3, which offers 120 hours of power; the lineSport, focusing on contemporary sportive aesthetics; the Souverain (or Souveraine, depending of the preceding noun's gender), with a range of complications, such as a minute repeater, a constant force tourbillon with dead-beat seconds, and a unique Chronomètre à Résonance with two escapements beating in resonance and providing chronometer precise timekeeping, especially in its most recent version, where it is equipped with a remontoir system to even out the mainspring's torque; and the Élégante collection. The latter is an electromechanical watch providing 8 to 18 years of autonomy, depending on whether it is in daily use or in sleeping mode. Though not purely mechanical, it is one of Journe's favorites, it would seem. The latest iteration is dedicated to Serge Cukrowicz, a long-time friend and business companion of the brand who died in 2021. His colorful sartorial habits are replicated in the straps and especially the swatch of 52 glass ceramic stones set on the bezel.

F.P. Journe's timepieces are mostly sold in dedicated boutiques.

MONTRES JOURNE SA
17 rue de l'Arquebuse
CH-1204 Geneva
Switzerland

TEL.:
+41-22-322-09-09

E-MAIL:
info@fpjourne.com

WEBSITE:
www.fpjourne.com

FOUNDED:
1999

NUMBER OF EMPLOYEES:
135

ANNUAL PRODUCTION:
850–900 watches

U.S. DISTRIBUTOR:
Montres Journe America
Epic Hotel
270 Biscayne Boulevard Way
Miami, FL 33131
305-572-9802
america@fpjourne.com

MOST IMPORTANT COLLECTIONS:
Souveraine, Octa, lineSport, Elégante, Classique
(Prices indicated are approximate)

Tourbillon Souverain

Movement: manually wound, F.P.Journe caliber 1519 in rose gold; ø 34.6 mm, height 10 mm; 32 jewels; 21,600 vph; vertical tourbillon with constant force; balance with 4 inertia weights; rose gold plate and bridges; 80-hour power reserve
Functions: hours, minutes, subsidiary dead-beat seconds; power reserve indicator
Case: platinum, ø 42 mm, height 13.6 mm; sapphire crystal; transparent case back; water-resistant to 3 atm
Band: calfskin, buckle
Remarks: rose gold clous de Paris guilloché dial made from gold bridges with Grand Feu enamel small dial on white gold
Price: $242,200

Elégante Gino's Dream

Movement: electromechanical, F.P.Journe caliber 1210; 28.5 x 28.3 mm, height 3.13 mm; 18 jewels; quartz frequency 32,768 Hz; autonomy: daily use up to 10 years, 18 years in standby mode
Functions: hours, minutes, subsidiary seconds; motion detector with inertia weight at 4:30
Case: titalyt-coated titanium, 48 x 40 mm, height 7.95 mm; bezel set with colored ceramic-glass stones; sapphire crystal; transparent case back; water-resistant to 3 atm
Band: rubber, folding clasp
Remarks: goes into standby mode after 35 minutes without motion, microprocessor keeps time, restarts automatically, sets time when watch put back on; comes with straps in colored rubber, luminescent dial; dial fully lumed
Price: $38,000
Variations: in titanium; orange rubber; comes in 40-mm x 35 mm version

Octa Divine – Boutique Edition

Movement: automatic, F.P.Journe caliber 1300.3 in rose gold; ø 33 mm, height 5.20 mm; 36 jewels; 21,600 vph; gold rotor, rose gold plate and bridges with guilloché; up to 160-hour power reserve of which 120 hours are chronometry guaranteed
Functions: hours, minutes, subsidiary seconds; large date (instant); moon phase; power reserve indicator
Case: platinum, ø 42 mm, height 10.7 mm; white gold and whitened silver dial; sapphire crystal; transparent case back; water-resistant to 3 atm
Band: titanium bracelet and folding clasp
Remarks: guilloché on dial; blued hands
Price: $54,000

FRANCK MULLER

Francesco "Franck" Muller has been considered one of the great creative minds in the industry ever since he designed and built his first tourbillon watch back in 1986. In fact, he never ceased amazing his colleagues and competition ever since, with his astounding timepieces that combined complications in a new and imaginative manner.

But a while ago the "master of complications" stepped away from the daily business of the brand, leaving space for the person who had paved young Muller's way to fame, Vartan Sirmakes. It was Sirmakes, previously a specialist in watch cases, who had contributed to the development of the double-domed, tonneau-shaped Cintrée Curvex case, with its elegant, 1920s retro look. He also presided over numerous complications, like the Crazy Hours, which shake up the notion of time itself. Franck Muller also created the Gigatourbillons, which are 20 millimeters across and are now appearing in various other collections. Lately, the brand even made a fast tourbillon that does a rotation in five seconds, which is not that simple, since speed also demands a more robust structure without sacrificing the delicacy of the mechanism.

Even a brand that prides itself on a traditional look must make some concessions to modern aesthetics. The more recent Vanguards have sought to make the traditional Art-Deco tonneau-shaped case so typical of the brand appear more modern and even trendy. Increasingly, Franck Muller has been using vivacious colors and playful dials, which in the somewhat stringent days of the post-pandemic seem to suggest entertaining lights at the end of the tunnel. The Crazy Hours still finds many fans. Another way to shake things up was making square or round watches, which stick out sharply in the midst of the curvy rectangles.

Franck Muller is vertically integrated, meaning that when you purchase a watch, it has been entirely conceived and built "in-house," from the strap to the caliber. In fact, Franck Muller seems to operate almost independently of other watchmakers. In 1997, Muller and Sirmakes founded the Franck Muller Group Watchland, which holds the majority interest in several other companies, ten of which are watch brands, like Backes & Strauss, Martin Braun, or Pierre Kunz. They exhibit in Geneva at the same time as many other brands but always seem to be in another dimension.

GROUPE FRANCK MULLER WATCHLAND SA
22, route de Malagny
CH-1294 Genthod
Switzerland

TEL.:
+41-22-959-88-88

E-MAIL:
contact@franckmuller.ch

WEBSITE:
www.franckmuller.com

FOUNDED:
1991

NUMBER OF EMPLOYEES:
approx. 500 (estimated)

U.S. DISTRIBUTOR:
Franck Muller USA, Inc
207 W. 25th Street, 8th Floor
New York, NY 10001
212-463-8898
www.franckmuller-usa.com

MOST IMPORTANT COLLECTIONS:
Giga Tourbillon, Aeternitas, Revolution, Evolution 3-1, Vanguard, Cintrée Curvex

Vanguard Crazy Hours Vegas Racing

Reference number: V 45 CH SQT RCG VEGAS CARBONE (ER)
Movement: automatic, Franck Muller caliber MVD FM 2800-SQT; ø 26.2 mm, height 5.2 mm; 27 jewels; 28,800 vph; finely finished movement with côtes de Genève and perlage on bridges and mainplate; bidirectional rotor; 42-hour power reserve
Functions: non-sequential instantaneously jumping hours, minutes, sweep seconds
Case: compressed carbon, 53.7 mm x 44 mm, height 15.1 mm; sapphire crystal; transparent case back; water-resistant to 3 atm
Band: calfskin, pin buckle with black PVD
Price: $37,000; limited to 77 pieces

Vanguard Colorado Racing

Reference number: V 45 SC DT RCG 1000 COLORADO (ER)
Movement: automatic, FM caliber 2536-SCDT; ø 25.6 mm, height 3.60 mm; 25 jewels; 28,800 vph; finely finished movement with sunray brushing, and perlage on dial and mainplate; gold and rhodium plating on components; 42-hour power reserve
Functions: hours, minutes, sweep seconds; date
Case: stainless steel, 53.7 mm x 44 mm, height 12.7 mm; sapphire crystal; transparent case back; water-resistant to 3 atm
Band: calfskin and rubber, folding clasp
Price: $13,000

Vanguard Carbon

Reference number: V 45 SC DT COL DRM CARBONE NR (NR)
Movement: automatic, FM caliber 2536-SCDT; ø 25.6 mm, height 3.60 mm; 25 jewels; 28,800 vph; finely finished movement with côtes de Genève and perlage on mainplate; gold and rhodium plating on components; 42-hour power reserve
Functions: hours, minutes, sweep seconds; date
Case: carbon with green inserts, 53.7 mm x 44 mm, height 12.7 mm; sapphire crystal; water-resistant to 3 atm
Band: textile, folding clasp with black PVD coating
Price: $15,300

Vanguard Lady Slim Skeleton

Reference number: V 35 S AT SQT COL DRM (BC)
Movement: automatic, FM caliber 708-SQ-V35;
36.2 mm x 31 mm, height 4.4 mm; 25 jewels;
21,600 vph; finely finished skeletonized movement, with sunray brushing and perlage on mainplate; 42-hour power reserve
Functions: hours, minutes, sweep seconds
Case: rose gold, 46.3 mm x 35 mm, height 8.7 mm; white enamel coated inner bezel under sapphire crystal; transparent case back; water-resistant to 3 atm
Band: reptile skin, pin buckle
Price: $32,600

Curvex Carbon Flash

Reference number: CX 36 SC DT FLASH CARBONE TTNRBR
Movement: automatic, FM caliber 2536-SCDT;
ø 25.6 mm, height 3.6 mm; 25 jewels; 28,800 vph; finely finished movement with côtes de Genève and perlage; bidirectional decorated rotor; 42-hour power reserve
Functions: hours, minutes, sweep seconds; date
Case: carbon, 53.1 mm x 36 mm, height 10 mm; sapphire crystal; water-resistant to 3 atm
Band: Nylon, pin buckle
Remarks: case made of 150 layers of aerospace-grade carbon; microblasted dial
Price: $19,400
Variations: stainless steel

Cintree Curvex Nuance

Reference number: 7880 SC DT NUANCE
Movement: automatic, FM caliber 2536-SCDT;
ø 25.6 mm, height 3.6 mm; 25 jewels; 28,800 vph; finely finished movement with côtes de Genève and perlage; bidirectional decorated rotor; 42-hour power reserve
Functions: hours, minutes, sweep seconds; date
Case: rose gold, 50.4 mm x 36 mm, height 11.6 mm; sapphire crystal; transparent case back; water-resistant to 3 atm
Band: reptile skin, rose gold buckle
Remarks: stamped guilloché dial with sun pattern, 25 layers of lacquer
Price: $21,300

Vanguard Lady Slim Vintage

Reference number: V 35 S S6 AT FO VIN D (RS)
Movement: automatic, FM caliber 708-S6; ø 29.9 mm, height 3.73 mm; 25 jewels; 21,600 vph; finely finished skeletonized movement, with côtes de Genève, sunray brushing and perlage; 42-hour power reserve
Functions: hours, minutes, subsidiary seconds
Case: rose gold set with 308 brilliant-cut diamonds, 46.3 mm x 35 mm, height 9.2 mm; inner bezel under sapphire crystal; transparent case back; water-resistant to 3 atm
Band: calfskin, pin buckle set with 12 brilliant-cut diamonds
Price: $20,000

Curvex CX Piano

Reference number: CX 33 SC AT FO PIANO ACNR
Movement: automatic, FM caliber 2536-SC; ø 26.2 mm, height 3.6 mm; 25 jewels; 28,800 vph; 42-hour power reserve
Functions: hours, minutes, sweep
Case: stainless steel, 48.4 mm x 33 mm, height 9.1 mm; inner bezel under sapphire crystal; water-resistant to 3 atm
Band: black satin, pin buckle
Remarks: dial coated in 20 layers of lacquer
Price: $9,400
Variations: black-coated stainless steel ($9,770); rose or yellow gold ($18,100), gold with diamonds

Round Race Chronograph

Reference number: 7002 CC DT FO RACE
Movement: automatic, FM caliber MVT 7003;
ø 30.4 mm, height 7.9 mm; 25 jewels; 28,800 vph; 46-hour power reserve
Functions: hours, minutes, subsidiary seconds; chronograph; date
Case: stainless steel, ø 42 mm, height 9.55 mm; inner bezel under sapphire crystal; transparent case back; water-resistant to 3 atm
Band: reptile skin, pin buckle
Remarks: stamped dial coated in 25 layers of lacquer
Price: $15,800

Vanguard Carbon Damascus

Reference number: V 43 S6 SQT CARBONE AMS BL (NR)
Movement: hand-wound, FM caliber 1740-VS2; ø 37.6 mm x 35.75 mm, height 6 mm; 19 jewels; 18,000 vph; finely finished skeletonized movement, satin brushing on wheels, antimagnetic Damascus steel; 42-hour power reserve
Functions: hours, minutes, subsidiary seconds
Case: carbon in Damascus pattern, 52.7 mm x 42.5 mm, height 12.6 mm; sapphire crystal; transparent case back; water-resistant to 3 atm
Band: calfskin and Nylon, folding clasp with black PVD coating
Remarks: case made of 150 layers of two-tone aerospace-grade compressed carbon
Price: $43,700

Vanguard Yachting

Reference number: V 45 SC DT YACHT (BO) O
Movement: automatic, FM caliber 2536-SCDT; ø 25.6 mm, height 3.6 mm; 25 jewels; 28,800 vph; finely finished movement with côtes de Genève and perlage; bidirectional decorated rotor; 42-hour power reserve
Functions: hours, minutes, sweep seconds; date
Case: stainless steel, 53.7 x 44 mm, height 15.1 mm; sapphire crystal; water-resistant to 3 atm
Band: stainless steel bracelet with invisible folding clasp
Remarks: stamped guilloché dial with wind rose decoration
Price: $12,400
Variations: with blue, green, white, grey dials

Vanguard Open Back

Reference number: V 41 SC DT FO (BU)
Movement: automatic, FM caliber 720; ø 33.79 mm x 33.12 mm, height 5.18 mm; 25 jewels; 21,600 vph; finely finished movement with côtes de Genève and perlage; bidirectional decorated rotor; 42-hour power reserve
Functions: hours, minutes, sweep seconds; date
Case: rose gold with blue inserts, 49.95 mm x 41 mm, height 12.2 mm; sapphire crystal; transparent case back; water-resistant to 3 atm
Band: reptile skin, pin buckle
Remarks: stamped guilloché dial with sun pattern
Price: $21,600

Curvex CX Grand Central Tourbillon Skeleton

Reference number: CX36 T CTR SQT TTNRBR ACBLBR
Movement: automatic, FM caliber CX 36T-CTR-SQ; ø 40.45 mm x 32.1 mm, height 12.34 mm; 23 jewels; 18,000 vph; central 20-mm balance wheel, one-minute tourbillon, finely finished movement with côtes de Genève and perlage on mainplate; 96-hour power reserve
Functions: hours, minutes, tourbillon seconds
Case: titanium, 52.65 mm x 36 mm, height 12.4 mm; sapphire crystal; transparent case back; water-resistant to 3 atm
Band: reptile skin, pin buckle
Remarks: four-day power reserve, currently the largest one-minute tourbillon housed in a wristwatch
Price: $152,000
Variations: stainless steel

Master Jumper

Reference number: CX 38 MJ 5N ACBR
Movement: automatic, FM caliber 3100-C1; ø 43.45 mm x 31.4, height 6.55 mm; 25 jewels; 21,600 vph; finely finished movement with côtes de Genève and perlage; bidirectional decorated rotor; 42-hour power reserve
Functions: jumping hours, jumping central minutes, jumping date
Case: rose gold with blue inserts, 55.4 mm x 40.2 mm, height 10.8 mm; sapphire crystal; water-resistant to 3 atm
Band: reptile skin, pin buckle
Remarks: stamped clous de Paris spiral dial with Zapon varnish
Price: $76,400

Vanguard Colorado Grand 35th anniversary

Reference number: V 45 CC GD SQT RCG 1000 COLORADO (NR)
Movement: automatic, FM caliber 7002-V1GGDTC3; ø 36.5 mm x 34.3 mm, height 8.70 mm; 27 jewels; 28,800 vph; finely finished movement with sunray brushing, snailing, and perlage; 46-hour power reserve
Functions: hours, minutes, subsidiary seconds; chronograph; grand date
Case: yellow gold, 53.7 mm x 44 mm, height 12.7 mm; sapphire crystal; transparent case back; water-resistant to 3 atm
Band: calfskin rubber, pin buckle
Price: $42,400

Caliber FM 720

Automatic; bicolor rotor; single mainspring barrel, 42-hour power reserve
Functions: hours, minutes, sweep seconds; date
Diameter: 33.21 mm
Height: 5.18 mm
Jewels: 25
Balance: variable inertia, Nivarox hairspring
Frequency: 21,600 vph
Shock protection: Kif Elastor
Remarks: bead-blasted and satinated bridges, perlage on mainplate, côtes de Genève on bridges; 186 parts

Caliber FM CX 36T-CTR-SQ

Automatic; skeletonized rotor; Dual (stacked) mainspring barrel, central tourbillon; 96-hour power reserve
Functions: hours, minutes
Diameter: 32.1 mm
Height: 12.34 mm
Jewels: 52
Balance: variable inertia, Nivarox hairspring
Frequency: 28,800 vph
Shock protection: Kif Elastor
Remarks: polished and beveled steel parts, perlage on mainplate, côtes de Genève on bridges; 189 parts

Caliber FM 3480-QPSE

Automatic; dual (stacked) mainspring barrel, tourbillon, 72-hour power reserve
Functions: hours, minutes, sweep seconds; minute repeater with Westminster carillon on 4 gongs and on/off indicator; full calendar with moon phase, equation of time, leap year; power reserve indicator; 36 complications in all
Diameter: 41.40 mm x 34.40
Height: 13.65 mm
Jewels: 99
Balance: variable inertia, Nivarox hairspring
Frequency: 18,000 vph
Shock protection: Kif Elastor
Remarks: polished and beveled steel parts, perlage on mainplate, côtes de Genève on bridges; 1,489 parts

Caliber FM 1740-VS2

Hand-wound; skeletonized movement; dual mainspring barrel, 168-hour power reserve
Functions: hours, minutes, subsidiary seconds; date
Diameter: 37.6 mm x 35.75 mm
Height: 6 mm
Jewels: 28
Balance: variable inertia, Nivarox hairspring
Frequency: 18,000 vph
Shock protection: Kif Elastor
Remarks: polished, beveled and engraved steel parts, satin brushing on bridges; 175 parts

Caliber FM 2025

Hand-wound; skeletonized movement; four mainspring barrels; flying tourbillon with 5-second rotation; 45-hour power reserve
Functions: hours, minutes
Diameter: 39.6 mm x 33.2 mm
Height: 8.5 mm
Jewels: 19
Balance: variable inertia, Nivarox hairspring
Frequency: 21,600 vph
Shock protection: Kif Elastor
Remarks: polished and beveled steel parts, perlage on mainplate, bridges, and ratchets; 269 parts

Caliber FM 2110-TS

Hand-wound; skeletonized movement; dual stacked (four total) mainspring barrels; 20-mm flying tourbillon on ceramic ball-bearings; 45-hour power reserve
Functions: hours, minutes, tourbillon; power reserve indicator
Diameter: 39.6 mm x 33.2 mm
Height: 8.5 mm
Jewels: 28
Balance: variable inertia, Nivarox hairspring
Frequency: 18,000 vph
Shock protection: Kif Elastor
Remarks: polished and beveled steel parts, perlage on mainplate, bridges, and ratchets; 265 parts

FREDERIQUE CONSTANT

Peter and Aletta Stas, the Dutch couple who founded Frederique Constant, have always sought to make high-end watches for consumers without deep pockets. So high-end, in fact, that in 2004 they went public with their first movement produced entirely in-house and equipped with silicon components.

The brand was founded in 1988 and named for Aletta's great-grandmother Frederique Schreiner and Peter's great-grandfather Constant Stas. The couple parlayed affordable watches with very classic—i.e., not boat-rocking—design into a modern factory in Geneva's industrial Plan-les-Ouates.

Following the sale of the company to the Japanese Citizen Group (2016), Dutchman Niels Eggerding was named CEO of the Frederique Constant brand. The factory in Geneva was expanded in 2019 to almost double its original size. In 2021, Frederique Constant achieved a mechanical breakthrough, with a compact silicon escapement rather than a normal escapement with balance. The oscillator vibrates at a frequency of 288,000 vibrations per hour. The Slimline Monolithic Manufacture ticks ten times faster than most mechanical watches and appears to achieve far better chronometric results as well. The new escapement—a genuine horological innovation—can be viewed through an opening at 6 o'clock.

To date, Frederique Constant has developed 33 mechanical in-house calibers, in particular with major complications such as a tourbillon or perpetual calendar, but also with practical "minor" complications such as a flyback chronograph or a classic automatic movement with date and moon phase display.

Frederique Constant celebrated its 36th anniversary in 2024. The future is looking bright for this relatively young brand. In addition to its main collections, by which it aims to bring high-quality, affordable watchmaking to the market, the company has at the same time gradually expanded its product range to include more exclusive pieces for discerning collectorssuch as the Classic Tourbillon Manufacture with an aventurine dial.

FREDERIQUE CONSTANT SA
Chemin du Champ des Filles 32
CH-1228 Plan-les-Ouates (Geneva)
Switzerland

TEL.:
+41-22-860-0440

E-MAIL:
info@frederique-constant.com

WEBSITE:
us.frederiqueconstant.com

FOUNDED:
1988

NUMBER OF EMPLOYEES:
150

U.S. DISTRIBUTOR:
Alpina Frederique Constant USA
350 5th Avenue, 29th Floor
New York, NY 10118
646-438-8124
customercare@usa.frederiqueconstant.com

MOST IMPORTANT COLLECTIONS/PRICE RANGE:
Manufacture collection / from approx. $3,195 to $44,995; Highlife collection / from approx $2,295 to $48,995; Classics Collection / from approx $1,095 to $2,850

Classic Tourbillon Manufacture

Reference number: FC-980AV3H8
Movement: automatic, caliber FC-980 in-house caliber; ø 30 mm, 33 jewels; 28,800 vph; one-minute tourbillon; silicon escape wheel and anchor, finely finished movement; 38-hour power reserve
Functions: hours, minutes, subsidiary seconds (on the tourbillon cage)
Case: white gold, ø 39 mm, height 10.99 mm; sapphire crystal, transparent case back, water-resistant to 3 atm
Band: reptile skin, folding clasp
Remarks: Limited to 36 pieces
Price: $39,995

Classic Worldtimer Manufacture

Reference number: FC-718KWM4H6
Movement: automatic, caliber FC-718 in-house caliber; ø 30mm, 26 jewels; 28,800 vph; finely finished movement; 38-hour power reserve
Functions: hours, minutes, seconds; date by hand; worldtimer
Case: stainless steel, ø 42 mm, height 12.15 mm; transparent case back; water-resistant to 5 atm
Band: leather, folding clasp
Price: $4,695

Classic Moonphase Date Manufacture

Reference number: FC-716S3H9
Movement: automatic, caliber FC-716; ø 30 mm, height 6.2 mm; 26 jewels; 28,800 vph; finely finished movement; 72-hour power reserve
Functions: hours, minutes, sweep seconds; date, moon phase
Case: rose gold, ø 40 mm, height 11.78 mm; sapphire crystal; transparent case back; water-resistant to 3 atm
Band: reptile skin, folding clasp
Price: $17,995; limited to 150 pieces

Classic Moonphase Date Manufacture

Reference number: FC-716GR3H6
Movement: automatic, caliber FC-716; ø 30 mm, height 6.2 mm; 26 jewels; 28,800 vph; finely finished movement; 72-hour power reserve
Functions: hours, minutes, sweep seconds; date, moon phase
Case: stainless steel, ø 40 mm, height 11.78 mm; sapphire crystal; transparent case back; water-resistant to 5 atm
Band: reptile skin, folding clasp
Price: $4,095

Classic Moonphase Date Manufacture

Reference number: FC-716S3H6
Movement: automatic, caliber FC-716; ø 30 mm, height 6.2 mm; 26 jewels; 28,800 vph; finely finished movement; 72-hour power reserve
Functions: hours, minutes, sweep seconds; date, moon phase
Case: stainless steel, ø 40 mm, height 11.78 mm; sapphire crystal; transparent case back; water-resistant to 5 atm
Band: reptile skin, folding clasp
Price: $4,095

Classic Moonphase Date Manufacture

Reference number: FC-716N3H6
Movement: automatic, caliber FC-716; ø 30 mm, height 6.2 mm; 26 jewels; 28,800 vph; finely finished movement; 72-hour power reserve
Functions: hours, minutes, sweep seconds; date, moon phase
Case: stainless steel, ø 40 mm, height 11.78 mm; sapphire crystal; transparent case back; water-resistant to 5 atm
Band: reptile skin, folding clasp
Price: $4,095

Classic Date Manufacture

Reference number: FC-706B3H6
Movement: automatic, caliber FC-706; ø 30 mm, height 6.2 mm; 26 jewels; 28,800 vph; finely finished movement; 72-hour power reserve
Functions: hours, minutes, sweep seconds; date
Case: stainless steel, ø 40 mm, height 11.78 mm; sapphire crystal; transparent case back; water-resistant to 5 atm
Band: reptile skin, folding clasp
Price: $3,495

Classic Date Manufacture

Reference number: FC-706S3H6
Movement: automatic, FC-706 caliber; ø 30 mm, height 6.2 mm; 26 jewels; 28,800 vph; finely finished movement; 72-hour power reserve
Functions: hours, minutes, sweep seconds; date
Case: stainless steel, ø 40 mm, height 11.78 mm; sapphire crystal; transparent case back; water-resistant to 5 atm
Band: reptile skin, folding clasp
Price: $3,495

Highlife Perpetual Calendar Manufacture

Reference number: FC-775G4NH6B
Movement: automatic, caliber FC-775; ø 30.5 mm, height 6.67 mm; 26 jewels; 28,800 vph; 38-hour power reserve
Functions: hours, minutes; perpetual calendar with date, weekday, month, moon phase, leap year
Case: stainless steel, ø 41 mm, height 12.65 mm; sapphire crystal; transparent case back; water-resistant to 10 atm
Band: stainless steel, folding clasp
Price: $9,895

Highlife Chronograph Automatic

Reference number: FC-391GR4NH6
Movement: automatic, caliber FC-391 (based on La Joux-Perret L110), ø 30.4 mm, height 7.6 mm; 26 jewels; 28,800 vph; 60-hour power reserve
Functions: hours, minutes; subsidiary seconds; chronograph, date
Case: stainless steel, ø 41 mm, height 14.22 mm; sapphire crystal; transparent case back; water-resistant to 10 atm
Band: leather, buckle with additional stainless-steel bracelet
Price: $3,895

Classics Premiere

Reference number: FC-301N3B6
Movement: automatic, caliber FC-301 (La Joux-Perret G100 base); ø 25.6 mm, height 4.45 mm; 26 jewels; 28,800 vph; 68-hour power reserve
Functions: hours, minutes, sweep seconds
Case: stainless steel, ø 38.5 mm, height 10.67 mm; sapphire crystal; transparent case back; water-resistant to 5 atm
Band: calfskin, pin buckle
Price: $2,195

Classics Premiere

Reference number: FC-301S3B5
Movement: automatic, caliber FC-301 (La Joux-Perret G100 base); ø 25.6 mm, height 4.45 mm; 26 jewels; 28,800 vph; 68-hour power reserve
Functions: hours, minutes, sweep seconds
Case: yellow gold-plated stainless steel, ø 38.5 mm, height 10.67 mm; sapphire crystal; transparent case back; water-resistant to 5 atm
Band: calfskin, pin buckle
Price: $2,395

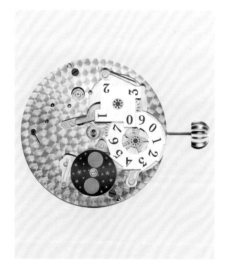

Caliber FC-980-4

Automatic; 1-minute tourbillon; single mainspring barrel, 38-hour power reserve
Functions: hours, minutes, subsidiary seconds
Diameter: 30 mm
Height: 5.7 mm
Jewels: 33
Balance: silicon
Frequency: 28,800 vph
Hairspring: flat hairspring
Shock protection: Incabloc
Remarks: perlage on mainplate, beveling, circular graining, flanks drawing, mirror polishing decorations

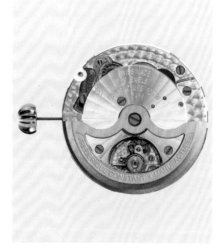

Caliber FC-706

Automatic; single mainspring barrel, 72-hour power reserve
Base caliber: FC-710
Functions: hours, minutes, sweep seconds; date
Diameter: 30 mm
Height: 6.2 mm
Jewels: 26
Frequency: 28,800 vph
Hairspring: flat hairspring with fine adjustment
Shock protection: Incabloc
Remarks: perlage on mainplate, blued screws, gold-plated and skeletonized rotor

Caliber FC-716

Automatic; single mainspring barrel, 72-hour power reserve
Base caliber: FC-710
Functions: hours, minutes, sweep seconds; date, moon phase
Diameter: 30 mm
Height: 6.2 mm
Jewels: 26
Frequency: 28,800 vph
Hairspring: flat hairspring with fine adjustment
Shock protection: Incabloc
Remarks: perlage on mainplate, blued screws, gold-plated and skeletonized rotor

GARRICK WATCHMAKERS

Britain has contributed enormously to the development of watchmaking, so it's hardly astonishing to find that the country is home to a growing number of brands vying on the international markets. Garrick Watchmakers is one of them. It was founded in 2013 in Devon by David Brailsford together with Simon Michlmayr, one of the top English watchmakers. The aim of these two men was to revive the old tradition of English watchmaking and to achieve the greatest possible vertical integration in the construction of their watches.

Wherever possible, Garrick either manufactures in its own workshop in Norwich, Norfolk or purchases from English suppliers. The company goes so far as to make its own hands, which is rare in the industry, since hands are very time-consuming to manufacture. The elaborately designed dials, too, are also entirely made in-house. Even cases are produced in England.

In the beginning Garrick had to delve deep into the history of English watchmaking and precision mechanics to regain the necessary knowledge to realize his vision. While the first models were still based on a Unitas caliber, the Portsmouth was presented in 2016, the first of what are now six of the company's own *manufacture* calibers. The same year saw the appearance of the Regulator, which uses its 42-millimeter case for three subdials and an opening on the free-sprung balance designed and built by the company. The so-called Trinity balance is made of a nonmagnetic alloy, Sircumet. To adjust the rate, the balance wheel is equipped with rim screws. The hairspring's position can be changed as well. In addition to genuine enamel dials, Garrick specializes in guilloché and finely engraved dials that appear in several of the S series, which have been released recently in 38-millimeter cases.

Garrick Watchmakers build no more than seventy watches every year. Thanks to its vertical manufacturing and the fact that each Garrick is made to order, customers are free to get some parts customized and create unique pieces. When ordering, make sure you check lead-time, though, because these are handmade pieces.

GARRICK WATCHMAKERS
Unit 2, Fletcher Way, Norwich, Norfolk
NR3 3ST
England

TEL.:
+44 (0)1603-327272

E-MAIL:
info@garrick.co.uk

WEBSITE:
www.garrick.co.uk

FOUNDED:
2013

EMPLOYEES:
9

ANNUAL PRODUCTION:
70 watches maximum

DISTRIBUTION:
Direct sales

MOST IMPORTANT COLLECTIONS/PRICE RANGE:
Regulator and S series / £2,500 to £30,000; prices only in pounds sterling

S7

Movement: hand-wound, Garrick caliber BF-04 (modified Unitas 6425); ø 29.4 mm, height 4.6 mm; 19 jewels; 21,600 vph; finely finished movement with black polishing; hand-polished and screw-mounted chatons; 47-hour power reserve
Functions: hours, minutes, subsidiary seconds
Case: stainless steel, ø 38 mm, height 9 mm; sapphire crystal; transparent case back; water-resistant to 10 atm
Band: reptile skin, pin buckle
Remarks: heat-blued hands; hand-made guilloché
Price: £6,500
Variations: engine turned dials

S2

Movement: manually wound, Garrick caliber UT-G06; 21 jewels; 21,600 vph; heat-blued cheater ring; gold or silver frosted finish; screw-mounted, hand-polished chatons; 45-hour power reserve
Functions: hours, minutes, sweep dead-beat seconds
Case: stainless steel, ø 42 mm, height 10 mm; sapphire crystal; transparent case back; water-resistant to 10 atm
Band: reptile skin or calfskin; pin buckle
Remarks: heat-blued chapter ring and hands; options for personalization
Price: £19,000
Variations: gold case; calfskin, buffalo, or ostrich strap

S3

Movement: manually wound, Garrick UT-G04 caliber; ø 36 mm, height 4.5 mm; 19 jewels; 18,000 vph; free-sprung balance; 45-hour power reserve
Functions: hours, minutes, subsidiary seconds; power reserve indicator
Case: stainless steel, ø 42 mm, height 11 mm; sapphire crystal; water-resistant to 3 atm
Band: reptile skin (or leather), pin buckle
Remarks: openworked dial with blued chapter rings
Price: £32,995

GIRARD-PERREGAUX

This venerable watch *manufacture* headquartered in La Chaux-de-Fonds is one of those with a very long history. It all began in 1791, though the genuinely successful part of the story is concentrated in the second half of the nineteenth century, 1867 to be precise, when Girard-Perregaux contributed a piece of watchmaking history with the aesthetically and technically sophisticated "Tourbillon with three golden bridges." Girard-Perregaux maintained its position at the forefront of Swiss watchmaking in the twentieth century with one of the first wrist-worn men's watches, as well as several pioneering achievements in mechanical watchmaking.

Italian entrepreneur Luigi ("Gino") Macaluso helped the brand achieve new greatness after 1992. In the wake of the renaissance of the mechanical watch, Girard-Perregaux managed to establish itself as a luxury manufacturer around the turn of the millennium. Following Macaluso's death in 2011, the company was purchased by the international Kering Group until it was taken over by its own management team led by CEO Patrick Pruniaux in the spring of 2022.

The tourbillon—in increasingly modern guises—remains the brand's focus, but along with the vintage trend and, no doubt, some nostalgia for the rational, elegant watches of older days, Girard-Perregaux decided to modernize the Laureato a few years ago, a collection that was first introduced in 1975. It is considered one of the icons of the 1970s thanks to its sporty, striking aesthetics, octagonal bezel over a round base, and metal bracelet seamlessly integrated into the case. The recently rebuilt and modernized *manufacture* in La Chaux-de-Fonds quickly produced several remarkable creations based on the distinctive sports watch.

Girard-Perregaux has also released a number of special editions to pay tribute to the brand's long-term partnership with the British sports car manufacturer Aston Martin and the Formula 1 team, such as the Neo Bridges Aston Martin Edition, a skeletonized watch with sporty, green NAC-coated bridges, the British racing team's color.

GIRARD-PERREGAUX
1, Place Girardet
CH-2300 La Chaux-de-Fonds
Switzerland

TEL.:
+41-32-911-3333

WEBSITE:
www.girard-perregaux.com

FOUNDED:
1791

U.S. DISTRIBUTOR:
Girard-Perregaux
Tradema of America, Inc.
7900 Glades Road, Suite 200
Boca Raton, FL 33434
833-GPWATCH
www.girard-perregaux.com

MOST IMPORTANT COLLECTIONS/PRICE RANGE:
Laureato / Vintage 1945 / Neo / approx. $7,500 to $625,000; ww.tc / $12,300 to $23,800; GP 1966 / $7,500 to $291,000

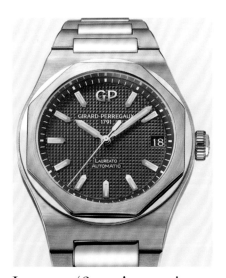

Laureato 42mm Automatic
Reference number: 81010-11-431-11A
Movement: automatic, GP caliber 01800-0013; ø 30 mm, height 3.97 mm; 28 jewels; 28,800 vph; 54-hour power reserve
Functions: hours, minutes, sweep seconds; date
Case: stainless steel, ø 42 mm, height 10.68 mm; sapphire crystal; transparent case back; water-resistant to 10 atm
Band: stainless steel, double folding clasp
Price: $14,300

Laureato Chronograph 42mm
Reference number: 81020-11-131-11A
Movement: automatic, GP caliber 03300-0137/0138/0141; ø 25.95 mm, height 6.5 mm; 63 jewels; 28,800 vph; 46-hour power reserve
Functions: hours, minutes, subsidiary seconds; chronograph; date
Case: stainless steel, ø 42 mm, height 12.01 mm; sapphire crystal; water-resistant to 10 atm
Band: stainless steel, double folding clasp
Price: $18,600

Laureato Chronograph Ti49
Reference number: 81020-21-3263-1CM
Movement: automatic, GP caliber 03300-0137/0138/0141; ø 25.95 mm, height 6.5 mm; 63 jewels; 28,800 vph; 46-hour power reserve
Functions: hours, minutes, subsidiary seconds; chronograph; date
Case: titanium, ø 42 mm, height 12.01 mm; sapphire crystal; water-resistant to 10 atm
Band: titanium, triple folding clasp
Price: $19,400

Laureato 38mm Automatic

Reference number: 81005-11-3154-1CM
Movement: automatic, GP caliber 03300; ø 25.95 mm,
height 3.36 mm; 27 jewels; 28,800 vph; oscillating mass
in rose gold; 46-hour power reserve
Functions: hours, minutes, sweep seconds; date
Case: stainless steel, ø 38 mm, height 10 mm; sapphire
crystal; transparent case back; water-resistant to
10 atm
Band: stainless steel, triple folding clasp
Price: $14,900

Laureato 42mm Skeleton

Reference number: 81015-11-001-11A
Movement: automatic, GP caliber 01800-0006;
ø 30 mm, height 4.16 mm; 25 jewels; 28,800 vph;
balance wheel with variable inertia, rose-gold rotor, fully
skeletonized movement; 54-hour power reserve
Functions: hours, minutes, subsidiary seconds
Case: stainless steel, ø 42 mm, height 10.68 mm;
sapphire crystal; transparent case back; water-resistant
to 10 atm
Band: stainless steel, triple folding clasp
Remarks: skeletonized dial
Price: $43,600

Neo Bridges Aston Martin Edition

Reference number: 84000-21-3236-5CX
Movement: automatic, GP caliber 08400-2164;
ø 32 mm, height 5.45 mm; 29 jewels; 21,600 vph;
symmetrical skeleton construction; NAC-coated
mainplate, bridges with PVD; micro-rotor; 48-hour
power reserve
Functions: hours, minutes
Case: titanium with black DLC, ø 45 mm, height
12.18 mm; sapphire crystal; transparent case back;
water-resistant to 3 atm
Band: rubber, triple folding clasp
Remarks: special edition for the collaboration with the
sports car maker and racing team Aston Martin
Price: $37,700; limited to 250 pieces

Neo Constant Escapement

Reference number: 93510-21-1930-5CX
Movement: hand-wound, GP caliber 09200; ø 39.5 mm,
height 7.4 mm; 29 jewels; 21,600 vph; patented
escapement with constant force system with two
escape wheels and a silicon impulse leaf spring, two
mainsprings with 4 winding springs; COSC-certified
chronometer; 168-hour power reserve
Functions: hours, minutes, sweep seconds; linear power
reserve indicator
Case: titanium, ø 45 mm, height 14.8 mm; sapphire
crystal; transparent case back; water-resistant to 3 atm
Band: rubber, triple folding clasp
Price: $99,600

Free Bridge Meteorite

Reference number: 82000-11-3259-5CX
Movement: automatic, GP caliber 01800-1170;
ø 36.2 mm, height 5.94 mm; 23 jewels; 28,800 vph;
54-hour power reserve
Functions: hours, minutes
Case: stainless steel, ø 44 mm, height 12.2 mm;
sapphire crystal; transparent case back; water-resistant
to 3 atm
Band: calfskin, triple folding clasp
Remarks: dial with meteorite elements
Price: $25,700

Laureato Absolute Light & Shade

Reference number: 81071-43-2022-1CX
Movement: automatic, GP caliber 01800-0006;
ø 30 mm, height 4.16 mm; 25 jewels; 28,800 vph;
balance wheel with variable inertia, rhodium-plated,
rose-gold rotor, fully skeletonized movement; 54-hour
power reserve
Functions: hours, minutes, subsidiary seconds
Case: sapphire crystal, ø 44 mm, height 11.56 mm; bezel
mounted on the case with 8 titanium screws; sapphire
crystal; transparent case back; water-resistant to 3 atm
Band: rubber, folding clasp in titanium
Price: $99,600

GLASHÜTTE ORIGINAL

Is there a little nostalgia creeping into the designers at Glashütte Original? Or is it just understated ecstasy for older looks? The retro touches that started appearing again a few years ago with the Sixties Square Tourbillon are still in vogue as the company delves into its own past for inspiration, such as the use of a special silver treatment on dials.

Glashütte Original *manufacture* roots go back to the mid-nineteenth century, though the name itself came later. The company, which had a sterling reputation for precision watches, became subsumed in the VEB Glashütter Uhrenbetriebe, a group of Glashütte watchmakers and suppliers who were collectivized as part of the former East German system. After reunification, the company took up its old moniker of Glashütte Original, and in 1995, the *manufacture* released an entirely new collection. Later, it purchased Union Glashütte. In 2000, the Swiss Swatch Group acquired the whole company and invested in expanding the production space at Glashütte Original headquarters. The company decided to separate out Union Glashütte, whose models are not distributed in the USA, by the way.

Manufacturing depth has reached 95 percent. All movements are designed by a team of experienced in-house engineers, while the components they comprise, such as plates, screws, pinions, wheels, levers, spring barrels, balance wheels, and tourbillon cages, are manufactured in the upgraded production areas. These parts are lavishly finished by hand before assembly by a group of talented watchmakers. Even dials are in-house. Among the highlights of its catalogue is the Senator Chronometer, which boasts second and minute hands that automatically jump to zero when the crown is pulled, allowing for extremely accurate time setting. Recently, the Senator Chronometer Tourbillon was released featuring some virtuoso watchmaking, including a positional error compensation of the flying going train, and the balance wheel and tourbillon cage can be stopped by a pull on the crown. Another sustained pull sets the tip of the seconds index on the tourbillon cage to zero, i.e., pointing vertically upwards.

GLASHÜTTER UHRENBETRIEB GMBH
Altenberger Strasse 1
D-01768 Glashütte
Germany

TEL.:
+49-350-53-46-0

E-MAIL:
info@glashuette-original.com

WEBSITE:
www.glashuette-original.com

FOUNDED:
1951 foundation as VEB Glashütter Uhrenbetriebe
1990 privatization and registration as Glashütter Uhrenbetrieb GmbH

U.S. DISTRIBUTOR:
Glashütte Original
The Swatch Group (U.S.), Inc.
1200 Harbor Boulevard
Weehawken, NJ 07087
201-271-1400

MOST IMPORTANT COLLECTIONS/PRICE RANGE:
Senator, Pano, Spezialist, SeaQ, Senator, Vintage, Ladies / $4,900 to $152,300

Senator Chronometer Tourbillon

Reference number: 1-58-06-01-03-61
Movement: hand-wound, Glashütte Original caliber 58-06; ø 36.6 mm, height 8.99 mm; 85 jewels; 21,600 vph; flying 1-minute tourbillon with flyback switch and exact indexing of the minute hand; silicon hairspring; DIN-tested chronometer; 70-hour power reserve
Functions: hours and minutes (off-center), subsidiary seconds (on the tourbillon cage); day/night indication, power reserve indicator
Case: platinum, ø 42 mm, height 12.6 mm; sapphire crystal; transparent case back; water-resistant to 5 atm
Band: reptile skin, double folding clasp
Remarks: limited to 50 pieces
Price: $175,500

Senator Moon Phase Skeleton

Reference number: 1-49-13-15-04-30
Movement: hand-wound, Glashütte Original caliber 49-13; ø 35 mm, height 5.8 mm; 35 jewels; 28,800 vph; fully skeletonized and finely finished movement; 40-hour power reserve
Functions: hours, minutes, subsidiary seconds; power reserve indicator; moon phase
Case: white gold, ø 42 mm, height 11.2 mm; sapphire crystal; transparent case back; water-resistant to 3 atm
Band: reptile skin, folding clasp
Remarks: skeletonized dial
Price: $42,200

PanoMaticCalendar

Reference number: 1-92-09-02-05-62
Movement: automatic, Glashütte Original caliber 92-09; ø 34.8 mm, height 7.65 mm; 53 jewels; 28,800 vph; screw balance with 4 gold regulating screws, indexless adjustment, hand-engraved balance bridge, Glashütte three-quarter plate with ribbing, skeletonized rotor with gold oscillating mass; 100-hour power reserve
Functions: hours and minutes (off-center), subsidiary seconds; annual calendar with panorama date, month (retrograde), moon phase
Case: rose gold, ø 42 mm, height 12.4 mm; sapphire crystal; transparent case back; water-resistant to 5 atm
Band: reptile skin, double folding clasp
Price: $31,000
Variations: in platinum (limited to 150 pieces, $41,000)

PanoMaticLunar

Reference number: 1-90-02-23-35-61
Movement: automatic, Glashütte Original caliber 90-02; ø 32.6 mm, height 7 mm; 47 jewels; 28,800 vph; screw balance with 18 weight screws, duplex swan-neck fine regulator, hand-engraved balance cock, Glashütte three-quarter plate with ribbing, blued screws, skeletonized rotor with gold oscillating mass, finely finished movement; 42-hour power reserve
Functions: hours and minutes (off-center), subsidiary seconds; panorama date, moon phase
Case: red gold, ø 40 mm, height 12.7 mm; sapphire crystal; transparent case back; water-resistant to 5 atm
Band: reptile skin, folding clasp
Price: $22,700
Variations: in stainless steel ($11,200)

PanoMaticInverse

Reference number: 1-91-02-01-05-62
Movement: automatic, Glashütte Original caliber 91-02; ø 38.2 mm, height 7.1 mm; 49 jewels; 28,800 vph; Glashütte three-quarter plate with ribbing, screw balance with 18 weight screws, duplex swan-neck fine regulator; inverted movement architecture, hand-engraved balance cock, skeletonized rotor with gold oscillating mass, finely finished movement; 42-hour power reserve
Functions: hours and minutes (off-center), subsidiary seconds; panorama date
Case: red gold, ø 42 mm, height 12.3 mm; sapphire crystal; transparent case back; water-resistant to 5 atm
Band: reptile skin, folding clasp
Price: $27,900
Variations: in stainless steel ($15,400)

Senator Excellence Perpetual Calendar

Reference number: 1-36-12-02-05-62
Movement: automatic, Glashütte Original caliber 36-12; ø 32.2 mm, height 7.35 mm; 49 jewels; 28,800 vph; silicon hairspring, screw balance with 4 regulating screws, swan-neck fine regulator, Glashütte three-quarter plate with ribbing, blued screws, skeletonized gold rotor, finely finished movement; 100-hour power reserve
Functions: hours, minutes, sweep seconds; perpetual calendar with panorama date, weekday, month, moon phase, leap year
Case: red gold, ø 42 mm, height 12.8 mm; sapphire crystal; transparent case back; water-resistant to 5 atm
Band: reptile skin, folding clasp
Price: $35,800
Variations: in stainless steel ($22,800)

Senator Excellence Panorama Date Moon Phase

Reference number: 1-36-24-02-02-64
Movement: automatic, Glashütte Original caliber 36-24; ø 32.2 mm, height 6.7 mm; 43 jewels; 28,800 vph; silicon hairspring, screw balance with 4 regulating screws, swan-neck fine regulator, Glashütte three-quarter plate with ribbing, blued screws, skeletonized rotor with gold oscillating mass, finely finished movement; 100-hour power reserve
Functions: hours, minutes, sweep seconds; panorama date, moon phase
Case: stainless steel, ø 40 mm, height 12.2 mm; sapphire crystal; transparent case back; water-resistant to 5 atm
Band: textile, folding clasp
Price: $11,900
Variations: in rose gold ($22,900)

Senator Chronograph Panorama Date

Reference number: 1-37-01-05-02-36
Movement: automatic, Glashütte Original caliber 37-01; ø 31.6 mm, height 8 mm; 65 jewels; 28,800 vph; screw balance with 4 regulating screws, swan-neck spring to regulate beat; mainplate with ribbing, blued screws, skeletonized gold rotor, finely finished movement; 70-hour power reserve
Functions: hours, minutes, subsidiary seconds; power reserve indicator; flyback chronograph; panorama date
Case: stainless steel, ø 42 mm, height 14.6 mm; sapphire crystal; transparent case back; water-resistant to 10 atm
Band: textile, folding clasp
Price: $14,500
Variations: with calfskin strap; with stainless steel bracelet ($15,700)

Senator Cosmopolite

Reference number: 1-89-02-05-02-64
Movement: automatic, Glashütte Original caliber 89-02; ø 39.2 mm, height 8 mm; 63 jewels; 28,800 vph; Glashütte three-quarter plate, screw balance with 4 regulating screws, swan-neck spring to regulate rate, hand-engraved balance bridge; 72-hour power reserve
Functions: hours, minutes, subsidiary seconds; additional 12-hour display (second time zone), world time display with 35 time zones, day/night indicator for home time and local time, power reserve indicator; panorama date
Case: stainless steel, ø 44 mm, height 14 mm; sapphire crystal; transparent case back; water-resistant to 5 atm
Band: textile, folding clasp
Price: $22,600
Variations: with reptile skin strap; in red gold ($39,400)

Sixties Subsidiary Seconds

Reference number: 1-39-60-01-01-04
Movement: automatic, Glashütte Original caliber 39-60; ø 26.2 mm, height 5.9 mm; 30 jewels; 28,800 vph; swan-neck fine adjustment, Glashütte three-quarter plate with ribbing, skeletonized rotor with gold oscillating mass, finely finished movement; 40-hour power reserve
Functions: hours, minutes, subsidiary seconds
Case: rose gold, ø 42 mm, height 12.4 mm; sapphire crystal; transparent case back; water-resistant to 3 atm
Band: reptile skin, pin buckle
Price: $16,700

Sixties Chronograph Annual Edition

Reference number: 1-39-34-06-22-04
Movement: automatic, Glashütte Original caliber 39-34; ø 30.04 mm, height 7.2 mm; 51 jewels; 28,800 vph; swan-neck fine adjustment, skeletonized rotor with gold oscillating mass, finely finished movement; 40-hour power reserve
Functions: hours, minutes, subsidiary seconds; chronograph
Case: stainless steel, ø 42 mm, height 12.4 mm; sapphire crystal; transparent case back; water-resistant to 3 atm
Band: textile, pin buckle
Price: $9,100

Serenade Luna

Reference number: 1-35-14-05-15-04
Movement: automatic, Glashütte Original caliber 35-14; ø 26 mm, height 3.8 mm; 32 jewels; 28,800 vph; swan-neck fine adjustment, silicon hairspring, Glashütte three-quarter plate with ribbing; finely finished movement; 60-hour power reserve
Functions: hours, minutes, sweep seconds; moon phase
Case: red gold, ø 32.5 mm, height 8.9 mm; bezel in rose gold, set with 48 diamonds; sapphire crystal; transparent case back; crown with diamond; water-resistant to 3 atm
Band: reptile skin, folding clasp
Remarks: dial set with 20 brilliant-cut diamonds; mother-of-pearl moon phase
Price: $22,700

SeaQ Chronograph

Reference number: 1-37-23-02-81-36
Movement: automatic, Glashütte Original caliber 37-23; ø 34.2 mm, height 8 mm; 47 jewels; 28,800 vph; screw balance with 4 regulating screws, swan-neck spring to regulate the rate; mainplate with ribbing, blued screws, skeletonized gold rotor, finely finished movement; 70-hour power reserve
Functions: hours, minutes, subsidiary seconds; flyback chronograph; panorama date
Case: stainless steel, ø 43.2 mm, height 16.95 mm; unidirectional bezel with ceramic insert, with 0-60 scale; sapphire crystal; transparent case back; screw-down crown; water-resistant to 30 atm
Band: textile, pin buckle
Price: $14,700

SeaQ Panorama Date

Reference number: 1-36-13-03-90-34
Movement: automatic, Glashütte Original caliber 36-13; ø 32.2 mm, height 6.7 mm; 39 jewels; 28,800 vph; silicon hairspring, screw balance with 4 regulating screws, indexless regulating system, Glashütte three-quarter plate with ribbing, blued screws, skeletonized gold rotor, finely finished movement; 100-hour power reserve
Functions: hours, minutes, sweep seconds; panorama date
Case: rose gold, ø 43.2 mm, height 15.65 mm; unidirectional bezel with ceramic insert, with 0-60 scale; sapphire crystal; transparent case back; screw-down crown; water-resistant to 30 atm
Band: textile, folding clasp
Price: $26,100

SeaQ

Reference number: 1-39-11-06-80-33
Movement: automatic, Glashütte Original caliber 39-11; ø 26 mm, height 4.3 mm; 25 jewels; 28,800 vph; swan-neck fine adjustment, Glashütte three-quarter plate with ribbing, skeletonized rotor with heavy-metal oscillating mass, finely finished movement; 40-hour power reserve
Functions: hours, minutes, sweep seconds; date
Case: stainless steel, ø 39.5 mm, height 12.5 mm; unidirectional bezel with ceramic insert, with 0-60 scale; sapphire crystal; screw-down crown; water-resistant to 20 atm
Band: rubber, folding clasp
Price: $9,400
Variations: with synthetic strap ($9,400); with stainless steel bracelet ($10,300)

Caliber 37

Automatic; single spring barrel, 70-hour power reserve
Functions: hours, minutes, subsidiary seconds; power
reserve indicator; flyback chronograph; panorama date
Diameter: 31.6 mm
Height: 8 mm
Jewels: 65
Balance: screw balance with 4 regulating screws
Frequency: 28,800 vph
Hairspring: flat hairspring, swan-neck fine adjustment
of the rate
Remarks: finely finished movement, chamfered
edges, polished steel parts, blued screws, mainplate
with Glashütte ribbing, skeletonized rotor with gold
oscillating mass

Caliber 58-06

Hand-wound; flying 1-minute tourbillon with balance
stop and indexed reset; single mainspring barrel,
70-hour power reserve
Functions: hours and minutes (off-center), subsidiary
seconds (on the tourbillon cage); day/night indicator,
power reserve indicator
Diameter: 36.6 mm
Height: 8.99 mm
Jewels: 85
Balance: screw balance screw balance
Frequency: 21,600 vph
Hairspring: silicon
Remarks: three-quarter plate with Glashütte ribbing,
blued screws, stop wheel with double sunburst ribbing,
hand-engraved structural parts; 572 parts

Caliber 58-08

Hand-wound; swan-neck fine adjustment; balance stop
and indexed reset; single spring barrel, 44-hour power
reserve
Functions: hours, minutes, subsidiary seconds; day/
night indication, power reserve indicator; panorama
date
Diameter: 35 mm
Height: 6.47 mm
Jewels: 58
Balance: screw balance with 18 weight screws
Frequency: 28,800 vph
Hairspring: Anachron
Shock protection: Incabloc
Remarks: silver-plated mainplate, galvanic grey,
planetary, double sunburst on winding wheel, screw-
mounted white-gold chatons; 572 parts

Caliber 89-02

Automatic; second-stop system; single mainspring
barrel, 72-hour power reserve
Functions: hours, minutes, subsidiary seconds; second
time zone, world time display with 35 time zones, day/
night indicator, power reserve indicator; panorama date
Diameter: 39.2 mm
Height: 8 mm
Jewels: 63
Balance: screw balance with 4 regulating screws
Frequency: 28,800 vph
Hairspring: flat hairspring, duplex swan-neck fine
adjustment for rate and beat
Shock protection: Incabloc
Remarks: very finely finished movement, screw-
mounted gold chatons, hand-engraved balance cock

Caliber 49-13

Hand-wound; swan-neck fine adjustment, stop-seconds
mechanism; single mainspring barrel, 40-hour power
reserve
Functions: hour and minute, subsidiary seconds (off-
center); power reserve indicator; moon phase
Diameter: 35 mm
Height: 5.8 mm
Jewels: 35, including 5 in screw-mounted gold chatons
Balance: screw balance with 18 weight screws
Frequency: 28,800 vph
Hairspring: Nivarox
Shock protection: Incabloc
Remarks: very finely finished movement, skeletonized
and engraved, polished steel parts

Caliber 92-09

Automatic; two spring barrels, 100-hour power reserve
Functions: hours and minutes (off-center), subsidiary
seconds; annual calendar with panorama date, month
(retrograde), moon phase
Diameter: 34.8 mm
Height: 7.65 mm
Jewels: 53
Balance: screw balance with 4 regulating screws
Frequency: 28,800 vph
Hairspring: flat hairspring
Remarks: very finely finished movement, chamfered
edges, polished steel parts, mainplate with Glashütte
ribbing, blued screws, off-center skeletonized rotor, with
21ct gold oscillating mass

GRAHAM

In the mid-1990s, unusual creations gave an old English name in watchmaking a brand-new life. In the eighteenth century, George Graham perfected the cylinder escapement and the dead-beat escapement with a temperature compensated pendulum, and he built an orrery, a mechanical model of the solar system. Graham certainly earned the right to be considered one of the big wheels in watchmaking history.

Despite his merits in the development of precision timekeeping, it was the mechanism he invented to measure short times on clocks (a kind of chronograph) that became the trademark of his wristwatch company. It consisted of a second set of hands that could be engaged to or disengaged from the constant flow of energy of the movement. Not surprisingly, the current Graham collection includes quite a few fascinating chronograph variations.

In 2000, the company released the Chronofighter, with its striking thumb-controlled lever mechanism—a modern twist on a function designed for World War II British fighter pilots, who couldn't activate the crown button of their flight chronographs with their thick gloves on. The company has also started a special series to "give back," as it were. Made of a special carbon, this U.S. Navy SEAL Chronofighter also features a special camo look designed to help hide soldiers from satellite cameras. A part of the sales of these watches will go to the nonprofit Navy SEAL Foundation.

And as was to be expected, the carbon Chronofighters, which are much lighter than the stainless-steel versions, are now available as a separate line. And in 2024, the company reached way back into a pre-Graham past to design a Chronofighter pulsometer watch inspired from the 1920s.

The Fortress line has also been designed in the same military look but without the prominent lever on the side. Instead, the chronograph functions are selected by a single pusher that is on the left-hand side of the watch, housed in a large onion-shaped crown.

GRAHAM
Boulevard des Eplatures 38
CH-2300 La Chaux-de-Fonds
Switzerland

TEL.:
+41-32-910-9888

E-MAIL:
info@graham1695.com

WEBSITE:
www.graham1695.com

FOUNDED:
1995

NUMBER OF EMPLOYEES:
approx. 30

ANNUAL PRODUCTION:
5,000–7,000 watches

U.S. DISTRIBUTOR:
Graham Watchmakers
169 East Flagler Street, Suite 932
Miami, FL 33131
305-890-6409
m.leemon@graham1695.com

MOST IMPORTANT COLLECTIONS:
Chronofighter, Fortress, Geo.Graham, Silverstone, Swordfish

Chronofighter Vintage Bronze & Green

Reference number: 2CVAK.G02A
Movement: automatic, Graham caliber G1747; ø 30 mm, height 8 mm; 25 jewels; 28,800 vph; 48-hour power reserve
Functions: hours, minutes, subsidiary seconds; chronograph; date and weekday
Case: bronze, ø 44 mm, height 12 mm; sapphire crystal; transparent case back; crown and pusher with finger lever on the left side; water-resistant to 10 atm
Band: calfskin, pin buckle
Price: $7,950
Variations: various straps and dials

Fortress GMT City

Reference number: 2FOBC.R01A
Movement: automatic, Graham caliber G1725; ø 25.6 mm, height 3.8 mm; 26 jewels; 28,800 vph; 42-hour power reserve
Functions: hours, minutes, sweep seconds; additional 24-hour display (second time zone)
Case: stainless steel, ø 44 mm; unidirectional bezel with ceramic insert, with reference cities; sapphire crystal; transparent case back; crown with integrated pusher to set the GMT hand; water-resistant to 10 atm
Band: calfskin, pin buckle
Remarks: limited to 50 pieces
Price: $6,450
Variations: various dial colors

Chronofighter Vintage Pulsometer

Reference number: 2VCS.G09A
Movement: automatic, Graham caliber G1718; ø 30 mm, height 8 mm; 25 jewels; 28,800 vph; 48-hour power reserve
Functions: hours, minutes, subsidiary seconds; chronograph; date and weekday
Case: stainless steel, ø 44 mm; sapphire crystal; transparent case back; crown and pusher with finger lever on the left side; water-resistant to 10 atm
Band: calfskin, pin buckle
Remarks: pulsometer scale on the dial
Price: $6,450; limited to 250 pieces
Variations: with blue strap and dial (limited to 250 pieces)

GRAND SEIKO

In 2017, Shinji Hattori, president of the Seiko Watch Company, announced that the Grand Seiko line had become a separate *manufacture* brand with a very clear identity.

For the brand's fiftieth anniversary in 2010, the Grand Seiko collection was given a host of new models and started being sold in the European market.

What makes the Grand Seiko collection special is the "Spring Drive" technology invented by a Seiko engineer. It took twenty-eight years to perfect. It's mostly mechanical but with a small, crucial electronic regulating element to tame the energy from the mainspring. The caliber has been continuously improved over time, notably with the use of a special alloy called SPRON, used for the mainspring and the hairspring.

Recent models based on that platform include the Spring Drive Chronograph with the automatic caliber 9R86 with ratchet wheel control and vertical chronograph clutch. The caliber 9S86 Hi-Beat vibrates at 36,000 vph.

It's no surprise, then, that classic watch fans have welcomed the Grand Seikos into their midst. The look is just retro enough to hint at the company's original watches of the 1960s, and the innovations are vigorous enough to keep the brand in the public eye. In 2022, the high-end skeletonized constant-force tourbillon named "Kodo," which means "heartbeat" in Japanese, drew a lot of welcome attention. Indeed, its carefully tuned escapement sounds like a beating heart.

The Evolution 9 collection was created in search of the ideal wristwatch. It features an innovative design that is entirely in keeping with the Grand Seiko style of 1967.

The 9SA4 is a new hand-wound caliber running at a frequency of 36,000 vph. The new caliber with 47 jewels features a power reserve indicator on the movement side and the in-house double impulse escapement, which is also used in the 9SA5 with automatic winding. In contrast to the latter, the architecture of the gear train in the hand-wound version has been reworked to achieve greater manual winding efficiency, among other things. In practice, the full power reserve of 80 hours can be achieved with 15 percent fewer crown rotations.

The shape of the case, which comes from the Evolution 9 collection, is reminiscent of the Grand Seiko classic 44GS, but has been significantly modernized.

SEIKO HOLDINGS
Ginza, Chuo, Tokyo
Japan

WEBSITE:
www.grand-seiko.com

FOUNDED:
1960

NUMBER OF EMPLOYEES:
90,000 (for the entire holding)

U.S. DISTRIBUTOR:
Grand Seiko Corporation of America
1111 MacArthur Boulevard
Mahwah, NJ 07430
201-529-5730
info@grand-seiko.us.com
www.grand-seiko.us.com

MOST IMPORTANT COLLECTIONS/PRICE RANGE:
Elegance, Sport, Heritage / approx. $5,000 to $59,000

Heritage 62GS Spring Drive "Shunbun"

Reference number: SBGA413G
Movement: automatic, Grand Seiko caliber 9R65; ø 30 mm, height 5.1 mm; 30 jewels; electromagnetic "tri-synchro regulator" escapement with sliding wheel; antimagnetic to 4,800 A/m; 72-hour power reserve
Functions: hours, minutes, sweep seconds; power reserve indicator; date
Case: titanium, ø 40 mm, height 12.8 mm; sapphire crystal; transparent case back; screw-down crown; water-resistant to 10 atm
Band: titanium, folding clasp, with safety lock
Price: $6,900

Heritage Spring Drive

Reference number: SBGA211
Movement: automatic, Grand Seiko caliber 9R65; ø 30 mm, height 5.1 mm; 30 jewels; electromagnetic "tri-synchro regulator" escapement with sliding wheel; antimagnetic to 4,800 A/m; 72-hour power reserve
Functions: hours, minutes, sweep seconds; power reserve indicator; date
Case: titanium, ø 41 mm, height 12.5 mm; sapphire crystal; transparent case back; screw-down crown; water-resistant to 10 atm
Band: titanium, folding clasp, with safety lock
Price: $6,600

Heritage 62GS Mechanical Hi-Beat 36,000 "Sakura-Wakaba"

Reference number: SBGH343
Movement: automatic, Grand Seiko caliber 9S85; ø 31.6 mm, height 5.18 mm; 37 jewels; 36,000 vph; antimagnetic to 4,800 A/m; 55-hour power reserve
Functions: hours, minutes, sweep seconds; date
Case: titanium, ø 38 mm, height 12.9 mm; sapphire crystal; transparent case back; screw-down crown; water-resistant to 10 atm
Band: titanium, folding clasp, with safety lock
Price: $7,300

Evolution 9 Spring Drive 5 Days "Suwa"

Reference number: SLGA021
Movement: automatic, Grand Seiko caliber 9RA2; ø 31.6 mm, height 5.18 mm; 38 jewels; electromagnetic "tri-synchro regulator" escapement with sliding wheel; antimagnetic to 4,800 A/m; 120-hour power reserve
Functions: hours, minutes, sweep seconds; date
Case: stainless steel, ø 40 mm, height 11.8 mm; sapphire crystal; transparent case back; screw-down crown; water-resistant to 10 atm
Band: stainless steel, folding clasp
Price: $9,300

Evolution 9 Hi-Beat 36,000 "White Birch"

Reference number: SLGW003
Movement: hand-wound, Grand Seiko caliber 9SA4; ø 31.6 mm, height 5.18 mm; 47 jewels; 36,000 vph; antimagnetic to 4,800 A/m; 80-hour power reserve
Functions: hours, minutes, sweep seconds
Case: titanium, ø 38.6 mm, height 10 mm; sapphire crystal; transparent case back; water-resistant to 3 atm
Band: reptile skin, folding clasp, with safety lock
Price: $10,500

Evolution 9 Spring Drive 5 Days "Atera Valley"

Reference number: SLGA025
Movement: automatic, Grand Seiko caliber 9RA2; ø 31.6 mm, height 5.18 mm; 38 jewels; electromagnetic "tri-synchro regulator" escapement with sliding wheel; antimagnetic to 4,800 A/m; 120-hour power reserve
Functions: hours, minutes, sweep seconds; date
Case: titanium, ø 40 mm, height 11.8 mm; sapphire crystal; transparent case back; screw-down crown; water-resistant to 10 atm
Band: titanium, triple folding clasp
Price: $10,500

Elegance Hi-Beat 36,000 GMT

Reference number: SBGM221
Movement: automatic, Grand Seiko caliber 9S66; ø 28.4 mm; 35 jewels; 36,000 vph; antimagnetic to 4,800 A/m; 72-hour power reserve
Functions: hours, minutes, sweep seconds; additional 24-hour display (second time zone); date
Case: stainless steel, ø 39.5 mm, height 13.7 mm; sapphire crystal; transparent case back; water-resistant to 3 atm
Band: reptile skin, folding clasp, with safety lock
Price: $4,900

Elegance Spring Drive "Omiwatari"

Reference number: SBGY007
Movement: hand-wound, Grand Seiko caliber 9S64; ø 28.4 mm; 24 jewels; electromagnetic "tri-synchro regulator" escapement with sliding wheel; antimagnetic to 4,800 A/m; 72-hour power reserve
Functions: hours, minutes, sweep seconds
Case: stainless steel, ø 38.5 mm, height 10.2 mm; sapphire crystal; transparent case back; water-resistant to 3 atm
Band: reptile skin, folding clasp, with safety lock
Price: $8,300

Elegance hand-wound

Reference number: SBGW301
Movement: hand-wound, Grand Seiko caliber 9S64; ø 28.4 mm; 24 jewels; 28,800 vph; antimagnetic to 4,800 A/m; 72-hour power reserve
Functions: hours, minutes, sweep seconds
Case: stainless steel, ø 37.3 mm, height 11.7 mm; sapphire crystal; transparent case back; water-resistant to 3 atm
Band: reptile skin, pin buckle
Price: $4,800

GUINAND

Guinand is one of those watch brands that does not make too much brouhaha in the business, but rather maintains its base of faithful clients, who know an affordable, readable, reliable watch when they see one. It was founded in 1865, in Les Brenets, Switzerland, just north of the watch hub, Le Locle. Early on, the company focused on chronographs and managed to survive for quite a while. Thanks to solid manufacturing capacity and a focus on, among other things, pilot watches, the company drew the attention of Helmut Sinn, who was just starting his own company in Frankfurt and needed a partner with expertise in chronographs. In the 1990s, Helmut Sinn bought Guinand, but in 2015, the company became independent again.

Today, Guinand continues to manufacture high-quality mechanical wristwatches in small-ish batches but always using the quality components. All models are conceived, developed, designed, and manufactured in-house. And thanks to a focus on development, the timepieces are always at the cutting edge of technology. Any special functions requiring modification of the movements are usually designed in-house. A current example is the chronograph caliber GUI-02 with day/night indication using a central 24-hour hand. For the pilot's chronographs, Guinand has developed a case that meets very high standards with a triple-sealed crown and FKM-R sealing system as well as a specially hardened rotating bezel mounted on ball-bearings. "Classical" these days means taking a look back, which is part of the brand's design codes. In 2024, it released the Monte-Carlo Rally, which recalls those bicompax dials with clear sun-brushing from the 1960s known as "pandas."

Guinand attaches importance to craftsmanship in the manufacture of its watches. Each watch is assembled by a single watchmaker and then goes through quality control and a final test lasting several days, after which a final inspection certificate is issued. The watches are only sold in the company's own showrooms and via the manufacturer's own online store, which is one way of keeping prices affordable for watches that are very well made. This direct sales model also enables more personal contact with the customer.

GUINAND GMBH
Hausener Weg 61
D-60489 Frankfurt am Main
Germany

TEL:
+49-69-780-099

E-MAIL:
vertrieb@guinand-uhren.de

WEBSITE:
www.guinand-uhren.de

FOUNDED:
1865

NUMBER OF EMPLOYEES:
6

ANNUAL PRODUCTION:
Around 1000 watches

DISTRIBUTION:
Direct sales online or in the showroom

MOST IMPORTANT COLLECTIONS/PRICE RANGE:
Pilot watches, chronographs, divers and dress watches / starting around $1,500

Pilot Chrono FR

Reference number: 40.50.X.03.Tricompax.FR
Movement: automatic, Sellita caliber SW510A; ø 30 mm, height 7.9 mm; 27 jewels; 28,800 vph; finely decorated movement; 60-hour power reserve
Functions: hours, minutes, subsidiary seconds; chronograph; date
Case: stainless steel, ø 40.7 mm, height 15.2 mm; black bidirectional bezel with hard coating and 0-60 scale; sapphire crystal; transparent case back; screw-in crown; water-resistant to 20 atm
Band: stainless steel, folding clasp
Price: $2,100
Variations: with calfskin strap ($1,960)

Flieger Chrono Greyline

Reference number: 40.50.X.03.Tricompax.Greyline
Movement: automatic, caliber GUI-02 (based on Sellita SW510A); ø 30 mm, height 8.15 mm; 27 jewels; 28,800 vph; decorated movement; 60-hour power reserve
Functions: hours, minutes, subsidiary seconds; additional 24-hour display (2nd time zone); chronograph; date
Case: stainless steel, ø 40.7 mm, height 15.2 mm; black bidirectional bezel with hard coating and 0-24 scale; sapphire crystal; transparent case back; screw-in crown; water-resistant to 20 atm
Band: calfskin, pin buckle
Price: $2,200
Variations: with stainless steel bracelet ($2,360)

Monte-Carlo Rallye

Reference number: 40.50.X.16.Rally
Movement: automatic, Sellita caliber SW510A; ø 30 mm, height 7.9 mm; 27 jewels; 28,800 vph; finely decorated movement; 60-hour power reserve
Functions: hours, minutes, subsidiary seconds; chronograph; date
Case: stainless steel, ø 40.7 mm, height 15.2 mm; black bidirectional bezel with hard coating and 0-60 scale; sapphire crystal; transparent case back; screw-in crown; water-resistant to 20 atm
Band: calfskin, pin buckle
Price: $2,500
Variations: with stainless steel bracelet ($2,700)

HABRING²

The name Habring² stands for Maria Kristina Habring and her husband, Richard. This very gifted, fun, and creative couple have been manufacturing fine mechanical works of art in a small workshop in Austria's Völkermarkt. "You get two for one," Richard jokes with the ease of someone whose name, when uttered, triggers sage nodding. Before setting off on his own, he had a very distinguished career at IWC developing a split-seconds chronograph.

The couple's first watch labeled with their own name came out in 2004: a simple three-handed watch based on a refined and unostentatiously decorated ETA pocket watch movement, the Unitas 6498-1. The exceptional quality visible in every detail made Habring² an instant success among connoisseurs.

Since then, they have worked on a wide range of products, notably their movements, like the Caliber A09, which is available in both a manual and a bidirectionally wound automatic version, or the versatile A11, which appears in numerous models with a few iterations. All the little details that differentiate this caliber are either especially commissioned or are made in-house. Its sporty version drives a pilot's watch.

Also more or less in-house are the components of Habring²'s Seconde Foudroyante, with the foudroyante mechanism fed by a separate spring barrel. For the twentieth anniversary of the IWC double chronograph, Habring² built a limited, improved edition. The movement, based on the ETA 7750 "Valjoux," was conceived in 1991-1992 with an additional module between the chronograph and automatic winder.

Suffice to say, the four-member team's technical sophistication is remarkable. They do not shy away from modern materials like silicon, or technologies, or ion etching. In 2024, they designed a brand-new sports watch in a medium format that stylistically breaks away from the established patterns, with the strict geometric circle of the bezel contrasting with the soft roundness of the case. The brushed stainless-steel case and the polished surfaces on the sides emphasize the handcrafted aspect of the surface finish. The watch is equipped with the Hermès manufacture caliber H1912 with automatic winding.

HABRING UHRENTECHNIK OG
Hauptplatz 16
A-9100 Völkermarkt
Austria

TEL.:
+43-4232-51-300

E-MAIL:
info@habring.com

WEBSITE:
www.habring2.com

FOUNDED:
1997

NUMBER OF EMPLOYEES:
7

ANNUAL PRODUCTION:
300 watches

U.S. RETAILERS:
Martin Pulli (USA-East)
215-508-4610
www.martinpulli.com

BRANDON SKINNER (USA-WEST)
760-765-5657
www.horologybythesea.com

MOST IMPORTANT COLLECTIONS/PRICE RANGE:
Felix / from $5,800; Erwin / from $7,200; Doppel Felix / from $9,800; COS Felix / from $8,900

Oskar Pointer Date and Moon
Reference number: Oskar Pointer Date and Moon
Movement: hand-wound, Habring caliber A11Ups; ø 30 mm, height 5.5 mm; 18 jewels; 28,800 vph; tangential screws for fine adjustment; antimagnetic escapement; finely finished movement; 48-hour power reserve
Functions: hours, minutes, subsidiary seconds; date, moon phase
Case: stainless steel, ø 38.5 mm, height 9 mm; sapphire crystal; transparent case back; water-resistant to 3 atm
Band: calfskin, buckle
Price: $7,650

Josef
Reference number: Josef
Movement: hand-wound, Habring caliber AGSP; ø 30 mm, height 6.25 mm; 21 jewels; 28,800 vph; tangential screws for fine adjustment; antimagnetic escapement; finely finished movement; 48-hour power reserve
Functions: hours (off-center), minutes, subsidiary seconds (jumping); power reserve indicator
Case: stainless steel, ø 38.5 mm, height 8.4 mm; sapphire crystal; transparent case back; water-resistant to 3 atm
Band: calfskin, pin buckle
Price: $8,400

Felix Sport
Reference number: Felix Sport
Movement: hand-wound, Habring caliber A11B; ø 30 mm, height 4.2 mm; 18 jewels; 28,800 vph; Triovis-fine regulator; finely finished movement; 48-hour power reserve
Functions: hours, minutes, subsidiary seconds
Case: stainless steel, ø 38.5 mm, height 7 mm; sapphire crystal; transparent case back; water-resistant to 3 atm
Band: calfskin, pin buckle
Price: $5,500
Variations: various bands and dials

Erwin Tuxedo

Reference number: Erwin
Movement: hand-wound, Habring caliber A11MS;
ø 30 mm, height 5.7 mm; 21 jewels; 28,800 vph;
antimagnetic escapement; finely finished movement;
48-hour power reserve
Functions: hours, minutes, sweep seconds (jumping)
Case: stainless steel, ø 38.5 mm, height 9 mm; sapphire
crystal; transparent case back; water-resistant to 3 atm
Band: stainless steel, folding clasp
Price: $6,800
Variations: various dials

Chrono-Felix

Reference number: Chrono-Felix
Movement: hand-wound, Habring caliber A11C-H1;
ø 30 mm, height 6.5 mm; 25 jewels; 28,800 vph;
tangential screws for fine adjustment; antimagnetic
escapement; monopusher for chronograph functions;
finely finished movement; 48-hour power reserve
Functions: hours, minutes, subsidiary seconds;
chronograph
Case: stainless steel, ø 38.5 mm, height 11 mm;
sapphire crystal; transparent case back; water-resistant
to 5 atm
Band: calfskin, pin buckle
Price: $7,900
Variations: various dials

Chrono-Felix Top Second

Reference number: Chrono-Felix Top Second
Movement: hand-wound, Habring caliber A11C-H1;
ø 30 mm, height 7 mm; 25 jewels; 28,800 vph;
tangential screws for fine adjustment; antimagnetic
escapement; monopusher for chronograph functions;
finely finished movement; 48-hour power reserve
Functions: hours, minutes, rate display (blinking
seconds dot); chronograph
Case: stainless steel, ø 38.5 mm, height 11 mm;
sapphire crystal; transparent case back; water-resistant
to 3 atm
Band: textile, pin buckle
Price: $8,975

Doppel 38

Reference number: Doppel38
Movement: hand-wound, Habring caliber A11R-H1;
ø 30 mm, height 7 mm; 27 jewels; 28,800 vph;
tangential screws for fine adjustment; antimagnetic
escapement; monopusher for chronograph functions;
finely finished movement; 48-hour power reserve
Functions: hours, minutes, subsidiary seconds; split-
seconds chronograph
Case: stainless steel, ø 38.5 mm, height 11.5 mm;
sapphire crystal; transparent case back; water-resistant
to 3 atm
Band: calfskin, pin buckle
Price: $10,300
Variations: various dials

Doppel 38

Reference number: Doppel38
Movement: hand-wound, Habring caliber A11R-H1;
ø 30 mm, height 7 mm; 27 jewels; 28,800 vph;
tangential screws for fine adjustment; antimagnetic
escapement; monopusher for chronograph functions;
finely finished movement; 48-hour power reserve
Functions: hours, minutes, subsidiary seconds; split-
seconds chronograph
Case: stainless steel, ø 38.5 mm, height 11.5 mm;
sapphire crystal; transparent case back; water-resistant
to 3 atm
Band: textile, pin buckle
Price: $10,300
Variations: various dials

Chrono-Felix Perpetual

Reference number: Chrono-Felix Perpetual
Movement: hand-wound, Habring caliber A11CP;
ø 30 mm, height 7.3 mm; 25 jewels; 28,800 vph;
tangential screws for fine adjustment; antimagnetic
escapement; monopusher for chronograph functions;
48-hour power reserve
Functions: hours, minutes; chronograph; perpetual
calendar with date, weekday, month, moon phase, leap
year
Case: stainless steel, ø 38.5 mm, height 12 mm;
sapphire crystal; transparent case back; water-resistant
to 3 atm
Band: calfskin, pin buckle
Price: $26,500

HAGER

Keeping it simple is the best way to get things going. Hager, owned and operated by American service veteran Pierre "Pete" Brown, is simply named after Hagerstown where the company was started in 2009. The business model was equally streamlined: create high-quality and affordable automatic watches accessible to those who have never experienced the joy of owning a mechanical watch. The look: rugged and refined, for individuals with a sense of adventure in their bones.

It began with sports watches, classic divers. They were designed by Brown and his small team in Hagerstown. All the cues are there for the watch connoisseur, the brushed and polished cases with beveled edges, two-tiered stadium dial, with brass markers and hands outlined in black and coated with Super-LumiNova. The domed sapphire crystal, 120-click ceramic bezel and 24 click GMT ceramic bezels are also enhanced with Super-LumiNova. The cases are rated at 20 atm, meaning they are good for more than just washing the dishes. Inside them beats one of a variety of automatic winding Swiss and Japanese mechanical movements that are both encased and regulated in the USA. Lately, Hager has started making its own movements by using trusty ETA calibers as a basis.

Since its modest beginnings, Hager has expanded its line of watches and styles without, however, abandoning the sportive touch. For the elegant, yet casual dresser needing an everyday time-telling tool, there is the Pheon (an arrowhead), with a sandwich dial, or the square Interceptor, which was commissioned by a friend, Tom Wotring, whose father had flown an interceptor aircraft for a record number of hours. Affordable luxury, one might say. "We aren't just selling watches," he says, "we are selling the experience of owning a luxury timepiece." The fact that a Hager was chosen by the CIA to celebrate the Company's 75th anniversary says a lot. And in 2024, Brown, a Freemason, brought out a special for the lodges.

HAGER WATCHES
36 South Potomac Street
Suite 204
Hagerstown, MD 21740

TEL.:
240-232-2172

E-MAIL:
info@hagerwatches.com

WEBSITE:
www.hagerwatches.com

FOUNDED:
2009

NUMBER OF EMPLOYEES:
2

ANNUAL PRODUCTION:
1,000 to 1,500 watches

MOST IMPORTANT COLLECTIONS/PRICE RANGE:
Commando, GMT Aquamariner, U2, Interceptor, Pheon / $550 to $3,000

Diplomat Freemason Edition

Reference Number: 21007
Movement: automatic, caliber MD7082 (base ETA 2895 clone stamped and assembled USA); ø 25.6 mm, height 4.35 mm; 28,800 vph; 27 jewels; 42-hour power reserve
Functions: hours, minutes, subsidiary seconds
Case: stainless steel with rose gold PVD; ø 40 mm, height 9.3 mm; screw-in crown; sapphire crystal; transparent case back; water-resistant to 5 atm
Band: leather, pin buckle
Price: $895
Variations: multiple color convex sunburst patterned dials

Hager National Security Agency (NSA) Echelon Limited Edition

Reference Number: 2025LE
Movement: quartz, GA2100 caliber digital
Functions: hours, minutes, seconds; date; world timer, stop watch, 5 daily alarm; LED light, hand shift feature (hands move out of the way to show digital display contents)
Case: stainless steel; ø 43.5 mm x 51 mm, height 12 mm; custom NSA case back; water resistant to 3 atm
Band: stainless steel with 2-button clasp and 2-button slidelock extension quick release system
Price: $650
Variations: blue/black ceramic insert with blue fumé dial; red/blue ceramic insert with blue fumé dial; black/sand ceramic insert with green fumé dial

Aquamariner SSN

Reference number: 6203N
Movement: automatic, Miyota 8215 caliber; ø 26 mm; height 5.67 mm; 21 jewels; 21,600 vph; 40 hours power reserve
Functions: hours, minutes, sweep seconds; date
Case: stainless steel ø 41 mm, height 13 mm; screw-in crown; unilateral bezel with blue ceramic insert; sapphire crystal; screwed-down case back; water-resistant to 30 atm
Band: stainless steel, folding clasp with slide lock extension
Price: $650
Variations: blue dial and blue ceramic insert; gilt dial and ceramic gilt insert

HAMILTON

Hamilton Watch Co. was founded in 1892 in Lancaster, Pennsylvania, and, within a very brief period, grew into one of the world's largest *manufactures*. Around the turn of the twentieth century, every second railway employee in the United States was carrying a Hamilton watch in his pocket, not only to make sure the trains were running punctually, but also to assist in coordinating them and organizing schedules. And during World War II, the American army officers' kits included a service Hamilton.

Hamilton is the sole survivor of the large U.S. watchmakers—though only as a brand within the Swiss Swatch Group. At one time, Hamilton had itself owned a piece of the Swiss watchmaking industry in the form of the Büren brand in the 1960s and 1970s. As part of a joint venture with Heuer-Leonidas, Breitling, and Dubois Dépraz, Hamilton-Büren also made a significant contribution to the development of the automatic chronograph.

Shortly before, Hamilton, which had pioneered a tuning-fork watch, took the new movement technology and housed it in a modern case created by renowned industrial designer Richard Arbib. The triangular Ventura took the watch world by storm in 1957, in what was truly a frenzy of innovation that benefited the brand especially in the U.S. market. The American spirit of freedom and belief in progress this model evokes, something reflected in Hamilton's current marketing, are taken quite seriously by its designers—even those working in Biel, Switzerland. Today's collections are more focused on ostentatious "adventure" and aviator watches. But the brand also continues to create revamped versions of its classics, like the aforementioned Ventura and the digital PSR.

HAMILTON INTERNATIONAL LTD.
Mattenstrasse 149
CH- 2503 Biel/Bienne
Switzerland

TEL.:
+41-32-343-4004

E-MAIL:
info@hamiltonwatch.com

WEBSITE:
www.hamiltonwatch.com
shop.hamiltonwatch.com

FOUNDED:
1892

U.S. DISTRIBUTOR:
Hamilton
Swatch Group (US), Inc.
703 Waterford Way, Suite 450
Miami, FL 33126
800-234-8463
Hamilton.US@swatchgroup.com

PRICE RANGE:
between approx. $500 and $2,800

Khaki Aviation Pilot 42mm

Reference number: H64635560
Movement: automatic, Hamilton caliber H-30 (ETA C07.621 base); ø 25.6 mm, height 5.05 mm; 25 jewels; 21,600 vph; 80-hour power reserve
Functions: hours, minutes, sweep seconds; date and weekday
Case: stainless steel, ø 42 mm, height 12 mm; sapphire crystal; screw-down crown; water-resistant to 10 atm
Band: calfskin, pin buckle
Price: $1,045

Khaki Field Murph 38mm

Reference number: H70405710
Movement: automatic, Hamilton caliber H-10 (ETA C07.611 base); ø 25.6 mm, height 4.6 mm; 25 jewels; 21,600 vph; 80-hour power reserve
Functions: hours, minutes, sweep seconds
Case: stainless steel, ø 38 mm, height 11.1 mm; sapphire crystal; water-resistant to 10 atm
Band: calfskin, pin buckle
Price: $945

Jazzmaster Open Heart Auto

Reference number: H32675570
Movement: automatic, Hamilton caliber H-10 (ETA C07.611 base); ø 25.6 mm, height 4.6 mm; 25 jewels; 21,600 vph; 80-hour power reserve
Functions: hours, minutes, sweep seconds
Case: stainless steel, ø 40 mm, height 11.05 mm; sapphire crystal; transparent case back; water-resistant to 5 atm
Band: calfskin, pin buckle
Remarks: partly skeletonized dial
Price: $1,045
Variations: various colors and strap types

HANHART

The reputation of this rather special company really goes back to the twenties and thirties. At the time, the brand manufactured affordable and robust stopwatches, pocket watches, and chronograph wristwatches. These core timepieces were what the fans of instrument watches wanted, and so they were thrilled as the company slowly abandoned its quartz dabbling of the eighties and reset its sights on the brand's rich and honorable tradition. A new collection was in the wings, raising expectations of great things to come. Support by the shareholding Gaydoul Group provided the financial backbone to get things moving.

Hanhart managed to rebuild a name for itself with a foot in Switzerland and the other in Gütenbach in southern Germany, but it began to drift after the 2009 recession. Following bankruptcy, the company reorganized under the name Hanhart 1822 GmbH and moved everything to its German hometown. It has also returned to its stylistic roots: the characteristic red start/stop pusher graces the new collections, even on the bi-compax chronos of the Racemasters, which come with a smooth bezel. Pilots' chronographs have never lost any of their charm, either, and Hanhart was already making them in the 1930s, notably the Caliber 41 and the Tachy Tele, with asymmetrical pushers and the typical red pusher. These timepieces have to survive extreme conditions, like shocks and severe temperature fluctuations. Hanhart's long tradition and expertise with flyers' chronographs struck a chord with the Austrian Army. It ordered a special edition of the Primus series decorated with the coat-of-arms of the Austrian Airforce on the dial and certified by the military. The 417 ES series is another military-themed watch, one that served as a chronograph for the German air force at the time of its reconstruction.

HANHART 1882 GMBH
Hauptstrasse 33
D-78148 Gütenbach
Germany

TEL.:
+49-7723-93-44-0

FAX:
+49-7723-93-44-40

E-MAIL:
info@hanhart.com

WEBSITE:
www.hanhart.com

FOUNDED:
1882 in Diessenhofen, Switzerland; in Germany since 1902

NUMBER OF EMPLOYEES:
22

ANNUAL PRODUCTION:
approx. 1,000 chronographs and 30,000 stopwatches

U.S. DISTRIBUTOR:
WatchBuys 888-333-4895
www.watchbuys.com

MOST IMPORTANT COLLECTIONS/PRICE RANGE:
Mechanical stopwatches / from approx. $600; Pioneer / from approx. $1,070; Primus / from approx. $2,400

417 ES "Moby Dick"
Reference number: H721.202-0210
Movement: hand-wound, Sellita caliber SW510; ø 30 mm, height 7.9 mm; 23 jewels; 28,800 vph; 58-hour power reserve
Functions: hours, minutes, subsidiary seconds; chronograph
Case: stainless steel, ø 42 mm, height 13.3 mm; bidirectional bezel with reference marker; sapphire crystal; water-resistant to 10 atm
Band: calf leather, pin buckle
Price: $2,280

Preventor9 S Limited Production
Reference number: 762.210-0010
Movement: automatic, Sellita caliber SW200 with Dubois Dépraz module; ø 25.6 mm, height 4.6 mm; 30 jewels; 28,800 vph; 38-hour power reserve
Functions: hours, minutes, subsidiary seconds
Case: stainless steel with black PVD coating, titanium; ø 40 mm, height 12.05 mm; sapphire crystal; water-resistant to 10 atm
Band: calf leather, pin buckle
Remarks: limited to 100 pieces in 2024
Price: $1,270

Pioneer 417 ES 1954
Reference number: H701.210-7010
Movement: hand-wound, Sellita caliber SW510 M; ø 30 mm, height 7.9 mm; 23 jewels; 28,800 vph; 58-hour power reserve
Functions: hours, minutes, subsidiary seconds; chronograph
Case: stainless steel, ø 39 mm, height 13.3; bidirectional bezel, with reference markings; sapphire crystal; water-resistant to 10 atm
Band: calfskin, pin buckle
Remarks: anti-magnetic to 16,000 A/m
Price: $2,280

HAUTLENCE

Time can be read in so many ways. Back in 2004, after spending years in the Swiss watch industry, Guillaume Tetu and Renaud de Retz decided that their idea for tracking it was new and unique. They were not watchmakers, but they knew whom to bring on board for the genesis of Hautlence, an anagram of Neuchâtel, the town where their small company made its debut. And soon, the first HL model was produced: a large, rectangular timepiece with the ratios of a television set and a lively and visible mechanical life, with connecting rods between a retrograde minute and an hour chain, and other mechanical oddities.

But the road to finding that ideal balance between intricate engineering and design and public perception is often rocky. Fast forward to the 2020s…Hautlence is now a (founding) member of MELB Holding, headed by two men steeped in the watch business, Georges-Henri Meylan (formerly of Audemars Piguet) and former Breguet CFO Bill Muirhead. The industrial look with the "television" proportions has become the only Hautlence shape, though it has been given a more distinctive shape, with rounded edges. The use of blue rubber straps has also given the company a clear profile. More importantly, engineering has evolved and become more subtle, though no less complicated.

This all led to the "Sphere," with a ball-shaped jumping hour display and retrograde minutes.

At the 2023 Grand Prix d'Horlogerie in Geneva, the watch captured the Innovation Prize. In the meantime, the Series 2 has been released. The dial is a granular rose gold covering, looking like a sandy backdrop to the blue minute numerals.

Two other collections, the Linear Series 1 and the Vagabonde, allow the company to experiment with other complications, like tourbillons, or with designs and finishing that can fit on the space afforded by the "television set." Hautlence has always been willing to shock with their designs, and in 2024, the company released the Retrovision '47, which looks like an old radio. The tourbillon is hidden behind a grill reminiscent of a speaker and the dial resembles a frequency display. Thanks to luminescent material, the watch is quite visible in dark places.

HAUTLENCE
Rundbuckstrasse 10
CH - 8212 Neuhausen am Rheinfall
Switzerland

TEL.
+41-32-924-00-60

E-MAIL:
info@hautlence.com

WEBSITE:
www.hautlence.com

FOUNDED:
2004

NUMBER OF EMPLOYEES:
10

ANNUAL PRODUCTION:
150–200 watches

U.S. DISTRIBUTOR:
Westime
8569 Westime Sunset Boulevard
West Hollywood, CA 90069
310-289-0808
info@westime.com
www.westime.com

MOST IMPORTANT COLLECTIONS:
Concepts d'Exception, Vagabonde Series 4, Linear Series 1

HL Sphere Series 02
Reference number: BA80-ST01
Movement: manually wound, in-house A80; ø 39.6 mm x 32.6 mm x 12.3 mm; 37 jewels; 21,600 vph; components decorated and finished by hand; 72-hour power reserve
Functions: spherical jumping hours, retrograde minutes
Case: steel with anthracite PVD coating; 50.8 mm × 43 mm, height 15.6 mm (10.9 mm without sapphire crystal); polished and engraved steel crown; transparent case back; water-resistant to 10 atm
Band: black rubber, steel pin buckle with anthracite PVD coating
Remarks: spherical hour with braked retrograde minute system; intermediate sapphire dial with minute numerals in Globolight; rhodium-plated brass, grained plate
Price: $75,900; limited to 28 pieces

Retrovision '47
Reference number: ED20-SP00
Movement: automatic, in-house D20 caliber; ø 32 mm, height 5.5 mm; 39 jewels; 21,600 vph; double hairspring tourbillon (behind the grill) with bidirectional pawl winding system; decorated and finished by hand; 72-hour power reserve
Functions: Hours and minutes
Case: hand-painted titanium; 44.4 mm x 39.2 mm x 12.1 mm
Band: red calf leather, steel pin buckle
Price: $66,000; limited to 10 pieces

HLXX
Reference number: CA20-TI00
Movement: manually wound, in-house A20 caliber; ø 37.3 x 29.9 mm, height 5.3 mm; 21,600 vph; 24 jewels; movement decorated with Geneva stripes and finished by hand; 40-hour power reserve
Functions: jumping hours on sapphire disc, retrograde minutes
Case: titanium; 45.0 mm x 37.0 mm x 11.75 mm; crown with rubber ring; beveled sapphire crystal; water-resistant to 10 atm
Band: black rubber, titanium clasp
Remarks: complex dial construction, skeletonized and rhodium-plated brass base dial, intermediate tinted sapphire dial with applied minute numerals in Globolight®
Price: $43,900; limited to 20 pieces

HEDONE WATCH

In the many and often endless deliberations by professional and amateur thinkers, the branch of philosophy known as hedonism often gets a bad name. This is partly due to the fact that it seems to fly in the face of a capitalist work ethic that demands suffering. Yet, there is something to say about taking pleasure in life itself. After all, what would be the point of living otherwise?

The question is: Does the name Hedone mean anything special in Chinese? No, says Jacky Wong, it's a reference to hedonism, having a positive attitude, and doing things with good humor and fun.

By the same token, one of the brand's most noticeable—or iconic—models is the Philosophe, which borrows the famous yin-yang symbol from Daoism for the design of the dial. On the one side is the yin principle, the receptive, passive principle, third dimensional existence, perhaps. The oscillating balance, which appears on the dial as well is the active principle, the yang, the spiritual. The day/night indicator is also a reminder of this duality.

Hedone founder and CEO Jacky Wong literally grew up with watches, spending summer vacations with his father at his watch factory. His dream was to follow in the paternal footsteps, so for the past twenty years, he has been involved in watches. "End users often buy into a brand, or follow a designer label, and the actual aesthetics and function of the timepieces often becomes the secondary concern," he said in an interview. "I want to correct that, and bring back affordable, beautiful watches that are truly a joy to own."

Armed with a team that can rework and assemble movements and watches in-house, Wong has explored several aesthetic avenues. The Architect line features a sober dial with a clever day and month date appearing on two parallel slits on the dial. The Sculpteur collection is a classic skeleton watch, a kind of complication the brand has extended to the ladies' watches, which feature a bridge shaped like a rose. Finally, Wong has a line of hand-painted dials celebrating the Hong Kong movie scene, which has made a number of cult movies already.

HEDONE COMPANY
Flat A-6, 9th Floor,
Block A, Mai Hing Industrial Building,
16-18 Hing Yip Street,
Kwun Tong, Kowloon,
Hong Kong

TEL.:
+852-234-184-36

EMAIL:
info@hedone-watch.com

WEBSITE:
www.hedone-watch.com

NUMBER OF EMPLOYEES:
8

DISTRIBUTION:
Online sales and through the company website

MOST IMPORTANT COLLECTIONS AND PRICES:
Philosophe, Sculpteur, Architect, La Rose / $485 to $1,200

Hong Kong Watch

Movement: automatic, Ronda R150 caliber, ø 26.00 mm, height 4.40 mm; 25 jewels; 28,800 vph; 40-hour power reserve
Functions: hours, minutes, sweep seconds; day/date on two arched apertures
Case: stainless steel; ø 42 mm, height 10.8 mm; sapphire crystal; transparent case back; water-resistant to 5 atm
Band: calfskin, pin buckle
Remarks: dial with hand-painted scenes from Hong Kong movies
Price: on request
Variations: various color schemes

Philosophe

Reference number: H1001.0001
Movement: automatic, HM8202 caliber, ø 31.00 mm, height 5.75 mm; 20 jewels; 21,600 vph; rotor decorated with côtes de Genève; escapement on the dial; 36 hours power reserve
Functions: hours, minutes; day/night indicator
Case: stainless steel; ø 44 mm, height 12.5 mm; sapphire crystal; transparent case back; water-resistant to 3 atm
Band: calfskin, pin buckle
Price: $485
Variations: various color schemes

Sculpteur

Reference number: H4102.0006
Movement: hand-wound, HM7130; ø 36.60 mm, height 4.23 mm, 17 jewels; 21,600 vph; skeletonized movement, with blue PVD on bridges; 42-hour power reserve
Functions: hours, minutes
Case: stainless steel, ø 42 mm, height 10.8 mm; sapphire glass, transparent case back, water-resistant to 5 atm
Band: calfskin, pin buckle
Price: $1,160
Variations: with various colored bridges ($1,250)

HERMÈS

Thierry Hermès's timing was just right. When he founded his saddlery in Paris in 1837, France's middle class was up and coming and spending money on beautiful things and activities like horseback riding. Hermès became a household name and a symbol of good taste—not too flashy, not trendy, but quite useful. The advent of the automobile gave rise to luggage, bags, headgear, and soon Hermès, still in family hands today, diversified its range of products—foulards, fashion, porcelain, glass, perfume, and gold jewelry are active parts of its portfolio.

Watches were a natural natural, especially with the advent of the wristwatch in the years prior to World War I. Hermès even had a timepiece that could be worn on a belt. But some time passed before the company engaged in "real" watchmaking. In 1978, La Montre Hermès opened its watch manufactory in Biel.

Hermès went all in to acquire genuine expertise on watchmaking. "Our philosophy is all about the quality of time," says CEO Laurent Dordet. "It's about imagination; we want people to dream." The way there was through "poetic" complications that allowed the company to navigate between classy but plain watches and finely finished timepieces bristling with complications. These are sometimes done in collaboration with external designers and movement makers—the recent Arceau Le Temps Voyageur (time as traveler), a collaboration with Chronode in Le Locle is one example.

Hermès has watches with unusual hand movements with different speeds, hands that can be stopped, fascinating moon phase and time zone displays, or charming countdown functions. In 2023, the brand presented the modern H08 chronograph in an unusual combination of materials, namely, a carbon case and a titanium crown.

In 2024, a completely new sports watch appeared in the portfolio in a medium-size format that breaks away stylistically from the established patterns, with the strict geometric circle of the bezel contrasting with the soft roundness of the case. The brushed stainless-steel shell appears to have been sketched by hand, while the polished surfaces on the sides emphasize the handcrafted aspect of the surface finish.

LA MONTRE HERMÈS SA
Erlenstrasse 31A
CH-2555 Brügg
Switzerland

TEL.:
+41-32-545-0400

E-MAIL:
lmh.reception@hermes.com

WEBSITE:
www.hermes.com

FOUNDED:
1978

NUMBER OF EMPLOYEES:
344

U.S. DISTRIBUTOR:
Hermès of Paris, Inc.
55 East 59th Street
New York, NY 10022
800-441-4488
www.hermes.com

MOST IMPORTANT COLLECTIONS/PRICE RANGE:
Arceau, Cape Cod, Faubourg, Galop d'Hermès, Heure H, H08, Cut, Klikti, Kelly, Medor, Slim d'Hermès / $2,800 to $600,000

Cut

Reference number: 403190WW00
Movement: automatic, Hermès caliber H1912; ø 23.9 mm, height 3.7 mm; 28 jewels; 28,800 vph; finely finished movement; 50-hour power reserve
Functions: hours, minutes, sweep seconds
Case: stainless steel, ø 36 mm; sapphire crystal; transparent case back; water-resistant to 10 atm
Band: stainless steel, double folding clasp
Price: $7,350
Variations: various cases and dials; with rubber strap

Cut

Reference number: 403249WW00
Movement: automatic, Hermès caliber H1912; ø 23.9 mm, height 3.7 mm; 28 jewels; 28,800 vph; finely finished movement; 50-hour power reserve
Functions: hours, minutes, sweep seconds
Case: stainless steel, ø 36 mm; bezel in rose gold; sapphire crystal; transparent case back; crown in rose gold; water-resistant to 10 atm
Band: stainless steel with rose-gold middle links, double folding clasp
Price: $15,500
Variations: various cases and dials; with rubber strap

Cut

Reference number: 403267WW00
Movement: automatic, Hermès caliber H1912; ø 23.9 mm, height 3.7 mm; 28 jewels; 28,800 vph; finely finished movement; 50-hour power reserve
Functions: hours, minutes, sweep seconds
Case: stainless steel, ø 36 mm; bezel in rose gold set with 56 diamonds; sapphire crystal; transparent case back; crown in rose gold; water-resistant to 10 atm
Band: rubber, pin buckle
Price: $16,300
Variations: various cases and dials; with stainless steel-/rose- gold bracelet

Arceau Duc Attelé

Reference number: 403928WW00
Movement: hand-wound, Hermès caliber H1926;
ø 34 mm, height 16 mm; 54 jewels; 36,000 vph;
triple axis tourbillon with 25-second, 60-second, and
300-second rotation; open, sapphire-crystal chime
bridge; finely finished movement; 48-hour power
reserve
Functions: hours, minutes; minute repeater
Case: titanium, ø 43 mm; sapphire crystal; transparent
case back; water-resistant to 3 atm
Band: reptile skin, folding clasp
Remarks: guilloché dial with visible chiming mechanism
(hammers and gongs) inspired from a historic design by
Henri d'Origny from 1978
Price: $395,000; limited to 24 pieces

Arceau Chorus Stellarum

Reference number: 403493WW00
Movement: automatic, Hermès caliber H1837; ø 26 mm,
height 3.7 mm; 28,800 vph; finely finished movement;
50-hour power reserve
Functions: hours, minutes; animated automaton
("jacquemarts") activated by a pusher at 9 o'clock
Case: white gold, ø 41 mm; sapphire crystal; transparent
case back; water-resistant to 3 atm
Band: reptile skin, pin buckle
Remarks: inspired from a historic design by Henri
d'Origny from 1978
Price: $153,400; limited to 6 pieces

H08

Reference number: 060124WW00
Movement: automatic, Hermès caliber H1837; ø 26 mm,
height 3.7 mm; 28 jewels; 28,800 vph; 45-hour power
reserve
Functions: hours, minutes, sweep seconds; date
Case: titanium and rose gold, 39 mm x 39 mm; bezel
in ceramic; sapphire crystal; crown in ceramic; water-
resistant to 10 atm
Band: rubber, double folding clasp
Price: $15,900
Variations: with textile strap

Arceau Belles du Mexique

Reference number: 403414WW00
Movement: automatic, Hermès caliber H1912;
ø 23.9 mm, height 3.7 mm; 28 jewels; 28,800 vph; finely
finished movement; 50-hour power reserve
Functions: hours, minutes
Case: white gold, ø 38 mm, height 3.7 mm; bezel set
with 82 diamonds; sapphire crystal; transparent case
back; water-resistant to 3 atm
Band: reptile skin, pin buckle
Remarks: dial with hand-painted miniatures; limited to
12 pieces
Price: $74,000

Arceau Grand Tralala Brides et Mors

Reference number: 403428WW00
Movement: automatic, Hermès caliber H1912;
ø 23.9 mm, height 3.7 mm; 28 jewels; 28,800 vph; finely
finished movement; 50-hour power reserve
Functions: hours, minutes, subsidiary seconds
Case: rose gold, ø 34 mm, height 3.7 mm; bezel set with
64 diamonds; sapphire crystal; transparent case back;
water-resistant to 3 atm
Band: reptile skin, pin buckle
Remarks: dial set with 110 diamonds
Price: $47,250
Variations: with black dial and strap

Kelly

Reference number: 056854WW00
Movement: quartz
Functions: hours, minutes
Case: rose gold, set with 43 diamonds, 16 mm x 16 mm;
sapphire crystal; water-resistant to 3 atm
Band: rose gold, folding clasp set with 221 diamonds
Remarks: case as a detachable "padlock" on a rose-gold
Price: $37,600
Variations: with rose-gold strap fully set with diamonds;
in stainless steel

H. MOSER & CIE.

H. Moser & Cie has been making a name for itself in the industry as a serious watchmaker, though not averse to flashes of humor, like the Swiss Mad (sic) Watch made of Vacherin cheese it presented in 2017 (the cheese for the case is mixed with a hardening resin). And there's the Swiss Alp watch, made to look like an Apple Watch, but with all the essential Moser codes: streamlined design, top-notch technical implementation.

The company was originally founded in Le Locle in 1825 by one Heinrich Moser (1805–1874), from Schaffhausen, at the tender age of twenty-one. Soon after, he moved to Saint Petersburg, Russia, where ambitious watchmakers were enjoying a good market. In 1828, H. Moser & Cie. was brought to life—a brand later resuscitated in modern times by a group of investors and watch experts together with Moser's great-grandson, Roger Nicholas Balsiger.

With the support of a host of Swiss and German specialists, the company returned to quality fundamentals. Its claim to fame is movements that contain a separate, removable escapement module supporting the pallet lever, escape wheel, and balance. The latter is fitted with the Straumann spring, made by Precision Engineering, another one of the Moser Group companies.

This small company has considerable technical know-how, which is probably what attracted MELB Holding, owners of Hautlence, as an investor. Under a new CEO, the brand redefined its style: understatement, soft tones, humor, and subtle technicity. A buy-in to the Genevan movement maker Agenhor will no doubt extend the company's technical abilities.

Moser & Cie.'s three core collections—Endeavour, Venturer, and Pioneer—feature "clean" dials in solid colors, including the blackest black, called Vantablack. The month hand on the Endeavour is a mere arrowhead in the center of the dial that points to the hours, which double as the months. The minimalism extends to watches that would otherwise clamor for more complexity. The Streamliner collection will celebrate its fifth anniversary in 2025 and can be considered a successful modernization. Collaborations have also kept the brand fresh, notably in 2024 with the iconoclastic Underdog brand.

H. MOSER & CIE
Rundbuckstrasse 10
CH-8212 Neuhausen am Rheinfall
Switzerland

TEL.:
+41-52-674-0050

E-MAIL:
info@h-moser.com

WEBSITE:
www.h-moser.com

FOUNDED:
1828

NUMBER OF EMPLOYEES:
80+

ANNUAL PRODUCTION:
approx. 2,000 watches

U.S. DISTRIBUTOR:
Melb Americas
info@melb-americas.com
917-974-8245

MOST IMPORTANT COLLECTIONS/PRICE RANGE:
Endeavour / approx. $17,500 to $352,000; Pioneer / approx. $14,200 to $86,900; Streamliner / approx. $21,900 to $175,000; Heritage / approx. $15,300 to $290,000; concept watches

Streamliner Small Seconds Blue Enamel

Reference number: 6500-1200
Movement: automatic, Moser caliber HMC 500; ø 30 mm, height 4.5 mm; 26 jewels; 21,600 vph; escapement with Straumann hairspring platinum micro-rotor; 74-hour power reserve
Functions: hours, minutes, subsidiary seconds
Case: stainless steel, ø 39 mm, height 10.9 mm; sapphire crystal; transparent case back; water-resistant to 12 atm
Band: stainless steel, triple folding clasp
Remarks: enamel dial
Price: $32,900

Streamliner Tourbillon Skeleton

Reference number: 6814-1200
Movement: automatic, Moser caliber HMC 814; ø 32 mm, height 5.5 mm; 28 jewels; 21,600 vph; exchangeable escapement with a flying 1-minute tourbillon, Straumann double hairspring, completely skeletonized mainplate and ridges, and oscillating mass; 72-hour power reserve
Functions: hours, minutes
Case: stainless steel, ø 40 mm, height 12.1 mm; sapphire crystal; transparent case back; screw-down crown; water-resistant to 12 atm
Band: stainless steel, triple folding clasp
Remarks: skeletonized dial
Price: $86,900

Streamliner Concept Minute Repeater Tourbillon

Reference number: 6905-1200
Movement: hand-wound, HMC 905 caliber, ø 33 mm, height 9.62 mm; 35 jewels; 21,600 vph; exchangeable escapement with a flying 1-minute tourbillon, skeletonized tourbillon bridge, fine finishing on movement; 90-hour power reserve
Functions: hours, minutes, minute repeater
Case: stainless steel, ø 42.3 mm, height 14.4 mm; sapphire crystal; transparent case back; water-resistant to 5 atm
Band: stainless steel, triple folding clasp
Remarks: hammers and gongs arranged on the dial side; enamel dial; limited to 50 pieces
Price: $296,000

Streamliner Centre Seconds Purple Haze

Reference number: 6201-1201
Movement: automatic, Moser caliber HMC 201; ø 32 mm, height 5.5 mm; 27 jewels; 21,600 vph; escapement with Straumann hairspring; 72-hour power reserve
Functions: hours, minutes, sweep seconds
Case: stainless steel: ø 40 mm, height 12.1 mm; sapphire crystal; transparent case back; screw-down crown; water-resistant to 12 atm
Band: stainless steel, triple folding clasp
Price: $24,000
Variations: with a grey dial

Endeavour Perpetual Calendar "Passion Fruit"

Reference number: 1800-1200
Movement: hand-wound, Moser caliber HMC 800; ø 34 mm, height 6.3 mm; 32 jewels; 18,000 vph; exchangeable escapement with Straumann hairspring, "flash calendar" functions correctable forward and backward; twin spring barrels; fine finishing on movement; 168-hour power reserve
Functions: hours, minutes, subsidiary seconds; power reserve indicator; perpetual calendar with large date and small sweep month display; leap year display (movement side)
Case: stainless steel, ø 42 mm, height 12.8 mm; sapphire crystal; transparent case back; water-resistant to 3 atm
Band: kudu leather, folding clasp
Remarks: collaboration between H. Moser & Cie. and Studio UnderdOg; purple lacquer and fumé Grand Feu enamel dial
Price: $64,500 as a set with the Studio UnderdOg 03Series PassiOn Fruit (limited to 100 pieces)

03Series PassiOn Fruit

Reference number: 03OFB
Movement: hand-wound, Sellita caliber SW 510 M; ø 30 mm, height 6.3 mm; 23 jewels; 28,800 vph; monopusher chronograph; 63-hour power reserve
Functions: hours, minutes, subsidiary hacking seconds; chronograph with 30-minute totalizer
Case: stainless steel, ø 38.5 mm, height 12.6 mm; sapphire crystal; transparent case back; water-resistant to 3 atm
Band: calfskin, folding clasp
Remarks: collaboration between H. Moser & Cie. and Studio UnderdOg; purple lacquer and fumé Grand Feu enamel dial
Price: $64,500 as a set with Endeavour Perpetual Calendar "Passion Fruit" (limited to 100 pieces)

Pioneer Centre Seconds Concept Citrus Green

Reference number: 3201-1204
Movement: automatic, Moser caliber HMC 201; ø 32 mm, height 5.5 mm; 27 jewels; 21,600 vph; escapement with Straumann hairspring; 72-hour power reserve
Functions: hours, minutes, sweep seconds
Case: stainless steel: ø 42.8 mm, height 10.6 mm; sapphire crystal; transparent case back; screw-in crown; water-resistant to 12 atm
Band: rubber, pin buckle
Price: $15,900
Variations: various straps

Pioneer Retrograde Seconds Midnight Blue

Reference number: 3250-1200
Movement: automatic, Moser caliber HMC 201; ø 32 mm, height 6.5 mm; 31 jewels; 21,600 vph; movement with Moser strip decoration; escapement with Straumann hairspring; 72-hour power reserve
Functions: hours, minutes, retrograde seconds (at 6 o'clock)
Case: stainless steel; ø 42.8 mm, height 14.2 mm; sapphire crystal; transparent case back; screw-in crown; water-resistant to 12 atm
Band: rubber, pin buckle
Remarks: midnight-blue fumé dial
Price: $21,900
Variations: comes with leather strap or stainless-steel bracelet

Pioneer Tourbillon Arctic Blue

Reference number: 3804-1208
Movement: automatic, Moser caliber HMC 804; ø 32 mm, height 5.5 mm; 21,600 vph; exchangeable escapement with Straumann double hairspring, flying one-minute tourbillon, skeletonized bridges with black PVD, oscillating mass in red gold; 72-hour power reserve
Functions: hours, minutes
Case: stainless steel, ø 42.8 mm, height 10.8 mm; sapphire crystal; transparent case back; screw-in crown; water-resistant to 12 atm
Band: rubber, folding clasp
Price: $54,900
Variations: various straps

Endeavour Chinese Calendar Limited Edition

Reference number: 1210-0400
Movement: automatic, Moser caliber HMC 210; ø 32 mm, height 8.1 mm; 33 jewels; 21,600 vph; exchangeable escapement with Straumann hairspring, finely finished movement; 72-hour power reserve
Functions: hours, minutes, subsidiary seconds; date, Chinese calendar with month, moon phase, leap month, year
Case: red gold, ø 40 mm, height 13 mm; sapphire crystal; transparent case back; water-resistant to 3 atm
Band: reptile skin, folding clasp
Remarks: limited to 100 pieces
Price: $74,800

Endeavour Chronograph H. Moser X Massena Lab

Reference number: 1220-1200
Movement: automatic, Moser caliber HMC 220; ø 32 mm, height 8.4 mm; 51 jewels; 21,600 vph; exchangeable escapement with Straumann hairspring, bidirectional pawl winding system; finely finished with Moser stripes; 72-hour power reserve
Functions: hours, minutes, subsidiary seconds; chronograph (with 45-minute counter); tachymetric scale
Case: stainless steel, ø 41 mm, height 13.3 mm; sapphire crystal; transparent case back; water-resistant to 3 atm
Remarks: blue fumé dial with sunburst pattern
Band: kudu leather, pin buckle
Price: $27,600; limited to 100 pieces

Heritage Dual Time

Reference number: 8809-1200
Movement: automatic, Moser caliber HMC 809; ø 32 mm, height 6 mm; 27 jewels; 21,600 vph; 72 hours power reserve
Functions: hours, minutes, sweep seconds; additional 12-hour display (second time zone); date
Case: stainless steel, ø 42 mm, height 11.6 mm; sapphire crystal; transparent case back; water-resistant to 3 atm
Band: kudu leather, buckle
Remarks: burgundy dial with sunburst pattern
Price: $21,900

Caliber HMC 812

Hand-wound; exchangeable escapement with gold pallet lever and escape wheel; "flash calendar" functions correctable forward and backward; twin 2 spring barrels; 168-hour power reserve
Functions: hours, minutes, sweep seconds; power reserve indicator; perpetual calendar with date, sweep month, leap year indicator on movement side
Diameter: 34 mm
Height: 6.3 mm
Jewels: 33
Balance: glucydur
Frequency: 18,000 vph
Hairspring: Straumann
Shock protection: Incabloc

Caliber HMC 500

Automatic; platinum micro-rotor; double spring barrel, 74-hour power reserve
Functions: hours, minutes, subsidiary seconds
Diameter: 30 mm
Height: 4.5 mm
Jewels: 26
Frequency: 21,600 vph
Balance spring: Straumann
Remarks: finely finished movement

Caliber HMC 210

Automatic; exchangeable escapement; double spring barrel, 72-hour power reserve
Functions: hours, minutes, subsidiary seconds; date, Chinese calendar with month, moon phases, leap month, year
Diameter: 32 mm
Height: 8.1 mm
Jewels: 33
Frequency: 21,600 vph
Balance spring: Straumann
Remarks: red-gold oscillating mass; finely finished movement

HUBLOT

Ever since Hublot moved into a new, modern, spacious factory building in Nyon, near Geneva, the brand has evolved with stunning speed. The growth has been such that Hublot has even built a second factory, which is even bigger than the first. The ground-breaking ceremony took place on March 3, 2014, and the man holding the spade was then-Hublot chairman Jean-Claude Biver, who now also heads LVMH Group's Watch Division.

Hublot grew and continues to grow thanks to a combination of innovative watchmaking and vigorous communication. It was together with current CEO Ricardo Guadalupe that Biver developed the idea of fusing different and at times incompatible materials in a watch: carbon composite and gold, ceramic and steel, denim and diamonds. In 2011, the brand introduced the first scratchproof precious metal, an alloy of gold and ceramic named "Magic Gold." In 2014, Hublot came out with a watch whose dial is made of osmium, one of the world's rarest metals. Using a new patented process, Hublot has also implemented a unique concept of cutting wafer-thin bits of glass that are set in the open spaces of a skeletonized movement plate.

The "art of fusion" tagline drove the brand into all sorts of technical and scientific partnerships and created a buzz that is ongoing, apparently, regardless of the economic environment. Hublot's concept is based on the idea of "being the first, different and unique." To achieve that goal, it has associated its name with major sports events and brands, and has created technoid, martial, exuberant, eye-burning timepieces that holler rather than merely display the time.

The models in the constantly expanding Classic Fusion Original collection look like good old friends. With their clean lines and reduced dimensions, they are very similar to the original Hublot timepieces from the 1980s. *La Montre des Montres* (MDM) is what Hublot inventor Carlo Crocco once called his creation, "the watch of all watches." In any case, the watches, which are also available in classic precious metals, form a stylistic counterpoint to the frenzied, colorful, effusive devices for which the brand is known.

HUBLOT SA
Chemin de la Vuarpillière 33
CH-1260 Nyon
Switzerland

TEL.:
+41-22-990-9000

E-MAIL:
info@hublot.ch

WEBSITE:
www.hublot.com

FOUNDED:
1980

NUMBER OF EMPLOYEES:
over 800 worldwide

ANNUAL PRODUCTION:
approx. 50,000 watches

U.S BRANCH:
2455 E Sunrise Blvd, #402
Fort Lauderdale, FL 33304
954-568-9400

MOST IMPORTANT COLLECTIONS/PRICE RANGE:
Big Bang / $11,000 to $1,053,000; Classic Fusion
/ $5,200 to $474,000; Manufacture Piece (MP) /
$82,000 to $579,000

MP-10 Tourbillon Weight Energy System Titanium

Reference number: 910.NX.0001.RX
Movement: hand-wound, caliber HUB 9013; 66 jewels;1-minute tourbillon, mounted at 35°; two moving linear winding weights; 48-hour power reserve
Functions: hours and minutes (shown on black anodized aluminum drums), subsidiary seconds (on the tourbillon cage); power reserve indicator
Case: titanium, 41.4 mm x 54.1 mm, height 22.4 mm; sapphire crystal; transparent case back; water-resistant to 3 atm
Band: rubber, folding clasp
Price: $275,000; limited to 50 pieces

MP-11 14-Day Power Reserve Water Blue Sapphire

Reference number: 911.JL.0129.RX
Movement: hand-wound, caliber HUB 9011; ø 34 mm, height 10.95 mm; 39 jewels; 28,800 vph; 7 mainsprings stacked perpendicular to the mechanism axes, force deflection via helical gears; anthracite-coated bridges; 336-hour power reserve
Functions: hours and minutes (off-center); power reserve indicator
Case: sapphire crystal, ø 45 mm, height 14.4 mm; bezel mounted to case with 6 titanium screws; sapphire crystal; transparent case back; water-resistant to 3 atm
Band: rubber, folding clasp
Remarks: sapphire crystal-dial
Price: $171,000; limited to 50 pieces

Big Bang Unico Green Saxem

Reference number: 441.JG.4990.RT
Movement: automatic, caliber HUB 1280 "Unico"; ø 30.4 mm, height 6.75 mm; 43 jewels; 28,800 vph; 72-hour power reserve
Functions: hours, minutes, subsidiary seconds; flyback chronograph; date
Case: synthetic sapphire ("Saxem"), ø 42 mm, height 14.5 mm; bezel mounted to case with 6 titanium screws; sapphire crystal; transparent case back; water-resistant to 5 atm
Band: rubber, folding clasp
Price: $121,000; limited to 100 pieces

Big Bang Unico Dark Green Ceramic

Reference number: 441.GX.5210.RX
Movement: automatic, caliber HUB 1280 "Unico 2"; ø 30.4 mm, height 6.75 mm; 43 jewels; 28,800 vph; 72-hour power reserve
Functions: hours, minutes, subsidiary seconds; flyback chronograph; date
Case: ceramic, ø 42 mm, height 14.5 mm; bezel mounted to case with 6 titanium screws; sapphire crystal; transparent case back; water-resistant to 10 atm
Band: rubber, folding clasp
Price: $24,100

Big Bang Unico Orange Ceramic

Reference number: 441.CU.5910.RX
Movement: automatic, caliber HUB 1280 "Unico 2"; ø 30.4 mm, height 6.75 mm; 43 jewels; 28,800 vph; 72-hour power reserve
Functions: hours, minutes, subsidiary seconds; flyback chronograph; date
Case: ceramic, ø 42 mm, height 14.5 mm; bezel mounted to case with 6 titanium screws; sapphire crystal; transparent case back; water-resistant to 10 atm
Band: rubber, folding clasp
Price: $29,600; limited to 250 pieces

Big Bang Integral Time Only Titanium 38mm

Reference number: 457.NX.7170.NX
Movement: automatic, caliber HUB 1115 (Sellita SW300-1a base); ø 25.6 mm, height 3.6 mm; 25 jewels; 28,800 vph; 48-hour power reserve
Functions: hours, minutes, sweep seconds; date
Case: titanium, ø 38 mm, height 9.4 mm; bezel mounted to case with 6 titanium screws; sapphire crystal; transparent case back; water-resistant to 10 atm
Band: titanium, folding clasp
Price: $13,100
Variations: comes in various colors

Big Bang Integral Time Only King Gold 38mm

Reference number: 457.OX.1280.OX
Movement: automatic, caliber HUB 1115 (Sellita SW300-1a base); ø 25.6 mm, height 3.6 mm; 25 jewels; 28,800 vph; 48-hour power reserve
Functions: hours, minutes, sweep seconds; date
Case: rose gold, ø 38 mm, height 9.4 mm; bezel mounted to case with 6 titanium screws; sapphire crystal; transparent case back; water-resistant to 10 atm
Band: rose gold, folding clasp
Price: $47,100
Variations: comes in various colors

Big Bang Integral Time Only Black Magic 38mm

Reference number: 457.CX.1270.CX
Movement: automatic, caliber HUB 1115 (Sellita SW300-1a base); ø 25.6 mm, height 3.6 mm; 25 jewels; 28,800 vph; 48-hour power reserve
Functions: hours, minutes, sweep seconds; date
Case: ceramic, ø 38 mm, height 9.4 mm; bezel mounted to case with 6 titanium screws; sapphire crystal; transparent case back; water-resistant to 10 atm
Band: ceramic, folding clasp
Price: $15,300

Big Bang Integrated Time Only Blue Indigo Ceramic 40mm

Reference number: 456.EX.5129.EX
Movement: automatic, caliber HUB 1710 (Zenith Elite 670 base); ø 26.2 mm, height 3.7 mm; 27 jewels; 28,800 vph; 50-hour power reserve
Functions: hours, minutes, sweep seconds; date
Case: ceramic, ø 40 mm, height 9.35 mm; bezel mounted to case with 6 titanium screws; sapphire crystal; transparent case back; water-resistant to 10 atm
Band: ceramic, folding clasp
Remarks: sapphire crystal-dial
Price: $20,800; limited to 200 pieces

Big Bang Integrated Time Only Sky Blue Ceramic 40mm

Reference number: 456.EX.5120.EX
Movement: automatic, caliber HUB 1710 (Zenith Elite 670 base); ø 26.2 mm, height 3.7 mm; 27 jewels; 28,800 vph; 50-hour power reserve
Functions: hours, minutes, sweep seconds; date
Case: ceramic, ø 40 mm, height 9.35 mm; bezel mounted to case with 6 titanium screws; sapphire crystal; transparent case back; water-resistant to 10 atm
Band: ceramic, folding clasp
Remarks: sapphire crystal-dial
Price: $20,800; limited to 200 pieces

Classic Fusion Tourbillon Orlinski Sky Blue

Reference number: 505.ES.5129.RX.ORL24
Movement: hand-wound, caliber HUB 6021; ø 34 mm, height 5.7 mm; 25 jewels; 21,600 vph; 1-minute tourbillon; fully skeletonized movement; 115-hour power reserve
Functions: hours, minutes; power reserve indicator
Case: ceramic, ø 45 mm, height 12 mm; bezel mounted to case with 6 titanium screws; sapphire crystal; transparent case back; water-resistant to 3 atm
Band: rubber, folding clasp
Price: $99,000; limited to 30 pieces

Classic Fusion Tourbillon Orlinski Yellow Ceramic

Reference number: 505.CY.119Y.RX.ORL24
Movement: hand-wound, caliber HUB 6021; ø 34 mm, height 5.7 mm; 25 jewels; 21,600 vph; 1-minute tourbillon; fully skeletonized movement; 115-hour power reserve
Functions: hours, minutes; power reserve indicator
Case: ceramic, ø 45 mm, height 12 mm; bezel mounted to case with 6 titanium screws; sapphire crystal; transparent case back; water-resistant to 3 atm
Band: rubber, folding clasp
Price: $99,000; limited to 30 pieces

Spirit of Big Bang Tourbillon 5-Day Power Reserve Carbon Orange

Reference number: 645.QO.4710.RX
Movement: hand-wound, caliber HUB 6020; ø 31.65 mm, height 5.7 mm; 25 jewels; 21,600 vph; 1-minute tourbillon; skeletonized movement; 115-hour power reserve
Functions: hours and minutes (off-center); power reserve indicator
Case: carbon with micro-glass fibers, 42 mm x 51 mm, height 15.3 mm; bezel mounted to case with 6 titanium screws; sapphire crystal; transparent case back; water-resistant to 3 atm
Band: rubber, folding clasp
Price: $105,000; limited to 50 pieces

Spirit of Big Bang Steel Rainbow

Reference number: 682.SX.9900.LR.0999
Movement: automatic, caliber HUB 1120 (Sellita SW300-1 base); ø 25.6 mm, height 3.6 mm; 25 jewels; 28,800 vph; 40-hour power reserve
Functions: hours, minutes, sweep seconds; date
Case: stainless steel, set with 96 colored stones, ø 32 mm, height 11.1 mm; bezel set with 58 colored stones, mounted to case with 6 titanium screws; sapphire crystal; water-resistant to 10 atm
Band: rubber with reptile skin insert, folding clasp
Remarks: dial set with 339 precious stones
Price: $75,800

Spirit of Big Bang Steel Full Pavé

Reference number: 682.SX.9000.RX.1604
Movement: automatic, caliber HUB 1120 (Sellita SW300-1 base); ø 25.6 mm, height 3.6 mm; 25 jewels; 28,800 vph; 40-hour power reserve
Functions: hours, minutes, sweep seconds; date
Case: stainless steel, set with 96 synthetic diamonds, ø 32 mm, height 11.1 mm; bezel set with 58 synthetic diamonds, mounted to case with 6 titanium screws; sapphire crystal; water-resistant to 10 atm
Band: rubber, folding clasp
Remarks: dial set with 339 diamonds
Price: $36,200

Square Bang Unico Titanium Blue

Reference number: 821.NX.5170.RX
Movement: automatic, caliber HUB 1280 "Unico 2"; ø 30.4 mm, height 6.75 mm; 43 jewels; 28,800 vph; mainplate and bridges with grey coating; 72-hour power reserve
Functions: hours, minutes, subsidiary seconds; chronograph; date
Case: titanium, 42 mm x 42 mm, height 14.7 mm; bezel mounted to case with 6 titanium screws; sapphire crystal; screw-down crown; water-resistant to 10 atm
Band: rubber, folding clasp
Price: $24,100
Variations: different case variants

Square Bang Unico King Gold Blue

Reference number: 821.OX.5180.RX
Movement: automatic, caliber HUB 1280 "Unico 2"; ø 30.4 mm, height 6.75 mm; 43 jewels; 28,800 vph; mainplate and bridges with grey coating; 72-hour power reserve
Functions: hours, minutes, subsidiary seconds; chronograph; date
Case: rose gold, 42 mm x 42 mm, height 14.7 mm; bezel mounted to case with 6 titanium screws; sapphire crystal; screw-down crown; water-resistant to 10 atm
Band: rubber, folding clasp
Price: $44,900
Variations: different case variants

Square Bang Unico Full Magic Gold

Reference number: 821.MX.0130.RX
Movement: automatic, caliber HUB 1280 "Unico 2"; ø 30.4 mm, height 6.75 mm; 43 jewels; 28,800 vph; mainplate and bridges with grey coating; 72-hour power reserve
Functions: hours, minutes, subsidiary seconds; chronograph; date
Case: gold-ceramic alloy ("Magic Gold"), 42 mm x 42 mm, height 14.7 mm; bezel mounted to case with 6 titanium screws; sapphire crystal; screw-down crown; water-resistant to 10 atm
Band: rubber, folding clasp
Price: $42,700
Variations: different case variants

Caliber HUB 9011

Hand-wound; 7 mainsprings stacked perpendicular to the mechanism axes, force deflection via helical gears; 336-hour power reserve
Functions: hours and minutes (off-center); power reserve indicator
Diameter: 34 mm
Height: 10.95 mm
Jewels: 39
Frequency: 28,800 vph
Hairspring: silicon hairspring
Shock protection: Incabloc
Remarks: anthracite-colored mainplate and bridges; 270 parts

Caliber HUB 1280

Automatic; column wheel control of chronograph functions; silicon pallet lever and escapement, removable escapement; double-pawl automatic winding (Pellaton system), winding rotor with ceramic ball bearing; single spring barrel; 72-hour power reserve
Functions: hours, minutes, subsidiary seconds; flyback chronograph; date
Diameter: 30 mm
Height: 6.75 mm
Jewels: 43
Balance: glucydur
Frequency: 28,800 vph
Balance spring: flat hairspring with fine adjustment
Shock protection: Incabloc
Remarks: 354 parts

Caliber HUB 6035

Automatic; flying 1-minute tourbillon; off-center microrotor, skeletonized movement; single mainspring barrel, 72-hour power reserve
Functions: hours, minutes
Diameter: 34 mm
Height: 5.7 mm
Jewels: 26
Balance: glucydur
Frequency: 21,600 vph
Hairspring: flat hairspring with fine adjustment
Shock protection: Incabloc
Remarks: 282 parts

ITAY NOY

Our relationship to precious objects is complex and ultimately reveals as much about ourselves as about the object. Itay Noy's collections, always limited editions, are each unique in their look and feel. No doubt about it: his watches will foster conversations with the outside world and with the wearer as well. They are each a talking piece for the public, a touchstone for the owner.

Noy, who hails from and lives in Israel, began his journey into watchmaking around 2000 with the City Squares model, which shows time on the backdrop of a map of the owner's favorite or native city. In 2013, Noy showcased a square watch run on a Technotime automatic movement with a face-like dial—well before another famous watchmaker did the same—that changes with the movement of the hands, a tongue-in-cheek reminder of our daily communication with our phones and the meaning of the frame.

Exploring this intimacy between the watch and the owner is an endless source of inspiration for Noy, a jeweler by trade who, with time, as it were, has begun reaching into the engineer's magic box. He has even worked on a bespoke movement with a Swiss firm.

An attempt to woo time itself is demonstrated in the Time Tone collection with another "dynamic dial," to use Noy's term. This watch gives the owner the choice of a colored disk acting as an hour hand that only he or she will know, while the minute hand does its work in the center of the dial.

Not having any brand managers breathing down his neck has given Noy the freedom to create all sorts of ways of displaying time. For instance, the Full Month shows the date or the moon appearing through a circle of digits carved into the dial. ReOrder has the hours digitally flashing on a sandwich dial, haphazardly it would seem. Another rearrangement of the time comes with the Time Quarters, whose dial is divided into four independent quadrants. As for Part Time, the most recent production, it does the most logical thing: dividing the dial in two, or, day and night.

ITAY NOY
19 Mazal Arieh,
Old Jaffa
Israel

TEL.:
+972-352-473-80

FAX:
+972-352-473-81

E-MAIL (FOR CUSTOMER QUESTIONS):
studio@itay-noy.com

WEBSITE:
www.itay-noy.com

FOUNDED:
2000

NUMBER OF EMPLOYEES:
4

ANNUAL PRODUCTION:
150

DISTRIBUTION:
Please contact Studio Itay Noy for information.
www.itay-noy.com

MOST IMPORTANT COLLECTIONS/PRICE RANGE:
Time Quarters, ReOrder, Full Month, Chrono Gears,
Part Time and Seven-Day Cycle / $2,800–$16,800

Shabbat

Reference number: SDC-SHABBAT
Movement: automatic, INS200; ø 29 mm, height 5.05 mm; 26 jewels; 28,800 vph; 38-hour power reserve
Functions: hours, minutes, sweep seconds, quick-set date, and day window
Case: stainless steel, ø 40 mm, height 8.4 mm; sapphire crystal; screw-down case back; water-resistant to 5 atm
Band: leather, folding clasp
Price: $4,900; limited edition and numbered 77 pieces

Identity Hebrew

Reference number: ID-HEB.BL
Movement: automatic, ETA caliber 2824-2; ø 25.6 mm, height 4.6 mm; 25 jewels; 28,800 vph; 38-hour power reserve
Functions: hours, minutes, sweep seconds, quick-set date window
Case: stainless steel, ø 42.4 mm, height 10 mm; sapphire crystal; screw-down case back; water-resistant to 5 atm
Band: leather, folding clasp
Price: $2,800; limited to 99 numbered pieces
Variations: black or brown leather band

Night Flight Jerusalem

Reference number: NF.Jerusalem
Movement: hand-wound, ETA caliber 6497-1; ø 36.6 mm, height 4.5 mm; 17 jewels; 18,000 vph; 38-hour power reserve
Functions: hours, minutes, subsidiary seconds
Case: stainless steel with black PVD, ø 44 mm, height 12 mm; sapphire crystal dome; transparent case back; water-resistant to 5 atm
Band: leather, double folding clasp
Remarks: dial made of layers of lacquer combined with gold
Price: $16,800
Variations: different cities around the world available

Seven-Day Cycle

Reference number: SDC.WT
Movement: automatic, INS200 caliber; ø 29 mm, height 5.05 mm; 26 jewels; 28,800 vph; 38-hour power reserve
Functions: hours, minutes, sweep seconds, quick-set date, and day window
Case: stainless steel, ø 40 mm, height 8.4 mm; sapphire crystal; screw-down case back; water-resistant to 5 atm
Band: hand-made leather band; double folding clasp
Price: $4,900; limited to 77 numbered pieces

Full Month

Reference number: FM-NUM.WT
Movement: automatic, IN.VMF5400 caliber; ø 30 mm, height 3 mm; 29 jewels; 21,600 vph; extra-thin micro-rotor; 48-hour power reserve
Functions: hours, minutes, subsidiary seconds; full date window
Case: stainless steel, 40 mm x 44 mm, height 7.44 mm; sapphire crystal; transparent case back; water-resistant to 5 atm
Band: hand-made leather band, double folding clasp
Price: $12,800; limited to 18 numbered pieces
Variations: black or brown leather band

ReOrder

Reference number: RO.WT
Movement: hand-wound, IN.IP13 caliber; ø 36.6 mm, height 5.5 mm; 20 jewels; 21,600 vph; 42-hour power reserve
Functions: dynamic dial with 12 digit-shaped windows indicating the hours, minutes, and central seconds
Case: stainless steel, ø 44 mm, height 12 mm; sapphire crystal; transparent case back; water-resistant to 5 atm
Band: hand-made leather band, double folding clasp
Price: $6,800; limited to 24 numbered pieces
Variations: blue, white, and gold plated

Part Time

Reference number: PT-DN.BL
Movement: hand-wound, IN.DD&6498-1 caliber; ø 36.6mm, height 5.2 mm; 17 Jewels; 21,600 vph; 46-hour power reserve
Functions: analog hours from 6am-6pm, and from 6pm-6am; moon disk, sun disk, minutes, subsidiary seconds
Case: stainless steel, ø 41.6 mm x 44.6 mm, height 10.6 mm; sapphire crystal; transparent case back; water-resistant to 5 atm
Band: leather band, double folding clasp
Price: $6,800; limited edition of 24 numbered pieces
Variations: blue or black

Celestial Time

Reference number: CT.W
Movement: hand-wound, IN.AR caliber; ø 36.6 mm, height 5.5 mm; 20 jewels; 18,000 vph; 46-hour power reserve
Functions: dynamic dial with zodiac hour disc, minutes, and sweep seconds
Case: stainless steel, ø 44 mm, height 12 mm; sapphire crystal dome; transparent case back; water-resistant to 5 atm
Band: handmade leather band, double folding clasp
Price: $5,800; limited edition of 24 numbered pieces
Variations: Western or Chinese zodiac signs

Time Quarters

Reference number: TT.4C
Movement: hand-wound, IN.AR caliber; ø 36.6 mm, height 5.5 mm; 20 jewels; 18,000 vph; power reserve 46 hours.
Functions: dynamic dial with 4 time-display windows indicating, hours, minutes, and central seconds
Case: stainless steel, ø 44 mm, height 12 mm; sapphire crystal; transparent case back; water-resistant to 5 atm
Band: hand-made leather band, double folding clasp
Price: $6,800; limited edition of 24 numbered pieces
Variations: yellow, red, green or 4-color time-displays

IWC

It was an American who laid the cornerstone for an industrial watch factory in Schaffhausen—now environmentally state-of-the-art facilities. In 1868, Florentine Ariosto Jones, a watchmaker and engineer from Boston, moved to then low-wage Switzerland to open the International Watch Company Schaffhausen.

Jones was a talented designer, who had a significant influence on the development of watch movements. Soon, he gave IWC its own seal of approval, the *Ingenieursmarke* (Engineer's Brand), a standard it still maintains today. The company has maintained its codes more or less ever since. The portfolio includes the rugged and sportive Pilot and Big Pilot watches, the refined Da Vincis, elegant Portofinos, and complicated Portugieser, which was named for two Portuguese fellows who went to Schaffhausen to commission a super-precise watch.

IWC movements include the Jones caliber, named for the IWC founder, and the pocket watch caliber 89, introduced in 1946 as the creation of then technical director Albert Pellaton. Four years later, Pellaton created the first IWC automatic movement. In 2020, IWC decided to equip all the Portuguese models with in-house calibers, including the automatic 52000 and 82000 caliber families, which use Pellaton or double-pawl winding mechanisms.

While pilot's watches play an important role in IWC's portfolio, with the broad Top Gun line including some models in ceramic cases, the flagship model is undoubtedly the Portugieser. The reference 325 from 1939, which was in fact a pocket watch inside a wristwatch case, was inspired by the early observation watches for seafaring. With its large, high-precision movements and easy-to-read dials, the Portugieser embodies IWC's heritage in the field of technical and professional watches.

The DNA of an instrument can also be recognized in the top model of the current collection, the Eternal Calendar with its secular calendar display and the unprecedented accuracy of the moon phase display, which is programmed to last an incredible 45 million years. The IWC Portugieser Eternal Calendar is thus the ultimate proof of the brand's great goal: engineering beyond time.

INTERNATIONAL WATCH CO.
Baumgartenstrasse 15
CH-8201 Schaffhausen
Switzerland

TEL.:
+41-52-635-6565

E-MAIL:
info@iwc.com

WEBSITE:
www.iwc.com

FOUNDED:
1868

NUMBER OF EMPLOYEES:
approx. 750

U.S. DISTRIBUTOR:
IWC North America
645 Fifth Avenue, 5th Floor
New York, NY 10022
800-432-9330

MOST IMPORTANT COLLECTIONS/PRICE RANGE:
Da Vinci, Pilot's, Portugieser, Ingenieur, Aquatimer, Pallweber / approx. $4,000 to $260,000

Ingenieur Automatic 40

Reference number: IW328901
Movement: automatic, IWC caliber 32111; ø 28.2 mm, height 3.77 mm; 21 jewels; 28,800 vph; finely finished with côtes de Genève; 120-hour power reserve
Functions: hours, minutes, sweep seconds; date
Case: stainless steel, ø 40 mm, height 10.7 mm; bezel mounted to case with five visible screws; sapphire crystal; water-resistant to 10 atm
Band: stainless steel, folding clasp with fine adjustment
Remarks: antimagnetic to 40,000 A/m using soft iron core
Price: $11,700
Variations: various dial colors; in titanium ($14,600)

Ingenieur Automatic 40

Reference number: IW328903
Movement: automatic, IWC caliber 32111; ø 28.2 mm, height 3.77 mm; 21 jewels; 28,800 vph; finely finished with côtes de Genève; 120-hour power reserve
Functions: hours, minutes, sweep seconds; date
Case: stainless steel, ø 40 mm, height 10.7 mm; bezel mounted to case with five visible screws; sapphire crystal; water-resistant to 10 atm
Band: stainless steel, folding clasp with fine adjustment
Remarks: antimagnetic to 40,000 A/m using soft iron core
Price: $11,700
Variations: various dial colors; in titanium ($14,600)

Ingenieur Automatic 40

Reference number: IW328904
Movement: automatic, IWC caliber 32111; ø 28.2 mm, height 3.77 mm; 21 jewels; 28,800 vph; finely finished with côtes de Genève; 120-hour power reserve
Functions: hours, minutes, sweep seconds; date
Case: titanium, ø 40 mm, height 10.7 mm; bezel mounted to case with five visible screws; sapphire crystal; water-resistant to 10 atm
Band: titanium, folding clasp with fine adjustment
Remarks: antimagnetic to 40,000 A/m using soft iron core
Price: $14,600
Variations: in stainless steel with various dial colors ($11,700)

Portugieser Automatic 42

Reference number: IW501701
Movement: automatic, IWC caliber 52011; ø 37.8 mm, height 7.5 mm; 31 jewels; 28,800 vph; Pellaton winding system; finely finished with côtes de Genève; 168-hour power reserve
Functions: hours, minutes, subsidiary seconds; power reserve indicator; date
Case: stainless steel, ø 42.4 mm, height 12.9 mm; sapphire crystal; transparent case back; water-resistant to 5 atm
Band: reptile skin, folding clasp
Price: $13,500
Variations: red gold case ($25,000)

Portugieser Perpetual Calendar 44

Reference number: IW503701
Movement: automatic, IWC caliber 52616; ø 37.8 mm, height 9 mm; 54 jewels; 28,800 vph; Breguet hairspring, gold oscillating mass; 168-hour power reserve
Functions: hours, minutes, subsidiary seconds; power reserve indicator; perpetual calendar with date, weekday, month, moon phase, year display (four digits)
Case: red gold, ø 44.4 mm, height 14.9 mm; sapphire crystal; transparent case back; water-resistant to 5 atm
Band: reptile skin, folding clasp
Price: $46,500

Portugieser Eternal Calendar

Reference number: IW505701
Movement: automatic, IWC caliber 52640; ø 37.8 mm, height 9 mm; 54 jewels; 28,800 vph; Breguet hairspring, gold oscillating mass; 168-hour power reserve
Functions: hours, minutes, subsidiary seconds; power reserve indicator; perpetual calendar with date, weekday, month, double moon phase, year display
Case: platinum, ø 44.4 mm, height 14.9 mm; sapphire crystal; transparent case back; water-resistant to 5 atm
Band: reptile skin, folding clasp
Remarks: the secular perpetual calendar takes the irregularities of the Gregorian calendar until the year 3999; the moon phase displays have been deemed accurate for 45 million years.
Price: $150,000

Portugieser Chronograph

Reference number: IW371624
Movement: automatic, IWC caliber 69355; ø 30 mm, height 7 mm; 27 jewels; 28,800 vph; finely finished with côtes de Genève; 46-hour power reserve
Functions: hours, minutes, subsidiary seconds; chronograph
Case: stainless steel, ø 41 mm, height 13.1 mm; sapphire crystal; water-resistant to 3 atm
Band: reptile skin, double folding clasp
Price: $8,400

Portugieser Automatic 42

Reference number: IW501705
Movement: automatic, IWC caliber 52011; ø 37.8 mm, height 7.5 mm; 31 jewels; 28,800 vph; Pellaton winding system; finely finished with côtes de Genève; 168-hour power reserve
Functions: hours, minutes, subsidiary seconds; power reserve indicator; date
Case: stainless steel, ø 42.4 mm, height 13 mm; sapphire crystal; transparent case back; water-resistant to 5 atm
Band: reptile skin, folding clasp
Price: $13,500

Portugieser Perpetual Calendar 44

Reference number: IW503704
Movement: automatic, IWC caliber 52616; ø 37.8 mm, height 9 mm; 54 jewels; 28,800 vph; Breguet hairspring, gold oscillating mass; 168-hour power reserve
Functions: hours, minutes, subsidiary seconds; power reserve indicator; perpetual calendar with date, weekday, month, moon phase, year display (four digits)
Case: white gold, ø 44.4 mm, height 14.9 mm; sapphire crystal; transparent case back; water-resistant to 5 atm
Band: reptile skin, folding clasp
Price: $47,500

Portugieser Chronograph

Reference number: IW371625
Movement: automatic, IWC caliber 69355; ø 30 mm, height 7 mm; 27 jewels; 28,800 vph; finely finished with côtes de Genève; 46-hour power reserve
Functions: hours, minutes, subsidiary seconds; chronograph
Case: red gold, ø 41 mm, height 13.1 mm; sapphire crystal; water-resistant to 3 atm
Band: reptile skin, double folding clasp
Price: $19,200

Portugieser Automatic 42

Reference number: IW501707
Movement: automatic, IWC caliber 52011; ø 37.8 mm, height 7.5 mm; 31 jewels; 28,800 vph; Pellaton winding system; finely finished with côtes de Genève; 168-hour power reserve
Functions: hours, minutes, subsidiary seconds; power reserve indicator; date
Case: red gold, ø 42.4 mm, height 12.9 mm; sapphire crystal; transparent case back; water-resistant to 5 atm
Band: reptile skin, folding clasp
Price: $26,700

Portugieser Perpetual Calendar 44

Reference number: IW503702
Movement: automatic, IWC caliber 52616; ø 37.8 mm, height 9 mm; 54 jewels; 28,800 vph; Breguet hairspring, gold oscillating mass; 168-hour power reserve
Functions: hours, minutes, subsidiary seconds; power reserve indicator; perpetual calendar with date, weekday, month, moon phase, year display (four digits)
Case: red gold, ø 44.4 mm, height 14.9 mm; sapphire crystal; transparent case back; water-resistant to 5 atm
Band: reptile skin, folding clasp
Price: $46,500

Pilot's Watch Chronograph 41 Top Gun Oceana

Reference number: IW389404
Movement: automatic, IWC caliber 69380; ø 30 mm, height 7.9 mm; 33 jewels; 28,800 vph; 46-hour power reserve
Functions: hours, minutes, subsidiary seconds; chronograph; date and weekday
Case: ceramic, ø 41.9 mm, height 15.5 mm; sapphire crystal; transparent case back; screw-down crown; water-resistant to 10 atm
Band: rubber with textile insert, pin buckle
Price: $11,700

Pilot's Watch Chronograph Top Gun Edition Lake Tahoe

Reference number: IW389105
Movement: automatic, IWC caliber 69380; ø 30 mm, height 7.9 mm; 33 jewels; 28,800 vph; 46-hour power reserve
Functions: hours, minutes, subsidiary seconds; chronograph; date and weekday
Case: ceramic, ø 44.5 mm, height 15.7 mm; sapphire crystal; transparent case back; screw-down crown; water-resistant to 8 atm
Band: rubber with textile insert, pin buckle
Price: $12,500

Big Pilot's Watch Perpetual Calendar Top Gun Ceratanium

Reference number: IW503604
Movement: automatic, IWC caliber 52615; ø 37.8 mm, height 9 mm; 54 jewels; 28,800 vph; Pellaton winding; 168-hour power reserve
Functions: hours, minutes, subsidiary seconds; power-reserve indicator; perpetual calendar with date, weekday, month, moon phase, year display (four digits)
Case: special alloy based on ceramic and titanium (Ceratanium), ø 46.2 mm, height 15.4 mm; sapphire crystal; transparent case back; screw-in crown; water-resistant to 6 atm
Band: Ceratanium, folding clasp
Price: $56,700

Caliber 32111

Automatic; second-stop system; single mainspring barrel, 120-hour power reserve
Functions: hours, minutes, sweep seconds; date
Diameter: 28.2 mm
Height: 3.77 mm
Jewels: 21
Frequency: 28,800 vph
Remarks: finely finished with côtes de Genève; 163 parts

Caliber 59210

Hand-wound; single mainspring barrel, 192-hour power reserve
Functions: hours, minutes, subsidiary seconds; power reserve indicator; date
Diameter: 37.8 mm
Height: 5.8 mm
Jewels: 30
Balance: glucydur with variable inertia
Frequency: 28,800 vph
Hairspring: Breguet
Shock protection: Incabloc

Caliber 82200

Automatic; double-pawl winding (Pellaton system); single mainspring barrel, 60-hour power reserve
Functions: hours, minutes, subsidiary seconds
Diameter: 30 mm
Height: 6.6 mm
Jewels: 31
Frequency: 28,800 vph
Hairspring: flat hairspring
Remarks: finely finished movement with perlage and côtes de Genève

Caliber 69355

Automatic; column-wheel control of the chronograph functions; single mainspring barrel, 46-hour power reserve
Functions: hours, minutes, subsidiary seconds; chronograph
Diameter: 30 mm
Height: 7.9 mm
Jewels: 27
Balance: glucydur
Frequency: 28,800 vph
Hairspring: flat hairspring
Remarks: finely finished movement with perlage and côtes de Genève

Caliber 52615

Automatic; double-pawl winding (Pellaton system) with ceramic wheels; two spring barrels, 168-hour power reserve
Functions: hours, minutes, subsidiary seconds; power reserve indicator; perpetual calendar with month, weekday, date, double moon phase (for northern and southern hemispheres), year display (four digits)
Diameter: 37.8 mm
Height: 9 mm
Jewels: 54
Balance: with variable inertia
Frequency: 28,800 vph
Hairspring: Breguet
Shock protection: Incabloc

Caliber 89361

Automatic; double-pawl winding (Pellaton system), column-wheel control of chronograph functions; single spring barrel, 68-hour power reserve
Base caliber: 89000
Functions: hours, minutes, subsidiary seconds; flyback chronograph; date
Diameter: 30 mm
Height: 7.46 mm
Jewels: 38
Balance: glucydur with variable inertia
Frequency: 28,800 vph
Hairspring: flat hairspring
Shock protection: Incabloc
Remarks: concentric chronograph totalizer for minutes and hours

JAEGER-LECOULTRE

The Jaeger-LeCoultre *manufacture* has had a long and tumultuous history. In 1833, Antoine LeCoultre opened his own workshop for the production of gearwheels. Having made his fortune, he then did what many other artisans did; in 1866, he had a large house built and brought together all the craftspeople needed to produce timepieces, from the watchmakers to the turners and polishers. He outfitted the workshop with the most modern machinery of the day, all powered by a steam engine. "La Grande Maison" was the first watch *manufacture* in the Vallée de Joux.

At the start of the twentieth century, the grandson of the company founder, Jacques-David LeCoultre, built slender, complicated watches for the Paris manufacturer Edmond Jaeger. The Frenchman was so impressed with these that, after a few years of fruitful cooperation, he engineered a merger of the two companies.

In the 1970s, the German VDO Group (later Mannesmann) took over the company and helped it weather the quartz crisis.

Thanks to its inclusion in the Richemont stable, Jaeger-LeCoultre continued to grow. A vast array of calibers (around 1,400), including minute repeaters, tourbillons, and other *grandes complications*, a lubricant-free movement, and more than 400 patents, tell their own story. Today, it is the largest employer in the Vallée de Joux—just as it was back in the 1860s. The most enduring collection produced by the brand is probably the Reverso, which can swivel around to show a second watch face on the back. The 2023 production shows that the Reverso still has life.

But Jaeger-LeCoultre also boasts other iconic collections, like the Master, the Polaris, and the Atmos. That's because the brand has always managed to unify technical wizardry with a very fine sense of aesthetics, which is expressed in many models illustrating the many métiers d'art from the watch world. The Master Grande Tradition Perpetual Calendar, for example, or the Grande Complication, which displays sidereal time combined with a minute repeater that rings on sapphire crystal gongs soldered to the sapphire crystal itself for a more penetrating sound. Another horological masterwork is the Duomètre Heliotourbillon Perpetual featuring a triple-axis tourbillon with two different rotation times.

MANUFACTURE JAEGER-LECOULTRE
Rue de la Golisse, 8
CH-1347 Le Sentier
Switzerland

TEL.:
+41-21-852-0202

E-MAIL:
info@jaeger-lecoultre.com
client.relations.us@jaeger-lecoultre.com

WEBSITE:
www.jaeger-lecoultre.com

FOUNDED:
1833

NUMBER OF EMPLOYEES:
Around 1,400

ANNUAL PRODUCTION:
approx. 75,000 watches

U.S. DISTRIBUTOR:
Jaeger-LeCoultre
645 Fifth Avenue
New York, NY 10022
1-877-552-1833
www.jaeger-lecoultre.com

MOST IMPORTANT COLLECTIONS/PRICE RANGE:
Atmos / starting at $7,100; Duomètre / starting at $41,700; Master / starting at $7,250; Polaris / starting at $7,250; Rendez-Vous / starting at $7,850; Reverso / starting at $4,750

Reverso Hybris Artistica Calibre 179

Reference number: Q39424E1
Movement: hand-wound, JLC caliber 179; 26.2 x 41 mm, height 6.85 mm; 52 jewels; 21,600 vph; spherical double-axis tourbillon with different rotational speeds (60 and 12.6 secs.), Gyrolab escapement with hemispheric hairspring; 40-hour power reserve
Functions: hours, minutes, subsidiary seconds (on the tourbillon cage); additional 24-hour display (2nd time zone on the rear),
Case: pink gold, 31 x 51.2 mm, height 13.63 mm; sapphire crystal; water-resistant to 3 atm
Band: reptile skin, double folding clasp
Remarks: case turns and swivels 180°; limited to 10 pieces
Price: $530,000

Reverso Tribute Duoface Tourbillon

Reference number: Q392242J
Movement: hand-wound, JLC caliber 847; dimension 17.2 x 22 mm, height 3.9 mm; 31 jewels; 21,600 vph; "two-sided" flying tourbillon with hidden operation; 38-hour power reserve
Functions: hours, minutes; additional time indication (2nd time zone on the rear), day/night indication
Case: pink gold, 27.4 x 45.5 mm, height 9.15 mm; sapphire crystal; water-resistant to 3 atm
Band: reptile skin, double folding clasp
Remarks: case turns and swivels 180°
Price: $138,000

Reverso Tribute Chronograph

Reference number: Q389257J
Movement: hand-wound, JLC caliber 860; 17.2 x 22 mm, height 5.5 mm; 38 jewels; 28,800 vph; column-wheel control of the chronograph functions; 52-hour power reserve
Functions: hours, minutes; additional time indication (2nd time zone) and chronograph on the rear
Case: pink gold, 29.9 x 49.4 mm, height 11.14 mm; sapphire crystal; water-resistant to 3 atm
Band: reptile skin, pin buckle
Remarks: case turns and swivels 180° come with additional calfskin strap
Price: $38,300
Variations: in stainless steel ($25,000)

Reverso Tribute Chronograph

Reference number: Q389848J
Movement: hand-wound, JLC caliber 860; 17.2 x 22 mm, height 5.5 mm; 38 jewels; 28,800 vph; column wheel control of chronograph functions; 52-hour power reserve
Functions: hours, minutes; additional time display (second time zone) and chronograph on the rear
Case: stainless steel, 29.9 mm x 49.4 mm, height 11.14 mm; sapphire crystal; water-resistant to 3 atm
Band: reptile skin, double folding clasp
Remarks: case turns and swivels 180°; comes with extra calfskin strap
Price: $25,000
Variations: in red gold ($38,800)

Reverso Tribute Monoface Small Seconds

Reference number: Q713257J
Movement: hand-wound, JLC caliber 822/2; 17.2 x 22 mm, height 2.94 mm; 19 jewels; 21,600 vph; 42-hour power reserve
Functions: hours, minutes, subsidiary seconds
Case: red gold, 27.4 mm x 45.6 mm, height 7.56 mm; sapphire crystal; water-resistant to 3 atm
Band: calfskin, pin buckle
Remarks: case turns and swivels 180°; comes with extra calfskin / textile strap
Price: $22,700
Variations: with silver or red dial; in stainless steel ($10,600)

Reverso Tribute Monoface Small Seconds

Reference number: Q713256J
Movement: hand-wound, JLC caliber 822/2; 17.2 x 22 mm, height 2.94 mm; 19 jewels; 21,600 vph; 42-hour power reserve
Functions: hours, minutes, subsidiary seconds
Case: red gold, 27.4 mm x 45.6 mm, height 7.56 mm; sapphire crystal; water-resistant to 3 atm
Band: calfskin and textile, pin buckle
Remarks: case turns and swivels 180°; comes with extra calfskin strap
Price: $22,700
Variations: with black or silver dial; in stainless steel ($10,600)

Reverso Tribute Monoface Small Seconds

Reference number: Q7132521
Movement: hand-wound, JLC caliber 822/2; 17.2 x 22 mm, height 2.94 mm; 19 jewels; 21,600 vph; 42-hour power reserve
Functions: hours, minutes, subsidiary seconds
Case: red gold, 27.4 mm x 45.6 mm, height 7.56 mm; sapphire crystal; water-resistant to 3 atm
Band: calfskin and textile, pin buckle
Remarks: case turns and swivels 180°; comes with extra calfskin strap
Price: $22,700
Variations: with black or red dial; in stainless steel ($10,600)

Reverso Tribute Monoface Small Seconds

Reference number: Q713842J
Movement: hand-wound, JLC caliber 822/2; 17.2 x 22 mm, height 2.94 mm; 19 jewels; 21,600 vph; 42-hour power reserve
Functions: hours, minutes, subsidiary seconds
Case: stainless steel, 27.4 mm x 45.6 mm, height 8.5 mm; sapphire crystal; water-resistant to 3 atm
Band: calfskin and textile, double folding clasp
Remarks: case turns and swivels 180°
Price: $10,600
Variations: in red gold ($22,700)

Duometre Heliotourbillon Perpetual

Reference number: Q6202420
Movement: hand-wound, JLC caliber 388; ø 34.3 mm, height 11.15 mm; 89 jewels; 28,800 vph; triple-axis tourbillon with different rotation times (2x30, 1x60 seconds), two separate geartrains for time display and complications, each with its own spring barrel; 46-hour power reserve
Functions: hours and minutes (off-center); power reserve indicator (for each spring barrel); perpetual calendar with large date, weekday, month, moon phase, year display (four digits)
Case: red gold, ø 44 mm, height 14.7 mm; sapphire crystal; transparent case back; water-resistant to 3 atm
Band: reptile skin, pin buckle
Price: $438,000; limited to 20 pieces

Duometre Chronograph Moon

Reference number: Q622656J
Movement: hand-wound, JLC caliber 391; ø 34.3 mm, height 8.24 mm; 54 jewels; 21,600 vph; two separate gearworks for the time and the complications each with their own spring barrel; 50-hour power reserve
Functions: hours and minutes (off-center); "flashing" sixth of a second; day/night indicator, power reserve indicator (for each spring barrel); chronograph; moon phase display
Case: platinum, ø 42.5 mm, height 14.2 mm; sapphire crystal; transparent case back; water-resistant to 5 atm
Band: reptile skin, pin buckle
Price: $86,000

Duometre Chronograph Moon

Reference number: Q622252J
Movement: hand-wound, JLC caliber 391; ø 34.3 mm, height 8.24 mm; 54 jewels; 21,600 vph; two separate gearworks for the time and the complications each with their own spring barrel; 50-hour power reserve
Functions: hours and minutes (off-center); "flashing" sixth of a second; day/night indicator, power reserve indicator (for each spring barrel); chronograph; moon phase display
Case: red gold, ø 42.5 mm, height 14.2 mm; sapphire crystal; transparent case back; water-resistant to 5 atm
Band: reptile skin, pin buckle
Price: $70,000

Duometre Quantième Lunaire

Reference number: Q604848J
Movement: hand-wound, JLC caliber 381; ø 34.3 mm, height 8.24 mm; 42 jewels; 21,600 vph; two separate gearworks for the time and the complications each with their own spring barrel; 50-hour power reserve
Functions: hours and minutes (off-center); "flashing" sixth of a second; power reserve indicator (for each spring barrel); date, moon phase
Case: stainless steel, ø 42.5 mm, height 13.05 mm; sapphire crystal; transparent case back; water-resistant to 5 atm
Band: reptile skin, double folding clasp
Price: $44,300

Master Ultra Thin Perpetual Calendar

Reference number: Q114258J
Movement: automatic, JLC caliber 868AA; ø 26 mm, height 4.72 mm; 54 jewels; 28,800 vph; 70-hour power reserve
Functions: hours, minutes, sweep seconds; perpetual calendar with date, weekday, month, moon phase, year display (four digits)
Case: red gold, ø 39 mm, height 9.2 mm; sapphire crystal; transparent case back; water-resistant to 5 atm
Band: reptile skin, pin buckle
Price: $40,700

Master Ultra Thin Perpetual Calendar

Reference number: Q1142510
Movement: automatic, JLC caliber 868AA; ø 26 mm, height 4.72 mm; 54 jewels; 28,800 vph; 70-hour power reserve
Functions: hours, minutes, sweep seconds; perpetual calendar with date, weekday, month, moon phase, year display (four digits)
Case: red gold, ø 39 mm, height 9.2 mm; sapphire crystal; transparent case back; water-resistant to 5 atm
Band: reptile skin, pin buckle
Price: $40,700
Variations: with blue dial and strap; bezel set with diamonds ($47,900)

Master Ultra Thin Perpetual Calendar

Reference number: Q1142501
Movement: automatic, JLC caliber 868AA; ø 26 mm, height 4.72 mm; 54 jewels; 28,800 vph; 70-hour power reserve
Functions: hours, minutes, sweep seconds; perpetual calendar with date, weekday, month, moon phase, year display (four digits)
Case: red gold, ø 39 mm, height 9.2 mm; bezel set with 60 diamonds; sapphire crystal; transparent case back; water-resistant to 5 atm
Band: reptile skin, pin buckle
Price: $47,900
Variations: without diamonds ($40,700)

Master Ultra Thin Perpetual Calendar

Reference number: Q114842J
Movement: automatic, JLC caliber 868AA; ø 26 mm, height 4.72 mm; 54 jewels; 28,800 vph; 70-hour power reserve
Functions: hours, minutes, sweep seconds; perpetual calendar with date, weekday, month, moon phase, year display (four digits)
Case: stainless steel, ø 39 mm, height 9.2 mm; sapphire crystal; transparent case back; water-resistant to 5 atm
Band: reptile skin, double folding clasp
Price: $28,500
Variations: in red gold ($40,700); in red gold with bezel set with diamonds ($47,900)

Master Ultra Thin Moon

Reference number: Q1368480
Movement: automatic, JLC caliber 925AA; ø 26 mm, height 4.9 mm; 30 jewels; 28,800 vph; 70-hour power reserve
Functions: hours, minutes, sweep seconds; date, moon phase
Case: stainless steel, ø 39 mm, height 10.04 mm; sapphire crystal; transparent case back; water-resistant to 5 atm
Band: reptile skin, double folding clasp
Price: $11,900
Variations: in red gold ($23,700)

Polaris Perpetual Calendar

Reference number: Q908268J
Movement: automatic, JLC caliber 868AA; ø 26 mm, height 4.72 mm; 54 jewels; 28,800 vph; 70-hour power reserve
Functions: hours, minutes, sweep seconds; perpetual calendar with date, weekday, month, moon phase, year display (four digits)
Case: red gold, ø 42 mm, height 11.97 mm; sapphire crystal; transparent case back; water-resistant to 10 atm
Band: rubber, double folding clasp
Price: $52,500

Polaris Perpetual Calendar

Reference number: Q9088180
Movement: automatic, JLC caliber 868AA; ø 26 mm, height 4.72 mm; 54 jewels; 28,800 vph; 70-hour power reserve
Functions: hours, minutes, sweep seconds; perpetual calendar with date, weekday, month, moon phase, year display (four digits)
Case: stainless steel, ø 42 mm, height 11.97 mm; sapphire crystal; transparent case back; water-resistant to 10 atm
Band: stainless steel, double folding clasp
Price: $36,100

Polaris Perpetual Calendar

Reference number: Q908263J
Movement: automatic, JLC caliber 868AA; ø 26 mm, height 4.72 mm; 54 jewels; 28,800 vph; 70-hour power reserve
Functions: hours, minutes, sweep seconds; perpetual calendar with date, weekday, month, moon phase, year display (four digits)
Case: red gold, ø 42 mm, height 11.97 mm; sapphire crystal; transparent case back; water-resistant to 10 atm
Band: rubber, double folding clasp
Remarks: comes with extra reptile skin strap
Price: $52,500

Polaris Geographic

Reference number: Q9078640
Movement: automatic, JLC caliber 939; ø 26 mm, height 4.9 mm; 34 jewels; 28,800 vph; 70-hour power reserve
Functions: hours, minutes, sweep seconds; additional 12-hour display (second time zone), world time display, day/night indicator, power reserve indicator
Case: stainless steel, ø 42 mm, height 11.54 mm; crown-activated ring with reference cities; sapphire crystal; water-resistant to 10 atm
Band: textile, double folding clasp
Remarks: comes with extra rubber strap
Price: $16,100

Caliber 860

Hand-wound; column-wheel control chronograph functions; single mainspring barrel, 52-hour power reserve
Functions: hours, minutes; additional 12-hour display (second time zone, on the rear); chronograph with retrograde minutes totalizer (on the rear)
Dimensions: 17.2 mm x 22 mm
Height: 5.5 mm
Jewels: 38
Balance: glucydur
Frequency: 28,800 vph
Remarks: skeletonized movement; 300 parts

Caliber 956AA

Automatic; automatic movement for the watch and alarm function; single mainspring barrel, 44-hour power reserve
Functions: hours, minutes, sweep seconds; alarm; date
Diameter: 28 mm
Height: 7.47 mm
Jewels: 24
Balance: glucydur
Frequency: 28,800 vph
Hairspring: flat hairspring
Remarks: perlage on mainplate, bridges with côtes de Genève, fixture for a resonance case back; 271 parts

Caliber 899AC

Automatic; silicon escapement; gold rotor; single mainspring barrel, 70-hour power reserve
Functions: hours, minutes, sweep seconds; date
Diameter: 26 mm
Height: 3.7 mm
Jewels: 32
Frequency: 28,800 vph
Remarks: perlage on mainplate, bridges with côtes de Genève; 218 parts

Caliber 866AA

Automatic; silicon escapement; gold rotor; single mainspring barrel, 70-hour power reserve
Functions: hours, minutes, subsidiary seconds; full calendar with date, weekday, month, moon phase
Diameter: 26 mm
Height: 5.65 mm
Jewels: 34
Balance: glucydur
Frequency: 28,800 vph
Remarks: perlage on mainplate, bridges with côtes de Genève

Caliber 945

Hand-wound; silicon anchor with integrated pallets, flying tourbillon rotates with dial in 56 minutes (sidereal time, star time); single spring barrel, 48-hour power reserve
Functions: hours, minutes, hours, quarter hour and minute repeater; perpetual calendar with, date, month, celestial map with zodiac signs
Diameter: 34.7 mm
Height: 12.62 mm
Jewels: 49
Balance: screw balance
Frequency: 28,800 vph
Hairspring: flat hairspring
Remarks: repetition with "trebuchet" hammers to strengthen the impulses; 527 parts

Caliber 925AA

Automatic; single mainspring barrel, 70-hour power reserve
Functions: hours, minutes, sweep seconds; date, moon phase
Diameter: 26 mm
Height: 4.9 mm
Jewels: 30
Frequency: 28,800 vph
Remarks: 245 parts

Caliber 751

Automatic; column-wheel control of the chronograph functions; two spring barrels, 65-hour power reserve
Functions: hours, minutes, subsidiary seconds; chronograph
Diameter: 26.2 mm
Height: 5.7 mm
Jewels: 37
Balance: screw balance with 4 weights
Frequency: 28,800 vph
Hairspring: flat hairspring
Shock protection: Kif
Remarks: 262 parts

Caliber 822/2

Hand-wound; single mainspring barrel, 42-hour power reserve
Functions: hours, minutes, subsidiary seconds
Dimensions: 17.2 mm x 22 mm
Height: 2.94 mm
Jewels: 19
Balance: screw balance
Frequency: 21,600 vph
Hairspring: flat hairspring

Caliber 925/2

Automatic; single mainspring barrel, 70-hour power reserve
Functions: hours, minutes, sweep seconds; date, moon phase
Diameter: 26 mm
Height: 4.9 mm
Jewels: 30
Frequency: 28,800 vph
Remarks: 245 parts

Caliber 978F

Automatic; 1-minute tourbillon; gold rotor; single mainspring barrel, 45-hour power reserve
Functions: hours, minutes, subsidiary seconds (on the tourbillon cage); date hand (jumping hand from the 15th to the 16th of the month)
Diameter: 30 mm
Height: 7.2 mm
Jewels: 33
Balance: glucydur screw balance
Frequency: 28,800 vph
Hairspring: Breguet hairspring
Shock protection: Kif
Remarks: perlage on mainplate, bridges with côtes de Genève; 302 parts

Caliber 868/A2

Automatic; single mainspring barrel, 70-hour power reserve
Functions: hours, minutes, sweep seconds; perpetual calendar with date, weekday, month, moon phase, year display (four digits)
Diameter: 26 mm
Height: 4.72 mm
Jewels: 46
Balance: glucydur
Frequency: 28,800 vph
Remarks: 332 parts

Caliber 868/1

Automatic; single mainspring barrel, 38-hour power reserve
Functions: hours, minutes, sweep seconds; perpetual calendar with date, weekday, month, moon phase, year display (four digits)
Diameter: 27.8 mm
Height: 4.72 mm
Jewels: 46
Balance: glucydur
Frequency: 28,800 vph
Remarks: 336 parts

JÖRG SCHAUER

Jörg Schauer's watches are first and foremost cool. The cases have been carefully finished and the look is well planned to draw the eye without being too noisy. After all, he is a perfectionist and leaves nothing to chance. He works on every single case himself, polishing and performing his own brand of magic for as long as it takes to display his personal touch. This time-consuming process is one that Schauer believes is absolutely necessary. "I do this because I place a great deal of value on the fact that my cases are absolutely perfect," he explains. "I can do it better than anyone, and I would never let anyone else do it for me."

Schauer, a goldsmith by training, has been making watches since 1990. He began by doing one-off pieces in precious metals for collectors and then opened his business and simultaneously moved to stainless steel. His style is to produce functional, angular cases with visibly screwed-down bezels and straightforward dials in plain black or white. Forget finding any watch close to current trends in his collection; Schauer only builds timepieces that he genuinely likes. Purchasing a Schauer is not that easy. He has chosen a strategy of genuine quality over quantity and only produces about 50 watches annually. This includes special watches like the One-Hand Durowe, running on a modified Unitas made by the movement manufacturer Durowe, which Schauer acquired in 2002. It has been revived as the One-Hand 44. And lately he has extended his line of chronographs named Kulisse," which means something like "back stage."

His production structure is a vital part of his success and includes prototyping, movement modification, finishing, case production, dial painting and printing—all done in Schauer's own workshop in Engelsbrand. He prefers to find any needed outside support among regional specialists.

JÖRG SCHAUER
Durowe GmbH
Jörg Schauer
Pforzheimer Straße 41
75331 Engelsbrand
Germany

TEL.:
+49-(0)7235-975-87 45

E-MAIL:
info@durowe.com

WEBSITE:
www.durowe.com

FOUNDED:
1990

NUMBER OF EMPLOYEES:
2

ANNUAL PRODUCTION:
Approx. 50 watches

DISTRIBUTION:
Direct sales; online shop; please contact the address in Germany

One-Hand Jubiläum
Movement: automatic, ETA caliber 2824-2; ø 25.6 mm, height 4.6 mm; 25 jewels; 28,800 vph; fine finishing, special engraved rotor; 38-hour power reserve
Functions: hours (each line stands for five minutes)
Case: stainless steel, ø 42 mm, height 10.2 mm; bezel fixed with 12 screws; sapphire crystal; transparent case back; water-resistant to 5 atm
Band: rubber, folding clasp
Remarks: limited to 100 pieces
Price: $2,200
Variations: with metal link bracelet ($2,500)

Chronograph Kulisse Edition 10 Jubiläum
Movement: automatic, ETA caliber 7753; ø 30 mm, height 7.9 mm; 25 jewels; 28,800 vph; with decorative ribbing and blued screws; 48-hour power reserve
Functions: hours, minutes, subsidiary seconds; chronograph; date
Case: stainless steel, ø 42 mm, height 14.9 mm; bezel fixed with 12 screws; sapphire crystal; transparent case back; water-resistant to 5 atm
Band: reptile skin, folding clasp
Remarks: limited to 130 pieces
Price: $4,500
Variations: with metal link bracelet ($4,800), with manual winding ($4,900);

Chronograph Kulisse Edition 9
Movement: automatic, ETA caliber 7751; ø 30 mm, height 7.9 mm; 25 jewels; 28,800 vph; with decorative ribbing and blued screws; 48-hour power reserve
Functions: hours, minutes, subsidiary seconds; chronograph; moonphase, day, month, date
Case: stainless steel, ø 42 mm, height 14.9 mm; bezel fixed with 12 screws; sapphire crystal; transparent case back; water-resistant to 5 atm
Band: calfskin, folding clasp
Price: $5,400
Variations: with metal link bracelet ($5,800); with manual winding ($5,800); with white dial

JS WATCH CO.

When they weren't pillaging Europe and terrorizing populations from the British Isles to Russia, the Vikings were in fact a very hardworking and talented bunch. And when not roaming about, they tended their fields, herds, and houses, and, as a number of exhibitions in the past twenty years have shown, they made jewelry. Their work in this field was remarkable and fed their commercial supply chains, to use a modern term.

Iceland is where many descendants of the Norsemen live—a rugged and stark landscape, with over three hundred volcanoes and long winter nights. The ability to design and create fine jewelry lives on, and since 2003, the tiny country with a population of over 387,000 has been producing watches as well, thanks to four friends: designer Grimkell Sigurþórsson, watchmakers Sigurður Gilbertsson and Gilbert Guðjónsson, and Júlíus Heiðarsson.

Their first launch in 2005 of one hundred watches sold out within half a year, and so they persisted, using Swiss or German parts and movements, but creating watches with some unique features paying tribute to their small but very intriguing country. The "assortment chronometer" movements provide solid performance and standard decoration, meaning lower prices but good quality. The timepieces are inspired and named after an event, place, or year in Iceland or Icelandic history. "We made the Sif N.A.R.T., which was named for the first helicopter of Iceland's Coast Guard rescue teams and the North Atlantic Rescue Timer," says Sigurþórsson, now the Director of Design and Marketing of the tiny company. One of the latest models celebrating local stars is the Fraternitas Islandica, which was made for the island's Freemasons, as the little symbol at 6 o'clock and the Templar cross at 12 o'clock indicate.

The Gilbert collection pays tribute to the company's own watchmaker, Gilbert Guðjónsson, with sober, almost self-effacing timepieces. In the Vinland line, one finds a complicated chronograph collection sporting a tachymeter scale. To appeal to different tastes, there is a choice of dials, including one in red and black, a hint at the lava running under this mysterious country. The second Vinland, a special edition, has a rich guilloché dial and Norse engravings on the mainplate visible through the case back.

JS WATCH CO. REYKJAVIK
Laugavegur 62
101 Reykjavik
Iceland

TEL.:
+354-551-05-00

E-MAIL:
info@jswatch.com

WEBSITE:
www.jswatch.com

FOUNDED:
2003

NUMBER OF EMPLOYEES:
5

ANNUAL PRODUCTION:
500 pieces

DISTRIBUTION:
Retail and direct sales
info@jswatch.com
+354-551-41-00

PRICE RANGE:
$1,978 to $14,147

101 Black Diamond

Reference number: 101-32-8
Movement: automatic, Soprod caliber M100; ø 25.60 mm, height 3.60 mm; 25 jewels; 28,800 vph; "assortment chronometer" fine-tuning for near-COSC rating; 42-hour power reserve
Function: central hours, minutes, subsidiary seconds; date
Case: stainless steel, 32 mm, height 10.3 mm; sapphire crystal; transparent case back; water-resistant to 5 atm
Band: stainless steel milanaise mesh, folding clasp
Price: $4,142
Variations: leather, reptile skin, and pin buckle

101 10 Year Edition

Reference number: 101-10-3
Movement: automatic, Soprod caliber M100; ø 25.60 mm, height 3.60 mm; 25 jewels; 28,800 vph; "assortment chronometer" fine-tuning for near-COSC rating; 42-hour power reserve
Function: central hours, minutes, sweep seconds; date
Case: stainless steel, 38.5 mm, height 10 mm; fluted bezel; sapphire crystal; transparent case back; water-resistant to 5 atm
Band: calfskin, pin buckle
Price: $2,215
Variations: ostrich leather, reptile skin, stainless steel bracelet

Fraternitas Islandica

Reference number: FRA-38-1
Movement: automatic, Soprod caliber M100; ø 25.60 mm, height 3.60 mm; 25 jewels; 28,800 vph; "assortment chronometer" fine-tuning for near-COSC rating; 42-hour power reserve
Function: central hours, minutes, sweep seconds; date
Case: stainless steel, 38.5 mm, height 10 mm; sapphire crystal; transparent case back; water-resistant to 5 atm
Band: calfskin, pin buckle
Price: $2,466

JUNGHANS

The town of Glashütte in Saxony was already a watchmaking name to be reckoned with when Erhard Junghans (b. 1823) founded his factory in 1861 in Schramberg, a small town in the Black Forest. His son Arthur then developed it into a large-scale production site on the American industrial model. At the height of its success, the factory employed nearly three thousand men and women making nine thousand wall clocks and alarm clocks daily.

In the boom years after World War II, the company, with its logo featuring a star, produced mainly wristwatches. It went on to ring in modern times with its own solar and radio-controlled watches. Junghans was twice the official timekeeper at the Olympic Games.

In 2009, Dr. Hans-Jochem Steim, a successful entrepreneur and political figure from Schramberg, purchased the company, which had gone bankrupt. An infusion of cash allowed it to set up a new production and distribution schedule. Today, the brand boasts an extensive collection of high-quality wristwatches, ranging from genuine icons of design to major classics, all the way to sporty chronographs. In 2018, the company opened a watch- and clockmaking museum in the restored *Terrassenbau*, a century-old, terraced, industrial construction that allowed Junghans employees to work with strong natural lighting. All watches are designed, manufactured, and assembled in this historic building.

In the same year, Junghans came out with a brand-new radio-controlled movement, the Caliber J101, designed to mix high-tech with a classic look. To satisfy a broad market, Junghans manufactures quartz and mechanical watches, all in a sober Bauhaus idiom. Some of the most popular models include the Meister S, a sporty, masculine watch, and a series of watches that combine the radio-controlled Caliber J101 with the latest in solar technology, all packaged in the traditional Junghans look. A brand-new time signal enables rapid synchronization with a smartphone thanks to a specially developed app.

UHRENFABRIK JUNGHANS
GmbH & Co. KG
Geisshaldenstrasse 49
D-78713 Schramberg

TEL.:
+49-742-218-0

E-MAIL:
info@junghans.de

WEBSITE:
www.junghans.de

FOUNDED:
1861

NUMBER OF EMPLOYEES:
127

ANNUAL PRODUCTION:
approx. 60,000 watches

U.S. DISTRIBUTOR:
DKSH Luxury & Lifestyle North America Inc.
9-D Princess Road
Lawrenceville, NJ 08648
609-750-8800

MOST IMPORTANT COLLECTIONS/PRICE RANGE:
Meister, Max Bill by Junghans, MEGA, 1972
Competition, Form / from approx. $395 to $2,500;
special pieces up to $17,000

Pilot Chronoscope

Reference number: 27/3493.00
Movement: automatic, caliber J880.4 (ETA 2892-A2 base with Dubois Dépraz module); ø 30 mm, height 7.6 mm; 49 jewels; 28,800 vph; rhodium-plated movement, blued screws, rotor with ribbing; 42-hour power reserve
Functions: hours, minutes, subsidiary seconds; chronograph
Case: stainless steel, ø 43.3 mm, height 14.4 mm; bidirectional bezel, with 0-60 scale; sapphire crystal; water-resistant to 10 atm
Band: calfskin, pin buckle
Price: $2,890

Pilot Chronoscope

Reference number: 27/3492.00
Movement: automatic, caliber J880.4 (ETA 2892-A2 base with Dubois Dépraz module); ø 30 mm, height 7.6 mm; 49 jewels; 28,800 vph; rhodium-plated movement, blued screws, rotor with ribbing; 42-hour power reserve
Functions: hours, minutes, subsidiary seconds; chronograph
Case: stainless steel, ø 43.3 mm, height 14.4 mm; bidirectional bezel, with 0-60 scale; sapphire crystal; water-resistant to 10 atm
Band: calfskin, pin buckle
Price: $2,790

Pilot Automatic

Reference number: 27/4495.00
Movement: automatic, caliber J800.1.6 (Sellita SW261 base); ø 25.6 mm, height 4.6 mm; 26 jewels; 28,800 vph; rhodium-plated movement, blued screws, rotor with ribbing; 38-hour power reserve
Functions: hours, minutes, subsidiary seconds; date
Case: stainless steel, ø 43.3 mm, height 12.5 mm; bidirectional bezel, with 0-60 scale; sapphire crystal; water-resistant to 10 atm
Band: calfskin, pin buckle
Price: $2,260

Meister Chronoscope

Reference number: 27/4223.02
Movement: automatic, caliber J880.1 (Sellita
SW500 base); ø 30 mm, height 7.9 mm; 25 jewels;
28,800 vph; rhodium-plated movement, blued screws,
rotor with ribbing; 48-hour power reserve
Functions: hours, minutes, subsidiary seconds;
chronograph; date and weekday
Case: stainless steel, ø 40.7 mm, height 13.9 mm;
sapphire crystal; transparent case back; water-resistant
to 5 atm
Band: ostrich skin, pin buckle
Price: $2,590

Meister Chronoscope

Reference number: 27/4429.46
Movement: automatic, caliber J880.1 (Sellita
SW500 base); ø 30 mm, height 7.9 mm; 25 jewels;
28,800 vph; rhodium-plated movement, blued screws,
rotor with ribbing; 48-hour power reserve
Functions: hours, minutes, subsidiary seconds;
chronograph; date and weekday
Case: stainless steel, ø 40.7 mm, height 13.9 mm;
sapphire crystal; transparent case back; water-resistant
to 5 atm
Band: stainless steel, folding clasp
Price: $2,690

Meister Automatic

Reference number: 27/4416.02
Movement: automatic, caliber J800.1 (Sellita
SW200-1 base); ø 25.6 mm, height 4.6 mm; 26 jewels;
28,800 vph; rhodium-plated movement, blued screws,
rotor with ribbing; 38-hour power reserve
Functions: hours, minutes, sweep seconds; date
Case: stainless steel, ø 40.4 mm, height 10.9 mm;
sapphire crystal; transparent case back; water-resistant
to 5 atm
Band: ostrich skin, pin buckle
Price: $1,550
Variations: with stainless steel bracelet and black dial
($1,600)

Pilot Automatic

Reference number: 27/4491.00
Movement: automatic, caliber J800.1.6 (Sellita
SW261 base); ø 25.6 mm, height 4.6 mm; 26 jewels;
28,800 vph; rhodium-plated movement, blued screws,
rotor with ribbing; 38-hour power reserve
Functions: hours, minutes, subsidiary seconds; date
Case: stainless steel with black DLC, ø 43.3 mm, height
12.5 mm; bidirectional bezel, with 0-60 scale; sapphire
crystal; water-resistant to 10 atm
Band: calfskin, pin buckle
Price: $2,260

Meister S Automatic

Reference number: 27/4210.44
Movement: automatic, caliber J800.4 (Basis ETA 2836-
2); ø 25.6 mm, height 3.8 mm; 25 jewels; 28,800 vph;
rhodium-plated movement, blued screws, rotor with
engraved logo; 38-hour power reserve
Functions: hours, minutes, sweep seconds; date and
weekday
Case: stainless steel, ø 40.5 mm, height 13 mm;
sapphire crystal; screw-down crown; water-resistant
to 20 atm
Band: stainless steel, folding clasp
Price: $2,190

Meister S Automatic

Reference number: 27/4211.00
Movement: automatic, caliber J800.4 (Basis ETA 2836-
2); ø 25.6 mm, height 3.8 mm; 25 jewels; 28,800 vph;
rhodium-plated movement, blued screws, rotor with
engraved logo; 38-hour power reserve
Functions: hours, minutes, sweep seconds; date and
weekday
Case: stainless steel, ø 40.5 mm, height 13 mm;
sapphire crystal; screw-down crown; water-resistant
to 20 atm
Band: rubber with calfskin inlay, folding clasp
Price: $2,090
Variations: with stainless steel bracelet and anthracite
dial ($2,190)

Form A Chronoscope

Reference number: 27/4370.00
Movement: automatic, caliber J880.1 (Sellita SW500 base); ø 30 mm, height 7.9 mm; 25 jewels; 28,800 vph; 48-hour power reserve
Functions: hours, minutes, subsidiary seconds; chronograph; date and weekday
Case: stainless steel with black PVD, ø 42 mm, height 13.7 mm; sapphire crystal; transparent case back; water-resistant to 5 atm
Band: calfskin, pin buckle
Price: $2,260
Variations: various index and strap colors

Form A Chronoscope

Reference number: 27/4371.02
Movement: automatic, caliber J880.1 (Sellita SW500 base); ø 30 mm, height 7.9 mm; 25 jewels; 28,800 vph; 48-hour power reserve
Functions: hours, minutes, subsidiary seconds; chronograph; date and weekday
Case: stainless steel with black PVD, ø 42 mm, height 13.7 mm; sapphire crystal; transparent case back; water-resistant to 5 atm
Band: calfskin, pin buckle
Price: $2,260
Variations: various index and strap colors

Form A Chronoscope

Reference number: 27/4473.00
Movement: automatic, caliber J880.1 (Sellita SW500 base); ø 30 mm, height 7.9 mm; 25 jewels; 28,800 vph; 48-hour power reserve
Functions: hours, minutes, subsidiary seconds; chronograph; date and weekday
Case: stainless steel with black PVD, ø 42 mm, height 13.7 mm; sapphire crystal; transparent case back; water-resistant to 5 atm
Band: calfskin, pin buckle
Price: $2,260
Variations: with black strap

Max Bill Regulator Bauhaus

Reference number: 27/4493.02
Movement: automatic, caliber J800.5 (Sellita SW266-1 base); ø 25.6 mm, height 4.6 mm; 25 jewels; 28,800 vph; 38-hour power reserve
Functions: hours (off-center), minutes, subsidiary seconds; date
Case: stainless steel, ø 40 mm, height 10.9 mm; sapphire crystal; transparent case back; water-resistant to 3 atm
Band: calfskin, pin buckle
Price: $2,750

Max Bill Automatic Bauhaus

Reference number: 27/4308.02
Movement: automatic, caliber J800.1 (Sellita SW200-1 base); ø 25.6 mm, height 4.6 mm; 26 jewels; 28,800 vph; 38-hour power reserve
Functions: hours, minutes, sweep seconds; date
Case: stainless steel with black PVD, ø 38 mm, height 10 mm; sapphire crystal; transparent case back; water-resistant to 5 atm
Band: calfskin, pin buckle
Price: $1,600
Variations: in stainless steel without PVD, with white dial ($1,550)

Max Bill Chronoscope Bauhaus

Reference number: 27/4303.02
Movement: automatic, caliber J880.2 (Sellita SW500 base); ø 30 mm, height 7.9 mm; 25 jewels; 28,800 vph; 48-hour power reserve
Functions: hours, minutes; chronograph; date
Case: stainless steel, ø 40 mm, height 14.4 mm; sapphire crystal; transparent case back; water-resistant to 5 atm
Band: calfskin, pin buckle
Price: $2,600
Variations: as a regulator version ($2,750)

KLEYNOD

Watches were a common gift in the former Soviet Union, so it may not come as a great surprise that millions of timepieces of all types were manufactured during that period. Today, many can be found for sale online. They are appreciated for their rugged looks, the identifiable symbols (like the red star), and their robust construction. Several big names dominate, of course, Vostok, Sturmanskie, Raketa, among others. Most are still with us these days as new brands appear using the old tools.

Among the more recent enterprises is the Kyiv Watch Factory, founded in 1997 in the Ukrainian capital. It was the manufacturing hub for the Russian brand Poljot, among others. Perhaps more famous, in Ukraine at least, was the making of a watch for Ukrainian astronaut Leonid Kadeniuk, who was on the international STS-87 mission that was carried out by the space shuttle Columbia. In 2002, the company decided to create a distinct brand of its own. They chose the name Kleynod, which derives from the German *Kleinod*, or Polish *klejnot*, an old word for "gem."

The output is divided into six main collections. For the sake of affordability, the movements used are mostly quartz, but a fair number of the watches do come equipped with Swiss-made mechanical movements by Ronda or Sellita. Still, they are all under the $1,000-dollar mark.

Perhaps more interestingly though are the motifs on the dials that reflect a pride in the country's long history. The 3, 6, 9, and 12 appearing on the dial of the Kleynods of Independence collection may hardly be recognizable at first because they have been stylized to look like the *tryzub*, the distinctive Ukrainian trident, on a guilloché background, which originates back in the mists of the nation's history. The numerals of the Classic model also mirror the style of the *tryzub*, though the dial is far simpler.

As for the recent Antonov "Mriya" watch, its size is a tribute to the famously outsized cargo aircraft built by the eponymous Ukrainian company and known for its ability to land pretty much anywhere.

KLEYNOD UKRAINIAN WATCHES
Kyrylivska Street 69
Kyiv, 04080
Ukraine

TEL.:
+38-067-223-1085

E-MAIL:
trade@kleynod.ua

WEBSITE:
www.kleynodwatches.com

FOUNDED:
2002

NUMBER OF EMPLOYEES:
100

ANNUAL PRODUCTION:
approx. 90,000 watches

U. S. DISTRIBUTOR:
V2Com Commerce LLC
775 Bloomfield Ave, Suite 1B
Clifton, New Jersey 07012
973-272-8251
kleynodusa@gmail.com

MOST IMPORTANT COLLECTIONS/PRICE RANGE
Mechanical and quartz: Antonov (quartz) / Classic / Embroidery / Kleynods of Independence / Football Collection / Kleynod Forces; up to $785

AN-225 "Mriya"

Reference number: AN-225/1988
Movement: quartz, caliber Ronda 7003.I; ø 33.8 mm, height 5.6 mm; 5 jewels
Functions: hours, minutes, sweep seconds, large date, day (retrograde)
Case: stainless steel, ø 54.2 mm, height 52 mm; sapphire crystal; dial with guilloche and plated signs with luminescent coating; water-resistant to 10 atm
Band: leather, normal clasp
Price: $725

Kleynods of Independence

Reference number: K 10-606
Movement: automatic, Sellita caliber SW-200-1; ø 25.6 mm, height 4.6 mm; 26 jewels; 28,800 vph; 41-hour power reserve
Functions: hours, minutes, sweep seconds
Case: stainless steel with gold plating (IPG), 46 mm x 32 mm, height 12 mm; sapphire crystal; water-resistant to 5 atm
Band: IPG steel and leather, folding clasp
Remarks: guilloché on dial with Ukrainian trident coat of arms
Price: $805; limited to 2500 pieces
Variations: comes in stainless steel, with white dial; comes with extra leather strap

Men's watch

Reference number: K30-636
Movement: automatic, Sellita caliber SW-200-1; ø 25.6 mm, height 4.6 mm; 26 jewels; 28,800 vph; 41-hour power reserve
Functions: hours, minutes, sweep seconds; date
Case: stainless steel with gold plating (IPG), ø 44 mm, height 12 mm; sapphire crystal; water-resistant to 5 atm
Band: leather, folding clasp
Remarks: guilloché on dial with Ukrainian trident coat of arms in the center
Price: $890; limited to 300 pieces
Variations: in stainless steel, with white dial; comes with extra leather strap

KOBOLD

Like many others in the field, Michael Kobold had already developed an interest in the watch industry in childhood. As a young man, he found a mentor in Chronoswiss founder Gerd-Rüdiger Lang, who encouraged him to start his own brand. This happened in 1998 when Kobold was nineteen years of age and still a student at Carnegie Mellon University.

Today, after twenty-five years, Kobold Watch Company is paying homage to mentor Lang with a re-imagined version of master watchmaker Gerd-R. Lang's iconic Kairos, which had its debut in 1986. It is not surprising for a company whose motto is "Embrace Adventure" that explorers such as Sir Ranulph Fiennes, whom Guinness Book of World Records describes as "the world's greatest living explorer," and mountaineers such as Reinhold Messner and David Breashears wear these mechanical instruments as well.

The brand's centerpiece is the Soarway collection and the fabled Soarway case, which was originally created in 1999 by Sir Ranulph, Gerd-R. Lang, and company founder Kobold, himself an avid mountain climber.

Kobold's love of the Himalayas has driven his commitment to the people of Nepal. In 2015, he launched the Soarway Foundation/Engage Nepal, which today is run by the former US ambassador to Nepal. His love of that country is also behind the Fire Truck Expedition as a way to supply the mountain-clad country with key firefighting equipment.

Kobold has contributed to the renaissance of American watchmaking with in-house CNC machining of the cases and in-house assembly. At one point there was even talk of an in-house movement. After Gerd-R. Lang passed away, however, Kobold acquired over 15,000 of the late watchmaker's movements. "By combining Rüdiger's vintage movements with watchcases he designed such as the Kairos and Convertible, we now have a perfect solution while at the same time paying tribute to my late friend and mentor," says Kobold.

KOBOLD TIME GMBH
Willibald-Alexis-Strasse 18
D-10965 Berlin
Germany

TEL.:
+49-151-105-500-10
1-877-SOARWAY

E-MAIL:
info@koboldwatch.com

WEBSITE:
www.koboldwatch.com

FOUNDED:
1998

NUMBER OF EMPLOYEES:
8

ANNUAL PRODUCTION:
maximum 2,500 watches

DISTRIBUTION:
factory-direct, select retailers
1-877-SOARWAY

MOST IMPORTANT COLLECTION/PRICE RANGE:
Soarway, Phantom, SMG / $2,650 to $48,000

25th Anniversary Chronograph

Reference number: KD 2143211
Movement: automatic, ETA 7750; ø 25.6 mm, height 7.9 mm; 25 jewels; 28,800 vph; fully skeletonized; côtes de Genève, perlage, engraved and skeletonized gold-plated rotor; 46-hour power reserve
Functions: hours, minutes, subsidiary seconds; date; chronograph
Case: stainless steel, ø 37 mm, height 15 mm; sapphire crystal; exhibition case back; water-resistant to 3 atm
Band: alligator strap, screw-locked buckle
Remarks: fully skeletonized movement, limited to 25 pieces
Price: $14,500

Kairos Field Watch

Reference number: KD 2853
Movement: automatic, Foerster F. 197; ø 26.5 mm, height 5.2 mm; 25 jewels; 18,000 vph; 36-hour power reserve
Functions: hours, minutes, sweep seconds
Case: stainless steel, 19 components, ø 38 mm, height 12 mm; screwed-in crown; screwed-down exhibition case back; screw-locked lug bars, water-resistant to 3 atm
Band: canvas strap, screw-locked buckle
Price: $525

Convertible

Reference number: KD 2803
Movement: automatic, ETA 2670; ø 17.5 mm, height 4.8 mm; 17 jewels; 28,800 vph; with côtes de Genève, perlage, engraved and skeletonized gold-plated rotor; 39-hour power reserve
Functions: hours, minutes, sweep seconds
Case: stainless, 43 x 27 mm, height 9 mm; screw-locked lug bars; sapphire crystal; screwed-down case back; water-resistant to 3 atm
Band: calfskin, screw-locked buckle
Price: $4,650

Richard E. Byrd II Field Watch

Reference number: KD 2863
Movement: automatic, ETA 2824-A2; ø 36 mm, height 3.6 mm; 21 jewels; 28,800 vph; 38-hour power reserve
Functions: hours, minutes, sweep seconds
Case: stainless steel, 19 components, ø 40 mm, height 12 mm; sapphire crystal; screwed-down exhibition case back; crown; screw-locked lug bars, water-resistant to 10 atm
Band: canvas strap, screw-locked buckle
Price: $750

Seal Ceramic James Gandolfini—Meteorite dial

Reference number: KD 842121C
Movement: automatic, ETA 2892-A2; ø 36 mm, height 3.6 mm; 21 jewels; 28,800 vph; 42-hour power reserve
Functions: hours, minutes, sweep seconds
Case: ceramic, ø 44 mm, height 17.0 mm; unidirectional rotating bezel with 60-minute divisions; antireflective sapphire crystal; screwed-in crown; screwed-down case back; water-resistant to 100 atm
Band: rubber, signed buckle
Price: $8,500; limited to 51 pieces
Variations: varied dials, including Mount Everest summit rock, malachite, turquoise

SMG-2

Reference number: KD 5546142
Movement: automatic, Caliber ETA 2893-A2; ø 26.2 mm, height 4.1 mm; 21 jewels; 28,800 vph; 40-hour power reserve
Functions: hours, minutes, sweep seconds; 2nd time zone; date
Case: stainless steel, ø 43 mm, height 12.75 mm; unidirectional bezel with 0-60 scale; antireflective sapphire crystal; screwed-down case back; screwed-in crown; water-resistant to 20 atm
Band: rubber, buckle
Price: $6,450

Phantom SL Chronograph

Reference number: KD 7934552
Movement: automatic, ETA 7750; ø 25.6 mm, height 7.9 mm; 25 jewels; 28,800 vph; côtes de Genève, perlage, engraved and skeletonized gold-plated rotor; 46-hour power reserve
Functions: hours, minutes, subsidiary seconds; date, day; chronograph
Case: titanium, ø 40.5 mm, height 17 mm; bezel with tachymeter scale (blank bezel optional); screw-down crown; sapphire crystal; screw-down case back; water-resistant to 20 atm
Band: reptile skin, buckle
Price: $3,450

Arctic Diver

Reference number: KD 9652155
Movement: automatic, ETA 2824; ø 25.6 mm, height 4.6 mm; 25 jewels; 28,800 vph; côtes de Genève, perlage, engraved gold-plated rotor; soft iron core; 38-hour power reserve
Functions: hours, minutes, sweep seconds; date (optional)
Case: DLC-coated titanium, ø 44.5 mm, height 15 mm; unidirectional bezel with 60-minute divisions (blank bezel optional); screw-down crown; sapphire crystal; screw-down case back; water-resistant to 50 atm
Band: rubber, buckle
Price: $5,650

Soarway Diver

Reference number: KD 1113145
Movement: automatic, ETA 2892; ø 25.6 mm, height 3.6 mm; 25 jewels; 28,800 vph; côtes de Genève, perlage, engraved and skeletonized gold-plated rotor; 42-hour power reserve
Functions: hours, minutes, sweep seconds; date (optional)
Case: DLC-coated stainless steel, ø 40.5 mm, height 10 mm; unidirectional bezel with 60-minute divisions; screw-down crown; sapphire crystal; screw-down case back; water-resistant to 30 atm
Band: canvas, buckle
Price: $5,950

KUDOKE

Stefan Kudoke, a watchmaker from Frankfurt an der Oder, has made a name for himself as an extremely skilled and imaginative creator of timepieces. He apprenticed with two experienced watchmakers and graduated as the number one trainee in the state of Brandenburg. This earned him a stipend from a federal program promoting gifted individuals. He then moved on to one of the large *manufactures* in Glashütte, where he refined his skills in its workshop for complications and prototyping. At the age of twenty-two, with a master's diploma in his pocket, he decided to get an MBA and then devote himself to building his own company.

His guiding principle is individuality, and that is not possible to find in a serial product. So Kudoke began building unique pieces. By realizing the special wishes of customers, he manages to reflect each person's uniqueness in each watch. And he has produced some genuinely outstanding timepieces, like the ExCentro1 and 2 or more recently a watch with an octopus that seems to be climbing out of the case. Even his more minimalistic pieces, like the KUDOKE 1 and 2 are deeply thought-out. They come in carefully chosen, yet toned-down colors, like anthracite, that interact subtly with the shapes.

Kudoke has divided his output into two clear categories: HANDwerk, meaning crafts, and referring to straight watchmaking, like the KUDOKE 3, and KUNSTwerk, which means artwork and refers mostly to his engravings. The latter category gives him the opportunity to work his specialties, like engraving and goldsmithing. Under his creative hand, edges might be turned into graceful bodies, or a plate fragment might be turned into figures and garlands. His creativity has earned him a Grand Prix d'Horlogerie de Genève (GPHG) prize in the "Petite Aiguille" category in 2019 and once again in 2024 for his KUDOKE 3 Salmon. The small family-run company was one of the very few German brands to win this "Oscar" of the watch industry with its successful KUDOKE 2 model.

KUDOKE UHREN
Tannenweg 5
D-15236 Frankfurt (Oder)
Germany

TEL.:
+49-335-280-0409

E-MAIL:
info@kudoke.eu

WEBSITE:
www.kudoke.eu

FOUNDED:
2007

NUMBER OF EMPLOYEES:
4

ANNUAL PRODUCTION:
150 watches

DISTRIBUTION:
Contact the brand directly for information

PRICE RANGE:
between approx. $4,500 and $32,000

Kudoke 2
Reference number: SK-036
Movement: hand-wound, Kudoke caliber 1-Version 24h; ø 30 mm, height 5.05 mm; 18 jewels; 28,800 vph; hand-engraved and finished; 46-hour power reserve
Functions: hours, minutes; additional 24-hour display
Case: stainless steel, ø 39 mm, height 10.7 mm; sapphire crystal; transparent case back
Band: calfskin, pin buckle
Remarks: hand-engraved celestial disk and galvanically treated in three colors
Price: $12,090

Kudoke 3
Reference number: SK-037
Movement: hand-wound, Kudoke caliber 1; ø 30 mm, height 4.3 mm; 18 jewels; 28,800 vph; hand-engraved and finished; 46-hour power reserve
Functions: hours (incremental display), minutes
Case: stainless steel, ø 39 mm, height 10.3 mm; sapphire crystal; transparent case back
Band: calfskin, pin buckle
Price: $10,090

Kudoke Infinity
Reference number: SK-035
Movement: hand-wound, Kudoke caliber 1; ø 30 mm, height 4.3 mm; 18 jewels; 28,800 vph; hand-engraved and finished; 46-hour power reserve
Functions: hours, minutes
Case: stainless steel, ø 39 mm, height 10.3 mm; sapphire crystal; transparent case back
Band: calfskin, pin buckle
Remarks: gold-flow dial;
Price: $15,280; limited to 12 pieces per year

LAURENT FERRIER

A rock rolling along a riverbed or being buffeted by coastal surf will, over time, achieve a kind of perfect shape, streamlined, flowing, smooth. It will usually become a comfortable touchstone for the human hand—a fine pebble, or *galet* in French. And that is the name given to the watches made by Laurent Ferrier in Geneva, Switzerland. The name refers to the special look and feel of the cases, which are just one hallmark of this very unusual, yet classical, watch brand.

Laurent Ferrier is a real person, the offspring of a watchmaking family from the Canton of Neuchâtel, and a trained watchmaker. As a young man he had a passion for cars, too, and even raced seven times at the 24 Hours of Le Mans. In 2009, after thirty-five years of employment at Patek Philippe working on new movements, Ferrier decided he had been shaped enough by his industry. He gathered up his deep experience and founded his own enterprise. He was joined by his son, Christian Ferrier, a watchmaker in his own right, and fellow former race driver François Sérvanin.

In 2023, the Grand Sport Tourbillon Pursuit picked up the Tourbillon Prize at the Geneva "grand prix," the GPHG. Like other models in the collection, this one uses a natural escapement with a double hairspring, ensuring greater accuracy (a technical idea going back to Breguet). The tourbillon is once again concealed on the movement side, keeping the dial free of clutter.

The flagship Galet keeps evolving and being used to house different complications, like a second time zone. The Classic Auto Sandstone keeps the *galet* shape with a copper-hued dial that whispers "vintage." And after the 2023 prize for the Tourbillon Pursuit, Laurent Ferrier picked up a second prize in 2024 for the Classic Moon Silver in red gold, this time in the Calendar and Astronomy category.

LAURENT FERRIER
Route de Saint Julien 150
CH-1228 Plan-les-Ouates
Switzerland

TEL.:
+41-22-716-3388

E-MAIL:
info@laurentferrier.ch

WEBSITE:
www.laurentferrier.ch

FOUNDED:
2010

NUMBER OF EMPLOYEES:
12

ANNUAL PRODUCTION:
135

U.S. DISTRIBUTOR:
Cellini Jewelers
430 Park Avenue
at 56th Street
New York, NY 10022
212.888.0505
800.CELLINI
Contact@CelliniJewelers.com

MOST IMPORTANT COLLECTIONS/PRICE RANGE:
Variations of the Galet / from $40,000 to $345,000

Classic Auto Sandstone

Reference number: LCF046.AC.B2G1
Movement: automatic, Laurent Ferrier caliber LF270.01; ø 31.6 mm, height 4.85 mm; 28,800 vph; 31 jewels; platinum off-center micro-rotor; natural lever escapement with double escape wheel; finely decorated bridges and mainplate; 72-hour power reserve
Functions: hours, minutes, subsidiary seconds; date
Case: stainless steel, ø 40 mm, height 11.94 mm; ball-shaped crown; sapphire crystal, transparent screwed-down case back; water-resistant to 12 atm
Band: calfskin with Alcantara lining, pin buckle
Remarks: satin-brushed coppery lacquer dial
Price: on request; limited to 20 pieces

Grand Sport Tourbillon Pursuit

Reference number: LCF044.T1.RN1
Movement: manually wound, Laurent Ferrier caliber LF619.01; ø 31.60, height 5.57 mm; 21,600 vph; 23 jewels; Swiss lever escapement, tourbillon with double balance spring; finely decorated bridges and mainplate; semi-instantaneous calendar with correction forward or backward; 80-hour power reserve
Functions: hours, minutes, subsidiary seconds; day, date
Case: titanium, ø 44 mm, height 13.40 mm; domed and tinted sapphire crystal; transparent case back; ball-shaped crown; water-resistant to 10 atm
Band: titanium, folding clasp
Remarks: the tourbillon is on the back in traditional style
Price: $190,000

Classic Micro-Rotor Evergreen

Reference number: LCF039.R5.G3N
Movement: hand-wound, Laurent Ferrier caliber LF126.02; ø 31.60 mm, height 6.30 mm; 21,600 vph; 25 jewels; silicon escapement, finely decorated bridges and mainplate; 80-hour power reserve
Functions: hours, minutes, subsidiary seconds; sweep date, day, month (with bidirectional correction); moon phase (corrector at 8:30)
Case: stainless steel, ø 40 mm, height 12.90 mm; ball-shaped crown; sapphire crystal front, transparent case back; water-resistant to 3 atm
Band: nubuck, pin buckle
Price: $80,000
Variations: red-gold case ($90,000)

LEICA

Alongside fine watchmaking, the manufacture of cameras has always been regarded as one of the highest disciplines of precision manufacturing. Leica Camera AG's decision to develop its own wristwatch collection was therefore a natural step. After all, the Leica M series still generates hosannas of admiration amongst connoisseurs of fine cameras. They are compact, silent, extremely precise, and robust. Applying the same quality to a wristwatch was simply a matter of time.

In 2023, Leica launched the first two wristwatches designed and built from scratch. This followed several starts and restarts around 2018, with models listed as L1 and L2 appearing briefly on the market. Discreetly hidden on the winding crown of the ZM 1 and ZM 2 "timepieces" is the trademark red dot upon which Leica-users would normally see the company's name.

Having met with market approval, Leica came out with a second series, the Leica ZM 11. It is simpler and more conventional than its older siblings, but the high-quality surface finish of the titanium or stainless steel case is clearly top notch. The movement was developed by the Swiss manufacturer Chronode in Le Locle, a company that has been behind the success of many other brands. A special function inspired by the lens locking mechanism of a Leica camera is the rapid strap changing system, which provides a wide range of options for choosing the right watch strap for every occasion. The look of the ZM 11 can be easily changed by simply pressing that red "Leica" dot under the lug and replacing the sportive vulcanized rubber strap or elastic textile strap with an elegant titanium or stainless-steel bracelet.

Other aesthetic features from the cameras can be found in the details on the watches, including of course the shutter-like dial itself, which changes color when the watch is tilted. Note, too, the fine hands and indexes, the shape of the intricately crafted stainless-steel case, or the special fluting on the crowns (from the shutter button). The cambered sapphire crystal, of course, is reminiscent of Leica lenses.

Leica maintains a full-fledged watchmaking atelier at the company's Wetzlar site, where the timepieces are prepared for shipment and any warranty claims are handled. As for distribution, there are dedicated camera shops around the world.

ERNST LEITZ WERKSTÄTTEN GMBH
Am Leitz-Park 4
D-35578 Wetzlar
Germany

TEL.:
+49 6441-899-330

E-MAIL:
pr@ernst-leitz-werkstaetten.com

WEBSITE:
www.ernst-leitz-werkstaetten.com

FOUNDED:
2022

NUMBER OF EMPLOYEES:
7

DISTRIBUTION
Retail, direct sales
Leica Store LA
424-777-0341
leicastore.la@leica-camera.com
Leica Store
202-787-5900
leicastore.dc@leica-camera.com

MOST IMPORTANT COLLECTIONS/PRICE RANGE:
ZM 1 and ZM 2, monochrome versions, ZM 11 /
$10,000 to $15,500

ZM 1

Movement: hand-wound, Leica caliber ZM 1;
ø 35.75 mm, height 6.35 mm; 26 jewels; 28,800 vph;
automatic seconds zero reset; 60-hour power reserve
Functions: hours, minutes, subsidiary seconds; power-reserve indicator; date
Case: stainless steel, ø 41 mm, height 14.5 mm;
sapphire crystal; transparent case back; patented crown
with pusher that switches between winding and time-setting, with a switch indicator; water-resistant to 5 atm
Band: calfskin, pin buckle
Price: $10,000

ZM 2

Movement: hand-wound, Leica caliber ZM 2;
ø 35.75 mm, height 8.4 mm; 26 jewels; 28,800 vph;
automatic seconds zero reset; 60-hour power reserve
Functions: hours, minutes, subsidiary seconds;
additional 12-hour display (2nd time zone), day/night
indication, power reserve indicator (crown-activated
scale ring on the flange); date
Case: stainless steel, ø 41 mm, height 14.5 mm;
sapphire crystal; transparent case back; patented crown
with pusher that switches between winding and time-setting, with a switch indicator; water-resistant to 5 atm
Band: calfskin, pin buckle
Price: $13,480

ZM 11

Movement: automatic, Leica caliber LA-3001 (Chronode
C102 base); ø 30.4 mm, height 4.15 mm; 35 jewels;
28,800 vph; automatic seconds zero reset; 60-hour
power reserve
Functions: hours, minutes, sweep seconds; date
Case: titanium, ø 41 mm, height 13 mm; sapphire
crystal; transparent case back; water-resistant to
10 atm
Band: textile, pin buckle
Remarks: rapid strap changing system activated by a
red button (like the lens locking mechanism on Leica
cameras)
Price: $7,325
Variations: with titanium bracelet ($8,150); in stainless
steel with bracelet ($7,450); in stainless steel with
rubber or textile strap ($6,775)

LIP

Like the Vallée de Joux, or Geneva, or La Chaux-de-Fonds, the town of Besançon, France, was at one time a major watchmaking hub. It even has an observatory, which was once upon a time needed to set watches.

In 1867, Emmanuel Lipmann founded a small watchmaking enterprise in this booming town and, together with his sons, quickly established himself as a specialist in stopwatches. They were an innovative family. In 1904, Ernest Lipmann had Pierre and Marie Curie prepare a radium paint for dials. During the First World War, observation watches and chronographs equipped in this way were in great demand, but it was not until the 1930s that the brand took off with a mass-produced wristwatch caliber (T18).

In 1952, Fred Lipmann, who had been forced to change his name to Lip during the war under the Vichy Regime, released the first electromechanical wristwatch, and in the 1970s, Lip became the first European company to produce quartz watches in series. There were problems, however, with Japanese and American competition, the oil crisis in 1973, and the drop in the dollar exchange rate. The company had to file for bankruptcy. The unionized workers, however, resisted, and Lip became a household name for the workers' movement in France. And they won. A workers' committee transferred the company to collective self-management and hired the designer Roger Tallon, who, with the legendary Mach 2000, contributed significantly to the unexpected but brief rise of the Lip brand. After renewed economic troubles, however, Lip was restructured into a co-operative in the 1980s and liquidated in 1990.

At the turn of the millennium, the brand was revitalized using Chinese technology and by 2014 had returned to new production facilities at its former founding site in Besançon. Shortly afterwards, the first watches manufactured in France were unveiled, and since then, Lip has seen a steady rise in the favor of watch buyers. The interesting history of the brand, coupled with the distinctive aesthetics of the reinterpreted classics, and not least the very affordable prices of the product, even for well-equipped automatic watches, make Lip an insider tip for collectors and newcomers alike.

MONTRES LIP
Chemin des Maurapans
ZAC Valentin
F-25075 Besançon
France

TEL.:
+33-381-48-48-41

EMAIL:
lip@smb-horlogerie.com

WEBSITE:
www.lip.fr

FOUNDED:
1867/2014

NUMBER OF EMPLOYEES:
8

DISTRIBUTION:
Retail, webshop

PRICE RANGE:
$150 to $1,700

Mythic Titane Automatique

Reference number: 671658
Movement: automatic, Miyota 82S0; ø 26 mm, height 5.67 mm; 21 jewels; 21,600 vph; skeletonized movement with côtes de Genève on bridges; 41-hour power reserve
Functions: hours, minutes, sweep seconds
Case: titanium, 35 mm x 35 mm, height 10 mm; sapphire crystal; water-resistant to 5 atm
Band: brushed titanium, folding clasp
Remarks: original design by Prisca Briquet
Price: $935

Grande Nautic-Océan Automatique 41 mm

Reference number: 671854
Movement: automatic, Miyota caliber 8215; ø 25.6 mm, height 5.67 mm; 21 jewels; 21,600 vph; 38-hour power reserve
Functions: hours, minutes, sweep seconds (with stop-second); date
Case: stainless steel, ø 41 mm, height 12 mm; crown-activated inner rotating scale ring with 0-60 scale; sapphire crystal; transparent case back; water-resistant to 20 atm
Band: vulcanized rubber, pin buckle
Price: $575

Rallye Automatique Chronographe 42 mm

Reference number: 671821
Movement: automatic, Seiko caliber NE86; ø 28.6 mm, height 7.62 mm; 34 jewels; 28,800 vph; bidirectional rotor with côtes de Genève; column wheel control of chronograph functions, with vertical clutch; 45-hour power reserve
Functions: hours, minutes, subsidiary seconds; date; chronograph with minute totalizer; tachymeter scale
Case: stainless steel, 42 mm, height 13 mm; sapphire crystal; water-resistant to 5 atm
Band: calfskin, pin buckle
Remarks: inspired by the "Ninja" model of the late 1960s thus named because of the white mask around the subsidiary dials; screw-down case back with engraving of Bugatti T35
Price: $1,655; limited to 999 pieces

LONGINES

The Longines winged hourglass logo is the world's oldest trademark, according to the World Intellectual Property Organization (WIPO). Since its founding in 1832, the brand has manufactured somewhere in the region of 35 million watches, making it one of the genuine heavyweights of the Swiss watch world. In 1983, Nicolas G. Hayek merged the two major Swiss watch manufacturing groups ASUAG and SIHH into what would later become the Swatch Group. Longines, the leading ASUAG brand, barely missed capturing the same position in the new concern; that honor went to Omega, the SIHH frontrunner. However, from a historical and technical point of view, this brand has what it takes to be at the helm of any group. Was it not Longines that equipped polar explorer Roald Amundsen and air pioneer Charles Lindbergh with their watches? It has also been the timekeeper at many Olympic Games and is a major sponsor at many other sports events, from riding to archery.

Longines now has an impressive portfolio of in-house calibers in stock, from simple manual winders to complicated chronographs. Thanks to this stock, it can supply Swatch Group with anything from cheap, thin quartz watches to heavy gold chronographs and calendars with quadruple retrograde displays. In addition to elegant ladies' watches and modern sports watches such as the HydroConquest and Spirit collections, remakes of great classics, the company has made a point of remaking models from its own history through the Heritage collection. For example, the Ultra-Chron, with its high-speed oscillating movement, has been reissued exclusively for Longines with modern technology. There is also a detailed replica of a pilot's watch from the 1930s, whose special feature is an internal reference time index that can be adjusted via the rotating bezel. In 2024, the striking Legend Diver Watch, with its inner, crown-activated rotating bezel for setting the dive time, is being presented with new dial variants.

LONGINES WATCH CO.
Rue des Longines 8
CH-2610 St-Imier
Switzerland

TEL.:
+41-32-942-5425

E-MAIL:
info@longines.com

WEBSITE:
www.longines.com

FOUNDED:
1832

NUMBER OF EMPLOYEES:
worldwide approx. 2000

U.S. DISTRIBUTOR:
Longines
The Swatch Group (U.S.), Inc.
Longines Division
703 Waterford Way, Ste. 450
Miami, FL 33126
786-725-5393
www.longines.com

MOST IMPORTANT COLLECTIONS/PRICE RANGE:
The Longines Master Collection, Longines DolceVita, HydroConquest, Heritage Collection / from approx. $1,000 to $10,000

Pilot Majetek

Reference number: L2.838.1.53.2
Movement: automatic, Longines caliber L893.6 (based on ETA A31.501); ø 25.6 mm; 26 jewels; 25,200 vph; silicon hairspring, antimagnetic nickel-phosphorus escapement wheel and anchor (LIGA technology); 72-hour power reserve
Functions: hours, minutes, subsidiary seconds
Case: stainless steel, ø 42 mm, height 13.3; bidirectional bezel (under the crystal) with reference markings; sapphire crystal; screw-in crown; water-resistant to 10 atm
Band: textile, pin buckle
Remarks: modeled on a pilot's watch of the Czech air force ("Majetek")
Price: $5,000; limited to 1935 pieces

Spirit Flyback

Reference number: L3.821.1.53.6
Movement: automatic, Longines caliber L791.4 (Basis ETA A08.261); ø 30 mm, height 7.9 mm; 28 jewels; 28,800 vph; silicon hairspring, Column wheel control of the chronograph functions; COSC-certified chronometer; 68-hour power reserve
Functions: hours, minutes, subsidiary seconds; flyback chronograph
Case: titanium, ø 42 mm, height 17 mm; bidirectional bezel with ceramic insert, with 0-60 scale; sapphire crystal; transparent case back; screw-down crown; water-resistant to 10 atm
Band: titanium, double folding clasp
Price: $5,200

Spirit Flyback

Reference number: L3.821.5.59.2
Movement: automatic, Longines caliber L791.4 (Basis ETA A08.261); ø 30 mm, height 7.9 mm; 28 jewels; 28,800 vph; silicon hairspring, column wheel control of the chronograph functions; COSC-certified chronometer; 68-hour power reserve
Functions: hours, minutes, subsidiary seconds; flyback chronograph
Case: stainless steel, ø 42 mm, height 17 mm; yellow-gold bidirectional bezel with ceramic insert, with 0-60 scale; sapphire crystal; transparent case back; screw-down crown, yellow-gold crown and pushers; water-resistant to 10 atm
Band: calfskin, double folding clasp, with fine adjustment
Price: $6,500

Spirit Zulu Time

Reference number: L3.802.1.53.6
Movement: automatic, Longines caliber L844 (ETA A31.411 base); ø 25.6 mm, height 3.85 mm; 21 jewels; 25,200 vph; silicon hairspring, antimagnetic escapement (LIGA technology); COSC-certified chronometer; 72-hour power reserve
Functions: hours, minutes, sweep seconds (incremental setting of hour hand); additional 24-hour display (second time zone); date
Case: titanium, ø 39 mm, height 13.5 mm; bidirectional bezel with ceramic insert, with 0-24 scale; sapphire crystal; screw-down crown; water-resistant to 10 atm
Band: titanium, double folding clasp
Price: $4,275

Conquest Heritage Central Power Reserve

Reference number: L1.648.4.78.2
Movement: automatic, Longines caliber L896.5 (ETA A31.321 base); ø 25.6 mm; 21 jewels; 25,200 vph; silicon hairspring, antimagnetic escapement (LIGA technology); 72-hour power reserve
Functions: hours, minutes, sweep seconds; power reserve indicator; date
Case: stainless steel, ø 38 mm, height 12.3 mm; sapphire crystal; water-resistant to 5 atm
Band: reptile skin, pin buckle
Price: $3,800

Conquest Heritage Central Power Reserve

Reference number: L1.648.4.62.2
Movement: automatic, Longines caliber L896.5 (ETA A31.321 base); ø 25.6 mm; 21 jewels; 25,200 vph; silicon hairspring, antimagnetic escapement (LIGA technology); 72-hour power reserve
Functions: hours, minutes, sweep seconds; power reserve indicator; date
Case: stainless steel, ø 38 mm, height 12.3 mm; sapphire crystal; water-resistant to 5 atm
Band: reptile skin, pin buckle
Price: $3,800

Conquest Heritage Central Power Reserve

Reference number: L1.648.4.52.2
Movement: automatic, Longines caliber L896.5 (ETA A31.321 base); ø 25.6 mm; 21 jewels; 25,200 vph; silicon hairspring, antimagnetic escapement (LIGA technology); 72-hour power reserve
Functions: hours, minutes, sweep seconds; power reserve indicator; date
Case: stainless steel, ø 38 mm, height 12.3 mm; sapphire crystal; water-resistant to 5 atm
Band: reptile skin, pin buckle
Price: $3,800

Legend Diver

Reference number: L3.764.4.99.6
Movement: automatic, Longines caliber L888.5 (ETA A31.L11 base); ø 25.6 mm, height 3.85 mm; 21 jewels; 25,200 vph; silicon hairspring, antimagnetic escapement (LIGA technology); 72-hour power reserve
Functions: hours, minutes, sweep seconds
Case: stainless steel, ø 39 mm, height 12.7 mm; crown-activated inner ring with 0-60 scale; sapphire crystal; screw-down crown; water-resistant to 30 atm
Band: stainless steel, double folding clasp
Price: $3,300

Conquest

Reference number: L3.430.4.02.6
Movement: automatic, Longines caliber L888 (ETA A31.L01 base); ø 25.6 mm, height 3.85 mm; 21 jewels; 25,200 vph; silicon hairspring; 72-hour power reserve
Functions: hours, minutes, sweep seconds; date
Case: stainless steel, ø 34 mm, height 10.9 mm; sapphire crystal; transparent case back; water-resistant to 10 atm
Band: stainless steel, double folding clasp
Price: $2,075

Conquest

Reference number: L3.430.0.87.9
Movement: automatic, Longines caliber L888 (ETA A31.L11 base); ø 25.6 mm, height 3.85 mm; 21 jewels; 25,200 vph; silicon hairspring; 72-hour power reserve
Functions: hours, minutes, sweep seconds; date
Case: stainless steel, ø 40 mm, height 10.9 mm; bezel set with 48 diamonds; sapphire crystal; transparent case back; water-resistant to 10 atm
Band: rubber, double folding clasp, with fine adjustment
Remarks: dial set with 14 diamonds
Price: $4,100

Conquest

Reference number: L3.430.5.92.9
Movement: automatic, Longines caliber L888 (ETA A31.L11 base); ø 25.6 mm, height 3.85 mm; 21 jewels; 25,200 vph; silicon hairspring; 72-hour power reserve
Functions: hours, minutes, sweep seconds; date
Case: stainless steel, ø 34 mm, height 10.9 mm; bezel in rose gold; sapphire crystal; transparent case back; crown in rose gold; water-resistant to 10 atm
Band: rubber, double folding clasp
Price: $3,000

Conquest

Reference number: L3.720.4.92.6
Movement: automatic, Longines caliber L888 (Basis ETA A31.L11); ø 25.6 mm, height 3.85 mm; 21 jewels; 25,200 vph; silicon hairspring; 72-hour power reserve
Functions: hours, minutes, sweep seconds; date
Case: stainless steel, ø 38 mm, height 10.9 mm; sapphire crystal; transparent case back; water-resistant to 10 atm
Band: stainless steel, double folding clasp
Price: $2,075

Conquest

Reference number: L3.835.4.02.9
Movement: automatic, Longines caliber L898 (ETA A31.L21 base); ø 28 mm, height 6.35 mm; 37 jewels; 25,200 vph; silicon hairspring; 72-hour power reserve
Functions: hours, minutes, subsidiary seconds; chronograph
Case: stainless steel, ø 42 mm, height 14.3 mm; bezel set with ceramic insert; sapphire crystal; transparent case back; water-resistant to 10 atm
Band: rubber, double folding clasp, with fine adjustment
Price: $3,650

HydroConquest GMT

Reference number: L3.890.4.96.9
Movement: automatic, Longines caliber L844 (Basis ETA A31.411); ø 25.6 mm, height 3.85 mm; 21 jewels; 25,200 vph; silicon hairspring, antimagnetic escapement (LIGA technology); 72-hour power reserve
Functions: hours, minutes, sweep seconds (incremental setting of hour hands); additional 24-hour display (second time zone); date
Case: stainless steel, ø 43 mm, height 12.9 mm; unidirectional bezel with ceramic insert, with 0-60 scale; sapphire crystal; screw-down crown; water-resistant to 30 atm
Band: rubber, double folding clasp, with fine adjustment
Price: $2,775

HydroConquest GMT

Reference number: L3.890.4.56.6
Movement: automatic, Longines caliber L844 (Basis ETA A31.411); ø 25.6 mm, height 3.85 mm; 21 jewels; 25,200 vph; silicon hairspring, antimagnetic escapement (LIGA technology); 72-hour power reserve
Functions: hours, minutes, sweep seconds (incremental setting of hour hands); additional 24-hour display (second time zone); date
Case: stainless steel, ø 43 mm, height 12.9 mm; unidirectional bezel with ceramic insert, with 0-60 scale; sapphire crystal; screw-down crown; water-resistant to 30 atm
Band: stainless steel, double folding clasp
Price: $2,975

LOUIS ERARD

Once upon a time in the watchmaking workshops, there was a large clock that gave the minutes as the main time increment and the hours on a separate dial. This allowed the watchmakers to set and test the accuracy of the piece they were assembling. Over time, so-called regulator dials became popular with the public. It is said that train conductors preferred them because they needed accuracy to the minute.

Among the rare brands that have made regulator watches an important part of their output is Louis Erard. The company namesake (1893–1964), a watchmaker by trade, founded a watchmaking school in his native La Chaux-de-Fonds, and later a casing business for the thriving industry, and then a watchmaking company under his own name.

Erard's business acumen was as good as his technical skill. In the 1930s, he worked on the legendary Valjoux 72 chronograph movement, and in 1956, his company received the coveted right to manufacture movements. In fact, Louis Erard, the company, managed to weather the quartz crisis thanks to a careful modernization program in the 1970s launched by Erard's grandson.

In 1992, Louis Erard moved to Le Noirmont in the Jura Mountains. It had some trouble maintaining a profile, until Manuel Emch of Jaquet Droz and Romain Jérôme stepped in. The new directive was "make collecting affordable" mainly through daring collaborations with the likes of Alain Silberstein, Konstantin Chaykin, Massena Lab, Vianney Halter, and more. Collections are limited, and most watches are under $5,000 dollars. These watches seem to be finding customers amongst those seeking "something different," and because they are in limited editions (178 pieces), they do have a clear collector appeal.

The recipe for Louis Erard appears to be working, and the brand has woken up from a long sleep. It allows for lots of creativity and bold products that still depend on solid watchmaking. Those who keep a close eye on the industry are always curious to see what the little company up in the Jura will be producing next. They will have to note, however, that the collections have been renamed: 2300 for chronographs, Noirmont for regular watches, Noirmont X for the collaborations, and Noirmont métiers d'art to create a platform for the many decorative handcrafts.

LOUIS ERARD SA
Ouest 2
CH-2340 Le Noirmont
Switzerland

TEL.:
+41-32-957-65-30

E-MAIL:
info@louiserard.com

WEBSITE:
www.louiserard.com

FOUNDED:
1929

NUMBER OF EMPLOYEES:
15

ANNUAL PRODUCTION:
not specified

DISTRIBUTION/SALES:
Contact the company in Switzerland.
In the USA:
Exquisite Timepieces
4380 Gulfshore Blvd., N. Suite 800
Naples, FL 34103
239-666-8163
exquisitetimepieces.com

CELLINI JEWELERS
430 Park Ave
New York, NY 10022
212-888-0505
cellinijewelers.com

MOST IMPORTANT COLLECTIONS/PRICE RANGE:
2300 (chronographs), Noirmont, Noirmont X /
$1,000 to $5,000

Noirmont Le Régulateur Gravé Noir

Reference number: 85237AA89
Movement: automatic, Sellita SW266-1; ø 22 mm, height 5.60 mm; 31 jewels; 28,800 vph; open-worked oscillating weight with Louis Erard logo, 38-hour power reserve
Functions: hour disk, sweep minute, seconds disk
Case: stainless steel, ø 42 mm, height 12.25 mm; sapphire crystal; transparent case back; water-resistant to 5 atm
Band: calfskin, pin buckle
Remarks: first sector-type dial
Price: $4,500; limited to 178 pieces
Variations: with green minute track; in 39-millimeter case

Excellence Petite Seconde Guilloché

Reference number: 34248AA21.BVA150
Movement: automatic, Sellita SW266-1 (*élaboré* quality); ø 25.60 mm, height 5.60 mm; 31 jewels; 28,800 vph; finely finished movement; open-worked oscillating weight with Louis Erard logo, 38-hour power reserve
Functions: hours, minutes, subsidiary seconds
Case: stainless steel, ø 39 mm, height 12.82 mm; crown with fir-tree pattern; sapphire crystal; transparent case back; water-resistant to 5 atm
Band: calfskin, pin buckle, quick strap change system
Remarks: hand guilloché flinqué on dial center (draped guilloché), basket guilloché for hour track and subsidiary seconds dial
Price: $2,990; limited to 178 pieces in all
Variations: with slate dial

2300 Chronograph Sport Rainbow

Reference number: 78119TS32.BDF02
Movement: automatic, ETA 7750 Valjoux; ø 30 mm, height 7.9 mm; 25 jewels; 28,800 vph, finely finished chronograph movement; openworked oscillating weight, 48-hour power reserve
Functions: hours, minutes, subsidiary seconds; chronograph with tachymeter scale; date and weekday
Case: titanium, ø 44 mm, height 15 mm; sapphire crystal; bezel with ceramic insert; transparent, screw-down case back; water-resistant to 5 atm
Band: rubber (FKM), folding clasp with rapid change system
Remarks: rainbow colors as guide on the minute track
Price: $4,490; limited to 99 pieces
Variations: with blue-themed or orange/green-themed dial ($4,490); limited to 99 pieces each

LOUIS MOINET

There's always something happening at Louis Moinet, but what really boosted the brand was a rather special historic discovery: in the race to be the first to invent something new, Louis Moinet (1768–1853), it seems, emerged as the first maker of a chronograph. His *Compteur de tierces*, dating to 1816, was revealed to the public in 2013. This special chronograph counted one-sixtieth of a second with a frequency of 216,000 vph. It was built to make more accurate astronomical calculations.

The original Louis Moinet was a professor at the Academy of Fine Arts in Paris and president of the Société Chronométrique and was without a doubt one of the most inventive, multitalented men of his time. He worked with such eminent watchmakers as Breguet, Berthoud, Winnerl, Janvier, and Perrelet. Among his accomplishments is an extensive two-volume treatise on horology.

Following in such footsteps is hardly an easy task, but Jean-Marie Schaller and Micaela Bertolucci decided that their idiosyncratic creations were indeed imbued with the spirit of the great Frenchman. They work with a team of independent designers, watchmakers, movement specialists, and other suppliers to produce the most unusual wristwatches filled with clever functions and surprising details. The Jules Verne chronographs have hinged levers, for example, and the second hand on the Tempograph changes direction every ten seconds.

Increasingly, this independent-minded brand is exploring the worlds of astronomy, space travel, and science fiction, and it has been attracting a lot of attention. The Cosmopolis won a Guinness world record for being the watch "with the most meteorite inserts." The Black Moon and Moon Tech use rare lunar meteorites to depict the astronomical moon traveling on a central dome surrounded by a dial made from a microelectronic wafer. The marker for the current stage is the 3 o'clock index, which is covered by a bit of Kapton from the Apollo 11 mission. The Astronef line features two satellite tourbillons revolving at different speeds around the dial over a microelectronic wafer. As for the Time to Race, the customer can pick his or her number and color pattern, and that watch will then be unique. The mission at Louis Moinet is to make watches that tell stories.

LES ATELIERS LOUIS MOINET SA
Rue du Temple 1
CH-2072 Saint-Blaise
Switzerland

TEL.:
+41-32-753-6814

E-MAIL:
info@louismoinet.com

WEBSITE:
www.louismoinet.com

FOUNDED:
2005

U.S. DISTRIBUTOR:
Fitzhenry Consulting
1029 Peachtree Parkway, #346
Peachtree City, GA 30269
561-212-6812
Don@fitzhenry.com

MOST IMPORTANT COLLECTIONS:
Memoris, Sideralis, Tempograph Chrome,
Spacewalker, Ultravox; numerous unique pieces

Time to Race, Rosso Corsa
Reference number: LM-96.20.8R
Movement: automatic, Louis Moinet caliber LM 96; ø 30.40 mm, height 10.69 mm; 30 jewels; 28,800 vph; column-wheel control, monopusher chronograph; screw balance; oscillating mass with clous de Paris; mainplate with côtes de Genève; 48-hour power reserve
Functions: hours, minutes, subsidiary seconds, chronograph
Case: titanium, ø 40.7 mm, height 17.92 mm; sapphire crystal; screw-down transparent back; water-resistant to 5 atm
Band: rubber, folding clasp
Remarks: customers can choose their "lucky number" and one of several colors, so each piece is unique and will never be made again
Price: $36,000

Astronef
Reference number: LM-105.20.60
Movement: hand-wound, Louis Moinet caliber LM105; ø 38.50 mm, height 13.60 mm; 56 jewels; 21,600 vph; 2 spring barrels, one for each of the two satellite tourbillons rotating in opposite directions and at different rates, crossing paths 18 times per hour; each tourbillon has gold counterweights to ensure smooth rotation; 48-hour power reserve
Functions: hours, minutes
Case: titanium frame (ø 43.50 mm) with a sapphire crystal case, ø 41.60 mm, height 18.30 mm; transparent case back; water-resistant to 1 atm
Band: reptile skin, folding clasp
Price: $365,000; limited to 8 pieces

Cosmopolis
Reference number: LM-135.20.20
Movement: hand-wound, Louis Moinet caliber LM 135; ø 32 mm, height 5.70 mm; 26 jewels; 28,800 vph; 1-minute off-center flying tourbillon; two superimposed barrel springs arranged head to tail ("volte-face") to discharge energy simultaneously; 96-hour power reserve
Functions: hours, minutes
Case: titanium ø 40.7 mm, height 15.12 mm; domed sapphire crystal; water-resistant to 3 atm
Band: reptile skin, folding clasp
Remarks: this timepiece, featuring twelve distinct meteorites, holds the world record for "most meteorite inserts in a watch"
Price: $235,000; limited to 3 pieces

Starman

Reference number: LM-139.50.25
Movement: hand-wound, Louis Moinet caliber LM139;
ø 32 mm, height 5.70 mm; 26 jewels; 28,800 vph;
1-minute off-center flying tourbillon; two superimposed
barrel springs arranged head to tail ("volte-face")
to discharge energy simultaneously, 96-hour power
reserve
Functions: hours, minutes, seconds on tourbillon cage
Case: red gold, ø 47.4 mm, height 16.90 mm;
transparent case back; water-resistant to 3 atm
Band: reptile skin, folding clasp
Remarks: the planets on the rear can be positioned as
the owner would like
Price: $185,000; limited to 12 pieces

Jules Verne Mystery Island

Reference number: LM-135.50.V8
Movement: hand-wound, Louis Moinet caliber LM
135; ø 32 mm, height 5.70 mm; 26 jewels; 28,800 vph;
1-minute off-center flying tourbillon; two superimposed
barrel springs arranged head to tail ("volte-face")
to discharge energy simultaneously; 96-hour power
reserve
Functions: hours, minutes
Case: red gold, ø 40.7 mm, height 15.12 mm; sapphire
crystal; water-resistant to 3 atm
Band: reptile skin, folding clasp
Remarks: one of 8 unique pieces each with a different
slice of lapis lazuli in the dial center; hand-guilloché with
special translucid varnish
Price: $129,900

Tempograph Neo, Lapis Lazuli

Reference number: LM-125.10.20
Movement: automatic, Louis Moinet caliber LM 85;
ø 30.40 mm, height 8.29 mm; 36 jewels; 28,800 vph;
screw balance with 18 screws; partially skeletonized
movement, oscillating mass with clous de Paris, 48-hour
power reserve
Functions: hours, minutes, seconds (retrograde on
20-second scale with tricolored 1-minute counter on
subdial)
Case: stainless steel, ø 44 mm, height 14.75; water-
resistant to 5 atm
Band: rubber with alligator pattern, folding clasp
Price: $29,900; limited to 28 pieces

Black Moon

Reference number: LM-110.20.50
Movement: automatic, Louis Moinet caliber LM 110;
ø 30.4 mm, height 12.70 mm; 29 jewels; 28,800 vph;
astronomical moon, the full moon and the new moon
are represented by lunar meteorites placed on a domed
central disc; 48-hour power reserve
Functions: hours, minutes, seconds, moon
Case: titanium, ø 40.7 mm, height 17.92 mm; domed
sapphire crystal; water-resistant to 3 atm
Band: reptile skin, folding clasp
Price: $34,000, limited to 60 pieces

Moon Tech

Reference number: LM-111.20.01
Movement: automatic, Louis Moinet caliber LM 110;
ø 30.4 mm, height 12.70 mm; 29 jewels; 28,800 vph;
48-hour power reserve
Functions: hours, minutes, seconds; moon phase
Case: titanium, ø 40.7 mm, height 17.92 mm; domed
sapphire crystal; water-resistant to 3 atm
Band: reptile skin, folding clasp
Remarks: astronomical moon on domed central disc
(full and new moons of lunar meteorites), current phase
indicated at 3 o'clock by index covered with Kapton foil
from the Apollo 11 mission; silicon wafer microelectronic
circuits used for dial
Price: $37,000, limited to 11 pieces

Memoris Neo, Onyx

Reference number: LM-124.20.50
Movement: automatic, Louis Moinet caliber LM 84;
ø 30.40 mm, height 10.69 mm; 30 jewels; 28,800 vph;
column-wheel control, monopusher chronograph; screw
balance; oscillating mass with clous de Paris; 48-hour
power reserve
Functions: hours, minutes, subsidiary seconds,
chronograph
Case: titanium, ø 46 mm, height 16.82 mm; sapphire
crystal; screw-down transparent back; water-resistant
to 5 atm
Band: rubber with alligator pattern, folding clasp
Remarks: each timepiece comes with a pair of cufflinks
representing Louis Moinet's "compteur de tierce"
Price: $36,000, limited to 28 pieces

MAURICE LACROIX

The roots of the brand Maurice Lacroix run deep, all the way to the late nineteenth century, in fact. The name Maurice Lacroix, however, was chosen in 1975 and carried the brand to respectable international success. In 2011, DKSH (Diethelm Keller & SiberHegner), a Swiss holding company that specializes in international market expansions, became the majority shareholder. This has ensured Maurice Lacroix a strong position in all major markets, with flagship stores and its own boutiques.

Nevertheless, the heart of the company remains the production facilities in the highlands of the Jura, in Saignelégier and Montfaucon, where the brand built La Manufacture des Franches-Montagnes SA (MFM) outfitted with state-of-the-art technology to produce very specific individual parts and movement components.

The watchmaker can thank the clever interpretations of "classic" pocket watch characteristics for its steep ascent in the 1990s. Since then, the *manufacture* has redesigned the complete collection, banning every lick of Breguet-like bliss from its watch designs. In the upper segment, *manufacture* models such as the chronograph and the retrograde variations on Unitas calibers set the tone. In the lower segment, modern "little" complications outfitted with module movements based on ETA and Sellita are the kings. The brand is mainly associated with the hypnotically turning square wheel, the "roue carrée."

The Aikon collection has been gaining in popularity ever since its introduction in 2016. It has a sort of back-to-the-roots quality: precise timekeeping, high readability, and exceptionally comfortable wear. And like all other Maurice Lacroix watches, the Aikon offers a lot of perceived value. The latest creation in the Aikon family is a collaboration with Tide Ocean SA, a company with the mission of recycling and upcycling plastic collected from the oceans: The AIKON #tide comes in a variety of bright colors. The design is genuinely cool. The new Pontos S Diver has been competing with the Aikon, however. The professionally equipped diver's watch made way for the revived sports watch line in 2016, but now it is coming back—a little less martial than before but more wearable and still a "real diver's watch" from the thick sapphire crystal to the screw-down crown.

MAURICE LACROIX SA
Rue des Rangiers 21
2350 Saignelégier
Switzerland

TEL.:
+41- 43-434-66-66

E-MAIL:
info@mauricelacroix.com

WEBSITE:
www.mauricelacroix.com

FOUNDED:
1975

NUMBER OF EMPLOYEES:
about 150 worldwide

U.S. DISTRIBUTOR:
DKSH Premium Brand Distribution
Suite 21331 NE 17TH St
Miami, FL 33132
609-750-8800

MOST IMPORTANT COLLECTIONS/PRICE RANGE:
Aikon / $990 to $4,600; Les Classiques / $950 to $4,300; Eliros / $690 to $1,390; Fiaba (ladies') / $1,150 to $2,900; Pontos / $2,090 to $3,750; Masterpiece manufacture models / $6,250 to $14,900

Masterpiece Skeleton Label Noir

Reference number: MP7228-DLB04-090-2
Movement: hand-wound, caliber ML 134; 19 jewels; 18,000 vph; fully skeletonized movement; open barrel spring; 45-hour power reserve
Functions: hours, minutes, subsidiary seconds
Case: stainless steel with grey DLC (gunmetal), ø 43 mm, height 13 mm; bezel and crown with black DLC; sapphire crystal; transparent case back; water-resistant to 5 atm
Band: textile, double folding clasp
Price: $7,950; limited to 288 pieces

Masterpiece Triple Retrograde

Reference number: MP6538-SS001-110-1
Movement: automatic, Sellita caliber SW200-1 with ML291 module; ø 25.6 mm; 47 jewels; 28,800 vph; 38-hour power reserve
Functions: hours, minutes, subsidiary seconds; additional 24-hour display (retrograde); date and weekday (retrograde)
Case: stainless steel, ø 43 mm, height 14 mm; sapphire crystal; transparent case back; water-resistant to 5 atm
Band: calfskin, folding clasp
Price: $6,250
Variations: various straps and dials

Aikon Master Grand Date

Reference number: AI6118-DLB0B-330-2
Movement: automatic, caliber ML 331; ø 37.2 mm; 43 jewels; 18,000 vph; 50-hour power reserve
Functions: hours and minutes (off-center), subsidiary seconds; large date
Case: stainless steel with black DLC, ø 45 mm, height 15 mm; sapphire crystal; water-resistant to 10 atm
Band: rubber, double folding clasp
Remarks: comes with extra Nylon strap
Price: $9,600
Variations: various cases, straps, and dials

Aikon Automatic PVD

Reference number: AI6008-PVB00-330-2
Movement: automatic, caliber ML 115 (Sellita SW200-1 base); ø 25.6 mm, height 4.6 mm; 26 jewels; 28,800 vph; 38-hour power reserve
Functions: hours, minutes, sweep seconds
Case: stainless steel with grey DLC (gunmetal). ø 42 mm, height 11 mm; sapphire crystal; transparent case back; screw-down crown; water-resistant to 20 atm
Band: rubber, pin buckle
Price: $2,550; limited to 888 pieces

Aikon Automatic Chronograph Titanium

Reference number: AI6038-TT030-330-2
Movement: automatic, caliber ML 112 (ETA 7750 base); ø 30 mm, height 7.9 mm; 25 jewels; 28,800 vph; 48-hour power reserve
Functions: hours, minutes, subsidiary seconds; chronograph; date and weekday
Case: titanium, ø 44 mm, height 15 mm; sapphire crystal; transparent case back; screw-down crown; water-resistant to 20 atm
Band: rubber, pin buckle
Price: $4,350

Aikon Automatic Date 42 mm

Reference number: AI6008-SS002-630-1
Movement: automatic, caliber ML 115 (Sellita SW200-1 base); ø 25.6 mm, height 4.6 mm; 26 jewels; 28,800 vph; 38-hour power reserve
Functions: hours, minutes, sweep seconds; date
Case: stainless steel, ø 42 mm, height 11 mm; sapphire crystal; transparent case back; screw-down crown; water-resistant to 20 atm
Band: stainless steel, double folding clasp
Price: $2,300
Variations: various dial colors

Aikon Automatic Skeleton

Reference number: AI6007-SS002-030-1
Movement: automatic, caliber ML 115 (Sellita SW200-1 base); ø 25.6 mm, height 4.6 mm; 26 jewels; 28,800 vph; skeletonized movement; 38-hour power reserve
Functions: hours, minutes, sweep seconds
Case: stainless steel, ø 39 mm, height 11 mm; sapphire crystal; transparent case back; screw-down crown; water-resistant to 20 atm
Band: stainless steel, double folding clasp
Price: $3,850

Aikon Automatic Bronze

Reference number: AI6008-BRZ01-730-3
Movement: automatic, caliber ML 115 (Sellita SW200-1 base); ø 25.6 mm, height 4.6 mm; 26 jewels; 28,800 vph; 38-hour power reserve
Functions: hours, minutes, sweep seconds; date
Case: bronze, ø 42 mm, height 11 mm; sapphire crystal; transparent case back; screw-down crown; water-resistant to 20 atm
Band: calfskin, pin buckle
Price: $2,650; limited to 888 pieces

Aikon Chrono Quartz

Reference number: AI1118-SS002-230-1
Movement: quartz
Functions: hours, minutes, subsidiary seconds; chronograph; date
Case: stainless steel, ø 42 mm, height 11 mm; sapphire crystal; screw-down crown; water-resistant to 10 atm
Band: stainless steel, double folding clasp
Price: $1,400

MAURICE LACROIX

Aikon Automatic Date 35 mm

Reference number: AI6006-SS002-370-1
Movement: automatic, caliber ML 115 (Basis Sellita SW200-1); ø 25.6 mm, height 4.6 mm; 26 jewels; 28,800 vph; 38-hour power reserve
Functions: hours, minutes, sweep seconds; date
Case: stainless steel, ø 35 mm; sapphire crystal; transparent case back; screw-down crown; water-resistant to 20 atm
Band: stainless steel, double folding clasp
Remarks: dial with 8 diamond indexes
Price: $2,400
Variations: various dial colors

Aikon Quartz Colors

Reference number: AI1106-SS002-450-1
Movement: quartz
Functions: hours, minutes, sweep seconds; date
Case: stainless steel, ø 35 mm, height 9 mm; sapphire crystal; water-resistant to 10 atm
Band: stainless steel, double folding clasp
Remarks: dial with diamond indexes (56 diamonds)
Price: $1,350

Aikon Quartz

Reference number: AI1106-PVY13-170-1
Movement: quartz
Functions: hours, minutes, sweep seconds; date
Case: stainless steel, ø 35 mm, height 9 mm; bezel set with yellow-gold PVD-coated elements; sapphire crystal; water-resistant to 10 atm
Band: stainless steel with yellow-gold PVD-coated middle links, double folding clasp
Remarks: dial with diamond indexes (56 diamonds)
Price: $1,400

Pontos S Diver

Reference number: PT6248-BRZ01-330-3
Movement: automatic, caliber ML 115 (Sellita SW200-1 base); ø 25.6 mm, height 4.6 mm; 26 jewels; 28,800 vph; 38-hour power reserve
Functions: hours, minutes, sweep seconds; date
Case: Bronze, ø 42 mm, height 13 mm; crown-activated scale ring with 0-60 scale; sapphire crystal; screw-down crown; water-resistant to 30 atm
Band: calfskin, pin buckle
Price: $2,700; limited to 888 pieces

Pontos S Diver

Reference number: PT6248-SS00L-130-4
Movement: automatic, caliber ML 115 (Sellita SW200-1 base); ø 25.6 mm, height 4.6 mm; 26 jewels; 28,800 vph; 38-hour power reserve
Functions: hours, minutes, sweep seconds; date
Case: stainless steel, ø 42 mm, height 13 mm; crown-activated scale ring with 0-60 scale; sapphire crystal; screw-down crown; water-resistant to 30 atm
Band: rubber, pin buckle
Remarks: comes with extra white rubber strap
Price: $2,200

Pontos Day Date

Reference number: PT6358-SS002-334-1
Movement: automatic, caliber ML 143 (Sellita SW220 base); ø 25.6 mm, height 3.8 mm; 19 jewels; 28,800 vph; 38-hour power reserve
Functions: hours, minutes, sweep seconds; date and weekday
Case: stainless steel, ø 41 mm, height 11 mm; sapphire crystal; transparent case back; water-resistant to 10 atm
Band: stainless steel, double folding clasp
Price: $2,250

MB&F

In the world of alternative time-tellers, there is one prophet: Maximilian Büsser. After breaking away from brand constraints at Harry Winston, where he launched the Opus line, Büsser founded MB&F (that is, "and friends") with the mission of setting creators free. He acts as initiator and coordinator. His Horological Machines are developed and realized in cooperation with highly specialized watchmakers, inventors, and designers in an "idea collective" creating unheard-of mechanical timepieces of great inventiveness, complication, and exclusivity. The composition of this collective varies as much as each machine. Number 5 ("On the Road Again") is an homage to the 1970s, when streamlining rather than brawn represented true strength. The display in the lateral window is reflected by a prism. HM10 is engineering imitating nature, as the watch turns into a bulldog, with bulging, conical "eyes" that tell the time and jaws that open and close to tell you the power reserve.

Contrasting sharply with the modern productions are the Legacy Machines, which reach into horological history and reinterpret past mechanical feats. Even these, of late, have been showing some futuristic chromosomes, as it were. The incredibly complicated Sequential Evo, a collaboration with supreme watch wizard Stephen McDonnell, features two chronographs and a special switch, the "Twinverter," allowing for multiple time computations.

MB&F machines have won awards, several at the Grand Prix d'Horlogerie in different categories, and in 2022, the company clinched the Aiguille d'Or. Büsser is not himself a watchmaker, but his spirit, his deep knowledge of engineering, and his surefooted aesthetic instinct are always present in each new watch. They are also vented freely in the M.A.D. Galleries the world round, where one finds "mechanical art objects" that are beautiful, intriguing, technically impeccable, and sometimes perfectly useless. They have their own muse and serve as worthy companions to the sci-fi-inspired table clocks that MB&F produces with L'Epée 1839.

In-depth exploration of the possible in luxury watchmaking does require well-heeled companions, so in 2024, MB&F announced that Chanel Group had acquired a 25% stake in the company.

MB&F
Route de Drize, 2
CH-1227 Carouge
Switzerland

TEL.:
+41-22-786-3618

E-MAIL:
info@mbandf.com

WEBSITE:
www.mbandf.com

FOUNDED:
2005

NUMBER OF EMPLOYEES:
40

ANNUAL PRODUCTION:
approx. 350 watches

U.S. DISTRIBUTORS:
Westime Los Angeles and Miami
310-470-1388 (Los Angeles)
786-347-5353 (Miami)
info@westime.com
Provident Jewelry, Florida
561-747-4449; nick@providentjewelry.com
Stephen Silver, Redwood City (California)
650-325-9500; www.shsilver.com
Cellini, New York
212-888-0505; contact@cellinijewelers.com
Watches of Switzerland Las Vegas
702-792-0183, www.watchesofswitzerland.com

MOST IMPORTANT COLLECTIONS/PRICE RANGE:
Horological Machines / from $90,000; Legacy
Machines / from $64,000

Legacy Machine Sequential Flyback

Movement: hand-wound, MB&F caliber LM Sequential Flyback; ø 36.6 mm, height 12.6 mm; 63 jewels; 21,600 vph; dual spring barrel, inverted movement design with balance wheel hovering over the dial; dual chronograph mechanism with "twinverter" pushers to switch between modes; finely finished with côtes de Genève; 72-hour power reserve
Functions: hours and minutes (decentral); power reserve indicator; double chronograph with independent measurement and flyback function
Case: platinum, ø 44 mm, height 18.2 mm; sapphire crystal; transparent case back; screw-down crown; water-resistant to 3 atm
Band: reptile skin, folding clasp
Remarks: limited to 33 pieces
Price: $218,000

HM8 Mark 2

Movement: automatic, MB&F caliber HM8 (Girard-Perregaux base); 30.5 mm x 36.1 mm, height 7.2 mm; 30 jewels; 28,800 vph; gold rotor; disk display using a prism; 42-hour power reserve
Functions: hours (digital, jumping), minutes (digital)
Case: titanium with blue carbon Macrolon case cover, 41.5 mm x 47 mm, height 19 mm; sapphire crystal; transparent case back; water-resistant to 3 atm
Band: calfskin, pin buckle
Price: $78,000; limited to 33 pieces
Variations: with green or white case cover

Legacy Machine Perpetual EVO

Movement: hand-wound, MB&F caliber LM Perpetual; ø 36.6 mm, height 12.6 mm; 41 jewels; 18,000 vph; two spring barrels, inverted movement architecture with balance wheel hovering over the dial; finely finished with côtes de Genève; 72-hour power reserve
Functions: hours and minutes (off-center); power reserve indicator; perpetual calendar with date, weekday, month, leap year (retrograde)
Case: titanium, ø 44 mm, height 17.5 mm; sapphire crystal; transparent case back; water-resistant to 8 atm
Band: rubber, folding clasp
Price: $167,000
Variations: with green dial; in zirconium

MEISTERSINGER

MeisterSinger, headquartered in Münster, Germany, has made minimalism a hallmark of this brand, which was launched in 2001. Founder Manfred Brassler chose a look that, in many ways, returns to the very beginnings of watchmaking. Indeed, watch hands have different functions. The seconds hand is essentially there to tell that the watch is working, and the hour hand is essentially a slower minute hand, so the two can be pressed into service for a single function, thereby making space on the dial for the eye to wander.

MeisterSinger customers are looking for that combination of technical and cultural tradition of early watchmaking with Swiss-made quality and a uniquely purified design, which has earned the brand three dozen awards to date.

Looking at these ultimately simplified dials does tempt one to classify the one-hand watch as an archetype. The single hand simply cannot be reduced any further, and the 144 minutes for 12 hours around the dial do have a normative function of sorts. In other words, the watch does exactly what it's supposed to do. This applies to the looks as well: the unmistakable design elements make each MeisterSinger clearly recognizable, and that is what makes this brand's products so desirable.

By the same token, MeisterSinger also produces watches that deliver other functions without violating any of its codes. The collection includes models with day, date, power reserve, and moon phase displays, as well as hour strike. The new Pangaea Day Date 365 in historicizing style shows how effortlessly the design features of historical watches harmonize with the philosophy of MeisterSinger. The vintage Neo watch has been upgraded by replacing the previously used hard plexiglass with scratch-resistant sapphire crystal. The tried-and-true Unomat is given an even sportier look and an impressive luminosity thanks to the use of Lumicast. Unusual concepts, such as the Edition Passage, complete the 2024 collection.

MEISTERSINGER GMBH & CO. KG
Hafenweg 46
D-48155 Münster
Germany

TEL.:
+49-251-133-4860

E-MAIL:
info@meistersinger.de

WEBSITE:
www.meistersinger.de

FOUNDED:
2001

NUMBER OF EMPLOYEES:
13

ANNUAL PRODUCTION:
approx. 10,000 watches

U.S. DISTRIBUTOR:
Duber Time
1115 4th Street North Unit #B
Saint Petersburg, FL 33701
727-202-3262
damir@dubertime.com

PRICE RANGE:
from approx. $995 to $6,600

Pangaea Day Date
Reference number: PDD365901
Movement: automatic, Sellita caliber SW220; ø 25.6 mm, height 5.1 mm; 26 jewels; 28,800 vph; 38-hour power reserve
Functions: hours (each line marks a 5-minute increment); date and weekday
Case: stainless steel, ø 40 mm, height 11.7 mm; sapphire crystal; transparent case back; water-resistant to 5 atm
Band: calfskin, pin buckle
Price: $2,950
Variations: various dial colors

№ 03
Reference number: BM9908
Movement: automatic, Sellita caliber SW300-1; ø 25.6 mm, height 3.6 mm; 25 jewels; 28,800 vph; 42-hour power reserve
Functions: hours (each line marks a 5-minute increment)
Case: stainless steel, ø 38 mm, height 11 mm; sapphire crystal; water-resistant to 5 atm
Band: calfskin, pin buckle
Price: $2,250
Variations: with white or ivory dial

Stratoscope
Reference number: ST982G
Movement: automatic, MeisterSinger caliber MS-Luna (Sellita SW220-1 base); ø 25.6 mm, height 5.05 mm; 26 jewels; 28,800 vph; 38-hour power reserve
Functions: hours (each line marks a 5-minute increment); date, moon phase
Case: stainless steel, ø 43 mm, height 14.8 mm; sapphire crystal; transparent case back; water-resistant to 5 atm
Band: calfskin (saddle leather), folding clasp
Price: $4,899

№ 01

Reference number: AM903
Movement: hand-wound, Sellita caliber SW210; ø 25.6 mm, height 3.4 mm; 19 jewels; 28,800 vph; 42-hour power reserve
Functions: hours (each line marks a 5-minute increment)
Case: stainless steel, ø 43 mm, height 11.5 mm; sapphire crystal; water-resistant to 5 atm
Band: calfskin, pin buckle
Price: $2,500
Variations: with white or blue dial

Unomat

Reference number: UN902BLU
Movement: automatic, Sellita caliber SW400-1; ø 31 mm, height 4.67 mm; 26 jewels; 28,800 vph; anti-magnetic; 38-hour power reserve
Functions: hours (each line marks a 5-minute increment); date
Case: stainless steel, ø 43 mm, height 13.95 mm; sapphire crystal; screw-down crown; water-resistant to 30 atm
Band: rubber, pin buckle
Price: $2,750
Variations: with orange dial elements

Bell Hora

Reference number: BHO918G
Movement: automatic, MeisterSinger caliber MS-Bell (Sellita SW200-1 base with hour chime); ø 25.6 mm, height 6.9 mm; 26 jewels; 28,800 vph; 38-hour power reserve
Functions: hours (each line marks a 5-minute increment), acoustic hour chime (can be muted)
Case: stainless steel, ø 43 mm, height 14.95 mm; sapphire crystal; transparent case back
Band: calfskin, folding clasp
Price: $4,850
Variations: various dial colors

Neo

Reference number: NES901G
Movement: automatic, Sellita caliber SW200-1; ø 25.6 mm, height 4.6 mm; 26 jewels; 28,800 vph; 38-hour power reserve
Functions: hours (each line marks a 5-minute increment)
Case: stainless steel, ø 36 mm, height 10.5 mm; sapphire crystal; water-resistant to 5 atm
Band: calfskin, pin buckle
Price: $2,150
Variations: with blue or ivory dial

Edition Passage

Reference number: ED-PASSAGE
Movement: automatic, Sellita caliber SW200-1; ø 25.6 mm, height 4.6 mm; 26 jewels; 28,800 vph; 38-hour power reserve
Functions: hours (each line marks a 5-minute increment or 300 seconds)
Case: stainless steel, ø 43 mm, height 12.3 mm; sapphire crystal; transparent case back; water-resistant to 5 atm
Band: calfskin, pin buckle
Price: $2,500; limited to 100 pieces

Perigraph

Reference number: AM1008
Movement: automatic, Sellita caliber SW200-1; ø 25.6 mm, height 4.6 mm; 26 jewels; 28,800 vph; 38-hour power reserve
Functions: hours (each line marks a 5-minute increment); date (rotating disc display)
Case: stainless steel, ø 43 mm, height 12.3 mm; sapphire crystal; transparent case back; water-resistant to 5 atm
Band: calfskin, pin buckle
Price: $2,500
Variations: with white or ivory dial

MIDO

Among the legacies of World War I was the popularization of the wristwatch, which had freed up soldiers' and aviators' hands to fight and steer, respectively, and permitted artillery officers to coordinate barrages. And, not surprisingly, this led to a kind of reindustrialization of the watch industry. Among the earliest companies to appear on the scene was Mido, which was founded on November 11, 1918—Armistice Day—by Georges Schaeren in Solothurn, Switzerland. The name means "I measure" in Spanish.

At first, the brand produced colorful and imaginative watches that were well suited to the Roaring Twenties. But in the 1930s Mido began making more serious, robust, sportive timepieces better suited for everyday use. For the watch fan of today, water resistance and self-winding are normal. Mido, however, was already offering this functionality in the 1930s with the introduction of the Multifort. This Swiss manufacturer also developed a number of practical novelties like the Radiotime model (1939) and the Multicenterchrono (1941), which today have become genuine collectors' items.

In 1971 the Schaeren family sold the company to the General Watch Co. Ltd., a holding company belonging to ASUAG, which, in turn became the SMH and, ultimately, Swatch Group. Mido continues to produce mostly mechanical watches with about one-quarter of its production devoted to quartz movements. In 1998, Mido decided to revive some of its older watchmaking values. The Multifort, Commander, Battalion, and Baroncelli collections are each in their own way expressions of that mission. Nothing "in your face," just affordable timepieces with the basic hallmarks of a good Swiss watch, like côtes de Genève on the rotors and, in some cases, even COSC certification. The look can vary from classic and timeless diver's, like the Ocean Star family, to the Multiforts with, at times, the "television" look from the 1970s. The price-performance ratio is excellent.

MIDO SA
Chemin des Tourelles 17
CH-2400 Le Locle
Switzerland

TEL.:
+41 32 933 35 11

WEBSITE:
www.mido.ch

FOUNDED:
1918

NUMBER OF EMPLOYEES:
50 (estimated)

ANNUAL PRODUCTION:
over 100,000

U.S. DISTRIBUTOR:
Mido, division of The Swatch Group (U.S.) Inc.
703 Waterford Way, Suite 450
Miami, FL 33126
www.midowatches.com

MOST IMPORTANT COLLECTIONS/PRICE RANGES:
Baroncelli / $460 to $1,450; Commander / $710 to $2,000; Multifort / $620 to $2,230; Ocean Star / $890 to $1,900

Ocean Star 600 Chronometer
Reference number: M026.608.11.051.01
Movement: automatic, Mido caliber 80.821 COSC Si (ETA C07.821 base); ø 25.6 mm, height 5.22 mm; 25 jewels; 21,600 vph; silicon hairspring; rotor with côtes de Genève; COSC-certified chronometer; 80-hour power reserve
Functions: hours, minutes, sweep seconds; date
Case: stainless steel, ø 43.5 mm, height 14.05 mm; unidirectional bezel with ceramic insert, with 0-60 scale; sapphire crystal; screw-down crown, helium valve; water-resistant to 60 atm
Band: stainless steel, folding clasp, with extension link
Remarks: comes with extra rubber strap; certified according to the European diver's norm
Price: $1,780

Ocean Star GMT Special Edition
Reference number: M026.829.18.041.00
Movement: automatic, Mido caliber 80.661 (ETA C07.661 base); ø 25.6 mm, height 5.22 mm; 25 jewels; 21,600 vph; with côtes de Genève; 80-hour power reserve
Functions: hours (crown-switched jumping hand), minutes, sweep seconds; additional 24-hour display (second time zone); date
Case: stainless steel, ø 40.5 mm, height 13.4 mm; bidirectional bezel with aluminum insert with 0-24 hour scale; sapphire crystal; screw-down crown; water-resistant to 20 atm
Band: stainless steel, folding clasp
Remarks: comes with extra textile strap
Price: $1,460

Multifort M Freeze
Reference number: M038.430.11.041.00
Movement: automatic, Mido caliber 80.621 (ETA C07.621 base); ø 25.6 mm, height 5.22 mm; 25 jewels; 21,600 vph; with côtes de Genève; 80-hour power reserve
Functions: hours, minutes, sweep seconds; date and weekday
Case: stainless steel, ø 42 mm, height 11.99 mm; sapphire crystal; transparent case back; water-resistant to 10 atm
Band: stainless steel, folding clasp
Price: $960

Multifort TV Big Date

Reference number: M049.526.17.081.00
Movement: automatic, Mido caliber 80.651
(ETA C07.651 base); ø 28.8 mm, height 5.86 mm;
25 jewels; 21,600 vph; with côtes de Genève; 80-hour
power reserve
Functions: hours, minutes, sweep seconds; large date
Case: stainless steel, 40 mm x 39.2 mm, height
11.5 mm; sapphire crystal; transparent case back;
screw-down crown; water-resistant to 10 atm
Band: rubber, pin buckle
Price: $1,200

Ocean Star GMT Special Edition

Reference number: M026.629.11.041.00
Movement: automatic, Mido caliber 80.661
(ETA C07.661 base); ø 25.6 mm, height 5.22 mm;
25 jewels; 21,600 vph; with côtes de Genève; 80-hour
power reserve
Functions: hours (crown-switched jumping hand),
minutes, sweep seconds; additional 24-hour display
(second time zone); date
Case: stainless steel, ø 44 mm, height 13.43 mm;
unidirectional bezel with ceramic insert, with 0-60 scale;
sapphire crystal; screw-down crown; water-resistant
to 20 atm
Band: stainless steel, folding clasp
Remarks: comes with extra textile strap
Price: $1,460

Ocean Star 200 C Carbon Chronometer Limited Edition

Reference number: M042.431.77.081.00
Movement: automatic, Mido caliber 80 COSC Si
(ETA C07.821 base); ø 25.6 mm, height 5.22 mm;
25 jewels; 21,600 vph; silicon hairspring; COSC-certified
chronometer; 80-hour power reserve
Functions: hours, minutes, sweep seconds; date and
weekday
Case: stainless steel with black PVD, ø 42.5 mm, height
12.25 mm; unidirectional bezel with ceramic insert, with
0-60 scale; sapphire crystal; screw-down crown; water-
resistant to 20 atm
Band: rubber, folding clasp, with extension link
Remarks: carbon fiber dial
Price: $2,200; limited to 888 pieces

Multifort Patrimony Powerwind

Reference number: M040.407.11.041.00
Movement: automatic, Mido caliber 80.621
(ETA C07.621 base); ø 25.6 mm, height 5.22 mm;
25 jewels; 21,600 vph; 80-hour power reserve
Functions: hours, minutes, sweep seconds; date
Case: stainless steel, ø 40 mm, height 12.05 mm;
sapphire crystal; transparent case back; water-resistant
to 10 atm
Band: stainless steel, folding clasp
Price: $1,040

Commander Gradient

Reference number: M021.407.18.411.00
Movement: automatic, Mido caliber 80.611
(ETA C07.611 base); ø 25.6 mm, height 4.86 mm;
25 jewels; 21,600 vph; with côtes de Genève; 80-hour
power reserve
Functions: hours, minutes, sweep seconds; date
Case: stainless steel, ø 40 mm, height 10.8 mm;
sapphire crystal; transparent case back; water-resistant
to 5 atm
Band: textile, folding clasp
Remarks: smoky acrylic dial
Price: $970

Commander Lady

Reference number: M021.207.33.021.00
Movement: automatic, Mido caliber 72
(ETA A31.111 base); ø 25.6 mm, height 3.85 mm;
21 jewels; 25,200 vph; with côtes de Genève; 72-hour
power reserve
Functions: hours, minutes, sweep seconds; date
Case: stainless steel with yellow-gold PVD, ø 35 mm,
height 9.2 mm; sapphire crystal; transparent case back;
water-resistant to 5 atm
Band: stainless steel with yellow-gold PVD, folding clasp
Price: $1,310

MILUS

Milus is one of those brands that has had quite a journey in recent times. It was founded by Paul William Junod in Biel/Bienne and remained in family hands until the year 2002. A new era began then with the founding of Milus International SA under Jan Edöcs and with investments from the giant Peace Mark Group from Hong Kong.

Within a few years, the brand had made a new name for itself with a triple retrograde seconds module, which was developed together with the specialists at Agenhor in Geneva. And that made all the difference to the Milus image. In the 1970s, the brand had a reputation for jewelry. Now, however, it had become a genuine and respected watchmaker, one producing top-drawer horological complications that could compete quite boldly on a market. The TriRetrograde function is a Milus trademark and could be found in a host of models all named after constellations (Tirion, Merea, Zetios).

After the Peace Mark Group collapsed in 2008, Milus quickly found another investor in the Chow Tai Fook Group owned by Dr. Cheng Yu-tung. In 2011, Cyril Dubois took over at the head of the company. Quietly, but surely, the brand expanded on several fronts with the TriRetrogrades in the lead. Unfortunately, it had no staying power. And in 2017, Luc Tissot and his wife Katia bought the brand and started streamlining the portfolio. The strategy was simple: have three attractive collections on the affordable end of the price scale. Thus we find a robust, functional diver's watch, the Archimèdes with water-resistance to 30 atm. It was also built with a bezel under the sapphire crystal that can be turned using a separate crown and a helium valve. The entry-level LAB 01 features a modern fiberglass dial. And the third, the Snow Star, is all that's left from the old collections. It was originally made in the 1940s and given, so goes the story, to US Navy Pilots in the Pacific (along with other valuables like gold and jewelry) as part of "life barter kits." The model has been rebuilt and modernized. One can imagine that TriRetrograde mechanism will soon show up.

MILUS INTERNATIONAL SA
Rue de Reuchenette 19
CH-2502 Biel/Bienne
Switzerland

TEL.:
+41-32-344-3939

E-MAIL:
info@milus.com

WEBSITE:
www.milus.com

FOUNDED:
1919

DISTRIBUTION:
Contact company in Switzerland

MOST IMPORTANT COLLECTIONS/PRICE RANGE:
Snow Star / from approx. 1,970; Archimèdes by Milus / from approx. $2,200; LAB 01 / from approx. $1,200

Archimèdes by Milus

Reference number: MIH.01.002.YS
Movement: automatic, ETA 2892-A2; ø 25.6 mm, height 3.60 mm; 21 jewels; 28,800 vph; 42-hour power reserve
Functions: hours, minutes, sweep seconds; date
Case: stainless steel, ø 41 mm, height 11.9 mm; sapphire glass; bidirectional bezel; screw-in crown, helium valve; water-resistant to 30 atm
Band: rubber, pin buckle
Price: $2,290
Variation: with Milanese mesh bracelet

Snow Star

Reference number: MIH.02.003.904
Movement: automatic, ETA 2892-A2; ø 25.6 mm, height 3.60 mm; 21 jewels; 28,800 vph; 42-hour power reserve
Functions: hours, minutes, sweep seconds; date
Case: stainless steel, ø 39 mm, height 9.45 mm; sapphire crystal; water-resistant to 10 atm
Band: stainless steel, with safe release system
Remarks: replica of a watch that pilots had as a barter when flying over the Pacific during WW2
Price: $2,190
Variations: with calfskin band

LAB 01

Reference number: MIL.01.003
Movement: automatic, Sellita SW200; ø 26 mm, height 4.6 mm; 26 jewels; 28,800 vph; 38-hours power reserve
Functions: hours, minutes, sweep seconds
Case: stainless steel, ø 40 mm, height 9.5 mm; sapphire glass; water-resistant to 3 atm
Band: Milanese mesh, folding clasp
Remarks: fiberglass dial
Price: $1,130

MINASE

Successful companies frequently like to build a monument to their achievements. It might be a real structure, like the Chrysler Building in New York, or something more ephemeral, like an arts endowment. In 2005, Kyowa, a toolmaking enterprise founded in Japan in 1963, paid homage to its own skills in working on watch components by launching a watch brand. Its logo, appearing at 12 o'clock on some models, was inspired from a step drill.

Minase Watches was named after a small village some 250 miles north of Tokyo that was absorbed in that same year 2005 into the neighboring city of Yuzawa. Until recently, it produced no more than three hundred watches a year for the Japanese market, but lately it has begun widening its horizons internationally and its focus on a modern design and traditional Japanese decorative techniques has engendered an enthusiastic fan base.

The company's timepieces are all made according to *monozukuri* philosophy, a reference to excellent manufacturing practices. One technique used is *sallaz*, or block polishing, which gives a particularly sparkling polish. The stainless-steel bracelets have been inspired by complex Japanese wooden puzzles.

The brand has three basic collections, each of which expresses the company's dedication to traditional hand-finishing. The Five Windows features multiple sapphire crystals integrated into the cases to reveal each watch's complex case-in-case structure, the intricate dial, and the mechanism inside. The oversized date aperture creates visual space on the dial. A subcollection with two extra openings, the Seven Windows, occasionally becomes a canvas for limited editions decorated by select Japanese artists. Lacquerware specialist Junichi Hakose, for example, used the *maki-e urushi* technique—sap from the urushi tree, with gold sprinklings—to create a riveting pattern on one of the dials. In 2024, Hakose's workshop was destroyed in an earthquake, so the company announced some possible delays in delivery.

The Horizon line is more sportive, with an elegantly curved sapphire crystal covering an arched dial on a tonneau case. The Divido is far more classical, with a round dial in a slightly angular case.

MINASE
Company representation
H-Development Sarl
Ch. du Long-Champ 99
CH-2504 Biel/Bienne
Switzerland

TEL.:
+41-32-521-06-13

E-MAIL:
info@h-development.ch

WEBSITE:
www.minasewatches.ch
www.h-development.ch

FOUNDED:
2005

DISTRIBUTION:
Contact the representation in Switzerland

ANNUAL PRODUCTION:
approx. 500 pieces

MOST IMPORTANT COLLECTIONS/PRICE RANGE:
Five Windows, Seven Windows, Horizon, Divido,
Uruga / $3,800 to $6,000; special editions

Divido Urushi Makie Rubber

Reference number: VM14-RBKURE-SSD
Movement: automatic, KT7002 (ETA 2892 base);
ø 25.6 mm, height 3.6 mm; 28,800 vph; 21 jewels;
bridges with perlage and black-or coating; blued screws;
50-hour power reserve
Functions: hours, minutes, sweep seconds
Case: stainless steel, ø 40.6 mm, height 11 mm;
sapphire crystal, transparent case back; water-resistant
to 5 atm
Band: rubber, folding clasp
Remarks: dial features urushi makie technique
Price: $6,900
Variations: red, green or blue urushi makie dial, also
available with stainless steel bracelet or shibo urushi
dial, a mix of urushi lacquer and egg white

Horizon Steel

Reference number: VM12-M01NBL-SSB
Movement: automatic, KT7002 (ETA 2892 base);
ø 25.6 mm, height 3.6 mm; 28,800 vph; 21 jewels;
bridges with perlage and black-or coating; 50-hour
power reserve
Functions: hours, minutes, sweep seconds; date
Case: stainless steel, ø 51 mm x 38 mm, height 12 mm;
sapphire crystal, transparent case back; water resistant
to 5 atm
Band: stainless steel, folding clasp
Remarks: PVD dial
Price: $5,500
Variations: blue, black or grey dial, also available on
rubber strap

Windows Rose Gold

Reference number: VM15-CBKNGR-KYJ-rg
Movement: automatic, KT7002 (ETA 2892-A2 bases);
ø 25.6 mm, height 3.6 mm; 28,800 vph; 21 jewels;
bridges with perlage and black-or coating; 50-hour
power reserve
Functions: hours, minutes, sweep seconds; date
Case: yellow gold, ø 47 mm x 38 mm, height 13 mm;
domed box sapphire crystal (non-reflective coating)
on top, see-through sapphire case back and 5 sapphire
crystals at 12, 6 and 9 o'clock, and 2 at 3 o'clock;
transparent case back; water-resistant to 3 atm
Band: calfskin, folding clasp
Price: $23,800
Variations: with black dial; or with urushi lacquer
designs by Junichi Hakose

MING

It takes a certain courage to launch a new watch brand in a crowded market that is subject to emotional swings. Ming, however, is no ordinary brand. It is a cooperative enterprise made up of six watchmaking enthusiasts from around the world. Leading the team is Ming Thein, a well-known photographer, designer, corporate strategist, and watch fan. He hails from Malaysia. Added up, the Ming team computes to a total of eighty solid years' experience collecting watches of all sorts, from vintage pieces to avant-garde works of kinetic art, from robust ground-level timepieces to custom-made products in the six-figure range.

Each of their purchases always gave them a genuine feeling of value and happiness. The mission of the six brand founders was therefore to reconnect with that feeling of emotional excitement that comes from discovering an authentic diamond in the rough. Their strategy was to create a series of watches that are conscientiously finished and stand out thanks to some subtle details in the finishing and the design. These are not flashy pieces, but rather subtle seducers by dint of the details, like the carefully worked lugs or the modified ETA 7001 caliber, turning a fairly square assembly into a delicate and colorful ballet of gearwheels and bridges.

The year 2024 brought many kudos for the brand, notably a Grand Prix d'Horlogerie prize for the best sports watch for the Bluefin, a 38-millimeter diver's watch rated for 60 atm. It is in typical Ming minimalist style, though not as minimalist as the Minimalist watch, which has a series of lines in Polar White luminescent material in place of an hours track with markers. Another novelty is a cooperation with the Genevan company Agenhor, which years ago developed a central chronograph. This allows the 20.01 Series 3 to avoid subsidiary dials in favor of a very intricate dial made in collaboration with Femtoprint. It is made up of a borosilicate base with cavities filled with liquid Super-LumiNova that produce an intense glow in the dark.

HOROLOGER MING SDN BHD
B-3A-3, Sunway Palazzio
1 Jalan Sri Hartamas 3
50480 Kuala Lumpur
Malaysia

E-MAIL:
hello@ming.watch

WEBSITE:
www.ming.watch

FOUNDED:
August 2017

NUMBER OF EMPLOYEES:
6

DISTRIBUTION:
Online, direct to customer

ANNUAL PRODUCTION:
3000+ pieces

MOST IMPORTANT COLLECTIONS/PRICE RANGE:
20 series, 37 series; Special Projects, CHF 2,500 – CHF 60,000

37.02 Minimalist

Reference number: 3702M
Movement: automatic, Ming-customized Sellita caliber SW 300.M1; ø 25.6 mm, height 3.6 mm; 22 jewels; 28,800 vph; skeletonized bridges and customized rotor; hacking seconds; 45-hour power reserve
Functions: hours, minutes
Case: stainless steel, ø 38 mm, height 11 mm; domed sapphire crystal front and rear; water-resistant to 10 atm
Band: FKM rubber, pin buckle
Remarks: minimalist dial with Ming's own Polar White luminescent material on the hour track and blue Super-LumiNova on the hands
Price: $3,650

37.09 Bluefin

Reference number: 3709B
Movement: automatic, Ming-customized Sellita caliber SW 300.M1; ø 25.6 mm, height 3.6 mm; 22 jewels; 28,800 vph; skeletonized bridges and customized rotor; hacking seconds; 45-hour power reserve
Functions: hours, minutes, sweep seconds, timing dial
Case: stainless steel, ø 38 mm, height 12.8 mm; crown-activated rotating dial with 0-60 scale; sapphire crystal; transparent case back; water-resistant to 60 atm
Band: FKM rubber, pin buckle
Remarks: composite metal and laser-etched sapphire dial with inlaid ceramic Super-LumiNova
Price: $5,600

20.01 Series 3

Reference number: 2001S3
Movement: hand-wound, exclusive AgenGraphe caliber 6361.M1; ø 34 mm, height 5.65 mm; 18 jewels; 28,800 vph; double skeletonized spring barrels; central chronograph; anthracite skeletonized bridges with contrast rhodium circular brushing; 55-hour power reserve
Functions: hours, minutes; chronograph with sweep minute totalizer
Case: titanium and 18k rose-gold, ø 41.5 mm, height 14.2 mm; water-resistant to 5 atm
Band: goat leather, pin buckle in 18k rose-gold
Remarks: world's first fused borosilicate dial, with 600 individually hand-filled luminous voids
Price: $50,000

MK II

If vintage and unserviceable watches had their say, they would probably be naturally attracted to Mk II for the name alone, which is a military designation for the second generation of equipment. The company, which was founded by watch enthusiast and maker Bill Yao in 2002, not only puts retired designs back into service, but also modernizes and customizes them. Before the invention of the screw-down crown, diving watches were not nearly as reliably sealed, for example. And some beautiful old pieces were made with plated brass cases or featured Bakelite components, which are easily damaged or have aged poorly. The company substitutes these materials with modern counterparts and uses more reliable modern manufacturing methods and techniques to ensure a better outcome.

These are material issues that the team at Mk II handles with great care. They will not, metaphorically speaking, airbrush a Model-T. As genuine watch lovers themselves, they make sure that the final design is in the spirit of the watch itself, which still leaves a great deal of leeway for many iterations, given sufficient parts. In the company's output, vintage style and modern functionality are key. The watches are assembled by hand at the company's workshop in Pennsylvania—and subjected to a rigorous regimen of testing. The components are individually inspected, the cases tested at least three times for water resistance, and at the end the whole watch is regulated in six positions. The ready-to-wear collection is made in Japan and finished in the USA. These watches are robust, timeless, and, for the collector of lesser means, affordable.

MK II CORPORATION
303 W. Lancaster Avenue, #283
Wayne, PA 19087
USA

E-MAIL:
info@mkiiwatches.com

WEBSITES:
www.mkiiwatches.com
https://tornek-rayville.us/

FOUNDED:
2002

NUMBER OF EMPLOYEES:
3

ANNUAL PRODUCTION:
1,200 watches

DISTRIBUTION:
Direct to consumer sales

MOST IMPORTANT COLLECTIONS/PRICE RANGE:
Ready-to-Wear Collection / $500 to $995;
Benchcrafted Collection / $1,000 to $2,000

TR-660
Reference Number: CD02.2-TR660-1002AmK
Movement: automatic (hack setting), TMI caliber NH35 (made in Japan); ø 27.40 mm, height 5.32 mm; 24 jewels; 21,600 vph; 50-hour power reserve
Functions: hours, minutes, sweep seconds, date
Case: stainless steel, ø 40.00 mm, height 14.72 mm; unidirectional bezel with 0-120 scale; high domed sapphire crystal; screw-down case back and crown; water-resistant to 20 atm
Band: nylon, pin buckle
Price: $949
Variations: rubber strap, luminous acrylic inlay

Fulcrum 39
Reference Number: CD06.2-1001
Movement: automatic (hack setting), Miyota 9015 caliber (made in Japan); ø 26 mm, height 3.9 mm; 24 jewels; 28,800 vph; 42-hour power reserve
Functions: hours, minutes, sweep seconds, date
Case: stainless steel; ø 39.5 mm, height 14.1 mm; unidirectional bezel with 0-120 scale; high domed sapphire crystal; screw-down case back and crown; water-resistant to 20 atm
Band: stainless steel, folding clasp with extension clasp
Price: $995
Variations: rubber strap, luminous acrylic inlay

Type 7B "Blakjak"
Reference Number: CG07-1001F
Movement: automatic (hack setting), TMI caliber NH36 (made in Japan); ø 27.40 mm, height 5.32 mm; 24 jewels; 21,600 vph; 41-hour power reserve
Functions: hours, minutes, sweep seconds, day/date
Case: stainless steel, ø 42.50 mm, height 13.20 mm; unidirectional bezel with 0-120 scale; sapphire crystal; screw-down case back; screw-in crown; water-resistant to 20 atm
Band: stainless steel, folding clasp
Price: $895
Variations: rubber strap, 12-hour bezel inlay

MONTBLANC

Nicolas Rieussec (1781–1866) skillfully used the invention of a special chronograph—the "Time Writer," a device that released droplets of ink onto a rotating sheet of paper—to make a name for himself. Montblanc, once famous only for its exclusive writing implements, borrowed that name on its way to becoming a distinguished watch brand. Within a few years, it had created an impressive range of chronographs driven by in-house calibers: from simple automatic stop-watches to flagship pieces with two independent spring barrels for time and "time-writing."

In 2007, Richemont Group, owner of Montblanc, purchased a little *manufacture* called Minerva, and put it at the disposal of the company. Minerva, which was founded in Villeret in 1858, was already building keyless pocket watches in the 1880s, and went on to produce monopusher chronographs. Today, the Minerva Institute serves as a kind of think tank, a place where young watchmakers can absorb the old traditions and skills, as well as the wealth of experience and mindset of the masters.

Montblanc is maintaining the over 160-year Minerva tradition with four leading collections. The 1858 and the Heritage clearly draw inspiration from the company's past codes, with quotations from the 1920s and 1930s, like those salmon-colored dials. The Star Legacy and the TimeWalker lines allow Montblanc to explore some more complex complications packaged in more modern forms.

After focusing on the summit of Mont Blanc at 4810 meters (whereby, it does vary depending on the thickness of the coat of snow on its summit), the eponymous brand is now diving to adventurous depth—4810 meters under the sea. The latest diver's watch, the Iced Sea o Oxygen Deep 4810, has a reinforced case back and extra-thick sapphire crystal and is emptied of oxygen when screwed shut.

The second major innovation of late is the case barrel of the 1858 Geosphere CARBO2 o Oxygen, which is made of a very sintered material that binds CO_2 from biogas production and mineral waste from recycling factories. The composite has the feel of steel and a dark, mysterious look. The left-hand side of the case features an engraved profile of Mont Blanc covered with luminescent material.

MONTBLANC MONTRE SA
10, chemin des Tourelles
CH-2400 Le Locle
Switzerland

TEL.:
+41-32-933-8888

E-MAIL:
service@montblanc.com

WEBSITE:
www.montblanc.com

FOUNDED:
1997 (1858 Villeret, 1906 in Hamburg)

NUMBER OF EMPLOYEES:
worldwide approx. 3,000 (200 in Le Locle and Villeret)

U.S. DISTRIBUTOR:
Montblanc North America
645 Fifth Avenue, 7th Floor
New York, NY 10022
800-995-4810
www.montblanc.com

MOST IMPORTANT COLLECTIONS:
Heritage Chronométrie, Heritage Spirit, Meisterstück, Minerva, Nicolas Rieussec, 4810, TimeWalker, Collection Villeret, 1858 Collection, Iced Sea

1858 Geosphere Chronograph "Zero Oxygen" CARBO2

Reference number: 132300
Movement: automatic, caliber MB 29.27; ø 29.98 mm, height 9.11 mm; 33 jewels; 28,800 vph; 46-hour power reserve
Functions: hours, minutes; additional synchronously counter-rotating world time indicators for northern and southern hemispheres; chronograph; date
Case: carbon composite (Carbo2), ø 44 mm, height 17.1 mm; bidirectional bezel in stainless steel with ceramic insert, with points of the compass; sapphire crystal; water-resistant to 10 atm
Band: rubber with textile insert, triple folding clasp
Remarks: special case barrel made of carbon fiber combined with absorbed CO_2; filled with nitrogen
Price: $10,000

1858 Iced Sea Deep 4810

Reference number: 133268
Movement: automatic, caliber MB 29.29; ø 25.6 mm, height 4.6 mm; 26 jewels; 28,800 vph; COSC-certified chronometer; 120-hour power reserve
Functions: hours, minutes, sweep seconds; date
Case: titanium, ø 43 mm, height 19.4 mm; unidirectional bezel with ceramic insert, with 0-60 scale; sapphire crystal; screw-down crown; water-resistant to 481 atm
Band: rubber, folding clasp
Remarks: case filled with nitrogen, micro-structured, polished dial ("gratté-boisé")
Price: $10,000

The Unveiled Secret Minerva Monopusher Chronograph

Reference number: 133296
Movement: hand-wound, caliber MB M16.26; ø 37.5 mm, height 7.05 mm; 26 jewels; 18,000 vph; inverted movement with chronograph mechanism on the dial side; column-wheel control of the chronograph functions with monopusher; screw balance; 50-hour power reserve
Functions: hours, minutes, subsidiary seconds; chronograph
Case: stainless steel, ø 43 mm, height 14.18 mm; bezel in white gold; sapphire crystal; water-resistant to 3 atm
Band: reptile skin, triple folding clasp
Remarks: skeletonized dial
Price: $44,000; limited to 88 pieces

1858 Iced Sea Automatic Date

Reference number: 133300
Movement: automatic, caliber MB 24.17 (Sellita SW200 base); ø 25.6 mm, height 4.6 mm; 26 jewels; 28,800 vph; 38-hour power reserve
Functions: hours, minutes, sweep seconds; date
Case: bronze, ø 41 mm, height 12.9 mm; unidirectional bezel with ceramic insert, with 0-60 scale; sapphire crystal; water-resistant to 30 atm
Band: rubber, double folding clasp
Remarks: micro-structured, polished dial ("gratté-boisé")
Price: $3,915

1858 Iced Sea Automatic Date

Reference number: 132291
Movement: automatic, caliber MB 24.17 (Sellita SW200 base); ø 25.6 mm, height 4.6 mm; 26 jewels; 28,800 vph; 38-hour power reserve
Functions: hours, minutes, sweep seconds; date
Case: stainless steel, ø 41 mm, height 12.9 mm; unidirectional bezel with ceramic insert, with 0-60 scale; sapphire crystal; water-resistant to 30 atm
Band: stainless steel, double folding clasp
Remarks: micro-structured, polished dial ("gratté-boisé")
Price: $3,405

1858 Geosphere Chronograph "Zero Oxygen"

Reference number: 130811
Movement: automatic, caliber MB 29.27; ø 29.98 mm, height 9.11 mm; 33 jewels; 28,800 vph; 46-hour power reserve
Functions: hours, minutes; additional synchronously counter-rotating world time indicators for northern and southern hemispheres; chronograph; date
Case: titanium, ø 42 mm, height 12.8 mm; bidirectional bezel with ceramic insert, with points of the compass; sapphire crystal; water-resistant to 10 atm
Band: textile, triple folding clasp
Remarks: case filled with nitrogen
Price: $9,900

1858 Geosphere "Zero Oxygen"

Reference number: 130982
Movement: automatic, caliber MB 29.25 (Sellita SW300-1 base with Montblanc module); ø 25.6 mm; 26 jewels; 28,800 vph; 42-hour power reserve
Functions: hours, minutes; additional synchronously counter-rotating world time indicators for northern and southern hemispheres; date
Case: titanium, ø 42 mm, height 12.8 mm; bidirectional bezel with ceramic insert, with points of the compass; sapphire crystal; water-resistant to 10 atm
Band: titanium, double folding clasp
Remarks: case filled with nitrogen
Price: $7,600

1858 Iced Sea Automatic Date

Reference number: 129371
Movement: automatic, caliber MB 24.17 (Sellita SW200 base); ø 25.6 mm, height 4.6 mm; 26 jewels; 28,800 vph; 38-hour power reserve
Functions: hours, minutes, sweep seconds; date
Case: stainless steel, ø 41 mm, height 12.9 mm; unidirectional bezel with ceramic insert, with 0-60 scale; sapphire crystal; water-resistant to 30 atm
Band: stainless steel, double folding clasp
Remarks: micro-structured, polished dial ("gratté-boisé")
Price: $3,405
Variations: with rubber strap ($3,405)

The Unveiled Secret Minerva Monopusher Chronograph

Reference number: 131155
Movement: hand-wound, caliber MB M16.26; ø 37.5 mm, height 7.05 mm; 26 jewels; 18,000 vph; inverted movement structure with dial-side chronograph mechanism; column wheel control of chronograph functions using monopusher; screw balance; 50-hour power reserve
Functions: hours, minutes, subsidiary seconds; chronograph
Case: stainless steel, ø 43 mm, height 14.18 mm; bezel in white gold; sapphire crystal; water-resistant to 3 atm
Band: reptile skin, triple folding clasp
Remarks: skeletonized dial
Price: $39,500; limited to 88 pieces

1858 The Unveiled Timekeeper Minerva Limited Edition

Reference number: 130987
Movement: hand-wound, caliber MB M13.21; ø 29.5 mm, height 6.4 mm; 22 jewels; 18,000 vph; control of chronograph functions by rotating bezel; screw balance, hairspring with Phillips end curve; 60-hour power reserve
Functions: hours, minutes, subsidiary seconds; chronograph
Case: stainless steel, ø 42 mm, height 13.85 mm; unidirectional bezel in white gold, unidirectional rotating bezel to control chronograph functions; sapphire crystal; water-resistant to 3 atm
Band: reptile skin, triple folding clasp
Price: $43,500; limited to 100 pieces

1858 The Unveiled Timekeeper Minerva Limited Edition

Reference number: 130988
Movement: hand-wound, caliber MB M13.21; ø 29.5 mm, height 6.4 mm; 22 jewels; 18,000 vph; control of chronograph functions by rotating bezel; screw balance, hairspring with Phillips end curve; 60-hour power reserve
Functions: hours, minutes, subsidiary seconds; chronograph
Case: yellow gold ("lime gold"), ø 42.5 mm, height 13.85 mm; unidirectional bezel in white gold, unidirectional rotating bezel to control chronograph functions; water-resistant to 3 atm
Band: reptile skin, pin buckle
Price: $57,000; limited to 28 pieces

Star Legacy Automatic Date

Reference number: 130958
Movement: automatic, caliber MB 24.17 (Sellita SW200-1 base); ø 25.6 mm, height 4.6 mm; 26 jewels; 28,800 vph; 38-hour power reserve
Functions: hours, minutes, sweep seconds; date
Case: stainless steel, ø 39 mm, height 10.44 mm; sapphire crystal; transparent case back; water-resistant to 5 atm
Band: reptile skin, pin buckle
Price: $2,390; limited to 1786 pieces

Star Legacy Moonphase

Reference number: 130959
Movement: automatic, Montblanc caliber MB 24.31 (Sellita SW380 base); ø 25.6 mm, height 4.1 mm; 25 jewels; 28,800 vph; 50-hour power reserve
Functions: hours, minutes, sweep seconds; date, moon phase
Case: stainless steel, ø 42 mm, height 11.38 mm; sapphire crystal; transparent case back; water-resistant to 5 atm
Band: reptile skin, triple folding clasp
Remarks: limited to 1786 pieces
Price: $4,600

1858 Iced Sea Automatic Date

Reference number: 129372
Movement: automatic, caliber MB 24.17 (Sellita SW200 base); ø 25.6 mm, height 4.6 mm; 26 jewels; 28,800 vph; 38-hour power reserve
Functions: hours, minutes, sweep seconds; date
Case: stainless steel, ø 41 mm, height 12.9 mm; unidirectional bezel with ceramic insert, with 0-60 scale; sapphire crystal; water-resistant to 30 atm
Band: rubber, double folding clasp
Remarks: micro-structured, polished dial ("gratté-boisé")
Price: $3,205
Variations: with stainless steel bracelet ($3,205)

1858 Automatic Chronograph "Zero Oxygen"

Reference number: 130983
Movement: automatic, caliber MB 29.13 (Sellita SW510 base); ø 30 mm, height 7.9 mm; 27 jewels; 28,800 vph; 48-hour power reserve
Functions: hours, minutes, subsidiary seconds; chronograph
Case: stainless steel, ø 42 mm, height 12.8 mm; bidirectional bezel with ceramic insert, with markings of the compass; sapphire crystal; water-resistant to 10 atm
Band: stainless steel, double folding clasp
Remarks: case filled with pure nitrogen
Price: $5,200

Caliber MB M16.29

Hand-wound; column-wheel control of the chronograph functions using separate pushers; single mainspring barrel, 55-hour power reserve
Functions: hours, minutes, subsidiary seconds; chronograph
Diameter: 38.4 mm
Height: 6.3 mm
Jewels: 22
Balance: screw balance
Frequency: 18,000 vph
Hairspring: with Phillips end curve
Remarks: perlage on mainplate, rhodium-plated, bridges with côtes de Genèves gold-plated geartrain

Caliber MB M13.21

Hand-wound; column-wheel control of the chronograph functions; single mainspring barrel, 60-hour power reserve
Functions: hours, minutes, subsidiary seconds; chronograph
Diameter: 29.5 mm
Height: 6.4 mm
Jewels: 22
Balance: screw balance with weights
Frequency: 18,000 vph
Hairspring: with Phillips end curve
Shock protection: Incabloc
Remarks: German silver mainplate and bridges, rhodium-plated, partial perlage and hand-chamfered

Caliber MB 29.27

Automatic; single spring barrel, 46-hour power reserve
Functions: hours, minutes; second time zone, synchronously counter-rotating world time indicators for northern and southern hemispheres; chronograph; date
Diameter: 29.98 mm
Height: 9.11 mm
Jewels: 33
Frequency: 28,800 vph
Hairspring: flat hairspring
Remarks: perlage on mainplate, rhodium-plated

Caliber MB 29.22

Automatic; single mainspring barrel, 48-hour power reserve
Base caliber: Cartier 1904-PS MC
Functions: hours, minutes; additional 12-hour display (second time zone); perpetual calendar with date, weekday, month, moon phase, leap year
Diameter: 28.2 mm
Height: 4.95 mm
Jewels: 77
Frequency: 28,800 vph
Hairspring: flat hairspring
Remarks: 378 parts

Caliber MB M16.31

Hand-wound; column-wheel control of the chronograph functions over different pushers, swan-neck fine adjustment; single mainspring barrel, 50-hour power reserve
Functions: hours, minutes, subsidiary seconds; stop-seconds chronograph
Diameter: 38.4 mm
Height: 8.13 mm
Jewels: 22
Balance: screw balance with Breguet hairspring
Frequency: 18,000 vph
Hairspring: with Phillips end curve
Remarks: perlage on mainplate, rhodium-plated, bridges with côtes de Genève, gold-plated gear train; 262 parts

Caliber MB M29.24

Automatic; 1-minute tourbillon with external hairspring; two spring barrels, 48-hour power reserve
Functions: hours, minutes
Diameter: 30.6 mm
Height: 4.5 mm
Jewels: 27
Balance: screw balance with 18 weight screws
Frequency: 21,600 vph
Hairspring: flat hairspring
Remarks: gold microrotor, bridges with côtes de Genève

MÜHLE GLASHÜTTE

Family-run businesses are notoriously successful, especially as each generation must balance tradition with managing the challenges that time brings. Rob. Mühle & Sohn has been doing this for exactly 155 years. The company started as a manufacturer of precision measuring instruments and managed to survive the ups and downs of German history. Originally, this was for the local watch industry and the German School of Watchmaking. By the early 1920s, the firm was supplying the automobile industry, making speedometers, automobile clocks, tachometers, and other measurement instruments.

As a supplier for the Wehrmacht, it drew Soviet bombers during World War II and was then nationalized. After the fall of the Iron Curtain, Hans-Jürgen Mühle took the helm, followed, in 2007, by his son, Thilo Mühle. Just in time for the 155th anniversary, Thilo's children, Fanny and Dustin Mühle, took on more and more responsibility in the increasingly international family business.

The wristwatch line was launched as a sideline in mid-1994 but has now overtaken the nautical instruments for which Mühle was famous. Its collection comprises mechanical wristwatches at entry- and mid-level prices. For these, the company uses Swiss base movements that are equipped with such in-house developments as a patented woodpecker-neck regulation system and the Mühle rotor. The modifications are so extensive that they have led to the calibers having their own names. The traditional line named "R. Mühle & Sohn," introduced in 2014, is equipped with the RMK 1 and RMK 2 calibers. And there are other, somewhat less nautically inspired timepieces, like the Lunova series or the 29ers, which are simply elegant in an unspectacular way. While the watches are by and large in the sportive-elegant segment, the company has shown some boldness in the color of the dials and straps.

MÜHLE GLASHÜTTE GMBH
Nautische Instrumente und Feinmechanik
Altenberger Strasse 35
D-01768 Glashütte
Germany

TEL.:
+49-35053-3203-0

E-MAIL:
info@muehle-glashuette.de

WEBSITE:
www.muehle-glashuette.de

FOUNDED:
first founding 1869; second founding 1993

NUMBER OF EMPLOYEES:
47

U.S. DISTRIBUTOR:
Mühle Glashütte USA
920 Dr. MLK Jr. Street North
St. Petersburg, FL 33704
727-896-4278
www.muehleglashuetteusa.com

MOST IMPORTANT COLLECTIONS/PRICE RANGE:
mechanical wristwatches / approx. $1,300 to $5,400

Sportivo Active Chronograph

Reference number: M1-52-02-CK
Movement: automatic, Mühle caliber MU 9419 (Sellita SW510 base); ø 30 mm, height 7.9 mm; 25 jewels; 28,800 vph; woodpecker-neck regulator, Glashütte three-quarter plate, finely finished Mühle rotor with special Mühle finishing; 62-hour power reserve
Functions: hours, minutes, subsidiary seconds; chronograph; date
Case: stainless steel, ø 42.5 mm, height 15.5 mm; bidirectional bezel with ceramic insert, with 0-60 scale; sapphire crystal; transparent case back; screw-down crown; water-resistant to 30 atm
Band: rubber with textile overlay, pin buckle
Price: $4,199

Sportivo Compass Date

Reference number: M1-52-22-MB
Movement: automatic, Sellita caliber SW200-1; ø 25.6 mm, height 4.6 mm; 26 jewels; 28,800 vph; with woodpecker-neck regulator, finely finished Mühle rotor with special Mühle finishing; 41-hour power reserve
Functions: hours, minutes, sweep seconds; date
Case: stainless steel, ø 42.5 mm, height 11.4 mm; bidirectional bezel with ceramic insert, with compass scale; sapphire crystal; screw-down crown; water-resistant to 30 atm
Band: stainless steel, folding clasp, with extension link
Price: $2,849

S.A.R. Mission-Timer Titanium

Reference number: M1-51-03-KB
Movement: automatic, Sellita caliber SW400-1; ø 31 mm, height 4.67 mm; 26 jewels; 28,800 vph; with woodpecker-neck regulator, finely finished Mühle rotor with special Mühle finishing; 41-hour power reserve
Functions: hours, minutes, sweep seconds; date
Case: titanium, ø 43 mm, height 13 mm; bezel in ceramic; sapphire crystal; screw-down crown; water-resistant to 50 atm
Band: rubber, folding clasp, with extension link
Price: $3,249

S.A.R. Rescue-Timer

Reference number: M1-41-03-MB
Movement: automatic, Sellita caliber SW200-1;
ø 25.6 mm, height 4.6 mm; 26 jewels; 28,800 vph; with
woodpecker-neck regulator, finely finished Mühle rotor
with special Mühle finishing; 41-hour power reserve
Functions: hours, minutes, sweep seconds; date
Case: stainless steel, ø 42 mm, height 13.5 mm; bezel
with rubber insert; sapphire crystal; screw-down crown;
water-resistant to 100 atm
Band: stainless steel, folding clasp, with extension link
Price: $2,499
Variations: with rubber strap ($2,399); with full-lume
dial ($2,399)

29er Big

Reference number: M1-25-37-CB
Movement: automatic, Sellita caliber SW200-1;
ø 25.6 mm, height 4.6 mm; 26 jewels; 28,800 vph;
woodpecker-neck regulator, finely finished Mühle rotor
with special Mühle finishing; 41-hour power reserve
Functions: hours, minutes, sweep seconds; date
Case: stainless steel, ø 42.4 mm, height 11.3 mm;
sapphire crystal; transparent case back; screw-down
crown; water-resistant to 10 atm
Band: textile, pin buckle
Price: $1,899
Variations: with stainless steel bracelet ($1,949)

29er Zeigerdatum

Reference number: M1-25-32-CB
Movement: automatic, Sellita caliber SW221-1;
ø 25.6 mm, height 5.05 mm; 26 jewels; 28,800 vph;
woodpecker-neck regulator, finely finished Mühle rotor
with special Mühle finishing; 41-hour power reserve
Functions: hours, minutes, sweep seconds; date
Case: stainless steel, ø 42.4 mm, height 12.2 mm;
sapphire crystal; transparent case back; water-resistant
to 10 atm
Band: textile, pin buckle
Price: $1,999
Variations: with stainless steel bracelet ($2,149)

Panova Blau

Reference number: M1-40-72-MB
Movement: automatic, Sellita caliber SW200-1;
ø 25.6 mm, height 4.6 mm; 26 jewels; 28,800 vph;
woodpecker-neck regulator, finely finished Mühle rotor
with special Mühle finishing; 41-hour power reserve
Functions: hours, minutes, sweep seconds
Case: stainless steel, ø 40 mm, height 10.4 mm;
sapphire crystal; screw-down crown; water-resistant
to 10 atm
Band: stainless steel milanaise, folding clasp
Price: $1,299

Teutonia IV Moonphases

Reference number: M1-44-05-LB
Movement: automatic, Sellita caliber SW280-1;
ø 25.6 mm, height 5.4 mm; 26 jewels; 28,800 vph;
woodpecker-neck regulator, finely finished Mühle rotor
with special Mühle finishing; 41-hour power reserve
Functions: hours, minutes, sweep seconds; date, moon
phase
Case: stainless steel, ø 41 mm, height 12.6 mm;
sapphire crystal; transparent case back; water-resistant
to 10 atm
Band: calfskin, double folding clasp
Price: $2,899
Variations: with stainless steel bracelet ($3,049)

Teutonia II GMT

Reference number: M1-33-96-LB-II
Movement: automatic, Sellita caliber SW330-2;
ø 25.6 mm, height 4.1 mm; 21 jewels; 28,800 vph;
woodpecker-neck regulator, Glashütte three-quarter
plate, finely finished Mühle rotor with special Mühle
finishing; 56 hour power reserve
Functions: hours, minutes, sweep seconds; additional
24-hour display (second time zone); date
Case: stainless steel, ø 41 mm, height 10.6 mm;
sapphire crystal; transparent case back; water-resistant
to 10 atm
Band: calfskin, double folding clasp
Price: $2,949

NOMOS

Who says Germans have no sense of humor? The best of it is subtle enough to be accessible to the poets and thinkers (*Dichter und Denker*) with command of the language and its many dialects. At its apex, humor must be self-deprecatory and deadpan. This may be the reason for Nomos's global success. Ever since its founding in 1990 by Roland Schwertner and his associate Uwe Ahrendt, the company's marketing measures have harmonized with the product in a subtly playful and humorous manner.

Nomos Glashütte is now the number one producer of mechanical watches in Germany. It manufactures them in the best tradition of the German Werkbund and Bauhaus—research, design, and production work hand in hand. The emphasis on design meant that the brand needed its own calibers, and these are now wisely distributed throughout the thirteen model families with over one hundred variations that grace the company's portfolio. The one that made a loud splash, however, was the DUW 4401 (Deutsche Uhrenwerke Nomos Glashütte), equipped with the "Swing System," an in-house escapement with a spring "made in Germany." Unveiled in 2014, this caliber has gradually become the core regulating instrument for Nomos watches and been integrated into all the brand's movements. Its great advantage is thinness, which lets the company maintain its USP as it were: very elegant, unobtrusively attractive mechanical watches.

Speaking of design, of the over two hundred people who work at Nomos, about twenty or so are members of the Berlin-based company Berlinerblau and the others are spread out across the world, from Glashütte to New York, from Hong Kong and Shanghai to Lake Como in Italy. This aesthetic-philosophical scrim, as it were, has produced such genial watch families as the swimmer's watch Ahoi (as in "ship ahoy!"), with an optional synthetic strap like those that carry locker keys at Germany's public swimming pools. The Autobahn is a panegyric to Germany's favorite playground, the highway. Quirky dial colors are also part of the brand's mission. The Tangente watches now come in a slew of colors, each iteration with a special name as well. The recipe has, so far, earned the brand five stars from consumers and over 170 prizes for design and quality.

NOMOS GLASHÜTTE/SA
Roland Schwertner KG
Ferdinand-Adolph-Lange-Platz 2
01768 Glashütte
Germany

TEL.:
+49-35053-404-0

E-MAIL:
nomos@glashuette.com

WEBSITE:
nomos-glashuette.com

FOUNDED:
1990

NUMBER OF EMPLOYEES:
over 200

U.S. DISTRIBUTOR:
For the U.S. market, please contact:
NOMOS Glashuette USA Inc.
347 W. 36th St., Suite 600
New York, NY 10018
212-929-2575
contact@nomos-watches.com

MOST IMPORTANT COLLECTIONS/PRICE RANGE:
Ahoi, Autobahn, Club, Club Campus, Club Sport, Ludwig, Lux, Metro, Orion Tangente, Tangomat, Tetra, Zürich / from $1,440 to $10.920 (for gold models) / Lambda, $18,500

Club Sport neomatik 39 Smoke

Reference number: 764
Movement: automatic, Nomos caliber DUW 3001; ø 28.8 mm, height 3.2 mm; 27 jewels; 21,600 vph; three-quarter plate, finely finished movement; 43-hour power reserve
Functions: hours, minutes, subsidiary seconds
Case: stainless steel, ø 39.5 mm, height 8.5 mm; sapphire crystal; transparent case back; water-resistant to 20 atm
Band: stainless steel, folding clasp
Price: $3,700
Variations: with brown and beige-gold dial; with closed case back

Tangente neomatik 41 Update

Reference number: 180
Movement: automatic, Nomos caliber DUW 6101; ø 35.2 mm, height 3.6 mm; 27 jewels; 21,600 vph; three-quarter plate, finely finished movement; 42-hour power reserve
Functions: hours, minutes, subsidiary seconds; date
Case: stainless steel, ø 40.5 mm, height 7.8 mm; sapphire crystal; transparent case back; water-resistant to 5 atm
Band: horse leather, pin buckle
Price: $4,100

Ahoi neomatik 38 Date Sky

Reference number: 526
Movement: automatic, Nomos caliber DUW 6101; ø 33 mm, height 3.6 mm; 27 jewels; 21,600 vph; three-quarter plate, finely finished movement; 42-hour power reserve
Functions: hours, minutes, subsidiary seconds; date
Case: stainless steel, ø 38.5 mm, height 9.9 mm; sapphire crystal; transparent case back; screw-down crown; water-resistant to 20 atm
Band: textile, double folding clasp
Price: $4,320
Variations: with sand-colored dial; with stainless steel case back

Tangente 38 Date

Reference number: 130
Movement: hand-wound, Nomos caliber DUW 4101; ø 32.1 mm, height 2.8 mm; 23 jewels; 21,600 vph; three-quarter plate, finely finished movement; 42-hour power reserve
Functions: hours, minutes, subsidiary seconds; date
Case: stainless steel, ø 37.5 mm, height 6.8 mm; sapphire crystal; transparent case back; water-resistant to 3 atm
Band: horse leather, pin buckle
Price: $2,780

Tangente neomatik 41 Update nachtblau

Reference number: 182
Movement: automatic, Nomos caliber DUW 6101; ø 35.2 mm, height 3.6 mm; 27 jewels; 21,600 vph; three-quarter plate, finely finished movement; 42-hour power reserve
Functions: hours, minutes, subsidiary seconds; date
Case: stainless steel, ø 40.5 mm, height 7.8 mm; sapphire crystal; transparent case back; water-resistant to 5 atm
Band: horse leather, pin buckle
Price: $4,100

Ludwig neomatik 41 Date

Reference number: 262
Movement: automatic, Nomos caliber DUW 6101; ø 35.2 mm, height 3.6 mm; 27 jewels; 21,600 vph; three-quarter plate, finely finished movement; 42-hour power reserve
Functions: hours, minutes, subsidiary seconds; date
Case: stainless steel, ø 40.5 mm, height 7.7 mm; sapphire crystal; transparent case back; water-resistant to 5 atm
Band: horse leather, pin buckle
Price: $4,000

Orion neomatik 41 Date new black

Reference number: 366
Movement: automatic, Nomos caliber DUW 6101; ø 35.2 mm, height 3.6 mm; 27 jewels; 21,600 vph; three-quarter plate, finely finished movement; 42-hour power reserve
Functions: hours, minutes, subsidiary seconds; date
Case: stainless steel, ø 40.5 mm, height 9.4 mm; sapphire crystal; transparent case back; water-resistant to 5 atm
Band: horse leather, pin buckle
Price: $4,200

Metro neomatik 41 Update

Reference number: 1165
Movement: automatic, Nomos caliber DUW 6101; ø 35.2 mm, height 3.6 mm; 27 jewels; 21,600 vph; three-quarter plate, finely finished movement; 42-hour power reserve
Functions: hours, minutes, subsidiary seconds; date
Case: stainless steel, ø 40.5 mm, height 9.1 mm; sapphire crystal; transparent case back; water-resistant to 5 atm
Band: textile, pin buckle
Price: $4,660

Metro Date Gangreserve

Reference number: 1101
Movement: hand-wound, Nomos caliber DUW 4401; ø 32.1 mm, height 2.8 mm; 23 jewels; 21,600 vph; three-quarter plate, finely finished movement; 42-hour power reserve
Functions: hours, minutes, subsidiary seconds; power reserve indicator; date
Case: stainless steel, ø 37 mm, height 7.7 mm; sapphire crystal; transparent case back; water-resistant to 3 atm
Band: horse leather, pin buckle
Price: $3,780

NOMOS

Zürich Weltzeit nachtblau

Reference number: 807
Movement: automatic, Nomos caliber DUW 5201;
ø 31 mm, height 5.7 mm; 26 jewels; 21,600 vph; finely
finished movement; 42-hour power reserve
Functions: hours, minutes, subsidiary seconds; world
time display (second time zone)
Case: stainless steel, ø 39.9 mm, height 10.9 mm;
sapphire crystal; transparent case back; water-resistant
to 3 atm
Band: horse leather, pin buckle
Price: $6,100
Variations: with white dial

Tangente Sport neomatik 42 Date

Reference number: 580
Movement: automatic, Nomos caliber DUW 6101;
ø 35.2 mm, height 3.6 mm; 27 jewels; 21,600 vph; three-
quarter plate, finely finished movement; 42-hour power
reserve
Functions: hours, minutes, subsidiary seconds; date
Case: stainless steel, ø 42 mm, height 10.9 mm;
sapphire crystal; transparent case back; screw-down
crown; water-resistant to 30 atm
Band: stainless steel, folding clasp
Price: $4,980
Variations: with blue-black dial

Club Sport neomatik 42 date blau

Reference number: 782
Movement: automatic, Nomos caliber DUW 6101;
ø 35.2 mm, height 3.6 mm; 27 jewels; 21,600 vph; three-
quarter plate, finely finished movement; 42-hour power
reserve
Functions: hours, minutes, subsidiary seconds; date
Case: stainless steel, ø 42 mm, height 10.2 mm;
sapphire crystal; transparent case back; screw-down
crown; water-resistant to 30 atm
Band: stainless steel, folding clasp
Price: $3,960
Variations: with black dial

Club Sport neomatik petrol

Reference number: 745
Movement: automatic, Nomos caliber DUW 3001;
ø 28.8 mm, height 3.2 mm; 27 jewels; 21,600 vph; three-
quarter plate, finely finished movement; 43-hour power
reserve
Functions: hours, minutes, subsidiary seconds
Case: stainless steel, ø 37 mm, height 8.3 mm; sapphire
crystal; water-resistant to 20 atm
Band: stainless steel, folding clasp
Price: $3,150
Variations: with blue dial; with sapphire crystal back

Club Campus nonstop red

Reference number: 716
Movement: hand-wound, Nomos caliber Alpha;
ø 23.3 mm, height 2.6 mm; 17 jewels; 21,600 vph; three-
quarter plate, finely finished movement; 43-hour power
reserve
Functions: hours, minutes, subsidiary seconds
Case: stainless steel, ø 36 mm, height 8.2 mm; sapphire
crystal; water-resistant to 10 atm
Band: vegan suede, pin buckle
Price: $1,500
Variations: various dial colors

Club Campus 38 endless blue

Reference number: 724
Movement: hand-wound, Nomos caliber Alpha;
ø 23.3 mm, height 2.6 mm; 17 jewels; 21,600 vph; three-
quarter plate, finely finished movement; 43-hour power
reserve
Functions: hours, minutes, subsidiary seconds
Case: stainless steel, ø 38.5 mm, height 8.5 mm;
sapphire crystal; water-resistant to 10 atm
Band: vegan suede, pin buckle
Price: $1,650
Variations: various dial colors

Ludwig 33 noir

Reference number: 226
Movement: hand-wound, Nomos caliber Alpha; ø 23.3 mm, height 2.6 mm; 17 jewels; 21,600 vph; three-quarter plate, finely finished movement; 43-hour power reserve
Functions: hours, minutes, subsidiary seconds
Case: stainless steel, ø 32.8 mm, height 6.5 mm; sapphire crystal; water-resistant to 3 atm
Band: suede, pin buckle
Price: $1,700
Variations: with transparent case back

Orion 33 rosé

Reference number: 325
Movement: hand-wound, Nomos caliber Alpha; ø 23.3 mm, height 2.6 mm; 17 jewels; 21,600 vph; three-quarter plate, finely finished movement; 43-hour power reserve
Functions: hours, minutes, subsidiary seconds
Case: stainless steel, ø 32.8 mm, height 8.5 mm; sapphire crystal; transparent case back; water-resistant to 3 atm
Band: suede, pin buckle
Price: $1,940
Variations: as Orion 33 gold ($2,240)

Tetra "Die Fuchsteufelswilde"

Reference number: 425
Movement: hand-wound, Nomos caliber Alpha; ø 23.3 mm, height 2.6 mm; 17 jewels; 21,600 vph; three-quarter plate, finely finished movement; 43-hour power reserve
Functions: hours, minutes, subsidiary seconds
Case: stainless steel, 29.5 mm x 29.5 mm, height 6.3 mm; sapphire crystal; water-resistant to 3 atm
Band: vegan suede, pin buckle
Price: $2,080
Variations: various colors; with transparent case back ($2,320)

Caliber DUW 1001

Hand-wound; swan-neck fine adjustment; two spring barrels, 84-hour power reserve
Functions: hours, minutes, subsidiary seconds; power reserve indicator
Diameter: 32 mm
Height: 3.6 mm
Jewels: 29, including 5 in screw-mounted gold chatons
Balance: screw balance
Frequency: 21,600 vph
Hairspring: Nivarox 1A
Shock protection: Incabloc
Remarks: hand-engraved balance cock, beveled and polished edges, rhodium-plated surfaces with perlage and Glashütte ribbing

Caliber DUW 6101

Automatic; single mainspring barrel, 43-hour power reserve
Functions: hours, minutes, subsidiary seconds; date
Diameter: 35.2 mm
Height: 3.6 mm
Jewels: 27
Balance: in-house manufacture
Frequency: 21,600 vph
Hairspring: in-house manufacture, heat-blued
Shock protection: Incabloc
Remarks: three-quarter plate, rhodium-plated surfaces with perlage and Glashütte ribbing, gold-plated engravings

Caliber DUW 3001

Automatic; single mainspring barrel, 43-hour power reserve
Functions: hours, minutes, subsidiary seconds
Diameter: 28.8 mm
Height: 3.2 mm
Jewels: 27
Balance: in-house manufacture
Frequency: 21,600 vph
Hairspring: in-house manufacture, heat-blued
Shock protection: Incabloc
Remarks: three-quarter plate, rhodium-plated surfaces with perlage and Glashütte ribbing

NORQAIN

Norqain was founded in 2018 by CEO Ben Küffer in Nidau near Biel/Bienne, that industrial city at the foot of the Jura Mountains in Switzerland that is home to several watch companies and related enterprises. He invited a number of people as cofounders to form the Board of Directors, notably Ted Schneider, a member of the family that once owned Breitling, and Swiss ice hockey legend Mark Streit, a watch enthusiast and a good ambassador for the new brand. Marc Küffer, Ben's father, was named the Chairman of the Board. He, for his part, had over forty-five years of experience in the manufacturing of Swiss luxury watches and had served on the Board of the Federation of the Swiss Watch Industry for twenty-five years.

The idea was perhaps not terribly original, but in a complicated world with lots of marketing, a clearcut message is often worth a thousand words: affordable quality. The brand's mission statement, as it were, was to be new, open-minded, rebellious, quality time-giving, adventurous, independent, and niche-oriented, which spells Norqain. The logo, a kind of N, is also a stylized mountain peak, expressing the watches' connection to sports and adventure.

The company manufactures mechanical watches only, which are assembled by hand in the production facility in Tavannes, a village in the Jura. To ensure high quality, Norqain signed a long-term strategic collaboration with Kenissi in Le Locle, a finicky movement-maker that was founded by Tudor (of Rolex fame) and is twenty percent owned by Chanel. It's an exclusive club, but the fact that Kenissi manager Jean-Paul Girardin is a former Breitling executive surely helped secure the partnership.

The first results of this important alliance were two exclusive manufacture movements: the three-hand caliber NN20/1 and the GMT caliber NN20/2, both with a power reserve of seventy hours and chronometer certification. The three collections—Adventure, Freedom, and Independence—boast quite original, striking design elements. And the conceptual recipe behind the brand seems to have worked because Norqain has become a household name amongst connoisseurs.

MONTRES NORQAIN SA
Hauptstrasse 7
CH-2560 Nidau
Switzerland

TEL:
+41-32-505-31-55

E-MAIL:
info@norqain.com

WEBSITE:
norqain.com

FOUNDED:
2018

NUMBER OF EMPLOYEES:
40

ANNUAL PRODUCTION:
more than 1,000

DISTRIBUTION:
retailers, own shops

MOST IMPORTANT COLLECTIONS/PRICE RANGE:
Adventure, Freedom, Independence / around $2,000 to $5,000

Adventure Neverest Glacier
Reference number: NN1001SC2CA/IAGL109/150SS
Movement: automatic, Norqain caliber NN20/1 (Kenissi caliber base); ø 31.8 mm, height 6.5 mm; 27 jewels; 28,800 vph; COSC-certified chronometer; 70-hour power reserve
Functions: hours, minutes, sweep seconds
Case: stainless steel, ø 40 mm, height 12.55 mm; bidirectional bezel with ceramic insert with 0-60 scale; sapphire crystal; transparent case back; screw-down crown; water-resistant to 20 atm
Band: stainless steel, folding clasp, with fine adjustment
Remarks: structured dial inspired from glacier crevasses
Price: $4,190; limited to 300 pieces
Variations: with rubber strap ($3,950)

Independence Wild One Skeleton
Reference number: NNQ3000QBR2AS/B013/3W1RBR1.20BQ
Movement: automatic, Norqain caliber NN08S (Sellita SW200-1 base); ø 25.6 mm, height 4.6 mm; 26 jewels; 28,800 vph; fully skeletonized movement; 38-hour power reserve
Functions: hours, minutes, sweep seconds
Case: carbon fiber (NORTEQ) with titanium movement container and rubber shock absorbers, ø 42 mm, height 12.3 mm; sapphire crystal; transparent case back; screw-down crown, with rubber overlay; water-resistant to 20 atm
Band: rubber, pin buckle
Price: $5,790

Freedom 60 Chrono Sky Blue
Reference number: N2201S22C/IAA221/201SG
Movement: automatic, Norqain caliber NN19 (Sellita SW510a base); ø 30.4 mm, height 7.9 mm; 27 jewels; 28,800 vph; 62-hour power reserve
Functions: hours, minutes, subsidiary seconds; chronograph; date
Case: stainless steel, ø 40 mm, height 14.9 mm; sapphire crystal; transparent case back; screw-down crown; water-resistant to 10 atm
Band: stainless steel, folding clasp
Price: $4,550
Variations: with strap of Nortide recycled material ($4,320); with Perlon-rubber strap ($4,360)

NOVE

The most popular watch genre is the diver's watch and for good reason. First, these timepieces exude an aura of adventure, danger, and fun, mixed with a bit of lizard-brain survival, all wrapped in one. It's part of their history. After all, have they not served on the wrists of extra-tough special commandos in various countries? The other reason is of course reliability. As genuine tool watches, they must be built with great care and function extremely well, since the users depend on them to know how long they've been underwater and how much time they have left to perform their tasks.

Any brand wanting to release a new one will face the challenge of innovation and creating a viable USP. Nove, a brand stationed in Hong Kong but with production in Switzerland, came up with the idea of a thin diver's watch, the Trident, which clocks in at 6.2 millimeters thickness in quartz. A second diver, the Atlantean, was conceived with a large dose of Super-LumiNova on the dial, hands, and bezel for good visibility even in deep waters, and an interior bidirectional bezel that can be locked into place with a special hand lever. The diameter of the Atlantean II, released in 2024, has been reduced to a still-hefty 46 millimeters, down from 50.5!

To cover its market well, Nove also has a rather fresh-looking dress watches, including the clever dual-faced Gemini GMT watch, which reverses using a bespoke lever mechanism, and the Modena chronographs, for the sportive buyer.

Having fresh ideas might be part of the company DNA, ever since it was founded by Tiffany Meerovitsch in 2015 when she was just 19 years old and about to go to university to study art and later digital marketing. It was a natural passion for her. She grew up steeped in watchmaking while visiting her father's office at a watchmaking company. "He had me working on the assembly line, where I learned how to assemble a watch," she said in an interview. "Seeing all these beautiful designs got me fascinated with the idea of starting my own label with my own designs."

Nove watches are assembled in Switzerland using Swiss parts. They make use of Ronda and Sellita movements mostly.

NOVE
Swiss office:
Via ai Boschi 6,
CH-6855 Stabio
Switzerland

HONG KONG OFFICE:
NOVE Limited
Unit A, 3/F, Kingsway Industrial Building,
Phase 1, 167-175 Wo Yi Hop Road,
Kwai Chung, N.T., Hong Kong

EMAIL:
mkt@nove.com

WEBSITE:
www.nove.com

FOUNDED:
2015 (incorporated 2018)

NUMBER OF EMPLOYEES:
About 15 employees

DISTRIBUTION:
Webshop (see website)

MOST IMPORTANT COLLECTIONS / PRICE RANGE:
Atlantean, Atlantean II, Gemini, Trident / $280 to $2,000

Atlantean II

Reference number: N002-07
Movement: automatic, Sellita caliber SW 200-1; ø 25.6 mm, height 4.6 mm; 25 jewels; 28,800 vph; 41-hour power reserve
Functions: hours, minutes, sweep seconds; date
Case: stainless steel, ø 46 mm, height 13.9 mm; screw-down crown with guard lock; bidirectional, lever-activated inner bezel; sapphire crystal; transparent case back; water-resistant to 30 atm
Band: stainless steel, safety clasp with micro-adjustment
Remarks: quick-change strap system
Price: $880
Variations: with green or black bezel

Marine Automatic

Reference number: M002-07
Movement: automatic, Sellita caliber SW 200; ø 25.6 mm, height 4.6 mm; 25 jewels; 28,800 vph; 41-hour power reserve
Functions: hours, minutes, sweep seconds; date
Case: stainless steel with IP blue coating, ø 41.5 mm, height 13.05 mm; screw-down crown; IP Blue; sapphire crystal; transparent case back; water-resistant to 20 atm
Band: stainless steel, folding clasp
Price: $880
Variations: various colors

Modena 500

Reference number: O001-02
Movement: automatic, Sellita SW500a caliber; ø 30 mm; height 7.6 mm; 25 jewels; 28,800 vph; 62-hour power reserve
Functions: hours, minutes, subsidiary seconds; day, date; chronograph with tachymeter scale
Case: stainless steel, ø 44 mm, height 15.7 mm; screw-down crowns; sapphire crystal; transparent case back; water-resistant to 20 atm
Band: stainless steel, safety clasp with micro-adjustment
Price: $1,880; limited to 99 pieces

OMEGA

As the largest brand in the SSIH Group, Omega had an important role to play during the quartz crisis that hit the Swiss watch industry in the 1970s. The Société Suisse de l'Industrie Horlogère and the Allgemeine Schweizerische Uhrenindustrie AG (ASUAG) merged to form the founding company of the Swatch Group. It became the flagship brand of the entire group and therefore had a leading position in terms of design, technology, and functionality.

Technology and design are really the drivers of Omega's success. It became the first company to try out new materials, like titanium and ceramic, or complications like the central tourbillon or George Daniels's coaxial escapement.

The 15,000-gauss antimagnetic movement has now been used in many of the new products. And there is a plethora of new "Master Chronometer" movements, which meet the stringent COSC requirements plus the tests required by Switzerland's Federal Institute of Metrology (METAS). Swatch Group subsidiary Nivarox-FAR has finally mastered the production of the difficult, oil-free parts of the system designed by Englishman George Daniels, although the escapement continues to include lubrication, as the long-term results of "dry" coaxial movements are less than satisfactory.

The most enduring and iterated Omega model is the Seamaster, which was born in 1948. In 1957, Omega introduced the Seamaster 300 automatic for professional divers (or *plongeurs professionels* hence the name Ploprof). A special model was released to the public in 1971, the Seamaster Planet Ocean Ultra Deep, which is water-resistant to 600 atm. And 2023, the Seamaster's seventy-fifth anniversary was also celebrated with a series of seawater blue dials ("Summer Blue").

In 2024, Omega once again acted as the official timepiece of the Summer Olympics held in Paris. It was the occasion for special models, like a steel Seamaster 300M with a "Moonshine gold" bezel or a stainless-steel or gold Speedmaster Chronoscope. The highlight of the Olympic collection, however, was the Paris 2024 Bronze Gold Edition in the style of a classic T3 chronometer, albeit equipped with the extremely modern Master Chronometer caliber 8926.

OMEGA SA
Jakob-Stämpfli-Strasse 96
CH-2502 Biel/Bienne
Switzerland

TEL.:
+41-32-343-9211

E-MAIL:
info@omegawatches.com

WEBSITE:
www.omegawatches.com

FOUNDED:
1848

U.S. DISTRIBUTOR:
Omega
703 Waterford Way, Suite 920
Miami, FL 33126
800-766-6342
www.omegawatches.com

MOST IMPORTANT COLLECTIONS / PRICE RANGE:
Constellation, DeVille, Seamaster, Speedmaster / from $3,200

Speedmaster Moonwatch Professional

Reference number: 310.30.42.50.04.001
Movement: hand-wound, Omega caliber 3861; ø 27 mm, height 6.9 mm; 26 jewels; 21,600 vph; co-axial escapement, silicon hairspring; antimagnetic to 15,000 Gauss; METAS-certified chronometer; 50-hour power reserve
Functions: hours, minutes, subsidiary seconds; chronograph
Case: stainless steel, ø 42 mm, height 13.2 mm; bezel set with aluminum insert; sapphire crystal; water-resistant to 5 atm
Band: stainless steel, folding clasp
Price: $8,100

Speedmaster Super Racing

Reference number: 329.30.44.51.01.003
Movement: automatic, Omega caliber 9920; ø 32.5 mm, height 7.6 mm; 54 jewels; 28,800 vph; 2 mainsprings, co-axial escapement, silicon hairspring, antimagnetic to 15,000 Gauss; METAS-certified chronometer; 60-hour power reserve
Functions: hours, minutes, subsidiary seconds; chronograph; date
Case: stainless steel, ø 44.25 mm, height 14.9 mm; bezel set with ceramic insert; sapphire crystal; transparent case back; water-resistant to 5 atm
Band: stainless steel, double folding clasp
Price: $11,600

De Ville Trésor Power Reserve

Reference number: 435.53.40.22.02.001
Movement: hand-wound, Omega caliber 8935; ø 29 mm, height 4.9 mm; 30 jewels; 25,200 vph; 2 mainsprings, co-axial escapement, silicon hairspring, antimagnetic to 15,000 Gauss; METAS-certified chronometer; 72-hour power reserve
Functions: hours, minutes, subsidiary seconds; power reserve indicator
Case: yellow gold, ø 40 mm, height 10.07 mm; sapphire crystal; transparent case back; water-resistant to 3 atm
Band: reptile skin, pin buckle
Price: $20,600

Seamaster 300

Reference number: 234.92.41.21.10.001
Movement: automatic, Omega caliber 8912; ø 29 mm, height 5.5 mm; 38 jewels; 25,200 vph; 2 mainsprings, co-axial escapement, silicon hairspring, antimagnetic to 15,000 Gauss; METAS-certified chronometer; 60-hour power reserve
Functions: hours, minutes, sweep seconds
Case: bronze-gold alloy, ø 41 mm, height 14.4 mm; unidirectional bezel with ceramic insert, with 0-60 scale; sapphire crystal; transparent case back; screw-down crown; water-resistant to 30 atm
Band: calfskin, pin buckle
Price: $13,600
Variations: in stainless steel

Seamaster Diver 300M

Reference number: 210.30.42.20.01.001
Movement: automatic, Omega caliber 8800; ø 26 mm, height 4.6 mm; 35 jewels; 25,200 vph; co-axial escapement, silicon hairspring, antimagnetic to 15,000 Gauss; METAS-certified chronometer; 55-hour power reserve
Functions: hours, minutes, sweep seconds; date
Case: stainless steel, ø 42 mm, height 13.56 mm; unidirectional bezel with ceramic insert with 0-60 scale; sapphire crystal; transparent case back; screw-down crown, helium valve; water-resistant to 30 atm
Band: stainless steel, folding clasp
Price: $5,900
Variations: various cases, straps, and dials

Seamaster Diver "Black Black"

Reference number: 210.92.44.20.01.003
Movement: automatic, Omega caliber 8806; ø 26 mm, height 4.6 mm; 35 jewels; 25,200 vph; co-axial escapement, silicon balance wheel and hairspring, antimagnetic to 15,000 Gauss; METAS-certified chronometer; 55-hour power reserve
Functions: hours, minutes, sweep seconds
Case: ceramic, ø 43.5 mm, height 14.5 mm; unidirectional bezel, with 0-60 scale; sapphire crystal; screw-down crown, helium valve; water-resistant to 30 atm
Band: rubber, pin buckle
Price: $9,500

Seamaster Diver 300M

Reference number: 210.30.42.20.03.003
Movement: automatic, Omega caliber 8800; ø 26 mm, height 4.6 mm; 35 jewels; 25,200 vph; co-axial escapement, silicon balance wheel and hairspring, antimagnetic to 15,000 Gauss; METAS-certified chronometer; 55-hour power reserve
Functions: hours, minutes, sweep seconds; date
Case: stainless steel, ø 42 mm, height 13.56 mm; unidirectional bezel with ceramic insert, with 0-60 scale; sapphire crystal; screw-down crown, helium valve; water-resistant to 30 atm
Band: stainless steel, folding clasp, with extension link
Price: $6,300
Variations: various cases, straps, and dials

Seamaster Aqua Terra 150M Master Chronometer

Reference number: 220.10.41.21.03.005
Movement: automatic, Omega caliber 8900; ø 29 mm, height 5.5 mm; 39 jewels; 25,200 vph; two spring barrels, co-axial escapement, silicon balance wheel and hairspring, antimagnetic to 15,000 Gauss; METAS-certified chronometer; 60-hour power reserve
Functions: hours, minutes, sweep seconds; date
Case: stainless steel, ø 41 mm, height 13.2 mm; sapphire crystal; water-resistant to 15 atm
Band: stainless steel, double folding clasp
Price: $6,600

Seamaster Aqua Terra Worldtimer

Reference number: 220.32.43.22.10.001
Movement: automatic, Omega caliber 8938; ø 29 mm, height 6 mm; 38 jewels; 25,200 vph; co-axial escapement, silicon hairspring, antimagnetic to 15,000 Gauss; METAS-certified chronometer; 60-hour power reserve
Functions: hours, minutes, sweep seconds; world time display (second time zone); date
Case: stainless steel, ø 43 mm, height 14.1 mm; sapphire crystal; transparent case back; screw-down crown; water-resistant to 15 atm
Band: rubber, folding clasp
Price: $10,700
Variations: various dials and cases

Seamaster Planet Ocean Ultra Deep

Reference number: 215.30.46.21.06.001
Movement: automatic, Omega caliber 8912; ø 29 mm, height 5.5 mm; 38 jewels; 25,200 vph; 2 mainsprings, co-axial escapement, silicon hairspring, antimagnetic to 15,000 Gauss; METAS-certified chronometer; 60-hour power reserve
Functions: hours, minutes, sweep seconds
Case: stainless steel ("O-Megasteel"), ø 45.5 mm, height 18.12 mm; unidirectional bezel with ceramic insert, with 0-60 scale; sapphire crystal; screw-down crown; water-resistant to 600 atm
Band: stainless steel ("O-Megasteel"), folding clasp
Price: $12,300
Variations: with rubber strap; in titanium with textile strap ($13,600)

Seamaster Planet Ocean 600M

Reference number: 215.32.44.21.06.001
Movement: automatic, Omega caliber 8900; ø 29 mm, height 5.5 mm; 39 jewels; 25,200 vph; 2 mainsprings, co-axial escapement, silicon hairspring, antimagnetic to 15,000 Gauss; METAS-certified chronometer; 60-hour power reserve
Functions: hours, minutes, sweep seconds; date
Case: stainless steel, ø 43.5 mm, height 16.2 mm; unidirectional bezel with ceramic insert, with 0-60 scale; sapphire crystal; screw-down crown, helium valve; water-resistant to 60 atm
Band: rubber with textile overlay, folding clasp
Price: $7,100

Seamaster "Ploprof"

Reference number: 227.32.55.21.03.001
Movement: automatic, Omega caliber 8912; ø 29 mm, height 5.5 mm; 38 jewels; 25,200 vph; 2 mainsprings, co-axial escapement, silicon hairspring, antimagnetic to 15,000 Gauss; METAS-certified chronometer; 60-hour power reserve
Functions: hours, minutes, sweep seconds
Case: stainless steel ("O-Megasteel"), 55 mm x 45 mm, height 15.5 mm; unidirectional bezel with ceramic insert, with 0-60 scale; sapphire crystal; screw-down crown, helium valve; water-resistant to 120 atm
Band: rubber, pin buckle
Remarks: the (unofficial) name of the model is derived from "Plongeurs Professionels" (professional divers)
Price: $14,300

Constellation Master Chronometer

Reference number: 131.33.41.21.04.001
Movement: automatic, Omega caliber 8900; ø 29 mm, height 5.5 mm; 39 jewels; 25,200 vph; two spring barrels, co-axial escapement, silicon hairspring, antimagnetic to 15,000 Gauss; METAS-certified chronometer; 60-hour power reserve
Functions: hours, minutes, sweep seconds; date
Case: stainless steel, ø 41 mm, height 13.5 mm; sapphire crystal; transparent case back; water-resistant to 5 atm
Band: rubber with reptile skin overlay, folding clasp
Price: $7,100
Variations: various dials

Seamaster Aqua Terra 150M

Reference number: 220.10.38.20.01.004
Movement: automatic, Omega caliber 8800; ø 26 mm, height 4.6 mm; 35 jewels; 25,200 vph; co-axial escapement, silicon hairspring, antimagnetic to 15,000 Gauss; METAS-certified chronometer; 55-hour power reserve
Functions: hours, minutes, sweep seconds; date
Case: stainless steel, ø 38 mm, height 12.3 mm; sapphire crystal; water-resistant to 15 atm
Band: stainless steel, folding clasp
Price: $6,600

Speedmaster Moonwatch Professional

Reference number: 310.62.42.50.99.001
Movement: hand-wound, Omega caliber 3861; ø 27 mm, height 6.9 mm; 26 jewels; 21,600 vph; co-axial escapement, silicon hairspring, antimagnetic to 15,000 Gauss; METAS-certified chronometer; 50-hour power reserve
Functions: hours, minutes, subsidiary seconds; chronograph
Case: yellow gold ("Moonshine Gold"), ø 42 mm, height 13.2 mm; bezel set with ceramic insert; sapphire crystal; transparent case back; water-resistant to 5 atm
Band: rubber, folding clasp
Price: $32,400

Speedmaster Dark Side of the Moon "Apollo 8"

Reference number: 310.92.44.50.01.001
Movement: hand-wound, Omega caliber 3869; ø 27 mm, height 6.87 mm; 26 jewels; 21,600 vph; co-axial escapement, silicon hairspring, antimagnetic to 15,000 Gauss; mainplate and bridges with black coating; METAS-certified chronometer; 50-hour power reserve
Functions: hours, minutes, subsidiary seconds; chronograph
Case: ceramic, ø 44.25 mm, height 13 mm; sapphire crystal; transparent case back; water-resistant to 5 atm
Band: rubber, folding clasp
Remarks: mainplate and bridges with carefully designed structure of the moon's surface
Price: $14,300

Speedmaster Moonwatch Master Chronometer

Reference number: 310.30.42.50.01.001
Movement: hand-wound, Omega caliber 3861; ø 27 mm, height 6.9 mm; 26 jewels; 21,600 vph; co-axial escapement, silicon hairspring, antimagnetic to 15,000 Gauss; METAS-certified chronometer; 50-hour power reserve
Functions: hours, minutes, subsidiary seconds; chronograph
Case: stainless steel, ø 42 mm, height 13.2 mm; bezel set with aluminum insert; Hesalite glass; water-resistant to 5 atm
Band: stainless steel, folding clasp
Price: $7,000
Variations: with textile strap ($6,600)

Speedmaster Moonphase

Reference number: 304.33.44.52.03.001
Movement: automatic, Omega caliber 9904; ø 32.5 mm, height 8.35 mm; 54 jewels; 28,800 vph; 2 mainsprings, co-axial escapement, silicon hairspring, antimagnetic to 15,000 Gauss; METAS-certified chronometer; 60-hour power reserve
Functions: hours, minutes, subsidiary seconds; chronograph; date, moon phase
Case: stainless steel, ø 44.25 mm, height 16.85 mm; bezel set with ceramic insert; sapphire crystal; water-resistant to 10 atm
Band: reptile skin, folding clasp
Price: $11,200
Variations: various cases and dials

De Ville Trésor Small Seconds

Reference number: 435.53.40.21.11.002
Movement: hand-wound, Omega caliber 8927; ø 29 mm, height 4.9 mm; 29 jewels; 25,200 vph; 2 mainsprings, co-axial escapement, silicon hairspring, antimagnetic to 15,000 Gauss; METAS-certified chronometer; 72-hour power reserve
Functions: hours, minutes, subsidiary seconds
Case: rose gold ("Sedna gold"), ø 40 mm, height 10.7 mm; sapphire crystal; water-resistant to 3 atm
Band: calfskin, pin buckle
Price: $20,000

Seamaster Diver James Bond Edition

Reference number: 210.90.42.20.01.001
Movement: automatic, Omega caliber 8806; ø 26 mm, height 4.6 mm; 35 jewels; 25,200 vph; co-axial escapement, silicon hairspring, antimagnetic to 15,000 Gauss; METAS-certified chronometer; 55-hour power reserve
Functions: hours, minutes, sweep seconds
Case: titanium, ø 42 mm, height 13 mm; unidirectional bezel with aluminum insert, with 0-60 scale; sapphire crystal; screw-down crown, helium valve; water-resistant to 30 atm
Band: titanium milanaise mesh, folding clasp
Price: $10,000
Variations: with textile strap ($8,900)

Speedmaster '57

Reference number: 332.12.41.51.03.001
Movement: hand-wound, Omega caliber 9906; ø 32.5 mm, height 6.4 mm; 44 jewels; 28,800 vph; co-axial escapement, silicon hairspring; column-wheel control of chronograph functions; METAS-certified chronometer; 60-hour power reserve
Functions: hours, minutes, subsidiary seconds; chronograph; date
Case: stainless steel, ø 40.5 mm, height 13 mm; sapphire crystal; water-resistant to 10 atm
Band: calfskin, pin buckle
Price: $9,100
Variations: various straps and dials

Caliber 8800

Automatic; co-axial escapement, antimagnetic to 15,000 Gauss; METAS-certified chronometer; single mainspring barrel, 55-hour power reserve
Functions: hours, minutes, sweep seconds; date
Diameter: 26 mm
Height: 4.6 mm
Jewels: 35
Balance: silicon, without adjustment
Frequency: 25,200 vph
Hairspring: silicon
Shock protection: Nivachoc
Remarks: blackened screws

Caliber 321B

Hand-wound; Breguet hairspring; column wheel control of chronograph functions; single mainspring barrel, 55-hour power reserve
Base caliber: Lémania 2310
Functions: hours, minutes, subsidiary seconds; chronograph
Diameter: 27 mm
Height: 6.87 mm
Jewels: 17
Frequency: 18,000 vph
Remarks: New edition of historical movement used in first Speedmaster models; red gold-plated, finely finished

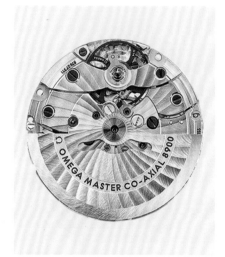

Caliber 8900

Automatic; co-axial escapement, antimagnetic to 15,000 Gauss; METAS-certified chronometer; two spring barrels, 60-hour power reserve
Functions: hours, minutes, sweep seconds; date
Diameter: 29 mm
Height: 5.5 mm
Jewels: 39
Balance: silicon, without adjustment
Frequency: 25,200 vph
Hairspring: silicon
Shock protection: Nivachoc
Remarks: mainplate, bridges and rotor with "arabesque" côtes de Genève; rhodium-plated mainsprings, blackened balance wheel and screws

Caliber 9900

Automatic; co-axial escapement; column wheel control of the chronograph functions; antimagnetic to 15,000 Gauss; METAS-certified chronometer; two spring barrels, 60-hour power reserve
Functions: hours, minutes, subsidiary seconds; chronograph; date
Diameter: 32.5 mm
Height: 7.6 mm
Jewels: 54
Balance: silicon, without adjustment
Frequency: 28,800 vph
Hairspring: silicon
Shock protection: Nivachoc
Remarks: mainplate, bridges and rotor with "arabesque" côtes de Genève, blackened balance wheel and screws

Caliber 8935

Hand-wound; co-axial escapement, antimagnetic to 15,000 Gauss; METAS-certified chronometer; two spring barrels, 72-hour power reserve
Functions: hours, minutes, subsidiary seconds; power reserve indicator
Diameter: 29 mm
Height: 5.5 mm
Jewels: 30
Balance: silicon, without adjustment
Frequency: 25,200 vph
Hairspring: silicon
Shock protection: Nivachoc
Remarks: mainplate and bridges with côtes de Genève, "Sednagold" balance bridge, blackened spring barrels, balance wheel and screws

Caliber 3861

Hand-wound; co-axial escapement, antimagnetic to 15,000 Gauss; METAS-certified chronometer; single mainspring barrel, 50-hour power reserve
Functions: hours, minutes, subsidiary seconds; chronograph
Diameter: 27 mm
Height: 6.87 mm
Jewels: 26
Frequency: 21,600 vph
Hairspring: silicon
Remarks: gold plated movement ("Moonshine Gold"); 240 parts

ORIS

Oris, located near Basel, Switzerland, since its founding in 1904, has stuck to its strategic guns for as long as it has existed: affordable quality. The result has been growing international success, now with a portfolio divided up into four "product worlds," each with its own distinct identity: aviation, motor sports, diving, and culture. In utilizing specific materials—a tungsten bezel for the divers, for example—and functions based on these types, Oris makes certain that each will fit perfectly into the world for which it was designed. Yet the heart of every watch houses a small, high-quality "high-mech" movement identifiable by the brand's standard red rotor.

A bold step came in 2014 with the in-house Caliber 110, a plain, but technically efficient, manually wound movement. It was made together with the engineers from the Technical College of Le Locle and features a 6-foot (1.8-meter) mainspring. Like clockwork, then, Oris produced further calibers, numbered 111, 112 (with GMT function), and 113.

In October 2020, the first wristwatches with the new Caliber 400 were launched. One goal in creating the movement was to eliminate problems even before they occur. COO Beat Fischli and his team spent five years researching and developing the movement in order to fulfil the previously established and defined criteria: five-day power reserve, special resistance to magnetic fields, chronometer accuracy, and high serviceability with long maintenance intervals of ten years. The Caliber 400 family debuted in the Aquis series but has already been used in various editions of the Big Crown and Divers Sixty-Five series.

For Oris, the 2024 model year is all about the latest Aquis. The brand's successful luxury diver's watch underwent a complete facelift, with a slimmer case; improved ergonomics; and a lot of visual detail work on the dial, hands, crown, and side protection. The stainless-steel cases are 41.5 and 43.5 mm in diameter. A version with a 36.5 mm diameter and slimmer bezel was introduced to give buyers a more elegant sportive watch. The new line also includes the patented Quick Strap Change system for fast, tool-free strap changes and a new folding clasp with integrated fine adjustment.

ORIS SA
Ribigasse 1
CH-4434 Hölstein
Switzerland

TEL.:
+41-61-956-1111

E-MAIL:
MyOris@oris.ch

WEBSITE:
www.oris.ch

FOUNDED:
1904

NUMBER OF EMPLOYEES:
210

U.S. DISTRIBUTOR:
Oris Watches USA
50 Washington Street, Suite 302
Norwalk, CT 06854
203-857-4769

MOST IMPORTANT COLLECTIONS/PRICE RANGE:
Divers Sixty-Five, Big Crown, Artelier, Aquis, ProPilot
/ approx. $1,300 to $10,300

Big Crown Caliber 473

Reference number: 01 473 7786 4065-07 5 19 22FC
Movement: hand-wound, Oris caliber 473; ø 30 mm; 27 jewels; 28,800 vph; 120-hour power reserve
Functions: hours, minutes, subsidiary seconds; power reserve indicator (on movement side); date
Case: stainless steel, ø 38 mm, height 11.8 mm; sapphire crystal; transparent case back; water-resistant to 5 atm
Band: deerskin, pin buckle
Price: $4,800

Oris X Cervo Volante

Reference number: 01 754 7779 4065-Set
Movement: automatic, Oris caliber 754 (Sellita SW200-1 base); ø 25.6 mm, height 4.6 mm; 26 jewels; 28,800 vph; 38-hour power reserve
Functions: hours, minutes, sweep seconds; date
Case: stainless steel, ø 38 mm, height 12.8 mm; sapphire crystal; transparent case back; water-resistant to 5 atm
Band: deerskin, pin buckle
Price: $2,500
Variations: with green or grey dial

ProPilot X Caliber 400 Laser

Reference number: 01 400 7778 7150-07 7 20 01TLC
Movement: automatic, Oris caliber 400; ø 30 mm, height 4.75 mm; 21 jewels; 28,800 vph; 120-hour power reserve
Functions: hours, minutes, sweep seconds
Case: titanium, ø 39 mm, height 12 mm; sapphire crystal; transparent case back; water-resistant to 10 atm
Band: titanium, folding clasp
Remarks: micro-laser engraving creates iridizing colors on titanium dial
Price: $5,500

ProPilot X Calibre 115

Reference number: 01 115 7759 7153-07 22 01TLC
Movement: hand-wound, Oris caliber 115; ø 34 mm,
height 6 mm; 38 jewels; 21,600 vph; skeletonized
movement; central, open spring barrel, 240-hour power
reserve
Functions: hours, minutes, subsidiary seconds; power
reserve indicator
Case: titanium, ø 44 mm, height 12.5 mm; sapphire
crystal; transparent case back; screw-down crown;
water-resistant to 10 atm
Band: titanium, folding clasp
Remarks: skeletonized dial
Price: $8,900
Variations: with calfskin strap

ProPilot X Kermit Edition

Reference number: 01 400 7778 7157-Set
Movement: automatic, Oris caliber 400; ø 30 mm,
height 4.75 mm; 21 jewels; 28,800 vph; 120-hour power
reserve
Functions: hours, minutes, sweep seconds; date
Case: titanium, ø 39 mm, height 12 mm; sapphire
crystal; water-resistant to 10 atm
Band: titanium, folding clasp
Remarks: Kermit the frog appears in the date aperture
on the first of each month
Price: $4,900

ProPilot Altimeter

Reference number: 01 793 7775 8764 Set
Movement: automatic, Oris caliber 793 (Sellita
SW300-1 base); ø 25.6 mm, height 3.6 mm; 25 jewels;
28,800 vph; 56-hour power reserve
Functions: hours, minutes, sweep seconds; altimeter
(barometric); date
Case: carbon fiber, ø 47 mm; sapphire crystal; water-
resistant to 10 atm
Band: textile, folding clasp
Price: $6,600

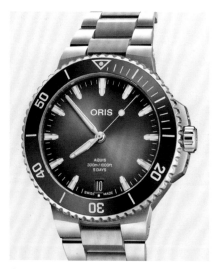

Aquis Date Calibre 400

Reference number: 01 400 7790 4135-07 8 23 02PEB
Movement: automatic, Oris caliber 400; ø 30 mm,
height 4.75 mm; 21 jewels; 28,800 vph; 120-hour power
reserve
Functions: hours, minutes, sweep seconds; date
Case: stainless steel, ø 43.5 mm, height 13.1 mm;
unidirectional bezel with ceramic insert, with 0-60 scale;
sapphire crystal; screw-down crown; water-resistant
to 30 atm
Band: stainless steel, folding clasp, with safety lock,
with extension link
Price: $4,100

Aquis Date Caliber 400

Reference number: 01 400 7790 4157-07 4 23 47EB
Movement: automatic, Oris caliber 400; ø 30 mm,
height 4.75 mm; 21 jewels; 28,800 vph; 120-hour power
reserve
Functions: hours, minutes, sweep seconds; date
Case: stainless steel, ø 43.5 mm, height 13.1 mm;
unidirectional bezel with ceramic insert with 0-60 scale;
sapphire crystal; screw-down crown; water-resistant
to 30 atm
Band: rubber, folding clasp
Price: $3,900

Aquis Date

Reference number: 01 733 7787 4135-07 4 22 35FC
Movement: automatic, Oris caliber 733 (Sellita
SW200-1 base); ø 25.6 mm, height 4.6 mm; 26 jewels;
28,800 vph; 41-hour power reserve
Functions: hours, minutes, sweep seconds; date
Case: stainless steel, ø 41.5 mm, height 12.9 mm;
unidirectional bezel with ceramic insert, with 0-60 scale;
sapphire crystal; transparent case back; screw-down
crown; water-resistant to 30 atm
Band: rubber, pin buckle, with extension link
Price: $2,500

Aquis Date Upcycle

Reference number: 01 733 7787 4150-07 8 22 04PEB
Movement: automatic, Oris caliber 733 (Sellita SW200-1 base); ø 25.6 mm, height 4.6 mm; 26 jewels; 28,800 vph; 41-hour power reserve
Functions: hours, minutes, sweep seconds; date
Case: stainless steel, ø 41.5 mm, height 12.9 mm; unidirectional bezel with ceramic insert, with 0-60 scale; sapphire crystal; transparent case back; screw-down crown; water-resistant to 30 atm
Band: stainless steel, folding clasp, with extension link
Remarks: dial made of recycled PET
Price: $2,800

Aquis Chronograph

Reference number: 01 771 7793 4155-07 8 23 01PEB
Movement: automatic, Oris caliber 771 (Sellita SW500-1 base); ø 30 mm, height 7.9 mm; 27 jewels; 28,800 vph; 62-hour power reserve
Functions: hours, minutes, sweep seconds; chronograph; date
Case: stainless steel, ø 43.5 mm, height 16.2 mm; unidirectional bezel, with 0-60 scale; sapphire crystal; transparent case back; screw-down crown; water-resistant to 30 atm
Band: stainless steel, folding clasp, with extension link
Price: $4,900

AquisPro 4000m

Reference number: 01 400 7777 7155-Set
Movement: automatic, Oris caliber 400; ø 30 mm, height 4.75 mm; 21 jewels; 28,800 vph; 120-hour power reserve
Functions: hours, minutes, sweep seconds; date
Case: stainless steel, ø 49.5 mm, height 23.4 mm; unidirectional bezel with ceramic insert with 0-60 scale; sapphire crystal; screw-down crown; water-resistant to 400 atm
Band: rubber, folding clasp, with safety lock, with extension link
Price: $6,600

Divers Sixty-Five Chronograph

Reference number: 01 771 7791 4054-07 8 20 18
Movement: automatic, Oris caliber 771 (Sellita SW500-1 base); ø 30 mm, height 7.9 mm; 27 jewels; 28,800 vph; 62-hour power reserve
Functions: hours, minutes, sweep seconds; chronograph
Case: stainless steel, ø 40 mm, height 15.4 mm; unidirectional bezel, with 0-60 scale; sapphire crystal; transparent case back; screw-down crown; water-resistant to 10 atm
Band: stainless steel, folding clasp, with extension link
Price: $4,600

Divers Sixty-Five Calibre 400

Reference number: 01 400 7774 4057-07 8 19 18
Movement: automatic, Oris caliber 400; ø 30 mm, height 4.75 mm; 21 jewels; 28,800 vph; 120-hour power reserve
Functions: hours, minutes, sweep seconds
Case: stainless steel, ø 38 mm, height 12.6 mm; unidirectional bezel, with 0-60 scale; sapphire crystal; transparent case back; screw-down crown; water-resistant to 10 atm
Band: stainless steel, folding clasp
Price: $3,900

Divers Sixty-Five Date

Reference number: 01 733 7707 4057-07 8 20 18
Movement: automatic, Oris caliber 733 (Sellita SW200-1 base); ø 25.6 mm, height 4.6 mm; 26 jewels; 28,800 vph; 41-hour power reserve
Functions: hours, minutes, sweep seconds; date
Case: stainless steel, ø 40 mm, height 12.8 mm; unidirectional bezel, with 0-60 scale; sapphire crystal; screw-down crown; water-resistant to 10 atm
Band: stainless steel, folding clasp, with extension link
Price: $2,700

PANERAI

Officine Panerai (in English: Panerai Workshops) joined the Richemont Group in 1997. Since then, it has made an unprecedented rise from an insider niche brand to a lifestyle phenomenon. The company, founded in 1860 by Giovanni Panerai, supplied the Italian navy with precision instruments. In the 1930s, the Florentine engineers developed a series of waterproof wristwatches that could be used by commandos under especially extreme and risky conditions. After 1997, under the leadership of Angelo Bonati, the company came out with a collection of oversize wristwatches, both stylistically and technically based on these historical models.

In 2002, Panerai opened a *manufacture* in Neuchâtel, and by 2005 it was already producing its own movements, the caliber family P.2000 and later the P.9000 family. The success of the verticalization of the brand led to the opening of a new *manufacture* in 2014, also in Neuchâtel, to bring development, manufacturing, assembly, and quality control under one roof. Around 250 people work in their respective areas of expertise in this light-filled building. The new environment brings together under one roof all the main processes and technical skills required to produce a watch of the highest quality. By opening the manufacturing process to the public, Panerai offers the opportunity to immerse oneself in a world of innovation and cutting-edge technology.

Parallel to consolidating, the brand has been steadily expanding its portfolio of new calibers.

Besides expanding the Panerai stable of calibers, the company has focused on the new sustainability trend among watch brands. The recent eLAB-ID concept watch bears the tagline "Do you want to be part of the solution?" It is made of over ninety-eight percent recycled materials: titanium for the case, sapphire for the glass, silicon for the escapement, PET bottles for the strap, Super-LumiNova for the dial. Only 30 pieces were produced, but Panerai has another solution, too: it uses recycled steel scrap for the case of the new Luminor Marina eSteel.

OFFICINE PANERAI
Viale Monza, 259
I-20126 Milan
Italy

TEL.:
+39-02-363-138

WEBSITE:
www.panerai.com

FOUNDED:
1860 in Florence, Italy

NUMBER OF EMPLOYEES:
Around 1,000 employees

U.S. DISTRIBUTOR:
Panerai
645 Fifth Avenue
New York, NY 10022
877-PANERAI
concierge.usa@panerai.com;
www.panerai.com

MOST IMPORTANT COLLECTIONS/PRICE RANGE:
Luminor / $5,000 to $25,000; Luminor / $8,000 to $30,000; Radiomir / $8,000 to $133,000; special editions / $10,000 to $125,000; clocks and instruments / $20,000 to $250,000

Submersible QuarantaQuattro Goldtech OroCarbo

Reference number: PAM02070
Movement: automatic, Panerai caliber P.900; ø 28.19 mm, height 4.2 mm; 23 jewels; 28,800 vph; 72-hour power reserve
Functions: hours, minutes, subsidiary seconds; date
Case: rose gold, ø 44 mm, height 13.35 mm; unidirectional composite material ("Carbotech") bezel, with 0-60 scale; sapphire crystal; crown with guard and hinged lever; water-resistant to 30 atm
Band: rubber, pin buckle
Price: $33,300

Luminor Submersible Marina Militare Carbotech

Reference number: PAM02979
Movement: automatic, Panerai caliber P.9010; ø 31 mm, height 6 mm; 31 jewels; 28,800 vph; 2 mainsprings, 72-hour power reserve
Functions: hours, minutes, subsidiary seconds; date
Case: composite material ("Carbotech"), ø 47 mm, height 15.45 mm; unidirectional bezel, with 0-60 scale; sapphire crystal; crown with guard and hinged lever; water-resistant to 30 atm
Band: rubber, folding clasp
Price: $20,200

Radiomir Tre Giorni

Reference number: PAM01334
Movement: hand-wound, Panerai caliber P.6000; ø 34.96 mm, height 4.5 mm; 19 jewels; 21,600 vph; 72-hour power reserve
Functions: hours, minutes
Case: stainless steel, ø 45 mm, height 10.5 mm; sapphire crystal; water-resistant to 10 atm
Band: calfskin, pin buckle
Price: $7,100

Radiomir Tre Giorni

Reference number: PAM01350
Movement: hand-wound, Panerai caliber P.6000;
ø 34.96 mm, height 4.5 mm; 19 jewels; 21,600 vph;
72-hour power reserve
Functions: hours, minutes
Case: stainless steel, ø 45 mm, height 10.5 mm;
sapphire crystal; water-resistant to 10 atm
Band: calfskin, pin buckle
Price: $7,100

Luminor Due

Reference number: PAM01248
Movement: automatic, Panerai caliber P.900;
ø 28.19 mm, height 4.2 mm; 23 jewels; 28,800 vph;
72-hour power reserve
Functions: hours, minutes, subsidiary seconds; date
Case: stainless steel, ø 38 mm, height 11.3 mm;
sapphire crystal; crown with guard and hinged lever;
water-resistant to 3 atm
Band: reptile skin, pin buckle
Price: $6,900

Luminor Due Luna Rossa

Reference number: PAM01381
Movement: automatic, Panerai caliber P.900;
ø 28.19 mm, height 4.2 mm; 23 jewels; 28,800 vph;
72-hour power reserve
Functions: hours, minutes, subsidiary seconds; date
Case: stainless steel, ø 42 mm, height 11.3 mm;
sapphire crystal; crown with guard and hinged lever;
water-resistant to 3 atm
Band: rubber with textile overlay, pin buckle
Price: $7,800

Luminor Due

Reference number: PAM01123
Movement: automatic, Panerai caliber P.900;
ø 28.19 mm, height 4.2 mm; 23 jewels; 28,800 vph;
72-hour power reserve
Functions: hours, minutes, subsidiary seconds; date
Case: stainless steel, ø 38 mm, height 11.3 mm;
sapphire crystal; crown with guard and hinged lever;
water-resistant to 3 atm
Band: stainless steel, folding clasp
Price: $7,700

Luminor Base Logo

Reference number: PAM01087
Movement: hand-wound, Panerai caliber P.6000;
ø 34.96 mm, height 4.5 mm; 19 jewels; 21,600 vph;
72-hour power reserve
Functions: hours, minutes
Case: stainless steel, ø 44 mm, height 13 mm; sapphire
crystal; crown with guard and hinged lever; water-
resistant to 10 atm
Band: rubber, pin buckle
Price: $5,600

Luminor Logo

Reference number: PAM01084
Movement: hand-wound, Panerai caliber P.6000;
ø 34.96 mm, height 4.5 mm; 19 jewels; 21,600 vph;
72-hour power reserve
Functions: hours, minutes, subsidiary seconds
Case: stainless steel, ø 44 mm, height 13 mm; sapphire
crystal; crown with guard and hinged lever; water-
resistant to 10 atm
Band: calfskin, pin buckle
Price: $6,100

Luminor Marina

Reference number: PAM01312
Movement: automatic, Panerai caliber P.9010; ø 31 mm, height 6 mm; 31 jewels; 28,800 vph; 2 mainsprings, 72-hour power reserve
Functions: hours, minutes, subsidiary seconds; date
Case: stainless steel, ø 44 mm, height 15.45 mm; sapphire crystal; crown with guard and hinged lever; water-resistant to 30 atm
Band: reptile skin, pin buckle
Price: $8,800

Submersible QuarantaQuattro

Reference number: PAM01229
Movement: automatic, Panerai caliber P.900; ø 28.19 mm, height 4.2 mm; 23 jewels; 28,800 vph; 72-hour power reserve
Functions: hours, minutes, subsidiary seconds; date
Case: stainless steel, ø 44 mm, height 13.35 mm; unidirectional bezel, with 0-60 scale; sapphire crystal; crown with guard and hinged lever; water-resistant to 30 atm
Band: rubber, pin buckle
Price: $9,900

Submersible QuarantaQuattro

Reference number: PAM01226
Movement: automatic, Panerai caliber P.900; ø 28.19 mm, height 4.2 mm; 23 jewels; 28,800 vph; 72-hour power reserve
Functions: hours, minutes, subsidiary seconds; date
Case: stainless steel, ø 44 mm, height 13.35 mm; unidirectional bezel, with 0-60 scale; sapphire crystal; crown with guard and hinged lever; water-resistant to 30 atm
Band: rubber, pin buckle
Price: $9,900

Radiomir Quaranta Goldtech

Reference number: PAM01026
Movement: automatic, Panerai caliber P.900; ø 28.19 mm, height 4.2 mm; 23 jewels; 28,800 vph; 72-hour power reserve
Functions: hours, minutes, subsidiary seconds; date
Case: rose gold, ø 40 mm, height 10.5 mm; sapphire crystal; transparent case back; water-resistant to 5 atm
Band: reptile skin, pin buckle
Price: $18,200

Luminor Chrono

Reference number: PAM01109
Movement: automatic, Panerai caliber P.9200; ø 31 mm, height 6.9 mm; 41 jewels; 28,800 vph; 42-hour power reserve
Functions: hours, minutes, subsidiary seconds; chronograph
Case: stainless steel, ø 44 mm, height 15.65 mm; sapphire crystal; crown with guard and hinged lever; water-resistant to 10 atm
Band: reptile skin, pin buckle
Remarks: comes with extra rubber strap
Price: $10,000

Luminor Due Luna Goldtech

Reference number: PAM01181
Movement: automatic, Panerai caliber P.900/MP; ø 28.19 mm, height 5.9 mm; 23 jewels; 28,800 vph; 72-hour power reserve
Functions: hours, minutes, subsidiary seconds; moon phase
Case: rose gold ("Goldtech"), ø 38 mm; sapphire crystal; transparent case back; crown with guard and hinged lever; water-resistant to 5 atm
Band: reptile skin, pin buckle
Remarks: mother-of-pearl dial
Price: $21,500

Caliber P.900

Automatic; single mainspring barrel, 72-hour power reserve
Functions: hours, minutes, subsidiary seconds; date
Diameter: 28.19 mm
Height: 4.2 mm
Jewels: 23
Balance: glucydur
Frequency: 28,800 vph
Shock protection: Incabloc
Remarks: 171 parts

Caliber P.9010

Automatic; two spring barrels arranged serially, 72-hour power reserve
Functions: hours, minutes, subsidiary seconds; date
Diameter: 31 mm
Height: 6 mm
Jewels: 31
Balance: glucydur
Frequency: 28,800 vph
Remarks: 200 parts

Caliber P.9012

Automatic; two spring barrels arranged serially, 72-hour power reserve
Functions: hours, minutes, subsidiary seconds; additional 12-hour display (second time zone), power reserve indicator; date
Diameter: 31 mm
Height: 6 mm
Jewels: 31
Balance: glucydur
Frequency: 28,800 vph
Shock protection: Incabloc
Remarks: 231 parts

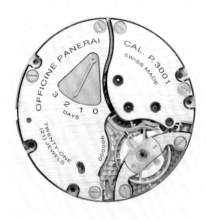

Caliber P.3001

Hand-wound; two spring barrels arranged serially, 72-hour power reserve
Functions: hours, minutes, subsidiary seconds; power reserve indicator (on the movement side)
Diameter: 37.2 mm
Height: 6.3 mm
Jewels: 21
Balance: glucydur
Frequency: 21,600 vph
Remarks: 213 parts

Caliber P.6000

Hand-wound; single mainspring barrel, 72-hour power reserve
Functions: hours, minutes, subsidiary seconds
Diameter: 34.9 mm
Height: 4.5 mm
Jewels: 19
Balance: glucydur
Frequency: 21,600 vph
Shock protection: Incabloc
Remarks: 110 parts

Caliber P.2005/T

Hand-wound; skeletonized movement; 1-minute tourbillon with rotating axis perpendicular to the balance pivot; triple spring barrel arranged serially, 144-hour power reserve
Functions: hours, minutes, subsidiary seconds; additional 24-hour display (second time zone), day/night indication, power reserve indicator (on movement side)
Diameter: 36.6 mm
Height: 10.05 mm
Jewels: 31
Balance: glucydur
Frequency: 28,800 vph
Remarks: 277 parts

PARMIGIANI

What began as the undertaking of a single man—a gifted watchmaker and reputable restorer of complicated vintage timepieces—in the small town of Fleurier in Switzerland's Val de Travers has now grown into an empire of sorts comprising several factories and more than 400 employees.

Michel Parmigiani is in fact just doing what he has done since 1976, when he began restoring vintage works. His output soon attracted the attention of the Sandoz Family Foundation, an organization established by a member of one of Switzerland's most famous families in 1964. The foundation bought 51 percent of Parmigiani Mesure et Art du Temps SA in 1996, turning what was practically a one-man show into a full-fledged and fully financed watch *manufacture.*

After the merger, Swiss suppliers were acquired by the partners, furthering the quest for horological autonomy. Atokalpa SA in Alle (Canton of Jura) manufactures parts such as pinions, wheels, and micro components. Bruno Affolter SA in La Chaux-de-Fonds produces precious metal cases, dials, and other specialty parts. Les Artisans Boitiers (LAB) and Quadrance et Habillage (Q&H) in La Chaux-de-Fonds manufacture cases out of precious metals and dials as well. Elwin SA in Moutier specializes in turned parts. In 2003, the movement development and production department officially separated from the rest as Vaucher Manufacture, now an autonomous entity with a sterling reputation.

Montre Hermès has also held a stake in Vaucher Manufacture, securing the supply of custom watchmaking technology and leather straps for its ambitious model policy.

Around the time of the firm's 25th anniversary, in 2021, Michel Parmigiani gradually withdrew from day-to-day operations, leaving the executive spot to CEO Guido Terreni. The collections were streamlined; outliers, like the Bugatti, were terminated, and importantly, the Tonda PF collection was redesigned and given new complications, including a time zone watch with a split-seconds (rattrapante) mechanism for rapidly resetting the second local time.

PARMIGIANI FLEURIER SA
Rue du Temple 11
CH-2114 Fleurier
Switzerland

TEL.:
+41-32-862-6630

E-MAIL:
info@parmigiani.ch

WEBSITE:
www.parmigiani.ch

FOUNDED:
1996

NUMBER OF EMPLOYEES:
425

ANNUAL PRODUCTION:
approx. 6,000 watches

U.S. DISTRIBUTOR:
Parmigiani Fleurier Distribution Americas LLC
2655 S. Le Jeune Road
Penthouse 1G
Coral Gables, FL 33134
305-260-7770; 305-269-7770

MOST IMPORTANT COLLECTIONS/PRICE RANGE:
Chronor, Kalpa, Tonda, Toric / approx. $15,000 to $80,000 for core collections, $300,000+ for haute horlogerie watches; no limit for unique models

Toric Petite Seconde
Reference number: PFC940-2010004-300181
Movement: hand-wound, Parmigiani caliber PF780; ø 28.4 mm, height 3.15 mm; 27 jewels; 28,800 vph; finely finished movement; 60-hour power reserve
Functions: hours, minutes, subsidiary seconds
Case: white gold, ø 40.6 mm, height 8.8 mm; sapphire crystal; transparent case back; water-resistant to 3 atm
Band: reptile skin, pin buckle
Remarks: white gold-dial
Price: $55,900
Variations: in rose gold ($48,400)

Toric Chronograph Rattrapante
Reference number: PFH951-2010001-300181
Movement: hand-wound, Parmigiani caliber PF361; ø 30.6 mm, height 8.45 mm; 35 jewels; 36,000 vph; skeletonized bridges; 65-hour power reserve; COSC-certified chronometer
Functions: hours, minutes, subsidiary seconds; stop-seconds chronograph
Case: rose gold, ø 42.5 mm, height 14.4 mm; sapphire crystal; transparent case back; water-resistant to 3 atm
Band: reptile skin, pin buckle
Price: $145,200; limited to 30 pieces

Toric Petite Seconde
Reference number: PFC940-2010001-300181
Movement: hand-wound, Parmigiani caliber PF780; ø 28.4 mm, height 3.15 mm; 27 jewels; 28,800 vph; finely finished movement; 60-hour power reserve
Functions: hours, minutes, subsidiary seconds
Case: rose gold, ø 40.6 mm, height 8.8 mm; sapphire crystal; transparent case back; water-resistant to 3 atm
Band: reptile skin, pin buckle
Remarks: rose gold-dial
Price: $48,400
Variations: in white gold ($55,900)

Tonda PF Sport Chronograph

Reference number: PFC931-1020003-400182
Movement: automatic, Parmigiani caliber PF070/6710;
ø 30.6 mm, height 6.95 mm; 42 jewels; 36,000 vph;
skeletonized rotor with rose gold-oscillating mass; finely
finished movement; 65-hour power reserve
Functions: hours, minutes, subsidiary seconds;
chronograph; date
Case: stainless steel, ø 42 mm, height 12.9 mm;
sapphire crystal; transparent case back; water-resistant
to 10 atm
Band: rubber, folding clasp
Price: $30,000

Tonda PF Minute Rattrapante

Reference number: PFC904-1020001-100182
Movement: automatic, Parmigiani caliber PF052;
ø 32 mm, height 4.9 mm; 32 jewels; 21,600 vph; micro-
rotor in rose gold, finely finished movement; 48-hour
power reserve
Functions: hours, minutes; additional adjustable minute
hand with push-button reset (rattrapante function)
Case: stainless steel, ø 40 mm, height 10.7 mm;
sapphire crystal; transparent case back; rose-gold
pusher; water-resistant to 6 atm
Band: stainless steel, folding clasp
Price: $31,800

Tonda PF GMT Rattrapante

Reference number: PFC905-1020001-100182
Movement: automatic, Parmigiani caliber PF051;
ø 30 mm, height 4.9 mm; 31 jewels; 21,600 vph; micro-
rotor in rose gold, finely finished movement; 48-hour
power reserve
Functions: hours, minutes; additional 12-hour display
(second time zone) with push-button reset (rattrapante
function)
Case: rose gold, ø 40 mm, height 10.7 mm; sapphire
crystal; transparent case back; rose-gold pusher; water-
resistant to 6 atm
Band: rose gold, folding clasp
Price: $65,600

Tonda PF Skeleton Platinum

Reference number: PFC912-2020003-200182
Movement: automatic, Parmigiani caliber PF777;
ø 30 mm, height 3.9 mm; 29 jewels; 28,800 vph; fully
skeletonized and blackened movement, rose-gold
skeletonized rotor; 60-hour power reserve
Functions: hours, minutes
Case: platinum, ø 40 mm, height 8.4 mm; sapphire
crystal; transparent case back; water-resistant to
10 atm
Band: platinum, folding clasp
Price: $125,800

Tonda PF Hijri Perpetual Calendar

Reference number: PFK999-2020001-200182
Movement: automatic, Parmigiani caliber PF009;
ø 33.8 mm, height 5.7 mm; 32 jewels; 28,800 vph;
platinum oscillating mass, finely finished movement;
48-hour power reserve
Functions: hours, minutes, sweep seconds; perpetual
calendar with date, weekday, month, moon phase
(according to the Islamic calendar)
Case: stainless steel, ø 42 mm, height 11.2 mm;
sapphire crystal; transparent case back; water-resistant
to 10 atm
Band: stainless steel, folding clasp
Price: $67,200

Tonda PF Gregorian Calendar

Reference number: PFC907-1020001-100182
Movement: automatic, Parmigiani caliber PF339;
ø 27.1 mm, height 5.5 mm; 32 jewels; 28,800 vph;
skeletonized rotor in rose gold; 50-hour power reserve
Functions: hours, minutes, sweep seconds; annual
calendar with date, weekday, month, moon phase
Case: stainless steel, ø 42 mm, height 11.1 mm; platinum
bezel; sapphire crystal; transparent case back; water-
resistant to 10 atm
Band: stainless steel, folding clasp
Price: $40,400

Tonda PF Micro Rotor Platinum

Reference number: PFC914-2020002-200182
Movement: automatic, Parmigiani caliber PF703; ø 30 mm, height 3 mm; 29 jewels; 21,600 vph; micro-rotor in platinum; 48-hour power reserve
Functions: hours, minutes; date
Case: platinum, ø 40 mm, height 7.8 mm; sapphire crystal; transparent case back; water-resistant to 10 atm
Band: platinum, folding clasp
Price: $92,800

Tonda PF Rose Gold Deep Ruby 36mm

Reference number: PFC804-2020001-200182
Movement: automatic, Parmigiani caliber PF777; ø 30 mm, height 3.9 mm; 29 jewels; 28,800 vph; skeletonized rotor in rose gold; 60-hour power reserve
Functions: hours, minutes
Case: rose gold, ø 36 mm, height 8.6 mm; sapphire crystal; transparent case back; water-resistant to 10 atm
Band: rose gold, double folding clasp
Remarks: dial with baguette-cut diamond indexes
Price: $58,000

Tonda PF Flying Tourbillon

Reference number: PFH921-2020002-200182
Movement: automatic, Parmigiani caliber PF517; ø 32 mm, height 3.4 mm; 29 jewels; 21,600 vph; flying 1-minute tourbillon; micro-rotor in platinum, finely finished movement; 48-hour power reserve
Functions: hours, minutes, subsidiary seconds (on the tourbillon cage)
Case: platinum, ø 42 mm, height 8.6 mm; sapphire crystal; transparent case back; water-resistant to 10 atm
Band: platinum, folding clasp in white gold
Price: $161,300; limited to 25 pieces

Tonda PF Sport Automatic

Reference number: PFC930-1020001-400182
Movement: automatic, Parmigiani caliber PF770/4100; ø 25.6 mm, height 3.9 mm; 29 jewels; 28,800 vph; skeletonized rotor with rose gold-oscillating mass, finely finished movement; 60-hour power reserve
Functions: hours, minutes, sweep seconds; date
Case: stainless steel, ø 41 mm, height 9.8 mm; sapphire crystal; transparent case back; water-resistant to 10 atm
Band: rubber, folding clasp
Price: $21,400

Tonda PF Micro Rotor Steel

Reference number: PFC914-1020001-100182
Movement: automatic, Parmigiani caliber PF703; ø 30 mm, height 3 mm; 29 jewels; 21,600 vph; micro-rotor in platinum; 48-hour power reserve
Functions: hours, minutes; date
Case: stainless steel, ø 40 mm, height 7.8 mm; sapphire crystal; transparent case back; water-resistant to 10 atm
Band: stainless steel, folding clasp
Price: $25,300

Tonda PF Micro Rotor No Date

Reference number: PFC914-1020021-100182
Movement: automatic, Parmigiani caliber PF703; ø 30 mm, height 3 mm; 29 jewels; 21,600 vph; micro-rotor in platinum; 48-hour power reserve
Functions: hours, minutes
Case: stainless steel, ø 40 mm, height 7.8 mm; sapphire crystal; transparent case back; water-resistant to 10 atm
Band: stainless steel, folding clasp
Price: $25,300

Caliber PF780

Hand-wound; single mainspring barrel, 60-hour power reserve
Functions: hours, minutes, subsidiary seconds
Diameter: 28.4 mm
Height: 3.15 mm
Jewels: 27
Frequency: 28,800 vph
Remarks: finely finished movement; 157 parts

Caliber PF361

Hand-wound; two column wheels; skeletonized movement architecture; rose-gold mainplate and bridges; single mainspring barrel, 65-hour power reserve
Functions: hours, minutes, subsidiary seconds; stop-seconds chronograph
Diameter: 30.6 mm
Height: 8.45 mm
Jewels: 35
Frequency: 36,000 vph
Remarks: 317 parts

Caliber PF070

Automatic; skeletonized bridges, skeletonized rotor in rose gold; single mainspring barrel, 65-hour power reserve; COSC-certified chronometer
Functions: hours, minutes, subsidiary seconds; chronograph; date
Diameter: 30.6 mm
Height: 6.95 mm
Jewels: 42
Frequency: 36,000 vph

Caliber PF703

Automatic; micro-rotor in platinum; single mainspring barrel, 48-hour power reserve
Functions: hours, minutes; date
Diameter: 30 mm
Height: 3 mm
Jewels: 29
Frequency: 21,600 vph
Remarks: 176 parts

Caliber PF051

Automatic; micro-rotor in rose gold; single mainspring barrel, 48-hour power reserve
Functions: hours, minutes; additional 12-hour display (second time zone) with pusher reset (rattrapante function)
Diameter: 30 mm
Height: 4.9 mm
Jewels: 31
Frequency: 21,600 vph
Remarks: 207 parts

Caliber PF517

Automatic; flying 1-minute tourbillon, micro-rotor in platinum; single mainspring barrel, 48-hour power reserve
Functions: hours, minutes, subsidiary seconds (on the tourbillon cage)
Diameter: 32 mm
Height: 3.4 mm
Jewels: 29
Frequency: 21,600 vph
Remarks: 205 parts

PATEK PHILIPPE

In the Swiss watchmaking landscape, Patek Philippe has a special status as the last independent family-owned business. The company originated in 1839 with two Polish émigrés to Switzerland, Count Norbert Antoine de Patek and Franciszek Czapek. In 1845, following the natural end of their contract, Patek sought another partner in the master watchmaker Jean Adrien Philippe, who had developed a keyless winding and time-setting mechanism. Ever since, Patek Philippe has been known for creating high-quality mechanical watches, some with extremely sophisticated complications. Even among its competition, the *manufacture* enjoys the greatest respect.

In 1932, Charles-Henri Stern took over the *manufacture*. His son Henri and grandson Philippe continued the tradition of solid leadership, steering the company through the notorious quartz crisis without ever compromising quality. The next in line, also Henri, heads the enterprise these days.

Producing an impressive 70,000-plus watches yearly demands ultramodern facilities. These were completed in 2019 in Plan-les-Ouates in Geneva, where various manufacturing activities can be performed under a single roof with an optimized workflow. The site is a complement to another industrial hub between La Chaux-de-Fonds and Le Locle, where case components are manufactured, cases are polished, and gem setting is done.

While Patek Philippe's main headquarters remains in Geneva, the *manufacture* no longer really has a need for that city's famed quality seal: all of its mechanical watches now feature the "Patek Philippe Seal," the criteria for which far exceed the requirements of the Poinçon de Genève and include specifications for the entire watch, not just the movement.

For those somewhat disappointed at the discontinuation of the famed Nautilus, the year 2024 brought a surprise—or shock, depending on your expectations. Patek announced a new watch, a square model, fairly thin, with rounded corners and a vague resemblance to the old Nautilus: the Cubitus. The effect was a lot of buzz, with some saying it was not what they would want from the venerable Genevans. This move into the casual-chic world is still being hotly discussed online, which may have been the aim.

PATEK PHILIPPE SA
Chemin du pont-du-centenaire 141
CH-1228 Plan-les-Ouates
Switzerland

TEL.:
+41-22-884-20-20

WEBSITE:
www.patek.com

FOUNDED:
1839

NUMBER OF EMPLOYEES:
approx. 2,000 (estimated)

ANNUAL PRODUCTION:
approx. 72,000 watches worldwide

U.S. DISTRIBUTOR:
Patek Philippe USA
45 Rockefeller Center, Suite 401
New York, NY 10111
212-218-1240

MOST IMPORTANT COLLECTIONS:
Aquanaut, Calatrava, Nautilus, Cubitus, complicated watches

Chronograph Perpetual Calendar

Reference number: 5270P-014
Movement: hand-wound, Patek Philippe caliber CH 29-535 PS Q; ø 32 mm, height 7 mm; 33 jewels; 28,800 vph; 55-hour power reserve
Functions: hours, minutes, subsidiary seconds; day/night indication; chronograph; perpetual calendar with date, weekday, month, moon phase, leap year
Case: platinum, ø 41 mm, height 12.4 mm; sapphire crystal; transparent case back; water-resistant to 3 atm
Band: reptile skin, folding clasp
Price: $218,820

Perpetual Calendar

Reference number: 5320G-011
Movement: automatic, Patek Philippe caliber 324 S Q; ø 32 mm, height 4.97 mm; 29 jewels; 28,800 vph; silicon Spiromax hairspring; gold rotor; 35-hour power reserve
Functions: hours, minutes, sweep seconds; day/night indicator; perpetual calendar with date, weekday, month, moon phase, leap year
Case: white gold, ø 40 mm, height 11.13 mm; sapphire crystal; transparent case back; water-resistant to 3 atm
Band: reptile skin, folding clasp
Remarks: comes with extra white-gold case back
Price: $97,580

Perpetual Calendar with Stop-Seconds Chronograph

Reference number: 5204G-001
Movement: hand-wound, Patek Philippe caliber CHR 29-535 PS Q; ø 32 mm, height 8.7 mm; 34 jewels; 28,800 vph; Breguet hairspring; 55-hour power reserve
Functions: hours, minutes, subsidiary seconds; stop-seconds chronograph; perpetual calendar with date, weekday, month, moon phase, leap year, day/night indication
Case: white gold, ø 40 mm, height 14.3 mm; sapphire crystal; transparent case back; water-resistant to 3 atm
Band: calfskin, folding clasp
Remarks: comes with extra white-gold case back
Price: $295,270

Nautilus Flyback Chronograph

Reference number: 5980/60G-001
Movement: automatic, Patek Philippe caliber CH 28-520 C/522; ø 30 mm, height 6.63 mm; 35 jewels; 28,800 vph; silicon Spiromax hairspring, gold rotor; 45-hour power reserve
Functions: hours, minutes, subsidiary seconds; flyback chronograph; date
Case: white gold, ø 40.5 mm, height 12.2 mm; sapphire crystal; transparent case back; screw-down crown; water-resistant to 3 atm
Band: calfskin, folding clasp
Price: $78,950

Cubitus

Reference number: 5821/1AR
Movement: automatic, Patek Philippe caliber 26 330 S C; ø 27 mm, height 3.3 mm; 30 jewels; 28,800 vph; Gyromax balance; silicon Spiromax hairspring, gold rotor; Patek Phillippe seal; 45-hour power reserve
Functions: hours, minutes, sweep seconds; date
Case: stainless steel and rose gold, ø 45 mm x 45 mm, height 8.3 mm; sapphire crystal; transparent case back; water-resistant to 3 atm
Band: composite fabric, folding clasp
Remarks: sunburst blue dial, horizontal embossment
Price: $61,280
Variations: in stainless steel ($41,240)

Cubitus

Reference number: 5822P
Movement: automatic, Patek Philippe caliber 240 PS CI J LU; ø 27 mm, height 3.3 mm; 30 jewels; 28,800 vph; Gyromax balance; silicon Spiromax hairspring, gold rotor; Patek Phillippe seal; 45-hour power reserve
Functions: hours, minutes, subsidiary seconds; large date, day; moon phase
Case: platinum, ø 45 mm x 45 mm, height 9.6 mm; pusher-activated ring with reference cities; sapphire crystal; transparent case back; water-resistant to 3 atm
Band: composite strap with fabric pattern, folding clasp
Remarks: sunburst blue dial, horizontal embossment; baguette-cut diamond on the bezel
Price: $88,380

Calatrava Pilot Travel Time Chronograph

Reference number: 5924G-010
Movement: automatic, Patek Philippe caliber 28-520 C FUS; ø 31 mm, height 6.95 mm; 34 jewels; 28,800 vph; Spiromax silicon hairspring, gold rotor; 45-hour power reserve
Functions: hours, minutes; additional 12-hour display (second time zone, crown-operated correction); flyback chronograph; date
Case: white gold, ø 42 mm, height 13.05 mm; sapphire crystal; transparent case back; water-resistant to 3 atm
Band: calfskin, pin buckle
Price: $78,360

Flyback Chronograph Annual Calendar

Reference number: 5905R-010
Movement: automatic, Patek Philippe caliber CH 28-520 QA 24H; ø 33 mm, height 7.68 mm; 37 jewels; 28,800 vph; silicon Spiromax hairspring, gold rotor; 45-hour power reserve
Functions: hours, minutes; flyback chronograph; annual calendar with date, weekday, month
Case: rose gold, ø 42 mm, height 14.03 mm; sapphire crystal; transparent case back; water-resistant to 3 atm
Band: reptile skin, pin buckle
Price: $77,770

Calatrava

Reference number: 6007G-001
Movement: automatic, Patek Philippe caliber 26-330 S C; ø 27 mm, height 3.3 mm; 30 jewels; 28,800 vph; silicon Spiromax hairspring, gold rotor; 35-hour power reserve
Functions: hours, minutes, sweep seconds; date
Case: white gold, ø 40 mm, height 9.17 mm; sapphire crystal; transparent case back; water-resistant to 3 atm
Band: calfskin with stamped carbon pattern, pin buckle
Price: $39,240

Calatrava

Reference number: 5226G-001
Movement: automatic, Patek Philippe caliber 26-330 S C; ø 27 mm, height 3.3 mm; 30 jewels; 28,800 vph; silicon Spiromax hairspring, gold rotor; 35-hour power reserve
Functions: hours, minutes, sweep seconds; date
Case: white gold, ø 40 mm, height 8.53 mm; sapphire crystal; transparent case back; water-resistant to 3 atm
Band: calfskin, pin buckle
Price: $41,710

Aquanaut Luce

Reference number: 5268/200R-010
Movement: automatic, Patek Philippe caliber 26-330 S C; ø 27 mm, height 3.3 mm; 30 jewels; 28,800 vph; Spiromax silicon hairspring, gold rotor; 35-hour power reserve
Functions: hours, minutes, sweep seconds; date
Case: rose gold, ø 38.8 mm, height 8.5 mm; bezel set with 48 diamonds; sapphire crystal; transparent case back; screw-down crown; water-resistant to 3 atm
Band: rubber, folding clasp
Price: $53,820

Calatrava Travel Time

Reference number: 5224R-001
Movement: automatic, Patek Philippe caliber 31-260 PS FUS 24H; ø 31.74 mm, height 3.7 mm; 44 jewels; 28,800 vph; silicon Spiromax hairspring, off-center platinum rotor; 48-hour power reserve
Functions: 24 hours, minutes, subsidiary seconds; second 24-hour display (second time zone, crown-operated correction)
Case: rose gold, ø 42 mm, height 9.85 mm; sapphire crystal; transparent case back; water-resistant to 3 atm
Band: calfskin, pin buckle
Price: $59,300

Alarm Travel Time

Reference number: 5520RG-001
Movement: automatic, Patek Philippe caliber AL 30-660 S C FUS; ø 31 mm, height 6.6 mm; 52 jewels; 28,800 vph; silicon Spiromax hairspring, gold rotor; 42-hour power reserve
Functions: hours, minutes, sweep seconds; additional 12-hour display (second time zone), day/night indicator (for home and local time); alarm; date
Case: rose gold, ø 42.2 mm, height 11.6 mm; sapphire crystal; transparent case back; water-resistant to 3 atm
Band: calfskin, pin buckle
Remarks: comes with extra rose-gold case back
Price: $259,240

Perpetual Calendar with Retrograde Date

Reference number: 5160/500R-001
Movement: automatic, Patek Philippe caliber 26-330 S QR; ø 28 mm, height 5.36 mm; 29 jewels; 28,800 vph; gold rotor; 35-hour power reserve
Functions: hours, minutes, sweep seconds; perpetual calendar with date (retrograde), weekday, month, moon phase, leap year
Case: rose gold, with hinged cover, ø 38 mm, height 11.81 mm; sapphire crystal; transparent case back; water-resistant to 3 atm
Band: reptile skin, folding clasp
Price: $202,090

In-line Perpetual Calendar

Reference number: 5236P-010
Movement: automatic, Patek Philippe caliber 31-260 PS QL; ø 34 mm, height 5.8 mm; 44 jewels; 28,800 vph; platinum micro-rotor; 38-hour power reserve
Functions: hours, minutes, subsidiary seconds; day/night indicator; perpetual calendar with date, weekday, month, moon phase, leap year
Case: platinum, ø 41.3 mm, height 11.07 mm; sapphire crystal; transparent case back; water-resistant to 3 atm
Band: reptile skin, folding clasp
Remarks: comes with extra platinum case back
Price: $141,400

World Time Watch with Date

Reference number: 5330G-001
Movement: automatic, Patek Philippe caliber 240 HU C; ø 30.5 mm, height 4.58 mm; 21,600 vph; gold rotor with guilloché; 38-hour power reserve
Functions: hours, minutes; world time display (second time zone); date
Case: white gold, ø 40 mm, height 11.57 mm; pusher-activated ring with reference cities; sapphire crystal; transparent case back; water-resistant to 3 atm
Band: calfskin, folding clasp
Remarks: world time display (switches backward and forward)
Price: $76,590

Annual Calendar Moon Phase

Reference number: 5396G-017
Movement: automatic, Patek Philippe caliber 26-330 S QA LU 24H; ø 33.3 mm, height 5.8 mm; 34 jewels; 28,800 vph; gold rotor; 35-hour power reserve
Functions: hours, minutes, sweep seconds; annual calendar with date, weekday, month, moon phase
Case: white gold, ø 38.5 mm, height 11.2 mm; sapphire crystal; transparent case back; water-resistant to 3 atm
Band: reptile skin, folding clasp
Price: $63,510

Golden Ellipse

Reference number: 5738/1R-001
Movement: automatic, Patek Philippe caliber 240; ø 27.5 mm, height 2.53 mm; 27 jewels; 21,600 vph; silicon Spiromax hairspring; gold micro-rotor; 48-hour power reserve
Functions: hours, minutes
Case: rose gold, 34.5 x 39.5 mm, height 5.9 mm; sapphire crystal; water-resistant to 3 atm
Band: rose gold, folding clasp
Remarks: new chain-style link bracelet made of over 300 links
Price: $61,010

Aquanaut Luce Annual Calendar

Reference number: 5261R-001
Movement: automatic, Patek Philippe caliber 26-330 S QA LU; ø 30 mm, height 5.32 mm; 34 jewels; 28,800 vph; Spiromax silicon hairspring, gold rotor; 35-hour power reserve
Functions: hours, minutes, sweep seconds; annual calendar with date, weekday, month, moon phase
Case: rose gold, ø 39.9 mm, height 10.9 mm; sapphire crystal; transparent case back; water-resistant to 3 atm
Band: composite material, folding clasp
Price: $63,750

Aquanaut Travel Time

Reference number: 5164G-001
Movement: automatic, Patek Philippe caliber 26-330 C FUS; ø 31 mm, height 4.82 mm; 29 jewels; 28,800 vph; Spiromax silicon hairspring; gold rotor; 35-hour power reserve
Functions: hours, minutes, sweep seconds; additional 12-hour display (second time zone), day/night indicator; date
Case: white gold, ø 40.8 mm, height 10.2 mm; sapphire crystal; transparent case back; screw-down crown; water-resistant to 3 atm
Band: composite material, folding clasp
Price: $63,040

Aquanaut Travel Time

Reference number: 5269R-001
Movement: quartz
Functions: hours, minutes, sweep seconds; additional 12-hour display (second time zone), day/night indicator
Case: rose gold, ø 38.8 mm, height 8.77 mm; sapphire crystal; screw-down crown; water-resistant to 3 atm
Band: composite material, folding clasp
Price: $35,350

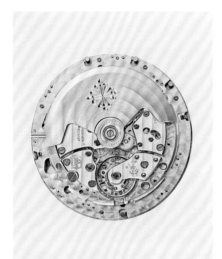

Caliber 324 S Q

Automatic; gold rotor; single mainspring barrel, 35-hour power reserve
Functions: hours, minutes, sweep seconds; day/night indicator; perpetual calendar with date, weekday, month, moon phase, leap year
Diameter: 32 mm
Height: 4.97 mm
Jewels: 29
Frequency: 28,800 vph

Caliber 26-330 S C

Automatic; gold rotor; single mainspring barrel, 35-hour power reserve
Functions: hours, minutes, sweep seconds; date
Diameter: 27 mm
Height: 3.3 mm
Jewels: 30
Balance: Gyromax
Frequency: 28,800 vph
Hairspring: silicon Spiromax
Remarks: 212 parts

Caliber CH 28-520 QA 24H

Automatic; gold rotor; single mainspring barrel, 45-hour power reserve
Functions: hours, minutes; flyback chronograph; annual calendar with date, weekday, month
Diameter: 33 mm
Height: 7.68 mm
Jewels: 37
Frequency: 28,800 vph
Hairspring: silicon Spiromax

Caliber 240 PS IRM C LU

Automatic; gold micro-rotor; single mainspring barrel, 38-hour power reserve
Functions: hours, minutes, subsidiary seconds; power reserve indicator; date, moon phase Diameter: 31 mm
Height: 3.98 mm
Jewels: 29
Balance: Gyromax, with 8 "masselotte" regulating screws
Frequency: 21,600 vph
Hairspring: silicon Spiromax
Shock protection: Kif
Remarks: 265 parts

Caliber AL 30-660 S C FUS

Automatic; gold rotor; single mainspring barrel, 42-hour power reserve
Functions: hours, minutes, sweep seconds; additional 12-hour display(second time zone), day/night indicator; alarm; date
Diameter: 31 mm
Height: 6.6 mm
Jewels: 52
Frequency: 28,800 vph
Hairspring: silicon Spiromax

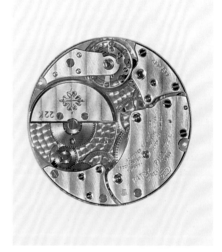

Caliber 240

Automatic; gold microrotor; single mainspring barrel, 48-hour power reserve
Functions: hours, minutes
Diameter: 27.5 mm
Height: 2.53 mm
Jewels: 27
Balance: Gyromax
Frequency: 21,600 vph
Hairspring: silicon Spiromax
Remarks: 161 parts

PAUL GERBER

In a world that often values hype more than the real thing, people like watchmaker Paul Gerber tend to get overlooked. And it's a shame because this man, who works out of his home in Zurich, has encyclopedic knowledge and experience of the industry. He has already developed a vast array of mechanisms and complications, including calendar movements, alarms, and tourbillons, for many brands. Gerber is the one who designed the complicated calendar mechanism for the otherwise minimalist MIH watch conceived by Ludwig Oechslin, curator of the International Museum of Horology (MIH) in La Chaux-de-Fonds and himself a watchmaker. To avoid cluttering a dial for a special customer, he recently devised a battery-run moon phase that fits in the watch strap. His work has twice appeared in *Guinness World Records*.

When his daily work for others lets up, Gerber gets around to building watches bearing his own name with such clever and rare complications as a retrograde second hand in an elegant thin case and a synchronously, unidirectional rotor system with miniature oscillating weights for his self-winding Retro Twin model. Gerber's works are usually limited editions.

After designing a tonneau-shaped manually wound wristwatch with a three-dimensional moon phase display, Gerber created a simple three-hand watch with an automatic movement conceived and produced completely in-house. It features a 100-hour power reserve and is wound by three synchronically turning gold rotors. Gerber also offers the triple rotor and large date features in a watch with an ETA movement and lightweight titanium case as a classic pilot watch design or in a version with a more modern dial (the Synchron model). The Model 41 has an optional complication that switches the second hand from sweep to dead-beat motion by way of a pusher at 2 o'clock.

Gerber is allegedly retired. But a watchmaker never really retires. Besides producing outstanding pieces, he also occasionally gives three-day workshops for people wanting to get a real feel for the work.

PAUL GERBER
Uhren-Konstruktionen
Bockhornstrasse 69
CH-8047 Zürich
Switzerland

TEL.:
+41-44-401-4569

E-MAIL:
info@gerber-uhren.ch

WEBSITE:
www.gerber-uhren.ch

FOUNDED:
1976

ANNUAL PRODUCTION:
up to 50 watches

U.S. DISTRIBUTOR:
Intro Swiss—Michel Schmutz
Michel Schmutz
6271 Corinth Rd.
Longmont, CO 80503
303-652-1520
introswiss@gmail.com

MOST IMPORTANT COLLECTIONS/PRICE RANGE:
mechanical watches / from approx. $6,750 to $27,000

Retrograd

Reference number: 152
Movement: manually wound, Gerber caliber 15 (base ETA 7001); ø 28 mm, 2.9 mm; 21 jewels; 21,600 vph
Functions: hours, minutes, subsidiary seconds (retrograde)
Case: yellow gold, ø 36 mm, height 8.5 mm; sapphire crystal; transparent case back; water-resistant to 3 atm
Band: reptile skin, buckle
Price: $12,950
Variations: rose gold $12,950

Modell 42

Reference number: 420 Triple Rotor-1
Movement: automatic, Gerber caliber 42 (base ETA 2824); ø 36 mm, height 6.1 mm; 25 jewels; 28,800 vph; automatic winding with 3 synchronously rotating gold rotors
Functions: hours, minutes, sweep seconds; large quick-set date
Case: titanium, ø 42 mm, height 12 mm; sapphire crystal; transparent case back; screw-in crown; water-resistant to 10 atm
Band: calfskin, buckle
Price: $6,750; limited to 46 pieces
Variations: 420 Triple Rotor-2 ($6,750)

Modell 42

Reference number: 420 DaN pilot
Movement: automatic, Gerber caliber 42 (base ETA 2824); ø 36 mm, height 6.1 mm; 25 jewels; 28,800 vph; automatic winding with 3 synchronously rotating gold rotors
Functions: hours, minutes, sweep seconds; day/night indicator; date
Case: titanium, ø 42 mm, height 12 mm; sapphire crystal; transparent case back; screw-in crown; water-resistant to 10 atm
Band: calfskin, buckle
Price: $7,100
Variations: 420 Triple Rotor-1 ($6,750); 420 Triple Rotor-2 ($6,750)

PEQUIGNET

The Jura mountains, which saddle Switzerland and France, are not only home to inventive and dogged craftspeople, notably watchmakers, on the Swiss side. In 1973, in Morteau, a small town close to the border, one Emile Pequignet founded a watch and jewelry company producing contemporary pieces that caught the spirit of the age and enjoyed fair success. In 2004, Pequignet himself retired and sold the brand to one Didier Leibundgut. This whole industry was bursting with energy, creating bigger and crazier watches. Pequignet steered a more conservative course and maintained its classic look. But it did develop its own *manufacture* movement, investing millions into the Calibre Royal.

The elaborate automatic movement is subject to eight patents. It can drive various functions, like a full calendar with moon phase or a power reserve indicator to tell the wearer how many of the 100 hours delivered by the large spring barrel have been used up. Since it does not need any modules, the movement is quite thin and can be configured for other functions quite easily. These functions are available in the Royale Sapphire collection.

The Calibre Royal reinvigorated the company, but it also cost inordinate amounts of money. The decade following was spent under the threat of liquidation. Finally, in December 2021, it was announced that a family fund had purchased the brand and the majority shareholder, Hugues Souparis, was now the new CEO. Morteau (pop. around 6,900) breathed a sigh of relief: maintaining the last independent French watch brand is a matter of honor in the region. And adding a tourbillon to their portfolio was definitely a good idea, since the development and manufacture of affordable, high-end movements in the Jura mountains means it can supply watch brands on both sides of the French-Swiss border with excellent calibers.

MONTRES PÉQUIGNET
1, rue du Bief
F-25503 Morteau
France

TEL:
+33 381 67 30 66

E-MAIL:
contact@pequignet.com

WEBSITE:
www.pequignet.com

FOUNDED:
1973

NUMBER OF EMPLOYEES:
50

U.S. DISTRIBUTOR
About Time Luxury Group
210 Bellevue Avenue
Newport, RI 02840
401-846-0598

MOST IMPORTANT COLLECTIONS / PRICE RANGE:
Men's and women's watches from $1,700 to $12,000

Royale Tourbillon
Reference number: 9035475
Movement: hand-wound, Calibre Royal Tourbillon; ø 34.5 mm, height 6.11 mm; 23 jewels; 21,600 vph; flying 1-minute tourbillon; finely finished movement; 88-hour power reserve
Functions: hours, minutes
Case: rose gold, ø 44 mm, height 11.7 mm; sapphire crystal; transparent case back; water-resistant to 5 atm
Band: reptile skin, pin buckle
Price: $78,000; limited to 24 pieces

Concorde Navy Blue
Reference number: 9040473
Movement: automatic, Calibre Initial; ø 25.6 mm, height 4.2 mm; 21 jewels; 28,800 vph; skeletonized winding rotor; 65-hour power reserve
Functions: hours, minutes, sweep seconds; date
Case: stainless steel, ø 40 mm, height 9.45 mm; sapphire crystal; transparent case back; water-resistant to 10 atm
Band: stainless steel, double folding clasp
Price: $4,800
Variations: with 36-millimeter case; various colors

Royale Saphir Green Jade
Reference number: 9010890
Movement: automatic, Calibre Royal; ø 30 mm, height 5.88 mm; 39 jewels; 21,600 vph; large spring barrel; finely finished with beveled edges and perlage; 88-hour power reserve
Functions: hours, minutes, subsidiary seconds; power reserve indicator; large date and weekday, moon phase
Case: stainless steel with black DLC, ø 42 mm, height 12.3 mm; sapphire crystal; transparent case back; water-resistant to 5 atm
Band: reptile skin, double folding clasp
Remarks: multipart sapphire-crystal dial
Price: $12,960; limited to 50 pieces
Variations: various colors (limited to 50 pieces each)

PERRELET

The Perrelet story will sound familiar to anyone who has read about Swiss watchmaking. Abraham-Louis Perrelet (1729–1826) was the son of a middle-class farmer from Le Locle who developed an interest in watchmaking early on in life. He was the first watchmaker in Le Locle to work on cylinder and duplex escapements, and there is a persistent rumor that he was responsible for a repeater that could be heard echoing in the mountains.

Many watchmakers who later became famous were at one time apprenticed to Perrelet, and some historians even suggest that Abraham-Louis Breguet was in this illustrious group. Suffice to say, Perrelet invented a great deal, including the "perpetual" watch from around 1770, a pocket watch that wound itself using the motion of the wearer.

When the brand hit the market in 1995, it came out with a double rotor and a movement, the P-181, which made waves in the industry. The Turbine soon followed, featuring a kind of jet engine fan that decoratively turns over the dial, creating all sorts of effects and giving lots of potential for creative designing. It was all creative and successful enough to attract the attention of Festina Group, which purchased the brand in 2004.

After a few years of silence, during which the company reorganized its distribution network, Perrelet returned to the watch world, having also made improvements to its automatic movements to ensure that their precision was at COSC level. The revised automatic P-411 still drives the LAB, cleverly designed to show the rotor just under a transparent dial. The Turbines are back, with that attractive hallmark animation on the dial, driven by the caliber P-331-MH with COSC certificate. The fan-shaped wheel on the upper part of the dial, which rotates at full speed depending on the movements of the wrist, creates fascinating and original visual effects depending on the decoration of the dial below. In 2024, the image that appears is a skull embossed in silver.

PERRELET SA
Rue Bubenberg 7
CH-2502 Biel/Bienne
Switzerland

TEL.:
+41-32-346-2626

FAX:
+41-32-346-2627

E-MAIL:
perrelet@perrelet.com

WEBSITE:
www.perrelet.com

FOUNDED:
brand founded in 1777, acquired by Festina Group in 2004

U.S. DISTRIBUTOR:
Perrelet USA
2937 SW 27th Avenue, Suite 102
Miami, FL 33133
305-588-3628
info@perreletusa.com

MOST IMPORTANT COLLECTIONS:
LAB, Turbine, First Class, Diamond Flower, Weekend

Weekend Skeleton

Reference number: A1306/3
Movement: automatic, Perrelet P-351-SQ caliber (based on Soprod); ø 25.6 mm, height 3.6 mm; 25 jewels; 28,800 vph; skeletonized mainplate and bridges, with anthracite NAC; microbeading; 42-hour power reserve
Functions: hours, minutes, sweep seconds
Case: stainless steel with black PVD, ø 39 mm, height 9.61 mm; sapphire crystal; transparent case back; water-resistant to 5 atm
Band: calfskin, pin buckle
Price: $2,050
Variations: with blue or black indices

LAB Peripheral Dual Time Big Date

Reference number: A110176
Movement: automatic, Perrelet caliber P-421; ø 34.8 mm, height 6.32 mm; 30 jewels; 28,800 vph hubless peripheral rotor on the dial side; 42-hour power reserve
Functions: hours, minutes, sweep seconds; additional 12-hour display (second time zone, complete set of hands) with day/night indication; large date
Case: stainless steel, ø 42 mm, height 13.51 mm; sapphire crystal; transparent case back; water-resistant to 5 atm
Band: calfskin, folding clasp
Remarks: oscillating mass of the hubless rotor visible on the dial side
Price: $5,480
Variations: with blue, silver, and black dial

Turbine Skull

Reference number: A1092/S1
Movement: automatic, Perrelet caliber P-331-MH (based on Soprod); ø 26.2 mm, height 3.6 mm; 25 jewels; 28,800 vph; 42-hour power reserve; COSC-certified chronometer
Functions: hours, minutes, sweep seconds
Case: stainless steel, ø 44 mm, height 12.65 mm; bezel in stainless steel with black PVD; sapphire crystal; transparent case back; water-resistant to 10 atm
Band: calfskin with rubber lining, folding clasp
Remarks: 12-blade turbine of anodized aluminum on the dial (no winding function), spins with wearer's movements revealing a relief, silver skull
Price: $5,000
Variations: in black, case with black PVD ($5,250)

PHOENIX WATCH COMPANY

Getting a brand off the ground always requires founders who know what they are doing. In the case of Phoenix, which saw the light of day in 2022, it was a trio of experts from three key areas of the industry: a collector, a certified master watchmaker, and a member of the watch industry's fourth estate, namely marketing. The first series of the brand is one of the very popular genres: pilot's watches in the form of a chronograph.

The first flight of the Phoenix, as it were, is the Eagle, released in 2023. Essentially, it is a series of three dials, all of which embrace the look and feel of a retro-mod pilot's chronograph, while using a combination of components that take advantage of modern technology and techniques, with respect to historical references.

Design is nothing if the mechanics running a watch are weak, so the company decided to outfit the watches with La Joux-Perret's caliber LJP 112. This particular movement is in fact an upgraded design based on the renowned Valjoux 7750 series. Improvements over the original include a power reserve extended to 60 hours, improved winding, stability, and shock resistance thanks to two additional ball bearings in the rotor system, and most critically, the transformation from a heart-cam system to a column-wheel control for the chronograph functions. The transparent case back allows one to see the well-decorated parts.

The unusual choice of an extra-tough authentic style acrylic crystal over the dial is interesting. It was chosen for its superior optical qualities and the fact that the material is functionally shatterproof. Acrylic (hesalite) crystals were de rigueur in the early days of watchmaking and are actually a better choice than sapphire in certain applications.

On the dial side, pilot's watches incorporate various telemeters, tachymeters, turn radius indicators, and even circular slide rules—not because they look interesting on the dial, but because they were needed as either primary or backup sources for critical calculations. Today these various scales are rarely used for their ostensible purpose, yet they continue on as inspired designs recalling a more analog age.

PHOENIX WATCH COMPANY
333 Washington Street, Suite 634
Boston, MA 02108
USA

TEL:
855-928-2411

EMAIL:
info@phoenixwatchco.com

WEBSITE:
www.phoenixwatchco.com

FOUNDED:
2022

ANNUAL PRODUCTION:
250 watches

MOST IMPORTANT COLLECTION/PRICE:
Eagle series / $4,680

Golden Eagle

Movement: automatic, La Joux-Perret caliber L112; ø 34.40 mm, height 7.90 mm; 26 jewels; 28,800 vph; rotor decorated with côtes de Genève; column-wheel control of chronograph; 60-hour power reserve
Functions: hours, minutes, subsidiary seconds; chronograph
Case: stainless steel; ø 44 mm, height 13.20 mm; extra-thick, shatterproof crystal; transparent case back; water-resistant to 5 atm
Band: calfskin, pin buckle
Price: $4,690; limited to 100 pieces

Strike Eagle

Movement: automatic, La Joux-Perret caliber L112; ø 34.40 mm, height 7.90 mm; 26 jewels; 28,800 vph; rotor decorated with côtes de Genève; column-wheel control of chronograph; 60-hour power reserve
Functions: hours, minutes, subsidiary seconds; chronograph
Case: stainless steel; ø 44 mm, height 13.20 mm; extra-thick, shatterproof crystal; transparent case back; water-resistant to 5 atm
Band: stainless steel milanaise mesh, folding clasp
Price: $4,690; limited to 100 pieces

American Eagle

Movement: automatic, La Joux-Perret caliber L112; ø 34.40 mm, height 7.90 mm; 26 jewels; 28,800 vph; rotor decorated with côtes de Genève; column-wheel control of chronograph; 60-hour power reserve
Functions: hours, minutes, subsidiary seconds; chronograph
Case: stainless steel; ø 44 mm, height 13.20 mm; extra-thick, shatterproof crystal; transparent case back; water-resistant to 5 atm
Band: calfskin, pin buckle
Price: $4,690; limited to 100 pieces

PIAGET

Piaget began making watch movements in the secluded Jura village of La Côte-aux-Fées in 1874. For decades, those movements were delivered to other watch brands. The *manufacture* itself, strangely enough, remained in the background. It wasn't until the 1940s that the Piaget family began to offer complete watches under their own name. Even today, Piaget, which long ago moved the business side of things to Geneva, still makes its watch movements at its main facility high in the Jura mountains.

In the late fifties, Piaget began investing in the design and manufacturing of ultrathin movements. This lends these watches the kind of understated elegance that became the company's hallmark. In 1957, Valentin Piaget presented the first ultrathin men's watch, the Altiplano, with the manual caliber 9P, which was 2 millimeters high. Shortly after, it came out with the 12P, an automatic caliber that clocked in at 2.3 millimeters.

The Altiplano has faithfully accompanied the brand for sixty years now. The movement has evolved over time. The 900P measures just 3.65 millimeters and is inverted to enable repairs, making the case back the mainplate with the dial set on the upper side.

Piaget is continuing to strive for thinner watches, even in the third millennium. The Altiplano Ultimate Concept, released in 2018, briefly set a world record as the thinnest mechanical watch with manual winding at two millimeters total height. It took four years of research and development.

In recent years, the Polo collection experienced expansion, with filigree skeleton versions of the two-hand watch and an ultra-thin perpetual calendar with a movement height of just four millimeters. A special treat was the detailed new edition of the Polo from the 1979 launch year, which was presented in honor of the brand's 150th anniversary year—flat and sporty as ever and, of course, made of solid gold.

PIAGET SA
CH-1228 Plan-les-Ouates
Switzerland

TEL.:
+41-32-867-21-21

E-MAIL:
info@piaget.com

WEBSITE:
www.piaget.com

FOUNDED:
1874

NUMBER OF EMPLOYEES:
900

ANNUAL PRODUCTION:
about 15,000 watches

U.S. DISTRIBUTOR:
Piaget North America
645 5th Avenue, 6th Floor
New York, NY 10022
212-909-4362
www.piaget.com

MOST IMPORTANT COLLECTIONS:
Altiplano, Polo S, Limelight, Possession

Polo Field
Reference number: G0A48022
Movement: automatic, Piaget caliber 1110P;
ø 25.58 mm, height 4 mm; 25 jewels; 28,800 vph;
perlage on mainplate, blued screws, finely finished with
côtes de Genève; 50-hour power reserve
Functions: hours, minutes, sweep seconds; date
Case: stainless steel, ø 42 mm, height 9.4 mm; sapphire
crystal; transparent case back; water-resistant to
10 atm
Band: rubber, folding clasp
Price: $12,900

Polo Chronograph
Reference number: G0A49024
Movement: automatic, Piaget caliber 1160P;
ø 25.58 mm, height 5.72 mm; 35 jewels; 28,800 vph;
perlage on mainplate, blued screws, finely finished with
côtes de Genève; 50-hour power reserve
Functions: hours, minutes; chronograph; date
Case: stainless steel, ø 42 mm, height 11.2 mm;
sapphire crystal; transparent case back; water-resistant
to 10 atm
Band: stainless steel, folding clasp
Price: $24,400

Polo Date
Reference number: G0A48021
Movement: automatic, Piaget caliber 1110P;
ø 25.58 mm, height 4 mm; 25 jewels; 28,800 vph;
perlage on mainplate, blued screws, finely finished with
côtes de Genève; 50-hour power reserve
Functions: hours, minutes, sweep seconds; date
Case: rose gold, ø 42.4 mm, height 9.4 mm; sapphire
crystal; transparent case back; water-resistant to
10 atm
Band: reptile skin, folding clasp
Price: $31,000

PIAGET

Polo 150 Years Anniversary Couple Watch 42mm

Reference number: G0A49023
Movement: automatic, Piaget caliber 1110P; ø 25.58 mm, height 4 mm; 25 jewels; 28,800 vph; perlage on mainplate, blued screws, finely finished with côtes de Genève; 50-hour power reserve
Functions: hours, minutes, sweep seconds; date
Case: stainless steel, ø 42.4 mm, height 9.4 mm; sapphire crystal; transparent case back; water-resistant to 10 atm
Band: rubber, folding clasp
Price: $14,700; limited to 300 pieces

Polo 150 Years Anniversary Couple Watch 36mm

Reference number: G0A49029
Movement: automatic, Piaget caliber 500P1; ø 20.5 mm, height 3.63 mm; 24 jewels; 28,800 vph; perlage on mainplate, blued screws, finely finished with côtes de Genève; 40-hour power reserve
Functions: hours, minutes, sweep seconds; date
Case: stainless steel, ø 36 mm, height 8.8 mm; bezel set with 60 diamonds; sapphire crystal; transparent case back; water-resistant to 5 atm
Band: rubber, folding clasp
Remarks: hour markers set with 36 diamonds
Price: $21,600; limited to 300 pieces

Polo Date 36mm

Reference number: G0A47017
Movement: automatic, Piaget caliber 500P1; ø 20.5 mm, height 3.4 mm; 26 jewels; 21,600 vph; finely finished movement; 40-hour power reserve
Functions: hours, minutes, sweep seconds; date
Case: rose gold, ø 36 mm, height 8.8 mm; bezel in rose gold set with 60 diamonds; sapphire crystal; transparent case back; crown in rose gold; water-resistant to 5 atm
Band: rose gold, folding clasp
Remarks: hour markers, set with 36 diamonds
Price: $53,500
Variations: various cases, straps, and dials

Polo Perpetual Calendar Ultra-Thin

Reference number: G0A48005
Movement: automatic, Piaget caliber 1255P; ø 29.9 mm, height 4 mm; 25 jewels; 21,600 vph; microrotor; perlage on mainplate, blued screws, finely finished with côtes de Genève; 42-hour power reserve
Functions: hours, minutes; perpetual calendar with date, weekday, month, moon phase, leap year
Case: stainless steel, ø 42 mm, height 8.65 mm; sapphire crystal; transparent case back; water-resistant to 3 atm
Band: stainless steel, folding clasp
Price: $60,000

Polo Skeleton

Reference number: G0A47008
Movement: automatic, Piaget caliber 1200S1; ø 29.9 mm, height 2.4 mm; 25 jewels; 21,600 vph; completely skeletonized movement, mainplate and bridges with green PVD; 44-hour power reserve
Functions: hours, minutes
Case: stainless steel, ø 42 mm, height 6.5 mm; sapphire crystal; transparent case back
Band: stainless steel, folding clasp
Price: $34,200
Variations: with blue PVD

Altiplano Ultimate Automatic

Reference number: G0A48125
Movement: automatic, Piaget caliber 910P; ø 41 mm, height 4.3 mm (including case and sapphire crystal); 30 jewels; 21,600 vph; inverted movement construction as a single unit with case, hubless peripheral rotor; 48-hour power reserve
Functions: hours and minutes (off-center)
Case: rose gold, ø 41 mm, height 4.3 mm; sapphire crystal
Band: reptile skin, pin buckle
Price: $36,000
Variations: in white gold ($37,100)

PILO & CO. GENÈVE

Brimming bank accounts held by mysterious and at times shady characters may not be Geneva's best-kept secret anymore, not in the age of leaks to the media. Far less known is the fact that Geneva is a veritable hub of all sorts of crafts, notably those associated with watchmaking, and they were at one time concentrated in the district of St. Gervais where the craftspeople were referred to as "Les Cabinotiers." Among them are little watch companies that continue to produce excellent timepieces and survive in the shadow of the big brands and groups that have also made the city their home.

One of these independent companies, Pilo & Co. Genève, will be celebrating its twenty-fifth anniversary in 2026. It was founded by Amarildo Pilo, who, while not of Swiss origin, has a very Genevan story. His father was an Albanian diplomat who was called back when the government in his native country changed at the end of the 1980s. His two sons stayed to continue their studies. Amarildo decided on an internship with a watch distributor and ended up becoming totally entranced with the watch world. In 2001, feeling he had the experience and the wherewithal, he launched his own brand.

Today, Pilo & Co. is represented throughout Switzerland and has found faithful customers in Europe and Asia. The company has three shops in Geneva. It produces a wide range of styles in quartz and mechanical. The sheer output allows for variety in the use of colors and shapes, from round to tonneau. The dials are often open-worked or fully skeletonized.

The portfolio has now grown to fifteen collections of affordable watches that combine good looks with the kind of workmanship expected from a Swiss brand. They include the Extraneō with a two-level dial and clean, traditional decoration, and most recently the high-end Corleone Evoluzione Superleggera, a bold chronograph in a rectangular carbon case with a cleverly shaped and domed and beveled sapphire crystal to increase the readability of the dial, which is made of a meteorite that displays a classic Widmanstätten pattern.

PILO & CO GENEVE
11 Faubourg-de-Cruseilles
CH-1227 Carouge
Switzerland

TEL.:
+41-22-328-0112

E-MAIL:
contact@pilo-watches.com

WEBSITE:
www.pilo-watches.com

FOUNDED:
2001

NUMBER OF EMPLOYEES:
7

DISTRIBUTION:
Contact main office in Geneva
contact@pilo-watches.com

MOST IMPORTANT COLLECTIONS/PRICE RANGE:
Mechanical and quartz watches: Allegra, Corleone, Doppio Orario, Illusione, Invidia, Montecristo, Tempo and Exceptional Pieces / $300 to $5,000

Extraneō
Reference number: P0573HAS MB
Movement: automatic, caliber Soprod P024; ø 25.60 mm, 4.6 mm; 25 jewels; 28,800 vph; 38-hour power reserve
Functions: hours, minutes, sweep seconds
Case: stainless steel, ø 40 mm, height 10.7 mm; sapphire crystal; stainless steel case back; water-resistant to 5 atm
Band: stainless steel
Price: $1,620

Corleone Superleggera
Reference number: P0558HACF
Movement: automatic, caliber Soprod 7750RM3H; ø 30.40 mm, 7.9 mm; 25 jewels; 28,800 vph; 42-hour power reserve
Functions: hours, minutes, subsidiary seconds; chronograph; date; power reserve indicator
Case: forged carbon, ø 45 mm x 54 mm, height 15 mm; sapphire crystal domed and beveled; transparent case back; water-resistant to 10 atm
Band: sailcloth, pin buckle
Remarks: meteorite dial
Price: $8,960; limited to 25 pieces

Pièce d'Exception
Reference number: P0611HABI MB
Movement: automatic, PW01 in-house caliber; ø 30 mm, height 7.8 mm; 27 jewels; 28,800 vph; finely finished movement with finely finished black oscillating mass; 42-hour power reserve
Functions: hours, minutes, subsidiary seconds; 24-hour display (second time zone); day, date; power reserve indicator
Case: stainless steel, ø 44 mm, height 12.87 mm; sapphire crystal; transparent case back; water-resistant to 5 atm
Band: stainless steel, folding clasp
Price: $5,980

PORSCHE DESIGN

In 1972, Professor Ferdinand Alexander Porsche founded his own design studio with the aim of creating technically inspired products beyond the world of vehicles. From the very beginning, Porsche Design was all about exploring new technical possibilities not only in watches but also in accessories. Just like the first Porsche 911, a key design object in recent history, the iconic Chronograph I was designed by Prof. F. A. Porsche. In 1972, the founder of Porsche Design followed a premise: "My aim was to create a watch to match the car."

The Chronograph I was a timeless sporty precision instrument whose design was derived from the dashboard gauges of the Porsche 911. It was the first time that the design, aesthetics, and functionality of a sports car were reproduced in a watch. The Chronograph I was also the world's first all-black wristwatch.

Porsche Design engineers still inspire themselves from the automobile industry when it comes to materials and functionality.

A cooperation with Porsche Motorsport allows the latest technologies and findings from the world of racing to be incorporated into the development of watches. Porsche Design relies on exclusive COSC-certified movements to drive its watches. In collaboration with the engineers at the Porsche Development Center in Weissach (Germany), the company has produced technical masterpieces and unique calibers that impose Porsche's high quality on the "sports cars on your wrist."

The calibers include Caliber 01.200, with a complex flyback mechanism; Caliber 04.110, with a very clever GMT switching mechanism; and two other calibers, 01.100 and 03.100. Among the newer collections is the Chronograph I, a boldly sportive line with special models, such as the Chronograph 1 – All Black Numbered Edition and Chronograph 1 Utility – Limited Edition.

The revolutionary "Custom-built Timepieces" program introduces the principle of vehicle configuration into the luxury watch segment. There are countless possible combinations to choose from, like the case with the bezel, the dial ring in over 140 different car colors, the strap made of vehicle leather with colored decorative stitching made of vehicle yarn, or the rotor with a rim look. Each watch is individually crafted by hand so that all details reflect the owner's aesthetic preferences.

PORSCHE LIFESTYLE GROUP
Groenerstrasse 5
D-71636 Ludwigsburg
Germany

TEL.:
+49-711-911-0

E-MAIL:
contact@porsche-design.us

WEBSITE:
www.porsche-design.com

FOUNDED:
1972

U.S. DISTRIBUTOR:
Porsche Design of America, Inc.
600 Anton Blvd., Suite 1280
Costa Mesa, CA 92626
770-290-7500
timepieces@porsche-design.us
www.porsche-design.com

MOST IMPORTANT COLLECTIONS:
Chronograph 1, custom-built timepieces with configurator, 1919 Collection, Chronotimer Flyback

Chronograph 1 – All Black Numbered Edition

Reference number: 6043.7.01.001.01.5
Movement: automatic, Porsche Design caliber WERK 01.140; ø 30 mm, height 7.9 mm; 25 jewels; 28,800 vph; 48-hour power reserve; COSC-certified chronometer
Functions: hours, minutes, subsidiary seconds; chronograph; date and weekday
Case: titanium with black titanium carbide coating, ø 40.8 mm, height 14.15 mm; sapphire crystal; transparent case back; screw-down crown; water-resistant to 10 atm
Band: titanium with black titanium carbide coating, folding clasp
Price: $9,650; limited to 1000 pieces per year

Chronograph 1 Utility – Limited Edition

Reference number: 6041.8.41.001.12.2
Movement: automatic, Porsche Design caliber WERK 01.240; ø 30 mm, height 7.9 mm; 25 jewels; 28,800 vph; 48-hour power reserve; COSC-certified chronometer
Functions: hours, minutes, subsidiary seconds; flyback chronograph; date and weekday
Case: titanium carbide, ø 42.7 mm, height 15.5 mm; sapphire crystal; transparent case back; screw-down crown; water-resistant to 10 atm
Band: calfskin, folding clasp
Price: $13,000; limited to 250 pieces

Chronograph 1 – 50 Years 911 Turbo

Reference number: 6041.8.01.002.10.2
Movement: automatic, Porsche Design caliber WERK 01.240; ø 30 mm, height 7.9 mm; 25 jewels; 28,800 vph; 48-hour power reserve; COSC-certified chronometer
Functions: hours, minutes, subsidiary seconds; flyback chronograph; date and weekday
Case: titanium with black titanium carbide coating, ø 40.8 mm, height 15.5 mm; sapphire crystal; transparent case back; screw-down crown; water-resistant to 10 atm
Band: textile, folding clasp
Remarks: comes with extra titanium bracelet
Price: $12,000

Custom-built Chronograph

Movement: automatic, Porsche Design caliber WERK 01.100 (ETA 7750 base); ø 30 mm, height 7.9 mm; 25 jewels; 28,800 vph; 48-hour power reserve; COSC-certified chronometer
Functions: hours, minutes; rate control; chronograph; date
Case: titanium, ø 42 mm, height 15.33 mm; bezel with titanium carbide coating; sapphire crystal; transparent case back; screw-down crown; water-resistant to 5 atm
Band: calfskin, folding clasp
Remarks: watch can be personalized using the configurator
Price: $7,250
Variations: basic model price $6,250

Custom-built Globetimer

Movement: automatic, Porsche Design caliber WERK 04.110; ø 28.5 mm, height 6.94 mm; 26 jewels; 28,800 vph; 38-hour power reserve; COSC-certified chronometer
Functions: hours, minutes, sweep seconds; additional 24-hour display (second time zone), day/night indication; date
Case: titanium, ø 42 mm, height 14.68 mm; bezel set titanium carbide coating; sapphire crystal; screw-down crown; water-resistant to 5 atm
Band: calfskin, folding clasp
Remarks: watch can be personalized using the configurator with various customization options
Price: $6,800
Variations: basic model price $6,250

Sport Chrono Subsecond 39 Titanium & Black

Reference number: 6023.3.71.001.07.2
Movement: automatic, Porsche Design caliber WERK 03.200 (Sellita SW261 base); ø 25.6 mm, height 5.6 mm; 31 jewels; 28,800 vph; 38-hour power reserve; COSC-certified chronometer
Functions: hours, minutes, subsidiary seconds; date
Case: titanium, ø 39 mm, height 12.25 mm; sapphire crystal; screw-down crown; water-resistant to 10 atm
Band: calfskin, folding clasp
Price: $5,350

Sport Chrono Subsecond 39 Titanium & Blue

Reference number: 6023.3.71.002.07.2
Movement: automatic, Porsche Design caliber WERK 03.200 (Sellita SW261 base); ø 25.6 mm, height 5.6 mm; 31 jewels; 28,800 vph; 38-hour power reserve; COSC-certified chronometer
Functions: hours, minutes, subsidiary seconds; date
Case: titanium, ø 39 mm, height 12.25 mm; sapphire crystal; screw-down crown; water-resistant to 10 atm
Band: calfskin, folding clasp
Price: $5,350

1919 Globetimer UTC All Black

Reference number: 6023.4.02.005.07.2
Movement: automatic, Porsche Design caliber WERK 04.110; ø 28.5 mm, height 6.94 mm; 26 jewels; 28,800 vph; 38-hour power reserve; COSC-certified chronometer
Functions: hours, minutes, sweep seconds; additional 24-hour display (second time zone), day/night indication; date
Case: titanium with black titanium carbide coating, ø 42 mm, height 14.9 mm; sapphire crystal; screw-down crown; water-resistant to 10 atm
Band: calfskin, folding clasp
Price: $6,350

1919 Globetimer UTC All Titanium Blue

Reference number: 6023.4.05.002.05.5
Movement: automatic, Porsche Design caliber WERK 04.110; ø 28.5 mm, height 6.94 mm; 26 jewels; 28,800 vph; 38-hour power reserve; COSC-certified chronometer
Functions: hours, minutes, sweep seconds; additional 24-hour display (second time zone), day/night indication; date
Case: titanium, ø 42 mm, height 14.9 mm; sapphire crystal; screw-down crown; water-resistant to 10 atm
Band: titanium, folding clasp
Price: $6,590

RADO

Rado is a relatively young brand, especially for a Swiss one. The company, which grew out of the Schlup clockwork factory, launched its first watches in 1957, but it achieved international fame only five years later, in 1962, when it surprised the world with a revolutionary invention. Rado's oval DiaStar was the first truly scratch-resistant watch ever, sporting a case made of a ceramic and tungsten carbide alloy. In 1985, its parent company, the Swatch Group, decided to put Rado's know-how and extensive experience in developing materials to good use, and from then on, the brand intensified its research activities at its home in Lengnau, Switzerland, and continued to produce only watches with extremely hard cases.

Rado distinguishes between two ceramic variants The first is high-tech ceramic, which is heated to 1,450 °C and cools to a hard, durable surface. The second is plasma high-tech ceramic, which involves heating the watch case and bracelet links once again, but this time to 20,000 °C until the surface melts into a glass-hard layer.

The continuous research into hard materials has produced generations of collections of watches made of experimental ceramics. In 2011, for example, they produced the ultra-light Ceramos, which went into the D-Star collection. Obviously, Rado also holds more than thirty patents.

A special material is worth nothing without a strict design code. The reborn diving watch classic, Captain Cook, is one way to present the modern ceramic development from the alchemist's kitchen of Comadur, a sister company within the Swatch Group.

Another is the eye-catching True Square collection, a comfortably wearable timepiece with a 38-millimeter edge length. It is available in black or in metallic shiny plasma ceramic. Further, the True Square and Captain Cook models as well as the brand-new DiaStar Original are now available with exclusive skeleton movements from the Group's sister company ETA.

RADO UHREN AG
Bielstrasse 45
CH-2543 Lengnau
Switzerland

TEL.:
+41-32-655-6111

E-MAIL:
info@rado.com

WEBSITE:
www.rado.com
store.us.rado.com

FOUNDED:
1957

NUMBER OF EMPLOYEES:
approx. 470

U.S. DISTRIBUTOR:
Rado
The Swatch Group (U.S.), Inc.
703 Waterford Way, Suite 450
Miami, FL 33126
786-725-5393

MOST IMPORTANT COLLECTIONS/PRICE RANGE:
Hyperchrome / from approx. $1,100; Diamaster / from approx. $1,500; Integral / from approx. $2,000; True Square / from approx. $1,400; Centrix / from approx. $800; Coupole Classic / from approx. $1,000; Tradition / from approx. $2,000

Captain Cook High-Tech Ceramic Skeleton

Reference number: R32150162
Movement: automatic, ETA caliber R808; ø 25.6 mm, height 4.74 mm; 25 jewels; 21,600 vph; skeletonized mainplate; 80-hour power reserve
Functions: hours, minutes, sweep seconds
Case: ceramic, ø 43 mm, height 14.6 mm; unidirectional bezel with rose-gold PVD, with ceramic insert with 0-60 scale; sapphire crystal; transparent case back; screw-down crown; water-resistant to 30 atm
Band: ceramic, titanium triple folding clasp
Price: $4,400

Captain Cook

Reference number: R32154208
Movement: automatic, ETA caliber R763; ø 25.6 mm, height 4.74 mm; 25 jewels; 21,600 vph; 80-hour power reserve
Functions: hours, minutes, sweep seconds; date
Case: stainless steel, ø 42 mm, height 12.3 mm; unidirectional bezel with ceramic insert, with 0-60 scale; sapphire crystal; screw-down crown; water-resistant to 30 atm
Band: textile, pin buckle
Remarks: comes with stainless steel and leather strap
Price: $2,700

Captain Cook High-Tech Ceramic Skeleton Limited Edition

Reference number: R32152209
Movement: automatic, ETA caliber R808; ø 25.6 mm, height 4.74 mm; 25 jewels; 21,600 vph; skeletonized mainplate; 80-hour power reserve
Functions: hours, minutes, sweep seconds
Case: ceramic, ø 43 mm, height 14.6 mm; unidirectional bezel with ceramic insert, with 0-60 scale; sapphire crystal; screw-down crown; water-resistant to 30 atm
Band: rubber, folding clasp
Price: $4,450; limited to 250 pieces

Centrix Open Heart

Reference number: R30029942
Movement: automatic, ETA caliber R734; ø 25.6 mm, height 4.74 mm; 25 jewels; 21,600 vph; skeletonized mainplate; 80-hour power reserve
Functions: hours, minutes, sweep seconds
Case: stainless steel with rose-gold PVD, ø 35 mm, height 11.1 mm; sapphire crystal; transparent case back; water-resistant to 5 atm
Band: stainless steel with rose-gold PVD and ceramic elements, folding clasp
Remarks: openworked dial, set with diamonds
Price: $3,650

Centrix Open Heart

Reference number: R30012202
Movement: automatic, ETA caliber R734; ø 25.6 mm, height 4.74 mm; 25 jewels; 21,600 vph; skeletonized mainplate; 80-hour power reserve
Functions: hours, minutes, sweep seconds
Case: stainless steel, ø 39.5 mm, height 11.3 mm; sapphire crystal; transparent case back; water-resistant to 5 atm
Band: stainless steel with ceramic elements, folding clasp
Remarks: openworked dial
Price: $2,400

Rado HyperChrome Chronograph Limited Edition

Reference number: R32022152
Movement: automatic, ETA caliber R650; ø 28.6 mm, height 6.1 mm; 37 jewels; 28,800 vph; 47-hour power reserve
Functions: hours, minutes, subsidiary seconds; chronograph; date
Case: ceramic (plasma-treated), ø 45 mm, height 13 mm; sapphire crystal; water-resistant to 10 atm
Band: ceramic (plasma-treated), triple folding clasp
Price: $4,850; limited to 999 pieces

Rado True Square x Kunihiko Morinaga

Reference number: R27086172
Movement: automatic, ETA caliber R734; ø 25.6 mm, height 4.74 mm; 25 jewels; 21,600 vph; skeletonized mainplate; 80-hour power reserve
Functions: hours, minutes, sweep seconds
Case: ceramic, 38 x 44.2 mm, height 9.7 mm; sapphire crystal; transparent case back; water-resistant to 5 atm
Band: ceramic, titanium triple folding
Remarks: dial with photo-chrome effect, which changes color depending on the light; perlage on partly skeletonized mainplate
Price: $2,700

Rado True Round Open Heart

Reference number: R27107172
Movement: automatic, ETA caliber R734; ø 25.6 mm, height 4.74 mm; 25 jewels; 21,600 vph; skeletonized mainplate; 80-hour power reserve
Functions: hours, minutes, sweep seconds
Case: ceramic, ø 40 mm, height 10.4 mm; sapphire crystal; transparent case back; water-resistant to 5 atm
Band: ceramic, titanium triple folding clasp
Remarks: skeletonized dial
Price: $2,500

Rado True Round Open Heart

Reference number: R27115022
Movement: automatic, ETA caliber R734; ø 25.6 mm, height 4.74 mm; 25 jewels; 21,600 vph; skeletonized mainplate; 80-hour power reserve
Functions: hours, minutes, sweep seconds
Case: ceramic, ø 40 mm, height 10.4 mm; sapphire crystal; transparent case back; water-resistant to 5 atm
Band: ceramic, titanium triple folding clasp
Remarks: skeletonized dial; sapphire crystal with dichroic effect
Price: $2,500

RAKETA

The city of Saint Petersburg, known as Russia's cultural capital, is not that old. Its founding goes back to Czar Peter I, later known as "the Great," who was intent on modernizing his country and decided to have a city built that would face the West and reflect Western values. It was a costly enterprise, especially in lives, since the builders were serfs and the swampy area was rife with disease, but in the end, he got his city. He had a fleet built as well and, in 1721, opened a lapidary known as Petrodvorets (or Peter's Palace), which would later prepare precious stones for the czars.

That factory has had many lives in its three-hundred-year history. Since 1949, after restoration following destruction during World War II, it has been producing watches, first under the name Pobeda (Victory) and Zvezda (Star). On April 12, 1961, Yuri Gagarin orbited Earth once in the Vostok 1 spacecraft, opening the way to human space exploration. The following year saw the launch of the Raketa (rocket) brand at the Petrodvorets factory, which had quite a success with Soviet citizenry.

When David Henderson-Stewart, a young English businessman, visited the factory in 2010, the shine had gone under the onslaught of the free market. A few stalwart employees kept the home fires burning, but everything was run down. Though not from the watch world—an innocence he credits for his spontaneous decision and commitment—he saw the potential. Investors were found, experts brought in, and Raketa was put back into business with several collections all made totally in-house and visually unique. Soviet-era or Russian iconography are the main themes. There are military style 24-hour watches, like the Polar. And there are models honoring some of the artistic movements of the revolutionary era, like the Avant-Garde, or the Copernicus, which celebrates the great scientific revolution launched by the man who determined the heliocentric structure of the Solar System.

RAKETA WATCH FACTORY LTD
Sankt-Peterburgskiy prospekt, 60
198516 St. Petersburg, Peterhof
Russia

TEL.:
+7-926-304-0591

E-MAIL:
info@raketa.com

WEBSITE:
www.raketa.com

FOUNDED:
1721 / 1961

DISTRIBUTION:
Contact the company

MOST IMPORTANT COLLECTIONS/PRICE RANGE:
Avant-Garde, Space Launcher, Copernicus, Polar, Russian Code / $800 to $3,750

Avant-Garde
Reference number: W-13-16-10-0292
Movement: automatic, Raketa caliber 2615; ø 26 mm, height 6.8 mm; 24 jewels; 18,000 vph; bidirectional rotor with laser-made Neva waves decoration and nanocoating; 40-hour power reserve
Functions: hours, minutes, sweep seconds
Case: stainless steel, ø 39.5 mm, height 15.78 mm; crown with ruby cabochon; sapphire crystal; transparent case back (mineral glass); water-resistant to 5 atm
Band: leather, buckle
Price: $1,795

Polar
Reference number: W-12-19-30-0300
Movement: automatic, Raketa caliber 2624A; ø 26mm, height 6.8 mm; 24 jewels; 18,000 vph; hand-made Neva waves decoration and nanocoating; 40-hour power reserve
Functions: 24-hour watch, minutes, sweep seconds
Case: stainless steel, ø 41.6 mm, height 14.9 mm; screw-down crown with ruby cabochon; sapphire crystal; transparent case back; water-resistant to 20 atm
Band: stainless steel, pin buckle
Price: $1,750

Copernicus
Reference number: W-13-16-30-0307
Movement: automatic, Raketa caliber 2615; ø 26 mm, height 6.8 mm; 24 jewels; 18,000 vph; bidirectional gold-plated rotor with Neva waves decoration and nanocoating; 40-hour power reserve
Functions: hours, minutes, sweep seconds
Case: stainless steel, ø 39.5 mm, height 15.78 mm; crown with ruby cabochon; sapphire crystal; transparent case back (mineral glass); water-resistant to 5 atm
Band: stainless steel, folding clasp
Remarks: aventurine and agate dial
Price: $1,980
Variations: various strap colors

RESERVOIR

One of the most logical inspirations for watches is the humble gauge, and for good reason. It usually has a similar shape to a watch (round), and it serves to depict a certain event or action using a pointing device and numerals. It must also be legible at a glance. In addition, gauges tend to be found precisely where a mechanical process is taking place, and that excites the imagination of any person who appreciates the mesmerizing synergism of gears, cams, rackets, and other parts.

While gauges and meters are used fairly frequently as elements in watchmaking, only a few brands have actually made them the centerpiece of their design strategy. Reservoir, a French brand founded in 2017 by François Moreau, has taken this object mirroring to the nth degree, one could say. Connoisseurs of vintage British cars will easily spot the resemblance of many models to the odometers in the Mini Morris: a big round dial with a fuel gauge at the lower end. Since gauges usually have a single pointer, many Reservoir models have a retrograde minute hand with jumping hours in a separate window below the center. This basic dial serves as a visual pattern for three separate lines inspired by air, land, and sea, with "land" focused mostly on cars.

Lately, Reservoir has collaborated with a number of outside forces to create special editions. One partner is Monza Design, for example, and the other is the brand developer and e-commerce platform Heroes. The latter's raven symbol appears on the case-back of a 390 Fastback that looks like the speedometer of a 1960s pony car, those compact sports cars that were all the rage. Another collaboration was with the elite tactical French police force "Groupe d'intervention de la Gendarmerie nationale" or, to use the unnerving acronym, GIGN.

For its movements, which require some dexterity to manufacture, Reservoir uses basic ETA La Joux-Perret calibers with special modifications built by Télôs, an exclusive movement and module maker in La Chaux-de-Fonds that specializes in implementing the ideas, no matter how wild, of horological dreamers.

RESERVOIR WATCH SAS
138, rue du Faubourg Saint-Honoré
F-75008 Paris
France

TEL:
+33 (0)1 42 89 11 79

E-MAIL:
contact@reservoir-watch.com

WEBSITE:
www.reservoir-watch.com

FOUNDED:
2017

NUMBER OF EMPLOYEES:
10

U. S. DISTRIBUTOR:
Online sales
Timeless Distribution
contactUSA@reservoir-watch.com
305-588-3628

MOST IMPORTANT COLLECTIONS/PRICE RANGE:
Cars, Aeronautics, Marine, Music, Comics by Reservoir / from $3,800

Monza Design 325y

Reference number: RSV01.MD/138.YL
Movement: automatic, caliber RSV-240 based on La Joux-Perret LP G100; ø 25.6 mm, height 4.45 mm; 24 jewels; 28,800 vph, 56-hour power reserve
Functions: retrograde minutes, jumping hours; power reserve indicator
Case: stainless steel; ø 43 mm, height 14 mm; sapphire crystal; transparent case back; screw-down crown; water-resistant to 5 atm
Band: stainless steel, pin buckle
Remarks: collaboration with Monza Design of race-car fame; comes with extra rubber strap with tire imprint
Price: $5,400
Variations: black dial with red power reserve; red dial and black power reserve

390 Fastback x Heroes

Reference number: RSV01.3F/133.HR
Movement: automatic, caliber RSV-240 based on La Joux-Perret LP G100; ø 25.6 mm, height 4.45 mm; 24 jewels; 28,800 vph, 56-hour power reserve
Functions: retrograde minutes, jumping hours
Case: stainless steel with black PVD; ø 41.5 mm, height 12 mm; screw-down crown; water-resistant to 5 atm
Band: leather, folding clasp
Remarks: dial design inspired from the speedometer of a 1967 "Pony Car" and its V8 engine known as the 390
Price: $3,950; limited to 66 pieces
Variations: in black ($5,750)

RESERVOIR watch x GIGN

Reference number: RSV02.GY/135
Movement: automatic, caliber RSV-240 based on La Joux-Perret LP G100; ø 25.6 mm, height 4.45 mm; 24 jewels; 28,800 vph, 56-hour power reserve
Functions: retrograde minutes, jumping hours; power reserve indicator
Case: stainless steel; ø 42 mm, height 13 mm; sapphire crystal; transparent case back; screw-down crown; water-resistant to 5 atm
Band: canvas and leather, folding clasp
Remarks: tribute to 50 years (1974–2024) of the elite French police force GIGN
Price: $5,400; limited to 192 pieces

RESSENCE

Belgian Benoît Mintiens had the luck of the newcomer at Baselworld 2010. He showed up at the last minute and found some space to show a strange watch he had conceived, with an almost two-dimensional dial. He returned in 2011 with the Type 1001. It consisted of a large rotating dial carrying a hand that pointed to a minute track on the bezel. Hours, small second, and a day/night indication rotated on dedicated subsidiary dials. All who beheld it were mesmerized. He sold all fifty of his models off the bat.

The mechanics behind the Ressence watches—the name is a compounding of "Renaissance of the Essential"—are simple: a stripped-down and rebuilt ETA 2824 leaves the minute wheel as the main driver of the other wheels.

In a bid to improve readability, he immersed the dial section in oil, giving the displays a very contemporary two-dimensional look, much like an electronic watch. The movement had to be kept separate from the oil and was connected to the dial using magnets and a set of superconductors and a Faraday cage to protect the movement from magnetism. Baffles compensate for the expanding and contracting of the oil due to temperature shifts. The Type 3 also lost the crown, the only obstacle to making a perfectly smooth watch, in favor of a clever setting and winding mechanism controlled by the case back.

The variations on the theme have been emerging from the Ressence studio at a regular pace. He started experimenting discreetly with the design, produced a diver's watch chic enough to wear for any occasion, and went a bit electronic with a thing called the e-Crown, which allows the wearer to reset the time electronically by discreetly tapping twice on the watch's crystal. Mintiens always preserves the special charm that comes from their rounded, gently curved shape on all sides without a glass holder rim. The curvature of the surface has a radius of 12.5 centimeters, which is approximately the half-diameter of a bowling ball. Lately, the dials have received carefully chosen colorings, or mosaics of luminous substance.

RESSENCE WATCHES
Meirbrug 1
2000 Antwerp
Belgium

TEL.:
+32-3-446-0060

E-MAIL:
hello@ressence.be

WEBSITE:
www.ressencewatches.com

FOUNDED:
2010

U.S. DISTRIBUTOR:
Totally Worth It (TWI2, Inc.)
76 Division Avenue
Summit, NJ 07901-2309
201-894-4710
724-263-2286
info@totallyworthit.com

COLLECTION PRICES:
Type 1: $20,600; Type 2: $48,800; Type 3: $42,200; Type 5: $35,800; Type 8: 15,000; Type 9: $14,900

Type 1°

Movement: hand-wound, ROCS 1.3 (modified ETA 2892 caliber); ø 32 mm; 40 jewels; 28,800 vph; case back for winding and time setting; 27 gearwheels; 36-hour power reserve
Functions: hours, minutes, subsidiary seconds (Ressence Orbital Convex System: peripheral minute dial with rotating satellites); weekday (off-center, orbiting)
Case: titanium, ø 42.7 mm, height 11 mm; sapphire crystal; winding and time setting using the case back; splash-resistant to 1 atm
Price: $20,100
Variations: various dial colors; 41 mm diameter case

Type 9 Grey

Movement: automatic, ROCS 3.5 (modified ETA 2824-2 caliber); ø 32 mm; 47 jewels; 28,800 vph; case back for winding and time setting; 20 gearwheels; 36-hour power reserve
Functions: hours, minutes
Case: polished titanium, ø 39 mm, height 11 mm; sapphire crystal; water-resistant to 1 atm
Band: synthetic, buckle
Price: $14,900
Variation: Aqua (blue)

Type 8 Indigo

Movement: automatic, ROCS 8.1 (Modul, base ETA 2892/2); ø 32 mm; 31 jewels; 28,800 vph; case back for winding and time setting; gear train with 20 gearwheels; 36-hour power reserve.
Functions: hours, minutes; Ressence Orbital Convex System (ROCS) peripheral minute dial with 1 rotating satellite
Case: titanium, ø 42.9 mm, height 11 mm; sapphire crystal; splash-resistant to 1 atm
Band: leather, buckle
Price: $15,000
Variations: in sage green and blue

RGM

The traditional values of hard work and persistence are alive and well in Roland Murphy, founder of RGM, one of the U.S.'s most famous and exclusive watch companies. Murphy, born in Maryland, went through the watchmaker's drill, studying at the Bowman Technical School, then in Switzerland, and finally working with Swatch before launching his own business in 1992 in Pennsylvania, which could be considered a kind of "watch valley."

The secret to his success, however, has always been to stay in touch with fundamental American values and icons. His first watch, the Signature, resurrected vintage pocket watch movements developed by Hamilton. The Railroad series today is run on restored Hamilton movements. His second big project was the Caliber 801, the first "high-grade mechanical movement made in series in America since Hamilton stopped production of the 992 B in 1969," Murphy shares with a grin. This was followed by an all-American-made watch, the Pennsylvania Tourbillon.

And so, model by model, Murphy continues to expand his "Made in U.S.A." portfolio. "You cannot compare us to the big brands," says Murphy. "We are small and specialized, the needs are different. We work directly with the customer." This may account for the brand's diversity. There are retro-themed watches, sports-themed watches (honoring baseball or chess), a diver's water-resistant to 70 atm, and the series 400 chronograph with a pulsometer and extra-large subdials for visibility.

Of late, Murphy has turned to the many crafts associated with watchmaking, notably engine-turned guilloché. The many other crafts associated with watchmaking are gradually entering his portfolio, such as cloisonné enamel motifs, Grand Feu enameling, or hand-painted images on mother of pearl. The Lady RGM is one such timepiece. It comes in a 28-millimeter case with a guilloché on mother-of-pearl dial.

These crafts can appear anywhere in RGM's collections. In 2023, for example, the Model 25 featured a stone marquetry dial depicting a tiger. In 2024, inspired by a series of outstanding prints by John James Audubon from the first half of the nineteenth century, Murphy launched a "Birds of America" series, which begins with the glossy ibis from that collection. And if these examples are not enough, RGM offers customization services.

RGM WATCH COMPANY
801 W. Main Street
Mount Joy, PA 17552
USA

TEL.:
717-653-9799

E-MAIL:
sales@rgmwatches.com

WEB:
www.rgmwatches.com

FOUNDED:
1992

NUMBER OF EMPLOYEES:
12

ANNUAL PRODUCTION:
200–300 watches

DISTRIBUTION:
RGM deals directly with customers
sales@rgmwatches.com

MOST IMPORTANT COLLECTION/PRICE RANGE:
Pennsylvania Series (completely made in the U.S.) /
range of different models $2,500 to $125,000

Model 150-B

Movement: automatic, RGM-modified Unitas caliber 6498; ø 36.6 mm, height 4.5 mm; 17 jewels; 18,000 vph; rhodium finish with perlage and côtes de Genève; up to 56-hour power reserve
Functions: hours, minutes, subsidiary seconds
Case: stainless steel, ø 42 mm, height 10.5 mm; sapphire crystal; transparent case back; water-resistant to 5 atm
Band: leather, pin buckle
Remarks: blue radiant dial
Price: $3,250
Variations: black dial

Model 25 "Birds of America"

Reference number: Model 25
Movement: automatic, RGM-modified ETA caliber 2892-A2 with solid gold in-house rotor; ø 25.6 mm; 23 jewels; 28,800 vph; rhodium finish with perlage and côtes de Genève; 56-hour power reserve
Functions: hours, minutes, sweep seconds
Case: stainless steel, ø 40 mm, height 10.4 mm; sapphire crystal; transparent case back; water-resistant to 5 atm
Band: calfskin, buckle
Remarks: miniature of ibis, reproduced from "Birds of America" plates from John James Audubon
Price: $17,900

Lady RGM

Movement: hand-wound, RGM modified ETA-Peseux 7001 caliber-Sellita caliber 300-1; ø 23.3 mm, height 2.5 mm; 17 jewels; 21,600 vph; rhodium finish with côtes de Genève; up to 56-hour power reserve
Functions: hours, minutes
Case: rose gold, ø 28 mm, height 7.7 mm; sapphire crystal; transparent case back; water-resistant to 5 atm
Band: leather, pin buckle
Remarks: guilloché on mother-of-pearl dial
Price: $13,000
Variations: dial in silver; as Pilot ($2,950)

RICHARD MILLE

Mille never stops delivering the wow to the watch world with what he calls his "race cars for the wrist." He is not an engineer, however, but rather a marketing expert who earned his first paychecks in the watch division of the French defense, automobile, and aerospace concern Matra in the early 1980s. "I have no historical relationship with watchmaking whatsoever," says Mille, "and so I have no obligations either. The mechanics of my watches are geared towards technical feasibility."

His early work was with the wizards at Audemars Piguet Renaud & Papi (APRP) in Le Locle, who would take on the Mille challenge. Audemars Piguet even tested some of those scandalous innovations—materials, technologies, functions—in a Richard Mille watch before daring to use them in its own collections (Tradition d'Excellence).

In 2007, Audemars Piguet finally became a shareholder in Richard Mille, and so the three firms are now closely bound. The assembly of the watches is done in the Franches-Montagnes region in the Jura, where Richard Mille and his partner Dominique Guenat opened the firm Horométrie around two decades ago. These days, the watch business is in the hands of daughter Amanda and son Alexandre, so that the father has more time for his racing cars.

To keep its fans happy, the brand enjoys exploring the lunatic fringe of the technically possible. A collaboration with Airbus Corporate Jets gave rise to a case made of a lightweight titanium-aluminum alloy used in turbines. The superlight and tough material called graphene, developed at the University of Manchester, also found its way to Horométrie and McLaren. Richard Mille timepieces have survived on wrists of elite athletes, like tennis star Rafael Nadal and sprinter Yohan Blake. Anything that moves really fast seems to catch Mille's eye. In a collaboration with Ferrari, his company reengineered the whole idea of watchmaking to produce a 1.75-millimeter miracle (as thick as a quarter) that is even fairly shock-resistant. Not the thinnest anymore, but still quite an achievement.

RICHARD MILLE
c/o Horométrie SA
11, rue du Jura
CH-2345 Les Breuleux
Switzerland

TEL.:
+41-32-959-4353

E-MAIL:
info@richardmille.ch

WEBSITE:
www.richardmille.com

FOUNDED:
2000

ANNUAL PRODUCTION:
approx. 4,600 watches

U.S. DISTRIBUTOR:
Richard Mille Americas
8701 Wilshire Blvd.
Beverly Hills, CA 90211
310-205-5555

Richard Mille watches are priced in Swiss francs.

RM UP-01 Ferrari

Reference number: RM UP-01
Movement: hand-wound, Richard Mille caliber RMUP-01; 41.45 x 28.85 mm, height 1.18 mm; 23 jewels; 28,800 vph; modified lever escapement; titanium mainplate and bridges; 45-hour power reserve
Functions: hours, minutes
Case: titanium, 51 mm x 39 mm, height 1.75 mm; sapphire crystal (2 sapphire crystals, 0.2 and 0.4 mm thick)
Band: rubber, pin buckle
Remarks: winding crown and selector (winding, hand-setting) placed between the back and top plate
Price: CHF 1,700,000; limited to 150 pieces

RM 65-01 Automatic Split-Seconds Chronograph

Reference number: RM 65-01 titanium
Movement: automatic, caliber RMAC4; 31.78 mm x 29.98 mm, height 8.69 mm; 51 jewels; 36,000 vph; fully skeletonized titanium mainplate and bridge; automatic declutchable rotor with adjustable inertia; 60-hour power reserve
Functions: minutes, subsidiary seconds; crown mode display; stop-seconds chronograph; date
Case: carbon composite (Carbon TPT), 44.5 mm x 50 mm, height 16.1 mm; sapphire crystal; transparent case back; crown with selector function; switchable pusher for rapid winding; water-resistant to 5 atm
Band: rubber, pin buckle
Price: CHF 313,000

RM 72-01 Lifestyle Flyback Chronograph Automatic

Reference number: RM 72-01
Movement: automatic, caliber CRMC1; 29.10 mm x 31.25 mm, height 6.05 mm; 39 jewels; 28,800 vph; completely skeletonized titanium movement and bridges; free-sprung balance wheel with variable inertia; 50-hour power reserve
Functions: hours, minutes, subsidiary seconds; crown mode display; flyback chronograph; large date
Case: titanium, 38.4 mm x 47.34 mm, height 11.68 mm; sapphire crystal; transparent case back crown with selector function; water-resistant to 5 atm
Band: rubber, pin buckle
Price: CHF 204,000
Variations: in red gold; in white or black ceramic and red gold; in black or white ceramic

RM 30-01 Automatic

Reference number: RM 30-01
Movement: automatic, caliber RMAR2; 29.45 mm x 31.25 mm, height 5.41 mm; 38 jewels; 28,800 vph; skeletonized titanium movement, 2 mainsprings, automatic declutchable rotor with adjustable inertia; 55-hour power reserve
Functions: hours, minutes, sweep seconds; power reserve indicator, rotor clutch function indicator; crown mode display; large date
Case: red gold, 42 mm x 50 mm, height 14.15 mm; sapphire crystal; transparent case back; water-resistant to 5 atm
Band: rubber, pin buckle
Price: CHF 230,000
Variations: with ceramic case

RM 67-01 Automatic Extra Thin

Reference number: RM 67-01
Movement: automatic, Richard Mille caliber CRMA6; 29.1 mm x 31.25 mm, height 3.6 mm; 25 jewels; 28,800 vph; titanium mainplate and bridges; platinum winding rotor; 50-hour power reserve
Functions: hours, minutes; crown function indicator; date
Case: white gold, 38.7 mm x 47.5 mm, height 7.75 mm; bezel and case middle set with baguette diamonds; sapphire crystal; transparent case back; water-resistant to 3 atm
Band: rubber, folding clasp
Price: CHF 693,000
Variations: without precious stones

RM 17-01 Manual Winding Tourbillon

Reference number: RM 17-01
Movement: hand-wound, Richard Mille caliber RM017; 29.45 mm x 31.25 mm, height 4.65 mm; 23 jewels; 21,600 vph; 1-minute tourbillon with ceramic capstone; skeletonized titanium mainplate; 70-hour power reserve
Functions: hours, minutes; power reserve indicator, crown function indicator
Case: red gold, 40.1 mm x 48.15 mm, height 13.08 mm; bezel with snowflake-set diamonds; sapphire crystal; transparent case back; crown with torque limiter; water-resistant to 5 atm
Band: rubber, pin buckle
Price: CHF 921,000
Variations: without precious stones

RM 037 Automatic White Gold Snow Set

Reference number: RM 037
Movement: automatic, Richard Mille caliber CRMA1; 22.9 mm x 28 mm, height 4.82 mm; 25 jewels; 28,800 vph; skeletonized movement; winding rotor with variable geometry; 50-hour power reserve
Functions: hours, minutes, crown function indicator; large date
Case: white gold, 34.4 mm x 52.2 mm, height 12.5 mm; bezel with snowflake-set diamonds; sapphire crystal; transparent case back; pusher with selector function
Band: rubber, pin buckle
Remarks: dial center set with diamonds (snowflake setting)
Price: CHF 345,000

RM 07-01 Automatic Onyx and Diamonds

Reference number: RM 07-01
Movement: automatic, Richard Mille caliber CRMA2; 22 mm x 29.9 mm, height 4.92 mm; 25 jewels; 28,800 vph; fully skeletonized and plasma-treated titanium mainplate and bridges; skeletonized red-gold rotor with adjustable inertia and winding performance; 50-hour power reserve
Functions: hours, minutes
Case: ceramic (TZP), 31.4 mm x 45.66 mm, height 11.85 mm; bezel set with diamonds; sapphire crystal; transparent case back; water-resistant to 5 atm
Band: rubber, folding clasp
Remarks: onyx dial, center set with diamonds
Price: CHF 241,000

RM 07-01 Automatic Intergalactic Bright Night

Reference number: RM 07-01
Movement: automatic, Richard Mille caliber CRMA2; 22 mm x 29.9 mm, height 4.92 mm; 25 jewels; 28,800 vph; fully skeletonized and plasma-treated titanium mainplate and bridges, balance with 4 regulating screws, skeletonized red-gold rotor with adjustable inertia and winding performance; 50-hour power reserve
Functions: hours, minutes
Case: carbon fiber (TPT), 31.4 mm x 45.66 mm, height 11.85 mm; bezel and case middle set with diamonds; sapphire crystal; transparent case back; water-resistant to 5 atm
Band: carbon fiber (TPT); folding clasp
Remarks: central dial set with diamonds
Price: CHF 241,000,
Variations: "Starry Night"; "Misty Night"; "Dark Night"

ROBOT

When brainstorming a name for a new line of watches to be produced by his company, Bohematic, entrepreneur Josef Zajíček decided to tap the Czech Republic's long and rich literary culture and call the line Robot. Few probably know that the word is originally Czech and refers to hard work. As such, it is related to the German word, which in older German meant burdensome work or tedium.

Be that as it may, the name—for the Czech people and those who know the nation's literature—will immediately recall the science fiction play *R.U.R* (it stands for Rossum's Universal Robots) by the famous writer Karel Čapek, written in 1920. In it, Čapek describes androids created by humans to serve them. And that describes what all timepieces do quite well.

Robot watches are manufactured in Nové Město nad Metují, a small town in northern Czechia that is known for several industries, including precision engineering and watchmaking. The company was founded in 2018 by Zajíček, with a design studio named Olgoj Chorchoj and a team of experienced watchmakers, designers, and craftsmen. Most of the brand's watches run on La Joux-Perret calibers.

Their inspiration is quite simply the nation's rich industrial culture. The Aerodynamic, for example, pays tribute to the Tatra 77—the world's first aerodynamically shaped mass-produced car. The Minor series is also inspired by motorsports, with one series dedicated to Brazilian racing legend Emerson Fittipaldi, who drove in both Formula One and IndyCar in the 1970s.

The latest collection is a tribute to the L-39 Albatros, a legendary Czech training jet, probably the profile of which is drawn on the dial at 9 o'clock. Launched in 1968, the Albatros was widely used by Warsaw Pact nations, and is still in use today in various iterations, including as a jet for private fliers.

But Robot has also produced elegant dress watches that are expressions of pure design for design sake, like the Ida for women, and the Aplos line, which can be worn by anyone.

ROBOT WATCH
Bohematic s.r.o.
Maiselova 2
101 00 Prague
Czech Republic

TEL.:
+420-722-977-256

E-MAIL:
info@bohematic.cz

WEBSITE:
www.robot-watch.com

FOUNDED:
2018

NUMBER OF EMPLOYEES:
16

ANNUAL PRODUCTION:
approx. 200 watches

DISTRIBUTION:
direct sales; online shop; please contact the company directly

COLLECTIONS/PRICE RANGE:
Various models / $4,000 to $10,000

Minor Emerson Fittipaldi Limited Edition

Reference number: 2001LE03
Movement: automatic, La Joux-Perret caliber LJP 8120; ø 30.4 mm, height 7.9 mm; 26 jewels; 28,800 vph; 55-hour power reserve
Functions: hours, minutes, subsidiary seconds; chronograph; date
Case: sand-blasted titanium with black PVD, ø 44 mm, height 15 mm; bidirectional bezel with 0-12 scale; sapphire crystal; transparent case back; water-resistant to 10 atm
Band: hand-made calfskin, pin buckle
Remarks: each dial hand signed by F1 and IndyCar legend Emerson Fittipaldi
Price: $6,280; limited to 100 pieces

Aerodynamic Titanium Green

Reference number: 2101ST07
Movement: manual, La Joux-Perret caliber LJP 7513; ø 33 mm, height 4.5 mm; 33 jewels; 28,800 vph; partially skeletonized movement, bridges with sunburst pattern; 192-hour power reserve
Functions: hours, minutes, subsidiary seconds; power-reserve indicator; date
Case: sand-blasted titanium, ø 39 mm, height 12.2 mm; sapphire crystal; transparent case back; water-resistant to 5 atm
Band: hand-made calfskin, pin buckle
Price: $7,190
Variations: various dial colors

Minor Bronze Aura PVD

Reference number: 2001ST05
Movement: automatic, La Joux-Perret caliber LJP 8120; ø 30.4 mm, height 7.9 mm; 26 jewels; 28,800 vph; 55-hour power reserve
Functions: hours, minutes, subsidiary seconds; chronograph; date
Case: titanium with bronze PVD, ø 44 mm, height 15 mm; bidirectional bezel, with 12 divisions; sapphire crystal; transparent case back; water-resistant to 10 atm
Band: hand-made calfskin, pin buckle
Remarks: fine perforation on dial
Price: $5,820

Albatros Silver

Reference number: 2401ST01
Movement: hand-wound, ROBOTF1S0 caliber by
La Joux-Perret caliber LJP 8120; ø 30.4 mm, height
7.9 mm; 33 jewels; 21,600 vph; 8-day power reserve
Functions: hours, minutes, subsidiary seconds; power
reserve indicator, date
Case: stainless steel, ø 44 mm, height 11.5 mm;
sapphire crystal; transparent case back; water-resistant
to 10 atm
Band: textile with leather NATO strap, pin buckle
Price: $6,730

Spectra

Reference number: 2402ST01
Movement: hand-wound, Robot caliber based on La
Joux-Perret G100; ø 25.6 mm, height 4.45; 24 jewels;
28,800 vph; 68-hour power reserve
Functions: hours, minutes, sweep second; date
Case: stainless steel, ø 39 mm, height 10.3; sapphire
crystal; water resistance 5 atm
Band: textile, pin buckle
Price: $2,500

IDA AURA

Reference number: 2301ST04
Movement: automatic, La Joux-Perret caliber G100;
ø 25.6 mm, height 4.45 mm; 24 jewels; 28,800 vph;
68-hour power reserve
Functions: hours, minutes, sweep seconds; date
Case: stainless steel, with IP DLC, ø 39 mm, height
10.5 mm; sapphire crystal; transparent case back;
water-resistant to 5 atm
Band: leather, pin buckle
Price: $3,100
Variations: various cases and dials

Graphic Analog – Silver

Reference number: 2202ST01
Movement: automatic, La Joux-Perret caliber G100;
ø 25.6 mm, height 4.45 mm; 24 jewels; 28,800 vph;
68-hour power reserve
Functions: hours, minutes, sweep seconds; date
Case: stainless steel, ø 42 mm, height 12 mm; sapphire
crystal; transparent case back; water-resistant to 5 atm
Band: textile, pin buckle
Remarks: rectangles on dial with luminous mass
Price: $4,000

Flieger Friday

Reference number: 2201PE01
Movement: automatic, La Joux-Perret caliber G100;
ø 25.6 mm, height 4.45 mm; 24 jewels; 28,800 vph;
68-hour power reserve
Functions: hours, minutes, sweep seconds
Case: stainless steel, ø 39 mm, height 10.3 mm;
sapphire crystal; transparent case back; water-resistant
to 5 atm
Band: calfskin, pin buckle
Price: $2,280; limited to 50 pieces

Graphic Sutnar Orbis

Reference number: 1901LE12
Movement: automatic, La Joux-Perret caliber G100;
ø 25.6 mm, height 4.45 mm; 24 jewels; 28,800 vph;
68-hour power reserve
Functions: hours, minutes, sweep seconds; date
Case: stainless steel, ø 42 mm, height 12 mm; sapphire
crystal; transparent case back; water-resistant to 5 atm
Band: calfskin, pin buckle
Remarks: gold electroplated hands
Price: $5,370; limited to 12 pieces

ROLEX

Essentially, the Rolex formula for success has always been "what you see is what you get"—and plenty of it. For over a century now, the company has made wristwatch history without a need for *grandes complications*, perpetual calendars, tourbillons, or exotic materials. And its output in sheer quantity is phenomenal at not quite a million watches per year. But make no mistake about it: the quality of these timepieces is legendary.

For as long as anyone can remember, this brand has held the top spot in the COSC's statistics, and year after year Rolex delivers just about half of all the official institute's successfully tested mechanical chronometer movements. The brand has also pioneered several fundamental innovations: Rolex founder Hans Wilsdorf invented the hermetically sealed Oyster case in the 1920s, which he later outfitted with a screwed-in crown and an automatic movement wound by rotor. Shock protection, water resistance, the antimagnetic Parachrom hairspring, and automatic winding are some of the virtues that make wearing a Rolex timepiece much more comfortable and reliable. As for movements, the automatic caliber 3255 features new materials (nickel-phosphorus), special micromanufacturing technology (LIGA) to make the pallet fork and balance wheel of the Chronergy escapement, and a barrel spring that can store up more energy than ever. Rolex also uses what it calls "Oyster" steel, an alloy of 904L steel, and puts some models on a "Jubilee" bracelet that is five links wide, giving it extra suppleness.

Rolex watches are produced in four different locations in Switzerland. Headquarters in Geneva handles final assembly and quality control and sales. All development, manufacturing, and quality control is done a few miles away in Plan-les-Ouates. Jewel-setting and dial-making are done in the Chêne-Bourg district of Geneva, and movements come from a factory in Biel/Bienne.

Meanwhile the company has built up representation in nearly one hundred countries in the world, with over thirty subsidiaries with customer service centers. The vast network also includes around four thousand watchmakers trained according to Rolex's own standards, who work in the branch offices or at the dealers themselves.

ROLEX SA
Rue François-Dussaud 3
CH-1211 Geneva 26
Switzerland

WEBSITE:
www.rolex.com

FOUNDED:
1908

NUMBER OF EMPLOYEES:
over 2,000 (estimated)

ANNUAL PRODUCTION:
approx. 1,000,000 watches (estimated)

U.S. DISTRIBUTOR:
Rolex Watch U.S.A., Inc.
650 Fifth Avenue
New York, NY 10019
212-758-7700
www.rolex.com

Oyster Perpetual GMT-Master II

Reference number: 126710GRNR
Movement: automatic, Rolex caliber 3285; ø 28.5 mm, height 6.4 mm; 31 jewels; 28,800 vph; Parachrom hairspring, Paraflex shock protection, Chronergy escapement, glucydur balance wheel with Microstella regulating bolts; 70-hour power reserve; COSC-certified chronometer
Functions: hours (crown-activated setting in 1-hour steps), minutes, sweep seconds; additional 24-hour display (2nd time zone); date
Case: stainless steel, ø 40 mm, height 13 mm; bidirectional bezel with ceramic insert, with 0-24 scale; sapphire crystal; screw-down crown; water-resistant to 10 atm
Band: Oyster stainless steel, folding clasp, with extension link
Price: $10,700
Variations: with Jubilee bracelet ($10,900)

Oyster Perpetual GMT-Master II

Reference number: 126710BLNR
Movement: automatic, Rolex caliber 3285; ø 28.5 mm, height 6.4 mm; 31 jewels; 28,800 vph; Parachrom hairspring, Paraflex shock protection, Chronergy escapement, glucydur balance wheel with Microstella regulating bolts; 70-hour power reserve; COSC-certified chronometer
Functions: hours (crown-activated setting in 1-hour steps), minutes, sweep seconds; additional 24-hour display (second time zone); date
Case: stainless steel, ø 40 mm, height 13 mm; bidirectional bezel set with ceramic insert and 24-hour scale; sapphire crystal; screw-down crown; water-resistant to 10 atm
Band: Jubilee stainless steel, folding clasp, extension link
Price: $10,900
Variations: with Oyster bracelet ($10,700)

Oyster Perpetual Deepsea

Reference number: 136668LB
Movement: automatic, Rolex caliber 3235; ø 29.1 mm; 31 jewels; 28,800 vph; Parachrom hairspring, Paraflex shock protection, Chronergy escapement, glucydur balance wheel with Microstella regulating bolts; 70-hour power reserve; COSC-certified chronometer
Functions: hours, minutes, sweep seconds; date
Case: yellow gold, ø 44 mm; unidirectional bezel with ceramic insert, with 0-60 scale; sapphire crystal; screw-down crown, helium valve; water-resistant to 390 atm
Band: Oyster yellow gold, folding clasp, with safety lock, extension link, and fine adjustment
Remarks: heaviest diver's watch, at 322 grams
Price: $54,200

Oyster Perpetual Sea-Dweller

Reference number: 126603
Movement: automatic, Rolex caliber 3235; ø 29.1 mm; 31 jewels; 28,800 vph; Parachrom hairspring, Chronergy escapement, glucydur balance wheel with Microstella regulating bolts; 70-hour power reserve; COSC-certified chronometer
Functions: hours, minutes, sweep seconds; date
Case: stainless steel, ø 43 mm, height 13.8 mm; unidirectional bezel in yellow gold with ceramic insert with 0-60 scale; sapphire crystal; screw-down crown, helium valve; water-resistant to 122 atm
Band: Oyster stainless steel with yellow gold elements, folding clasp, with safety lock, extension link, and fine adjustment
Price: $18,600
Variations: in stainless steel ($13,250)

Oyster Perpetual Submariner Date

Reference number: 126610LV
Movement: automatic, Rolex caliber 3230; ø 29.1 mm; 31 jewels; 28,800 vph; Parachrom hairspring, Paraflex shock protection, Chronergy escapement, glucydur balance wheel with Microstella regulating bolts; 70-hour power reserve; COSC-certified chronometer
Functions: hours, minutes, sweep seconds; date
Case: stainless steel, ø 41 mm, height 12.5 mm; unidirectional bezel with ceramic insert, with 0-60 scale; sapphire crystal; screw-down crown; water-resistant to 30 atm
Band: Oyster stainless steel, folding clasp, with extension link
Price: $10,800
Variations: in white gold ($43,700) with blue Cerachrom bezel

Oyster Perpetual Submariner

Reference number: 124060
Movement: automatic, Rolex caliber 3230; ø 29.1 mm; 31 jewels; 28,800 vph; Parachrom hairspring, Paraflex shock protection, Chronergy escapement, glucydur balance wheel with Microstella regulating bolts; 70-hour power reserve; COSC-certified chronometer
Functions: hours, minutes, sweep seconds
Case: stainless steel, ø 41 mm, height 12.5 mm; unidirectional bezel with ceramic insert, with 0-60 scale; sapphire crystal; screw-down crown; water-resistant to 30 atm
Band: Oyster stainless steel, folding clasp, with extension link
Price: $9,100

Oyster Perpetual Cosmograph Daytona

Reference number: 126506
Movement: automatic, Rolex caliber 4131; ø 30.5 mm, height 6.5 mm; 44 jewels; 28,800 vph; Parachrom hairspring, Paraflex shock protection, Chronergy escapement; 72-hour power reserve; COSC-certified chronometer
Functions: hours, minutes, subsidiary seconds; chronograph
Case: platinum, ø 40 mm, height 12.8 mm; Cerachrom bezel; sapphire crystal; transparent case back; screw-down crown and pushers; water-resistant to 10 atm
Band: Oyster platinum, folding clasp, with safety lock, with extension link
Price: $77,800
Variations: with diamond dial ($84,100)

Oyster Perpetual Cosmograph Daytona

Reference number: 126500LN
Movement: automatic, Rolex caliber 4131; ø 30.5 mm, height 6.5 mm; 44 jewels; 28,800 vph; Parachrom hairspring, Paraflex shock protection, Chronergy escapement; 72-hour power reserve; COSC-certified chronometer
Functions: hours, minutes, subsidiary seconds; chronograph
Case: stainless steel, ø 40 mm, height 12.8 mm; Cerachrom bezel; sapphire crystal; screw-down crown and pushers; water-resistant to 10 atm
Band: Oyster stainless steel, folding clasp, with safety lock and extension link
Price: $15,100
Variations: with black dial

Oyster Perpetual Cosmograph Daytona

Reference number: 126515LN
Movement: automatic, Rolex caliber 4131; ø 30.5 mm, height 6.5 mm; 44 jewels; 28,800 vph; Parachrom hairspring, Paraflex shock protection, Chronergy escapement; 72-hour power reserve; COSC-certified chronometer
Functions: hours, minutes, subsidiary seconds; chronograph
Case: rose gold (Everose), ø 40 mm, height 12.8 mm; Cerachrom bezel; sapphire crystal; screw-down crown and pushers; water-resistant to 10 atm
Band: rubber Oysterflex, folding clasp, with fine adjustment
Price: $33,500
Variations: in white gold ($33,500)

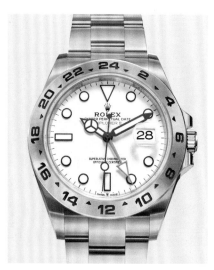

Oyster Perpetual Explorer II

Reference number: 226570
Movement: automatic, Rolex caliber 3285; ø 28.5 mm; 31 jewels; 28,800 vph; Parachrom hairspring, Paraflex shock protection, Chronergy escapement, glucydur balance wheel with Microstella regulating bolts; 70-hour power reserve; COSC-certified chronometer
Functions: hours (crown-activated setting in 1-hour steps), minutes, sweep seconds; additional 24-hour display (second time zone); date
Case: stainless steel, ø 42 mm; sapphire crystal; screw-down crown; water-resistant to 10 atm
Band: Oyster stainless steel, folding clasp, with extension link
Price: $9,650
Variations: with black dial

Oyster Perpetual Explorer 40

Reference number: 224270
Movement: automatic, Rolex caliber 3230; ø 29.1 mm; 31 jewels; 28,800 vph; Parachrom hairspring, Paraflex shock protection, Chronergy escapement, glucydur balance wheel with Microstella regulating bolts; 70-hour power reserve; COSC-certified chronometer
Functions: hours, minutes, sweep seconds
Case: stainless steel, ø 40 mm; sapphire crystal; screw-down crown; water-resistant to 10 atm
Band: Oyster stainless steel, folding clasp, with extension link
Price: $7,700

Oyster Perpetual Air-King

Reference number: 126900
Movement: automatic, Rolex caliber 3230; ø 28.5 mm; 31 jewels; 28,800 vph; Parachrom hairspring, Paraflex shock protection, Chronergy escapement, glucydur balance wheel with Microstella regulating bolts; 70-hour power reserve; COSC-certified chronometer
Functions: hours, minutes, sweep seconds
Case: stainless steel, ø 40 mm, height 11.6 mm; sapphire crystal; screw-down crown; water-resistant to 10 atm
Band: Oyster stainless steel, folding clasp, with safety lock, with extension link
Price: $7,450

Oyster Perpetual Sky-Dweller

Reference number: 336935
Movement: automatic, Rolex caliber 9002; ø 33 mm, height 8 mm; 40 jewels; 28,800 vph; Parachrom hairspring, Paraflex shock protection, glucydur balance wheel with Microstella regulating bolts; 72-hour power reserve; COSC-certified chronometer
Functions: hours, minutes, sweep seconds; additional 24-hour display (second time zone); annual calendar with date, month
Case: rose gold (Everose), ø 42 mm, height 14.1 mm; bidirectional bezel to control the functions; sapphire crystal; screw-down crown; water-resistant to 10 atm
Band: rose gold (Everose) Jubilee, folding clasp with fine adjustment
Price: $54,000
Variations: in yellow gold ($51,000)

Oyster Perpetual Yacht-Master 42

Reference number: 226658
Movement: automatic, Rolex caliber 3235; ø 29.1 mm, height 6 mm; 31 jewels; 28,800 vph; Parachrom hairspring, Paraflex shock protection, Chronergy escapement; 48-hour power reserve; COSC-certified chronometer
Functions: hours, minutes, sweep seconds; date
Case: yellow gold, ø 42 mm, height 11.9 mm; bidirectional bezel set with ceramic insert with 0-60 scale; sapphire crystal; screw-down crown; water-resistant to 10 atm
Band: Oysterflex rubber, folding clasp, with safety lock and fine adjustment
Price: $30,300

Oyster Perpetual Yacht-Master 42

Reference number: 226627
Movement: automatic, Rolex caliber 3235; ø 29.1 mm, height 6 mm; 31 jewels; 28,800 vph; Parachrom hairspring, Paraflex shock protection, Chronergy escapement; 48-hour power reserve; COSC-certified chronometer
Functions: hours, minutes, sweep seconds; date
Case: titanium RLX, ø 42 mm, height 11.9 mm; bidirectional bezel set with ceramic insert with 0-60 scale; sapphire crystal; screw-down crown; water-resistant to 10 atm
Band: titanium RLX, folding clasp, with fine adjustment
Price: $14,050

Oyster Perpetual Datejust 41

Reference number: 126300
Movement: automatic, Rolex caliber 3235; ø 29.1 mm;
31 jewels; 28,800 vph; Parachrom hairspring, Paraflex
shock protection, Chronergy escapement, glucydur
balance wheel with Microstella regulating bolts; 70-hour
power reserve; COSC-certified chronometer
Functions: hours, minutes, sweep seconds; date
Case: stainless steel, ø 41 mm, height 11.6 mm; sapphire
crystal; screw-down crown; water-resistant to 10 atm
Band: Jubilee stainless steel, folding clasp, with
extension link
Price: $8,300

Oyster Perpetual Datejust 41

Reference number: 126333
Movement: automatic, Rolex caliber 3235; ø 29.1 mm;
31 jewels; 28,800 vph; Parachrom hairspring, Paraflex
shock protection, Chronergy escapement, glucydur
balance wheel with Microstella regulating bolts; 70-hour
power reserve; COSC-certified chronometer
Functions: hours, minutes, sweep seconds; date
Case: stainless steel, ø 41 mm, height 11.6 mm; yellow-
gold bezel and crown; sapphire crystal; screw-down
crown; water-resistant to 10 atm
Band: Jubilee stainless steel with yellow-gold elements,
folding clasp, with extension link
Price: $14,750

Oyster Perpetual Day-Date 40

Reference number: 228235
Movement: automatic, Rolex caliber 3255; ø 29.1 mm,
height 5.4 mm; 31 jewels; 28,800 vph; Parachrom
hairspring, Paraflex shock protection, Chronergy
escapement, glucydur balance wheel with Microstella
regulating bolts; 70-hour power reserve; COSC-certified
chronometer
Functions: hours, minutes, sweep seconds; date and
weekday
Case: rose gold (Everose), ø 40 mm, height 11.6 mm;
sapphire crystal; screw-down crown; water-resistant
to 10 atm
Band: rose gold (Everose) President bracelet, hidden
folding clasp
Remarks: "ombré" dial with color gradient
Price: $43,200
Variations: in white or yellow gold

Perpetual 1908

Reference number: 52508
Movement: automatic, Rolex caliber 7140; ø 28.5 mm,
height 4.05 mm; 38 jewels; 28,800 vph; Syloxi-
hairspring, Paraflex shock protection, Chronergy
escapement; 66-hour power reserve; COSC-certified
chronometer
Functions: hours, minutes, subsidiary seconds
Case: yellow gold, ø 39 mm, height 9.5 mm; sapphire
crystal; transparent case back; water-resistant to 5 atm
Band: reptile skin, double folding clasp
Price: $23,000
Variations: with black dial

Perpetual 1908

Reference number: 52509
Movement: automatic, Rolex caliber 7140; ø 28.5 mm,
height 4.05 mm; 38 jewels; 28,800 vph; Syloxi
hairspring, Paraflex shock protection, Chronergy
escapement; 66-hour power reserve; COSC-certified
chronometer
Functions: hours, minutes, subsidiary seconds
Case: white gold, ø 39 mm, height 9.5 mm; sapphire
crystal; transparent case back; water-resistant to 5 atm
Band: reptile skin, double folding clasp
Price: $24,200
Variations: with white dial

Perpetual 1908

Reference number: 52506
Movement: automatic, Rolex caliber 7140; ø 28.5 mm,
height 4.05 mm; 38 jewels; 28,800 vph; Syloxi
hairspring, Paraflex shock protection, Chronergy
escapement; 66-hour power reserve; COSC-certified
chronometer
Functions: hours, minutes, subsidiary seconds
Case: platinum, ø 39 mm, height 9.5 mm; sapphire
crystal; transparent case back; water-resistant to 5 atm
Band: reptile skin, double folding clasp
Remarks: dial with guilloché
Price: $30,900

Caliber 3235

Automatic; optimized Chronergy escapement, nickel-phosphorus pallet lever and escape wheel (LIGA process); single mainspring barrel, 70-hour power reserve; COSC-certified chronometer
Functions: hours, minutes, sweep seconds; date
Diameter: 28.5 mm
Height: 6 mm
Jewels: 31
Balance: glucydur with Microstella regulating bolts
Frequency: 28,800 vph
Hairspring: Parachrom-Breguet hairspring
Shock protection: Paraflex
Remarks: used in Datejust

Caliber 3255

Automatic; optimized Chronergy escapement, nickel-phosphorus pallet lever and escape wheel (LIGA process); single mainspring barrel, 70-hour power reserve; COSC-certified chronometer
Functions: hours, minutes, sweep seconds; date and weekday
Diameter: 29.1 mm
Height: 5.4 mm
Jewels: 31
Balance: glucydur with Microstella regulating bolts
Frequency: 28,800 vph
Hairspring: Parachrom-Breguet hairspring
Shock protection: Paraflex
Remarks: used in Day-Date 40 also in Day-Date 36 models

Caliber 4131

Automatic; optimized Chronergy escapement, nickel-phosphorus pallet lever and escape wheel (LIGA process); single mainspring barrel, 72-hour power reserve; COSC-certified chronometer
Functions: hours, minutes, subsidiary seconds; chronograph
Diameter: 30.5 mm
Height: 6.5 mm
Jewels: 44
Balance: glucydur with Microstella regulating bolts
Frequency: 28,800 vph
Hairspring: Parachrom-Breguet hairspring
Shock protection: Paraflex
Remarks: used in Daytona model

Caliber 4161

Automatic; single mainspring barrel, 72-hour power reserve; COSC-certified chronometer
Base caliber: caliber 4130
Functions: hours, minutes, subsidiary seconds; programmable regatta countdown with memory
Diameter: 31.2 mm
Height: 8.05 mm
Jewels: 42
Balance: glucydur with Microstella regulating bolts
Frequency: 28,800 vph
Hairspring: Parachrom-Breguet hairspring
Shock protection: Kif
Remarks: used in Yacht-Master II model

Caliber 7140

Automatic; optimized Chronergy escapement, nickel-phosphorus pallet lever and escape wheel (LIGA process); single mainspring barrel, 66-hour power reserve; COSC-certified chronometer
Functions: hours, minutes, subsidiary seconds
Diameter: 28.5 mm
Height: 4.05 mm
Jewels: 38
Balance: glucydur with Microstella regulating bolts
Frequency: 28,800 vph
Hairspring: Parachrom hairspring
Shock protection: Paraflex
Remarks: used in Perpetual 1908 model

Caliber 9002

Automatic; optimized Chronergy escapement, nickel-phosphorus pallet lever and escape wheel (LIGA process); single mainspring barrel, 72-hour power reserve; COSC-certified chronometer
Functions: hours, minutes, sweep seconds; additional 24-hour display (second time zone); annual calendar with date, month
Diameter: 33 mm
Height: 8 mm
Jewels: 40
Balance: glucydur with Microstella regulating bolts
Frequency: 28,800 vph
Hairspring: Parachrom-Breguet hairspring
Shock protection: Kif
Remarks: used in Sky-Dweller model

SCHAUMBURG WATCH

If you are searching for a brand whose brand strategy is anti-brand, then Schaumburg is your brand. Frank Dilbakowski is the owner of this small watchmaking business in Rinteln, Westphalia, which has been producing very unusual timepieces at affordable prices since 1998. The name Schaumburg comes from the surrounding region. The firm has gained a reputation for high-performance timepieces for rugged sports and professional use. But expect to be surprised. The portfolio includes such pieces as the chronometer line Aquamatic, with water resistance to 1,000 meters, and the Aquatitan models, secure to 2,000 meters (200 atm). If you are into the worn-down-industrial look, there is the SteamPunk & Co. collection, with watches that really look as if they had been buried in someone's garden and have now been unearthed and cleaned up, but not restored. It is an unusual way of surfing the vintage wave.

The patinaed look should not be a deterrent, because Dilbakowski has prioritized robust and traditional watchmaking. The Rinteln workbenches produce the plates and bridges and provide all the finishing as well (perlage, engraving, skeletonizing). Some of the bracelets, cases, and dials are even manufactured in-house, but the base movements come from Switzerland and are reworked in house and even given a special ribbing.

Besides unadorned one-hand watches like the recent Squarematic Unique, which mixes 1970s-style modernity with a little rusty steampunk, the current portfolio of timepieces includes such outstanding pieces as a whole series of special moon phases, like the Lucky MooN. Dilbakowski does not only look back to industrial days. Lately, he has started using cork as a material, a tip of the hat to sustainability. By the same token, he created a watch with a fine, blued meteorite dial, also a trend these days. Bottom line: Schaumburg is a courageous brand, and one that needs a bit of boldness to invest in. But it does produce genuinely eye-catching pieces.

SCHAUMBURG WATCH
Kirchplatz 5 and 6
D-31737 Rinteln
Germany

TEL.:
+49-5751-923-351

E-MAIL:
info@schaumburgwatch.com

WEBSITE:
www.schaumburgwatch.com

FOUNDED:
1998

NUMBER OF EMPLOYEES:
9

ANNUAL PRODUCTION:
not specified

DISTRIBUTION:
Retail

U.S. DISTRIBUTOR:
Schaumburg Watch
About Time Luxury Group
210 Bellevue Avenue
Newport, RI 02840
401-846-0598
nicewatch@aol.com

MOST IMPORTANT COLLECTIONS/PRICE RANGE:
mechanical wristwatches / approx. $1,500 to $13,000

SolSequor

Reference number: SolSequor
Movement: automatic, caliber SW-11 (base MAB 88); ø 25.6 mm, height 3.6 mm; 25 jewels; 28,800 vph; perlage on movement, côtes de Genève on the rotor; 42-hour power reserve
Functions: hours, minutes; date; sunrise and sunset display
Case: stainless steel, ø 43 mm, height 12.5 mm; sapphire crystal; transparent case back; water-resistant to 5 atm
Band: calfskin, buckle
Remarks: thermally-patinated hands, cams, and dial
Price: $6,700

Natural Wonders Meteorite

Reference number: Natural Wonders Meteorite
Movement: hand-wound, caliber SW-07.1 (modified Unitas 6498); ø 36.6 mm, height 4.5 mm; 17 jewels; 18,000 vph; Schaumburg three-quarter plate and Schaumburg ribbing; extensively skeletonized and decorated dial and movement; 46-hour power reserve
Functions: hours (5-minute indices)
Case: stainless steel, ø 42 mm, height 10 mm; sapphire crystal; transparent case back, water-resistant to 5 atm
Band: vegan cork, pin buckle
Remarks: thermally colored meteorite dial with Widmanstätten pattern
Price: $2,700

Lucky MooN

Reference number: Lucky MooN
Movement: automatic, SW-20ALM Chronoflex; ø 25.6 mm, height 4.6 mm; 26 jewels; 28,800 vph; Etachron balance, Nivarox hairspring and mainspring; 42-hour power reserve
Functions: hours, minutes; sweep seconds, moon phase
Case: stainless steel, ø 41 mm, height 10.5 mm; sapphire crystal; water-resistant to 5 atm
Band: vegan cork, pin buckle
Price: $1,890

SCHWARZ ETIENNE

When Raffaello Radicchi, who hails from Perugia, Italy, spoke about his business, he describes it as if it were a little shop. Ask him why he went into watchmaking, he answers, "I was allergic to metal and could only wear a gold watch." Subtext: He could not afford a gold watch, so he founded a watch company.

Radicchi was a genuine maverick and a lone figure in this somewhat hermetic industry. He arrived in Switzerland at eighteen and worked as a mason. He retrained as a carpenter and started buying and renovating homes, and soon he was earning some serious money. In the early aughts, an acquaintance bought up a watch brand in La Chaux-de-Fonds and suggested that Radicchi buy the building that came with it. The brand, once a big name in the industry and a supplier of movements (to Chanel, among others), had originally been founded by Paul Schwarz and Olga Etienne.

By 2008, Radicchi owned the whole package. He understood that the company needed independence to survive. Having many outstanding local suppliers to partner with was a good start. But Schwarz Etienne needed movements, so the company set out to make their own, and by 2015 it had three. These calibers now drive the company's watches, including a tourbillon, that are classical in look, yet very modern-technical, thanks to the inverted movement construction that puts the off-center microrotor on the dial. They've recently started appearing in the watches of other brands as well, notably Ming.

For all its traditionalism, the brand still maintains a feeling of youthful creativity with a lot of good and bold humor rarely found in the industry. The Roswell's case, for example, is shaped like a comic-book UFO. And for all its classic layout, the dial of the Roma series can sometimes become asymmetrical, like the 2023 Geometry series (designed by Eric Giroux) exhibiting four dial quadrants that all seem to clash with each other. Success these days also means being redone via a collaboration with Label Noir as a black-themed watch, which is what happened to the technically complex Petite Seconde Rétrograde Tourbillon.

SCHWARZ ETIENNE SA
Boulevard des Éplatures 16
2300 La Chaux-de-Fonds
Switzerland

TEL.:
+41-32-967-9420

E-MAIL:
info@schwarz-etienne.ch

WEBSITE:
www.schwarz-etienne.com

FOUNDED:
1902

NUMBER OF EMPLOYEES:
22
Annual production:
300 to 500

DISTRIBUTION:
Contact company for information.
Retailers in the USA
Esperluxe – Boston, MA
Exquisite Timepieces – Naples, FL
Goldsmith Complications – Delray, FL
Manfredi Jewels – Greenwich, CT
Oster Jewelers – Denver, CO
Rostovsky Watches – Beverly Hills, CA
Retailers in Canada
Kaufmann de Suisse – Montreal

MOST IMPORTANT COLLECTIONS:
La Chaux-de-Fonds, Fiji, Geometry, Roma, Roswell, special editions

Geometry Cherry

Reference number: WROGEOMA67SSVEBCLTD
Movement: automatic, Schwarz Etienne caliber ASE 200.02 with micro-rotor; finely finished movement; ø 30.40 mm, height 5.35 mm; 33 jewels; 21,600 vph; 86-hour power reserve
Functions: hours, minutes, subsidiary seconds
Case: stainless steel, ø 39 mm, height 11 mm; sapphire crystal; water-resistant to 5 atm
Band: calfskin, triple folding clasp
Remarks: gold dial with cherry red coloring, with asymmetric sections with clous de Paris and guilloché decoration
Price: $25,140; limited to 50 pieces
Variations: grey and blue dial

Label Noir x Schwarz Etienne

Movement: automatic, Schwarz Etienne caliber TSE PSR 122.00; ø 30.40 mm, height 7.05 mm; 40 jewels; 21,600 vph; 1-minute flying tourbillon; specially blackened bridges and dial (with côtes de Genève); inverted movement design with micro-rotor on dial side: 72 hour power reserve
Functions: off-center hours, minutes, subsidiary seconds (retrograde)
Case: stainless steel, ø 44 mm, height 13.70 mm; sapphire crystal; transparent case back; water-resistant to 5 atm
Band: textile, folding clasp
Remarks: original Schwarz-Etienne model entirely reworked in a sleek modern black style, including black Super-LumiNova on the hands
Price: on request; unique piece
Variations: original in red-gold case ($90,000)

Fiji

Reference number: WFI04MA01RBW01-A
Movement: automatic, Schwarz Etienne Caliber ASE 200.00 with micro-rotor; ø 30.40 mm, height 5.35 mm; 33 jewels; 21,600 vph; 86-hour power reserve
Functions: hours, minutes, subsidiary seconds as animated floral display
Case: red gold, ø 38 mm, height 10.76 mm; red gold crown; sapphire crystal; water-resistant to 5 atm
Band: calfskin, pin buckle with gold treatment
Remarks: case set with 512 diamonds, dial with 236, comes with second buckle set with 54 diamonds
Price: $63,420
Variations: black dial

SEIKO

Seiko is definitely among the great enterprises dominating the universe of watches, and it has reached that spot by what business people call innovation, i.e, by keeping a hand on the pulse of the zeitgeist and producing quality. Founder Kintaro Hattori had it right when he distilled his strategy into a single phrase: "Always be one step ahead of the others." Accordingly, Seiko's history is dotted with major milestones. There is the first quartz wristwatch in 1969 and the market launch of the "Spring Drive" technology in 1999. The robust sports watches in the Prospex collection, which Seiko offers in many variations, have always enjoyed great popularity, delighting not only sports fans with their precision and reliability.

Key to the quality is in-house production of everything, from caliber development to the production of parts and the assembly of all components. Seiko diving watches have now been around for almost 60 years and have evolved from the first titanium case for diving to the invention of the "accordion" bracelet and the single-shell construction of the case with shock protection. The company introduced many important innovations and actively contributed to the DIN standard for diving watches.

Exactly 100 years ago, the first wristwatch was launched on the market under the Seiko name, and naturally the anniversary is being celebrated with many new products. The Japanese aesthetic is particularly evident in the Presage collection, with its handcrafted dials made of porcelain or enamel. They combine traditional craftsmanship with the nation's outstanding industrial expertise in the manufacture of mechanical watches.

Seiko recently breathed new life into another collection. The King Seiko line has its origins in the 1950s. At that time, Seiko decided to introduce a brand within the brand that focused on the production of high-quality and particularly precise watches. An internal competition was organized with the clear objective of creating the world's best watch. And so, in addition to Grand Seiko (now an independent brand), King Seiko was created as a collection for the highest demands.

SEIKO HOLDINGS
Ginza, Chuo, Tokyo
Japan

WEBSITE:
www.seikowatches.com

FOUNDED:
1881

U.S. DISTRIBUTOR:
Seiko Corporation of America
1111 MacArthur Boulevard
Mahwah, NJ 07430
201-529-5730
custserv@seikousa.com
www.seikousa.com

MOST IMPORTANT COLLECTIONS/PRICE RANGE:
Astron / approx. $1,850 to $3,400; Presage / approx. $425 to $4,500; Prospex / approx. $395 to $6,000

Prospex 1965 Heritage Diver's
Reference number: SPB453J1
Movement: automatic, Seiko caliber 6R55; ø 27.4 mm, height 4.95 mm; 24 jewels; 21,600 vph; 72-hour power reserve
Functions: hours, minutes, sweep seconds; date
Case: stainless steel (super hard-coated), ø 40 mm, height 13 mm; unidirectional bezel, with 0-60 scale; sapphire crystal; screw-down crown; water-resistant to 30 atm
Band: stainless steel (super hard-coated), folding clasp, with safety lock, with extension link
Price: $1,300

Presage Classic
Reference number: SPB463J1
Movement: automatic, Seiko caliber 6R55; ø 27.4 mm, height 4.95 mm; 24 jewels; 21,600 vph; 72-hour power reserve
Functions: hours, minutes, sweep seconds; date
Case: stainless steel (super hard-coated), ø 40.2 mm, height 13 mm; sapphire crystal; transparent case back; water-resistant to 10 atm
Band: stainless steel (super hard-coated), folding clasp
Price: $1,000

King Seiko KS1969
Reference number: SJE109J1
Movement: automatic, Seiko caliber 6L35; ø 25.6 mm, height 3.7 mm; 26 jewels; 28,800 vph; 45-hour power reserve
Functions: hours, minutes, sweep seconds; date
Case: stainless steel, ø 39.4 mm, height 9.9 mm; sapphire crystal; water-resistant to 5 atm
Band: stainless steel, double folding clasp
Price: $3,100

Prospex 1965 Marinemaster Heritage Diver's

Reference number: SJE099J1
Movement: automatic, Seiko caliber 6L37 (6L35 base); ø 25.6 mm, height 3.7 mm; 26 jewels; 28,800 vph; 45-hour power reserve
Functions: hours, minutes, sweep seconds; date
Case: stainless steel, (super-hard coated), ø 39.5 mm, height 12.3 mm; unidirectional bezel, with 0-60 scale; sapphire crystal; transparent case back; screw-down crown; water-resistant to 20 atm
Band: stainless steel (super hard-coated), folding clasp, with safety lock, with extension link
Remarks: modern reinterpretation of the first diver from 1965
Price: $2,800

Seiko Prospex Speedtimer Automatic Chronograph

Reference number: SRQ047J1
Movement: automatic, Seiko caliber 8R48; ø 28.6 mm, height 7.5 mm; 34 jewels; 28,800 vph; 45-hour power reserve
Functions: hours, minutes, subsidiary seconds; chronograph; date
Case: stainless steel (super hard-coated), ø 42 mm, height 14.6 mm; sapphire crystal; water-resistant to 10 atm
Band: stainless steel (super hard-coated), folding clasp
Price: $2,500

Presage Cocktail Time GMT

Reference number: SSK041J1
Movement: automatic, Seiko caliber 4R34; ø 27.4 mm, height 5 mm; 24 jewels; 21,600 vph; antimagnetic to 4800 A/m; 41-hour power reserve
Functions: hours, minutes, sweep seconds; additional 24-hour display (second time zone); date
Case: stainless steel, ø 40.5 mm, height 12.8 mm; acrylic glass; transparent case back; water-resistant to 5 atm
Band: calfskin, folding clasp
Price: $595

Presage Craftmanship Series "Urushi" GMT

Reference number: SPB447J1
Movement: automatic, Seiko caliber 6R54; ø 27.4 mm, height 5.3 mm; 24 jewels; 21,600 vph; 72-hour power reserve
Functions: hours, minutes, sweep seconds; additional 24-hour display (second time zone); date
Case: stainless steel (super hard-coated), ø 40.2 mm, height 12.4 mm; sapphire crystal; transparent case back; water-resistant to 10 atm
Band: calfskin, folding clasp
Remarks: dial with Japanese urushi lacquer
Price: $1,750

Astron GPS Solar

Reference number: SSJ013J1
Movement: quartz, Seiko caliber 3X62; solar cell on the dial for power generation
Functions: hours, minutes, sweep seconds; power reserve indicator, airplane mode; perpetual calendar with date
Case: titanium (super hard-coated), ø 41.2 mm, height 12 mm; sapphire crystal; water-resistant to 10 atm
Band: titanium (super hard-coated), folding clasp
Price: $2,000

5 Sports SKX GMT "Sports Style"

Reference number: SSK035K1
Movement: automatic, Seiko caliber 4R34; ø 27.4 mm, height 5 mm; 24 jewels; 21,600 vph; 41-hour power reserve
Functions: hours, minutes, sweep seconds; additional 24-hour; date
Case: stainless steel, ø 42.5 mm, height 13.6 mm; bidirectional bezel, with 0-24 scale; acrylic glass; transparent case back; water-resistant to 10 atm
Band: stainless steel, folding clasp, with safety lock
Price: $470

SHANGHAI WATCH

One of China's most popular brands of watches bears the name of the country's most cosmopolitan-chic city, Shanghai, and is also one of the oldest in the country. The history of Shanghai Watch goes back to 1955.

When Mao Zedong took over China in December 1949, the country had basically been at war with itself and Japan for over 22 years. Much had changed since the end of the Qing Dynasty in 1911, except for the envisioned necessities of the population, the so-called "Three Great Things," a sewing machine, a bicycle, and a watch. The latter was especially important to run a country efficiently, be that in the military, transportation, or industrial sectors. In 1955, in a bid to end foreign dependence on watches and create a domestic industry, the government launched a competition amongst Chinese cities to start a native watch industry. Teams of watchmakers gathered about and went to work. Tianjin (now Sea-Gull) actually came first, but Shanghai took a little more time and retro-engineered a Swiss movement using Japanese and Soviet parts. Their watch, the A581, went on to become an icon: simple, functional, and quite elegant. It launched production in 1955.

The Shanghai Watch factory, a stylized image of which is used for the logo, is still manufacturing to this day in its original historic building. The design of its first watch has been upgraded to suit more modern tastes, but the functional look is still dominant. Today, they use Swiss or Chinese calibers and have even come out with an in-house movement.

To celebrate the 70th anniversary of the A581, which coincides with the 75th anniversary of the People's Republic of China, Shanghai Watch has released a special collection named Originate 1955. Other models in the portfolio include the Artistic collection that explores Chinese culture and handcrafts, like a reinterpretation of the Magpies and Prunus painting by the eighteenth-century artist Ding Liangxian. In the same collection is a tourbillon combined with a mysterious meteorite dial driven by an in-house movement.

SHANGHAI WATCHES COMPANY LTD
201, Yulin Rd.
Yangpu District
Shanghai
China

TEL.:
+86-400-821-6812

E-MAIL:
bd.shby@shwatch.cn

WEBSITE:
https://www.shwatch.cn

DATE FOUNDED:
1955

U.S. DISTRIBUTOR/RETAIL STRUCTURE:
Contact the company for information

MOST IMPORTANT COLLECTIONS/PRICE RANGE:
Originate, Metropolitan, Artistic / $500 to $5,500

Originate in 1955 Collection 70th Anniversary Limited Edition

Reference number: S5002.1801.014.08
Movement: automatic, (Sea-Gull caliber ST2130), ø 26 mm, height 4.8 mm; 28 jewels; 28,800 vph; 42-hour power reserve
Functions: hours, minutes, sweep seconds; date
Case: stainless steel, ø 39 mm, height 10.95 mm; sapphire crystal; 70th anniversary signature on case back; screw-in crown; water-resistant to 5 atm
Band: stainless steel, folding clasp, plus a canvas strap
Remarks: replica of the first Shanghai watch made by the People's Republic of China in 1955
Price: $680; limited to 700 pieces

Magpies and Prunus

Reference number: S1001.1404.031.09
Movement: automatic, Sellita SW300 caliber; ø 25.6 mm, height 4.6 mm; 25 jewels; 28,800 vph; hacking seconds; 56-hour power reserve
Functions: hours, minutes
Case: stainless steel with PVD rose gold, ø 36 mm, height 10.05 mm; sapphire crystal; transparent; screw-in crown; water-resistant to 5 atm
Band: leather, pin buckle
Remarks: red mother of pearl with gold carving
Price: $3,000
Variations: with black or white mother-of-pearl dial

Galactic Tourbillon Meteorite Watch

Reference number: S1300.6844.122.18
Movement: manual winding movement, Shanghai caliber F3B; ø 33 mm, height 5.6 mm; 30 jewels; 28,800 vph; eccentric-tourbillon; 40-hour power reserve
Functions: hours, minutes, subsidiary seconds at 9 o'clock; power reserve indicator at 4 o'clock
Case: stainless steel with PVD rose gold, ø 42 mm, height 13.50 mm; sapphire crystal; transparent case back; water-resistant to 5 atm
Band: reptile skin, folding clasp
Price: $5,050

SINN

Pilot and flight instructor Helmut Sinn began manufacturing watches in Frankfurt am Main because he thought the pilot's watches on the market were too expensive. The resulting combination of top quality, functionality, and a good price-performance ratio turned out to be an excellent sales argument. There is hardly another source that offers watch lovers such a sophisticated and reasonable collection of sporty watches, many conceived to survive in extreme conditions by conforming to German DIN industrial norms.

The company remains in Frankfurt (in the Sossenheim district) where its headquarters and manufacturing space are in a two-story building that is the pride of the brand. In 1994, Lothar Schmidt took over leadership, and his product developers began looking for inspiration in other industries and the sciences.

Special Sinn technology includes moisture-proofing cases by pumping in an inert gas like argon. Other Sinn innovations include the Diapal (a lubricant-free lever escapement), the Hydro (an oil-filled diver's watch), and tegiment processing (for hardened steel and titanium surfaces). The latest innovation is a patent-pending alloy of bronze with a sixth of gold mixed in, goldbronze 125.

Having noticed a lack of norms for aviator watches, Schmidt negotiated a partnership with the Aachen Technical University to create the *Technischer Standard Fliegeruhren* (TESTAF, or Technical Standard for Pilot's Watches), which is housed at the Eurocopter headquarters.

Sinn also joined forces with two German watch companies, the Sächsische Uhrentechnologie Glashütte (SUG) and the Uhren-Werke-Dresden (UWD). The latter produced the outstanding UWD 33.1 caliber with Sinn as chaperone.

All these moves brought the company enough wherewithal to open new headquarters in the Sossenheim district of Frankfurt. The building offers nearly 25,000 square feet of space, most of which is devoted to assembly and manufacturing. At the heart of the two-story construction is a grandiose atrium with a skylight offering lots of natural light. The roof was also turned into an open-air terrace.

SINN SPEZIALUHREN GMBH
Wilhelm-Fay-Strasse 21
D-65936 Frankfurt/Main
Germany

TEL.:
+49-69-9784-14-200

E-MAIL:
info@sinn.de

WEBSITE:
www.sinn.de

FOUNDED:
1961

NUMBER OF EMPLOYEES:
approx. 135 (at the Frankfurt location)

ANNUAL PRODUCTION:
approx. 14,000 watches

U.S. DISTRIBUTOR:
WatchBuys
888-333-4895
www.watchbuys.com

MOST IMPORTANT COLLECTIONS/PRICE RANGE:
Financial District, U-Models, Diapal / from approx.
$1,500 to $17,000

903 St HB

Reference number: 903.095
Movement: automatic, La Joux-Perret caliber L 112; ø 30.4 mm, height 7.9 mm; 26 jewels; 28,800 vph; column wheel control of chronograph functions; antimagnetic according to the German industrial norm (DIN); 60-hour power reserve
Functions: hours, minutes, subsidiary seconds; chronograph
Case: stainless steel, ø 41 mm, height 14.5 mm; bidirectional bezel, with integrated slide rule and tachymeter scale; sapphire crystal; transparent case back; screw-down crown; water-resistant to 20 atm
Band: calfskin, pin buckle
Remarks: comes with extra stainless-steel bracelet
Price: $4,170; limited to 500 pieces
Variations: with black or blue dial

903 St II

Reference number: 903.090
Movement: automatic, La Joux-Perret caliber L 110; ø 30.4 mm, height 7.9 mm; 26 jewels; 28,800 vph; column wheel control of chronograph functions; antimagnetic according to the German industrial norm (DIN); 60-hour power reserve
Functions: hours, minutes, subsidiary seconds; chronograph; date
Case: stainless steel, ø 41 mm, height 14.5 mm; bidirectional bezel, with integrated slide rule and tachymeter scale; sapphire crystal; transparent case back; screw-down crown; water-resistant to 20 atm
Band: stainless steel, folding clasp
Price: $4,160
Variations: as 903 St B E II with dark-blue dial

903 St B E II

Reference number: 903.091
Movement: automatic, La Joux-Perret caliber L 110; ø 30.4 mm, height 7.9 mm; 26 jewels; 28,800 vph; column wheel control of chronograph functions; antimagnetic according to the German industrial norm (DIN); 60-hour power reserve
Functions: hours, minutes, subsidiary seconds; chronograph; date
Case: stainless steel, ø 41 mm, height 14.5 mm; bidirectional bezel, with integrated slide rule and tachymeter scale; sapphire crystal; transparent case back; screw-down crown; water-resistant to 20 atm
Band: calfskin, pin buckle
Price: $3,780
Variations: as 903 ST II with black dial

U50 Hydro S

Reference number: 1051.020
Movement: quartz
Functions: hours, minutes, sweep seconds; date
Case: tegimented submarine steel, with black hard coating, ø 41 mm, height 11.8 mm; unidirectional bezel, with 0-60 scale; sapphire crystal; screw-down crown; water-resistant to 500 atm
Band: silicone, folding clasp, with safety lock
Remarks: completely oil-filled case, almost unlimited pressure resistance; certified according to the European diver's norm
Price: $3,510
Variations: in submarine steel without black hard coating ($3,330); in submarine steel with black-coated bezel ($3,430)

T50 GBDR

Reference number: 1052.020
Movement: automatic, Sellita caliber SW300-1; ø 25.6 mm, height 3.6 mm; 25 jewels; 28,800 vph; 42-hour power reserve
Functions: hours, minutes, sweep seconds; date
Case: titanium (bead-blasted), ø 41 mm, height 12.3 mm; unidirectional goldbronze bezel, with 0-60 scale; sapphire crystal; screw-down crown; water-resistant to 50 atm
Band: titanium, folding clasp, with extension link
Remarks: dehumidifying technology (protective gas)
Price: $4,830

T50

Reference number: 1052.010
Movement: automatic, Sellita caliber SW300-1; ø 25.6 mm, height 3.6 mm; 25 jewels; 28,800 vph; 42-hour power reserve
Functions: hours, minutes, sweep seconds; date
Case: titanium (bead-blasted), ø 41 mm, height 12.3 mm; unidirectional bezel, with 0-60 scale; sapphire crystal; screw-down crown; water-resistant to 50 atm
Band: textile, pin buckle
Remarks: dehumidifying technology (protective gas)
Price: $3,960

EZM 13.1

Reference number: 613.011
Movement: automatic, Sinn caliber SZ02 (Basis Concepto C99001); ø 30.4 mm, height 7.9 mm; 28 jewels; 28,800 vph; antimagnetic, finely finished movement; 46-hour power reserve
Functions: hours, minutes, subsidiary seconds; chronograph; date
Case: stainless steel, ø 41 mm, height 15 mm; sapphire crystal; screw-down crown; water-resistant to 50 atm
Band: stainless steel, folding clasp, with extension link
Remarks: dehumidifying technology (protective gas)
Price: $3,820
Variations: with silicone or calfskin strap ($3,570)

EZM 12

Reference number: 112.010
Movement: automatic, ETA caliber 2836-2; ø 25.6 mm, height 5.05 mm; 25 jewels; 28,800 vph; antimagnetic according to the German industrial norm (DIN); protected from magnetism to 80.000 A/m; 38-hour power reserve
Functions: hours, minutes, sweep seconds; date and weekday
Case: tegimented stainless steel, ø 44 mm, height 14 mm; bidirectional bezel, with 0-60 scale (countdown); crown-activated ring with 0-60 scale (up-counting); sapphire crystal; water-resistant to 20 atm
Band: silicone, folding clasp
Remarks: developed for the air paramedics; with pulse rotor scale; dehumidifying technology (protective gas)
Price: $4,180

104 St Sa I MG

Reference number: 104.0131
Movement: automatic, Sellita caliber SW220-1; ø 25.6 mm, height 5.05 mm; 26 jewels; 28,800 vph; antimagnetic according to the German industrial norm (DIN); 38-hour power reserve
Functions: hours, minutes, sweep seconds; date and weekday
Case: stainless steel, ø 41 mm, height 11.9 mm; bidirectional bezel, with 0-60 scale; sapphire crystal; transparent case back; screw-down crown; water-resistant to 20 atm
Band: textile, pin buckle
Price: $1,690
Variations: with blue or black dial ($1,690)

356 Flieger Klassik AS E

Reference number: 356.0202
Movement: automatic, Sellita caliber SW510;
ø 30.4 mm, height 7.9 mm; 27 jewels; 28,800 vph;
antimagnetic according to the German industrial norm
(DIN); 56-hour power reserve
Functions: hours, minutes, subsidiary seconds;
chronograph
Case: stainless steel, ø 38.5 mm, height 15.6 mm;
acrylic glass; screw-down crown; water-resistant to
10 atm
Band: calfskin, pin buckle
Price: $2,780
Variations: as a Klassik W with white dial

356 Flieger Klassik W

Reference number: 356.0201
Movement: automatic, Sellita caliber SW510;
ø 30.4 mm, height 7.9 mm; 27 jewels; 28,800 vph;
antimagnetic according to the German industrial norm
(DIN); 56-hour power reserve
Functions: hours, minutes, subsidiary seconds;
chronograph
Case: stainless steel, ø 38.5 mm, height 15.6 mm;
acrylic glass; screw-down crown; water-resistant to
10 atm
Band: stainless steel, folding clasp
Price: $3,070
Variations: with black dial; with calfskin strap ($2,780)

103 St Diapal

Reference number: 103.0616
Movement: automatic, La Joux-Perret caliber 8000;
ø 30.4 mm, height 7.9 mm; 28 jewels; 28,800 vph; oil-
free escapement (Diapal), column-wheel control of the
chronograph functions; antimagnetic according to the
German industrial norm (DIN); 46-hour power reserve
Functions: hours, minutes, subsidiary seconds;
additional 12-hour display (second time zone);
chronograph; date
Case: stainless steel, ø 41 mm, height 17.2 mm;
bidirectional bezel, with 0-60 scale; sapphire crystal;
transparent case back; crown and screw-down pushers;
water-resistant to 20 atm
Band: stainless steel, folding clasp
Remarks: dehumidifying technology (protective gas)
Price: $4,610
Variations: in titanium ($4,780)

3006 Jagduhr

Reference number: 3006.010
Movement: automatic, Concepto caliber C99002;
ø 30.4 mm, height 7.9 mm; 25 jewels; 28,800 vph;
antimagnetic according to the German industrial norm
(DIN); 46-hour power reserve
Functions: hours, minutes, subsidiary seconds;
additional 24-hour display; chronograph; date, weekday,
month, moon phase
Case: tegimented stainless steel, ø 44 mm, height
15.5 mm; sapphire crystal; transparent case back;
screw-down crown; water-resistant to 20 atm
Band: calfskin, pin buckle
Remarks: dehumidifying technology (protective gas)
Price: $5,970

910 SRS

Reference number: 910.020
Movement: automatic, ETA caliber 7750 (modified);
ø 30 mm, height 8.4 mm; 25 jewels; 28,800 vph; column
wheel control of chronograph functions; antimagnetic
according to the German industrial norm (DIN), finely
finished movement; 46-hour power reserve
Functions: hours, minutes, subsidiary seconds; flyback
chronograph; date
Case: stainless steel, ø 41.5 mm, height 15.5 mm;
sapphire crystal; transparent case back; water-resistant
to 10 atm
Band: horse leather, pin buckle
Price: $4,520

717

Reference number: 717.010
Movement: automatic, Sinn caliber SZ01 (Basis
Concepto C99001); ø 30.4 mm, height 8.5 mm;
28 jewels; 28,800 vph; sweep stopwatch second and
minute hands; 46-hour power reserve
Functions: hours, minutes, subsidiary seconds;
chronograph; date
Case: tegimented stainless steel, with black hard
coating, ø 45 mm, height 15.3 mm; sapphire crystal;
screw-down crown; water-resistant to 20 atm
Band: calfskin, pin buckle
Remarks: dehumidifying technology (protective gas)
Price: $5,860

105 St Sa UTC W

Reference number: 105.021
Movement: automatic, Sellita caliber SW330-2; ø 25.6 mm, height 4.1 mm; 25 jewels; 28,800 vph; antimagnetic according to the German industrial norm (DIN); 42-hour power reserve
Functions: hours, minutes, sweep seconds; additional 24-hour display (second time zone); date
Case: stainless steel, ø 41 mm, height 11.9 mm; bidirectional bezel, with 0-24 scale; sapphire crystal; transparent case back; screw-down crown; water-resistant to 20 atm
Band: textile, pin buckle
Price: $2,380

556 A

Reference number: 556.014
Movement: automatic, Sellita caliber SW200-1; ø 25.6 mm, height 4.6 mm; 26 jewels; 28,800 vph; antimagnetic according to the German industrial norm (DIN); 38-hour power reserve
Functions: hours, minutes, sweep seconds; date
Case: stainless steel, ø 38.5 mm, height 11 mm; sapphire crystal; transparent case back; screw-down crown; water-resistant to 20 atm
Band: calfskin, pin buckle
Price: $1,380
Variations: with red seconds hand ($1,670); with mother-of-pearl dial ($1,930)

1739 Ag B

Reference number: 1739.021
Movement: automatic, Sellita caliber SW300-1; ø 25.6 mm, height 3.6 mm; 25 jewels; 28,800 vph; 42-hour power reserve
Functions: hours, minutes
Case: stainless steel with silver alloy, ø 39 mm, height 9.1 mm; sapphire crystal; transparent case back; screw-down crown; water-resistant to 10 atm
Band: calfskin, pin buckle
Price: $2,870
Variations: without silver alloy, with silver-plated dial ($2,290); without silver alloy, with black dial ($2,290)

6068

Reference number: 6068.010
Movement: automatic, Sellita caliber SW300-1; ø 25.6 mm, height 3.6 mm; 25 jewels; 28,800 vph; antimagnetic according to the German industrial norm (DIN); 50-hour power reserve
Functions: hours, minutes, sweep seconds; date
Case: stainless steel, ø 38.5 mm, height 12 mm; crown-activated sing with 0-12 scale; sapphire crystal; transparent case back; water-resistant to 10 atm
Band: stainless steel, double folding clasp
Remarks: comes with leather strap
Price: $2,970
Variations: with blue dial

6012

Reference number: 6012.010
Movement: automatic, Sinn caliber SZ06 (ETA 7751 base); ø 30.4 mm, height 7.9 mm; 25 jewels; 28,800 vph; antimagnetic according to the German industrial norm (DIN); 42-hour power reserve
Functions: hours, minutes, subsidiary seconds; chronograph; full calendar with date, weekday, month, moon phase
Case: stainless steel, ø 41.5 mm, height 14.5 mm; sapphire crystal; transparent case back; water-resistant to 10 atm
Band: calfskin, pin buckle
Remarks: comes with extra stainless-steel bracelet
Price: $6,240

434 St GG B

Reference number: 434.032
Movement: quartz, ETA caliber E64.101; antimagnetic according to the German industrial norm (DIN)
Functions: hours, minutes, sweep seconds
Case: stainless steel, ø 34 mm, height 8 mm; bezel in yellow gold; sapphire crystal; water-resistant to 10 atm
Band: stainless steel, double folding clasp
Remarks: Q-technology (protection from electromagnetic impulses)
Price: $2,140
Variations: with black dial; with stainless steel bezel ($1,340)

SPEAKE MARIN

So many brands these days bear the name of great watchmakers from the distant past. Speake-Marin is an exception, because founder Peter Speake-Marin is very much alive but is no longer connected with his company, other than through his name and style.

This dyed-in-the-wool independent from Essex, England, moved to Le Locle, Switzerland, in 1996 to work with Renaud et Papi, at which point he set about making his own pieces. A dual-train tourbillon (the Foundation Watch) opened the door to the prestigious A.H.C.I.

Speake-Marin's watches have a strong connection to the industry's traditions. The topping tool logo suggests the expert handicraft that goes into making a watch, rather than hyper-modern CNC machines. He has also had his skilled fingers in a number of iconic timepieces, like the HM1 of MB&F, the Chapter One for Maîtres du Temps, and the Harry Winston Excenter Tourbillon.

The baton was passed to Christelle Rosnoblet in 2012—and then with more finality in 2017 when Peter Speake-Marine decided to step out completely. She had the delicate task of keeping the old fans happy while letting the brand take on a more distinct identity. The "old bottles," one might say are elements like the small seconds dial at 1:30, which also gives space to a retrograde date on the One & Two tourbillon collection. There is, too, the conical crown and the famous Piccadilly case, now remodeled. By the same token, the modernizations are hardly subtle. The company makes sure it is working with experienced partners, like the Cercle des Horlogers platform and industry stars like Eric Giroud. The Ripples dials, with their deep, lacquered engravings, show what happens when a strong wind begins blowing on traditional côtes de Genève.

In 2024, a Ripples Skeleton was released that was much thinner and therefore required the reconstruction of the movement. Speake Marin doesn't shy away from bold colors either, like minty greens, or a very Mediterranean terracotta.

Worthy of note, too, is the brand's commitment to charity work, hence this year a watch made for the TimeForArt auction organized by the Swiss Institute of New York. It depicts the Gapstow Bridge in Central Park done with miniature painting on both sides of a mother-of-pearl dial.

SPEAKE-MARIN
Avenue de Miremont 33C
1206 Geneva
Switzerland

TEL.:
+41-21-695-26-55

E-MAIL:
info@speake-marin.com

WEBSITE:
www.speake-marin.com

FOUNDED:
2002

NUMBER OF EMPLOYEES:
9

ANNUAL PRODUCTION:
400 watches

U.S. SALES:
Watches of Switzerland
844-4USAWOS
jkloiber@battalionpr.com

MOST IMPORTANT COLLECTIONS:
One & Two, Art Series, Vintage, Haute Horlogerie

Ripples Skeleton

Reference number: 604020150
Movement: automatic, SMA-07 caliber; ø 35.75 mm, height 3.25 mm; 31 jewels; 36,000 vph; tungsten micro-rotor; finely finished skeletonized movement; 52-hour power reserve
Functions: hours, minutes, subsidiary seconds
Case: stainless steel, ø 40.3 mm, height 6.3 mm; sapphire crystal; transparent case back; screw-down crown; water-resistant to 5 atm
Band: stainless steel, folding clasp with micro-adjustment
Remarks: new case design, heat-blued hands
Price: $35,000; limited to 60 pieces

One & Two Openworked Dual Time Terracotta

Reference number: 414209020
Movement: automatic, SMA02 caliber; ø 34 mm, height 6.6 mm; 36 jewels; 28,000 vph; integrated micro-rotor; openworked dial, 52-hour power reserve
Functions: hours, minutes, subsidiary seconds; 24-hour time zone with day/night indication; retrograde date
Case: titanium, ø 42 mm, height 12.35 mm; sapphire crystal; transparent case back; water-resistant to 3 bars
Band: rubber, pin buckle
Price: $36,700; limited to 28 pieces
Variations: in various color themes; in 38-mm case

Promenade in New York

Reference number: 914219550
Movement: automatic, SMA-03 caliber; ø 30 mm, height 3.9 mm; 31 jewels; 28,800 vph; micro-rotor; 52-hour power reserve
Functions: hours, minutes, subsidiary seconds
Case: titanium, ø 42 mm, height 10.05 mm; sapphire crystal; screw-down case back; water-resistant to 3 atm
Band: calfskin, pin buckle
Remarks: micropainted image of the Gapstow Bridge in Central Park on both sides of the mother-of-pearl dial
Price: unique piece made for charity auction

STOWA

When a watch brand organizes a museum for itself, it is usually with good reason. Stowa may not be the biggest fish in the horological pond, but it has been since 1927, and its products are excellent illustrations of German watchmaking culture. Stowa was founded by Walter Storz—hence the name—in Pforzheim. After the war, with the premises destroyed, Storz opened a factory in Rheinfelden on the Swiss border. Later it opened a second production facility in a suburb of Pforzheim, Engelsbrand, and in 2023, finally, moved back to Pforzheim itself.

Stowa is thus one of the few German brands to have operated without interruption since its start, albeit with a new owner as of 1990. It even managed to survive the quartz crisis of the 1970s, during which Europe was flooded with cheap watches from Asia and many traditional German watchmakers were put out of business. Storz managed to keep Stowa going, but even a quality fanatic has to pay a price during times of trouble; with huge input from his son, Werner, Storz restructured the company so that it was able to begin encasing reasonably priced quartz movements rather than being strictly an assembler of mechanical ones.

Another watchmaker, Jörg Schauer, took over the brand in 1996. Spurred on by the success of his own brand, he focused on mechanics from the very beginning. Collaboration with designer Hartmut Esslinger, the founder of Frog Design, resulted in a modern design language that is expressed above all in the Flieger collection. After twenty-five years, Jörg Schauer sold the Stowa watch brand to the Tempus Arte Group, which includes Lang & Heyne Dresden and the affiliated Uhren-Werke-Dresden (UWD) and Leinfelder Uhren in Munich. The group also holds a stake in customization specialist Blaken.

STOWA GMBH & CO. KG
Gewerbepark 16
D-75331 Engelsbrand
Germany

TEL.:
+49-7082-942630

E-MAIL:
info@stowa.com

WEBSITE:
www.stowa.com

FOUNDED:
1927

NUMBER OF EMPLOYEES:
20

ANNUAL PRODUCTION:
around 4,500 watches

DISTRIBUTION:
Direct sales; please contact the company in Germany during business hours
Note: Please check the daily euro/dollar exchange rate for accurate prices

Flieger Verus 36
Reference number: FliegerVerus36
Movement: automatic, Sellita caliber SW200-1; ø 25.6 mm, height 4.6 mm; 26 jewels; 28,800 vph; 38-hour power reserve
Functions: hours, minutes, sweep seconds
Case: stainless steel, ø 36 mm, height 11.3 mm; sapphire crystal; transparent case back; water-resistant to 5 atm
Band: calfskin, pin buckle
Price: $1,035
Variations: with date function; with movement in "top" quality ($1,175); with hand-wound movement ($1,200)

Flieger Classic 40
Reference number: FliegerKlassik40
Movement: automatic, Sellita caliber SW200-1; ø 25.6 mm, height 4.6 mm; 26 jewels; 28,800 vph; 38-hour power reserve
Functions: hours, minutes, sweep seconds
Case: stainless steel, ø 40 mm, height 10.2 mm; sapphire crystal; transparent case back; water-resistant to 5 atm
Band: calfskin, pin buckle
Price: $1,360
Variations: with hand-wound movement ($1,385); with date function

Flieger Bronze Vintage Baumuster "B" 40
Reference number: FliegerBronzeVintageBauB40
Movement: automatic, Sellita caliber SW200-1; ø 25.6 mm, height 4.6 mm; 26 jewels; 28,800 vph; 38-hour power reserve
Functions: hours, minutes, sweep seconds
Case: bronze, ø 40 mm, height 10.2 mm; sapphire crystal; transparent case back; water-resistant to 5 atm
Band: calfskin, pin buckle
Price: $1,580
Variations: with date function; with hand-wound movement ($1,600)

Marine Classic 40 Arabic

Reference number: MarineKlassik40arabisch
Movement: automatic, Sellita caliber SW200-1; ø 25.6 mm, height 4.6 mm; 26 jewels; 28,800 vph; 38-hour power reserve
Functions: hours, minutes, sweep seconds
Case: stainless steel, ø 40 mm, height 10.2 mm; sapphire crystal; transparent case back; water-resistant to 5 atm
Band: calfskin, pin buckle
Price: $930
Variations: with date function; with movement in "top" quality ($1,070); with hand-wound movement ($1,090)

Marine Original Bronze Vintage Roman

Reference number: MarineOriginalBronzeVintage
Movement: hand-wound, ETA caliber 6498-1; ø 37.2 mm, height 4.5 mm; 17 jewels; 18,000 vph; screw balance, swan-neck fine adjustment, côtes de Genève, blued screws; 46-hour power reserve
Functions: hours, minutes, subsidiary seconds
Case: bronze, ø 41 mm, height 12.1 mm; sapphire crystal; transparent case back; water-resistant to 5 atm
Band: calfskin, pin buckle
Price: $1,950
Variations: with Arabic numerals

Antea Classic KS

Reference number: AnteaKlassikKS
Movement: hand-wound, ETA caliber 7001; ø 23.8 mm, height 2.5 mm; 17 jewels; 21,600 vph; 38-hour power reserve
Functions: hours, minutes, subsidiary seconds
Case: stainless steel, ø 35.5 mm, height 6.9 mm; sapphire crystal; transparent case back; water-resistant to 3 atm
Band: calfskin, pin buckle
Price: $1,310
Variations: with stainless-steel milanaise bracelet ($1,390)

Tempora Big Eye Black

Reference number: TemporaBigEyeschwarz
Movement: automatic, Sellita caliber SW510; ø 30 mm, height 7.9 mm; 27 jewels; 28,800 vph; 56-hour power reserve
Functions: hours, minutes, subsidiary seconds; chronograph; date
Case: stainless steel with black coating, ø 44 mm, height 16 mm; sapphire crystal; water-resistant to 10 atm
Band: calfskin, folding clasp
Price: $3,260
Variations: in various colors

Partitio Klassik Black

Reference number: PartitioKlassikschwarz
Movement: automatic, Sellita caliber SW200-1; ø 25.6 mm, height 4.6 mm; 26 jewels; 28,800 vph; 38-hour power reserve
Functions: hours, minutes, sweep seconds
Case: stainless steel, ø 37 mm, height 10.9 mm; sapphire crystal; water-resistant to 5 atm
Band: calfskin, pin buckle
Price: $975
Variations: with hand-wound movement ($1,140)

Prodiver Mauritius Limited

Reference number: ProdiverMauritiusLimited
Movement: automatic, Sellita caliber SW200-1; ø 25.6 mm, height 4.6 mm; 26 jewels; 28,800 vph; 38-hour power reserve
Functions: hours, minutes, sweep seconds; date
Case: titanium, ø 42 mm, height 15.6 mm; unidirectional bezel with ceramic insert, with 0-60 scale; sapphire crystal; screw-down crown; water-resistant to 100 atm
Band: rubber, folding clasp, with safety lock
Price: $1,960

TAG HEUER

Measuring speed accurately in ever greater detail was always the goal of TAG Heuer, a company founded in 1860 in St. Imier, Switzerland, by Edouard Heuer. With this in mind, the brand strove for a number of technical milestones, including the first automatic chronograph caliber with a microrotor, created in 1969 with Hamilton-Büren, Breitling, and Dubois Dépraz. That was before Techniques d'Avant Garde (TAG), a high-tech firm, bought the company.

In 1999, TAG Heuer became part of LVMH Group and in addition to producing its own watches also later served as an extended workbench for companion brands Zenith and Hublot.

TAG Heuer has continued to break world speed records for mechanical escapements. For example, the Caliber 360 combined a standard movement with a 360,000-vph (50-Hz) chronograph mechanism able to measure hundredths of a second. And then there is the MikrotourbillonS, which features a separate chronograph escapement driven at a breakneck 360,000 vph.

TAG Heuer, now under CEO Frédéric Arnault, son of LVMH owner Bernard Arnault, is evolving along several lines. One is to re-release Heuer classics in more modern garb. The Heuer 02 manufacture caliber, for example, is a redeveloped chronograph movement. In addition to cooperations with the sports car manufacturer Porsche and the commitment to Formula 1 (with Red Bull Racing), the company relaunched a streamlined Aquaracer, a watch with a distinctive dodecagonal rotating bezel.

In 2023, TAG Heuer redesigned the classic Carrera, adding a high-domed sapphire box crystal and double flange. It was the 60th anniversary of the hit model, which has again become a chronograph trendsetter.

The new Monaco Split-Seconds Chronograph developed in collaboration with movement manufacturer Vaucher in 2023, on the other hand, was a look to the future. 2024 saw the debut of a new Monaco as a category of sports watch, which TAG Heuer intends to expand and cultivate in the coming years. The combination of *haute horlogerie* and sports watches has kept design departments on their toes, meeting a steep rise in customer demands. Head of Movement Development, Carole Forestier-Kasapi, has been working on optimizing her existing movements for some time now and consistently implements the requirements of this "new normal" in all new designs.

TAG HEUER
Branch of LVMH SA
6a, rue L.-J.-Chevrolet
CH-2300 La Chaux-de-Fonds
Switzerland

TEL.:
+41-32-919-8164

E-MAIL:
info@tagheuer.com

WEBSITE:
www.tagheuer.com

FOUNDED:
1860

NUMBER OF EMPLOYEES:
Around 2,000 internationally

ANNUAL PRODUCTION:
Est. 400,000

U.S. DISTRIBUTOR:
TAG Heuer/LVMH Watch & Jewelry USA
966 South Springfield Avenue
Springfield, NJ 07081
973-467-1890

MOST IMPORTANT COLLECTIONS/PRICE RANGE:
TAG Heuer Carrera, Monaco, Aquaracer, Formula 1, Connected, Autovia / from approx. $1,450 to $35,000

Connected Calibre E4 45 mm

Reference number: SBR8A14.BT6317
Movement: quartz, Qualcomm Snapdragon 4100+Smartwatch processor with Google's Wear-OS; 330mAh lithium-ion battery
Functions: hours, minutes, seconds (digital); world time display, pulse sensors, compass, speed; near-field communication (NFC), microphone; various micro-apps available; date
Case: stainless steel, ø 45 mm; bezel with ceramic insert; sapphire crystal; water-resistant to 5 atm
Band: silicone, folding clasp
Price: $1,450

Aquaracer Professional 200 Solargraph

Reference number: WBP1315.BA0005
Movement: quartz, TAG Heuer caliber TH50-01
Functions: hours, minutes, sweep seconds; date
Case: stainless steel, ø 34 mm, height 9.7 mm; unidirectional bezel, with 0-60 scale; sapphire crystal; screw-down crown; water-resistant to 20 atm
Band: stainless steel, folding clasp
Remarks: solar cell power supply (integrated in the dial)
Price: $2,150
Variations: various colors

Aquaracer Professional 200 Solargraph

Reference number: WBP1311.BA0005
Movement: quartz, TAG Heuer caliber TH50-01
Functions: hours, minutes, sweep seconds; date
Case: stainless steel, ø 34 mm, height 9.7 mm; unidirectional bezel, with 0-60 scale; sapphire crystal; screw-down crown; water-resistant to 20 atm
Band: stainless steel, folding clasp
Remarks: solar cell power supply (integrated in the dial)
Price: $2,150
Variations: various colors

Carrera Chronograph Dato

Reference number: CBS2211.FC6545
Movement: automatic, TAG Heuer caliber TH20-07; ø 32 mm, height 6.9 mm; 33 jewels; 28,800 vph; column-wheel control of chronograph function; 80-hour power reserve
Functions: hours, minutes; chronograph; date
Case: stainless steel, ø 39 mm, height 13.86 mm; sapphire crystal; transparent case back; water-resistant to 10 atm
Band: reptile skin, folding clasp
Price: $6,550

Carrera Chronograph Tourbillon

Reference number: CBS5011.FC6566
Movement: automatic, TAG Heuer caliber TH20-09; ø 32 mm, height 6.9 mm; 33 jewels; 28,800 vph; 1-minute tourbillon; column-wheel control of chronograph function; 65-hour power reserve
Functions: hours, minutes; chronograph
Case: stainless steel, ø 42 mm, height 14.33 mm; sapphire crystal; transparent case back; water-resistant to 10 atm
Band: reptile skin, folding clasp
Price: $24,050

Carrera Skipper

Reference number: CBS2241.FN8023
Movement: automatic, TAG Heuer caliber Heuer 02; ø 31 mm, height 6.9 mm; 33 jewels; 28,800 vph; 80-hour power reserve
Functions: hours, minutes, subsidiary seconds; chronograph; date
Case: rose gold, ø 39 mm, height 13.9 mm; sapphire crystal; transparent case back; water-resistant to 10 atm
Band: textile, folding clasp
Price: $21,500

Carrera Chronograph

Reference number: CBS2216.BA0041
Movement: automatic, TAG Heuer caliber Heuer 02; ø 31 mm, height 6.9 mm; 33 jewels; 28,800 vph; 80-hour power reserve
Functions: hours, minutes, subsidiary seconds; chronograph; date
Case: stainless steel, ø 39 mm, height 13.86 mm; sapphire crystal; transparent case back; water-resistant to 10 atm
Band: stainless steel, folding clasp
Price: $6,650

Carrera Skipper

Reference number: CBS2213.FN6002
Movement: automatic, TAG Heuer caliber Heuer 02; ø 31 mm, height 6.9 mm; 33 jewels; 28,800 vph; column-wheel control of chronograph function; 80-hour power reserve
Functions: hours, minutes, subsidiary seconds; chronograph; date
Case: stainless steel, ø 39 mm, height 13.9 mm; sapphire crystal; transparent case back; water-resistant to 10 atm
Band: textile, folding clasp
Price: $6,750

Carrera Date

Reference number: WBN2350.BD0000
Movement: automatic, TAG Heuer caliber 7 (Sellita SW300 base); ø 25.6 mm, height 3.6 mm; 25 jewels; 28,800 vph; 56-hour power reserve
Functions: hours, minutes, sweep seconds; date
Case: stainless steel, ø 36 mm, height 10.2 mm; bezel in rose gold; sapphire crystal; transparent case back; crown in rose gold; water-resistant to 5 atm
Band: stainless steel with rose-gold middle links, folding clasp
Price: $4,950
Variations: various cases, straps, and dials

Monaco Split-Seconds Chronograph

Reference number: CBW2181.FC8322
Movement: automatic, TAG Heuer caliber TH81-00; 52 jewels; 36,000 vph; skeletonized rotor; 65-hour power reserve
Functions: hours, minutes, subsidiary seconds; stop-seconds chronograph
Case: titanium with black DLC, 41 mm x 41 mm, height 15.2 mm; sapphire crystal; transparent case back; water-resistant to 3 atm
Band: calfskin with textile overlay, double folding clasp
Remarks: skeletonized dial; case back of sapphire box glass
Price: $138,000

Monaco Split-Seconds Chronograph

Reference number: CBW2182.FC8339
Movement: automatic, TAG Heuer caliber TH81-00; 52 jewels; 36,000 vph; skeletonized rotor; 65-hour power reserve
Functions: hours, minutes, subsidiary seconds; stop-seconds chronograph
Case: titanium, 41 mm x 41 mm, height 15.2 mm; sapphire crystal; transparent case back; water-resistant to 3 atm
Band: calfskin with textile overlay, double folding clasp
Remarks: skeletonized dial; case back of sapphire box glass
Price: $138,000

Monaco Calibre 11

Reference number: CAW211P.FC6356
Movement: automatic, TAG Heuer caliber 11 (Sellita SW300 base with 2006 module by Dubois Dépraz); ø 30 mm, height 7.3 mm; 59 jewels; 28,800 vph
Functions: hours, minutes, subsidiary seconds; chronograph; date
Case: stainless steel, 39 mm x 39 mm, height 14.5 mm; sapphire crystal; transparent case back; water-resistant to 10 atm
Band: calfskin, folding clasp
Price: $8,100

Monza Flyback Chronometer

Reference number: CR5090.FN6001
Movement: automatic, TAG Heuer caliber Heuer 02; ø 31 mm, height 6.9 mm; 33 jewels; 28,800 vph; COSC-certified chronometer; 80-hour power reserve
Functions: hours, minutes, subsidiary seconds; flyback chronograph; date
Case: carbon composite, ø 42 mm, height 16 mm; sapphire crystal; transparent case back; screw-down crown; water-resistant to 10 atm
Band: textile, folding clasp
Price: $14,250

Formula 1 Chronograph

Reference number: CAZ201G.BA0876
Movement: automatic, TAG Heuer caliber 16 (Sellita SW500 base); ø 30.4 mm, height 7.9 mm; 25 jewels; 28,800 vph; 42-hour power reserve
Functions: hours, minutes, subsidiary seconds; chronograph; date
Case: stainless steel, ø 44 mm, height 15 mm; bezel with ceramic insert; sapphire crystal; screw-down crown; water-resistant to 20 atm
Band: stainless steel, folding clasp
Price: $3,800
Variations: various colors and strap types

Formula 1 Chronograph

Reference number: CAZ2012.BA0970
Movement: automatic, TAG Heuer caliber 16 (Sellita SW500 base); ø 30.4 mm, height 7.9 mm; 25 jewels; 28,800 vph; 42-hour power reserve
Functions: hours, minutes, subsidiary seconds; chronograph; date
Case: stainless steel, ø 44 mm, height 15 mm; bezel with ceramic insert; sapphire crystal; screw-down crown; water-resistant to 20 atm
Band: stainless steel ceramic central links, folding clasp
Price: $4,100
Variations: various colors and strap types

TEMPTION

Klaus Ulbrich is something of a grand seigneur of the German watch design scene. Since he laid the cornerstones of his watch brand Temption in 1996, he has seen numerous fashion trends come and go. Ulbrich is an engineer with special training in the construction of watches and movements, and right from the start, he intended to develop timekeepers that were modern in their aesthetics but not subject to the whims of zeitgeist. The design behind all Temption models is inspired by two contrasting stylistic movements: the modernist design codes of the Irish architect Eileen Gray (1878–1976) and the fascinating Japanese concept of *wabi sabi*, the aesthetics of passing time and its impact on the world we create.

Ulbrich sketches all the watches himself. The watches are designed, manufactured, assembled, tested, and later serviced at the company headquarters in Herrenberg, a town just to the east of the Black Forest. The vertical integration of the production facilities means that the company can also make individual parts.

Imitators of Ulbrich's design approaches did not last long in most cases, but the Temption collection remained unaffected, and classics such as the "chronograph with complication," CGK204, still exemplify what he once called the "information pyramid": the time display is in the foreground, followed by the date and the chronograph functions. The brand lettering and logo are completely irrelevant in this environment, which is why they are printed almost invisibly in glossy on matte. Incidentally, this works just as well on white dials as it does on black ones.

TEMPTION GMBH
Raistinger Str. 46
D-71083 Herrenberg
Germany

TEL.:
+49-7032-977-954

E-MAIL:
ftemption@aol.com

WEBSITE:
www.temption.info

FOUNDED:
1997

NUMBER OF EMPLOYEES:
4

ANNUAL PRODUCTION:
700 watches

U.S. DISTRIBUTOR:
Debby Gordon
3306 Arrow Creek Dr.
Granbury, TX 76049
debby@temptionusa.com
Toll-free number: 1-888-400-4293

MOST IMPORTANT COLLECTIONS/PRICE RANGE:
automatics (three-hand), GMT, chronographs, and chronographs with complications / approx. $1,900 to $3,300

CM05

Reference number: 05SST2892
Movement: automatic, Temption caliber T15.1 (Soprod A10 base (or if requested ETA 2892-A2); ø 25.6 mm, height 3.6 mm; 21 jewels; 28,800 vph; finely finished movement; 42-hour power reserve
Functions: hours, minutes, sweep seconds; date
Case: stainless steel, ø 42 mm, height 10.8 mm; sapphire crystal; transparent case back; screw-down crown; water-resistant to 10 atm
Band: stainless steel, double folding clasp, with safety lock
Price: $1,880

Chronograph CGK204 White

Reference number: 204V2316BSST
Movement: automatic, Temption caliber T18.1 (based on ETA 7751); ø 30 mm, height 7.8 mm; 25 jewels; 28,800 vph; finely finished movement; 42-hour power reserve
Functions: hours, minutes, subsidiary seconds; additional 24-hour display (2nd time zone); chronograph; full calendar with date, weekday, month, moon phase
Case: stainless steel, ø 43 mm, height 14 mm; sapphire crystal; transparent case back; screw-in crown and pushers, with coral cabochons; water-resistant to 10 atm
Band: calfskin, folding clasp
Price: $2,950
Variations: with rubber strap

Chronograph CGK205-Blau V2

Reference number: 205V2316BSST
Movement: automatic, Temption caliber T18.1 (based on ETA 7751); ø 30 mm, height 7.8 mm; 25 jewels; 28,800 vph; finely finished movement; 42-hour power reserve
Functions: hours, minutes, subsidiary seconds; additional 24-hour display; chronograph; full calendar with date, weekday, month, moon phase
Case: stainless steel, ø 43 mm, height 14 mm; sapphire crystal; transparent case back; screw-in crown and pushers, with colored cabochons; water-resistant to 10 atm
Band: calfskin, folding clasp
Remarks: comes with additional stainless steel link bracelet
Price: $3,300

TISSOT

There is Swiss-made, and then there is the Swiss Watch, as a kind of unobtrusive yet clearly defined icon you will see on many a Swiss wrist. That's a Tissot. The company was founded in 1853 in the town of Le Locle in the Jura mountains. In the century that followed, it gained international recognition for its Savonnette pocket watch. And even when the wristwatch became popular in the early twentieth century, time and again Tissot managed to attract attention to its products. To this day, the Banana Watch of 1916 and its first watches in the art deco style (1919) remain design icons of that epoch. The watchmaker has always been at the top of its technical game as well: the first antimagnetic watch (1930), the first mechanical plastic watch (Astrolon, 1971), and its touch-screen T-Touch (1999) all bear witness to Tissot's remarkable capacity for finding unusual and modern solutions.

Today, Tissot belongs to the Swatch Group and serves as the group's entry-level brand. The brand has been cultivating a sportive image of late, expanding into everything from basketball to superbike racing, from ice hockey to fencing—and water sports, of course. Partnerships with several NBA teams have been signed, notably with the Houston Rockets, Chicago Bulls, and Washington Wizards in October 2018. The chronograph Couturier line is outfitted with the new ETA chronograph caliber C01.211. This caliber features several plastic parts: another step in simplifying, and lowering the cost of, mechanical movements.

The revival of the Tissot PRX from the late seventies was a spectacular success for the brand three years ago. The PRX Powermatic exhibits the lines of the original launched in 1978, which is characterized by the stylistic unity of the watch case and bracelet and adapts them only slightly for the use of automatic movements instead of the then-fashionable (and thinner) quartz movements. In 2022, the PRX Chronograph became the flagship of the new collection, also equipped with contemporary high-performance mechanical movements, while maintaining attractive prices.

TISSOT SA
Chemin des Tourelles, 17
CH-2400 Le Locle
Switzerland

TEL.:
+41-32-933-3111

E-MAIL:
info@tissot.ch

WEBSITE:
www.tissotwatches.com

FOUNDED:
1853

U.S. DISTRIBUTOR:
Tissot
The Swatch Group (U.S.), Inc.
703 Waterford Way
Suite 450
Miami, FL 33126
www.us.tissotshop.com

MOST IMPORTANT COLLECTION/PRICE RANGE
Ballade / from $925; T-Touch / from $850; NBA Collection / from $375; Chemin des Tourelles / from $795; Seastar from $495; Swissmatic from $395

PRX Automatic Chronograph
Reference number: T137.427.11.091.00
Movement: automatic, ETA caliber A05.231; ø 30 mm, height 7.9 mm; 27 jewels; 28,800 vph; 60-hour power reserve
Functions: hours, minutes, subsidiary seconds; chronograph; date
Case: stainless steel, ø 42 mm, height 14.54 mm; sapphire crystal; transparent case back; water-resistant to 10 atm
Band: stainless steel, double folding clasp
Price: $1,895
Variations: various dial colors

PRX Automatic Chronograph
Reference number: T137.427.11.011.01
Movement: automatic, ETA caliber A05.H31; ø 30 mm, height 7.9 mm; 27 jewels; 28,800 vph; 60-hour power reserve
Functions: hours, minutes, subsidiary seconds; chronograph; date
Case: stainless steel, ø 42 mm, height 14.5 mm; sapphire crystal; transparent case back; water-resistant to 10 atm
Band: stainless steel, double folding clasp
Price: $1,895
Variations: various dial colors

PRX Powermatic 80
Reference number: T137.407.11.091.01
Movement: automatic, ETA caliber Powermatic 80 (ETA 2824-2 base); ø 25.6 mm, height 4.74 mm; 23 jewels; 21,600 vph; 80-hour power reserve
Functions: hours, minutes, sweep seconds; date
Case: stainless steel, ø 40 mm, height 10.93 mm; sapphire crystal; transparent case back; water-resistant to 10 atm
Band: stainless steel, folding clasp
Price: $725
Variations: various cases, straps, and dials

PRX Powermatic 80

Reference number: T137.407.11.051.01
Movement: automatic, ETA caliber Powermatic 80 (ETA 2824-2 base); ø 25.6 mm, height 4.74 mm; 23 jewels; 21,600 vph; 80-hour power reserve
Functions: hours, minutes, sweep seconds; date
Case: stainless steel, ø 40 mm, height 10.93 mm; sapphire crystal; transparent case back; water-resistant to 10 atm
Band: stainless steel, folding clasp
Price: $725
Variations: various cases, straps, and dials

PRX Powermatic 80

Reference number: T137.407.11.351.01
Movement: automatic, ETA caliber Powermatic 80 (ETA 2824-2 base); ø 25.6 mm, height 4.74 mm; 23 jewels; 21,600 vph; 80-hour power reserve
Functions: hours, minutes, sweep seconds; date
Case: stainless steel, ø 40 mm, height 10.93 mm; sapphire crystal; transparent case back; water-resistant to 10 atm
Band: stainless steel, folding clasp
Price: $725
Variations: various cases, straps, and dials

PR516 Mechanical Chronograph

Reference number: T149.459.21.051.00
Movement: hand-wound, ETA caliber A05.291; ø 30 mm, height 7.3 mm; 26 jewels; 28,800 vph; 60-hour power reserve
Functions: hours, minutes, subsidiary seconds; chronograph
Case: stainless steel, ø 41 mm, height 13.7 mm; sapphire crystal; transparent case back; water-resistant to 10 atm
Band: stainless steel, double folding clasp
Price: $1,850
Variations: comes with a quartz movement, in three different colors

Seastar 1000 Powermatic 80

Reference number: T120.807.11.091.00
Movement: automatic, ETA caliber Powermatic 80 (ETA 2824-2 base); ø 25.6 mm, height 4.74 mm; 23 jewels; 21,600 vph; 80-hour power reserve
Functions: hours, minutes, sweep seconds; date
Case: stainless steel, ø 40 mm, height 12.48 mm; unidirectional bezel with ceramic insert, with 0-60 scale; sapphire crystal; screw-down crown; water-resistant to 30 atm
Band: stainless steel, double folding clasp
Price: $750
Variations: with grey dial; in stainless steel with black PVD ($795)

Seastar 1000 Powermatic 80

Reference number: T120.807.11.051.00
Movement: automatic, ETA caliber Powermatic 80 (ETA 2824-2 base); ø 25.6 mm, height 4.74 mm; 23 jewels; 21,600 vph; 80-hour power reserve
Functions: hours, minutes, sweep seconds; date
Case: stainless steel, ø 40 mm, height 12.48 mm; unidirectional bezel with ceramic insert, with 0-60 scale; sapphire crystal; screw-down crown; water-resistant to 30 atm
Band: stainless steel, double folding clasp
Price: $750
Variations: with blue dial; in stainless steel with black PVD ($795)

Seastar 1000 Powermatic 80

Reference number: T120.807.33.051.00
Movement: automatic, ETA caliber Powermatic 80 (ETA 2824-2 base); ø 25.6 mm, height 4.74 mm; 23 jewels; 21,600 vph; 80-hour power reserve
Functions: hours, minutes, sweep seconds; date
Case: stainless steel with black PVD, ø 40 mm, height 12.48 mm; unidirectional bezel with ceramic insert, with 0-60 scale; sapphire crystal; screw-down crown; water-resistant to 30 atm
Band: stainless steel with black PVD, double folding clasp
Price: $795
Variations: in stainless steel ($750)

TOURBY WATCHES

In an industry and a world that tries hard to attract attention at times by fairly spectacular means, Tourby Watches has been gathering a solid following and fan club, notably in the U.S.A., by keeping everything simple and elegant. The company, which is headquartered in the town of Wetter in Westphalia, Germany, manufactures mechanical wristwatches whose design is inspired by classic models. Among its famous pieces is a pilot's watch made especially for the dangerous deployments of the Strike Fighters Weapons School Pacific, a U.S. Navy training school for fighter pilots.

The story began when Erdal Yildiz inherited a pocket watch from his grandfather. The Unitas movement inside was in need of serious revision. So, he looked around for a proper watchmaker and was soon enamored with the craft itself. The world of mechanical watches became a genuine passion during his studies. He then contacted a number of suppliers in Germany and Switzerland, and in 2007 founded his own brand. The name Tourby has nothing to do with tourbillons, which his company does not manufacture. Rather, it is Yildiz's nickname. It was short and memorable, and the domain name was still available!

All raw materials are purchased from top-notch suppliers in Germany and Switzerland. Some of the parts are ready to use on delivery; others need to be reworked in the company's own workshops in the cities of Bochum and Hagen. The cases are finished by hand, for example, as are the movements—all Swiss ETA calibers—which are extensively decorated, along with the dials, at least in part. The leather straps are stitched by hand. Final assembly, quality control, and after-sales service are all done by the company. Erdal Yildiz ensures that they are adjusted to chronometer precision (top grade).

Tourby Watches produces series, but also does made-to-order pieces. The customer can choose his or her case, dial, hands, strap, and even the movement with its decoration. Another option is skeletonization. It's a good way to get hold of a unique piece.

TOURBY WATCHES
Königstrasse 78
D-58300 Wetter an der Ruhr
Hagen in Westfalen
Germany

TEL:
+49 176 83118382

E-MAIL:
info@tourbywatches.com

WEBSITE:
www.tourbywatches.com

FOUNDED:
2007

NUMBER OF EMPLOYEES:
5

ANNUAL PRODUCTION:
500

DISTRIBUTION:
Tourby deals directly with customers

MOST IMPORTANT COLLECTIONS/PRICE RANGE:
Lawless Diver / from $1,400; Art Deco Classic / from $1,800; Ottoman / from $1,575; Planetarium / $9,000; special set

Old Military Enamel
Reference number: 1410
Movement: hand-wound, ETA caliber 6498-2; ø 37 mm, height 4.5 mm; 17 jewels, 21,600 vph, skeletonized movement, adjusted in 5 positions, côtes de Genève, double sunburst wheels, blued screws, blued swan-neck fine adjustment, 60-hour power reserve
Functions: hours, minutes, subsidiary seconds
Case: stainless steel, 40.5 mm, height 10.6 mm, vaulted sapphire crystal, transparent case back, water-resistant to 5 atm
Band: reptile skin, pin buckle
Remarks: silver dial
Price: $3,000
Variations: comes in three sizes (40, 43, and 45 mm)

Gemstone turquoise
Reference number: 8020
Movement: hand-wound, ETA caliber 6498-2; ø 37 mm, height 4.5 mm; 17 jewels, 21,600 vph, skeletonized movement, adjusted in 5 positions, côtes de Genève, double sunburst wheels, blued screws, blued swan-neck fine adjustment, 60-hour power reserve
Functions: hours, minutes
Case: stainless steel, 40.5 mm, height 10.6 mm, vaulted sapphire crystal, transparent case back, water-resistant to 5 atm
Band: reptile skin, pin buckle
Remarks: stone dial
Price: $4,000
Variations: lapis lazuli or aventurine dial

Aventurine Enamel Automatic
Reference number: 8003
Movement: automatic, ETA caliber 2824-2; ø 25.6 mm, height 4.6 mm; 25 jewels, 28,800 vph, chronometer-rated, skeletonized movement and dial, 40-hour power reserve
Functions: hours, minutes, sweep seconds
Case: stainless steel, 37 mm, height 11 mm; sapphire crystal, transparent case back, water-resistant to 10 atm
Band: reptile skin, pin buckle
Remarks: aventurine dial
Price: $3,000

Art Deco

Reference number: 2040
Movement: hand-wound, ETA caliber 6498-2; ø 37 mm, height 4.5 mm; 17 jewels, 21,600 vph, skeletonized movement, adjusted in 5 positions, côtes de Genève, double sunburst wheels, blued screws, blued swan-neck fine adjustment, 60-hour power reserve
Functions: hours, minutes, subsidiary seconds
Case: stainless steel, ø 43 mm, height 10.4 mm, arched sapphire crystal, transparent case back, water-resistant to 5 atm
Band: reptile skin, pin buckle
Remarks: silver dial
Price: $3,000
Variations: comes in three sizes (40, 43 and 45 mm)

Skeleton

Reference number: 3002
Movement: hand-wound, ETA caliber 6498-1; ø 37 mm, 17 jewels, 18,000 vph, adjusted in 5 positions, hand-engraved, blued screws, skeletonized movement, 50-hour power reserve
Functions: hours, minutes
Case: stainless steel, ø 40.5 mm, height 10.6 mm, arched sapphire crystal, transparent case back, water-resistant to 5 atm
Band: leather, pin buckle
Remarks: completely engraved by hand
Price: $4,500
Variations: different case dimensions (40, 43 and 45 mm)

Art Deco Chrono Salmon Dial

Reference number: 2500
Movement: automatic, ETA caliber 7753; ø 30 mm, 27 jewels, 28,800 vph, adjusted in 5 positions, chronometer-rated; skeletonized movement, 44-hour power reserve
Functions: hours, minutes, small second, stop-seconds, stop minutes, stop hours, date
Case: stainless steel, ø 40 mm, height 14 mm, sapphire crystal, transparent case back, water-resistant to 5 atm
Band: rubber, pin buckle
Price: $4,500
Variations: rose gold

Lawless GMT 40

Reference number: 6230
Movement: self-winding, ETA caliber 2893-2; ø 25.6 mm, 21 jewels, 28,800 vph, adjusted in 5 positions, chronometer-rated, skeletonized movement, 42-hour power reserve
Functions: hours, minutes, sweep seconds, additional 24-hour display (2nd time zone)
Case: stainless steel, ø 40 mm, height 11.8 mm, sapphire crystal, rotating bezel, water-resistant to 20 atm
Band: steel bracelet, pin buckle
Price: $2,000
Variations: black dial

Lawless Blue

Reference number: 6301
Movement: automatic, ETA caliber 2824-2; ø 25.6 mm, height 4.6 mm; 28,800 vph, chronometer-rated, skeletonized movement and dial, 40-hour power reserve
Functions: hours, minutes, sweep seconds, date
Case: stainless steel, ø 37 mm, height 11 mm, sapphire crystal, transparent case back, water-resistant to 20 atm
Band: rubber strap, pin buckle
Price: $2,500
Variations: black dial

Pilot Automatic Blue

Reference number: 1310.1
Movement: automatic, ETA caliber 2824-2; ø 25.6 mm, height 4.6 mm; 28,800 vph, chronometer-rated, skeletonized movement and dial, 40-hour power reserve
Functions: hours, minutes, sweep seconds
Case: stainless steel, ø 43 mm, height 12 mm; sapphire crystal, water-resistant to 20 atm
Band: leather, pin buckle
Price: $1,650
Variations: black dial

TOWSON WATCH COMPANY

Spencer Shattuck was thirteen when he wrote an eighth-grade thesis on watchmaking. His key source was a week-long hang-out with George Thomas and Hartwig Balke, two passionate and highly experienced watchmakers. Even though they had been close to retirement, these two men founded Towson Watch Company.

In 2020, while still a student, Shattuck bought the 25% share of Towson that had been owned by Marylander Kevin Plank, founder of the sports apparel company Under Armour. Netflix should pay attention, because this could be material for a series.

Like so many dyed-in-the-wool watchmakers, Thomas and Balke didn't market their achievements loudly. But Thomas's first tourbillon pocket watches are displayed at the National Watch and Clock Museum in Columbia, Pennsylvania. And in 1999, Balke made a chronograph, the STS-99 Mission (now simply the Mission), for a NASA astronaut. The two also restored a venerable watch belonging to Philip Melanchthon, friend and fellow traveler of Martin Luther. In 2009, Thomas was invited to open up a pocket watch belonging to President Lincoln, which revealed a secret message: "Jonathan Dillon April 13 – 1861 Fort Sumpter was attacked by the rebels on the above date. J Dillon."

Towson watches have a clear retro feel. They also pay tribute to local sites, like the Choptank or Potomac rivers, and things like Baltimore's Pride II schooner, with a case shaped like the company logo, and the Martin M-130 flying boat, with a chronograph replicating exactly the standard colors of old pilot watches.

For Spencer Shattuck the challenge has been to refresh the brand without losing its inherent charm and to make it better known to a broader public. The latest models show the way: the Cadet and Recruits connect to Baltimore's importance in naval history. The Choptank has been altered somewhat to make it less bulky, and its characteristic case has been further streamlined into a new line, the Talbot, which is a 10-millimeter thin dress watch with a wavy guilloché dial—excellent choice for a port city—that comes in two colors, a serious blue and a bright, salmony pink.

TOWSON WATCH CO.
502 Dogwood Lane
Towson, MD 21286
USA

TEL.:
410-823-1823

FAX:
410-823-8581

E-MAIL:
towsonwatchco@aol.com

WEBSITE:
www.twcwatches.com

FOUNDED:
2000

NUMBER OF EMPLOYEES:
4

ANNUAL PRODUCTION:
200 watches

DISTRIBUTION:
Retail

MOST IMPORTANT COLLECTIONS/PRICE RANGE:
Cadet and Recruit, Choptank, Martin, Mission, Pride II, Potomac, Skipjack, Talbot / $1,695 to $9,400

Talbot

Reference number: EP250
Movement: automatic, Sellita SW200-1; ø 26 mm; height 4.60 mm; 26 jewels; 28,800 vph; finely finished movement with côtes de Genève on rotor, perlage on mainplate, blued screws; 38-hour power reserve
Functions: hours, minutes, sweep second; date
Case: stainless steel; 37 mm x 33 mm; height 10 mm; sapphire crystal; transparent back with sapphire crystal; water-resistant to 5 atm
Band: stainless steel, folding clasp.
Price: $2,400; limited to 100 pieces

Talbot Pink

Movement: automatic; Sellita SW200-1-2; ø 26 mm; height 4.60 mm; 26 jewels; 28,800 vph; finely finished movement with côtes de Genève on rotor, perlage on mainplate, blued screws; 38-hour power reserve
Functions: hours, minutes, sweep second; date
Case: stainless steel; 37 mm x 33 mm; height 10 mm; sapphire crystal; transparent back with sapphire crystal; water-resistant to 5 atm
Band: stainless steel, folding clasp.
Price: $2,400; limited to 100 pieces

Choptank

Reference number: E250-2
Movement: automatic, ETA caliber 7751 Valjoux; ø 30 mm; height 7.9 mm; 25 jewels; 28,800 vph; finely decorated with côtes de Genève, blued screws and hands; day correction system; 48-hour power reserve
Functions: hours, minutes, subsidiary second; full calendar with day, weekday, sweep date; moon phase; 24-hour display; chronograph
Case: stainless steel; dimension 40 mm x 44 mm; height 13.5 mm; sapphire crystal at front; transparent screwed-down case back; water resistant to 5 atm
Band: calfskin; folding clasp
Price: $4,700; limited to 250 pieces

Half-Skelly

Reference number: HS100
Movement: hand-wound, Unitas caliber 6498; ø 36.6 mm; height 4.5 mm; 17 jewels; 18,000 vph; partially skeletonized movement, black-coated mainplate; 46-hour power reserve
Functions: hours; minute; subsidiary second
Case: stainless steel; ø 42 mm; height 10.8 mm; domed sapphire crystal; screwed transparent case back; water-resistant to 5 atm
Band: calf leather, buckle
Remarks: silver dial rings; dial and components guilloché by Jochen Benzinger
Price: $9,500
Variations: white dial; with stainless steel mesh bracelet

Martin M-130

Reference number: CC100
Movement: automatic, ETA caliber 7750 Valjoux, ø 30 mm; height 7.9 mm; 25 jewels; 28,800 vph; fine finishing with côtes de Genève; 48-hour power reserve
Functions: hours, minutes, subsidiary second, chronograph, date
Case: stainless steel, ø 42 mm, height 13.5 mm, sapphire crystal, screwed-down case back, water resistant to 5 atm
Band: leather, folding clasp
Remarks: case back with engraving of famous China Clipper flying boat from the 1930s built by the Glenn B. Miller company
Price: $3,745
Variations: stainless steel mesh bracelet ($4,250)

Mission Series 2

Reference number: MM250-2
Movement: automatic ETA caliber 7750; ø 30 mm, height 7.9 mm; 25 jewels; 28,800 vph; fine finishing with blued screws, perlage, and côtes de Genève; chronometer-grade regulation; 48-hour power reserve
Functions: hours, minutes, subsidiary seconds; chronograph with tachymeter scale; date
Case: stainless steel, ø 42 mm, height 13 mm, sapphire crystal, screwed transparent case back with sapphire crystal, water resistant to 5 atm
Band: calf leather, orange stitching, folding clasp
Price: $2,895; limited to 100 pieces

Cadet

Reference number: CR250
Movement: automatic, Sellita caliber SW200; ø 26; height 4.60 mm; 21 jewels; 28,800 vph; finely finished with côtes de Genève on rotor, perlage on mainplate, blued screws; 42-hour power reserve
Functions: hours (with inside military time track), minutes, sweep seconds; date
Case: satin-finished stainless steel; ø 41 mm; height 10.5 mm; sapphire crystal; screwed transparent back with sapphire crystal; water-resistant to 5 atm
Band: calf leather, folding clasp
Price: $1,625; limited to 250 pieces

Recruit

Reference number: CR250
Movement: automatic, Sellita caliber SW200; ø 26; height 4.60 mm; 21 jewels; 28,800 vph; finely finished with côtes de Genève on rotor, perlage on mainplate, blued screws; 42-hour power reserve
Functions: hours (with inside military time track), minutes, sweep seconds; date
Case: satin-finished stainless steel; ø 41 mm; height 10.5 mm; sapphire crystal; screwed transparent back with sapphire crystal; water-resistant to 5 atm
Band: calf leather, folding clasp
Price: $1,695; limited to 250 pieces
Variations: as Cadet

North.er

Reference number: NP250
Movement: automatic, ETA caliber 2893-2; ø 25.6 mm, height 4.1 mm; 24 jewels; 28,800 vph; 48-hour power reserve
Functions: hours, minutes, sweep seconds; date; 2nd time zone hand
Case: stainless steel, ø 42 mm, height 13.5 mm; sapphire crystal, transparent case back, water-resistant to 5 atm
Band: calfskin, folding clasp
Price: $2,425

TRILOBE

Gautier Massonneau, son of an architect and an interior designer, has a natural attraction to shapes. Still in his 20s, and just cutting his teeth in the world of infrastructure financing, he decided to buy himself a watch but couldn't find any that met his expectations.

He stumbled upon a timeless and transcultural form, the trefoil, an arrangement of "leaves" with powerful symbolic value. Indeed, the number 3, or the triangle, suggests completion. Do we not live in a world of three dimensions? And there is the past, the present, and the future; the religious trinities; and any story that must have a beginning, middle, and an end.

The beating heart is the off-center seconds disc, an open-worked six-leaved trefoil. The other leaves, a minute ring and an hour ring, radiate outwards across the dial, like water on a still pond, or the light of the sun. A poetic image is reflected in the name as well: Les Matinaux (the morning people), a collection of poems by René Char.

To realize the module for his first model, Massonneau turned to Jean-François Mojon and his company Chronode in Le Locle, Switzerland. Together, they created the X-Centric caliber, which is based on an ETA movement, and they managed to get the rings to turn without rubbing each other. For clients seeking a customized watch, there is a "Secret" version, which lets them choose a constellation of Super-LumiNova stars on a dark blue sky reflecting a precise time precious to the owner.

The second Trilobe collection also plays with turning subdials and rings. The Nuit Fantastique is inspired by the story of a nobleman's crazy night in Vienna, a story by Austrian author Stefan Zweig, famous for his obsessive characters. And in 2022, Massoneau presented Une Folle Journée (a crazy day), also a literary reference, amongst others, to the *Marriage of Figaro.* (Mozart's famous opera, which was based on a play called *La Folle Journée* by Pierre Beaumarchais) In 2023, the "crazy day" reappeared with 150 diamonds on the hour, minute, and seconds rails set using a unique, invisible technique.

All three collections appear in different cases or with various finishings. The latest color is called dune, a kind of sandy beige with a grainy look, like a beach.

TRILOBE
Trilobe Watches SAS
18 rue Volney
75002, Paris
France

TEL.:
+33-1-4233-5296

E-MAIL:
cercles@trilobewatches.com

WEBSITE:
www.trilobe.com

FOUNDED:
2019

NUMBER OF EMPLOYEES:
8

ANNUAL PRODUCTION:
approx. 700 pieces

U.S. DISTRIBUTOR:
Totally Worth It (TWI2, Inc.)
76 Division Avenue
Summit, NJ 07901-2309
201-894-4710
724-263-2286
info@totallyworthit.com

MOST IMPORTANT COLLECTIONS/PRICE RANGE:
Les Matinaux, La Nuit Fantastique, Une Folle Journée
/ $8,800 to $39,500; jewel versions up to $180,000

Une Folle Journée, Dune Rose Gold

Reference number: UFJ02GD
Movement: automatic, X-Centric caliber; ø 35.2 mm, height 5.78 mm; 33 jewels; 28,800 vph; micro-rotor; dial composed of three off-center concentric circles; 48-hour power reserve
Functions: hours, minutes, subsidiary seconds on rotating discs with fixed indices
Case: rose gold, ø 40.5 mm, height 10.2 mm (17.8 mm incl. the domed sapphire crystal); transparent case back; water-resistant to 5 atm
Band: reptile skin, pin buckle
Remarks: time displayed 10 mm above the dial on rotating rings set with 150 diamonds using a special setting technique
Price: $39,500
Variations: with diamond on time rings ($170,000); in titanium ($22,900)

Les Matinaux Secret L'Heure Exquise

Reference number: LM011LS
Movement: automatic, X-Centric caliber; ø 35.2 mm, height 5.78 mm; 33 jewels; 28,800 vph; microrotor; 48-hour power reserve
Functions: hours, minutes, subsidiary seconds; moon phase
Case: titanium, ø 40.5 mm, height 8.8 mm; sapphire crystal; transparent case back; water-resistant to 5 atm
Band: reptile skin, pin buckle
Remarks: three off-center concentric and rotating rings for hour, minute and seconds; the watch can be personalized by placing a constellation on the dial reflecting a special date in the buyer's life
Price: $18,000
Variations: comes with 38.5-mm case; in rose-gold case ($28,800); with calfskin strap

Nuit Fantastique Dune

Reference number: NF05DG
Movement: automatic, X-Centric caliber; ø 35.2 mm, height 5.78 mm; 33 jewels; 28,800 vph; 48-hour power reserve
Functions: hours, minutes, subsidiary seconds
Case: titanium, ø 40.5 mm, height 9.2 mm; sapphire crystal; transparent case back; water-resistant to 5 atm
Band: reptile skin, pin buckle
Remarks: sand-colored (dune) grained dial, clous de Paris on seconds disk
Price: $10,600
Variations: white or black dial (Lumière and Ombre); with barley-grain guilloché

TUDOR

Rolex founder Hans Wilsdorf started Tudor in 1946 as a second brand to offer the legendary reliability of his watches at a more affordable price. Tudor still benefits from the same industrial platform as Rolex, especially in cases and bracelets, assembly, and quality assurance, not to mention distribution and after-sales. However, the movements themselves are usually delivered by ETA and "Tudorized" according to the company's own aesthetics and technical criteria.

After coming out of the shadows in 2007, the company had an easy time registering with consumers with the Heritage Black Bay, especially considering the trend towards 1970s nostalgia. The first edition of the model with a wine-red bezel was followed by numerous variants with and without a rotating bezel, and with a GMT function. The latter was the second new development by the Rolex sister brand after the three-hand manufacture calibers. In the summer of 2021, Tudor finally presented a brand-new surprise: the Black Bay Ceramic is the first model to feature a ceramic case and a completely magnetic field-resistant movement. As a result, the Black Bay Ceramic even passes the stringent Swiss METAS magnetism test, making Tudor the second brand (after Omega) with a Master Chronometer certificate.

As for movements, the MT-5621 made its debut in the simple North Flag and as the MT-5612 in the Pelagos models. The M5601/5602 calibers, with three hands and a date, were followed by an attractive automatic chronograph. The Tudor calibers are produced by the movement manufacturer Kenissi, a joint venture with Breitling, among others. The movement of the automatic chronograph, which is basically a Breitling caliber B01, is also "shared" with this brand.

After launching various Black Bay models made of unusual case materials, Tudor invested in the development of the Pelagos special FXD model for professional use with integrated strap bars. Two special editions for various sports, like professional cycling, or Formula One, use this system, and they also boast bezels inlaid with carbon fiber. Price-conscious Tudor fans will be delighted with the Ranger, which is a basic three-hander but done with great attention to detail.

MONTRES TUDOR SA
Rue François-Dussaud 3-5-7
1211 Geneva 26
Switzerland

TEL.:
+41-22-302-2200

WEBSITE:
www.tudorwatch.com

FOUNDED:
1946

U.S. DISTRIBUTOR:
Tudor Watch U.S.A., LLC
665 Fifth Avenue
New York, NY 10022
212-897-9900
www.tudorwatch.com

MOST IMPORTANT COLLECTIONS AND PRICE RANGE:
Black Bay, Heritage, Pelagos, Ranger / $2,700 to $7,000

Black Bay Monochrome

Reference number: 7941A1A0NU
Movement: automatic, Tudor caliber MT5602-U; ø 31.8 mm, height 6.5 mm; 25 jewels; 28,800 vph; silicon hairspring, antimagnetic gear train components; Master Chronometer (METAS) certification; COSC-certified chronometer; 70-hour power reserve
Functions: hours, minutes, sweep seconds
Case: stainless steel, ø 41 mm, height 13.6 mm; unidirectional bezel with aluminum numeral disc, with 0-60 scale; sapphire crystal; screw-down crown; water-resistant to 20 atm
Band: five-link stainless steel, folding clasp, with fine adjustment
Price: $4,250
Variations: with three-link bracelet ($4,150); with rubber strap ($3,950)

Black Bay 54

Reference number: 79000N
Movement: automatic, Tudor caliber MT5400; ø 26 mm, height 4.99 mm; 27 jewels; 28,800 vph; silicon hairspring; COSC-certified chronometer; 70-hour power reserve
Functions: hours, minutes, sweep seconds
Case: stainless steel, ø 37 mm; unidirectional bezel with aluminum numerals disc, with 0-60 scale; sapphire crystal; screw-down crown; water-resistant to 20 atm
Band: stainless steel, folding clasp, with extension link
Remarks: inspired by the first Tudor diver's watch numbered 7922
Price: $3,900
Variations: with textile or leather strap ($3,700)

Black Bay Ceramic Blue

Reference number: 79210CNU
Movement: automatic, Tudor caliber MT5602-1U; ø 31.8 mm, height 6.5 mm; 25 jewels; 28,800 vph; silicon hairspring, antimagnetic gear train components; Master Chronometer (METAS) certification; COSC-certified chronometer; 70-hour power reserve
Functions: hours, minutes, sweep seconds
Case: ceramic, ø 41 mm, height 14.4 mm; unidirectional bezel with ceramic numerals disc, with 0-60 scale; sapphire crystal; screw-down crown; water-resistant to 20 atm
Band: calfskin and rubber, stainless-steel folding clasp with black PVD
Remarks: special edition to support the Visa Cash App RB Formula One Team with the dial in the team color, blue; comes with extra textile strap
Price: $5,150

Black Bay 58 GMT

Reference number: 7939G1A0NRU
Movement: automatic, Tudor caliber MT5450-U; ø 30.3 mm, height 6.14 mm; 34 jewels; 28,800 vph; silicon hairspring, antimagnetic gear train components; Master Chronometer (METAS) certification; COSC-certified chronometer; 65-hour power reserve
Functions: hours (crown activated jumping hours), minutes, sweep seconds; additional 24-hour display (second time zone); date
Case: stainless steel, ø 39 mm; bidirectional bezel with bicolor number disc in aluminum, with 0-24 scale; sapphire crystal; screw-down crown; water-resistant to 20 atm
Band: stainless steel, folding clasp, with fine adjustment
Price: $4,600
Variations: with rubber strap with folding clasp ($4,400)

Black Bay 58 18K

Reference number: 79018V
Movement: automatic, Tudor caliber MT5400; ø 30.3 mm, height 5 mm; 27 jewels; 28,800 vph; silicon hairspring; COSC-certified chronometer; 70-hour power reserve
Functions: hours, minutes, sweep seconds
Case: yellow gold, ø 39 mm; unidirectional bezel with aluminum insert, with 0-60 scale; sapphire crystal; transparent case back; screw-down crown; water-resistant to 20 atm
Band: yellow gold, folding clasp, with fine adjustment
Price: $32,100

Black Bay 41

Reference number: 79680
Movement: automatic, Tudor caliber MT5601; ø 33.8 mm, height 6.5 mm; 25 jewels; 28,800 vph; silicon hairspring; COSC-certified chronometer; 70-hour power reserve
Functions: hours, minutes, sweep seconds
Case: stainless steel, ø 41 mm; sapphire crystal; screw-down crown; water-resistant to 10 atm
Band: stainless steel, five rows of links, folding clasp, with fine adjustment
Price: $4,125
Variations: with blue dial ($4,125); also with 31-,36- or 39-mm diameter

Black Bay Pro

Reference number: 79470
Movement: automatic, Tudor caliber MT5652; ø 31.8 mm, height 7.52 mm; 28 jewels; 28,800 vph; silicon hairspring; COSC-certified chronometer; 70-hour power reserve
Functions: hours (crown activated jumping hours), minutes, sweep seconds; additional 24-hour display (second time zone); date
Case: stainless steel, ø 39 mm; with 0-24 scale; sapphire crystal; screw-down crown; water-resistant to 20 atm
Band: stainless steel, folding clasp, with safety lock
Price: $4,225
Variations: with calfskin, rubber, or textile strap ($3,900)

Black Bay Chrono

Reference number: 79360N
Movement: automatic, Tudor caliber MT5813; ø 30.4 mm, height 7.23 mm; 41 jewels; 28,800 vph; silicon hairspring, balance wheel with variable inertia; COSC-certified chronometer; 70-hour power reserve
Functions: hours, minutes, subsidiary seconds; chronograph; date
Case: stainless steel, ø 41 mm; bezel with aluminum numeral disc; sapphire crystal; screw-down crown and pushers; water-resistant to 20 atm
Band: stainless steel, folding clasp, with safety lock
Remarks: comes with extra textile strap
Price: $5,550
Variations: with leather or textile strap ($5,225); with white dial

Ranger

Reference number: 79950
Movement: automatic, Tudor caliber MT5402; ø 26 mm, height 4.99 mm; 27 jewels; 28,800 vph; silicon hairspring; COSC-certified chronometer 70-hour power reserve
Functions: hours, minutes, sweep seconds
Case: stainless steel, ø 39 mm; sapphire crystal; screw-down crown; water-resistant to 10 atm
Band: rubber/leather, folding clasp, with safety lock
Price: $2,975
Variations: with textile strap ($2,975); with stainless-steel link bracelet ($3,300)

Pelagos LHD

Reference number: 25610TNL
Movement: automatic, Tudor caliber MT5612LHD;
ø 31.8 mm, height 6.5 mm; 25 jewels; 28,800 vph;
silicon hairspring; COSC-certified chronometer; 70-hour
power reserve
Functions: hours, minutes, sweep seconds; date
Case: titanium, ø 42 mm; unidirectional stainless-
steel bezel with ceramic numeral disc, with 0-60 scale;
sapphire crystal; screw-down crown, helium valve;
water-resistant to 50 atm
Band: titanium, folding clasp, with safety lock, with
extension link, with fine adjustment
Remarks: comes with rubber strap
Price: $5,025

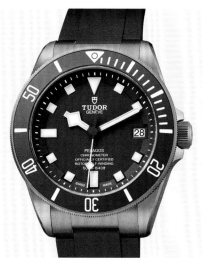

Pelagos

Reference number: 25600TB
Movement: automatic, Tudor caliber MT5612;
ø 31.8 mm, height 6.5 mm; 26 jewels; 28,800 vph;
silicon hairspring; COSC-certified chronometer; 70-hour
power reserve
Functions: hours, minutes, sweep seconds; date
Case: titanium, ø 42 mm; unidirectional titanium bezel
with ceramic numeral disc, insert, with 0-60 scale;
sapphire crystal; screw-down crown, helium valve;
water-resistant to 50 atm
Band: rubber, pin buckle, with extension link
Remarks: comes with additional titanium link bracelet
Price: $5,025
Variations: with black dial

Pelagos FXD Chrono Cycling Edition

Reference number: 25827KN
Movement: automatic, Tudor caliber MT5813;
ø 30.4 mm, height 7.23 mm; 41 jewels; 28,800 vph;
silicon hairspring; column wheel control; COSC-certified
chronometer; 70-hour power reserve
Functions: hours, minutes, subsidiary seconds;
chronograph; date
Case: carbon composite, ø 43 mm; sapphire crystal;
screw-down crown; water-resistant to 10 atm
Band: textile, pin buckle
Remarks: fixed lug bars (tear-safe); special edition to
support professional cycling
Price: $5,275

Caliber MT5602-U

Automatic; antimagnetic gear train components;
Master Chronometer (METAS) certification; single
mainspring barrel; COSC-certified chronometer;
70-hour power reserve
Functions: hours, minutes, sweep seconds
Diameter: 31.8 mm
Height: 6.5 mm
Jewels: 25
Balance: glucydur screw balance
Frequency: 28,800 vph
Hairspring: silicon
Related calibers: MT5601/5612 (encasing diameter
33.8/31.8 mm) without antimagnetic components

Caliber MT5402

Automatic; single mainspring barrel; COSC-certified
chronometer; 70-hour power reserve
Functions: hours, minutes, sweep seconds
Diameter: 26 mm
Height: 4.99 mm
Jewels: 27
Balance: glucydur screw balance
Frequency: 28,800 vph
Hairspring: silicon

Caliber MT5813

Automatic; single mainspring barrel; COSC-certified
chronometer; 70-hour power reserve
Functions: hours, minutes, subsidiary seconds;
chronograph; date
Diameter: 30.4 mm
Height: 7.23 mm
Jewels: 41
Balance: glucydur screw balance
Frequency: 28,800 vph
Hairspring: silicon

TUTIMA

The name Glashütte is synonymous with watches in Germany. The area, also known for precision engineering, already had quite a watchmaking industry going when World War I closed off markets, followed by the hyperinflation of the early twenties. To rebuild the local economy, a conglomerate was created to produce finished watches, under the leadership of jurist Dr. Ernst Kurtz, consisting of the movement manufacturer UROFA Glashütte AG and UFAG. The top watches were given the name Tutima, derived from the Latin *tutus*, meaning whole, sound. Among the brand's most famous timepieces was a pilot's watch that set standards in terms of aesthetics and functionality.

A few days before World War II ended, Kurtz left Glashütte and founded Uhrenfabrik Kurtz in southern Germany. A young businessman and former employee of Kurtz by the name of Dieter Delecate is credited with keeping the manufacturing facilities and the name Tutima going even as the company sailed through troubled waters. In founding Tutima Uhrenfabrik GmbH in Ganderkesee, this young, resolute entrepreneur prepared the company's strategy for the coming decades.

Delecate has had the joy of seeing Tutima return to its old home and vertically integrated operations, meaning it is once again a genuine *manufacture*. In 2013, Tutima proudly announced a genuine made-in-Glashütte movement (at least 50 percent must be produced in the town), Caliber 617. Tutima Glashütte has started reviving the great watchmaking crafts that have made the region world famous. Among these horological treats is the Hommage minute repeater and the three-hand Patria, which comes in a noble steel or gold case with a blue dial. For a genuine vintage feeling, the brand introduced the Tempostopp, a flyback chronograph run on the Caliber 659, a replica of the legendary Urofa Caliber 59 from the 1940s with a few necessary improvements in the details. More contemporary is the Saxon One line with a range of classic complications. And then there are the military-inspired models for everyday usage based on military watches, like the M2 Coastline, of lightweight titanium but with soft edges that will not ruin a silk shirt cuff.

TUTIMA UHRENFABRIK GMBH NDL. GLASHÜTTE
Altenberger Strasse 6
D-01768 Glashütte
Germany

TEL.:
+49-35053-320-20

E-MAIL:
info@tutima.com

WEBSITE:
www.tutima.com

FOUNDED:
1927

NUMBER OF EMPLOYEES:
approx. 60

U.S. DISTRIBUTOR:
Tutima USA, Inc.
P.O. Box 983
Torrance, CA 90508
1-TUTIMA-1927
info@tutimausa.com
www.tutima.com

MOST IMPORTANT COLLECTIONS/PRICE RANGE:
Patria, Saxon One, M2, Grand Flieger, Hommage /
approx. $1,650 to $29,500

M2 Pioneer

Reference number: 6451-03
Movement: automatic, Tutima caliber 521 (ETA 7750 base); ø 30 mm, height 7.9 mm; 25 jewels; 28,800 vph; sweep minute counter; rotor with gold seal; 48-hour power reserve
Functions: hours, minutes, subsidiary seconds; additional 24-hour display; chronograph; date
Case: titanium, ø 46.5 mm, height 16 mm; bidirectional bezel, with 0-60 scale; sapphire crystal; screw-down crown; water-resistant to 30 atm
Band: titanium, folding clasp
Remarks: soft-iron core for protection from magnetism
Price: $5,380

M2 Seven Seas S

Reference number: 6155-04
Movement: automatic, Tutima caliber 330 (ETA 2836-2 base); ø 25.6 mm, height 5.05 mm; 25 jewels; 28,800 vph; rotor with gold seal; 38-hour power reserve
Functions: hours, minutes, sweep seconds; date
Case: stainless steel, ø 44 mm, height 13 mm; unidirectional bezel with ceramic insert, with 0-60 scale; sapphire crystal; screw-down crown; water-resistant to 50 atm
Band: stainless steel, folding clasp
Price: $2,350

Saxon One Chronograph ZSM

Reference number: 6421-09
Movement: automatic, Tutima caliber 521 (ETA 7750 base); ø 30 mm, height 7.9 mm; 25 jewels; 28,800 vph; sweep minute counter; rotor with gold seal; 48-hour power reserve
Functions: hours, minutes, subsidiary seconds; additional 24-hour display; chronograph; date
Case: stainless steel, ø 43 mm, height 15.7 mm; bidirectional bezel, with 0-60 scale; sapphire crystal; transparent case back; screw-down crown; water-resistant to 20 atm
Band: rubber, pin buckle
Price: $6,300; limited to 100 pieces

Flieger Legacy T5 Automatic Chronograph

Reference number: 6405-03
Movement: automatic, Tutima caliber 310 (Sellita SW500 base); ø 30 mm, height 7.9 mm; 25 jewels; 28,800 vph; rotor with gold seal; 62-hour power reserve
Functions: hours, minutes, subsidiary seconds; chronograph; date
Case: titanium, ø 41 mm, height 16.1 mm; sapphire crystal; transparent case back; screw-down crown; water-resistant to 10 atm
Band: calfskin, folding clasp
Price: $4,300

Grand Flieger Airport Chronograph

Reference number: 6407-03
Movement: automatic, Tutima caliber 310 (ETA 7750 base); ø 30 mm, height 7.9 mm; 25 jewels; 28,800 vph; rotor with gold seal; 48-hour power reserve
Functions: hours, minutes, subsidiary seconds; chronograph; date and weekday
Case: stainless steel, ø 41 mm, height 16 mm; unidirectional bezel with ceramic insert, with 0-60 scale; sapphire crystal; transparent case back; screw-down crown; water-resistant to 20 atm
Band: calfskin with textile overlay, folding clasp
Price: $3,900

Grand Flieger Airport Automatic

Reference number: 6107-05
Movement: automatic, Tutima caliber 330 (ETA 2836-2 base); ø 25.6 mm, height 5.05 mm; 25 jewels; 28,800 vph; rotor with gold seal; 38-hour power reserve
Functions: hours, minutes, sweep seconds; date and weekday
Case: stainless steel, ø 41 mm, height 13 mm; unidirectional bezel with ceramic insert, with 0-60 scale; sapphire crystal; transparent case back; screw-down crown; water-resistant to 20 atm
Band: calfskin with textile overlay, folding clasp
Price: $2,500

Lady Sky

Reference number: 6705-22
Movement: automatic, Tutima caliber 335 (Sellita SW200-1 base); ø 25.6 mm, height 4.6 mm; 25 jewels; 28,800 vph; 41-hour power reserve
Functions: hours, minutes, sweep seconds; date
Case: stainless steel, ø 34 mm, height 10.1 mm; bezel in yellow gold; sapphire crystal; transparent case back; screw-down crown; water-resistant to 5 atm
Band: stainless steel with yellow-gold PVD-coated middle links, folding clasp
Price: $3,640

Patria Dual Time

Reference number: 6601-02
Movement: hand-wound, Tutima caliber 619; ø 31 mm, height 4.78 mm; 20 jewels; 21,600 vph; screw balance screw balance and Breguet hairspring; Glashütte three-quarter plate; 3 gold chatons, winding wheels with click; finely finished gold-plated movement; 65-hour power reserve
Functions: hours, minutes, subsidiary seconds; additional 12-hour display (second time zone)
Case: rose gold, ø 43 mm, height 11.2 mm; sapphire crystal; transparent case back; water-resistant to 5 atm
Band: reptile skin, pin buckle
Price: $19,500

The Patria

Reference number: 6600-04
Movement: hand-wound, Tutima caliber 617; ø 31 mm, height 4.78 mm; 20 jewels; 21,600 vph; screw balance screw balance and Breguet hairspring; Glashütte three-quarter plate; winding wheels with click; finely finished gold-plated movement; 65-hour power reserve
Functions: hours, minutes, subsidiary seconds
Case: rose gold, ø 43 mm, height 11.2 mm; sapphire crystal; transparent case back; water-resistant to 5 atm
Band: reptile skin, pin buckle
Price: $17,800

ULYSSE NARDIN

Ulysse Nardin celebrated 175 years in 2021, though a few of those years were dormant. It was Rolf Schnyder who revived the venerable brand after the quartz crisis. At one time it had a reputation for marine chronometers and precision watches. Schnyder had the luck to meet the multitalented Dr. Ludwig Oechslin, who developed a host of innovations for Ulysse Nardin, from intelligent calendar movements to escapement systems. He was the first to use silicon and synthetic diamonds. In fact, just about every Ulysse Nardin has become famous for some spectacular technical innovation, be it the Moonstruck with its stunning moon phase accuracy or the outlandish Freak series that more or less does away with the dial.

After Schnyder's death in 2011, the brand developed a strategy of partnerships and acquisitions, notably of the enameler Donzé Cadrans SA, which gave rise to the Marine Chronometer Manufacture, powered by the Caliber UN-118.

In 2014, the French luxury group Kering, owner of Sowind (Girard-Perregaux), purchased Ulysse Nardin. The two companies were neighbors in La Chaux-de-Fonds, Switzerland, and this has created synergies. Ulysse Nardin continued developing clever solutions such as a new blade-driven anchor escapement and the regatta countdown watch with a second hand that runs counterclockwise first before running clockwise like a conventional chronograph once the race has started.

A joint venture with Sigatec in Sion and its sister company, Mimotec, which specialize in lithogalvanics (LIGA) and processing silicon, allowed Ulysse Nardin to continue developing its advanced technologies. Specialties such as the dual Ulysse escapement in the "Freak" model or the Ulysse anchor escapement in the tourbillon caliber 178 with the flying bearing of the anchor made of silicon would not have been feasible without the new manufacturing possibilities and materials.

Kering Group's sell-off of Ulysse Nardin and Girard-Perregaux in a management buyout under the guidance of Patrick Pruniaux, CEO of both brands, is bringing the two watch brands even closer together. As both companies are based in La Chaux-de-Fonds, the exploitation of production synergies, for example, is obvious. For the moment, the two brands have kept on producing unconventional watches.

ULYSSE NARDIN SA
3, rue du Jardin
CH-2400 Le Locle
Switzerland

TEL.:
+41-32-930-7400

WEBSITE:
www.ulysse-nardin.com

FOUNDED:
1846

U.S. DISTRIBUTOR:
Ulysse Nardin Inc.
7900 Glades Rd., Suite 200
Boca Raton, FL 33434
646 500 8664
usa@ulysse-nardin.com

MOST IMPORTANT COLLECTIONS:
FREAK Collection, Blast Collection, Marine Collection and Diver Collection; Dual Time (also ladies' watches); complications and métiers d'art (alarm clocks, perpetual calendar, tourbillons, minute repeaters, jacquemarts, astronomical watches, enamel, micropainting)

Marine Torpilleur
Reference number: 1183-310/43
Movement: automatic, caliber UN-118; ø 31.6 mm, height 6.45 mm; 50 jewels; 28,800 vph; "DIAMonSIL" escapement, silicon hairspring; 60-hour power reserve; COSC-certified chronometer
Functions: hours, minutes, subsidiary seconds; power reserve indicator; date
Case: stainless steel, ø 42 mm, height 13 mm; sapphire crystal; transparent case back; screw-down crown; water-resistant to 5 atm
Band: reptile skin, folding clasp
Price: $9,000
Variations: with white dial; with rubber or textile strap; with stainless-steel milanaise bracelet

Marine Torpilleur Moonphase
Reference number: 1192-310-0A/1A
Movement: automatic, caliber UN-119; ø 31.6 mm, height 6.2 mm; 45 jewels; 28,800 vph; "DIAMonSIL" escapement, silicon hairspring; 60-hour power reserve; COSC-certified chronometer
Functions: hours, minutes, subsidiary seconds; power reserve indicator; moon phase
Case: rose gold, ø 42 mm, height 13 mm; sapphire crystal; transparent case back; screw-down crown; water-resistant to 5 atm
Band: reptile skin, folding clasp
Price: $23,800

Marine Torpilleur Tourbillon
Reference number: 1283-310-0AE/1A
Movement: automatic, caliber UN-128; ø 31.6 mm, height 7.4 mm; 36 jewels; 28,800 vph; flying 1-minute tourbillon; silicon escapement and hairspring; 60-hour power reserve
Functions: hours, minutes; power reserve indicator
Case: stainless steel, ø 42 mm, height 11.93 mm; sapphire crystal; transparent case back; screw-down crown; water-resistant to 5 atm
Band: reptile skin, folding clasp
Price: $46,400
Variations: in rose gold with black dial ($63,200)

Marine Torpilleur Dual Time

Reference number: 3343-320-3A/1A
Movement: automatic, caliber UN-24; ø 25.6 mm, height 5.35 mm; 23 jewels; 28,800 vph
Functions: hours, minutes, subsidiary seconds; additional 24-hour display (second time zone); large date
Case: stainless steel, ø 42 mm, height 13 mm; ceramic bezel; sapphire crystal; transparent case back; screw-down crown; water-resistant to 5 atm
Band: reptile skin, folding clasp
Price: $12,000

Diver Net Azur

Reference number: 1183-170-2B/3A
Movement: automatic, caliber UN-118; ø 31.6 mm, height 6.45 mm; 50 jewels; 28,800 vph; "DIAMonSIL" escapement, silicon hairspring; 60-hour power reserve; COSC-certified chronometer
Functions: hours, minutes, subsidiary seconds; power reserve indicator; date
Case: composite material (recycled fishing nets and carbon), ø 44 mm, height 14.81 mm; bidirectional bezel in recycled stainless-steel bezel with carbon insert, with 0-60 scale; sapphire crystal; screw-down crown; water-resistant to 30 atm
Band: recycled plastic, pin buckle
Remarks: ceramic glass
Price: $13,300

Diver Net OPS

Reference number: 1183-170-8A/3B
Movement: automatic, caliber UN-118; ø 31.6 mm, height 6.45 mm; 50 jewels; 28,800 vph; "DIAMonSIL" escapement, silicon hairspring; 60-hour power reserve; COSC-certified chronometer
Functions: hours, minutes, subsidiary seconds; power reserve indicator; date
Case: composite material (recycled fishing nets and carbon), ø 44 mm, height 14.81 mm; bidirectional bezel in recycled stainless-steel bezel with carbon insert, with 0-60 scale; sapphire crystal; screw-down crown; water-resistant to 30 atm
Band: rubber, folding clasp
Price: $13,300
Variations: with pin buckle; with textile strap ($13,300)

Diver Chronograph

Reference number: 1503-170-3/93
Movement: automatic, caliber UN-150; ø 31 mm, height 6.75 mm; 25 jewels; 28,800 vph; silicon escapement; 48-hour power reserve
Functions: hours, minutes, subsidiary seconds; chronograph; date
Case: titanium, ø 44 mm, height 16.1 mm; unidirectional bezel, with 0-60 scale; sapphire crystal; transparent case back; screw-down crown; water-resistant to 30 atm
Band: rubber, pin buckle
Price: $13,100
Variations: with textile strap ($11,200); with stainless steel bracelet ($13,800); in rose gold ($41,700)

Diver X Skeleton OPS

Reference number: 3723-170-1A/3A
Movement: automatic, caliber UN-372; 23 jewels; 21,600 vph; "DIAMonSIL" escapement, silicon hairspring; mainplate skeletonized; 72-hour power reserve
Functions: hours, minutes, sweep seconds
Case: titanium, ø 44 mm, height 15.7 mm; unidirectional bezel with carbon composite insert, with 0-60 scale; sapphire crystal; transparent case back; screw-down crown; water-resistant to 20 atm
Band: rubber, folding clasp
Price: $26,400
Variations: with azure or white strap; with textile strap

Blast Skeleton X

Reference number: 3713-260-3/03
Movement: hand-wound, caliber UN-371; ø 37 mm, height 5.86 mm; 23 jewels; 18,000 vph; skeletonized movement; two spring barrels; silicon balance wheel and hairspring; 96-hour power reserve
Functions: hours, minutes
Case: titanium, ø 42 mm, height 10.85 mm; bezel set with blue PVD; sapphire crystal; transparent case back; water-resistant to 5 atm
Band: rubber, pin buckle
Price: $22,200
Variations: with reptile skin strap; carbon; in titanium

Blast Tourbillon

Reference number: 1725-400-3A/02
Movement: automatic, caliber UN-172; ø 36.4 mm, height 6.1 mm; 25 jewels; 18,000 vph; flying 1-minute tourbillon; micro-rotor in platinum; silicon escapement; fully skeletonized movement; 72-hour power reserve
Functions: hours, minutes
Case: rose gold and DLC-coated titanium, ø 45 mm, height 11 mm; bezel in DLC-coated titanium; sapphire crystal; transparent case back; water-resistant to 5 atm
Band: rubber, folding clasp
Price: $67,300
Variations: with reptile skin strap; with satin strap

Blast Hourstriker

Reference number: 6215-400-3A/02
Movement: automatic, caliber UN-621; ø 35.5 mm, height 10.8 mm; 46 jewels; 28,800 vph; flying 1-minute tourbillon, silicon escapement; platinum micro-rotor (manual winding for the chime), 60-hour power reserve
Functions: hours, minutes, "au-passage" hour and half-hour striking on request
Case: rose gold, barrel section of DLC-coated titanium, ø 45 mm; sapphire crystal; transparent case back; water-resistant to 3 atm
Band: rubber, folding clasp
Price: $109,700
Variations: with reptile skin band

Freak X

Reference number: 2305-270/02
Movement: automatic, caliber UN-230; ø 34.5 mm, height 10.1 mm; 21 jewels; 28,800 vph; baguette movement on a peripheral carousel, silicon escapement, movement components are used as hands, crown-controlled conventional winding and hands-setting; 72-hour power reserve
Functions: hours, minutes
Case: rose gold and DLC-coated titanium, ø 43 mm, height 13.5 mm; sapphire crystal; transparent case back
Band: calfskin, folding clasp
Price: $36,900
Variations: with reptile skin strap; with black DLC; in titanium

Freak ONE

Reference number: 2405-500-2A/3D
Movement: automatic, caliber UN-240; ø 34.5 mm, height 10.1 mm; 21 jewels; 21,600 vph; baguette movement on a rotating carousel, movement components are used as hands; "DIAMonSIL" pallet lever and escape wheel, silicon balance wheel and hairspring; 90-hour power reserve
Functions: hours, minutes
Case: titanium with black DLC, ø 44 mm, height 13.3 mm; bezel in rose gold; sapphire crystal; transparent case back
Band: rubber, folding clasp
Remarks: high efficiency patented "Grinder" automatic winding
Price: $68,600

Freak ONE OPS

Reference number: 2403-500-8A/3A
Movement: automatic, caliber UN-240; ø 34.5 mm, height 10.1 mm; 21 jewels; 21,600 vph; baguette movement on a rotating carousel, movement components are used as hands; "DIAMonSIL" pallet lever and escape wheel, silicon balance wheel and hairspring; 90-hour power reserve
Functions: hours, minutes
Case: titanium with black DLC, ø 44 mm, height 13.3 mm; carbon composite bezel; sapphire crystal; transparent case back; water-resistant to 3 atm
Band: rubber with textile insert, folding clasp
Remarks: high efficiency, patented "Grinder" automatic winding
Price: $66,800
Variations: with bicolor rubber strap

Freak S Nomad

Reference number: 2513-500LE-4A-GUI/3A
Movement: automatic, caliber UN-251; ø 34.5 mm, height 10.1 mm; 22 jewels; 28,800 vph; baguette movement on a rotating carousel dual Ulysse escapement, double silicon balance wheel with torque weights, movement components are used as hands; 72-hour power reserve
Functions: hours, minutes
Case: titanium, case barrel of carbon composite, ø 45 mm, height 16.65 mm; bezel in PVD-coated titanium; sapphire crystal; transparent case back; water-resistant to 3 atm
Band: rubber with textile overlay, folding clasp
Price: $148,300; limited to 99 pieces
Variations: with reptile skin strap

URWERK

Many watchmakers make unique pieces, but Felix Baumgartner and designer Martin Frei are in and of themselves unique. Their products are immediately recognizable, their ultra-technical style—never losing sight of the visual codes they laid down when they founded their company in 1997—has always been the source of eye-popping mechanisms. It's all in the name, a play on the words *Uhrwerk*, for movement, and *Urwerk*, meaning a sort of primal mechanism. Their specialty is inventing surprising time indicators featuring digital numerals that rotate like satellites and display the time in a relatively linear depiction on a small "dial" at the front of the flattened case, which could almost—but not quite—be described as oval. Their inspiration goes back to the so-called night clock of the eighteenth-century Campanus brothers, but the realization is purely *2001: A Space Odyssey*.

Urwerk's debut was with the Harry Winston Opus 5. They went on to create and invent all sorts of new ways of displaying time not always based on the satellite idea. The Black Cobra displayed time using cylinders, which also required clever ways to recoup energy for driving the heavy components. With each return to the drawing board, Baumgartner and Frei find new ways to explore what has now become an unmistakable form, using high-tech materials, like aluminum titanium nitride (AlTiN), or a gold-silver alloy known as electrum, or finding new functions for the owner to play with.

Urwerk is continually pushing the envelope, even by its own standards. In 2023, Frei and Baumgartner came up with the 100V Stardust. It featured a complication that let the minute hand track the distance a human being standing on the Equator travels on rotating Earth and at the same time the journey of Earth around the sun. The new 100V, driven by the 12.02 and named LightSpeed, shows the journey of light from the sun to all eight planets. Next to that is the uniquely shaped EMC SR-71, inspired by the world's fastest stealth surveillance plane, the Blackbird. Finally, the Scorpion extends the range of models with animal names. The poisonous tail is in fact the digital hours that pop up inside the retrograde minutes arrow. A comment on the passage of time killing us all.

URWERK SA
Bourg du Four 5
CH-1204 Geneva
Switzerland

TEL:
+41-22-900-2027

E-MAIL:
info@urwerk.com

WEBSITE:
www.urwerk.com

FOUNDED:
1995

ANNUAL PRODUCTION:
150 watches

U.S. DISTRIBUTOR:
Ildico Inc.
8701 Wilshire Blvd.
Beverly Hills, CA 90211
310-205-5555

UR-150 Scorpion Dark

Movement: automatic, caliber UR 50.01; 28,800 vph; 38 jewels; finely finished movement with circular graining and shot-blasting; 43-hour power reserve
Functions: satellite hours, minutes
Case: stainless steel with anthracite PVD, 52.31 mm x 42.49 mm, height 14.79 mm; sapphire crystal; screw-down crown; transparent case back; water-resistant to 5 atm
Band: rubber, pin buckle
Price: $105,000; limited to 30 pieces
Variations: Titan version with titanium case ($103,000)

UR-100V LightSpeed

Movement: automatic, caliber UR 12.02; 28,800 vph; 40 jewels; with air-brake control; aluminum carousel; carousel and baseplates in ARCAP alloy; finely finished movement with circular graining and shot-blasting; 48-hour power reserve
Functions: satellite hours (on beryllium-bronze Geneva crosses), minutes; display of light's distance from sun to eight planets of the solar system
Case: carbon, 51.73 mm x 43 mm, height 14.55 mm; sapphire crystal; screw-down crown; transparent case back; water-resistant to 5 atm
Band: rubber, folding clasp
Price: $76,000

EMC SR-71

Movement: hand-wound, UR EMC; 28,800 vph; ARCAP P40 balance; integrated optical sensor for rate monitoring to compare with referential oscillator (16,000,000 Hz), triggered by pusher; adjustment screw on movement side; power from microgenerator with collapsible winding handle on the case side; double spring barrel; 80 hours power reserve
Functions: hours and minutes (off-center), subsidiary seconds; power reserve display, rate precision display
Case: titanium with black DLC coating, 49.57 mm x 51 mm, height 15.8 mm; sapphire crystal; functional elements, rate fine-tuning screw on the back; water-resistant to 3 atm
Band: NATO-style Nylon and leather, Velcro fastening
Price: $176,000

VACHERON CONSTANTIN

The origins of this oldest continuously operating watch *manufacture* can be traced back to 1755 when Jean-Marc Vacheron opened his workshop in Geneva. His highly complex watches were particularly appreciated by clients in Paris. The development of such an important outlet for horological works there had a lot to do with the emergence of a wealthy class around the powerful French court. The Revolution put an end to all the financial excesses of that market, however, and the Vacheron company suffered as well, until the arrival of marketing wizard François Constantin in 1819.

Fast-forward to the late twentieth century: the brand with the Maltese cross logo had evolved into a tradition-conscious keeper of *haute horlogerie* under the aegis, starting in the mid-1990s, of the Vendôme Luxury Group (today's Richemont SA).

Today, most of its basic movements are made in-house at the production facilities and headquarters in Plan-les-Ouates and the workshops in Le Brassus in Switzerland's Jura region. Products range from the world's most complicated watch, like the 57260, to the finely crafted Les Cabinotiers and Traditionnelle collections. For daily use, there are the Overseas models, and the entry-level collection, the Fiftysix, with a basic movement and no Geneva Seal.

When not looking ahead, Vacheron Constantin is looking back to its great feats of the past, which have their own family, Les Collectionneurs. Among the favorites is a revisited American 1921 model, now made from 100-year-old spare parts and components and manufactured with 100-year-old tools. This watchmaking icon with its boldly oblique dial differs from the current models in the 1921 collection in that the dial and crown are tilted to the left.

Most customers of the brand prefer to remain anonymous, but one spectacular one-off timepiece has now been named after its owner for the first time in a long time. William Robert Berkley, an American insurance entrepreneur, ordered the world's most complicated portable mechanical watch from the company. Among numerous other complications, "The Berkley" pocket watch has a perpetual Chinese calendar, a tricky combination of solar and lunar calendars with countless irregularities. Its movement has a record-breaking number of 2877 individual parts.

VACHERON CONSTANTIN
Chemin du Tourbillon
CH-1228 Plan-les-Ouates
Switzerland

TEL.:
+41-22-930-2005

E-MAIL:
info@vacheron-constantin.com

WEBSITE:
www.vacheron-constantin.com

FOUNDED:
1755

NUMBER OF EMPLOYEES:
approx. 800

U.S. DISTRIBUTOR:
Vacheron Constantin
645 Fifth Avenue
New York, NY 10022
877-701-1755

MOST IMPORTANT COLLECTIONS:
Patrimony, Traditionnelle, Métiers d'Art, Overseas, Fiftysix, Historiques and Égérie, Harmony, Patrimony, Traditionnelle, Historiques, Métiers d'Art, Malte, Overseas, Égérie, FiftySix, Quai de l'Île, unique pieces. As well as unique and bespoke timepieces from its Les Cabinotiers department

Traditionnelle Tourbillon

Reference number: 6000T/000P-H025
Movement: automatic, Vacheron Constantin caliber 2160/1; ø 31 mm, height 5.65 mm; 30 jewels; 18,000 vph; 1-minute tourbillon; peripheral, gold oscillating mass; 80-hour power reserve; Geneva Seal
Functions: hours, minutes, subsidiary seconds (on the tourbillon cage)
Case: platinum, ø 41 mm, height 10.4 mm; sapphire crystal; transparent case back; water-resistant to 3 atm
Band: reptile skin, folding clasp
Price: on request

Traditionnelle Tourbillon Retrograde Date Openface

Reference number: 6010T/000R-B638
Movement: automatic, Vacheron Constantin caliber 2162 R31; ø 31 mm, height 6.25 mm; 30 jewels; 18,000 vph; 1-minute tourbillon; peripheral gold oscillating mass; 72-hour power reserve; Geneva Seal
Functions: hours, minutes, subsidiary seconds (on the tourbillon cage); date (retrograde)
Case: rose gold, ø 41 mm, height 11.07 mm; sapphire crystal; transparent case back; water-resistant to 3 atm
Band: reptile skin, folding clasp
Price: $200,000

Overseas Tourbillon

Reference number: 6000V/210T-H032
Movement: automatic, Vacheron Constantin caliber 2160; ø 31 mm, height 5.65 mm; 30 jewels; 18,000 vph; 1-minute tourbillon; hubless peripheral winding rotor; 80-hour power reserve; Geneva Seal
Functions: hours, minutes, subsidiary seconds (on the tourbillon cage)
Case: titanium, ø 42.5 mm, height 10.39 mm; sapphire crystal; transparent case back; water-resistant to 5 atm
Band: rubber, triple folding clasp
Remarks: comes with extra titanium and calfskin strap with pin buckle
Price: $140,000

Overseas Self-Winding

Reference number: 4520V/210R-B967
Movement: automatic, Vacheron Constantin caliber 5100; ø 30.6 mm, height 4.7 mm; 37 jewels; 28,800 vph; gold rotor; 60-hour power reserve; Geneva Seal
Functions: hours, minutes, sweep seconds; date
Case: rose gold, ø 41 mm, height 10.69 mm; sapphire crystal; transparent case back; screw-down crown; water-resistant to 15 atm
Band: rose gold bracelet with triple-blade quick-release folding clasp
Remarks: comes with extra rubber and calfskin strap and pin buckle
Price: $60,500

Overseas Dual-Time

Reference number: 7920V/210R-B965
Movement: automatic, Vacheron Constantin caliber 5110 DT/2; ø 30.6 mm, height 6 mm; 37 jewels; 28,800 vph; 60-hour power reserve; Geneva Seal
Functions: hours, minutes, sweep seconds; additional 12-hour display (second time zone), day/night indicator; date
Case: rose gold, ø 41 mm, height 12 mm; sapphire crystal; transparent case back; screw-down crown; water-resistant to 15 atm
Band: rose gold bracelet with triple-blade quick-release folding clasp
Remarks: soft-iron core for antimagnetic protection; comes with extra rubber and calfskin strap and pin buckle
Price: $75,500

Overseas Chronograph

Reference number: 5500V/210A-B686
Movement: automatic, Vacheron Constantin caliber 5200; ø 30.6 mm, height 6.6 mm; 54 jewels; 28,800 vph; column wheel control of chronograph functions; gold rotor; 52-hour power reserve; Geneva Seal
Functions: hours, minutes, subsidiary seconds; chronograph; date
Case: stainless steel, ø 42.5 mm, height 13.7 mm; sapphire crystal; transparent case back; screw-down crown and pushers; water-resistant to 15 atm
Band: stainless steel bracelet with triple-blade quick-release folding clasp
Remarks: comes with extra rubber and calfskin skin strap and pin buckle
Price: $35,600

Overseas Perpetual Calendar Ultra-Thin

Reference number: 4300V/220R-B064
Movement: automatic, Vacheron Constantin caliber 1120 QP/1; ø 29.6 mm, height 4.05 mm; 36 jewels; 19,800 vph; 40-hour power reserve; Geneva Seal
Functions: hours, minutes; perpetual calendar with date, weekday, month, moon phase, leap year
Case: rose gold, ø 41.5 mm, height 8.1 mm; sapphire crystal; transparent case back; water-resistant to 5 atm
Band: rose gold bracelet with triple-blade quick-release folding clasp
Remarks: soft-iron core for anti-magnetic protection; comes with extra rubber calfskin skin strap and pin buckle
Price: $115,000
Variations: in pink gold with silver and blue dial, also in white gold with blue dial

Historiques 222

Reference number: 4200H/222J-B935
Movement: automatic, Vacheron Constantin caliber 2455/2; ø 26.2 mm, height 3.6 mm; 27 jewels; 28,800 vph; 40-hour power reserve; Geneva Seal
Functions: hours, minutes; date
Case: yellow gold, ø 37 mm, height 7.95 mm; sapphire crystal; transparent case back; water-resistant to 5 atm
Band: yellow gold with triple-blade folding clasp
Remarks: gently modernized reedition for the 45th anniversary of the "222"
Price: $74,000

Historiques American 1921

Reference number: 82035/000R-9359
Movement: hand-wound, Vacheron Constantin caliber 4400AS; ø 28.6 mm, height 2.8 mm; 21 jewels; 28,800 vph; 65-hour power reserve; Geneva Seal
Functions: hours, minutes, subsidiary seconds
Case: rose gold, 40 mm x 40 mm, height 8.06 mm; sapphire crystal; transparent case back; water-resistant to 3 atm
Band: alligator leather, pin buckle
Remarks: based on a historic model from 1921
Price: $40,400

Patrimony Moon Phase Retrograde Date

Reference number: 4010U/000G-H070
Movement: automatic, Vacheron Constantin caliber 2460 R31L; ø 27.2 mm, height 5.4 mm; 27 jewels; 28,800 vph; 40-hour power reserve; Geneva Seal
Functions: hours, minutes; date (retrograde), moon phase
Case: white gold, ø 42.5 mm, height 9.7 mm; sapphire crystal; transparent case back; water-resistant to 3 atm
Band: reptile skin, pin buckle
Price: $49,400

Patrimony Hand-Wound

Reference number: 1410U/000R-H018
Movement: hand-wound, Vacheron Constantin caliber 1440; ø 22.1 mm, height 2.6 mm; 19 jewels; 28,800 vph; 42-hour power reserve; Geneva Seal
Functions: hours, minutes
Case: rose gold, ø 39 mm, height 7.7 mm; sapphire crystal; water-resistant to 3 atm
Band: reptile skin, pin buckle
Price: $25,200
Variations: in white gold

Patrimony Automatic

Reference number: 85180/000J-9231
Movement: automatic, Vacheron Constantin caliber 2450 Q6/3; ø 25.6 mm, height 3.6 mm; 27 jewels; 28,800 vph; 40-hour power reserve; Geneva Seal
Functions: hours, minutes, sweep seconds; date
Case: yellow gold, ø 40 mm, height 8.55 mm; sapphire crystal; water-resistant to 3 atm
Band: reptile skin, pin buckle
Price: $31,800
Variations: in white gold ($28,570)

Patrimony Perpetual Calendar Ultra-Thin

Reference number: 43175/000R-B519
Movement: automatic, Vacheron Constantin caliber 1120 QP/1; ø 29.6 mm, height 4.05 mm; 36 jewels; 19,800 vph; skeletonized rotor with gold oscillating mass; 40-hour power reserve; Geneva Seal
Functions: hours, minutes; perpetual calendar with date, weekday, month, moon phase, leap year
Case: rose gold, ø 41 mm, height 8.91 mm; sapphire crystal; transparent case back; water-resistant to 3 atm
Band: reptile skin, folding clasp
Price: $88,000
Variations: in pink gold with silver dial

Traditionelle Complete Calendar

Reference number: 4010T/000R-B344
Movement: automatic, Vacheron Constantin caliber 2460 QCL/1; ø 29mm, height 5.4 mm; 27 jewels; 28,800 vph; 40-hour power reserve; Geneva Seal
Functions: hours, minutes, sweep seconds; full calendar with date, weekday, month, moon phase
Case: rose gold, ø 41 mm, height 10.72 mm; sapphire crystal; transparent case back; water-resistant to 3 atm
Band: reptile skin, pin buckle
Price: $45,300
Variations: in white gold with grey dial

Fiftysix Complete Calendar

Reference number: 4000E/000R-B438
Movement: automatic, Vacheron Constantin caliber 2460 QCL/1; ø 29 mm, height 5.4 mm; 27 jewels; 28,800 vph; 40-hour power reserve; Geneva Seal
Functions: hours, minutes, sweep seconds; full calendar with date, weekday, month, moon phase
Case: rose gold, ø 40 mm, height 11.6 mm; sapphire crystal; transparent case back; water-resistant to 3 atm
Band: reptile skin, pin buckle
Price: $44,500
Variations: in pink gold with brown dial and in stainless steel with silver or blue dial

Overseas Self-Winding

Reference number: 4605V/200R-B969
Movement: automatic, Vacheron Constantin caliber 1088/1; ø 20.8 mm, height 3.83 mm; 26 jewels; 28,800 vph; gold rotor; 40-hour power reserve
Functions: hours, minutes, sweep seconds; date
Case: rose gold, ø 35 mm, height 9.33 mm; bezel set with 90 round-cut diamonds; sapphire crystal; transparent case back; water-resistant to 15 atm
Band: rose gold bracelet with triple folding clasp
Remarks: comes with extra rubber and calfskin strap and pin buckle
Price: $58,500
Variations: in stainless steel ($30,500)

Overseas Self-Winding

Reference number: 4605V/200A-B971
Movement: automatic, Vacheron Constantin caliber 1088/1; ø 20.8 mm, height 3.83 mm; 26 jewels; 28,800 vph; gold rotor; 40-hour power reserve
Functions: hours, minutes, sweep seconds; date
Case: stainless steel, ø 35 mm, height 9.33 mm; bezel set with 90 round-cut diamonds; sapphire crystal; transparent case back; water-resistant to 15 atm
Band: stainless steel, folding clasp
Remarks: comes with extra rubber and calfskin strap and pin buckle
Price: $30,500

Traditionnelle Perpetual Calendar Ultra-Thin

Reference number: 4305T/000G-B948
Movement: automatic, Vacheron Constantin caliber 1120 QP; ø 29.6 mm, height 4.05 mm; 36 jewels; 19,800 vph; 40-hour power reserve; Geneva Seal
Functions: hours, minutes; perpetual calendar with date, weekday, month, moon phase, leap year
Case: white gold, ø 36.5 mm, height 8.43 mm; bezel and lugs set with 76 round-cut diamonds; sapphire crystal; transparent case back; crown with diamond; water-resistant to 3 atm
Band: reptile skin, pin buckle set with 17 round-cut diamonds
Price: $88,000

Traditionnelle Moon Phase

Reference number: 83570/000G-9916
Movement: hand-wound, Vacheron Constantin caliber 1410 AS; ø 26 mm, height 4.2 mm; 22 jewels; 28,800 vph; 40-hour power reserve; Geneva Seal
Functions: hours, minutes, subsidiary seconds; power reserve indicator; moon phase
Case: white gold, ø 36 mm, height 9.1 mm; bezel and lugs set with 81 round-cut diamonds; sapphire crystal; transparent case back; crown with diamond; water-resistant to 3 atm
Band: reptile skin, pin buckle
Remarks: mother-of-pearl dial
Price: $45,000
Variations: in rose gold, and in white gold with snow-set dial

Égérie Moon Phase

Reference number: 8005F/000R-H030
Movement: automatic, Vacheron Constantin caliber 1088 L; ø 30 mm, height 5.03 mm; 26 jewels; 28,800 vph; 40-hour power reserve
Functions: hours, minutes, sweep seconds; moon phase
Case: rose gold, ø 37 mm, height 10.08 mm; bezel set with 58 round-cut diamonds; sapphire crystal; transparent case back; crown with moonstone cabochon; water-resistant to 3 atm
Band: calfskin, pin buckle
Remarks: pink gold dial ring set with 36 round-cut diamonds; two extra leather straps
Price: $43,100; limited to 100 pieces

Égérie Moon Phase

Reference number: 8005F/000R-B958
Movement: automatic, Vacheron Constantin caliber 1088 L; ø 30 mm, height 5.03 mm; 26 jewels; 28,800 vph; 40-hour power reserve
Functions: hours, minutes, sweep seconds; moon phase
Case: rose gold, ø 37 mm, height 10.08 mm; bezel set with 58 round-cut diamonds; sapphire crystal; transparent case back; crown with moonstone cabochon; water-resistant to 3 atm
Band: reptile skin, pin buckle
Remarks: pink gold dial ring set with 36 round-cut diamonds; two extra reptile skin straps
Price: $39,300
Variations: with light-colored dial; in stainless steel

Caliber 2460 R31R7/3

Automatic; single mainspring barrel, 40-hour power reserve; Geneva Seal
Functions: hours, minutes; date and weekday; (retrograde)
Diameter: 27.2 mm
Height: 5.4 mm
Jewels: 27
Balance: glucydur
Frequency: 28,800 vph
Remarks: skeletonized gold rotor; 276 parts

Caliber 2460 QCL/1

Automatic; second stop; single mainspring barrel, 40-hour power reserve; Geneva Seal
Functions: hours, minutes, sweep seconds; full calendar with date, weekday, month
Diameter: 29 mm
Height: 5.4 mm
Jewels: 27
Balance: glucydur
Frequency: 28,800 vph
Remarks: gold rotor; 308 parts

Caliber 2460 R31L/2

Automatic; single mainspring barrel, 40-hour power reserve; Geneva Seal
Functions: hours, minutes; date (retrograde), moon phase
Diameter: 27.2 mm
Height: 5.4 mm
Jewels: 27
Balance: glucydur
Frequency: 28,800 vph
Remarks: gold rotor; 275 parts

Caliber 2162 R31

Automatic; hubless peripheral winding rotor; 1-minute tourbillon; two spring barrels, 72-hour power reserve; Geneva Seal
Functions: hours, minutes, subsidiary seconds (on the tourbillon cage); date (retrograde)
Diameter: 31 mm
Height: 5.65mm
Jewels: 30
Balance: glucydur
Frequency: 18,000 vph
Remarks: gold oscillating mass; 242 parts

Caliber 2455/2

Automatic; gold rotor; single mainspring barrel, 40-hour power reserve; Geneva Seal
Functions: hours, minutes; date
Diameter: 26.2 mm
Height: 3.6 mm
Jewels: 27
Balance: glucydur
Frequency: 28,800 vph
Remarks: 194 parts

Caliber 1120 QP

Automatic; extra thin construction; winding rotor with support ring; single mainspring barrel, 40-hour power reserve; Geneva Seal
Functions: hours, minutes; perpetual calendar with date, weekday, month, moon phase, leap year
Diameter: 29.6 mm
Height: 4.05 mm
Jewels: 36
Balance: glucydur
Frequency: 19,800 vph
Remarks: skeletonized rotor with gold oscillating mass; 276 parts

Caliber 1088 L

Automatic; swan-neck fine adjustment; single mainspring barrel, 40-hour power reserve; Geneva Seal
Functions: hours, minutes, sweep seconds
Diameter: 30 mm
Height: 5.03 mm
Jewels: 26
Balance: glucydur
Frequency: 28,800 vph
Hairspring: flat hairspring
Remarks: skeletonized gold rotor; 172 parts

Caliber 4400 AS

Hand-wound; single mainspring barrel, 65-hour power reserve; Geneva Seal
Functions: hours, minutes, subsidiary seconds
Diameter: 28.6 mm
Height: 2.8 mm
Jewels: 21
Balance: glucydur
Frequency: 28,800 vph
Remarks: perlage on mainplate, beveled edges, bridges with côtes de Genève; 127 parts

Caliber 1326

Automatic; two spring barrels, 48-hour power reserve
Functions: hours, minutes, sweep seconds; date
Diameter: 26.2 mm
Height: 4.3 mm
Jewels: 25
Balance: glucydur
Frequency: 28,800 vph
Hairspring: flat hairspring
Remarks: skeletonized er gold rotor; finely finished with côtes de Genève; 142 parts

Caliber 1003

Hand-wound; single spring barrel, 31-hour power reserve; Geneva Seal
Functions: hours, minutes
Diameter: 21.1 mm
Height: 1.64 mm
Jewels: 18
Balance: glucydur
Frequency: 18,000 vph
Remarks: currently the thinnest mechanical movement in production

Caliber 3300

Hand-wound; column wheel control of the chronograph functions, horizontal clutch; single mainspring barrel, 65-hour power reserve; Geneva Seal
Functions: hours, minutes, subsidiary seconds; power reserve indicator; chronograph with crown pusher
Diameter: 32.8 mm
Height: 6.7 mm
Jewels: 35
Balance: glucydur
Frequency: 21,600 vph
Remarks: 252 parts

Caliber 2260

Hand-wound; 1-minute tourbillon; four spring barrels, 336-hour power reserve; Geneva Seal
Functions: hours, minutes, subsidiary seconds (on the tourbillon cage); power reserve indicator
Diameter: 29.1 mm
Height: 6.8 mm
Jewels: 31
Balance: glucydur
Frequency: 18,000 vph
Remarks: 231 parts

VAN CLEEF & ARPELS

In 1999, while shopping around for more companies to add to its roster of high-end jewelers, Richemont Group decided to purchase Van Cleef & Arpels. The venerable brand had a lot of name recognition thanks in part to a host of internationally known customers, like Jacqueline Kennedy Onassis, whose two marriages each involved a Van Cleef & Arpels ring. It also had a reputation for the high quality of its workmanship with jewels and related crafts. It was Van Cleef & Arpels that came up with the mystery setting using a special rail and cut totally hidden from the casual eye.

Van Cleef & Arpels was a family business that came to be when a young stone cutter, Alfred van Cleef, married Estelle Arpels in 1896, and ten years later opened a business on Place Vendôme in Paris with Estelle's brother Charles. More of Estelle's brothers joined the firm, which was soon booming and serving, quite literally, royalty.

Watches were always a part of the portfolio. But after joining Richemont, Van Cleef now had the support of a very complete industrial portfolio that would allow it to make stunning movements that could bring dials to life. Most models today run on the Valfleurier Q020 movement exclusively developed for the company. But it was a collaboration with Jean-Marc Wiederrecht and Agenhor on the Pont des Amoureux with its stunning retrograde complication that became a standard for the brand. In 2022, the company came out with another stunner, the Heures Florales, which replicates the concept garden of Swedish botanist and taxonomist Carl Linnaeus, where time could be read according to which flowers are open. And Van Cleef has also looked to the sky for inspiration, with, for instance, a planetarium for the wrist, a collaboration with the eminent watchmaker, Christiaan van der Klaauw.

These poetic complications have continued to wow the public as works that exhibit genuine technical and artistic potential in watchmaking. It's hardly any wonder that in 2024, the company clinched three prizes at the GPHG: Artistic Crafts for the Lady Arpels Jour Enchanté, Ladies' Complication for the Brise d'Été, and Ladies' Watch for the Lady Jour Nuit.

VAN CLEEF & ARPELS
2, rue du Quatre-Septembre
F-75002 Paris
France

TEL.:
+33-1-70-70-36-56

WEBSITE:
www.vancleefarpels.com

FOUNDED:
1906

U.S. DISTRIBUTOR:
1-877-VAN-CLEEF

MOST IMPORTANT COLLECTIONS:
Charms; Pierre Arpels; Poetic Complications

Lady Arpels Brise d'Eté
Reference number: VCARPERU00
Movement: automatic, Valfleurier Q020 caliber developed by Van Cleef and Arpels with special module to create breeze animation; 36-hour power reserve
Functions: hours, minutes; day/night indicated by different butterfly colors on a 0-12 scale; pusher to activate the on-demand breeze complication
Case: white gold, ø 38 mm, height 13.15 mm; bezel set with round diamonds; transparent case back; water-resistant to 5 atm
Band: reptile skin, pin buckle
Remarks: butterflies tell time and flutter in the breeze along with the flowers; mother-of-pearl backdrop with flowers, grasses and butterflies made using vallonné, champlevé, and plique-à-jour enamel, with tsavorite and spessartite garnets and miniature painting
Price: $169,000

Lady Féerie Or Rose
Reference number: VCARPBNJ00
Movement: automatic, Valfleurier Q020 caliber developed by Van Cleef and Arpels; 36-hour power reserve
Functions: jumping hours and retrograde minutes with time-on-demand module
Case: rose gold, set with diamonds, ø 33 mm, height 12.6 mm; bezel and crown set with 137 diamonds; water-resistant to 3 atm
Band: reptile skin; rose gold buckle set with diamonds
Remarks: rose-gold ballerina with butterfly wings made with plique-à-jour enamel and diamonds; each dial is hand-made, set with around 364 diamonds, 12 sapphires, mother-of-pearl elements
Price: $106,000

Jour Enchanté
Reference number: VCARPBMA00
Movement: hand-wound, Valfleurier Q474 caliber developed by Van Cleef & Arpels; 38-hour power reserve
Functions: hours, minutes
Case: white gold, ø 41 mm; round diamond on crown; water resistant up to 3 atm
Band: reptile skin, pin buckle
Remarks: dial and watch case with 308 diamonds, 94 sapphires, 56 spessartites, 13 turquoises
Price: $357,000; limited to 8 pieces

VARIO WATCHES

Ivan Chua, who hails from Singapore, found his way to watches in a most unusual fashion. After studying to become an engineer, he started building websites at a time when everyone needed an online presence and web designers were fairly rare. He then decided to expand this ability and went on to study animation, after which he became a motion designer with some major media companies, like MTV, as clients.

Being in business—albeit, a reluctant manager by his own admission—he needed to check the time often, which meant pulling out his phone a lot. One day, he decided to resuscitate his old quartz watches and noticed that the straps were ill-matched, even ugly. So, he started making his own and then selling them. He soon realized that a nice strap should have a nice watch. So, finally, he launched Vario in 2016.

As an engineer with a well-trained eye, Ivan Chua's strategy is to design watches that attract without distracting. Next to a few quartz collections, he began producing a series of mechanical, military-themed watches that connect emotionally to dramas of the past with a little touch of humor. The 1918 Trench models resemble timepieces used by soldiers in the trenches, which became very popular following World War One. They sit on a bund strap, the numerals are large, promising good visibility in the dark, as do the broad cathedral hands. World War Two is the inspiration for the 1945 D12 Field Watch, specifically the robust timepieces made for soldiers by Swiss and British watchmakers. To pep up the dial a bit, the Super-LumiNova on the hands and numerals glows in different colors.

For the ИAVI collection (the reverse N is not a typo), Chua turned to the romance of the seafaring life. The dials are clearly inspired by the order telegraphs on older ships. The single *pomme* hand points not to the captain's requested speed, of course, but rather to numerals written out in full letters. The small seconds hand is either a compass hand or an anchor. Chua's attention to detail extends all the way to the crown, which is shaped like an old-fashioned sailor's cap. And if you are looking for a compass, it is engraved on the back.

VARIO
Orchard Plaza
150 Orchard Road, #07-05
Singapore 238841

E MAIL:
customer_service@vario.sg

WEBSITE:
www.vario.sg

FOUNDED:
2016

NUMBER OF EMPLOYEES:
1

MOST IMPORTANT COLLECTIONS/ PRICE RANGE:
1918 Trench, Medic, Pilot / approx. $388; 1945 D12 / approx. $368; Empire / approx. $298 to $698; VERSA / approx. $428

ИAVI Single Hand

Movement: automatic, Miyota 82s5 caliber; ø 26 mm, height 5.67 mm; 21 jewels; 21,600 vph; 42-hour power reserve
Functions: single hand for hours and minutes, subsidiary seconds
Case: stainless steel, ø 38 mm, height 12 mm; sapphire crystal; compass engraving on the case back; water-resistant to 10 atm
Band: calfskin, pin buckle
Remarks: wavy pattern on the dial
Price: $418
Variations: various dial colors; subsidiary seconds with anchor hand

1945 D12 Field

Movement: automatic, Miyota 82s5 caliber; ø 26 mm, height 5.67 mm; 21 jewels; 21,600 vph; 42-hour power reserve
Functions: hours, minutes, subsidiary seconds
Case: stainless steel, ø 37 mm, height 10.5 mm; sapphire crystal; screw-down crown; winding and setting crown at 4 o'clock; water-resistant to 10 atm
Band: cordura, pin buckle
Remarks: homage to the "Dirty Dozen," a set of watches made for soldiers fighting in World War Two
Price: $368
Variations: multiple dial colors

1918 Trench

Movement: automatic; Miyota 8N33 caliber; ø 26 mm, height 4.47 mm; 17 jewels; 21,600 vph; 42-hour power reserve
Functions: hours, minutes, sweep seconds
Case: stainless steel, ø 40 mm, height 12 mm; sapphire crystal; water-resistant to 5 atm
Band: calfskin, pin buckle
Price: $388
Variations: various dials and straps

VORTIC WATCH COMPANY

The U.S. watch industry produced some very fine timepieces back in the nineteenth century, like Ball, Elgin, Hamilton, and Waltham. So where did the millions of pocket watches go?

Enter R. T. Custer from Pennsylvania. He got wind of companies collecting just the cases of old pocket watches for their gold and silver, and throwing out the movements, dials, hands, and anything deemed worthless to the non-watch fan. So, he took some classes in industrial design, learned all about 3D printing, graduated, and moved out to Colorado. With crowd-funded seed money and a few friends, he started printing simple cases.

This process, known as upcycling, did not please one brand, Hamilton, whose name appears on some of the dials. It decided to use the staggering cash-power of its parent group, Swatch, to stomp out the upstart in Colorado. After five years of litigation, a judge at the Southern District of New York finally ended the absurd battle in Custer's favor, stating clearly that buyers were not about to be confused by the use of the old Hamilton parts in an upcycled watch. Vortic promptly did a victory lap with a Lancaster 065, using a Hamilton dial and caliber from 1930.

Vortic continues to explore the opportunities of modern technology to redo old movements. And each year brings new surprises, like the Springfield 069 with a secometer sub-dial. Even in their modern casings, these watches recall some of the grand old days of American history and business. The difference is subtle at times, but a glance at the Boston (with a Waltham engine) or the Springfield (with an Illinois movement), might be enough to see that while both are in "practical" style, the one is just a touch more elegant and might have belonged to the rider rather than the conductor. Finally, the Military Editions (with Hamiltons inside) are on black DLC.

Worth noting at this point: R.T. Custer has also launched Colorado Watch (see page 116) as a conduit for almost entirely U.S.-made watches.

VORTIC WATCH COMPANY
324 Jefferson St
Fort Collins, CO 80524
USA

TEL.:
855-285-7884

E-MAIL:
info@vorticwatches.com

WEBSITE:
www.vorticwatches.com

FOUNDED:
2013

NUMBER OF EMPLOYEES:
10

MOST IMPORTANT COLLECTIONS/PRICE RANGE:
American Artisan Series, Railroad Edition, Military Edition, "Convert Your Watch" service / $2,500 to $14,000

American Artisan Series "The Lancaster 061"

Movement: hand-wound, antique American Hamilton Watch Company movement (built in 1944, serial number: H24375), 10 size (ø 36 mm, height 4.5 mm); 21 jewels; côtes de Genève, gold sword hands; 30-hour power reserve
Functions: hours, minutes, subsidiary seconds
Case: stainless steel, ø 43 mm, height 10 mm; sapphire crystal; stainless steel crown; transparent case back; water-resistant to 5 atm
Band: calfskin, steel buckle
Price: $4,700

American Artisan Series "The Springfield 069"

Movement: hand-wound, Illinois Watch Company movement (built 1925, serial number 4613117); 12 size (ø 40 mm, height 5 mm); 19 jewels; rare "secometer" sub-dial with gold screws, gear train and accents; 36-hour power reserve
Functions: hours, minutes, subsidiary seconds
Case: bronze, ø 45 mm, height 12 mm; sapphire crystal; bronze crown; transparent case back; water-resistant to 5 atm
Band: leather, bronze buckle
Price: $5,500

Military Edition "Sixth Edition"

Movement: hand-wound, Hamilton movement (lot built from 1938 to 1945); 16 size (ø 40 mm, height 6.5 mm); 22 jewels; original antique hands with hacking sweep seconds in the original movement; 40-hour power reserve
Functions: hours, minutes, sweep seconds (hacking)
Case: stone-washed titanium, ø 49 mm; sapphire crystal; transparent case back; water-resistant to 5 atm
Band: military canvas with leather overlay, pin buckle
Remarks: comes with black calfskin strap
Price: $9,500; limited to 50 pieces
Variations: handprinted lume for dial

VOSTOK EUROPE

Vostok-Europe is a young brand with old roots. What started as a joint venture between the original Vostok company—a wholly separate entity—deep in the heart of Russia and a start-up in the newly minted European Union member nation of Lithuania has grown into something altogether different over the years. Over time, demand and the need for alternative complications expanded the portfolio of movements to include Swiss and Japanese ones. While the heritage of the Soviet watch industry is still evident in the inspirations and designs of Vostok-Europe, the watches built today have become favorites of extreme athletes the world over.

"Real people doing real things," is the mantra that Igor Zubovskij, managing director of the company, often repeats. "We don't use models to market our watches. Only real people test our watches in many different conditions."

That community of "real people" includes cross-country drivers in the Dakar Rally, one of the most famous aerobatic pilots in the world, a team of spelunkers who literally went to the bottom of the world in the Krubera Cave, and world free-diving champions. In 2020 the brand became the official watch of the SSN-571 Alumni Association and a part of the history of the world's first nuclear submarine.

In 2023, the brand celebrated its 20th birthday with a special model, and the 700th anniversary of the town of Vilnius, Lithuania, which, legend has it, was founded by the Iron Wolf, who came to Grand Duke Gediminas in a dream, which was interpreted as meaning he should found a town at the spot where he was hunting.

Vostok-Europe has never deviated from its design codes, and "big" is the number one qualification. Their watches are, however, robustly made and ensure professional dive quality. Some models use tritium tube technology for illumination, which offers about twenty-five years of constant lighting. The vertical tubes are placed in a kind of candleholder-shaped part for full 360-degree illumination.

KOLIZ VOSTOK CO. LTD.
Vytenio 22
LT-03229
Vilnius
Lithuania

TEL.:
+370-69805460

E-MAIL:
info@vostok-europe.com

WEBSITE:
www.vostok-europe.com

FOUNDED:
2003

NUMBER OF EMPLOYEES:
24

ANNUAL PRODUCTION:
30,000 watches

DISTRIBUTION:
Contact the company at the address above

MOST IMPORTANT COLLECTIONS/PRICE RANGE:
Energia / from $900; Atomic Age / from $999; N1 Rocket/ from $350

Energia
Reference number: YN84-575O540
Movement: automatic, Seiko Epson YN84 caliber; ø 27.4 mm, height 5.32 mm; 22 jewels; 21,600 vph; 41-hour power reserve
Functions: hours, minutes, sweep seconds; power reserve indication; 24-hour display
Case: bronze; ø 48 mm, height 17.3 mm; unidirectional bezel with 0-60 scale; hardened anti-reflective K1 mineral glass; screw-down crown; helium release valve; water-resistant to 20 atm
Band: calfskin, pin buckle
Remarks: "Trigalight" constant tritium illumination; changing tool, and dry box
Price: $1,199; limited to 3,000 numbered pieces
Variation: with silicone strap

Geležinis Vilkas (Iron Wolf)
Reference number: NH72-225E764
Movement: automatic TMI NH72 caliber; ø 27.4 mm; 24 jewels; 21,600 vph; skeletonized movement; 41-hours power reserve
Functions: hours, minutes, sweep seconds
Case: stainless steel; ø 46 mm, height 16.8 mm; unidirectional ceramic bezel with 0-60 scale, hardened K1 mineral glass; screw-down crown; water-resistant to 20 atm
Band: stainless steel, folding clasp
Remarks: inspired by the Iron Wolf legend and the founding of Vilnius, Lithuania, in 1323; luminous wolf on the underside of the crystal
Price: $739

Atomic Age Fermi Collection
Reference number: NH34-640A703
Movement: automatic TMI NH34 caliber; ø 27.40 mm; height 5.32; 24 jewels; 21,600 vph; 41-hour power reserve
Functions: hours, minutes, sweep seconds; second time zone; 24-hour display
Case: stainless steel; ø 48 mm, height 16 mm; hardened antireflective K1 mineral glass; screw-down crown; water-resistant to 30 atm
Band: leather, pin buckle
Remarks: "Trigalight" tritium illumination; comes with additional silicone strap, changing tool, and dry box
Price: $999; limited to 3,000 numbered pieces

N1 Rocket

Reference number: NH35-225A710
Movement: automatic, TMI NH35 caliber; ø 27.4 mm; height 5.32; 24 jewels; 21,600 vph; 41-hour power reserve
Functions: hours, minutes, sweep seconds
Case: stainless steel; ø 46 mm, height 16 mm; unidirectional bezel with 0-60 scale, hardened K1 mineral glass; screw-down crown; water-resistant to 20 atm
Band: calfskin, pin buckle
Price: $429; limited to 3,000 numbered pieces
Variations: with stainless steel bracelet or silicone strap

Space Race

Reference number: NH35-325B746
Movement: automatic TMI NH35 caliber; ø 27.40 mm; height 5.32; 24 jewels; 21,600 vph; 41-hour power reserve
Functions: hours, minutes, sweep seconds
Case: stainless steel with rose gold PVD; ø 46 mm, height 16 mm; unidirectional bezel with 0-60 scale; hardened K1 mineral glass; screw-down crown; water-resistant to 20 atm
Band: leather, pin buckle
Price: $419; limited to 3,000 numbered pieces
Variations: with stainless steel bracelet or silicone strap

Expedition North Pole

Reference number: YN55-597A729
Movement: automatic, S. Epson YN55 caliber; ø 29.36 mm; 22 jewels; 21,600 vph; 41-hours power reserve
Functions: hours, minutes, sweep seconds; pulsometer
Case: stainless steel; ø 48 mm, height 17.4 mm; bi-directional bezel with pulsometer and breath rates scales; hardened antireflective K1 mineral glass; screw-down crown; water-resistant to 20 atm
Band: stainless steel, folding clasp
Price: $519; limited to 3,000 numbered pieces
Variations: with stainless steel bracelet or silicone strap

Expedition South Pole

Reference number: YN55-592A760
Movement: automatic, S. Epson YN55 caliber; ø 29.36 mm; 22 jewels; 21,600 vph; 41-hour power reserve
Functions: hours, minutes, sweep seconds
Case: stainless steel; ø 43 mm, height 15.4 mm; hardened mineral glass; screw-down crown; water-resistant to 20 atm
Band: leather, pin buckle
Remarks: semi-transparent dial
Price: $399; limited to 3,000 numbered pieces
Variations: with stainless steel bracelet or silicone strap

Limousine

Reference number: NH38-560B682
Movement: automatic, TMI NH38 caliber; ø 27.4 mm, height 5.77 mm; 22 jewels; 21,600 vph; 40-hour power reserve
Functions: hours, minutes, sweep seconds; open heart
Case: rose gold, PVD plated; ø 43 mm, height 14 mm; hardened K1 mineral crystal; water-resistant to 5 atm
Band: leather, pin buckle
Price: $399
Variations: with stainless steel bracelet

Lunokhod

Reference number: NH35-620A634
Movement: automatic, TMI NH35 caliber; ø 27.4 mm, height 5.77 mm; 22 jewels; 21,600 vph; 40-hour power reserve
Functions: hours, minutes, sweep seconds
Case: stainless steel; ø 49 mm, height 17.5 mm; unidirectional bezel with 60-minute divisions; hardened antireflective K1 mineral glass; screw-down crown; helium release valve; water-resistant to 20 atm
Band: Leather and silicon straps
Remarks: "Trigalight" constant tritium illumination; comes with changing tool and dry box
Price: $799; limited to 3,000 numbered pieces
Variations: with stainless steel bracelet

VULCAIN

For ever so long, watchmakers or companies producing watches kept their names off the face of their products. So, it was not until 1894 that one Maurice Ditisheim put a name to the very fine pocket watches he had been producing in La Chaux-de-Fonds since 1858, the year he opened his little atelier. Among the timepieces in his portfolio were chronographs, a perpetual calendar, and a minute repeater.

Ditisheim understood that the world was bigger than Switzerland and he extended his networks abroad. His son Ernest-Albert took over in the 1890s and continued not only producing excellent watches but also promoting what was now a brand. He cleverly chose the name Vulcain, or Vulcan, the "patron saint," if you will, of all metal workers. The company became known as Vulcain & Volta in 1911, Vulcain & Studio in the 1950s, and finally, simply and lastly, Vulcain.

The Ditisheims saw the potential of the wristwatch early on and soon began making various models with in-house calibers. The company's major turning point came at the 1947 World's Fair, where it presented its Cricket wristwatch. The aptly named timepiece had an alarm built in that made a loud chirping sound thanks to a double soundboard. The fact that President Truman loved the watch started a tradition: every American president since, except George W. Bush, received a Cricket, even Donald Trump.

After years of ups and downs and changing hands, Vulcain seems to have found its feet again under the able management of Carla Duarte. The collections have been extended beyond the fabled Cricket to include the equally fabled Nautical and Skindiver diving watches. Modern production logistics and digital distribution channels have enabled more competitive pricing. Finally, while the vintage flavor is still present, these watches have a clearly modern look.

VULCAIN
Manufacture des montres Vulcain S.A.
Chemin des Tourelles 4
CH-2400 Le Locle
Switzerland

TEL:
+41-32-930-5370

E-MAIL:
info@vulcain.ch

WEBSITE:
www.vulcain.ch

FOUNDED:
1858

NUMBER OF EMPLOYEES:
7

ANNUAL PRODUCTION:
5000 watches

RETAIL:
Contact the company headquarters

MOST IMPORTANT COLLECTIONS/PRICE RANGE:
Cricket, Chronograph 1970s, Monopusher, Nautical, Salute, Skindiver Nautique / $1,500 to $6,000

Skindiver Nautique
Reference number: C6A2683
Movement: automatic, ETA caliber 2824-2; ø 25.6 mm, height 4.6 mm; 25 jewels; 28,800 vph; 42-hour power reserve
Functions: hours, minutes, sweep seconds
Case: stainless steel, ø 38 mm, height 12.2 mm; unidirectional bezel with ceramic insert with 0-60 scale; sapphire crystal; screw-down crown; water-resistant to 20 atm
Band: silicone (tropical), pin buckle
Price: $1,640
Variations: various straps and dials; with PVD-gold-plated case ($2,125); with bronze case ($2,280)

Grand Prix
Reference number: 530A2223
Movement: automatic, Landeron caliber L24; ø 25.6 mm, height 4.6 mm; 25 jewels; 28,800 vph; reconditioned historical clockwork from the 1970s; 40-hour power reserve
Functions: hours, minutes, sweep seconds
Case: stainless steel, ø 39 mm, height 12.7 mm; sapphire crystal; water-resistant to 5 atm
Band: calfskin, pin buckle
Price: $1,425
Variations: various straps and dials

Chronograph 1970's
Reference number: 640109
Movement: hand-wound, Sellita caliber SW510 M BH; ø 30.4 mm, height 7 mm; 25 jewels; 28,800 vph; 63-hour power reserve
Functions: hours, minutes, subsidiary seconds; chronograph
Case: stainless steel, ø 38 mm, height 12.4 mm; sapphire crystal; water-resistant to 5 atm
Band: calfskin, pin buckle
Price: $2,950
Variations: various straps and dials

WEMPE GLASHÜTTE

Ever since 2005, the global jewelry chain Gerhard D. Wempe KG has been putting out watches under its own name again. It was probably inevitable: Gerhard D. Wempe, who founded the company in the late nineteenth century in Oldenburg, was himself a watchmaker. And in the 1930s, the company also owned the Hamburg chronometer works that made watches for seafarers and pilots.

Today, while Wempe remains formally in Hamburg, its manufacturing is done in Glashütte. The move to the fully renovated and expanded Urania observatory in the hills above town was engineered by Eva-Kim Wempe, great-granddaughter of the founder. There, the company does all its after-sales service and tests watches using the strict German Industrial Norm (DIN 8319), with official blessings from the Saxon and Thuringian offices for measurement and calibration, and according to international norms paid out by the German Calibration Service. Among other criteria, a chronometer must be tested in the assembled state, which differs from the Swiss COSC certification method. In 2024, the production facility was expanded again so that a total of twenty-four watchmakers can be trained in the future.

The move to Glashütte coincided with a push to verticalize by creating a line of in-house movements reserved for the Chronometerwerke models, like the very retro Power Reserve or the Automatic Moonphase. The calibers, bearing the initials CW, are made in partnership with companies like Nomos in Glashütte or the Swiss workshop MHVJ. The second Wempe line is called Zeitmeister, or Master of Time. This collection uses more standard, but reworked, ETA or Sellita calibers. It meets all the requirements of the high art of watchmaking and, thanks to its accessible pricing, is attractive for budding collectors.

All models are in the middle price range, which the luxury watch industry has long shunned. In 2020, Wempe joined a large community of brands with sportive-elegant timepieces. The Iron Walker series is supposed to be inspired by the workers who built the great skyscrapers of New York in the 1920s. The line is characterized by the elegant bracelet that integrates almost seamlessly into the case. The skyscrapers are hinted at in the shape of the hands.

WEMPE GLASHÜTTE I./SA.
Herbert-Wempe-Platz 1
01768 Glashütte
Germany

TEL.:
+49 35053 312-0

E-MAIL:
info@wempe.de

WEBSITE:
www.wempe.com

FOUNDED:
1878

NUMBER OF EMPLOYEES:
845 worldwide; 78 at Wempe Glashütte I/SA

ANNUAL PRODUCTION:
4,000 watches

U.S. DISTRIBUTOR:
Wempe
700 Fifth Avenue
New York, NY 10019
212-397-9000
www.wempe.com

MOST IMPORTANT COLLECTIONS/PRICE RANGE:
Wempe Zeitmeister / approx. $1,000 to $4,700;
Wempe Chronometerwerke / approx. $6,000 to
$56,500; Wempe Iron Walker / $1,950 to $4,250

Iron Walker automatic 40
Reference number: WI 100037
Movement: automatic, Sellita caliber SW300-1a; ø 25.6 mm, height 3.6 mm; 25 jewels; 28,800 vph; ISO 3159 certified chronometer; 56-hour power reserve
Functions: hours, minutes, sweep seconds; date
Case: stainless steel, ø 40 mm, height 9 mm; sapphire crystal; water-resistant to 10 atm
Band: stainless steel, folding clasp, with safety lock
Price: $3,170
Variations: with 36-millimeter case

Iron Walker Automatic 40
Reference number: WI 100038
Movement: automatic, Sellita caliber SW300-1a; ø 25.6 mm, height 3.6 mm; 25 jewels; 28,800 vph; ISO 3159 certified chronometer; 56-hour power reserve
Functions: hours, minutes, sweep seconds; date
Case: stainless steel, ø 40 mm, height 9 mm; sapphire crystal; water-resistant to 10 atm
Band: stainless steel, folding clasp, with safety lock
Price: $3,170
Variations: with 36-millimeter case

Iron Walker Automatic 40
Reference number: WI 100039
Movement: automatic, Sellita caliber SW300-1a; ø 25.6 mm, height 3.6 mm; 25 jewels; 28,800 vph; ISO 3159 certified chronometer; 56-hour power reserve
Functions: hours, minutes, sweep seconds; date
Case: stainless steel, ø 40 mm, height 9 mm; sapphire crystal; water-resistant to 10 atm
Band: stainless steel, folding clasp, with safety lock
Price: $3,170
Variations: with 36-millimeter case

Iron Walker Chronograph 42

Reference number: WI 690015
Movement: automatic, ETA caliber 7753; ø 30 mm, height 7.9 mm; 27 jewels; 28,800 vph; DIN-certified chronometer; 54-hour power reserve
Functions: hours, minutes, subsidiary seconds; chronograph; date
Case: stainless steel, ø 42 mm, height 13 mm; bezel, sapphire crystal; water-resistant to 10 atm
Band: stainless steel, folding clasp
Price: $5,075; limited to 100 pieces

Zeitmeister Chronograph 42

Reference number: WI 690028
Movement: automatic, ETA caliber 7753; ø 30 mm, height 7.9 mm; 27 jewels; 28,800 vph; DIN-certified chronometer; 54-hour power reserve
Functions: hours, minutes, subsidiary seconds; chronograph; date
Case: stainless steel, ø 42 mm, height 16 mm; bezel, sapphire crystal; water-resistant to 5 atm
Band: calfskin, folding clasp
Remarks: limited to 100 pieces
Price: $3,045

Zeitmeister Fliegeruhr 45

Reference number: WM 690029
Movement: automatic, ETA caliber A07.161; ø 36.6 mm, height 3.6 mm; 27 jewels; 28,800 vph; DIN-certified chronometer; 48-hour power reserve
Functions: hours, minutes, sweep seconds; date
Case: stainless steel with black PVD, ø 45 mm, height 15 mm; sapphire crystal; water-resistant to 5 atm
Band: calfskin, pin buckle
Remarks: limited to 50 pieces
Price: $2,880

Chronometerwerke Automatic Moon Phase

Reference number: WG 100002
Movement: automatic, Wempe caliber CW5; ø 32.8 mm, height 6 mm; 35 jewels; 28,800 vph; screw balance with variable inertia; 2 mainsprings, three-quarter plate, hand-engraved balance cock, 6 gold chatons, finely finished tungsten micro-rotor with Glashütte ribbing; DIN-certified chronometer; 82-hour power reserve
Functions: hours, minutes, sweep seconds; date, moon phase
Case: stainless steel, ø 41 mm, height 11 mm; sapphire crystal; transparent case back; water-resistant to 3 atm
Band: reptile skin, pin buckle
Price: $8,025

Iron Walker Tide

Reference number: WI 210003
Movement: automatic, ETA caliber 2892-A2; ø 25.6 mm, height 3.6 mm; 21 jewels; 28,800 vph; ISO 3159 certified chronometer; 56-hour power reserve
Functions: hours, minutes, sweep seconds; date
Case: stainless steel, ø 42 mm, height 11 mm; crown-activated internal scale ring with the tide display; sapphire crystal; screw-down crown; water-resistant to 30 atm
Band: rubber, folding clasp, with safety lock
Price: $4,185

Iron Walker Automatic 40

Reference number: WI 110004
Movement: automatic, Sellita caliber SW300-1a; ø 25.6 mm, height 3.6 mm; 25 jewels; 28,800 vph; ISO 3159 certified chronometer; 56-hour power reserve
Functions: hours, minutes, sweep seconds; date
Case: stainless steel, ø 40 mm, height 9.75 mm; rose-gold bezel and crown; sapphire crystal; water-resistant to 10 atm
Band: stainless steel, folding clasp, with safety lock
Price: $5,770
Variations: with 36-millimeter case

YEMA

How difficult it is to live in the shadow of a great and geographically close competitor is illustrated by the little town of Morteau, population just under 7,000, in Burgundy, France. But in the world of watchmaking, it has quite a reputation. It lies in *Pays Horloger* (watch country), in a gentle valley traversed by the meandering Doubs River (hence the name, which means dead, or stagnant, water). Watchmaking came to the region and replaced agriculture as a source of income in the mid-1750s. Today, the town's school has an excellent reputation as an institution that supplies extremely talented workers to the entire industry, notably in Switzerland: Le Locle and La Chaux-de-Fonds, global hubs of Swiss watchmaking, are just a few miles away. Not surprisingly, it has two watch brands, one of which is Yema.

Quietly and steadily, Yema has been producing sports watches for divers, motor sports enthusiasts, pilots, and seafarers since 1948. Among its most important achievements was the first watch able to go 200 meters (660 feet) underwater. The Master Elements of the late 1970s let the user calculate speed, flying time, and the amount of fuel left in flight. And the Spationaute was the first French watch to reach space on the wrist of Jean-Loup Chrétien.

In 2009, the company was bought by a local group, Montres Ambre SA, which chose a flight forward strategy. Leveraging the long experience of its employees, it began manufacturing its own calibers, the Yema 2000 and Yema 3000 (GMT) as well as the Morteau 20. While the first two automatic movements are essentially based on the Swiss standard movements from ETA and Sellita in terms of architecture, dimensions, and rate performance, the Morteau 20 caliber is a modern, extra-thin automatic movement (3.7 millimeters!) with a bidirectional tungsten micro-rotor and 70-hour power reserve. The watches are then assembled and regulated in the company's own workshops using many individual parts manufactured in-house, though some parts are outsourced to French companies. Also done in Morteau are design, prototyping, and assembly.

YEMA WATCHES
1 rue Fontaine de l'Epine
F-25500 Morteau
France

TEL.:
+33-381-67-67-67

EMAIL:
privilege@yema.com

WEBSITE:
www.yema.com

FOUNDED:
1948

NUMBER OF EMPLOYEES:
60

DISTRIBUTION:
online

MOST IMPORTANT COLLECTIONS:
Superman, Navygraf, Yachtingraf, Meangraf, Rallygraf

Yachtingraf Tourbillon Mareographe
Reference number: 37.33.66.SN.U6
Movement: hand-wound, Calibre Manufacture Morteau CMM.30 (BCP base); ø 31 mm; 19 jewels; 21,600 vph; 1-minute tourbillon with free-sprung hairspring; black finishing on the movement (ALD); 105-hour power reserve
Functions: hours, minutes; tide indicator
Case: stainless steel, ø 42.5 mm, height 14.5 mm; unidirectional bezel set with sapphire crystal insert, with 0-60 scale; sapphire crystal; screw-down crown; water-resistant to 10 atm
Band: rubber, folding clasp
Price: $9,990; limited to 75 pieces for the 75th anniversary of the company

Skin Diver Slim Micro-Rotor
Reference number: 12.24.99.SN.M3
Movement: automatic, Calibre Manufacture Morteau CMM.20; ø 25.6 mm, height 3.7 mm; 33 jewels; 28,800 vph; tungsten micro-rotor; 70-hour power reserve
Functions: hours, minutes, sweep seconds
Case: stainless steel, ø 39 mm, height 10 mm; unidirectional bezel with 0-60 scale; sapphire crystal; screw-down crown; water-resistant to 30 atm
Band: stainless steel with scale-shaped links, folding clasp
Price: $2,249; limited edition

Navygraf Marine Nationale
Reference number: 21.14.55.SN.M
Movement: automatic, Calibre Manufacture Morteau CMM.10; ø 28 mm, height 4.2 mm; 27 jewels; 28,800 vph; 70-hour power reserve
Functions: hours, minutes, sweep seconds
Case: stainless steel, ø 39 mm, height 11 mm; unidirectional bezel, with 0-60 scale; sapphire crystal; screw-down crown; water-resistant to 30 atm
Band: stainless steel, folding clasp, with safety lock, with extension link
Price: $1,590

ZEITWINKEL

The independent brand Zeitwinkel, based in Saint-Imier, one of the hubs of the watch industry in Switzerland, is really not a run-of-the-mill enterprise. Its key attributes, ones that many manufacturers aspire to, is to create timepieces that are "timeless, simple, and sustainable." It sounds quite banal at first, but Zeitwinkel really means it. Because of that "timeless" parameter, the company feels no pressure to enter the rat race of producing new models like clockwork, but rather waits for the inspiration to come.

The models produced by Zeitwinkel (the name means "time angle") are deceptively classical. The simplest exemplar is a two-hand watch; the most complicated, the 273°, a three-hand timepiece with power reserve display and large date. The most decoration one will find on the dials is a spangling of stylized Ws, which is the inverted logo derived from the brand's proprietary typeface. The cases feature a delicate interplay of sandblasted and polished areas, but they are discreetly elegant, in a fairly "German" way, which comes as no surprise, because Zeitwinkel's founders, Ivica Maksimovic and Peter Nikolaus, hail from there. Some details will catch the eye, notably the extra-large subsidiary seconds dial and the aperture for the patented large date, found beside the 11 o'clock marker.

The most valuable part of the watches is their veritable *manufacture* movements, plates and bridges made of German silver, which is fairly rare in the business. All components are made in-house or come courtesy of longtime independent suppliers near Zeitwinkel's workshop in Saint-Imier, where all movements as well as all watches are assembled and regulated by hand.

A Zeitwinkel warhorse is the 273°, which comes with full-color dials or with a smokey sapphire dial that reveals the movement as if seen under water. The 188° line, a sober watch until recently, now comes in a variety of colors with matching rubber straps. As for the 240°, it, too, is understated, but the details are what count, like the carefully designed case and the 120-ray sunburst dial center.

Finally, in keeping with the company's ideals, you won't find any alligator in Zeitwinkel watch straps. Choices here are exclusively rubber, calfskin, or calfskin with an alligator-like pattern.

ZEITWINKEL MONTRES SA
Rue Pierre-Jolissaint 35
CH-2610 Saint-Imier
Switzerland

TEL.:
+41-32-940-17-71

E-MAIL:
info@zeitwinkel.ch

WEBSITE:
www.zeitwinkel.ch

FOUNDED:
2006

ANNUAL PRODUCTION:
Between 600 and 800 watches

U.S. DISTRIBUTOR:
Contact company directly for purchase or retailer addresses

MOST IMPORTANT COLLECTIONS/PRICE RANGE:
mechanical wristwatches / starting at around $14,500

240° Noir

Reference number: 240-23033-00
Movement: automatic, ZW0102 caliber; ø 30.4 mm, height 5.7 mm; 30 jewels; 28,800 vph; German silver three-quarter plate with côtes de Genève and perlage; polished screws and edges; "Black-Or" on plates and bridges; 72-hour power reserve
Functions: hours, minutes, sweep seconds
Case: stainless steel with DLC, ø 40.5 mm, height 12.1 mm; sapphire crystal; transparent case back; water-resistant to 10 atm
Band: rubber, folding clasp
Remarks: structured dial with 120 sunrays
Price: $19,250
Variations: grey, orange, red, and blue dials with matching rubber straps; grey PVD case

273° Saphir Bleu

Reference number: 273-45018-00
Movement: automatic, caliber ZW0103; ø 30.4 mm, height 8 mm; 49 jewels; 28,800 vph; German silver three-quarter plate and bridges, côtes de Genève, polished screws and edges; perlage on dial side; 72-hour power reserve
Functions: hours, minutes, subsidiary seconds; power reserve indicator; big date
Case: stainless steel, ø 42.5 mm, height 13.8 mm; sapphire crystal; transparent case back; water-resistant to 5 atm
Band: calfskin, folding clasp
Remarks: blue sapphire crystal dial
Price: $24,000
Variations: smoked sapphire dial; different bands

188° MAKS Red "Rouge Lobélie"

Reference number: 188-30023-00
Movement: automatic, caliber ZW0102; ø 30.4 mm, height 5.7 mm; 28 jewels; 28,800 vph; German silver three-quarter plate and bridges, with côtes de Genève and perlage, polished screws and edges; 72-hour power reserve
Functions: hours, minutes, subsidiary seconds
Case: stainless steel, ø 39 mm, height 11.6 mm; sapphire crystal; transparent case back; water-resistant to 5 atm
Band: calfskin, folding clasp
Remarks: detailed 3D logo structure in dial, covered by 20 layers of hand-applied lacquer
Price: $16,200
Variations: various dial colors; rubber strap

ZENITH

Zenith, still housed in a tall, light-bathed industrial building in Le Locle, Switzerland, was founded in 1865 by Georges Favre-Jacot as a small watch reassembly workshop. It has produced all kinds of watches in its long history, but its claim to fame is the El Primero caliber, the first wristwatch chronograph movement boasting automatic winding and a frequency of 36,000 vph, allowing for measurements of a tenth of a second. It was 1969, and only a few manufacturers had risked such a high oscillation frequency—and none of them with such complexity as the integrated chronograph mechanism and bilaterally winding rotor of the El Primero.

LVMH Group bought the brand in 1999, boosting its technical possibilities. Zenith was dusted off and modernized. The historic complex in Le Locle, which was put on UNESCO's World Heritage list in 2009, was thoroughly renovated. Over eighty different crafts are now practiced there, from watchmaking to design, from art to prototyping. Synergies with the Group companions Hublot and TAG Heuer produced the Defy 21, a complex chronograph movement based on the 36,000-vph El Primero. It features two separate gear trains and escapements for time and chronograph functions, respectively. The chronograph movement beats at 360,000 vph, allowing the hundredths of a second to be displayed. The other technical feat is the Zero G that keeps the escapement system in the horizontal position.

Re-releasing older models has led the company to promote a circular economy, whereby older models can be perfectly restored and remain in circulation. The original El Primero was also modernized and is now the Primero 3600 caliber, boasting a little more power reserve than the original.

This caliber is used in the latest Chronomaster Sport models, which come in titanium and stainless steel with a green dial and green bezel. The highlight, however, is the comeback of the long-awaited chronograph with triple calendar display. In the new Chronomaster Original Triple Calendar, Zenith combines the contemporary performance of the legendary automatic high-frequency chronograph movement with a classic full calendar and moon phase display— all in a compact, historically inspired, and distinctive Chronomaster design.

ZENITH SA
34, rue des Billodes
CH-2400 Le Locle
Switzerland

TEL.:
+41-32-930-6262

WEBSITE:
www.zenith-watches.com

FOUNDED:
1865

NUMBER OF EMPLOYEES:
over 330 employees worldwide

U.S. DISTRIBUTOR:
Zenith Watches
966 South Springfield Avenue
Springfield, NJ 07081
866-675-2079
contact.zenith@lvmhwatchjewelry.com

MOST IMPORTANT COLLECTIONS/PRICE RANGE:
Academy / from $80,900; Elite / from $4,700;
Chronomaster / from $6,700; Pilot / from $5,700;
Defy / from $5,900

Chronomaster Open
Reference number: 18.3300.3604/69.C823
Movement: automatic, Zenith caliber 3604; ø 30 mm, height 6.6 mm; 35 jewels; 36,000 vph; movement partially skeletonized over the regulating section; 60-hour power reserve
Functions: hours, minutes, subsidiary seconds; chronograph
Case: stainless steel, ø 39.5 mm, height 12.6 mm; sapphire crystal; transparent case back; water-resistant to 10 atm
Band: stainless steel, folding clasp
Price: $10,000
Variations: with rubber strap ($9,800)

Chronomaster Original Triple Calendar
Reference number: 03.3400.3610/39.M3200
Movement: automatic, Zenith caliber 3610 "El Primero"; ø 30 mm, height 7.73 mm; 35 jewels; 36,000 vph; 60-hour power reserve
Functions: hours, minutes, subsidiary seconds; chronograph; full calendar with date, weekday, month, moon phase
Case: stainless steel, ø 38 mm, height 12.6 mm; sapphire crystal; transparent case back; water-resistant to 5 atm
Band: stainless steel, folding clasp
Price: $13,900
Variations: with calfskin strap ($13,400)

Chronomaster Original Triple Calendar
Reference number: 03.3400.3610/38.C911
Movement: automatic, Zenith caliber 3610 "El Primero"; ø 30 mm, height 7.73 mm; 35 jewels; 36,000 vph; 60-hour power reserve
Functions: hours, minutes, subsidiary seconds; chronograph; full calendar with date, weekday, month, moon phase
Case: stainless steel, ø 38 mm, height 12.6 mm; sapphire crystal; transparent case back; water-resistant to 5 atm
Band: calfskin, folding clasp
Price: $13,400
Variations: with stainless steel bracelet ($13,900)

Defy Revival

Reference number: 03.A3648.670/21.M3648
Movement: automatic, Zenith caliber 670 "Elite";
ø 25.6 mm, height 3.88 mm; 27 jewels; 28,800 vph;
50-hour power reserve
Functions: hours, minutes, sweep seconds; date
Case: stainless steel, ø 37 mm, height 15.5 mm;
unidirectional bezel, with 0-60 scale; sapphire crystal;
water-resistant to 60 atm
Band: stainless steel, double folding clasp
Remarks: replica of a historic model from 1969
Price: $7,700

Defy Extreme Diver

Reference number: 95.9600.3620/21.I300
Movement: automatic, Zenith caliber
3620 "El Primero"; ø 30 mm, height 6.6 mm; 26 jewels;
36,000 vph; 60-hour power reserve
Functions: hours, minutes, sweep seconds; date
Case: titanium, ø 42.5 mm, height 15.5 mm;
unidirectional bezel in ceramic with 0-60 scale; sapphire
crystal; transparent case back; screw-down crown,
helium valve; water-resistant to 60 atm
Band: textile, folding clasp
Price: $11,300

Defy Skyline Chronograph

Reference number: 03.9500.3600/51.I001
Movement: automatic, Zenith caliber
3600 "El Primero"; ø 30 mm, height 6.6 mm; 35 jewels;
36,000 vph; 60-hour power reserve
Functions: hours, minutes, subsidiary seconds;
chronograph; date
Case: stainless steel, ø 42 mm; sapphire crystal;
transparent case back; water-resistant to 10 atm
Band: stainless steel, folding clasp
Remarks: comes with extra rubber strap
Price: $13,400
Variations: with black dial and white dial and
interchangeable rubber straps

Defy Skyline 36mm

Reference number: 03.9400.670/51.I001
Movement: automatic, Zenith caliber 670 "Elite";
ø 25.6 mm, height 3.88 mm; 27 jewels; 28,800 vph;
48-hour power reserve
Functions: hours, minutes, sweep seconds; date
Case: stainless steel, ø 36 mm, height 10.35 mm;
sapphire crystal; transparent case back; screw-down
crown; water-resistant to 10 atm
Band: stainless steel, folding clasp
Price: $8,700
Variations: with green or pink dial; with diamond bezel
($12,300)

Defy Skyline Skeleton

Reference number: 03.9300.3620/79.I001
Movement: automatic, Zenith caliber 3620 "El Primero";
ø 30 mm, height 6.6 mm; 26 jewels; 36,000 vph;
skeletonized movement; 60-hour power reserve
Functions: hours, minutes, subsidiary seconds
(10-second rotation)
Case: stainless steel, ø 41 mm, height 11.6 mm; sapphire
crystal; transparent case back; screw-down crown;
water-resistant to 10 atm
Band: rubber, folding clasp
Remarks: skeletonized dial; comes with extra blue
rubber strap
Price: $11,300

Defy Skyline Skeleton Ceramic

Reference number: 49.9300.3620/78.I001
Movement: automatic, Zenith caliber 3620 "El
Primero"; ø 30 mm, 26 jewels; 36,000 vph; skeletonized
movement; 60-hour power reserve
Functions: hours, minutes, subsidiary seconds
(10-second rotation)
Case: ceramic, ø 41 mm, height 11.6 mm; sapphire
crystal; transparent case back; screw-down crown;
water-resistant to 10 atm
Band: ceramic, folding clasp
Remarks: skeletonized dial
Price: $17,500

Defy Extreme Titanium

Reference number: 95.9100.9004/01.I001
Movement: automatic, Zenith caliber
9004 "El Primero"; ø 32 mm, height 7.9 mm; 53 jewels;
36,000 vph; separate chronograph construction
with separate escapement (360,000 vph) and power
management; Timelab-certified chronometer; 50-hour
power reserve
Functions: hours, minutes, subsidiary seconds; power
reserve indicator (for the chronograph function);
chronograph (indicates 100th of a second)
Case: titanium, ø 45 mm, height 15.4 mm; sapphire
crystal; transparent case back; water-resistant to
20 atm
Band: titanium, double folding clasp
Price: $18,600

Defy Extreme Mirror

Reference number: 03.9102.9004/90.I001
Movement: automatic, Zenith caliber
9004 "El Primero"; ø 32 mm, height 7.9 mm; 53 jewels;
36,000 vph; separate chronograph construction
with separate escapement (360,000 vph) and power
management; Timelab-certified chronometer; 50-hour
power reserve
Functions: hours, minutes, subsidiary seconds; power
reserve indicator (for the chronograph function);
chronograph (indicates 100th of a second)
Case: stainless steel, ø 45 mm, height 15.4 mm;
sapphire crystal; transparent case back; water-resistant
to 20 atm
Band: stainless steel, double folding clasp
Price: $26,900

Defy Skyline Tourbillon

Reference number: 03.9300.3630/51.I001
Movement: automatic, Zenith caliber 3630 "El
Primero"; ø 30 mm; 34 jewels; 36,000 vph; 1-minute
tourbillon; 60-hour power reserve
Functions: hours, minutes, subsidiary seconds (on the
tourbillon cage)
Case: stainless steel, ø 41 mm, height 11.6 mm; sapphire
crystal; transparent case back; screw-down crown;
water-resistant to 10 atm
Band: stainless steel, folding clasp
Price: $57,100

Pilot Automatic

Reference number: 03.4000.3620/21.I001
Movement: automatic, Zenith caliber 3620 "El
Primero"; ø 30 mm; 26 jewels; 36,000 vph; 60-hour
power reserve
Functions: hours, minutes, sweep seconds; date
Case: stainless steel, ø 40 mm, height 12.9 mm;
sapphire crystal; transparent case back; screw-down
crown; water-resistant to 10 atm
Band: rubber textile overlay, triple folding clasp
Remarks: comes with extra calfskin leather strap
Price: $7,800

Pilot Big Date Flyback

Reference number: 03.4000.3652/51.I003
Movement: automatic, Zenith caliber 3652 "El Primero";
ø 30 mm; 26 jewels; 36,000 vph; 60-hour power reserve
Functions: hours, minutes, subsidiary seconds; flyback
chronograph; large date
Case: stainless steel, ø 42.5 mm, height 14.3 mm;
sapphire crystal; transparent case back; screw-down
crown; water-resistant to 10 atm
Band: rubber with textile overlay, triple folding clasp
Remarks: comes with extra calfskin strap
Price: $11,800

Pilot Big Date Flyback

Reference number: 49.4000.3652/21.I001
Movement: automatic, Zenith caliber 3652 "El Primero";
ø 30 mm; 26 jewels; 36,000 vph; 60-hour power reserve
Functions: hours, minutes, subsidiary seconds; flyback
chronograph; large date
Case: ceramic, ø 42.5 mm, height 14.3 mm; sapphire
crystal; transparent case back; screw-down crown;
water-resistant to 10 atm
Band: with textile overlay, triple folding clasp
Remarks: comes with extra textile strap
Price: $13,900

Caliber 670 Elite

Automatic; skeletonized; single mainspring barrel, 50-hour power reserve
Functions: hours, minutes, sweep seconds; date
Diameter: 25.6 mm
Height: 3.88 mm
Jewels: 27
Balance: glucydur
Frequency: 28,800 vph
Hairspring: flat hairspring
Shock protection: Kif
Remarks: 187 parts

Caliber 400 El Primero

Automatic; column wheel control of the chronograph functions; single mainspring barrel, 50-hour power reserve
Functions: hours, minutes, subsidiary seconds; chronograph; date
Diameter: 30 mm
Height: 6.5 mm
Jewels: 31
Balance: glucydur
Frequency: 36,000 vph
Hairspring: flat hairspring
Shock protection: Kif
Remarks: 278 parts

Caliber 3600 El Primero

Automatic; silicon anchor and escape wheel; column wheel control of chronograph functions; single mainspring barrel, 60-hour power reserve; COSC-certified chronometer
Functions: hours, minutes, subsidiary seconds; chronograph; date
Diameter: 30 mm
Height: 6.6 mm
Jewels: 35
Balance: glucydur
Frequency: 36,000 vph
Hairspring: flat hairspring
Shock protection: Kif

Caliber 3610 El Primero

Automatic; silicon anchor and escape wheel; column wheel control of chronograph functions; single mainspring barrel, 60-hour power reserve; COSC-certified chronometer
Functions: hours, minutes, subsidiary seconds; chronograph; full calendar with date, weekday, month, moon phase
Diameter: 30 mm
Height: 7.73 mm
Jewels: 35
Balance: glucydur Frequency: 36,000 vph
Hairspring: flat hairspring
Shock protection: Kif
Remarks: 366 parts

Caliber 3620 El Primero

Automatic; silicon anchor and escape wheel; single mainspring barrel, 60-hour power reserve; COSC-certified chronometer
Functions: hours, minutes, subsidiary seconds; date
Diameter: 30 mm
Height: 6.6 mm
Jewels: 26
Balance: glucydur
Frequency: 36,000 vph
Hairspring: flat hairspring
Shock protection: Kif

Caliber 9004 El Primero

Automatic; independent chronograph mechanism with separate escapement (360,000 vph) and power management; COSC-certified chronometer; 2 hairsprings of nanotube carbon matrix, impervious to magnetic fields and temperature fluctuations; single spring barrel, 50-hour power reserve; Timelab-certified chronometer
Functions: hours, minutes, subsidiary seconds; power reserve indicator (for chronograph functions); chronograph displays 1/100th of a second
Diameter: 32.8 mm
Height: 7.9 mm
Jewels: 53
Balance: glucydur
Frequency: 36,000 vph
Shock protection: Kif
Remarks: 293 parts

ZEROO TIME CO.

Japan has a few very globally famous brands, like Casio, Citizen, and Seiko. But in their shadow, one finds a number of small brands doing excellent work as well: Zeroo Time, for example, was launched in 2017 by a watch designer named Syuu Kiryou, who prefers to go by the name SYUU, all caps. His experience in the watch industry had left him feeling that watches needed strong design but had to be affordable as well, even if they had serious complications, like tourbillons.

The T8 Orion Full Skeleton Tourbillon, for instance, is fully skeletonized, including an elongated sapphire crystal in the case middle to offer a lateral view into the watch. On the T-6 Quaser, the tourbillon appears in the middle surrounded by a ring, giving it a somewhat extra-terrestrial look. The transparent case back reveals a pinwheel côtes de Genève on the mainplate.

Special design involves cost, and Zeroo Time intended to make products that would draw attention and were mechanically reliable but would not ruin the buyer. "We want every watch lover to have one of our watches" says SYUU. "We are planning to develop our own movements in the future and create products that are a cross between Swiss and Japanese made."

The way to achieve the delicate cost-quality balance was, first, to crowdfund, and avoid many of the extraneous expenses from distribution and retailing. The second strategy was to source low-cost parts, for instance Sea-Gull movements from China, which are taken apart and rigorously worked over by a team of watchmakers in Japan, where the watches are assembled. In the meantime, these parts are in fact purchased and replicated in China. The company also uses Swiss STP calibers, notably in its M3 Lyra series.

Almost eight years in, Zeroo is making a name for itself. It is present in fifteen countries, including the USA. The designs are also becoming more independent from external inspiration. The latest model, the T9 UFO, comes in a sleek, mellifluous case, like a space vessel. Its clean dial gives stage center (at 6 o'clock) to a simple tourbillon that rotates like a UFO's reactor.

ZEROO TIME CO.
2-1-3, Naganuma-cho, Hachioji-shi, Tokyo, 192-0907
Japan

TEL.:
+81 50-3656-4608

EMAIL:
hshiba@zerootime.com

WEBSITE:
https://zerootime.com/en-global

FOUNDED:
2017

NUMBER OF EMPLOYEES:
10

ANNUAL PRODUCTION:
approx. 1,000 pieces

U.S. DISTRIBUTOR:
King Jewelers Tennessee
4121 Hillsboro Pike | Nashville, TN 37215
info@kingjewelers.com
KingJewelers.com
615-724-5464

MOST IMPORTANT COLLECTIONS/PRICE RANGE:
Zeroo T (Tourbillon) series / $3,000 to $5,000

T9 UFO Automatic Tourbillon

Reference number: ZT009SSBB
Movement: automatic, tourbillon caliber ZT09; ø 34.5 mm; height 7 mm; 35 jewels; 28,800 vph; 60-hour power reserve
Functions: hours, minutes
Case: stainless steel, 46 mm x 40 mm; height 14.5 mm; sapphire crystal; transparent case back; water-resistant to 3 atm
Band: rubber (FKM), folding buckle
Price: $3,300
Variations: with various color straps and cases

T4-01 The Archer Full Skeleton Tourbillon

Reference number: ZT004-01BBK
Movement: automatic, tourbillon caliber ZT01A; ø 33.5 mm; height 6.5 mm; 20 jewels; 28,800 vph; 60-hour power reserve
Functions: hours, minutes
Case: stainless steel, 48 mm x 41 mm; height 13 mm; sapphire crystal; transparent case back; water-resistant to 3 atm
Band: rubber (FKM), folding buckle
Price: $3,200
Variations: with various color straps and cases

T7 The Archer Skeleton Tourbillon

Reference number: ZT007SSV
Movement: automatic, tourbillon caliber ZT03; ø 33.5 mm; height 6.5 mm; 20 jewels; 28,800 vph; 60-hour power reserve
Functions: hours, minutes
Case: stainless steel, ø 46 mm, height 13 mm; sapphire crystal; transparent case back; water-resistant to 3 atm
Band: stainless steel, folding buckle
Price: $3,500
Variations: with various colored case and straps

ZERO WEST

Time, place, and history are the reference points for Zero West, a company founded in 2015 by Andrew Brabyn and Graham Collins, a leading graphic designer and an aerospace engineer, respectively. The company name itself refers to the coordinates of the Greenwich Royal Observatory. Their first watch was a statement; the Longitude L1 paid homage to an icon of British (or even world) horology: John Harrison's remarkable H4 maritime clock that managed to keep accurate time on a ship in 1761 and which contributed to the establishment of the Greenwich prime meridian by George Airy in 1851.

Meanwhile, the company has defined three core collections for their brand: automotive, aviation, and marine. The Lancaster DB-1, for example, recalls the plane's altimeter dial, and inside one finds a smelted disc from the bodywork of ED825, which was along for the famous "Dambusters" (Operation Chastise) raid in 1943, during which the RAF ricocheted special bombs on dams in the Ruhr region to try and cripple Nazi Germany's industrial production.

Another aviation model is the M1 Mosquito, which contains a piece of the crankshaft from a Mosquito. These agile airplanes, known as "Mossies," were made of plywood and ran on two Rolls-Royce Merlin engines. They were involved, among others, in the D-Day landings and in Operation Jericho, a raid to free French resistance fighters from a German prison camp.

The automotive portfolio covers machines on wheels, like the drive shaft of the 1958 race winning Aston Martin DBR1 driven by Stirling Moss and Tony Brooks. Anyone with a good train set has at least heard of the famous Flying Scotsman, a locomotive that was the first to reach 100 mph, on November 30, 1930. A section of its boiler tube is the guest of honor in the FS-1 Flying Scotsman.

The watches are designed and assembled at the company's workshop and headquarters on the South Coast of England. It is where the two founders do their historical research and brainstorm each new watch dial. It is also where Graham Collins makes the straps for the collections. Low volume ensures high quality. The geographical location on the dials and case back relates to the watch's theme. Each watch is powered by tried-and-true Swiss calibers, like the ETA 2824 and Valjoux 7750 for the chronographs.

ZERO WEST LTD
41 Bridgefoot Path
Emsworth
Hampshire
United Kingdom
PO10 7EB

TEL.:
+44 (0)1243-376-676

E-MAIL:
time@zerowest.co.uk

WEBSITE:
www.zerowest.watch

FOUNDED:
2015

NUMBER OF EMPLOYEES:
5

DISTRIBUTION:
Contact the manufacturer directly

MOST IMPORTANT COLLECTIONS:
Aviation (Spitfire S1/S2/S3), (Hurricane H1); Marine (Longitude L2); Motorsport (LS-2 Land Speed Bullhead, Flying Scotsman)

Lancaster

Reference number: DB-1
Movement: automatic, ETA 2824; ø 44 mm, height 14.1mm; 26 jewels; 28,800 vph, 41-hour power reserve
Functions: hours, minutes
Case: stainless steel with 8 polished vertically cut ball-nose flutes, ø 44 mm, height 14.1 mm; sapphire crystal, transparent case back; screw-in crown; transparent case back with view of metal disc from a Lancaster ED825 with serial number; water-resistant to 10 atm
Band: fluoroelastomer rubber strap, pin buckle
Remarks: dial inspired from an altimeter gauge from a Lancaster cockpit and paying tribute to Operation Chastise and the Lancaster plane ED825, 1 of 19 on that mission
Price: $3,970; limited to 200 pieces

Mosquito

Reference Number: M1
Movement: automatic, Sellita SW200-1 (top premium grade); ø 41mm, height 13.5 mm; 28,800 vph, 26 jewels; 41-hour power reserve
Functions: hours, minutes
Case: stainless steel, ø 41 mm, height 13.5 mm; screw-in crown; sapphire crystal; transparent case back with view of a disc cut from a WW2 Mosquito Merlin engine crankshaft (HX909) with serial number; water-resistant to 10 atm
Band: fluoroelastomer rubber strap, pin buckle
Remarks: Vintage inspired dial commemorating Operation Jericho a WW2 raid to free French resistance fighters; date and longitude positions where the mission took place
Price: $3,970; limited to 100 pieces

Flying Scotsman

Reference Number: FS-1
Movement: automatic, Sellita SW200-1 (top premium grade); ø 41 mm, height 13.1 mm; 28,800 vph, 26 jewels; 41-hour power reserve
Functions: hours, minutes
Case: black PVD stainless steel, ø 41mm, height 13.1mm; screw-in crown; sapphire crystal; transparent case back with view of disc from the original Flying Scotsman boiler tube with serial number; water-resistant to 10 atm
Band: fluoroelastomer rubber, pin buckle
Remarks: dial inspired from a locomotive gauge; latitude and longitude of Doncaster works where the Flying Scotsman was built, and date of completion printed at 6 o'clock; luminous minute track
Price: $3,970; limited to 100 pieces

CONCEPTO

The Concepto Watch Factory, founded in 2006 in La Chaux-de-Fonds, is the successor to the family-run company Jaquet SA, which changed its name to La Joux-Perret a little while ago and then moved to a different location on the other side of the hub of watchmaking. In 2008, Valérien Jaquet, son of the company founder Pierre Jaquet, began systematically building up a modern movement and watch component factory on an empty floor of the building.

Today, the Concepto Watch Factory employs eighty people in various departments, such as Development/Prototyping, Decoparts (partial manufacturing using lathes, machining, or wire erosion), Artisia (production of movements and complications in large series), as well as Optimo (escapements). In addition to the standard family of calibers, the C2000 (based on the Valjoux) and the vintage chronograph movement C7000 (the evolution of the Venus Caliber), the company's product portfolio includes various tourbillon movements (Caliber C8000) and several modules for adding onto ETA movements (Caliber C1000). A brand-new caliber series, the C3000, features a retrograde calendar and seconds, a power reserve indicator, and a chronograph. The C4000 chronograph caliber with automatic winding is currently in pre-series testing.

One of Concepto's greatest assets is its flexibility. Most of the company's movements are not sold off the shelf, as it were, but rather designed according to the specific requirements of watchmaking companies with regard to form or technical DNA. Some of these cooperations become long-term relationships. Complicated movements are assembled entirely and tested by the company's watchmakers, while others are sold as kits for assembly by the watchmakers. Annual production is somewhere between 30,000 and 40,000 units, with additional hundreds of thousands of components made for contract manufacturing.

1053

Automatic; inverted construction with dial-side escapement; bidirectional off-center winding rotor; single spring barrel; 42-hour power reserve
Functions: hours, minutes, subsidiary seconds (all off-center)
Diameter: 33 mm
Height: 3.75 mm
Jewels: 31
Balance: glucydur
Frequency: 28,800 vph
Balance spring: flat hairspring
Remarks: black finishing on movement

2904 (dial side)

Inverted construction with dial-side escapement; single spring barrel; 48-hour power reserve
Functions: hours, minutes, subsidiary seconds
Diameter: 30.4 mm
Height: 4.6 mm
Jewels: 31
Balance: screw balance
Frequency: 28,800 vph
Balance spring: flat hairspring

3041 Skeleton (dial side)

Hand-wound; skeletonized symmetrical construction; single spring barrel; 48-hour power reserve
Functions: hours, minutes
Diameter: 32.6 mm
Height: 5.5 mm
Jewels: 21
Balance: screw balance
Frequency: 28,800 vph
Balance spring: flat hairspring
Remarks: extensive personalization options for finishing and accessories

2000-RAC

Automatic; column wheel control of chronograph functions; stop-second system; single spring barrel; 48-hour power reserve
Functions: hours, minutes, subsidiary seconds; chronograph
Diameter: 30.4 mm; **Height**: 8.4 mm
Jewels: 26; balance: screw balance
Frequency: 28,800 vph
Balance spring: flat hairspring
Shock protection: Incabloc
Remarks: related calibers: 2000 (without control wheel); with two or three totalizers ("tricompax") with or without date; various additional displays (moon phase, retrograde date hand, additional 24-hour sweep hand, power reserve indicator)

8500

Hand-wound; 1-minute tourbillon; column wheel control of chronograph functions; single spring barrel; 50-hour power reserve
Functions: hours, minutes, subsidiary seconds; split-seconds chronograph
Diameter: 31.3 mm
Height: 7.2 mm
Jewels: 31
Balance: screw balance
Frequency: 21,600 vph
Balance spring: flat hairspring
Remarks: very fine movement finishing

8950-A

Automatic; 1-minute tourbillon; single spring barrel; 60-hour power reserve
Functions: hours, minutes
Diameter: 30.4 mm
Height: 6.7 mm
Jewels: 27
Balance: glucydur
Frequency: 28,800 vph
Balance spring: flat hairspring
Remarks: related caliber: 8950-M (manual winding); extensive personalization options for the finishing, accessories, and functions

8000 (dial side)

Hand-wound; 1-minute tourbillon; single spring barrel; 72-hour power reserve
Functions: hours, minutes
Diameter: 32.6 mm
Height: 5.7 mm
Jewels: 19
Balance: screw balance
Frequency: 21,600 vph
Balance spring: flat hairspring
Remarks: extensive personalization options for the finishing, accessories, and functions

8152

Automatic; 1-minute tourbillon; bridges and plate made of sapphire crystal; off-center, bidirectional rotor; single spring barrel; 72-hour power reserve
Functions: hours, minutes
Diameter: 32.6 mm
Height: 8.5 mm
Jewels: 25
Balance: screw balance
Frequency: 21,600 vph
Balance spring: flat hairspring
Remarks: extensive personalization options for the finishing, accessories, and functions

8600 (dial side)

Hand-wound; 1-minute tourbillon; double spring barrel; 72-hour power reserve
Functions: hours, minutes; minute repeater with carillon (3 gongs)
Diameter: 34.6 mm
Height: 6.45 mm
Jewels: 36
Balance: screw balance
Frequency: 21,600 vph
Hairspring: flat hairspring
Remarks: many customization options for finishing, equipment and functions

ETA

This Swatch Group movement manufacturer ETA produced millions of movements a year. The company offers a broad spectrum of automatic movements in various dimensions with different functions, chronograph mechanisms in varying configurations, pocket watch classics (Calibers 6497 and 98), and hand-wound calibers of days gone by (Calibers 1727 and 7001). Add to that an endless variety of quartz technology from inexpensive three-hand mechanisms to highly complicated multifunctional movements and futuristic ETA quartz mechanisms featuring autonomous energy creation using a rotor and generator.

For a while, the company was selling its products to anyone and everyone. Then, in 2002, ETA's management announced it would discontinue providing half-finished component kits for reassembly and/or embellishment to specialized workshops, and from 2010 they would only offer completely assembled and finished movements for sale. The Swiss Competition Commission known as CoCo, however, studied the issue, and a new deal was struck in 2013, phasing out sales to customers over a period of six years. ETA is already somewhat of a competitor of independent reassemblers such as Soprod, Sellita, La Joux-Perret, Dubois Dépraz, and others thanks to its diversification of available calibers, which has led many brands to counter by creating their own base movements.

The almost stereotypical accusation of ETA being "mass goods" is not justified, however, for it is a real art to manufacture filigreed micromechanical technology in consistently high quality. This is certainly one of the reasons why there have been very few movement factories in Europe that can compete with ETA, or that would want to. Since the success of Swatch—a pure ETA product—millions of Swiss francs have been invested in new development and manufacturing technologies. ETA now only supplies movements to sister companies in the Group, i.e., all Swatch Group brands below Omega. However, these are new generations of movements with, in part, components that are insensitive to magnetic fields (made of silicon or Nivachron).

The internal ETA caliber designations are no longer communicated externally; instead, each Swatch Group brand now assigns its own caliber numbers. The movements presented on these pages represent only a small part of the still huge caliber portfolio —mechanical and quartz— of the Swiss movement giant with production sites Switzerland.

Certina Powermatic 80

Automatic; ball bearing-mounted rotor, hacking seconds, indexless fine adjustment; single mainspring barrel, 80-hour power reserve
Base caliber: ETA C07611
Functions: hours, minutes, sweep seconds; date aperture
Diameter: 26 mm
Height: 4.6 mm
Jewels: 25
Balance: glucydur
Frequency: 21,600 vph
Hairspring: Nivachron
Shock protection: Nivachoc
Remarks: the Powermatic caliber used by many Swatch Group brands is based on the architecture of the reliable ETA 2824-2; also made with a silicon hairspring

Mido Caliber 80

Automatic; ball bearing-mounted rotor, hacking seconds, indexless fine adjustment; single mainspring barrel, 80-hour power reserve
Base caliber: ETA C07611
Functions: hours, minutes, sweep seconds; date aperture
Diameter: 26 mm
Height: 4.6 mm
Jewels: 25
Balance: glucydur
Frequency: 21,600 vph
Hairspring: Nivachron
Shock protection: Novodiac
Remarks: the Powermatic caliber used by many Swatch Group brands is based on the architecture of the reliable ETA 2824-2; also made with a silicon hairspring

Tissot Powermatic 80

Automatic; ball bearing-mounted Rotor, hacking seconds, indexless fine adjustment ; single mainspring barrel, 80-hour power reserve
Base caliber: ETA C07611
Functions: hours, minutes, sweep seconds; date aperture
Diameter: 26 mm
Height: 4.6 mm
Jewels: 25
Balance: glucydur
Frequency: 21,600 vph
Hairspring: Nivachron
Shock protection: Nivachoc
Remarks: the Powermatic caliber used by many Swatch Group brands is based on the architecture of the reliable ETA 2824-2; also made with a silicon hairspring

Hamilton H-31

Automatic; hacking seconds; single mainspring barrel, 60-hour power reserve
Base caliber: ETA 7753
Functions: hours, minutes, subsidiary seconds; chronograph; date aperture with pusher-activated quick-set correction
Diameter: 30.4 mm
Height: 7.9 mm
Jewels: 25
Balance: glucydur
Frequency: 28,800 vph
Hairspring: flat hairspring
Shock protection: Nivachoc
Remarks: improved "Valjoux" chronograph caliber with symmetrical tricompax arrangement of the totalizers

Rado R808 (dial side)

Automatic; skeletonized mainplate and bridges; ball bearing-mounted rotor, hacking seconds, indexless fine adjustment; single mainspring barrel, 80-hour power reserve
Base caliber: ETA C.07611
Functions: hours, minutes, sweep seconds
Diameter: 25.6 mm
Height: 4.74 mm
Jewels: 25
Balance: glucydur
Frequency: 21,600 vph
Hairspring: Nivachron
Shock protection: Nivachoc
Remarks: exclusively used in Rado's True Square Skeleton, DiaStar Original Skeleton and Captain Cook High-Tech Ceramic models; based on the Powermatic caliber

Union Glashütte UNG-56.01

Hand-wound; Glashütte three-quarter plate with ribbing; hacking seconds; ETACHRON index system; single mainspring barrel, 60-hour power reserve
Functions: hours, minutes, subsidiary seconds; power reserve indicator; date
Diameter: 30 mm
Height: 5.4 mm
Jewels: 20
Frequency: 28,800 vph
Hairspring: flat hairspring
Shock protection: Nivachoc
Remarks: ETA construction based on the Valgranges chronograph movement reassembled and finished in Glashütte without hacking seconds and automatic winding; used in the 1893 Johannes Dürrstein jubilee edition

Longines L791.4

Automatic; hacking seconds; single mainspring barrel, 60-hour power reserve
Base caliber: ETA A08.261
Functions: hours, minutes, subsidiary seconds; flyback chronograph; date aperture with pusher-activated quick-set correction
Diameter: 30.4 mm
Height: 7.9 mm
Jewels: 28
Balance: glucydur
Frequency: 28,800 vph
Hairspring: silicon
Shock protection: Nivachoc
Remarks: exclusively used in the Longines Spirit Flyback chronograph

Longines L896.5

Automatic; ball bearing-mounted Rotor, hacking seconds, indexless fine regulation; single mainspring barrel, 72-hour power reserve
Functions: hours, minutes, sweep seconds; power reserve indicator with two central disks; date aperture
Diameter: 26 mm
Jewels: 21
Balance: glucydur
Frequency: 25,200 vph
Hairspring: silicon
Shock protection: Nivachoc
Remarks: exclusively used in Longines' Conquest Heritage Central Power Reserve

Longines L844.5

Automatic; ball bearing-mounted rotor, hacking seconds, indexless fine regulation; single mainspring barrel, 72-hour power reserve
Base caliber: ETA A31.411
Functions: hours (stepwise setting by crown), minutes, sweep seconds; additional 24-hour display (second time zone); date aperture
Diameter: 25.6 mm
Height: 3.85 mm
Jewels: 21
Balance: glucydur
Frequency: 25,200 vph
Hairspring: silicon
Shock protection: Nivachoc
Remarks: exclusively used in the Longines Spirit Zulu Time and Master Collection GMT models

2892-A2

Automatic; ball bearing–mounted rotor; stop-seconds, ETACHRON regulating system; single spring barrel; 42-hour power reserve
Functions: hours, minutes, sweep seconds; quick-set date window
Diameter: 26.2 mm
Height: 3.6 mm
Jewels: 21
Balance: glucydur
Frequency: 28,800 vph
Balance spring: flat hairspring
Shock protection: Incabloc

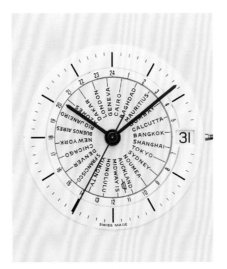

2893-1 (dial side)

Automatic; ball bearing rotor; stop-seconds, ETACHRON regulating system; 42-hour power reserve
Functions: hours, minutes, sweep seconds; quick-set date window at 3 o'clock; world time display via central disk
Diameter: 25.6 mm
Height: 4.1 mm
Jewels: 21
Frequency: 28,800 vph
Related calibers: 2893-2 (24-hour hand; 2nd time zone instead of world time disk); 2893-3 (only world time disk without date window)

2894-2

Automatic; ball bearing–mounted rotor; stop-seconds, ETACHRON regulating system; single spring barrel; 42-hour power reserve
Functions: hours, minutes, subsidiary seconds; chronograph; quick-set date window
Diameter: 28.6 mm
Height: 6.1 mm
Jewels: 37
Balance: glucydur
Frequency: 28,800 vph
Balance spring: flat hairspring
Shock protection: Incabloc
Related caliber: 2094 (diameter 23.9 mm, height 5.5 mm, 33 jewels)

2895-2 (dial side)

Automatic; ball bearing–mounted rotor; stop-seconds, ETACHRON regulating system; single spring barrel; 42-hour power reserve
Functions: hours, minutes, subsidiary seconds, at 6 o'clock; quick-set date window
Diameter: 26.2 mm
Height: 4.35 mm
Jewels: 27
Balance: glucydur
Frequency: 28,800 vph
Balance spring: flat hairspring
Shock protection: Incabloc

2896 (dial side)

Automatic; ball bearing rotor; stop-seconds, ETACHRON regulating system; 42-hour power reserve
Functions: hours, minutes, sweep seconds; power reserve display at 3 o'clock
Diameter: 25.6 mm
Height: 4.85 mm
Jewels: 21
Frequency: 28,800 vph

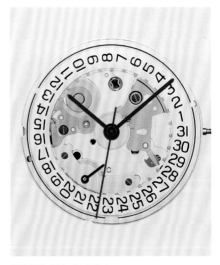

2897 (dial side)

Automatic; ball bearing–mounted rotor; stop-seconds, ETACHRON regulating system; single spring barrel; 42-hour power reserve
Functions: hours, minutes, sweep seconds; power reserve indicator; quick-set date window
Diameter: 26.2 mm
Height: 4.85 mm
Jewels: 21
Balance: glucydur
Frequency: 28,800 vph
Balance spring: flat hairspring
Shock protection: Incabloc

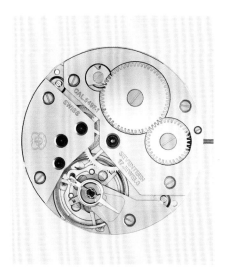

6497-1

Hand-wound; ETACHRON regulating system; single spring barrel; 46-hour power reserve
Functions: hours, minutes, subsidiary seconds
Diameter: 37.2 mm
Height: 4.5 mm
Jewels: 17
Frequency: 18,000 vph
Balance spring: flat hairspring
Remarks: pocket watch movement (Unitas model) in Lépine version with subsidiary seconds extending from the winding stem); as Caliber 6497-2 with 21,600 vph and 53-hour power reserve

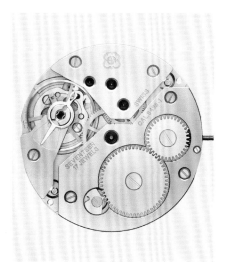

6498-1

Hand-wound; ETACHRON regulating system; single spring barrel; 46-hour power reserve
Functions: hours, minutes, subsidiary seconds
Diameter: 37.2 mm
Height: 4.5 mm
Jewels: 17
Frequency: 18,000 vph
Balance spring: flat hairspring
Remarks: pocket watch movement (Unitas model) in savonette version (subsidiary seconds at right angle to the winding stem); as Caliber 6498-2 with 21,600 vph and 53-hour power reserve

7001

Hand-wound; ultrathin construction; single spring barrel; 42-hour power reserve
Functions: hours, minutes, subsidiary seconds
Diameter: 23.7 mm
Height: 2.5 mm
Jewels: 17
Frequency: 21,600 vph
Balance spring: flat hairspring

7750 (dial side)

Automatic; stop-second system; single spring barrel; 42-hour power reserve
Functions: hours, minutes, subsidiary seconds; chronograph; quick-set date and weekday window
Diameter: 30.4 mm
Height: 7.9 mm
Jewels: 25
Balance: glucydur
Frequency: 28,800 vph
Balance spring: flat hairspring
Shock protection: Incabloc

7751 (dial side)

Automatic; stop-second system; single spring barrel; 42-hour power reserve
Functions: hours, minutes, subsidiary seconds; additional 24-hour display; chronograph; full calendar with date, weekday, month, moon phase
Diameter: 30.4 mm
Height: 7.9 mm
Jewels: 25
Balance: glucydur
Frequency: 28,800 vph
Balance spring: flat hairspring
Shock protection: Incabloc
Remarks: related caliber: 7754 with sweep 24-hour hand (2nd time zone)

7753

Automatic; stop-second system; single spring barrel; 42-hour power reserve
Functions: hours, minutes, subsidiary seconds; chronograph; quick-set date window with pusher
Diameter: 30.4
Height: 7.9 mm
Jewels: 25
Balance: glucydur
Frequency: 28,800 vph
Balance spring: flat hairspring
Shock protection: Incabloc
Remarks: variation of the Valjoux chronograph caliber with symmetrical "tricompax" layout of the totalizers

FESTINA SOPROD

The name Soprod stands for "Société de Production Horlogère" and refers to a company with a long tradition of movement-building, though, admittedly, mostly in quartz. It was founded in 1966, and later earned a favorable reputation as an external assembly company for ETA movements. Soprod continued enlarging its portfolio, adding customized decorations and finishings as a service and then building complete modules that could be used to enhance base movements.

Around the turn of the millennium, the company finally began to seriously develop its own calibers. The plan received an unexpected boost when ETA (Swatch Group) announced that, in the foreseeable future, they would no longer supply movement kits (*ébauches*) to external assemblers but would only supply end-customers directly. For then Swatch CEO Nicola Hayek, this would boost a reindustrialzation of the industry as larger groups would now be verticalizing their manufacturing. Aspiring watch companies would have to look elsewhere.

In the meantime, Soprod had become a member of the Swiss Festina Group, where it could provide extra capacities in the field of inexpensive quartz movements. But their mechanical division was growing steadily with two caliber lines (M and C) with over fifteen iterations. In 2011, at Baselworld, they presented their Alternance 10, or A10, which had the look and feel of the notoriously robust ETA 2892. As a base movement with a diameter of 25.6 millimeters, it fit inside in many cases, and Soprod already had a wide range of modules on tap to supplement it, like large dates, GMT, power reserves, and moon phases.

Expansion is the name of the game in a fluid market. Soprod continued making quartz movements and working on its mechanical calibers. In 2020 it launched the Newton line aimed at competing with another famous ETA caliber, the 2824-2, and with some of rival Sellita's products. It also ensured its own independence by starting to make its own escapement parts such as anchors, escape wheels, balance wheels, and hairsprings at its founding site in Les Reussilles in the Jura.

M100SQ

Automatic; skeletonized plate and bridges; bidirectional winding rotor, stop-second mechanism; single spring barrel, 42-hour power reserve
Functions: hours, minutes, sweep seconds; date with rapid correction
Diameter: 25.6 mm
Height: 3.6 mm
Jewels: 25
Frequency: 28,800 vph
Shock protection: Incabloc
Related calibers: M100 (standard version without skeletonization); M100 Balancier Visible (with openworked plate under the escapement parts)

M100

Automatic; bidirectional winding rotor, stop-second mechanism; single spring barrel, 42-hour power reserve
Functions: hours, minutes, sweep seconds; date with rapid correction
Diameter: 25.6 mm
Height: 3.6 mm
Jewels: 25
Frequency: 28,800 vph
Shock protection: Incabloc
Remarks: various regulation options (COSC, among others); various finishings (Optimal, Excellence, Manufacture)

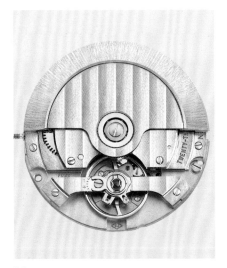

Newton

Automatic; in-house escapement and hairspring; unidirectional winding rotor, stop-second mechanism; single spring barrel, 44-hour power reserve
Functions: hours, minutes, sweep seconds; date, with rapid correction
Diameter: 25.6 mm
Height: 4.6 mm
Jewels: 23
Frequency: 28,800 vph
Shock protection: Incabloc
Remarks: with/without côtes de Genève

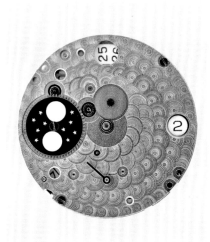

C105

Automatic; bidirectional winding rotor, stop-second mechanism; single spring barrel, 42-hour power reserve
Functions: hours, minutes, subsidiary seconds; date with rapid correction, moon phase Diameter: 25.6 mm
Height: 5.1 mm
Jewels: 33
Frequency: 28,800 vph
Shock protection: Incabloc

C110

Automatic; bidirectional winding rotor, stop-second mechanism; single spring barrel, 42-hour power reserve
Functions: hours, minutes, subsidiary seconds; date with rapid correction
Diameter: 25.6 mm
Height: 5.1 mm
Jewels: 29
Frequency: 28,800 vph
Shock protection: Incabloc

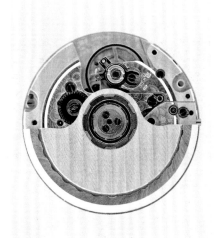

C115

Automatic; bidirectional winding rotor, stop-second mechanism; single spring barrel, 42-hour power reserve
Functions: hours, minutes, sweep seconds; additional 24-hour display (second time zone), power reserve display; date with rapid correction
Diameter: 25.6 mm
Height: 5.1 mm
Jewels: 33
Frequency: 28,800 vph
Shock protection: Incabloc

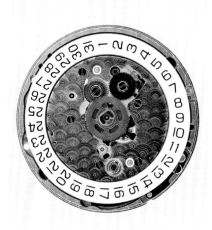

C125

Automatic; bidirectional winding rotor, stop-second mechanism; single spring barrel, 42-hour power reserve
Functions: hours, minutes, sweep seconds; additional 12-hour display (second time zone), day/night indication (with hour and minute at 6 o'clock); large date with rapid correction
Diameter: 25.6 mm
Height: 5.1 mm
Jewels: 25
Frequency: 28,800 vph
Shock protection: Incabloc

C120

Automatic; bidirectional winding rotor, stop-second mechanism; single spring barrel, 42-hour power reserve
Functions: hours, minutes, sweep seconds; additional 24-hour display (sweep second time zone); date, with rapid correction
Diameter: 25.6 mm
Height: 4.1 mm
Jewels: 25
Frequency: 28,800 vph
Shock protection: Incabloc

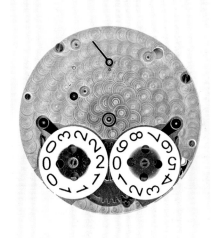

C130

Automatic; bidirectional winding rotor, stop-second mechanism; single spring barrel, 42-hour power reserve
Functions: hours, minutes, sweep seconds; power reserve display; large date with rapid correction
Diameter: 25.6 mm
Height: 5.1 mm
Jewels: 27
Frequency: 28,800 vph
Shock protection: Incabloc
Related calibers: C135 (with additional sweep 24-hour hand and date aperture); C140 (power reserve display und date aperture)

MANUFACTURE LA JOUX-PERRET

The re-industrialization of the caliber segment in Switzerland, brought about by some very confusing signals from Swatch Group and the Swiss government's Competition Commission, has created a number of opportunities for caliber builders who had until recently been operating in the shadow of ETA. Among them is Manufacture La Joux-Perret (MLJP), known primarily for its bespoke complication calibers for prestigious brands. It has now decided to enter the ready-to-wear caliber market in 2021 with the revised G100 three-hand automatic movement and the L100 automatic chronograph.

Due to their dimensions and specifications, both movements are suitable as replacements for the widely used 2824 and 7750 ("Valjoux") models, which will no longer be available to the watch industry in sufficient quantities after the expiry of the general supply obligation on the part of Swatch Group subsidiary ETA. The two MLJP calibers compete with Sellita's own high-volume movements SW200 and SW500, but they offer a greater amount of power reserve (68 and 60 hours, respectively) and partly better equipment (column-wheel control). Also in the standard portfolio of this caliber specialist is a classic-a hand-wound movement with the caliber number D100, whose architecture is strongly reminiscent of the pocket watch "Unitas" caliber. Its diameter, however, is only 23.3 millimeters.

MLJP has been part of the Citizen Group (Japan) since 2012. The company's headquarters and production facilities are located in La Chaux-de-Fonds, in the heart of watch country.

G100

Automatic; rotor on ball bearing, second stop; single spring barrel, 68-hour power reserve
Functions: hours, minutes, sweep seconds; date aperture
Diameter: 26 mm
Height: 4.45 mm
Jewels: 24
Balance: glucydur
Frequency: 28,800 vph
Hairspring: flat hairspring
Shock protection: Kif
Remarks: functionality and parts compatibility with ETA 2824-2; various display options, many customization options

L100

Automatic; column wheel control of chronograph functions; second stop; single spring barrel, 60-hour power reserve
Functions: hours, minutes, subsidiary seconds; chronograph; date and weekday aperture with rapid correction
Diameter: 30.4 mm
Height: 7.9 mm
Jewels: 26
Balance: Glucydur
Frequency: 28,800 vph
Hairspring: flat hairspring
Shock protection: Incabloc
Remarks: functionality and parts compatibility with ETA 7750; various display options, many customization options

T100

Hand-wound; flying 1-minute tourbillon; skeletonized movement; rhodium-plating; single mainspring barrel, 60-hour power reserve
Base caliber: LJP7814
Functions: hours, minutes
Diameter: 32.8 mm
Height: 4.4 mm
Jewels: 23
Balance: glucydur
Frequency: 28,800 vph
Hairspring: flat hairspring
Shock protection: Triovis

RONDA

Ronda is a Swiss company with a long tradition. It was founded by William Mosset, born in 1909 in the village of Hölstein, a man whose gift for micro-engineering declared itself early on when he invented a way to drill thirty-two holes in a metal plate in one operation and with great accuracy. The company was founded in 1946 in Lausen, a little town in the hinterlands of German-speaking Switzerland near Basel, where the first factory was built.

In the meantime the company has turned into a group with five subsidiaries: There are two production sites in Ticino, one in the Jura mountains, one operation in Thailand, and sales offices in Hong Kong. Overall, Ronda employs around 1,800 people in Switzerland and Asia.

The shareholders of the family enterprise, which is now in its second generation, value the company's absolute independence. This is undoubtedly a key advantage for the customer, since Ronda can continue defining its own strategy and can react decisively to customer needs.

That is why the company, which had already made a name for itself with quartz movements, decided to add a portfolio of automatic mechanical movements. The first product batches arrived on the market in early 2017; in the medium term, the mechanical Ronda Caliber R150 is to be produced in batches of six figures per year.

R150
Automatic; ball bearing–mounted rotor; stop-seconds, index for fine adjustment; single spring barrel; 40-hour power reserve
Functions: hours, minutes, sweep seconds; quick-set date
Diameter: 25.6 mm
Height: 4.4 mm
Jewels: 25
Frequency: 28,800 vph
Balance spring: flat hairspring
Shock protection: Incabloc

5040.B
Quartz; 54-month power reserve; single spring barrel
Functions: hours, minutes, subsidiary seconds; chronograph, with add and split function; large date
Diameter: 28.6 mm
Height: 4.4 mm
Jewels: 13

7004.P
Quartz; 48-month power reserve; single spring barrel
Functions: hours, minutes, subsidiary seconds; large date and weekday (retrograde)
Diameter: 34.6 mm
Height: 5.6 mm
Jewels: 6

SELLITA

Sellita was founded in 1950 by Pierre Grandjean in La Chaux- de- Fonds and is now one of the biggest reassemblers and finishers in the mechanical watch industry. On average, Sellita produces about one million automatic and hand- wound movements annually—a figure that represents about 25 percent of Switzerland's mechanical movement production, according to Miguel García, Sellita's president. Reassembly can be defined as the assembly and homologation of components to make a functioning movement. This is the type of work that ETA was very eager to outsource to companies back in the day in order to concentrate on manufacturing complete quartz movements and individual components for them.

Reassembly enterprises like Sellita rework and embellish components purchased from ETA according to their customers' wishes and can even complete smaller orders made by the company's estimated 350 clients.

When ETA announced that it would be halting its generous policy of selling its movement kits (*ébauches*) to companies outside the Swatch Group by the end of 2010, García, who has owned Sellita since 2003, reacted quickly by shifting production to the development and manufacturing of new in-house products. He planned and implemented a new line of movements based on the dimensions of the most popular ETA calibers. The strategy was aided by the fact that ETA's patents had expired.

Within just a few years, production capacity at the factory just outside La Chaux-de-Fonds doubled. Today, Sellita is by far the largest of the independent caliber makers in Switzerland. The company Sellita supplies the entire industry with "generic" calibers based on former ETA models. It has also designed and manufactured numerous standard movements with various complications. For a while, there were some growing pains, but for the past few years, Sellita has enjoyed a good reputation, and many start-up brands rely on them the way some brands formerly relied on ETA movements.

A newly created manufacturing division (AMT Manufacture SA) is now in charge of movements made according to customer specifications. These range from special requirements for their models, to unique technical specifications or finishings for the movements. It's a service that is being used with increasing frequency, since it enables smaller brands, in particular start-ups, to create individually designed timepieces.

SW100

Automatic; ball bearing-mounted rotor, hacking seconds; single mainspring barrel, 38-hour power reserve
Functions: hours, minutes, sweep seconds; date with fast correction
Diameter: 17.2 mm
Height: 4.8 mm
Jewels: 25
Balance: nickel or glucydur
Frequency: 28,800 vph
Hairspring: Nivaflex
Shock protection: Novodiac or Incabloc

SW200-1

Automatic; ball bearing-mounted rotor, hacking seconds; single mainspring barrel, 38-hour power reserve
Functions: hours, minutes, sweep seconds; date with fast correction
Diameter: 25.6 mm
Height: 4.6 mm
Jewels: 26
Balance: nickel or glucydur
Frequency: 28,800 vph
Hairspring: Nivaflex
Shock protection: Novodiac or Incabloc:
Related calibers: SW260-1 and SW261-1 (with subsidiary second at 6 o'clock), SW290-1 (with subsidiary second at 9 o'clock); SW220 (date and weekday)

SW300-1

Automatic; ball bearing-mounted rotor, hacking seconds; single mainspring barrel, 42-hour power reserve
Functions: hours, minutes, sweep seconds; date with fast correction
Diameter: 25.6 mm
Height: 3.6 mm
Jewels: 25
Balance: glucydur
Frequency: 28,800 vph
Hairspring: flat hairspring, Nivaflex
Shock protection: Incabloc
Related calibers: SW360-1 (with subsidiary second, height 4.35 mm, 31 jewels), SW330-2 (with additional 24-hour hand for second time zone)

SW210-1

Hand-wound; second stop; single mainspring barrel, 42-hour power reserve
Functions: hours, minutes, sweep seconds; date
Diameter: 25.6 mm
Height: 3.35 mm
Jewels: 18
Balance: nickel
Frequency: 28,800 vph
Hairspring: Nivaflex
Shock protection: Novodiac or Incabloc
Related calibers: SW216-1 (with subsidiary second and date)

SW400-1

Automatic; ball bearing-mounted rotor, hacking seconds; single mainspring barrel, 38-hour power reserve
Functions: hours, minutes, sweep seconds; date, with fast correction
Diameter: 31 mm
Height: 4.67 mm
Jewels: 26
Balance: nickel or glucydur
Frequency: 28,800 vph
Hairspring: Nivaflex
Shock protection: Novodiac or Incabloc
Remarks: technically like SW200, but with larger diameter; related caliber: SW461-1 (with subsidiary seconds)

SW400-1 S

Automatic; completely skeletonized movement; ball bearing-mounted rotor, second stop; single mainspring barrel, 42-hour power reserve
Functions: hours, minutes, sweep seconds; date with rapid correction
Diameter: 31 mm
Height: 4.67 mm
Jewels: 26
Balance: glucydur
Frequency: 28,800 vph
Hairspring: flat hairspring, Nivaflex
Shock protection: Incabloc
Remarks: various skeletonizations and finishings

SW500-M

Hand-wound; second stop; single mainspring barrel, 48-hour power reserve
Functions: hours, minutes, subsidiary seconds; chronograph; date and weekday with Fast correction
Diameter: 30 mm
Height: 7 mm
Jewels: 21
Balance: nickel or glucydur
Frequency: 28,800 vph
Hairspring: Nivaflex
Shock protection: Incabloc
Remarks: hand-wound version of the "Valjoux" construction

SW500-1

Automatic; ball bearing-mounted Rotor, second stop; single mainspring barrel, 48-hour power reserve
Functions: hours, minutes, subsidiary seconds; chronograph; date and weekday with Fast correction
Diameter: 30 mm
Height: 7.9 mm
Jewels: 25
Balance: nickel or glucydur
Frequency: 28,800 vph
Hairspring: Nivaflex
Shock protection: Incabloc
Related calibers: SW500 BV (bicompax without subsidiary seconds), SW510 (tricompax with symmetrical totalizer), SW510 BH (bicompax without hour totalizer), SW500/510 MP (single pusher), SW500/510 MPC (crown pusher)

SW562 S (dial side)

Automatic; crown pusher control of chronograph functions; ball bearing-mounted rotor, second stop; single mainspring barrel, 48-hour power reserve
Functions: hours, minutes, subsidiary seconds; chronograph
Diameter: 30 mm
Height: 6.9 mm
Jewels: 25
Balance: nickel or glucydur frequency: 28,800 vph
Hairspring: Nivaflex
Shock protection: Incabloc
Remarks: 1 mm thinner version of the SW500 chronograph (without date/weekday) with crown pusher control

WATCH YOUR WATCH

Mechanical watches are not only by and large more expensive and complex than quartzes, they are also a little high-maintenance, as it were. The mechanism within does need servicing occasionally—perhaps a touch of oil and an adjustment. Worse yet, the complexity of all those wheels and pinions engaged in reproducing the galaxy means that a user will occasionally do something perfectly harmless like wind his or her watch up only to find everything grinding to a halt. Here are some tips for dealing with these mechanical beauties for new watch owners and reminders for the old hands.

1. DATE CHANGES

Do not change the date manually (via the crown or pusher) on any mechanical watch—whether manual wind or automatic—when the time indicated on the dial reads between 10 and 2 o'clock. Although some better watches are protected against this horological quirk, most mechanical watches with a date indicator are engaged in the process of automatically changing the date between the hours of 10 p.m. and 2 a.m. Intervening with a forced manual change while the automatic date shift is engaged can damage the movement. Of course, you can make the adjustment between 10 a.m. and 2 p.m. in most cases—but this is just not a good habit to get into. When in doubt, roll the time past 12 o'clock and look for an automatic date change before you set the time and date. The Ulysse Nardin brand is notable, among a very few others, for in-house mechanical movements immune to this effect.

Bovet's barrier to pressing the wrong pusher.

2. CHRONOGRAPH USE

On a simple chronograph, start and stop are almost always the same button. Normally located above the crown, the start/stop actuator can be pressed at will to initiate and end the interval timing. The reset button, normally below the crown, is only used for resetting the chronograph to zero, but only when the chronograph is stopped—never while engaged. Only a "flyback" chronograph allows safe resetting to zero while running. With the chronograph engaged, you simply hit the reset button and all the chronograph indicators (seconds, minutes, and hours) snap back to zero and the chronograph begins to accumulate the interval time once again. In the early days of air travel this was a valuable complication as pilots would reset their chronographs when taking on a new heading—without having to fumble about with a three-step procedure with gloved hands.

Nota bene: Don't actuate or reset your chronograph while your watch is submerged—even if you have one of those that are built for such usage, like Omega, IWC, and a few other brands. Feel free to hit the buttons before submersion and jump in and swim while they run; just don't push anything while in the water.

3. CHANGING TIME BACKWARD

Don't adjust the time on your watch in a counterclockwise direction—especially if the watch has calendar functions. A few watches can tolerate the abuse, but it's better to avoid the possibility of damage altogether. Change the dates as needed (remembering the 10 and 2 rule above).

4. SHOCKS

Almost all modern watches are equipped with some level of shock protection. Best practices for the Swiss brands allow for a three-foot fall onto a hard wood surface. But if your watch is running poorly—or even worse has stopped entirely after an impact—do not shake, wind, or bang it again to get it running; take it to an expert for service as you may do even more damage. Sports like tennis, squash, or golf can have a deleterious effect on your watch, including flattening the pivots, overbanking, or even bending or breaking a pivot.

5. OVERWINDING

Most modern watches are fitted with a mechanism that allows the mainspring to slide inside the barrel—or stops it completely once the spring is fully wound—for protection against overwinding. The best advice here is just don't force it. Over the years, a winding crown may start to get "stickier" and more difficult to turn even when unwound. That's a sure sign it is due for service.

6. JACUZZI TEMPERATURE

Don't jump into the Jacuzzi—or even a steaming hot shower—with your watch on. Better-built watches with a deeper water-resistance rating typically have no problem with this scenario. However, take a 3 or 5 atm water-resistant watch into the Jacuzzi, and there's a chance the different rates of expansion and contraction of the metals and sapphire or mineral crystals may allow moisture into the case.

Panerai makes sure you think before touching the crown.

7. SCREW THAT CROWN DOWN (AND THOSE PUSHERS)!

Always check and double-check to ensure a watch fitted with a screwed-down crown is closed tightly. Screwed-down pushers for a chronograph—or any other functions—deserve the same attention. This one oversight has cost quite a few owners their watches. If a screwed-down crown is not secured, water will likely get into the case and start oxidizing the metal. In time, the problem can destroy the watch.

8. MAGNETISM

If your watch is acting up, running faster or slower, it may have become magnetized. This can happen if you leave your timepiece near a computer, cell phone, or some other electronic device. Many service centers have a so-called degausser to take care of the problem. A number of brands also make watches with a soft iron core to deflect magnetic fields, though this might not work with the stronger ones.

9. TRIBOLOGY

Keeping a mechanical timepiece hidden away in a box for extended lengths of time is not the best way to care for it. Even if you don't wear a watch every day, it is a good idea to run your watch at regular intervals to keep its lubricating oils and greases viscous. Think about a can of house paint: Keep it stirred and it stays liquid almost indefinitely; leave it still for too long and a skin develops. On a smaller level the same thing can happen to the lubricants inside a mechanical watch.

10. SERVICE

Most mechanical watches call for a three- to five-year service cycle for cleaning, oiling, and maintenance. Some mechanical watches can run twice that long and have functioned within acceptable parameters, but if you're not going to have your watch serviced at regular intervals, you do run the risk of having timing issues. Always have your watch serviced by a qualified watchmaker (see box), not at the kiosk in the local mall. The best you can expect there is a quick battery change.

Gary Girdvainis is the founder of Isochron Media LLC, publishers of WristWatch *and* AboutTime *magazines.*

Do it yourself at your own risk.

GLOSSARY

ANNUAL CALENDAR

The automatic allowances for the different lengths of each month of a year in the calendar module of a watch. This type of watch usually shows the month and date, and sometimes the day of the week (like this one by Patek Philippe) and the phases of the moon.

ANTIMAGNETIC

Magnetic fields found in common everyday places affect mechanical movements, hence the use of anti- or non-magnetic components in the movement. Some companies encase movements in antimagnetic cores such as Sinn's Model 756, the Duograph, shown here.

ANTIREFLECTION

A film created by steaming the crystal to eliminate light reflection and improve legibility. Antireflection functions best when applied to both sides of the crystal, but because it scratches, some manufacturers prefer to have it only on the interior of the crystal. It is mainly used on synthetic sapphire crystals. Dubey & Schaldenbrand applies antireflection on both sides for all of the company's wristwatches, such as this Aquadyn model.

AUTOMATIC WINDING

A rotating weight set into motion by moving the wrist winds the spring barrel via the gear train of a mechanical watch movement. Automatic winding was invented during the pocket watch era in 1770, but the breakthrough automatic winding movement via rotor began with the ball bearing Eterna-Matic in the late 1940s. Today we speak of unidirectional winding and bidirectionally winding rotors, depending on the type of gear train used. Shown is IWC's automatic Caliber 50611.

BALANCE

The beating heart of a mechanical watch movement is the balance. Fed by the energy of the mainspring, a tirelessly oscillating little wheel, just a few millimeters in diameter and possessing a spiral-shaped balance spring, sets the rhythm for the escape wheel and pallets with its vibration frequency. Today the balance is usually made of one piece of antimagnetic glucydur, an alloy that expands very little when exposed to heat.

BAR OR COCK

A metal plate fastened to the base plate at one point, leaving room for a gear wheel or pinion. The balance is usually attached to a bar called the balance cock. Glashütte tradition dictates that the balance cock be decoratively engraved by hand like this one by Glashütte Original.

BEVELING

To uniformly file down the sharp edges of a plate, bridge, or bar and give it a high polish. The process is also called *anglage*. Edges are usually beveled at a less than 45° angle to reflect light outwards. As the picture shows, this is painstaking work that needs the skilled hands and eyes of an experienced watchmaker or *angleur*.

BRIDGE

A metal plate fastened to the base plate at two points leaving room for a gear wheel or pinion. This vintage Favre-Leuba movement illustrates the point with three individual bridges.

CALIBER

A term, similar to type or model, that refers to different watch movements. Pictured here is Heuer's Caliber 11, the legendary automatic chronograph caliber from 1969. This movement was a coproduction jointly researched and developed for four years by Heuer-Leonidas, Breitling, and Hamilton-Büren. Each company gave the movement a different name after serial production began.

CARBON FIBER

A very light, tough composite material, carbon fiber is composed of filaments comprised of several thousand seven-micron carbon fibers held together by resin. The arrangement of the filaments determines the quality of a component, making each unique. Carbon fiber is currently being used for dials, cases, and even movement components.

CHAMPLEVÉ

A dial decoration technique, whereby the metal is engraved, filled with enamel, and baked, as in this cockatoo on a Cartier Tortue, enhanced with mother-of-pearl slivers.

CERAMIC

An inorganic, nonmetallic material formed by the action of heat and practically unscratchable. Pioneered by Rado, ceramic is a high-tech material generally made from aluminum and zirconia oxide. Today, it is used generally for cases and bezels and now comes in many colors.

CHRONOGRAPH

From the Greek *chronos* (time) and *graphein* (to write). Originally a chronograph literally wrote, inscribing the time elapsed on a piece of paper with the help of a pencil attached to a type of hand. Today this term is used for watches that show not only the time of day, but also certain time intervals via independent hands that may be started or stopped at will. Stopwatches differ from chronographs because they do not show the time of day. This exploded illustration shows the complexity of a Breitling chronograph.

CHRONOMETER

Literally, "measurer of time." As the term is used today, a chronometer denotes an especially accurate watch (one with a deviation of no more than 5 seconds a day for mechanical movements). Chronometers are usually supplied with an official certificate from an independent testing office such as the COSC. The largest producer of chronometers in 2008 was Rolex, with 769,850 officially certified movements. Chopard came in sixth with more than 22,000 certified L.U.C mechanisms, like the 4.96 in the Pro One model shown here.

COLUMN WHEEL

The component used to control chronograph functions within a true chronograph movement. The presence of a column wheel indicates that the chronograph is fully integrated into the movement. In the modern era, modules are generally used that are attached to a base caliber movement. This particular column wheel is made of blued steel.

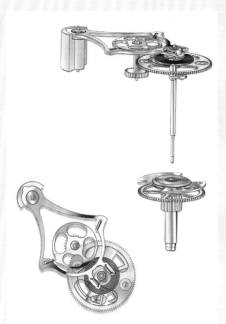

CONSTANT FORCE MECHANISM

Sometimes called a constant force escapement, it isn't really: in most cases this mechanism is "simply" an initial tension spring. It is also known in English by part of its French name, the *remontoir*, which actually means "winding mechanism." This mechanism regulates and portions the energy that is passed on through the escapement, making the rate as even and precise as possible. Shown here is the constant force escapement from A. Lange & Söhne's Lange 31— a mechanism that gets as close to its name as possible.

COSC

The Contrôle Officiel Suisse de Chronométrage, the official Swiss testing office for chronometers. The COSC is the world's largest issuer of so-called chronometer certificates, which are only otherwise given out individually by certain observatories (such as the one in Neuchâtel, Switzerland). For a fee, the COSC tests the rate of movements that have been adjusted by watchmakers. These are usually mechanical movements, but the office also tests some high-precision quartz movements. Those that meet the specifications for being a chronometer are awarded an official certificate as shown here.

CÔTES DE GENÈVE

Also called *vagues de Genève* and Geneva stripes. This is a traditional Swiss surface decoration comprising an even pattern of parallel stripes, applied to flat movement components with a quickly rotating plastic or wooden peg. Glashütte watchmakers have devised their own version of *côtes de Genève* that is applied at a slightly different angle, called Glashütte ribbing.

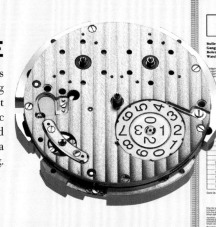

CROWN

The crown is used to wind and set a watch. A few simple turns of the crown will get an automatic movement started, while a manually wound watch is completely wound by the crown. The crown is also used for the setting of various functions, almost always including at least the hours, minutes, seconds, and date. A screwed-down crown like the one on the TAG Heuer Aquagraph pictured here can be tightened to prevent water entering the case or any mishaps while performing extreme sports such as diving.

EQUATION OF TIME

The mean time that we use to keep track of the passing of the day (24 hours evenly divided into minutes and seconds) is not equal to true solar time. The equation of time is a complication devised to show the difference between the mean time shown on one's wristwatch and the time the sun dictates. The Équation Marchante by Blancpain very distinctly indicates this difference via the golden sun-tipped hand that also rotates around the dial in a manner known to watch connoisseurs as *marchant*. Other wristwatch models, such as the Boreas by Martin Braun, display the difference on an extra scale on the dial.

ESCAPEMENT

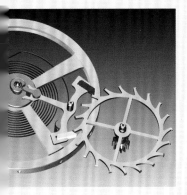

The combination of the balance, balance spring, pallets, and escape wheel, a subgroup which divides the impulses coming from the spring barrel into small, accurately portioned doses. It guarantees that the gear train runs smoothly and efficiently. The pictured escapement is one newly invented by Parmigiani, containing pallet stones of varying colors, though they are generally red synthetic rubies. Here one of them is a colorless sapphire, or corundum, the same geological material that ruby is made of.

FLINQUÉ

A dial decoration in which a guilloché design is given a coat of enamel, softening the pattern and creating special effects, as shown here on a unique Bovet.

GEAR TRAIN

A mechanical watch's gear train transmits energy from the mainspring to the escapement. The gear train comprises the minute wheel, the third wheel, the fourth wheel, and the escape wheel.

GLUCYDUR

Glucydur is a functional alloy of copper, beryllium, and iron that has been used to make balances in watches since the 1930s. Its hardness and stability allow watchmakers to use balances that were assembled at the factory and no longer required adjustment screws.

INDEX

A regulating mechanism found on the balance cock and used by the watchmaker to adjust the movement's rate. The index changes the effective length of the balance spring, thus making it move more quickly or slowly. This is the standard index found on an ETA Valjoux 7750.

JEWEL

To minimize friction, the hardened steel tips of a movement's rotating gear wheels (called pinions) are lodged in synthetic rubies (fashioned as polished stones with a hole) and lubricated with a very thin layer of special oil. These synthetic rubies are produced in exactly the same way as

sapphire crystal using the same material. During the pocket watch era, real rubies with hand-drilled holes were still used, but because of the high costs involved, they were only used in movements with especially quickly rotating gears. The jewel shown here on a bridge from A. Lange & Söhne's Double Split is additionally embedded in a gold chaton secured with three blued screws.

FLYBACK CHRONOGRAPH

A chronograph with a special dial train switch that makes the immediate reuse of the chronograph movement possible after resetting the hands. It was developed for special timekeeping duties such as those found in aviation, which require the measurement of time intervals in quick succession. A flyback may also be called a *retour en vol*. An elegant example of this type of chronograph is Corum's Classical Flyback Large Date shown here.

GUILLOCHÉ

A surface decoration usually applied to the dial and the rotor using a grooving tool with a sharp tip, such as a rose engine, to cut an even pattern onto a level surface. The exact adjustment of the tool for each new path is controlled by a device similar to a pantograph, and the movement of the tool can be controlled either manually or mechanically. Real *guillochis* (the correct term used by a master of guilloché) are very intricate and expensive to produce, which is why most dials decorated in this fashion are produced by stamping machines. Yvan Von Kaenel is one of the top guillocheurs still using a hand-controlled tool.

LIGA

The word LIGA is actually a German acronym that stands for lithography *(Lithografie)*, electroplating *(Galvanisierung)*, and plastic molding *(Abformung)*. It is a lithographic process exposed by UV or X-ray light that literally "grows" perfect micro components made of nickel, nickel-phosphorus, or 23.5-karat gold in a plating bath. The components need no finishing or trimming after manufacture.

LUMINOUS SUBSTANCE

Tritium paint is a slightly radioactive substance that replaced radium as a luminous coating for hands, numerals, and hour markers on watch dials. Watches bearing tritium must be marked as such, with the letter *T* on the dial near 6 o'clock. It has now for the most part been replaced by nonradioactive materials such as Super-LumiNova. Traser technology (as seen on these Ball timepieces) uses tritium gas enclosed in tiny silicate glass tubes coated on the inside with a phosphorescing substance. The luminescence is constant and will hold around twenty-five years.

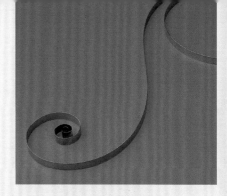

MAINSPRING

The mainspring, located in the spring barrel, stores energy when tensioned and passes it on to the escapement via the gear train as the tension relaxes. Today, mainsprings are generally made of Nivaflex, an alloy invented by Swiss engineer Max Straumann at the beginning of the 1950s. This alloy basically comprises iron, nickel, chrome, cobalt, and beryllium.

MINUTE REPEATER

A striking mechanism with hammers and gongs for acoustically signaling the hours, quarter hours, and minutes elapsed since noon or midnight. The wearer pushes a slide, which winds the spring. Normally a repeater uses two different gongs to signal hours (low tone), quarter hours (high and low tones in succession), and minutes (high tone). Some watches have three gongs, called a carillon. The Chronoswiss Répétition à Quarts is a prominent repeating introduction of recent years.

PERPETUAL CALENDAR

The calendar module for this type of timepiece automatically makes allowances for the different lengths of each month as well as leap years until the next secular year, which will occur in 2100. A perpetual calendar usually shows the date, month, and four-year cycle, and may show the day of the week and moon phase as well, as does IWC's Portugieser Eternal Calnedar of 2024, which can indicate leap years until 3999, for example.

PERLAGE

Surface decoration comprising an even pattern of partially overlapping dots, applied with a quickly rotating plastic or wooden peg, as shown here on the plates of Frédérique Constant's *manufacture* Caliber FC 910-1.

PLATE

A metal platform having several tiers for the gear train. The base plate of a movement usually incorporates the dial and carries the bearings for the primary pinions of the "first floor" of a gear train. The gear wheels are made complete by tightly fitting screwed-in bridges and bars on the back side of the plate. A specialty of the so-called Glashütte school, as opposed to the Swiss school, is the reverse completion of a movement not via different bridges and bars, but rather with a three-quarter plate. Glashütte Original's Caliber 65 (shown) displays a beautifully decorated three-quarter plate.

POWER RESERVE DISPLAY

A mechanical watch contains only a certain amount of power reserve. A fully wound modern automatic watch usually possesses between 36 and 42 hours of energy before it needs to be wound again. The power reserve display keeps the wearer informed about how much energy his or her watch still has in reserve, a function that is especially practical on manually wound watches with several days of possible reserve. The Nomos Tangente Power Reserve pictured here represents an especially creative way to illustrate the state of the mainspring's tension. On some German watches the power reserve is also displayed with the words "auf" and "ab."

PULSOMETER

A scale on the dial, flange, or bezel that, in conjunction with the second hand, may be used to measure a pulse rate. A pulsometer is always marked with a reference number—if it is marked with *gradué pour 15 pulsations*, for example, then the wearer counts fifteen pulse beats. At the last beat, the second hand will show what the pulse rate is in beats per minute on the pulsometer scale. The scale on Sinn's World Time Chronograph (shown) is marked simply with the German world *Puls* (pulse), but the function remains the same.

QUALITÉ FLEURIER

This certification of quality was established by Chopard, Parmigiani Fleurier, Vaucher, and Bovet Fleurier in 2004. Watches bearing the seal must fulfill five criteria, including COSC certification, passing several tests for robustness and precision, top-notch finishing, and being 100 percent Swiss-made (except for the raw materials). The seal appears here on the dial of the Parmigiani Fleurier Tonda 39.

RETROGRADE DISPLAY

A retrograde display shows the time linearly instead of circularly. The hand continues along an arc until it reaches the end of its scale, at which precise moment it jumps back to the beginning instantaneously. This Nienaber model not only shows the minutes in retrograde form, it is also a regulator display.

ROTOR

The rotor is the component that keeps an automatic watch wound. The kinetic motion of this part, which contains a heavy metal weight around its outer edge, winds the mainspring. It can either wind unilaterally or bilaterally (to one or both sides) depending on the caliber. The rotor from this Temption timepiece belongs to an ETA Valjoux 7750.

SAPPHIRE CRYSTAL

Synthetic sapphire crystal is known to gemologists as aluminum oxide (Al_2O_3) or corundum. It can be colorless (corundum), red (ruby), blue (sapphire), or green (emerald). It is virtually scratchproof; only a diamond is harder. The innovative Royal Blue Tourbillon by Ulysse Nardin pictured here features not only sapphire crystals on the front and back of the watch, but also actual plates made of both colorless and blue corundum within the movement.

SCREW BALANCE

Before the invention of the perfectly weighted balance using a smooth ring, balances were fitted with weighted screws to get the exact impetus desired. Today a screw balance is a subtle sign of quality in a movement due to its costly construction and assembly utilizing minuscule weighted screws.

349

SEAL OF GENEVA

Since 1886 the official seal of this canton has been awarded to Genevan watch *manufactures* who must follow a defined set of high-quality criteria that include the following: polished jewel bed drillings, jewels with olive drillings, polished winding wheels, quality balances and balance springs, steel levers and springs with beveling of 45 degrees and *côtes de Genève* decoration, and polished stems and pinions. The list was updated in 2012 to include the entire watch and newer components. Testing is done on the finished piece. The Seal consists of two, one on the movement, one on the case. The pictured seal was awarded to Vacheron Constantin, a traditional Genevan *manufacture*.

SILICIUM/SILICON

Silicon is an element relatively new to mechanical watches. It is currently being used in the manufacture of precision escapements. Ulysse Nardin's Freak has lubrication-free silicon wheels, and Breguet has successfully used flat silicon balance springs.

SKELETONIZATION

The technique of cutting a movement's components down to their weight-bearing basic substance. This is generally done by hand in painstaking hours of microscopic work with a small handheld saw, though machines can skeletonize parts to a certain degree, such as the version of the Valjoux 7750 that was created for Chronoswiss's Opus and Pathos models. This tourbillon created by Christophe Schaffo is additionally—and masterfully—hand-engraved.

SONNERIE

A variety of minute repeater that—like a tower clock—sounds the time not at the will of the wearer, but rather automatically (*en passant*), every hour (*petite sonnerie*), or quarter hour (*grande sonnerie*). Gérald Genta designed the most complicated sonnerie back in the early nineties. Shown is a recent model from the front and back.

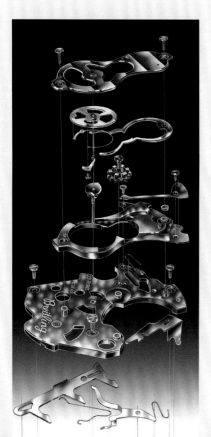

SPLIT-SECONDS CHRONOGRAPH

Also known in the watch industry by its French name, the *rattrapante* (exploded view at left). A watch with two second hands, one of which can be blocked with a special dial train lever to indicate an intermediate time while the other continues to run. When released, the split-seconds hand jumps ahead to the position of the other second hand. The PTC by Porsche Design illustrates this nicely.

SPRING BARREL

The spring barrel contains the mainspring. It turns freely on an arbor, pulled along by the toothed wheel generally doubling as its lid. This wheel interacts with the first pinion of the movement's gear train. Some movements contain two or more spring barrels for added power reserve.

SWAN-NECK FINE ADJUSTMENT

A regulating instrument used by the watchmaker to adjust the movement's rate in place of an index. The swan neck is especially prevalent in fine Swiss and Glashütte watchmaking (here, Lang & Heyne's Moritz model). Mühle Glashütte has varied the theme with its woodpecker's neck.

TACHYMETER

A scale on the dial, flange, or bezel of a chronograph that, in conjunction with the second hand, gives the speed of a moving object. A tachymeter takes a value determined in less than a minute and converts it into miles or kilometers per hour. For example, a wearer could measure the time it takes a car to pass between two mile markers on the highway. When the car passes the marker, the second hand will be pointing to the car's speed in miles per hour on the tachymetric scale.

TOURBILLON

A technical device invented by Abraham-Louis Breguet in 1801 to compensate for the influence of gravity on the balance of a pocket watch. The entire escapement is mounted on an epicyclic train in a "cage" and rotated completely on its axis over regular periods of time. This superb horological highlight is seen as a sign of technological know-how in the modern era. Harry Winston's Histoire de Tourbillon 4 is a spectacular example.

VIBRATION FREQUENCY (VPH)

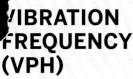

The spring causes the balance to oscillate at a certain frequency measured in hertz (Hz) or vibrations per hour (vph). Most of today's wristwatches tick at 28,800 vph (4 Hz) or 21,600 vph (3 Hz). Less usual is 18,000 vph (2.5 Hz). Zenith's El Primero (shown) was the first serial movement to beat at 36,000 vph (5 Hz), and the Breguet Type XXII runs at 72,000 vph.

WATER RESISTANCE

Water resistance is an important feature of any timepiece and is usually measured in increments of one atmosphere (atm or bar, equal to 10 meters of water pressure) or meters and is often noted on the dial or case back. Watches resistant to 100 meters are best for swimming and snorkeling. Timepieces resistant to 200 meters are good for scuba diving. To deep-sea dive there are various professional timepieces available for use in depths of 200 meters or more. The Hydromax by Bell & Ross (shown) is water-resistant to a record 11,000 meters.

 @wristwatchannual

Copyright © 2025 HEEL Verlag GmbH, Königswinter, Germany

English-language translation copyright © 2025 Abbeville Press,
655 Third Avenue, New York, NY 10017

Editor-in-chief: Peter Braun
Editor: Marton Radkai
Production manager: Louise Kurtz
Copy Editors: Cynthia K. Barton, Stephanie Sarkany
Composition: Erin Morris, Evergreen Design Studio
Project Management: Kourtnay King, Layman Poupard Publishing

For more information about advertising, please contact:
Gary Girdvainis
25 Gay Bower Road, Monroe, CT 06468
203-952-3522, garygeorgeg@gmail.com

ISBN 978-0-7892-1508-6

Twenty-sixth edition
10 9 8 7 6 5 4 3 2 1

Library of Congress Cataloging-in-Publication Data available upon request

For bulk and premium sales and for text adoption procedures, write to Customer Service Manager,
Abbeville Press, 655 Third Avenue, New York, NY 10017, or call 1-800-ARTBOOK.

Visit Abbeville Press online at www.abbeville.com.

ISBN 978-0-7892-1508-6 U.S. $39.95

EAN

9 780789 215086   53995